FIGHTING WORDS

FIGHTING WORDS

COMPETING VOICES FROM THE RUSSIAN REVOLUTION

Edited by Michael C. Hickey

GREENWOOD

AN IMPRINT OF ABC-CLIO, LLC
Santa Barbara, California • Denver, Colorado • Oxford, England

Library of Congress Cataloging-in-Publication Data

Competing voices from the Russian Revolution : fighting words / edited by Michael C. Hickey.
    p. cm.—(Fighting words)
Includes bibliographical references and index.
ISBN 978-0-313-38523-0 (hard copy : acid-free paper)—ISBN 978-0-313-38524-7 (ebook)
1. Soviet Union—History—Revolution, 1917–1921—Sources. 2. Soviet Union—History—Revolution, 1917–1921—Personal narratives. 3. Soviet Union—History—Revolution, 1917–1921—Social aspects—Sources. 4. Social conflict—Soviet Union—History—Sources. 5. Soviet Union—Politics and government—1917–1936—Sources. I. Hickey, Michael C.
  DK265.A5165   2011
  947.084′1—dc22   2010039676

ISBN: 978-0-313-38523-0
EISBN: 978-0-313-38524-7

15   14   13   12   11   1   2   3   4   5

This book is also available on the World Wide Web as an eBook.
Visit www.abc-clio.com for details.

Greenwood
An Imprint of ABC-CLIO, LLC

ABC-CLIO, LLC
130 Cremona Drive, P.O. Box 1911
Santa Barbara, California 93116-1911

This book is printed on acid-free paper ∞

Manufactured in the United States of America

This book is dedicated to the memory of my father,
Robert L. Hickey (1924–2009).

CONTENTS

SERIES FOREWORD

Fighting Words is a unique new series aimed at a broad audience, from college-level professors and undergraduates to high school teachers, students, and the general reader. Each volume in this series focuses on a unique historical controversy, told through first-hand accounts from the diverse perspectives of both the victors and the vanquished. The series is designed to introduce readers to a broad range of competing narratives about the past, giving voices to those often left silent in the secondary literature.

Each volume offers competing perspectives through relatively short primary documents, such as newspaper articles, contemporary chronicles, excerpts from participants' letters or memoirs, as well as other carefully selected sources; brief introductions provide the necessary background information and context to guide readers through the disparate accounts. Where necessary, key documents are reproduced in their entirety. However, most of the documents are brief in nature, and sharp in content, which will help to promote general classroom discussion and debate. The inclusion of vivid and colorful accounts from the participants themselves, combined with other primary sources from all sides, gives the series an exciting and engaging flavor.

The *Fighting Words* series is designed to promote meaningful discussion and debate about the past. Furthermore, the volumes in this series encourage readers to think critically about the evidence that historians use, or ignore, to reconstruct an understanding of that past. Each volume will challenge accepted assumptions about the topics covered, and readers will question the nature of primary sources, the motivations, agendas, and perspectives of the authors, and the silences inherent in all of the sources. Ultimately, readers will be left to ponder the question, whose history is this?

J. Michael Francis

About the Editor

MICHAEL C. HICKEY is a Professor of History at Bloomsburg University of Pennsylvania in Bloomsburg, PA. Dr. Hickey has published extensively on the 1917 Revolution in provincial Russia and on Russian-Jewish provincial communities in the Late Imperial and early Soviet periods.

About the Series Editor

DR. J. MICHAEL FRANCIS received his PhD in 1998 from the University of Cambridge, where he specialized in colonial Latin American history. Since then, he has taught at the University of North Florida, where he is an associate professor of history. He has written numerous articles on the history of early-colonial New Granada (Colombia). In 2006, he edited a three-volume reference work called *Iberia and the Americas: Culture, Politics, and History* (ABC-CLIO). His most recent book, *Invading Colombia: Spanish Accounts of the Gonzalo Jiménez de Quesada Expedition of Conquest*, was published in 2007 by Penn State University Press.

Dr. Francis serves as book review editor for the journal *Ethnohistory*, and series co-editor for *Latin American Originals* (Penn State University Press). He also sits on the advisory board of the University Press of Florida. In 2007, Dr. Francis was appointed as a research associate at the American Museum of Natural History in New York. At present, he is completing a new manuscript, entitled *Politics, Murder, and Martyrdom in Spanish Florida: Don Juan and the Guale Uprising of 1597*, which will be published by the American Museum of Natural History Press.

PREFACE

This book presents documents on public discussions and debates—fighting words—during the 1917 Russian Revolution. It illustrates the views of a wide range of revolutionary Russia's population. Some documents were written by political elites, like government officials and political party leaders; some were written by ordinary men and women who tilled fields, toiled in factories, worked in offices, or served in the military. All were written between July 1914 and mid-January 1918, with one exception—a short extract from a 1967 Soviet high school text that appears in chapter 8.

The book is divided into four parts. Part One (chapters 1 and 2) presents views on World War I, and covers the period from July 1914 through January 1917. Part Two (chapters 3–7) illustrates responses to the February Revolution, the aspirations of various social groups, and flash points of conflict in March–July 1917. Part Three (chapters 8–12) focuses on life in the provinces, perceptions of crisis, electoral politics, and flash points of conflict in July–October 1917. Part Four (chapters 13 and 14) presents debates over the October Revolution and the January 1918 meeting of the Constituent Assembly. Each part begins with an introductory essay that examines major events and developments and discusses historiographic issues. The introductions are followed by chapters of documents.

Each document has its own brief introduction that helps set the document in its historical context. In some cases, I have grouped closely related documents together as a single document set. The introductions to document sets give information on each individual document, and each is identified separately so that readers can distinguish among them. Most of the documents are from Russian-language newspapers (including several cartoons). The non-newspaper materials generally are from archival sources: some were published in documentary collections after 1917; others I have collected in the course of my own archival research. Most of the documents appear in their entirety, but I have cut redundant passages from many documents. Places where I have excised text are indicated with ellipses. In some documents, I have summarized long and complex passages; in such cases, my summaries are in square brackets. Several documents are transcriptions of public meetings, which include notations on interruptions to speeches, such as applause, or shouts from hecklers. To make the transcripts clearer for readers, I have indicated speakers' names in italics and placed the original stenographers' notes in parentheses.

With the exception of two meeting transcripts in chapter 13 that are composite texts assembled from multiple contemporary sources, each document in this book was reproduced on the basis of a single source text. Two documents—both in chapter 1—originally were written in English.

I have translated all the others from Russian texts, even when previous English translations existed. This allowed me to modulate the language so that readers will find it more familiar and to avoid minor errors or missed nuances in some older, standard translations. Roughly 70 percent of the documents appear here in English translation for the first time.

Readers should be aware of two other technical points regarding the documents. First, because the Russian language is written in the Cyrillic alphabet, rendering Russian words, names, and place names in the Latin alphabet used in English requires transliteration. This book uses the Library of Congress transliteration system, but I have spelled the names of a few very well-known people as they most often appear in English. Therefore, Russia's last tsar is referred to as Nicholas II, not Nikolai II, and the leader of the Provisional Government is referred to as Alexander Kerensky, not Aleksandr Kerenskii. A second point concerns dates. In this book, dates are always given according to the calendar then in use in Russia. Until February 1918, Russia was on the Julian calendar, which was 13 days behind the modern Gregorian calendar used in England, the United States, and elsewhere. Therefore, in this book the date on which Tsar Nicholas II stepped down from the throne is given as 2 March 1917, although in London or New York, the date was 15 March 1917.

The book also includes a Chronology of Major Events directly relevant to the documents, a map that indicates the location of many cities mentioned in the documents, a Biographical Glossary that provides information on many of the people mentioned in the documents, and a List of Further Readings.

ACKNOWLEDGMENTS

I would like to express my gratitude to *Fighting Words* series editor, Dr. Michael Francis, and to the staff at ABC-Clio for their patience in handling a book project that became much more complex than they had anticipated. Nina Emelianova, Director of the Smolensk Regional Archival Administration, granted me permission to reproduce archival documents. A sabbatical from Bloomsburg University gave me time to work on this project. Students in several of my courses at Bloomsburg University read versions of these translations, and their comments and questions helped me revise the manuscript. Among the many scholars who helped me on this project, I owe special thanks to Sarah Badcock, Olga Bertelson, Sally Boniece, Boris Lanin, Michael Melancon, Aaron Retish, M. Safa Saraçoğlu, and Rex A. Wade. Most of all, I thank Susan E. Stemont, who read and commented on multiple drafts of the entire manuscript, for her good counsel, patience, and unwavering love and support.

PART ONE
THE CONTEXT OF WORLD WAR I

This book begins with two chapters of documents from July 1914 to February 1917, documents that represent voices in conflict over World War I. Before turning to those documents, we need to survey ways historians have explained the origins of the revolution that broke out in Russia in February 1917. This survey is followed by a description of conditions in Russia during World War I, as background for the documents in chapters one and two.

Popular Views on the Causes of the February Revolution[1]

In late February 1917, a revolution erupted in Petrograd (Russia's capital city) that ended three centuries of the Romanov family's rule over Russia.[2] What caused that revolution? Popular histories, general textbooks, and television documentaries usually confidently tick off several factors: Russia's "hopeless backwardness"; the repressive, unjust rule of the Romanovs; the "iron will" of the revolutionaries (and especially of Bolshevik leader Lenin); the inept way that "weak-willed" Tsar Nicholas II and his "overbearing wife" Tsaritsa Alexandra ran the country during World War I. Popular histories also tend to devote a great deal of attention to the scandalous influence of the mystic Gregory Rasputin over the royal family, which is, after all, a fascinating story.

Specialists on the Origins of the February Revolution

The causes of the February Revolution typically mentioned in popular and general histories are important, but they often do not take into consideration insights from recent research by specialists on modern Russian history. It can take years for general or popular histories to incorporate shifts in the ways that specialists understand a topic, in part because the complex arguments of specialists can be difficult to summarize and "translate" into a popularized form. Most specialists on the revolution would not reject the list of "popular" ideas about the revolution's origins, but they would point out that the details are more complicated and often more contradictory.

For example, recent historians of the Russian Revolution generally agree that the state's organizational weaknesses and the country's relative economic underdevelopment help explain why Russia broke under the strain of modern "total" warfare in 1914–1917. But few specialists today describe Russia as exceptionally backward. It is now more common for historians to stress the similarities, as well as the differences, between developments in Russia and those elsewhere in Europe. Russia might have been on the eastern fringe of Europe, but it certainly was not isolated from the great economic, social, cultural, and intellectual transformations that swept the continent during what historians call "the long 19th century"

(1789–1914). In other words, specialists would press us to think about how causes of the Russian Revolution fit in the larger frameworks of European and world history.

When historians discuss the origins of major events like revolutions, they usually refer to "long-term" causes, "intermediate" causes, and "short-term" causes. In the case of the Russian Revolution, long-term causes would include factors like the effect of Russia's climate and soil conditions on the development of agriculture and settlement patterns; the ways that the empire's enormous size (it covered one-seventh of the Earth's dry land) and other geographic features shaped the state's development; the ramifications of serfdom (a form of compulsory unpaid agricultural labor), which persisted in Russia into the mid-19th century; and how deep patterns of Russian folk life and folk traditions shaped popular political culture. These issues are important to understanding modern Russian history, but they are beyond our scope here. When most historians discuss the intermediate causes of the February Revolution, they refer to developments in the late 18th and 19th centuries, and especially during the period from the Great Reforms of the 1860s—when the tsarist state sought to modernize Russia's economy and society by ending serfdom and instituting a number of other changes—up through World War I. By short-term causes, historians generally mean events and developments that accompanied World War I—the popular idea that "weak-willed" Nicholas II mishandled the war is an example of a short-term cause.

Specialists agree in a general way about what factors should be listed as causes of the February Revolution. What they do *not* agree on is the relative weight or importance of these causes. Of course, we could say that same thing about the origins of almost any major historical event. Historians who disagree over the origins of World War I, for example, really are arguing about the relative importance of several widely recognized causes. What follows is a summary of several intermediate-term factors often discussed in specialists' work on the revolution's origins.

The Tsar's Refusal to Give Up Autocratic Power

Until 1905, Russia's government was an autocracy—meaning that sovereignty and all legal state authority rested with a single person (the tsar or tsarina), whose power was not restrained or limited by a constitution. The regime fiercely resisted constitutional reforms that would weaken the autocrat's power. This meant that all opposition political activity was, by definition, revolutionary. In 1905, the regime's resistance to reform combined with the economic and social strains of war (Russia fought—and ultimately lost—a costly war against Japan in 1904–1905) to unleash a revolution. The 1905 Revolution forced the government to grant some political concessions, like a new set of Fundamental Laws and creation of an elected legislature (the State *Duma*). But in 1906–1914, the government took steps that undermined these concessions. Nicholas II still conceived of the state as autocratic. The persistence of autocratic rule is tied to each of the other factors discussed below.

The Problem of "Undergovernment"

Despite the great size and complexity of the tsarist state bureaucracy, Russia remained "undergoverned." The state generally lacked the means to efficiently collect taxes, administer the law, or implement policies effectively at the local level across much of the vast Russian Empire. The consequences of undergovernment became acutely clear at times of war, such as the Crimean War of 1853–1855, but also during Russo-Japanese War and, of course, during World War I. The Great Reforms of the 1860s were designed to preserve Russia's status as a great power, and this required that it solve the problem of undergovernment. The reforms abolished serfdom and reorganized the military, the court system, rural administration, municipal government, and the education system. More-over, they created a new network of local quasi-governmental institutions, the *zemstvos*, to provide education, medical, and other services at the local level. Zemstvso employees dedicated themselves to serving the people, but often found themselves frustrated by the tsarist state's reluctance to grant them professional autonomy, let alone to recognize the public's rights.

Although the Great Reforms fell far short of expectations held by much of the educated public (an important factor shaping the revolutionary movement), the government began back-peddling in the 1880s and implemented a series of "counterreforms." The government never extended the system of zemstvos and other institutions to the township level, nor did it institute the zemstvo reforms across the entire empire, so its ability to "penetrate" and rule the countryside remained limited. To this must be added the burdens of a bloated, costly, and often unresponsive bureau-cracy accustomed to arbitrary procedures and riddled by corruption.

The Tsarist Government's Reluctance to Grant Fundamental Civil Rights

The architects of the Great Reforms wanted to create a more dynamic society that would take greater responsibility for the implementation of government policies *without* giving society the power to make decisions about governance and *without* recognizing the civil rights of individuals. Specific sections of the population could vote for representatives in specific institutions—for example, property owners in cities could vote for the municipal governments (called *duma*s); peasants could vote for peasant deputies to the zemstvo assemblies, and aristocrats could elect assemblies of noblemen. But these institutions had little freedom to make policy, and counterreforms in the 1880s and 1890s reinforced tsarist authoritarianism. Until the 1905 Revolution, Russia had no elected legislative assembly and its people—who had no legally recognized civil rights—were the tsars' subjects rather than citizens.

The 1905 Revolution forced Tsar Nicholas II to concede further reforms. Russia's new Fundamental Laws did place limits on the autocracy, but Russia still did not have a constitution, properly speaking. The government took steps toward ensuring civil rights and agreed that legislation would be drafted by an elected State Duma. These concessions— along with the end of the Russo-Japanese War—helped the tsarist government reassert its authority. In 1906, as the government snuffed the last embers of the revolution, it undermined many revolutionary concessions and jury-rigged the State Duma electoral system to limit opposition. The post-1905 government did institute important reforms—the most significant of which were agrarian reforms associated with Prime Minister Petr Stolypin—but it also retained many characteristics of the pre-1905 authoritarian state. As a result, citizens often found their hard-won rights subordinated to the seemingly arbitrary caprice of the government.

The Disruptive Impact of Rapid Social Transformations

The Great Reforms of the 1860s accelerated the pace of economic and social change in ways that aggravated social tensions, magnified social grievances, and failed to satisfy the aspirations of those in the lower classes, most of whom lived in poverty.

One of the aims of the Great Reforms had been to promote the rapid industrial growth that was necessary for Russia to retain its status as a great power. The specifics of industrialization in Russia differed in some ways from industrialization in Western Europe. In Russia, for example, the state played a more direct role in economic development than in Great Britain, or even in Germany. Still, industrialization in Russia brought social problems and social stresses that were very much like the problems faced in other contemporary industrializing states. The men and women who toiled in Russia's factories and workshops, in its mines, and on its railroads experienced harsh working and living conditions, low wages, and a demeaning disciplinary regime reminiscent of industrialization elsewhere in Europe and in North America. If anything, the rapid pace of industrialization in Russia—where changes that took a century to develop in England were compressed into a few decades—made the process even more disruptive than in other European countries.

In Russia, as elsewhere, working people sought to organize and voice their aspirations and grievances through unions, political activity, and direct workplace action-like strikes. In many ways, the Russian context made its workers' movement even more militant than workers' movements elsewhere. At the dawn of the 20th century, workers in Russia had no legal labor unions and no legal forms of political representation through which they could voice their grievances. So workers—and especially workers who took seriously the socialist parties' criticisms of capitalism as an exploitive system—saw their struggle for a better life as inseparable from the struggle for rights against autocratic government. Wage-earning workers in the cities were a small minority of the empire's population (in 1897, about 11 million out of 125 million people), but they became a major political force during the 1905 Revolution. In 1905, Russia's urban workers participated vigorously in public life, through strikes and protests, but also through their own grassroots councils (called the soviets), trade unions, and a whole range of newly legalized clubs and other social organizations. The tsarist state severely limited the freedom of these organizations after it crushed the revolution in 1906. Unions and other workers' associations, for example, were legally banned from any political activities. Still, the workers' movement remained intertwined with the movement for revolutionary change.

At the dawn of the 20th century, Russia had some of the world's largest factories, and yet it remained an overwhelmingly rural country—indeed, it was the most rural of the major European states that engaged in World War I. People defined by the state as "peasants" accounted for about 80 percent of the population in 1897. Although some textbooks still make sweeping statements about Russian peasant isolation and backwardness, these are simplifications that few specialists today endorse. In the late 1800s, market forces, migration, and the spread of education were changing rural society in Russia, and by the early 1900s, literacy and consumer culture had made deep inroads in village life. The transformations taking place in the countryside were rife with contradictions. The Great Reforms had freed peasants from serfdom, but the state tied them legally to their village communities, restricted their freedom of movement, and forced them to pay special taxes (redemption fees) as compensation for their emancipation. The reforms hastened the integration of the countryside into the emerging market economy and opened new possibilities for peasants as producers of agricultural goods and as migratory wage laborers. The "traditionalism" of the village was challenged by young peasants' literacy, their access to consumer goods, and their exposure to urban fashions and values. At the same time, agriculture still depended on very traditional farming methods and produced small yields. Peasants believed that the serf reforms had provided them with too little land at too great a cost, and that it had left too much property under the control of the aristocratic landlords. Moreover, the reforms had apportioned land to the village communes rather than to individual households, and most contemporary commentators believed that this reinforced "backwards" modes of farming and put a drag on agricultural productivity.

After the Great Reforms, peasants could voice their grievances peacefully through the courts, as well as through petitions and appeals to the tsar and other officials (modes familiar from the prereform era). Peasant frustration and hostility toward the aristocratic landlords and toward the state also could take violent forms, such as attacks on the nobles' property. In 1905, rural violence became a mass phenomenon that shaped revolutionary politics. But peasants were not simply "primitive rebels." To a much greater extent than popular histories usually recognize, peasants also took part in peaceful organizational and political activities. And after the state used military force to bloodily repress the peasant rebellion in 1906, rural people continued to participate in political life, both locally and nationally (for example, through elections to the State Duma). From the peasants' perspective, though, the tsarist government did little to satisfy the rural population's grievances and aspirations. Many historians believe that the Stolypin agrarian reforms, which allowed peasants to form individual family farms by separating their land from that of the village community, actually heightened social tensions in the countryside. When pressed by crisis conditions, and when the state lost its ability to repress them, villagers readily rose up in rebellion against perceived injustices.

Weak Support for Liberalism and Conservative Monarchism

In Russia, the middle classes that had been the bulwark of liberalism and conservatism elsewhere in Europe proved relatively weak and politically fragmented. Policies imposed by the tsarist state limited the growth of Russia's middle classes and prevented them from congealing as a political force the way that the middle classes had in much of Western and Central Europe. Although Russia's middle classes had begun to exert themselves in public life in the early 1900s, and continued to do so after the 1905 Revolution, most historians conclude that they could not sustain a liberal reform movement as they had elsewhere in Europe.

Although liberalism generally is associated with the urban middle classes, in Russia there also was a phenomenon known as "gentry liberalism"—support among aristocratic landlords for constitutional reforms. The landowning nobility—which might be considered Russia's "ruling class," in that it had special legal privileges and status and provided the tsarist state with most of its functionaries—had seen its economic power and influence dwindle steadily during the 19th century. More important, nobles did not universally or unquestioningly support the government of Tsar Nicholas II. Since the mid-1800s, members of the nobility had made up the core of the liberal and socialist *intelligentsia*—the educated elements in society that were in the forefront of movements for social and political change. In 1905–1906, peasant unrest and threats to property rights pushed many gentry liberals further to the right, but Nicholas II still could not count on "his" nobles for the sort of powerful social and political support that the aristocratic landlords provided Wilhelm II in Germany. (Similar generalizations could be made about the clergy of Russia's official state religion, the Russian Orthodox Church; although the Church as an institution was considered a bulwark of tsarism, clergymen often championed social reforms and considered the state far too repressive.) Even the most conservative nobles and members of Russia's ultranationalist right-wing parties often found themselves at loggerheads with the tsarist government.

Broad Social Support for Revolutionary Political Ideas

In 19th-century Russia, a culture of political radicalism developed among the intelligentsia, which believed that revolutionary change was necessary to create a more just society. By the mid-1800s the educated elite (and especially reform-minded nobles) widely believed that that they owed a debt to the *narod*—the people, meaning the peasants who made up the overwhelming majority of Russia's population. The idea of service to the people became tied to the idea that Russia must enjoy liberty. For most members of the intelligentsia, this meant creating a constitutional regime that ensured individual civil rights; for some, it also meant socialism as defined by European Social Democrats (based on the principles of Marxism), or a populist form of agrarian socialism (based upon the model of the Russian village commune). Given the Romanov tsars' conception of their state as an autocracy, their reluctance to make fundamental political reform, and their intolerance of dissent, all these visions were implicitly revolutionary. For liberals in Russia to demand a constitution, civil rights, and elected legislative institutions amounted to demanding limits on the tsar's power that would end the autocracy. In 1905, the government granted concessions (Tsar Nicholas II's "October Manifesto") that fragmented the liberal opposition. But the largest liberal party, the Constitutional Democrats—called the Kadets— still demanded limits on the tsar's power that, if implemented, would amount to a political revolution.

Unlike the liberals, Russia's radical socialist political parties wished to overthrow both tsarism *and* capitalism. There were important differences between the ideologies and platforms of the two largest socialist parties— the populist SRs (the Party of Socialist Revolutionaries) and the Marxist Russian Social Democratic Labor Party (which split into two factions, the Mensheviks and the Bolsheviks). But together with the empire's many other, smaller socialist groups, they agreed that Russia needed a political revolution to create a republic that would secure civil liberties and democracy.[3] (Some liberals also insisted that Russia must be a republic, but most were willing to settle for a British-style constitutional monarchy). And the socialists went further still, insisting that true equality and freedom were impossible unless the capitalist economy and social system was overturned and replaced by some form of socialism.

Despite differences in ideology and culture, Russia's populist and Marxist revolutionaries had much in common. For example, Russian *Narodniki* (populists) read and studied the works of Karl Marx, and Russian Marxists read and studied the works of the *Nardonik* Nikolai Chernyshevskii. Party leaders in both camps generally came from the same intellectual and social milieu and shared common experiences as members of the revolutionary underground (the illegal revolutionary groups that sought to overthrow the tsarist order). Until World War I, they all generally agreed that Russia needed two revolutions. The first would clear away the tsarist regime and establish a "bourgeois" democratic republic with a capitalist economy; the second would overturn capitalism and create some sort of "toilers'" or "workers'" democracy with a socialist economy. They also agreed that the socialists must radicalize and organize the toilers (especially factory workers) toward the future revolution.

Factional disputes between the exiled socialist party leaders had relatively little influence on the day-to-day work of grassroots socialist activists—the people who were "on the ground" in Russia. In practice, party allegiances could have more to do with who had introduced you to socialist politics than with adherence to the details of party programs. People moved from party to party or considered themselves members of more than one party. Rivalries between factions existed, of course, and sometimes erupted into vicious disagreements. But such conflicts were less important than the common revolutionary cause, the struggle for a more equitable and more just social and political order.

Although party leaders often came from the intelligentsia, "ordinary people" played critical roles in the revolutionary movement. Factory workers, students, teachers, and peasant labor migrants—people whose names are often lost to history—were not simply passive recipients of propaganda and did not simply take directions from the socialist intelligentsia. In addition to studying the writings of Lenin and other intellectuals, historians also must consider why socialist doctrines resonated with the experiences of the lower classes and how people filtered the ideas and language of the socialists and blended it with other influences, such as their religious convictions. Workers' own understandings of socialism and social justice shaped their activism, guided their behavior during strikes and demonstrations, and conditioned their relations with other social groups (for instance, their hostility to the bourgeoisie—the property-owning middle class) and their relations with the tsarist state.

Growing Discontent among National Minorities

The Russian Empire was a multinational state. In 1897, the year of Russia's first modern census, native speakers of Russian accounted for only 45 percent of the empire's population (about 56 million of 125 million people). The Russian Empire included not only Eastern European territories, but also the Caucasus, Central Asia, and the vast expanse of Siberia. (Many historians describe the Russian Empire as composed of "internal" colonies, in contrast to the British or French empires, which controlled overseas colonies.) Contemporary critics of the tsarist government often referred to the Russian Empire as a "prison house of nations." Indeed, the Russian government brutally crushed the cultural, as well as political, independence of national, ethnic, and religious minorities and imposed a policy of "Russification." For example, tsarist laws restricted where Jews could live, where they could own land, what professions they could practice, and how many of them could attend universities. Many high-ranking tsarist state officials, including Tsar Nicholas II, were open and unapologetic antisemites, and it was widely believed that the tsarist government had a hand in waves of brutal anti-Jewish violence (the *pogroms*). The tsarist government's nationalities policy was complex, however, and differed depending on the region and the minority group. Policies toward Catholic Poles and Protestant Finns differed from those toward Muslim Turkic peoples or toward Jews. And in the dramatic case of Jews, recent studies have shown that tsarist government officials—for all of their vehement antisemitism—did not plan or organize the pogroms. That does not discount the importance of "the nationality question" to the revolution's origins. If anything, historians now are far more sensitive than in the past to the ways that ethnic identities and national consciousness shaped the revolution.

The Messy Issue of "Identity"

The attention that Russian historians pay to ethnic identities—and to "identities" more generally—reflects big trends in the historical profession in the late 20th century (the development of social history, labor history, women's history, and "new cultural" history). It once was common and acceptable for historians to make sweeping statements about the "Russian national character" or huge generalizations about the "dark [meaning primitive or ignorant] Russian peasantry." Most professional historians today soundly reject this sort of "essentialism," which often had racist overtones.

Moreover, historians are conscious that life is far more complicated than the categories that we create to describe it. Russia in 1914 was undergoing major social transformations. The law still identified people according to premodern legal "estates"—the nobles, the clergy, the peasants, the townspeople, the merchants, and so on. In some ways, these categories remained important and continued to shape how people thought about themselves and others. In other ways, they had become archaic. A "peasant" from rural Smolensk Province, for example, may have spent his entire adult life working in a factory in Moscow.

A person's sense of social identity—how that person defines himself or herself in relationship to others in society—can be complex. It can change over time, and it often depends on contexts. In the setting of his work, our peasant from Smolensk might think of himself as a Moscow worker or as skilled carpenter. But in other settings, he might define himself as a member of the fellow villagers' association of Iartsevo (a large village in Smolensk), or as an Orthodox Christian, or as a supporter of the Socialist Revolutionaries, or as a Russian. Historians recently have become particularly interested in the question of how ordinary people understand national identity.

Many historians argue that ordinary people in the Russian Empire, and particularly in urban Russia, had come to understand the world around them as divided into "us"—the lower classes (in Russian the *nizy*, or lower strata)—versus "them"—the privileged elite made up of nobles, bourgeois property owners, and state officials (in Russian the *verkhi*, or upper strata). Even when these adversarial conceptions of social identity did not strictly align with Marxist social class categories and divisions (proletarians—the property-less working class—versus the bourgeoisie—the property-owning, capitalist middle class), they still helped to undermine the tsarist order's authority and shaped the course of the 1917 Revolutions.

Did the Great War Hasten or Hinder Revolution?

Just as historians assign different weight to different long-term and intermediate-term causes of the revolution, they also disagree over the relative significance of short-term causes. Most short-term causes are associated with World War I, with the stresses that the war put on Russian society, the government's failure to organize the war effort effectively, and the importance of wartime corruption and scandals in undermining public faith in the tsar and his government. In the 1960s to 1980s, Russian historians were particularly divided over a speculative "what if?" question: What if Russia had not fought in World War I? Would the revolution have happened anyway, or could it have been avoided?

Russia faced serious long-term problems, but did those problems make revolution inevitable? Some historians have argued that Russia could have avoided revolution were it not for the Great War.[4] According to this view, the 1905 constitutional reforms and other government concessions set

Russia on the path toward gradual, peaceful reform and stability. It was the Great War that forced Russia from this path, exposed the regime's weaknesses, shattered public faith in the government and in the possibility of gradual change, and pushed the population past the brink of rebellion. This school of thought—sometimes described as the "optimistic" perspective—does not ignore long- and intermediate-term causes, but concludes that they were less important than the strains and stresses of war. During the Cold War, and even in some post–Cold War studies of historiography, the "optimistic" perspective is sometimes over-simplistically described as the "liberal" viewpoint.

In contrast to this "optimistic" perspective are the arguments of "conservative" historians who see cultural and intellectual trends as the Russian Revolution's central causes. These scholars stress Russia's traditions of authoritarian rule, but put relatively more emphasis on the role of intellectuals who believed that change could only come through violent revolution.[5] Ironically, this view had much in common with ideologically doctrinaire, state-sanctioned Communist histories in the Soviet Union, which credited Lenin's Bolshevik Party with leading Russia to the February Revolution and then guiding the masses toward the "inevitable" October Bolshevik Revolution. In both interpretations, the impact of World War I was of almost incidental significance compared with the will of the revolutionaries.

In the Soviet Union, those few historians whose rejected Communist Party–mandated simplifications still generally accepted Leninist interpretations of the revolution's origins, including the idea that the tsarist regime had been facing a "revolutionary situation" in 1914.[6] According to this argument, the revolutionary movement had been building momentum steadily since 1911, was accelerated by public outrage at a massacre of workers in Siberia's Lena Gold Fields in April 1912, and reached a peak in a workers' general strike in St. Petersburg (Petrograd) in July 1914. Historians in the Soviet Union generally argued that World War I delayed the outbreak of a revolution—in other words, that the tsarist government would have been overthrown in 1914 were it not for the war. According to this argument, the tsarist regime used the wartime situation to smash the workers' movement, the labor press, and the socialists' organizational networks. Soviet historians argued that it then took two years of great wartime suffering for the Russian peoples to create another "revolutionary situation," which finally brought down Tsar Nicholas II.

Just as there were parallels between the "conservative" and the doctrinaire Communist versions of history, there also were parallels between serious histories written in the Union of Soviet Socialist Republics and arguments made by historians in the United States and Western Europe. In the 1960s through the 1980s, many historians in the United States and Western Europe argued that pre-1914 political and social divisions in Russia overwhelmed progress toward peaceful reform. They often used the term "polarization" to describe these political and social divisions.[7] In prewar Russia, they argued, educated society (the *obshchestvo*) was deeply divided from the tsarist government. In other words, the two groups were at opposite poles (polarized), and very few people took the middle ground. At the same time, the privileged elites and the middle class (the *verkhi*) were deeply divided from the urban and rural lower classes (the *nizy*). Many historians argued that by 1914 this "dual polarization" had taken Russia to the brink of revolution, and that the Great War simply forestalled the inevitable. Advocates of this "social polarization paradigm" often are labeled "pessimists," because they infer that peaceful reform without revolution was improbable.[8]

This historiographic debate had its roots in disputes among revolutionary émigrés, but in a sense, it also was a product of the Cold War political environment, in that how one viewed the question often reflected one's view of the Soviet Union's historical legitimacy. In any case, relatively few historians took stark, "either-or" positions. Most specialists argued that the stresses and strains of war, rather than disrupting an otherwise stable system, provided the final blows to the already staggering autocratic regime.

The end of the Cold War and the collapse of the Soviet Union gave historians a chance to rethink many questions regarding the causes of the Russian Revolution. Historians not only gained access to previously unavailable archives and documents in Russia, but also turned their attention to previously understudied geographic regions and social groups. Since the 1990s, historians have been looking for new ways to understand the Russian Revolution and its place in history. One important recent trend among historians is to rethink how we divide the story of Russia's history into distinct chapters. Many historians now stress that instead of thinking of 1917 as a dividing line between two acutely different periods of history, it is better to think of the events of 1917 as a stage in a "continuum of crisis," which lasted from the onset of World War I until the end of the Russian Civil War.[9] Doing so has opened new insights on the relationship between developments in Russia and those elsewhere in wartime Europe, as well as continuities in state policies (such as policies toward grain collection and toward the surveillance of populations) that link the wartime tsarist state, the 1917 Provisional Government, the Bolshevik regime, and the anti-Bolshevik territorial governments of the Civil War period (the so-called Whites). It also has important implications for the study of revolutionary social history. One recent study, for example, has argued that during the war peasants developed new ways of thinking and interacting with the state that shaped their views of revolution in 1917 and then influenced their interactions with the Soviet government during the Civil War.[10]

A Brief Description of Russian Conditions during World War I

In July 1914, Tsar Nicholas II decided to mobilize the Russian Army against the Austro-Hungarians. For more than a decade, tensions had been building toward a general European war. The tsar's declaration—Russia's response to the complicated diplomatic crisis set off when a Serbian nationalist assassinated the Austrian Archduke Franz Ferdinand in the Bosnian city of Sarajevo on 28 June 1914—brought matters to a head. Germany responded by declaring war on Russia, which set off a chain reaction of war declarations. Dominos set up by prewar alliance systems crashed one upon another: Russia, Great Britain, France, and their allies now were at war against Germany, Austro-Hungary, and their allies (which from 1915 would include the Ottoman Turks). Many of the tsar's advisors thought Russia simply could not back down from this war, especially given its diplomatic failures since the humiliating Russo-Japanese War of 1904–1905. Most of them believed that the war would strengthen Russia's position in the European order and reinforce its role as the leader of the Slavic nations. A few expected that war would quell the strikes and student demonstrations that had been building in number and force in the first half of 1914. The conservative official Petr Durnovo, however, had warned the tsar that Russia was ill-prepared for a major war, that Russia's allies would let it bear the brunt of the conflict, and that the result could very well be collapse and revolution.

The declaration of war did bring a powerful, if brief, burst of patriotic support for the tsarist government. The Fourth State Duma, including the chief figures in the liberal opposition, pledged to support the government and voted to dissolve itself until the war's end. Both the tsar and State Duma leaders spoke of unity, of the need to set aside domestic disputes while defending the motherland from the Germans and Austro-Hungarians. The Russians—like their German enemies—described their cause as a just war against aggressors whose actions threatened European civilization. Across Europe, even the socialist parties urged patriotic support of their own governments and voted in favor of the war. In Russia, though, only a minority of the socialists took this position. Instead, most Russian social-ists condemned the war as an imperialist venture in which workers from different countries would butcher each other for a cause that enriched the capitalists. The war split Russia's already fractious socialists into hostile camps: the patriotic "defensists," who called for complete victory against the German enemy; socialists who opposed the "imperialist" war, but believed that Russia must defend itself from aggression; and radical anti-war activists, who argued that a Russian defeat would actually speed the revolution.

Once the war began, the Russian government moved quickly to arrest the antiwar socialists and cracked down on workers' organizations and the labor press. The war initially dampened the strike movement, but popular reactions to the government's mobilization efforts were mixed. There were great displays of patriotic fervor, helped along by carefully orchestrated prowar propaganda. But there also was abundant evidence of popular ambivalence and even open opposition to the war, including violent "disturbances" by peasants who resisted conscription or were unwilling to turn their horses over for military use.

Within six months, the human and economic costs of the war badly eroded whatever political capital the tsar's government had gained by declaring war. Russia had a huge army, but it was out-gunned and out-organized by the mechanized German forces. Russia did win some early victories in 1914, but its military casualties were appalling—in August 1914 alone the Germans killed, wounded, or captured more than 300,000 Russian soldiers in Eastern Prussia. In the fall, the German Army advanced almost to Warsaw. The Russians fared better against the Austro-Hungarians in Galicia, but by December 1914, the army was low on supplies, including artillery shells. The conflict had exposed the fragility of Russia's economy, which was ill suited and ill prepared for a sustained mechanized war. It also demonstrated the state bureaucracy's staggering capacity for mismanagement and the inadequacies of the reactionary appointees who oversaw Russia's military affairs. In early 1915, the tide of the war turned powerfully against the Russians. The Austrians pushed the Russian Army out of Galicia, and the Germans steadily drove through the empire's Polish and Lithuanian provinces. For Russians, this became known as the Great Retreat. Along with the retreating soldiers came millions of civilian refugees, including Jews who the Russian Army itself had brutally evacuated. By summer 1915, Russia faced a refugee crisis that compounded its already serious problems of transportation and food supply and that accentuated social tensions on the home front.

Among the civilian population, it was the peasantry who felt the pains of the war most sharply. Army mobilization dragged away nearly a third of all the men in the villages—about 1 million men per month were conscripted in 1914–1915. Conscription brought tragedy for hundreds of thousands of families. It altered life in the villages, as soldiers' wives often had to take up "male" roles as breadwinners and heads of households. And it created a shortage of labor that hampered Russia's already inefficient agrarian system. As the war continued, the amount of grain that actually made its way to market declined. Initially, at least, urban workers felt the burdens of war less than did villagers. For much of the war, skilled workers were exempted from military service, and for a time, wages actually increased. But as the war dragged on, working conditions worsened, employers demanded longer hours and more productivity, and inflation began to eat away at wage increases. Russian industry simply could not keep up with the needs of the army without a sharp decline in the availability of consumer goods. Prices for everyday items like sugar rose more quickly than did wages. In mid-1915 the number and intensity of strikes by urban workers and by farm laborers again began to rise, although they did not yet reach prewar levels. Scores of antiwar protests and goods riots broke out in the countryside, including dramatic, violent protests by women.

As living conditions in Russia declined, crowds vented their anger by attacking refugees and minorities, particularly Jews, who fell into both categories. At the same time, the brutal policies of commanders in territories occupied by the Russian Army fueled anti-Russian sentiments and nationalism. This was especially true in Poland, despite the Russian government's vague promise of a unified and semiautonomous Polish state, and in the Ukrainian districts of Galicia. In Transcaucasia, the military's treatment of the Azeri people as potential Turkish sympathizers aggravated ethnic tensions and ultimately aided the pan-Islamic movement (which called for the political unification and autonomy of predominantly Muslim territories); in Central Asia, the military's abuse of the Kazakh and Kirgiz peoples triggered a bloody but unsuccessful rebellion in 1916.

The military's abuse of the civilian population was one of several factors that pushed the leaders of the State Duma back into opposition. Convinced that the government could not run the war effort, the State Duma's liberals and moderates formed a Progressive Bloc in 1915. The State Duma then demanded that Nicholas II appoint new government ministers who would "enjoy the country's confidence." The tsar already had begun reorganizing his cabinet, several members of which had been the subject of embarrassing scandals involving corruption (and even accusations of complicity in spying for the Germans). Nicholas appointed several able civil servants, and some of the tsar's new ministers urged that he cooperate more fully with the State Duma. The government finally agreed to let zemstvo professionals and municipal government agencies form national "unions." Together with reenergized voluntary agencies, the Union of Zemstvos and the Union of Towns began to coordinate the war effort on the home front. Between the work of these agencies and new productivity in heavy industry, Russia actually was better prepared for war in early 1916 than it had been in 1914.

Still, the tsar and his closest advisors did not trust the State Duma, nor did the Duma's leaders have faith in the tsar's government. Nicholas II, urged on by his wife, Tsaritsa Alexandria, and by their "friend," the mystic Rasputin, replaced several able ministers with reactionaries whose records of service were, at best, dubious. In August 1915, Nicholas II decided to assume personal command of Russia's armed forces, against the objections of the State Duma. From the army's perspective, this seemed a blessing, at least at first, because the tsar allowed the general staff's most talented commanders to guide operations. In June 1916, forces commanded by General Brusilov scored major victories in Galicia. In late summer, though, the Brusilov Offensive collapsed, and Russia's armies were driven back yet again. War-weariness shattered the morale of Russia's soldiers and sailors, who deeply resented harsh military discipline. By late 1916, even top military commanders privately doubted the tsar's ability to guide Russia to victory.

War-weariness also magnified social tensions on the home front. By late summer 1916, the combination of peasant reluctance to give up their grain and government mishandling of the transportation and supply networks had created food shortages. In the fall, the government imposed food rationing, but speculation and hoarding drove up prices and eroded the average family's purchasing power. Angry women waiting in long lines for bread became a common sight in Russia's towns and cities. Peasants and urban workers compared their own plight with the privileges of propertied elites, who seemed immune from wartime hardships. (Expensive restaurants, for example, had been exempted from wartime prohibition and served alcohol to well-heeled customers). The number of strikes increased, and their length and intensity would continue to build through the winter months. And in late 1916, Russia was awash with rumors about German spies and the gluttony of "bourgeois" war profiteers. The most sordid rumors revolved around the Tsaritsa Alexandra, born a German princess, and her relationship with Rasputin.

As the 1916 military offensive collapsed, Nicholas II appointed a new crew of even more inept reactionaries and cronies of Rasputin to positions in his cabinet—including men rumored to have pro-German sympathies. State Duma members worried aloud about alleged German agents in the Imperial Court. During fall and winter 1916, relations between the tsar and the State Duma broke down almost completely, and even conservative State Duma members openly criticized the government's failure to lead. Key figures in the Progressive Bloc and in the military command began to privately discuss pressuring Nicholas II into appointing a new cabinet, one made up of leaders from the State Duma and the Union of Towns and Zemstvos. Some hoped to forced the tsar into giving the State Duma control over the government—in effect, turning Russia into a constitutional monarchy on the British model. In December 1916, conservative court insiders murdered Rasputin, an act that they hoped might save the tottering monarchy. But Nicholas and Alexandra reacted by digging in their heels, dismissing ministers who had cooperated with the State Duma, and appointing even more objectionable officials in their place.

By early 1917 rampant rumors, war-weariness, worsening living conditions, and the tsar's inept leadership had seriously undermined Nicholas II's political legitimacy. And when the monarchy's final crisis came in late February 1917, few people in Russia were willing to fight to preserve the Romanov dynasty.

CHAPTER ONE
THE WAR AND POLITICAL ELITES

DOCUMENT 1.1
MIKHAIL RODZIANKO, ADDRESS TO A SPECIAL SESSION OF THE FOURTH STATE DUMA, 26 JULY 1914[1]

On 26 July 1914, Tsar Nicholas II convened a special all-day session of the Fourth State Duma to display public support for Russia's war effort. At a presession reception at the tsar's Winter Palace, State Duma President Mikhail Rodzianko assured Nicholas II that all Russia would support the war effort. The following document is Rodzianko's opening speech to the special State Duma session, which reiterated his comments at the tsar's reception. The text is from a transcript printed in the official government newspaper, The Government Courier *(Pravitel'stvennyi vestnik). As in many such transcripts of meetings, interjections from the audience are indicated within parentheses.*

Gentlemen of the State Duma,

At this difficult hour for our motherland, the Emperor has convened the State Duma to demonstrate the Russian Tsar's oneness with his loyal people. At His Majesty's reception today, the State Duma responded to the Sovereign's call. We all know that Russia did not want war, and Russia's people have no desire for conquest. But fate has seen fit to drag us into this conflict, and now we face the enormous task of defending the State's integrity and unity.

In this maelstrom of events, unprecedented in world history, we are comforted by the majestic and dignified calm we all have exhibited. This calm keenly, and without wasted words, shows the whole world the strength and greatness of the Russian soul. (*Stormy applause and shouts from all sides:* "Bravo!" "Hurrah!")[2] Calmly, without boasting, we tell the invaders, "Hands off!" (*Applause, shouts from throughout the hall:* "Hurrah!") "We will not allow you to touch our Holy Russia!" Our people are good and peace-loving, but they are awesome and powerful when forced to defend themselves. (*Stormy applause.*) We will tell them, "Look here: you believe that we Russians are divided by conflict and hatred, but when danger threatens our common motherland, all boundless Russia's peoples become one family." (*Applause from all factions.*) The Russian giant shall not hang his head in discouragement, no matter what trials he may endure. He will bear it all on his powerful shoulders. And when we have driven out the enemy, then peace, prosperity, and happiness again will shine forth from our common indivisible motherland, in the full glory of its indestructible greatness. (*Continuous applause*)

Gentlemen of the State Duma! At this hour, our thoughts and wishes go out to our borders, where our courageous army and glorious navy move unhesitatingly into action. (*Applause from all the benches.*) Our thoughts are with our sons and brothers, whose inherent bravery personifies the greatness of our country. May the Lord God aid, strengthen, and protect them. We ardently desire our heroes' success and glory. It is the duty of we who remain at home to work continuously to care for families left without breadwinners. Let our army know that, not only in our words, but by our deeds, we will ensure that their families do not suffer hardships. (*Stormy, continuous applause and cries of,* "Bravo!")

DOCUMENT 1.2
DECLARATION OF SOCIAL DEMOCRATIC STATE DUMA
DEPUTIES ON THE WAR, 26 JULY 1914[3]

Not all State Duma members agreed with Rodzianko's pledge to support the war. The following document is a 26 July 1914 declaration by five Bolshevik and six Menshevik State Duma deputies.

A horrible unprecedented disaster has befallen the world's people. Millions of workers will be torn from peaceful labor, ruined, and pulled into a bloody whirlpool. Millions of families are doomed to hunger. War has begun.

When the European governments prepared for war, the European proletariat—led by the German workers—held fraternal protests against the ruling circles' preparations. In Russia, prewar persecution of the workers' press and workers' organizations prevented workers from openly protesting against the war. But Russian proletarians' hearts joined with those of European workers during the European proletariat's grand antiwar demonstrations.

We who represent Russia's working class consider it our duty to declare that the capitalist governments' policies of force and conquest reveal that all belligerent countries share responsibility for this war.[4] We declare that this war contradicts the sensibilities of conscious proletarian elements in Russia, as in the entire world.[5]

Unlike the ruling class, which accompanies its predatory policies with false cries of patriotism, the proletariat—as protector of freedom and the people's interests—will defend its honor and the great people's culture from all threats, internal or external. While the government calls for a united people, rightist circles have dragged Russia's people—like all peoples—into the war against their will. We must highlight the hypocrisy of these calls for unity.

The people cannot unite behind a government that does not act according to the people's will and enslaves the people. It cannot support the government when the popular masses—those whom war always mows down—have no rights, when the worker and peasant press is silenced, when workers' organizations are routed, when fighters for a free and happy people are imprisoned, and when troops and police fire on Petersburg's workers. Russia's peoples cannot unite behind a government that persecutes nationalities and makes them live in an atmosphere of violence and oppression.

The conscious proletariat in the belligerent countries will not join in war's madness and the barbaric debauchery it brings. We have the deep conviction that the proletariat's international solidarity will provide all mankind with a means to speedily end this war.

We believe that conditions for peaceful negotiations will come, not from the rapacious governments' diplomacy, but from their peoples, who will take matters into their own hands. We also hold the deep conviction that the war will finally open the European popular masses' eyes to the real source of the violence and oppression from which they suffer, and this current dreadful outbreak of barbarism will be the last.

DOCUMENT 1.3
"TO ALL RUSSIAN SOCIETY," A SOCIALIST REVOLUTIONARY ANTIWAR LEAFLET FROM KHARKOV, 17 AUGUST 1914[6]

The following document is a leaflet published by a Socialist Revolutionary group in the Ukrainian industrial city Kharkov. Historians sometimes call the Socialist Revolutionaries (SRs) a "peasants' party," but they had strong support among workers, students, and educated professionals. Like the Social Democrats, the SRs were divided into factions that differed over tactical issues. The war amplified these divisions: some senior SR leaders supported the war, while others vigorously condemned it. The authors of this leaflet belonged to an antiwar faction. Note that they use the term "democracy" to refer to the nonpropertied social classes.

"Through struggle, you will win back your rights."[7]

To All Russian Society: Citizens!

Terrible recent events in the world war have compelled the government to appeal to the people and to the State Duma—that phantom of a people's government—in a quest for unity and a search for support. The government has recognized that the state's might lay not in military force, but in internal order and unity. In its quest, the government has made promises that we must doubt, because their fulfillment would signify a turning point in Russian history. But these promises have blinded society, and the blinded people are ready to take a promissory note from a government that has never paid up in the past. A government that has not taken a single step toward meeting the democratic masses' demands— that gives only words, not concrete deeds—and has shamelessly refused to keep promises in the past.

Perhaps because of Russia's extraordinary position in current world events, those who have been blinded—the widest circles of Russia society—have forgotten their own liberation movement and their own vital demands. They abandoned these in a frenzied nightmare and replaced them with unrestrained Tsarism's fantasies of a slave Russia. The fog of international politics has clouded public activists' heads. Not a single free and honest voice has spoken against the ulcer that is the Russian autocracy. But we cannot remain silent. We cannot forget that the Russian Inquisition conducted by the Russian Tsar and his gang (who dragged Russia's people over war's terrible precipice) has spilled more blood than have the Germans. Those who authentically love the people, those who care for the people's domestic wellbeing and happiness, must be courageous and raise their voices against power.

You acknowledge society's power, you appeal to society for support, you give or allude to promises. But we demand proof. We demand actions—steps that meet Russia's democratic circles' demands halfway. You would liberate Galician Rus' from the "Schwabs."[8] But will you give the Galician Ukrainians the same rights that they have in Austria? Would you give Russians the same political privileges Kaiser Wilhelm has given German citizens? Where is the guarantee that victorious Russia will not again become a dark chasm, bereft of any freedom of thought? There is none.

This is what Russian society must say. This is what it must demand. With one voice, all Russia must lay out the following demands: a total political amnesty; universal electoral rights; freedom for the peasants' and workers' movement in all its forms; abolition of all nationality-based restrictions; democratization of town and zemstvo self-government.

Citizens! Abolish the militaristic poison. Out of love for the people, you must steer the ruling elites onto a path that can only lead to the people's complete and total liberation.

The Kharkov Group of the Party of Socialist Revolutionaries
Kharkov, 17 August 1914

DOCUMENT 1.4
GEORGII PLEKHANOV, "A LETTER OF EXPLANATION"[9]

The following document is a letter from Russia's senior Menshevik leader, Georgii Plekhanov, whose insistence on Russia's victory against "German and Austro-Hungarian aggression" set himself and his faction, Unity *(Edinstvo) to the right of most other Mensheviks. The letter appeared in* Speech *(Rech), the Petrograd newspaper of the liberal Party of People's Freedom (the Constitutional Democrats, or Kadets), on 15 October 1914. In the letter, Plekhanov refers to a speech he gave in Paris, at a send-off gathering for fellow Russian socialist émigrés who had volunteered to join the French Army in late July 1914.*

Comrades!

My friends in Russia inform me of comments (and, it should be said, inaccurate rumors) circulating in Russian society's democratic circles and among workers regarding my "parting words" to Russian comrades on the eve of their departure from Paris to enlist as volunteers in French Republican Army. Comrades in Russia have written me, and their sense of my "parting words" is filled with distortions and mistakes. To avoid misunderstanding, I must expound on the simple meaning of my "parting words."

They come to this—In Austria-Hungary and Germany's war against France, Belgium, and England, the interests of the *international proletariat and social progress* are with the latter three states. Therefore all concerned should wish for those states' victory. The comrades to whom I addressed these "parting words" fully agreed. That is why they took up arms to defend the French Republic.

At this event, I did not speak at all about "the war's Eastern Theater." But I did discuss Russia's interests in a conversation with a Russian professor, which was briefly noted in *The Russian Word*.[10] I have read this article, which is the source of the misunderstandings. In my comments to the professor . . . I said firmly that if Germany wins this war, it will make Russia into its economic vassal, and this would prevent Russia's further economic and socio-political development toward a democratic republic, a path that accords with our party's aims.

The article correctly said that in my conversation with the professor, I demonstrated the feelings of an "Ententist."[11] . . . In principle, I am against war. But now that war has begun, I cannot follow the council of Pushkin's Captain: "Sort out who is innocent and who is guilty, but punish both."[12] I wish for the defeat of the guilty, i.e., the aggressor. And I am deeply convinced that the aggressor is Germany and its ally, Austria-Hungary. Had my conversation with the Russian professor taken place after the German Army's truly barbaric deeds, such as its destruction of Leuven and bombardment of Reims Cathedral, then I would have wished for its defeat even more heatedly.[13]

DOCUMENT 1.5
VLADIMIR LENIN, "THE WAR AND SOCIAL DEMOCRACY"[14]

Vladimir Lenin, the Social Democrat Bolsheviks' leader, was in exile in Switzerland when the war began. He drafted the following document in August or early September 1914. After circulating among members of the Bolshevik Central Committee, a final draft appeared in the Geneva-based Bolshevik newspaper, Social-Democrat (Sotsial-Demokrat), *on 1 November 1914. Like many of Lenin's essays, it is a polemic against the other socialist factions. But it also contains arguments central to Lenin's wartime writings: condemnation of the Second Socialist International for failing to oppose the war; the claim that capitalist states were fighting an "imperialist war"; insistence that socialists use the war as a springboard for revolution; and "revolutionary defeatism"—the idea that military defeat would speed the Russian revolution.[15] Like other Russian Marxists, Lenin still believed Russia must overthrow tsarism and develop a bourgeois capitalist democracy before it could have a socialist revolution. (In 1915, Lenin began to argue that the war made a socialist revolution possible in Russia.) Lenin's 1914 position, though, was still radical enough for the tsarist government to strip Bolshevik State Duma members of parliamentary immunity and arrest them for treason. Like other socialists, Lenin used the term "the democracy" to refer to the laboring classes. In this document (and throughout this book), I have placed summarized text in brackets.*

After decades of preparation by all Europe's governments and bourgeois parties, the European War has begun. It was inevitable. The arms race, the intensified struggle between leading countries for markets in the latest (imperialist) stage of capitalist development, and the dynastic interests of East Europe's most backwards monarchies all have led to war. This war's real essence—its significance, its meaning—will be seizure of territories; subjugation of foreign nations; ruin of competing states and plunder of their wealth; diversion of the Russian, German, and other laboring masses' attention from domestic political crises; deception of workers with nationalism; and destruction of the worker-vanguard, so as to weaken the proletarian revolutionary movement.

It is the Social Democrats' primary responsibility to reveal the war's true significance, to unmercifully unmask the lies, sophisms, and "patriotic" phrases that the dominant classes—the landlords and bourgeoisie—spread in the war's defense.

The German bourgeoisie heads one belligerent camp. It deceives the working class and laboring masses by claiming that they fight to defend their country's freedom and culture, to destroy reactionary tsarism and liberate the peoples it oppresses. [Lenin goes on to argue that the German ruling classes will save tsarism to prevent revolution in Russia. Their real war aim is to plunder Serbia, France, and Belgium.] . . . The German bourgeoisie spreads fairy tales about a defensive war, but in reality has chosen to make war at the most opportune moment, when it can use the latest improvements in military technology and forestall the rearmament already planned by France and Russia.

The English and French bourgeoisies head the other belligerent camp. They deceive the working class and toiling masses by insisting that they fight to defend their countries' freedom and culture against German militarism and despotism. . . . In reality, the English and French bourgeoisies' aim is to seize Germany's colonies and destroy a rival whose rapid economic development has exceeded theirs. For this "noble" purpose, the "advanced" and "democratic" nations help primitive tsarism to tighten its stranglehold on Poland, the Ukraine, etc., and to intensify suppression of revolution in Russia.

[Lenin argues that the bourgeoisie in each belligerent country is disguising predatory war aims. Therefore socialist party leaders have betrayed the proletariat by supporting the war instead of directing workers' energy against their true enemy, the bourgeoisie.]

. . . The [Second] International's leaders have betrayed socialism by voting for war credits, repeating bourgeois-chauvinistic ("patriotic") slogans to justify and defend the war, joining bourgeois government cabinets in the belligerent countries, and so on. The most influential European socialist leaders and socialist newspapers take chauvinist, bourgeois, liberal positions that are not at all socialist.

[Lenin accuses the German and French socialist parties of having "disgraced socialism." He also refutes the German and Austrian Social Democrats' argument that the war is a struggle against tsarism. In reality, he says, Russia was on the verge of revolution when the war erupted, and the war will prolong the tsarist regime.]

Our party, the Russian Social Democratic Labor Party, is suffering great sacrifices because of the war. Our whole legal labor press has been shut down; most workers' organizations have been closed; and many of our comrades have been arrested and exiled. Still, our State Duma parliamentary representatives . . . considered it their absolute duty to *not* vote for war credits. Instead, they protested emphatically by walking out during the Duma session. They considered it their duty to brand the European governments' policies as imperialist. Despite the Tsarist government's heavy oppression, Russian worker-comrades are already publishing illegal proclamations against the war, fulfilling their duty to the democracy and the International.

[Lenin again attacks Social Democrats who supported the war and insists that socialists should "respond to any war declared by the bourgeois governments with increased propaganda in favor of civil war and social revolution." He accuses the Second International's leaders of reformist "opportunism" and abandoning revolutionary class struggle.]

Social Democrats' first duty in every country must be to fight chauvinism in that country. In Russia, chauvinism has been completely embraced by bourgeois liberals (the Kadets), by some Narodniks, right down to the Socialist Revolutionaries, and by "right" Social Democrats.[16] . . . From the international proletariat's perspective, it is impossible to determine the lesser evil for socialism: defeat of one group of belligerents or of the other. But from the standpoint of Russia's working class and toiling masses, we Russian Social Democrats cannot doubt that the lesser evil would be the defeat of the tsarist monarchy, a reactionary and barbarous government that oppresses the most nationalities and the most people in Europe and Asia.

. . . Because of Russia's great backwardness and because it has not yet had its bourgeois revolution, the Social Democrats' tasks still must be to establish three fundamental preconditions for democratic reconstruction: a democratic republic (with complete equality of rights and self-determination for all nationalities); confiscation of landowners' estates; and an eight-hour working day. But in the advanced countries, socialist revolution must be the slogan of the day. This becomes more and more urgent as the war's burdens weigh more and more on the proletariat's shoulders. . . . The greater the number of war victims, the clearer it will be to the laboring masses that the opportunists have betrayed the workers' cause; the clearer it will be that they must turn their weapons against their governments and bourgeoisie. The only proper socialist doctrine is to transform this imperialist war into a civil war. . . . That is the only way the proletariat can free itself from the chauvinist bourgeoisie's influence, the only way it can take rapid steps down the road toward authentic peoples' freedom, the road to socialism.

Long live the international workers' brotherhood against bourgeois chauvinism and patriotism in all countries!
Long live the Proletarian International, freed from opportunism!

The Central Committee of the Russian Social Democratic Labor Party

DOCUMENT 1.6
NIKOLAI AVKSENT'EV, "A YEAR OF STRUGGLES"[17]

Although the war accentuated intraparty tensions among the Socialist Revolutionaries (SRs) and Social Democrats (SDs), it also reinforced similarities that cut across party lines, as well as tendencies toward interparty cooperation (especially in Russia itself). In 1914 in Switzerland, exiled SR leaders Viktor Chernov and Mark Natanson took antiwar positions that anticipated Lenin's arguments. In Paris, other exiled SR leaders took a "defensist" position similar to Plekhanov's. In 1915, the SR and SD circles in Paris began publishing a newspaper, The Call (Prizyv), *to organize socialist support for Russia's war effort. In the following document—an essay from* The Call, *1 October 1915—right SR leader Nikolai Avksent'ev explains the* Prizyv *group's positions and answers its socialist critics.*

This year was hard for Russia. Russian troops at the front were thrown back in early summer. After that, the enemy steadily moved deep into the country. Hundreds of thousands of nearly unarmed Russian soldiers fell, deserted by their motherland. The Sukhomlinovs . . . and Miasoedovs brought the country to the brink of disaster.[18] The old order finally revealed its criminal essence. And it looks like it will carry Russia—which barely clings to life—with it into the abyss.

The only thing that can save Russia from ruin is a powerful and organized public, a powerful democracy—the great, decisive force in the contemporary battle between nations. But émigré revolutionary groups, which live in some other world, propagandize loudly in the name of "internationalism" and "defeatism." They tell the Russian democracy that the war is not its affair. They cry out that Russia's military forces are irrevocably broken. They call for their own country's defeat.

We cannot hesitate. The patriotic elements among Russia's socialists know they must exert all their influence to persuade the Russian democracy, to show it the proper path. It is their duty to take the initiative. [Avksent'ev explains that the "patriotic socialist émigrés" associated with *The Call* have adopted a common platform and share two fundamental beliefs on the war.]

First: socialists have the right and the responsibility to defend their country against aggression. Russian socialists, and the Russian democracy, have a whole-hearted interest in Russia's defense, not only because it is their duty to defend their motherland's independence, but also because participation in defense creates a durable organizational base for the struggle against the old order. In our platform, we wrote that "[t]he revolutionary democracy's struggle for general social and economic goals depends on its participants' efforts in national self-defense against hostile aggression. *The path that leads to victory is the path that leads to freedom.*" Therefore "Russia's liberation from its internal enemies (the old order and its defenders), will result from Russia's self-defense against foreign invasion—this is the great goal to which all other aims and considerations must be subordinated."

Second: In this great goal's behalf, we must unify all Russia's revolutionary democratic forces. They must have a single plan and a single impulse. . . .

Our united declaration, our call for unity, was met by angry retorts from the "internationalists" and "defeatists". . . . They call for a brotherhood of peoples, but they won't tolerate comradely cooperation between socialist parties. They insist on the right to be "custodians of the sacred temple." They angrily tell us, "Withdraw your proclamations!" The "panicky internationalists" [in the Bolsheviks'] camp accused Social Democrats who had joined "*Prizyv*" of uniting with people "outside the party." They describe our declaration as the "proclamation of a war party" and call for a break with us. The "internationalists" in the Socialist Revolutionaries' camp circulated a similar resolution to their party comrades. . . .

[Avksent'ev claims that his group actually represents the majority of activists in Russia, who want "the unification of the entire workers' socialist movement."] . . . Of course, our unification is hardly even a first step toward unifying the Russian socialist movement, which should be our dream and that of every Russian socialist worthy of the name. Of course, we have joined together for only one concrete task. Still, it has great significance. It demonstrates the possibility and profitability of *protracted common work*. . . . It is a first step toward mutual trust and comradeship. It is the result of *common* resolution, common activism. History will consider *these* facts; *these* facts provide a clear historical lesson.

[Avksent'ev dismisses the idea his position is an endorsement of the old regime. He repeats that *The Call*, not the internationalists, represents the mood of Russia's democratic forces. He cites several examples of successful interparty cooperation in the war effort and argues that these have pushed forward the democracy's struggle for civil rights.]

. . . The revolutionary democracy is on the correct path, the one we have strived toward. Of course, we do not arrogantly claim it does so *because of us*. But we feel happily confident that it is *with us*. We will be satisfied if our declaration played a role in setting it on this path. The revolutionary democracy is on the correct path. But its enemies are still strong. The dark forces of old Russia seek to disrupt the democracy's work, to reduce its power to oppose the foreign enemy, to extinguish its struggle for rights. A difficult, great task stands before us.

A people's best heroic traits are revealed in its efforts at defense. [Avksent'ev explains that for the ancient Greeks, the demigod Hercules embodied heroism.] . . . The Russian people and Russia's democratic warrior-heroes have a historic mission more difficult than the trials of Hercules. The Russian people must accomplish its feats simultaneously, rather than one after another. It must simultaneously clean the Augean stables of old order's remnants, break the iron chains that hold it, and battle against giants.[19] These difficult tasks at this complex hour in Russia's history demand great efforts from democratic Russia. But if inspired with confidence in its success, democratic Russia will be victorious. It truly holds the lever of action in its own hands.

We involuntary exiles—forcefully separated from the great matters that occupy our motherland—quiver as we watch the Russian democracy's strength and its struggle. As in previous years, we can only send it our very warmest brotherly greetings.

DOCUMENT 1.7
THE RUSSIAN PEOPLE'S UNION OF THE ARCHANGEL MICHAEL ON THE WAR, DECEMBER 1914[20]

The following document is an excerpt from a letter that circulated among members of the ultranationalist Russian People's Union of the Archangel

Michael in December 1914. The group had been created by right-wing politician Vladimir Purishkevich when he left the ultranationalist Union of Russian People in 1908. This document concerns an article in the patriotic newspaper Russian Citizen (Rossiiskii grazhdanin) *in which P. F. Bulatsel defended German Kaiser Wilhelm II and claimed Germany was not to blame for the war. This excerpt is from the letter's middle section, in which the organization's leaders reject "Germanophilia" and clarify their position on the war.[21] Charges of Germanophilia were of concern to the political right: rumors about German spies and German influence in the Imperial Court were rife during the war, and some liberal leaders claimed that the rightists wanted a separate peace with Germany.*

We, members of the Union of the Archangel Michael, are monarchists, in that we defend Russian Tsarism as an unrestricted Autocracy, which we consider the fundament and bulwark of culture in general and our Fatherland's military development in particular. There is a great gulf between our Russian monarchism and slavish admiration of the malicious Hohenzollern and Habsburg dynasties.[22] Our Union will welcome those dynasties' annihilation and humiliation as Russia's glory and the entire Christian world's triumph. And that is why the [Union's] Main Chamber considers it necessary to explain clearly that our monarchism is not in any way Germanophilic. . . .

DOCUMENT 1.8
A DIRECTIVE FROM SUPREME COMMANDER NIKOLAI NIKOLAEVICH ROMANOV, 7 JANUARY 1915; TSAR NICHOLAS II AS A FRONT SOLDIER[23]

When the war began, Tsar Nicholas II appointed his uncle, Grand Duke Nikolai Nikolaevich, as supreme commander.[24] The following document is a directive issued by the grand duke on 7 January 1915. It appeared in the February 1915 issue of The War: Chronicle and Commentary (Voina. Khronika i otkliki). *Such magazines presented carefully selected military news and patriotic photographs to bolster public support for the war. It is accompanied by an image from the magazine's cover in 1915: a photograph of Tsar Nicholas II in an infantry uniform with a rifle, as if ready to join the battle.*

The Supreme Commander's Directive No. 13, 7 January 1915, for General Distribution at His Imperial Highness' Order
Our enemies are resorting to proclamations and appeals to convince our troops in the combat zone to stop fighting. In this, the Austrians have exceeded the bounds of insolence, vileness, and high crimes. The Austrian Army has deliberately ordered its lower ranks to scatter among our troops, Holy Russia's brave sons, proclamations that our insolent enemies allege are from his Most Holy Imperial Majesty and bear his signature.

All loyal subjects know that in Russia everyone—from Supreme Commander to common soldier—unquestioningly obeys the holy and sovereign will of our dearly beloved Imperial Majesty, who is anointed by God and alone has authority to conduct or suspend the war.

Our enemies have concocted this base forgery, this most criminal business, because they cannot count on their own strength for success in the battlefield. Understand, Russian warrior-heroes, that our enemies have

"His Imperial Highness, His Majesty Emperor Nicholas Aleksandrovich in the uniform of the lower ranks." (*Voina. Khronika i otkliki* no. 6 (1915), cover.)

stooped to such a despicable low crime out of complete moral decay and because they absolutely can no longer carry on the fight in an honest battle. Believe firmly, that with God's help, our victorious army's deeds in forthcoming battles will give our unworthy enemy a decisive answer.

By my order, all people apprehended with such proclamations will be brought immediately before a field court and judged as state criminals under the strictest wartime laws.

—Adjutant General Nikolai

DOCUMENT 1.9
VASILII MAKLAKOV, "A TRAGIC SITUATION"[25]

The following document is an essay by liberal activist Vasilii Maklakov that appeared in The Russian Bulletin (Russkie vedomosti) *on 27 September 1915. To avoid censorship, Maklakov employed several plays on words. For example, he repeatedly uses the verb* pravit' *to mean "to steer," but it also means "to govern"; similarly, he uses the phrase* rodina mat' vasha *to mean "the mother who gave birth to you," but it also means "your motherland"). Readers would have understood this as Aesopian language thinly covering his political points.[26] Maklakov's allegory of passengers driven by an inept chauffeur appeared at the height of a political crisis, and readers would have recognized the driver as Tsar Nicholas II. Rumors were spreading that the notorious Grigorii Rasputin (1869–1916) and a "pro-German" faction around the Empress Alexandra were influencing the tsar's decisions. Liberals questioned the tsar's decision to take personal command of the army and criticized his ministerial appointments. Several of the monarchy's critics called on the tsar to form a new government drawn from parties in the Fourth State Duma. In September 1915, Prince Georgii L'vov, chairman of the Union of Towns and Zemstvos, proposed that the tsar appoint "a government that enjoys the nation's confidence." Nicholas flatly refused.*

New technology has created a new situation. To see this clearly, one cannot take it on directly, but must use allegory.

You are riding in an automobile along a steep, winding, narrow road. One wrong move and that's it, you're dead. The person dearest to you is in the automobile—the mother who gave birth to you. And suddenly you see that the chauffeur cannot steer. Perhaps he can't manage the car as it speeds down the mountain, or perhaps he simply doesn't know what is happening yet. But he is driving himself and you toward a wreck. If this continues, ruin is inevitable for him and for you. Fortunately, there are people in the automobile who know how to steer. One needs to take the wheel quickly. But changing seats while moving is difficult and dangerous. One second without anyone guiding the automobile, and it goes into the abyss.

There is no choice, though—you are headed into the breach. And the chauffeur won't budge. Perhaps he is blinded and cannot see or is feeble-minded and doesn't grasp what is happening. Or it could be from professional conceit or obstinacy. But he clings to the wheel and won't let go for anyone. What can be done now? Force him to give up his place? That might work were this a rustic cart or if these were ordinary times along a flat, quiet road. Then perhaps it would seem like salvation. But could it be done on this steep slope, on this mountain road? Would you have the dexterity or strength? In fact, *his* hands are on the wheel. He is driving the car now, and one wrong turn or awkward movement of his hands and the car is wrecked. You know this, but *he* knows it, too. And he is emboldened by your anxiety and your powerlessness: "They won't dare touch me!"

He is right: you don't dare touch him. Were you even more afraid and indignant, you might grab it. Forgetting the danger, forgetting yourself, you would find the strength to seize the wheel. But there would be a wreck anyway—and you would be making it happen. And this isn't just about you: your mother is riding with you, and she would perish along with you. You would be killing her, too.

You compose yourself. You will settle accounts with the chauffeur when the right time comes, when the danger has passed, when you are again on a flat stretch. Then you will take the wheel from the chauffeur. Moreover, you will not try to hinder him. You will even give him advice about how to drive. You will be driven, and that is what must be done.

But what if—after you have convinced yourself that you will survive—what if your mother, facing the danger, asks for your help, and, understanding your behavior, blames you for your impotence and indifference?

DOCUMENT 1.10
PAVEL MILIUKOV, "STUPIDITY OR TREASON?"[27]

The following document is a speech to the Fourth Russian State Duma by Kadet leader Pavel Miliukov on 1 November 1916. It came in the midst of a major political crisis occasioned by Russian military defeats, the breakdown of the food supply system, and eroding public faith in the tsar's leadership. In 1916, Nicholas II had appointed several ministers whom the Duma opposition considered incompetent reactionaries; moreover, several high-ranking officials had been accused of aiding the Germans or arrested for corruption. In fall 1916, the liberal Progressive Bloc called on the tsar to appoint a ministry "enjoying public confidence." [28] Because this fell far short of demanding a "responsible ministry"—a government that answered directly to the State Duma—at the 1 November Duma session the Menshevik Nikolai Chkheidze called the liberals the tsarist regime's dupes. In this speech, Miliukov responds to that charge and assails the tsar's failed government.

Gentlemen of the State Duma! I ascend the tribune today with a heavy heart. You all recall the circumstances under which the Duma gathered more than one year ago, on 19 July 1915. Our military failures had deeply impressed the Duma. These failures had been caused by military supply shortages, for which War Minister Sukhomlinov was found to blame.[29] Then, you will recall, the country—impressed by the great and universally evident danger—demanded unification of national forces and the creation of a national ministry enjoying the country's confidence. Then, you will recall, even the minister Gromykin recognized that "the war demands an enormous, extraordinary ascension of spirit and strength."

Then, you will recall, the regime yielded.[30] Then, ministers odious to society were removed before the Duma convened. Sukhomlinov, who the country considered a traitor (*Voices from the left*: "He is!") was removed. At the 28 July session, in response to the people's representatives' demands, Polivanov announced—to universal applause, as you will recall—the creation of an investigative commission that had taken the first steps toward prosecuting the former war minister.[31] Then, gentlemen, the public's actions were not in vain. Our army received what it needed, and the country went into war's second year as enthusiastically as it had the first.

Gentleman, what a difference there is now, in the war's 27th month! It is a difference of which I am particularly aware, having spent several months abroad. Now we face new problems, problems no less complex and serious, no less profound than those that faced us last in spring of last year. . . . As before, we strive for full victory. As before, we are ready to make any necessary sacrifice. And as before, we want to preserve national unity. But I say openly: our situation is different now. We have lost faith in the regime's ability to win the war (*Voices*: "That's right!"), since none of our attempts to reform and improve the regime have succeeded.

All the Allied states have invited the very best people from all parties to join their governments. . . . And what has our government done?

. . . Almost all cabinet members who might be considered trustworthy have systematically been forced from their posts, one after another. If previously our regime lacked necessary knowledge and talent, gentlemen, it now has sunken even lower level than in normal times in Russian history. (*Voices from the left*: "True. That's right.") The gulf between us and them has grown and become unbridgeable. (*Voices from the left*: "True.")

Gentlemen, then—a year ago—Sukhomlinov was investigated; now, he has been freed. (*Voices from the left*: "Shame.") Then, hated ministers were removed before the convocation. Now, their numbers have increased by one. (*Voice from the left*: "True!"; *from the right*: "Protopopov?")[32] Then, instead of appealing to the regime's reason and knowledge, we appealed to its patriotism and its conscience. But can we do that now? (*Voices from the left*: "Of course not!")

[Miliukov implies that former Foreign Affairs Minister Shturmer and his secretary, Manasevich-Manuilov, were German agents protected by pro-German elements in the Imperial Court.[33] After loud protests from the Duma's right wing, Miliukov accuses the ultranationalist parties of endorsing a separate peace with Germany to prevent a revolution allegedly planned by the left liberals. Rightist leaders responded by shouting that Miliukov was a "liar" and "slanderer."]

... Gentlemen, as you know, in addition to the previously cited memorandum, there have been several other notes on a range of different topics that develop the same ideas.... What we have here, gentlemen, is a fixation on a leftist revolution, a fixation that preoccupies each new cabinet member to the point of insanity. (*Voices from the left:* "Correct.") Everything gets sacrificed to this fixation—the lofty national passion to help in the war, the embryo of Russian freedom, and even relations with allies....

[Miliukov says recent government actions have shaken French and British confidence in Russia. He again alleges the figures close to the Russian Imperial Court are German agents and implies that Foreign Affairs Minister Shturmer and the recently appointed Interior Minister Protopopov shelter Russia's internal enemies.]

Yes, gentlemen, there is a great difference between our meeting with Goremykin on 15 July 1915 ... and this meeting today. These meetings bear no resemblance, just as there is no resemblance between the general conditions in our country [then and now]. Then we could speak about Duma legislation to organize the country. Had we been able to implement the laws we had drafted, including the law creating township-level zemstvos, then Russia would not be so helpless regarding food supply matters now.

That was then! And now, gentlemen, legislative issues are secondary. Now we all see and understand that this government cannot make laws, just as it cannot carry Russia to victory. (*Voices from the left*: "True.") Before, we presented evidence that without the participation of all the country's vital forces, the war cannot be managed at the front or supported in country's interior—that this required raising the people's enthusiasm.... Otherwise, the only alternative is repression, which actually increases the very danger that it is meant to prevent. Now, gentlemen, everyone understands that it is useless to return to the regime with arguments based upon evidence. Fear of their own people, of their own country, blinds them. Their goal now is to hasten the war's end, even without any gains, to eliminate the need for popular support. (*Voices from the left*: "Right.")

On 10 February 1916, I concluded a speech by stating that we would no longer appeal to "the regime's political wisdom" and would not wait for the government to satisfy our demands. Then, many thought my words excessively dark. Now, I will go further—perhaps these words will be brighter and more vivid. Now we say to the government, as we said in our Bloc's declaration: We will fight you. We will fight with all legal means until you step down. (*Voices from the left*: "Correct. Right.")

It is said that one government minister—and duma member Chkheidze overheard this accurately—upon learning the State Duma would discuss treason, shouted in agitation, "I may be a fool, but I am no traitor!" (*Laughter.*) Gentlemen, that minister's predecessor undoubtedly was clever, just as the previous foreign affairs minister was honest.[34] But now they are no longer in the cabinet. And for practical purposes, gentlemen, does it matter if this is a matter of stupidity or reason?

When you wait a whole year for an offensive in Romania, make preparations, and then—at the decisive moment—we have neither the troops nor a way to move them quickly because of bottlenecks on the roads—so yet again you have lost a good chance to strike a decisive blow in the Balkans—how do you explain it? Is it stupidity or treason? (*Voices from the left*: "They're the same thing.")

When, having been warned repeatedly . . . about German efforts to tempt the Poles and so add a million men to Wilhelm's army (I had spoken out about this as early as February), they deliberately ignore a thoughtful and honest minister's efforts and instead . . . resolve the matter by removing this same minister . . . Is that stupidity or treason?[35] (*Voices from the left*: "Treason!") Choose what you like. It is all the same.

When the Duma unceasingly insists that a successful struggle requires organizing the rear, but the regime continues to claim that organizing the country means organizing revolution and prefers chaos and disorganization—is that stupidity or treason? (*Voices from the left*: "That is treason." *Adzhemov*: "That is stupidity." *Laughter.*)[36]

Gentlemen, there is more. When, in the midst of general discontent and irritation, the regime stirs up popular unrest—it is a fact that the police department was involved in disturbances in factories this spring—when it provokes disturbances and provocations, knowing full well that this disrupts the war effort—is this done consciously or unconsciously?

When in the thick of war a single man at court undermines Russia's reputation and honor among the Allies (*Commotion*) . . . all we can say what is I said earlier: is this . . . (*Markov 2*: "Is your speech stupidity or treason?")[37] My speech serves the motherland, which is something you have not done! . . . (*Zamyslovskii*: "That is not right!")[38] It is hard to explain all this as simply stupidity.

Therefore one cannot fault the population if it reaches conclusions like those I have stated here . . . You understand, then, why today our only task must be to obtain the government's resignations. You ask, how can we fight them at a time of war? Understand, gentlemen, that they are a menace only at a time of war. They are a menace to the war. We fight them not for precisely that reason—at a time of war, in the war's name, and in the name of all that unites us. (*Voices from the left*: "Bravo." *Applause.*)

[Miliukov briefly breaks from his main theme to refute criticisms made earlier in session by the Menshevik deputy Chkhedzie.]

... We have many, many different reasons to be dissatisfied with the government. We can discuss them all in the future, if we have time. But all those different reasons come to one general point: the current government's ineptitude and malevolence. (*Voices from the left*: "Right.")

Therefore, gentlemen, in behalf of millions of victims who spilled torrents of blood, in the name of our national interests . . . and out of duty to the people who sent us here, we will fight until we win an authentically responsible government. Until we have a government defined by the three points of our common declaration: that all cabinet members alike understand the tasks now before us; that they agree and are ready to implement the State Duma majority's program; and that they answer to the State Duma majority, not only regarding its program, but in all their activities. A cabinet without these three characteristics will not enjoy the State Duma's confidence and must step down. (*Noisy applause. Voices*: "Bravo." *Loud and prolonged applause from the left, the center, and left section of the right.*)

DOCUMENT 1.11
A CONFIDENTIAL CONVERSATION WITH GENERAL
ALEKSEEV, EARLY NOVEMBER 1916[39]

The following document is a conversation with General Mikhail Alekseev as recounted by American scholar Frank Alfred Golder. Alekseev, a career officer who had led Russian forces in Galicia in 1914, became the tsar's chief of staff in September 1915. He retired after suffering a heart attack in November 1916.

Several months before the revolution the following confidential conversation took place between a journalist and Alekseev, the Russian Commander in Chief:

ALEKSEEV: I can get nothing from [the government ministers]. My supplies are decreasing. . . . It is even necessary to think about bread. We are already cutting down the [soldiers' rations]. [The government has] forgotten about food for the horses. . . .

JOURNALIST: What are you going to do about it?

A. What shall I do? With these people, there is nothing that can be done.

J. Have you said anything to the Tsar about it?

A. I have . . . but it does no good.

J. Why?

A. While you talk to him he pays attention, gets worked up, is eager to do something. . . . But as soon as he leaves you, he forgets about it. All kinds of pressure is brought to bear upon him. He is not a free man.

J. Is it true that the [Empress Alexandra] has much influence?

A. It is only too true. Her influence is irresistible. What is worse [is that] she never comes out in the open. She interferes with everybody, but works behind their backs. You never can tell what she will do next. Every time she comes [to Stavka], she makes new trouble.

J. Do the ministers ever consult you?

A. They come, they talk. What can they do? The honest ministers [resign] and the worthless remain. . . . If it were not for the war, I would resign too. If I should leave, what would [the untrustworthy ministers] do with the army? Do I not understand that Sturmer and Company are thinking only of an alliance with Germany? . . .⁴⁰

The home situation is serious. [Sturmer and Co.] are purposely instigating hunger disturbances in order to provoke a revolution so [they] have an excuse for breaking away from the Allies and [ending] the war. Our army is now in [position] to crush Germany, and without that there can be no real peace in Europe. But a permanent peace is not wanted by Sturmer and Protopopov. They wish to keep the people under the heel of a strong Germany. Apart from the Germans, no one will protect them from the revolution. The pity of it all is that at the head of the government there still are men who are interested in crushing the people.

DOCUMENT 1.12
TSARITSA ALEKSANDRA TO TSAR NICHOLAS II,
14 DECEMBER 1916⁴¹

The following document is a 14 December 1916 letter from Tsaritsa Alexandra to Tsar Nicholas II. During the war, the royal couple exchanged some 1,500 letters and telegrams. Nicky and Sunny, as they called one another, corresponded in English.⁴² Nicholas sent telegrams from Stavka (Supreme Headquarters), Alexandra sent letters from the Summer Palace at Tsarskoe Tselo near Petrograd. Alexandra's letters reflected deep-seated monarchical views (shared by Nicholas), and she frequently offered the tsar advice on state affairs. This specific letter was written during the political crisis of late 1916, when the tsar faced a growing chorus of demands that he form a new government. Alexandra particularly feared that a "responsible ministry" of liberal State Duma leaders and public figures like Prince L'vov would undercut the tsar's power.

Tsarskoe Selo, Dec. 14th, 1916

My beloved Sweetheart,

7 [below freezing] and thick snow. Scarcely slept this night again, remaining till luncheon in bed as all aches still & have a slight chill. Such loving thanks for [your] dear letter. Trepov was very wrong in putting off the duma now & wishing to call it beginning of January again, the result

being (which he, Rodzianko and all counted upon), that nobody goes home and all will remain fomenting, boiling in Petrograd. . . .[43]

[Alexandra reminds the tsar that Rasputin had urged him to disband the State Duma.]

. . . Trepov behaves now, as a traitor & is false as a cat—do not trust him, he concocts everything with Rodzianko together, it is only too well known. [Alexandra urges Nicholas to shut down the State Duma immediately and complains of treachery by Trepov, Rodzianko, and other public figures she considers to be enemies.]

. . . Be Peter the Great, John the Terrible, Emperor Paul—crush them all under you—now don't you laugh, noughty [sic] one—but I long to see you so with all those men who try to govern you—& it must be the contrary.[44]

[Alexandra notes her disgust at aristocratic women who criticize the tsar's policies. She compares them unfavorably to the ultranationalist Union of Russian People, which had sent her a telegram vowing support for the autocracy.] One is rotten, weak, immoral society—the other, healthy, right thinking, devoted subjects—& to these one must listen, their voice is Russia's & not society or the Duma's. One sees the right so clearly & they know the Duma ought to be closed and to them Trepov won't listen. If one does not listen to these ["right-thinking" devoted subjects], they will take things into their own hands to save you and more harm un-willingly may be done—then [sic] a simple word from you to close the Duma—but till February, if earlier—they will all stick here. I [could] hang Trepov for his bad councils . . .

[She rails against Trepov and insists that Nicholas follow Rasputin's advice and return to Petrograd at once to disband the State Duma.]

. . . I should have quietly & with clear conscience before the whole of Russia sent [Prince] L'vov to Siberia (one did so for far less grave acts), taken Samarin's rank away (he signed that paper [from] Moscow), Miliukov, Guchkov, & Polivanov to Siberia.[45] It is war and at such a time interior war is high treason, why don't you look at it like that, I really cannot understand. I am but a women, but my soul & brain tell me that it [would] be the saving of Russia—they sin far worse than anything that Sukhomilonov's ever did—Forbid [General] Brusilov etc. when they come to touch any political subject, fool who wants responsible cabinet, as Gregory [Rasputin] writes.

Remember even Mr. Phillipe said one dare not give constitution, as it would be [your] & Russia's ruin, & all true Russians say the same.[46] [She emphasizes that she considers it her wifely duty to advice Nicholas in this manner.]

Sweetheart, Sunshine of my life, if in battle you had to meet the enemy, you [would] never waver & go forth like a lion—be it now in the battle against a handful of brutes and republicans—be the Master, & all will bow down before you. [She recounts an "insolent" comment by an officer and her response.]

. . . We have been placed by God on a throne and we must keep it firm & give it over to our Son untouched—if you keep that in mind you will be remember to be the Sovereign—& how much easier for an autocratic sovereign than one who has sworn the Constitution . . .

[Alexandra notes that she must attend to their daughters.]

I kiss you & hold you tightly clasped to my breast, caress you, love you, can't sleep without you—bless you.

Ever [your] very own,
Wifey

THE WAR AND ORDINARY PEOPLE

DOCUMENT 2.1
A. DONSKOI, "FORWARD!"[1]

Russian newspapers and cheap popular magazines (like those in other countries at war) published scores of patriotic poems during World War I. The following document, a poem by A. Donskoi, appeared in Moscow's The Penny Journal (Zhurnal Kopeiki) *in fall 1914. Donskoi wrote similar verses for several newspapers in 1914–1917.* The Penny Journal *featured poems, essays, and illustrations depicting heroic Russian soldiers. This poem appeared above a photograph of Russian soldiers, bayonets fixed, charging at German cavalry. Donskoi repeats the phrase, "Forward, Comrades!" which is often linked to leftist politics. (In George Orwell's* Animal Farm, *for instance, the Stalin-like pig dictator is celebrated in a poem entitled, "Forward, Comrades!") In Donskoi's poem, though, "comrades" refers simply to "brothers in arms."*

"Forward!"

> Forward, comrades!
> Forward, comrades!
> To the enemy's gates!
> Our motherland calls.
>
> We will leave our homes.
> We will leave our fields.
> Forward, comrades!
> To the enemy's gates!
>
> Forward, comrades!
> And make our bitter enemies quake!
> We are defending the honor
> Of the Great Russian flag!
>
> Farewell, native home.
> Farewell, heavenly sky.
> We're leaving our soil.
> Our motherland calls!
>
> Farewell, father and mother!
> Farewell, my family!
> I am off to battle.
> But I am happy, I am lucky!
>
> Perhaps I will return
> From the fighting soon.
> Perhaps I will live to return
> To my dear motherland, Rus.

Forward, comrades!
Forward, comrades!
To the enemy's gate!
Our motherland calls.

You will suffer for a year.
It will be bloody. And when it is over
Our enemy will have pressed down upon us.
But we will have been victorious.

Russia is pure!
Russia is great!
Our Russian people
Is a thundering river!

And if it is roused,
Then enemies beware!
We will plant the Russian flag
On the enemy's soil.

Forward, comrades!
Forward, comrades!
We are all off for the fight.
Our motherland calls!

—Donskoi

DOCUMENT 2.2
PEASANT REACTIONS TO MILITARY
MOBILIZATION: POLICE REPORTS FROM
KAZAN AND STAVROPOL'[2]

The overwhelming majority of Russia's soldiers came from peasant villages for which the war presented great new burdens. The army conscripted nearly half the male rural labor force and requisitioned peasants' horses and livestock. In summer 1914, men and women in the many villages violently opposed conscription and requisition. The first document below is a 23 July 1914 report from the police commander in Kazan Province, an ethnically Tatar region on Volga River. It describes a violent rampage by mobilized reservists against estates owned by aristocratic landlords (in Russian, pomeshchiki). As was typical, the Provincial Governor responded by sending mounted police to put down the unrest. On 27 July, police reported that the unrest had subsided.[3] The second document is a 23 July 1914 police report about an attack against a zemstvo school in Stavropol' Province, in the North Caucasus region. Zemstvos were state agencies that provided rural communities with health care, education, and other vital services. Until 1917, zemstvo assemblies were elected using a voting system that favored the landlords. Although villagers generally trusted local teachers and zemstvo professionals, unequal elections and inequity in zemstvo taxes fostered hostility. In the war's first weeks, peasants angry at the military mobilization often vented their anger on zemstvo institutions.[4]

[Kazan Document]
Secret.

In my dispatch to the Department of Police (No. 9189, dated 22 July), I reported that the city of Kazan had been peaceful during the mobilization period.[5] On 22 July, there were continuous patriotic demonstrations all day and night. Yesterday it was announced that first category reserve companies would be called to active duty.

Reports are coming in from the counties that the reserve commands' lower ranks are committing local disorders on their way to Kazan. I received a short report that a party of reservists traveling from Chistopol' County set fire to hay at the manor of the landowner Lebedev, at Kaipy village in Laishev County. In Laishev County they also damaged property at Bestrel's estate, "Panovka," and at Frentsel's estate at Dershavino village. It is said their leaders promised to return and "destroy all" the landowners' manors.

On his Honor the Kazan governor's orders, a squadron of mounted police guards with officers has been dispatched to the locales in Laishev County where these disorders took place. His Honor also has entrusted me with dispatching forces to collect information. I will report more on this matter as soon as there is more information.

—[Police] Colonel Kalinin

[Stavropol' Document]
On 19 July at 12:00 in the village of Mikhailovsko, Stavropol' County, reservists at the military mobilization muster point began to shout that they were not going into the service and would not give up their horses. Then a crowd of about two hundred people walked to the zemstvo school construction site and started tearing building materials from the walls, doing almost a thousand rubles in damage.

The Stavropol' Provincial Governor sent mounted police guards under the Stavropol' County Police Chief's command, but not one of those guilty of the disorders has been found or apprehended. The reservists, on hearing that the guards were coming for them, quickly fled to the muster point in Stavropol' city and delivered the horses before the guards arrived.

—Colonel Gladyshevskii

DOCUMENT 2.3
A JEWISH LIBERAL VIEW OF THE WAR, JULY 1914[6]

The following document is an editorial from the liberal Jewish newspaper, New
Assent (Novyi voskhod), *on 24 July 1914. In Russia in 1914, Jews still did
not have the equal civil and citizenship rights they had achieved elsewhere in
Europe. Almost all the Russian Empire's 5 million Jewish subjects were legally
required to live in a western border zone known as the Pale of Settlement. Laws
restricted Jewish land ownership, entry into certain professions, and state school
admissions. Between 1880 and 1914, there had been several waves of popular
anti-Jewish hostility in Russia, including mass anti-Jewish riots* (pogroms) *in
1905–1906. Russian ultranationalists considered Jews untrustworthy aliens who
promoted revolution and supported the German enemy. Jewish liberals therefore
went to great lengths to demonstrate Jewish loyalty to Russia. This essay from*
New Assent *by a frequent contributor (identified only as S. P.) is an example
of these efforts. In 1915, the tsarist government closed the newspaper after its
editors protested military brutality toward Jews in districts near the front.*

The War.
. . . Russia's entire population, all its tribes and peoples, have been called to
the flag. At this great and unprecedented historic moment, all Russian-
Jews rise up as one to defend their country. Each of us will do our duty
for the fatherland—do it to the very end—steadfast and courageous,
conscientiously fulfilling our responsibilities.[7]

We have lived and grown up in Russia, and our ancestors' ashes rest
here. Unbreakable bonds tie Russian-Jews to Russia and remind us to
guard all our brothers' cherished lives. . . . We Russian-Jews are defenders
of our fathers' legacy and stalwarts of international Jewry. At the same
time, we have an unbreakable bond to the country in which we have lived
for hundreds of years. Nothing can separate us from it—not oppression,
not persecution, not conditions of any kind.

In the Imperial Manifesto declaring war, His Majesty explained that
"[i]n this terrible hour of our tribulation, we will forget internal conflicts."[8]
At this fateful moment, Russian-Jews think of these [conflicts] least of
all. In the general rush to defend the motherland, we stand shoulder
to shoulder with all Russia's population. Our courageous behavior will
demonstrate that we have no time for internal squabbles, no time to think
about profound insults against us.

. . . The enemy is on our soil, threatening our homes, our wives and
children. Fate has made the Pale of Jewish Settlement a theater of military
activity. The only experience comparable to this world war that we
Russian-Jews have lived though was Napoleon's invasion.[9] Then Russian-
Jews, who as a great mass had only recently been annexed to Russia,
displayed great patriotism and selfless devotion to the motherland.

. . . The Jewish people have always stood in the vanguard of fighters for humanity. Great ideals of law and equality have always made our people faithful warriors.[10]

At this historic moment, when our motherland is threatened by a foreign invasion, when a callous force has risen up in arms against the great ideals of humanity, Russian-Jewry courageously takes to the field of battle and does its sworn duty.

—S. P.

DOCUMENT 2.4
ANTON BOROVOI, "ON THE JEWISH QUESTION"[11]

The following document is a fall 1914 essay by Anton Borovoi from the Moscow magazine War and the Jews *(Voina i Evrei). Borovoi's title refers to the "Jewish Question," which in Russia actually meant two questions: should Jews be integrated into the "national body," and how could this be done? For a decade, liberals in the State Duma had tried, but failed, to abolish the Pale as a first step toward Jewish equal rights. Anti-Jewish attitudes still ran deep among Russian governmental and military elites and antisemitism was a key feature of ultranationalist politics in Russia (as across Europe). Liberal Jews hoped Jewish support for the war effort would pave the way for future reforms.*

War and the Jews *had a dual purpose: to reinforce Jewish patriotism and civic pride; and to contradict anti-Jewish stereotypes by demonstrating Jewish loyalty and Jewish contributions to the war effort. Each issue featured stories about heroic Jewish soldiers and photographs of Jews wounded or killed in action or decorated for bravery. Each opened with a short commentary on contemporary issues by a prominent Jewish activist or professional that balanced celebration of Jewish loyalty to Russia with criticisms of anti-Jewish government policies. This had been Jewish liberal leaders' approach from the war's first days. At the 26 July 1914 Fourth State Duma session, Naftali Friedman stressed that Jews, as "loyal sons of the fatherland" would fight to the last man to defend Russia, despite the "exceptionally harsh legal conditions in which [they] have lived and continue to live" in Russia.[12]*

Among the dozens of agonizing questions raised by the current war and new conditions of life, there is one that is perhaps the most disquieting for humanity. It is a question that should not even be among the issues facing the renewed Russia. It is the Jewish Question.

Nothing has demonstrated Jews' loyalty the way this war has. Jews are going to war with a simple goal and the same high spirits and expectations as the native Russian people. They have no regrets about shedding their blood for Russia. From the press, we all know of many cases in which soldier-Jews displayed rare initiative and unparalleled courage. Several have been honored with the highest possible decorations for their ingenuity on the field of battle. Jewish volunteers have been promoted to officers' rank. Meanwhile, we continue to see them burdened by lamentable injustices.

A wounded Jew is being taken to Moscow. In some remote *shtetl* in the Pale of Settlement, a telegram arrives: "I have been wounded. I am on train N to Moscow," or "I am wounded. I will be in Moscow."[13] Mother, father, and brother scrape together their last pennies. They are caught between worried agitation and their happiness that finally, despite his wounds, they will see their dear, beloved man. They rush off to travel hundreds of miles to Moscow.

But the wounded soldier's train still has not arrived. He is stuck in some station along the way, and he has not quite made it to Moscow. The family spends an agonizing day searching. Not knowing where he is, the relatives race about looking for the wounded hero at train stations and military evacuation points, at city and zemstvo organizations and private clinics.

But . . . as in the past, laws regulate the length of time that Jews can stay in the capital. Before the wounded soldier has even arrived, his family must return without having seen him.

You can see such dreadful injustices daily. Families return with their hopes dashed, fearing that they will never again see their wounded sons. How could this tragedy continue?

Could you imagine that now—when from Supreme Commander's lips we hear sage words about tolerance and brotherly love for oppressed humanity—such exclusionary laws, relics of the Middle Ages, remain in place, as if some disguised religious war were under way?[14] Polish society is now told by all sides: "Stop the boycott of the Jewish population; you are strong, reach out your hand first!"[15] It would shameful if Poland did this before we did.

Let rejuvenated Russia be the first to extend its hand![16] That would be a new and wonderful victory!

DOCUMENT 2.5
AN INTERCEPTED LETTER ON THE WAR
AND JEWS, 30 JULY 1914[17]

The following document is a letter intercepted by tsarist police in August 1914. The author is a Jew, identified only as David, in the Ukrainian city of Kharkov. The recipient, A. Z. Rotshtein, lived in Smorgon in Russian-ruled Lithuania. Both cities had large Jewish populations. Tsarist police routinely intercepted and read letters of people whom they suspected as revolutionaries. During the war, police also examined letters from ordinary civilians and soldiers, as well as correspondence of high-ranking military officers, State Duma deputies, and even high-ranking state officials. Not surprisingly, the police gave special attention to correspondence among Jews, who they considered "naturally" sympathetic to the Germans.

David refers to several events and figures in the history of Russian antisemitism. These include the Beillis Case, Russia's equivalent to France's Dreyfus Affair. In July 1911, Kiev police arrested Menachem Mendel Beillis for the alleged ritual murder of a Christian boy, whose blood he supposedly used to make Passover matzo. Several such "blood libel" cases took place in prewar Russia. In 1913, a jury acquitted Beillis, but his case became an international symbol of pervasive Russian antisemitism. David also refers to the antisemitic Russian ultranationalist politician, Vladimir Purishkevich.

The current war raises serious questions: will Germany's insolent fist have dominion over Europe? Will it be the master of the Near East? This is a war for rights and justice, for European culture. It will be terrible and long. Personally, I would like to see Russia get its comeuppance. It has it coming, for the pogroms, the Beillis Case, the Pale of Settlement, the oppression and persecution—for Jewish suffering and our tears. But it seems to me that this won't happen: it has become too strong and it has this alliance with England and France. . . .

Nonetheless we must live through this trial, my dear. Well, now Europe is kissing up to Pureshkevitch. What a remarkable time, what a marvelous paradox. How can they find such tenderness and sympathy for those who sowed hatred and reaped an abundant harvest of "ritual histories" and pogroms?[18] It really is funny, and at the same time it is tragic. Well, so Europe stands at the border, ready to defend [Russia's] honor and its dignity. And we are far from our fond home, Zion, from our life. [Russia] has given Jews nothing but restrictions. But now, because we are foreigners in solidarity with the Russians, they have resolved not to expel Jewish reservists' families from the Pale of Settlement. You must figure that they will do no more; in their opinion, this is all they can manage.

DOCUMENT 2.6
"THE SCOUT CALLED 'TIAPA': FROM AN OFFICER'S LETTER"[19]

The following story appeared in The War and Its Heroes: Our Wonder-Warriors in the War of 1914, *a book that depicted Russian soldiers' bravery, cunning, and self-sacrifice. The term wonder-warrior* (chudo-bogatyr) *in the book's title refers to champions in Russia folktales and fairytales. In 1914 and 1915, publishers like "Literacy"* (Gramotnost') *issued inexpensive books for a mass audience that glorified war heroes. This story's main character is a soldier nicknamed Tiapa, which has no equivalent in English. In Russian, it refers both to a heavy spade (tiapka or tiapa) that makes for slow work, and is the diminutive form for "dullard" (rastiapa). Therefore it suggests someone who is slow but hard working. The story gives Tiapa attributes common among "simple folk" who turn out to be wonder-warriors in folktales.*

"The Scout Called 'Tiapa': From an Officer's Letter"
Self-sacrifice has always been characteristic of our soldiers, and that is why we in the trenches are always calm: where philistine rational thought says "No!," the Russian soldier says "Yes!" The current aerometric war demands a great deal of us, but events prove our nation has an advantage despite new battle needs.[20] I will tell you about an interesting episode.

In a battle near L. a squadron of fifteen of our scouts found themselves behind enemy lines.[21] Nothing but German trenches stretched on all sides. It was impossible to return toward L. by road; they knew going that that way promised ruin. The soldiers set to considering: should they try their luck at slipping through, or advance further into the depths behind the enemy lines and hide out in the woods? The majority favored the latter proposal.

"Here's what I say, brothers!" said a hearty soldier nicknamed "Tiapa." He was given this name because he was heavy and slow.

"Well, what do you say, Tiapa?" the private first class grinned.

"Well, mister private first class sir, it would be good if we could stay in these trenches, praise God! That would really shake them!"

At first the private first class thought Tiapa said this simply out of laziness. But then, after looking him directly in the face, the private whistled knowingly.

"You're a good fellow, Tiapa!" he pronounced decisively. "Come on, boys, into the trenches!" Within a few minutes the soldiers had slipped into the German trenches, where they sat quietly.

Just a beat or two later, an entire company of German soldiers came barreling down the road where our scouts would still have been standing if not for Tiapa's initiative. Night fell.

Sitting in the trench, our scouts could hear the Germans' boots stamping as they marched by.

"Well, boys, get ready!" The private first class whispered. But Tiapa, who was sitting next to the private first class, tapped his hand.

"You must wait, mister private first class sir. There are more of them coming."

The private slapped himself on the forehead. "Ah! Confound it! Let's not rush out all confused! That's right, boys, wait!" And so they didn't come out of the trench.

Not half an hour had gone by when a second German company appeared. When the first German ranks had come to within about two hundred steps, the scouts opened fire.

Guessing that they had been cut off by Russians further down the road, the Germans began shooting in that direction, toward the German company that had already passed by. That first company, thinking that they were being shot at by Russians, returned fire.

And that is what private "Tiapa" had in mind when he proposed that his comrades stay in the German trenches.

DOCUMENT 2.7
A SOLDIER'S LETTER TO A MOSCOW ACQUAINTANCE CONCERNING THE WAR, 15 DECEMBER 1914[22]

During the war, police routinely inspected soldiers' letters as well as civilians' correspondence. The following document is a letter from an unidentified frontline soldier to an acquaintance named N. A. Rozhanskii at Moscow University.[23]

In Moscow you are enthusiastic, but here we are not. The struggle between enthusiasm and death is a struggle between most unequal forces. . . . We've been brutalized here. We can enjoy delicacies sent from Moscow. We can crack jokes and drink tea. But when we return from our positions, all we talk about is the previous battle or skirmish. We eat very quietly while they fire 10-inch artillery shells at our advanced positions: "They're not shooting at us, so we had better be quiet." Intellect says, "this is not good," but feeling—feeling is silent. We are happy when we see our own shells blowing up over our enemies' trenches. How do you keep your elevated ideals when your underwear is filthy . . . and when, moreover, you feel that those in the rear are disgusting parasites?

DOCUMENT 2.8
ALEKSANDR DNEPROVSKII, *A DESERTER'S NOTES*[24]

The following document is an excerpt from the diary of Aleksandr Dneprovskii, a well-read young man with literary pretentions. Dneprovskii was born in Ukraine in 1896. In spring 1915, he was conscripted into the Russian Army. In May 1916, Dneprovskii—a pacifist—deserted and fled for Kiev. This excerpt recalls his reaction to patriotic newspapers in 1916.

Every day *New Times* and other newspapers print articles about the war, patriotism, discipline, and spheres of influence in which lackeys inform us of "their brilliance."[25] Every day the newspaper jackals spew servility or are silent. Oh truth! Could the printed word have been invented for these blockheads? Every day tubs of printed slop are poured over the heads of long-suffering humanity! . . . Could this possibly continue infinitely? Is it possible that they will avoid punishment? That thunder will not smash their dishonest heads? If nothing in the world is lost, if all is reckoned, including the "tears of the youth," can their vileness go unpunished?

DOCUMENT 2.9
AN ANTIWAR STUDENT LEAFLET FROM
SMOLENSK, JANUARY 1915[26]

Teenagers played an important role in Russia's revolutionary movement in 1914–1917. The following document is a January 1915 essay in The Harbinger (Predvestnik), *an underground leaflet by teenage socialists in the western Russian city of Smolensk. Most of those involved knew one another from radical student circles (some were still students).*[27]

The Government and Society.

It has been seven months already since the great European conflagration ignited in the West and engulfed the European states, including Russia, in its flames. War had threatened the world for many years. During the 1913 Balkan War, war's terrible specter floated in the thick atmosphere of militarism. Who knows—had the democracies convened a congress, they might have prevented the current war. But now the war is a fact.

Russian society, roused from its long reactionary hibernation, was stunned with one blow of war's thunderous instruments and blinded by the flash of bayonets. Chauvinism's poison quickly corrupted the unprincipled philistines' souls and deadened their ability to perceive the nation's true enemies. The bourgeoisie rushed to join the country's reactionary forces; their "liberalism" was quickly reborn as chauvinism. Without a doubt, foreign events distracted people's attention from domestic developments. Russian's society's true shame is that it struck a hasty bargain with our vile government without even knowing the facts.

Here is how it began. Austro-Hungary declared war on Serbia. They said the cause was the murder of the Austrian crown's heir, Franz Ferdinand. Russia, feeling the atmosphere thickening, announced a partial mobilization on 16 July. On 17 July this became a full mobilization. Germany presented Russia with an ultimatum on demobilization. Then war was finally declared. On 26 July there was a "historic State Duma session," which signified all Russia's "unity." . . . Next came horridly rapid foreign events: first France and then Belgium (violating its neutrality) declared war on Germany. England intervened in the European conflict. Japan presented an ultimatum to Germany then declared war. Finally, Turkey intervened in the world war (probably thanks to Russian provocation).

All this happened so quickly that as soon as one event began to take shape, it would change, and several new events appeared. All eyes were on the West.

And what was happening in our country? Here, also, event after event flew by. Reaction took victorious steps forward. Everything achieved in the previous decade was strangled or cut off at the roots. The democratic press was eradicated. Workers' organizations were demolished. The democracy's leaders were arrested or went into exile. The socialist journals, *Russian Wealth* and *Legacies* vanished. . . .[28] Complete military censorship rules over the press, based on Article 87.[29] Only the Black Hundreds' and bourgeois newspapers—and there was very little difference between them to begin with—remained unscathed.[30] Those newspapers that still existed were caught up in a wild bacchanalia of chauvinism.

The press, bowing in admiration of the Russian diplomats' activities, constantly spouted slogans that are pretty words without foundation in truth. They told us fairytales about "the struggle of Slavism versus Germanism," about "united Russia," about "the unity of the tsar and the people," and about "the Russian struggle for freedom." And the philistines, eyes closed to the facts, were lulled into accepting these fairytales and believed the lies, believed every tune hummed by the boulevard newspapers. They filled their souls with sweet fantasies about Great Russia and its self-sacrificing battle for freedom . . .

But these slogans are not consistent with reality. In reality, we see that at the war's start there were Slavs in one camp—Russia and Serbia—and Germanic States in the other camp—Germany and Austria. The later states are Germanic in their dominant culture, if not in the composition of their populations (Austria is 56% Slavic). But any superficial fairytales about "Slavism" and "Germanism" fell apart when the world conflagration enveloped England, France, Belgium, Japan, and Turkey. Then it became clear that the war's causes lay not in national differences, but in the economic relations between belligerent countries. France had accounts to settle with Germany regarding territory taken in 1871 (Alsace and Lorraine). England had been lusting after Germany's colonies for decades. And Japan had its gaze fixed on [Shanghai].

When we look at Russia, the issues are more complex. Russia is trying to set its foot firmly on the Balkan Peninsula. This was the underlying aim of a series of wars between Russia and Turkey, particularly the wars of 1854 and 1877. Galicia and Poland attracted Russian diplomats' attention. But that would be difficult to manage with Germany, which was strong, and would not yield. Turkey, though—that was a different matter. There, it would be possible to get around obstacles. And Russia was very thankful to Turkey for intervening in the war. Of course, the war's territorial aims are tied to other issues—for instance, commercial treaties, dynastic affairs, etc. So the struggle of "Slavism versus Germanism" does not exist.

There is nothing of the kind, just as we have no constitution (although many are foaming at the mouth about returning to it).

The other, more serious, myth propagated by the bourgeois press is the myth of "United Russia." Those who read newspapers know that the bourgeois press has endorsed this idea, and they know what it is based on: "Miliukov has extended his hand to Purishkevich"; "All parties have united in patriotic demonstrations that sing the national anthem"; "Shmakov, in the strongest words has renounced his errors concerning the Jews," and so on.[31]

Yes, all these were facts. The Kadet Miliukov did take the Black Hundred Purishkevich's hand, and there were patriotic demonstrations. . . . But there is no "United Russia." It does not exist because not everyone in Russia has joined the Black-Hundreds chauvinists. . . . This is particularly clear now, when constitutional guarantees have been revoked and duma deputies (Bolshevik Social Democrats) have been arrested. Now, when there are mass arrests of workers and students and searches in the largest cities, like Petersburg and Moscow.

No! There cannot be a "United Russia," because the democracy is speaking out against the fratricidal war. In truth, had this outburst of pro-government patriotism been any more than a liberal gesture, there might have been "unity" among various political groups. But there is none . . . To speak of the "unity of the tsar and the people" now would require several reforms. Despite the artillery's thunder and the people's moans, the Russian tsar in his great "heart of hearts" is one with the Black Hundreds and will continue his reactionary policies. . . .

Oh, of course, the Russian bureaucratic government has always fought for "freedom," from the most distant past up to this pathetic struggle. Take a look at this progressive government! In the name of freedom, it destroyed the Turkish constitution (in 1877). In the name of freedom, it fought a war with Japan. In the name of our great freedom (yes, for us, all of us), it amputated the constitution won in the great 1905 Russian revolution. And now, in freedom's name, it is destroying everything in the country that resembles free thought. So, to distract society's attention from their "freedom-loving" actions, they lull us to sleep with fairytales about "German atrocities" and fill the philistines' souls with malicious nationalistic tendencies.

Comrades! Should we take the path of chauvinism, the path of the unprincipled and the narrow-minded now, when our brothers' blood is being shed in the West? Now, when the flames of reaction are burning in our country? No, comrades! We must not bear the people's suffering and moans silently. We must not be passive when all the reactionary dark forces are pushing down on us. We will prepare for the new events already unfolding before our eyes. We will prepare, so that the great Russian revolution does not take us by surprise! The war is gradually creating its own negation. The bourgeoisie and the bureaucracy have put nooses around their own necks by creating fairytales and acting under the din of patriotism. We will be prepared, so that when the moment is right we can accomplish a great feat in mankind's history. Join your voice to the voices of Russia's best people. Look into the eyes of Russian arbitrariness, the eyes of an autocracy stained by Russian blood, and say:

Down with the war!
Long live the brotherhood of peoples!

DOCUMENT 2.10
PEASANT WOMEN PETITION THE WAR
MINISTER, MAY 1916[32]

The following document is a 14 May 1916 letter to War Minister Dmitrii Shuvaev by authors who identified themselves as the "League of Unfortunate Peasant Women" in Moscow. There seems to be no other trace of this "League" in the historical record. Like many peasant women (especially soldiers' wives), the authors resented conscription, military requisition of livestock and grain, and shortages of sugar and other staples.

What is going on? We, peasant women of the Russian soil, have given the government our husbands, our sons, our brothers, our fathers. And now that is not enough for the government. It is going to exterminate us with hunger. No bread, no meat, no sugar, no anything. They've begun taking our cattle and our very last breadwinners. How are we supposed to support ourselves and our children? How are we supposed to live? In the end, the government is going to ruin us and give it all to the Germans. Protect us! We will write, we will cry out, "Our government has stolen everything!" We will write to our husbands, brothers, fathers in the trenches. We will pass the word to them. Save us, save us from the corrupt and treacherous government soon, before we are all dead. Most of all, come save us from the treasonous ministers. If you do not take measures, we will all rise up . . . Act on our demands now and do not delay. Give us bread. Down with the war. Down with the treacherous, treasonous ministers and the entire government.

DOCUMENT 2.11
SOLDIERS' WIVES PETITION THE AGRICULTURE
MINISTER, DECEMBER 1916[33]

The following document is a petition from soldiers' wives (soldatki) *in the village of Gavrina, in Tobol'sk Province in western Siberia. The women sent their petition to Count A. A. Bobrinskii, who Nicholas II had appointed as agriculture minister in August 1916. In November 1916, though, the tsar had replaced Bobrinskii with Aleksandr Rittikh. The petition's stilted and formal language suggests the hand of a low-level clerk familiar with conventions of bureaucratic supplications— probably the Dmitrii Oparin who signed the document for those women who were illiterate. Peasants often asked a clerk, teacher, or priest to write up their documents, so the language would sound "official." This document concerns use of war prisoners as farmworkers, which also was not unusual. By late 1916, more than 500,000 prisoners of war were assigned to field work in the Russian Empire.*

To his Most High Majesty, Minister of Agriculture Count Bobrinskii.
From soldiers' wives: Praskov'a Milhailova, Ustin'ia Gabova, Stepanida Gabova, Arina Vaganova, Maria Mikhailova, Stepanida Popova, Dar'ia Popova, Stepanida Punigova, and Nastas'ia Lushkova, of the village of Gavrina, Bezpukovsk township, Ishimsk county, Tobol'sk province.

A Petition

We have the honor of humbly requesting that Your Most High Majesty give your subordinates instructions on delivering war prisoners for winter and summer work. . . . On 20 November of this year, a directive was sent to peasant authorities in the 6th district about removing 75 war prisoners who had been employed in our Bezrukovsk Township.

All were taken from our village of Gavrina. We, soldiers' wives with little children, remain without laborers during the wintertime. The winter in the present year is severe. Hay must be taken to the district treasury officer, who is far away. There are no workers, and it is impossible to hire anyone at any wage. Could it be that the government would put us in this position? We greatly thank the government for giving us aid. But do so in a manner that supports and does not diminish our farming. We have had to reduce sowings because of the shortage of working hands. All we have remaining in the village are 60-year old men.

Do not let our request go unanswered. Give orders to provide us with war prisoners for work.

> Signed by: Praskov'ia Mikhailovna Mikhailova, Ustin'ia Gabova, Stepanida Punigova, Dar'ia Popova, Stepanida Popova; and for others who are illiterate, their names written down at their request by Dmitrii Zrastovich Oparin.

DOCUMENT 2.12
A SOLDIER'S LETTER ON THE MOOD AMONG
FRONT SOLDIERS, JANUARY 1917[34]

The following document is another letter intercepted by the police, sent by a frontline soldier (whose name was illegible) to Feodor Filippov, a platoon commander in the 177th Reserve Infantry Regiment's Third Company. We know nothing more of either the sender or the recipient, but the two were well acquainted (the author addresses Filippov by the diminutive, "Fedia"). The content suggests they knew one another from populist political circles.

The author uses the Russian term "burzhui." The word is derived from the word "bourgeois," but it did not refer as much to the "bourgeoisie" in a specific economic sense as it did to anyone whose wealth, profession, appearance, or political views were associated with the upper classes (the verkhi). *Calling someone* burzhui *inferred that they were vulgar and did not care for the common good. Near the letter's end, the author uses the phrase "land and freedom"—one the main slogans of the revolutionary populist movement. "Land" in this case meant land redistribution to the peasantry—land to those who worked it.*

17 January 1917

Dear comrade Fedia!

I send you holiday greetings, for the birth of Christ and for the New Year. Dear comrade, I know that you have your own crushing grief, and we must bear such grief. It has been ordered that the war will not end until there is a complete victory. And we are concerned, you know, about how we will be fed—one lentil at lunch and one at dinner. Dear comrade, tell your soldiers, so they know, that we must come out against the war . . .

Tell them: Comrades, it is time to come to one's senses. We have endured enough hunger and cold. Now our wives, mothers, fathers, and children are suffering from hunger. Assure them that our weapons will be used against our government and against all the Russian *burzhui*, who drink our blood and have been basking in the sun like snakes.

Ask them: Comrades, how could we not be fed up with being so far from our homes and our families, when each minute the threat of death makes us burrow into the earth like a beetle in shit . . . ? We don't know what we are defending! It isn't our own property that we are defending, and it won't be.

Tell them: Comrades, we are all being crippled. It is time. It is time for us to come to our senses. We are not fighting the Germans for the sake of freedom . . . We must have land and freedom.

Farewell, comrade.

P. S. Please, Mister Censor, kind sir! Let this letter pass, because you also know that we are being slaughtered like sheep in the war. You must know this.

DOCUMENT 2.13
FACTORY WORKERS' NEEDS IN SMOLENSK PROVINCE, JANUARY AND EARLY FEBRUARY 1917[35]

In January and February 1917, the number of striking workers in Petrograd rose steadily with each week. These strikes would coalesce into a general strike and help bring down the Romanov Dynasty in late February. Workers' chief complaints were shortages of goods and high prices for staples like bread, sugar, and kerosene. At the same time, factory managers faced serious shortages of the raw materials necessary to sustain production. The tsarist government administration understood the danger posed by shortages.

In late January 1917, the Senior Factory Inspector in Smolensk Province solicited information from local factory managers on supply needs. The following document set presents replies to these inquiries. The documents are arranged as they appear in the original archival file, not the chronological order in which they were written. The first is a report to the factory inspector by A. Khar'khov, manager of the I. Sokolov Lumber Mill, dated 1 February 1917. The second is from flour-mill owner E. Borobnikov, dated 31 January 1917. The third is from William Gerhard, owner of the Gerhard Textile Factory, also dated 1 February 1917.[36] The final report, from Sergei Reshetnikov, owner of a large textile machine parts factory, is dated 3 February 1917.[37] The authors address the factory inspector using capital letters (for example, "His Honor" and "You"), as was typical in formal correspondence with tsarist state officials.

To His Honor, the Factory Inspector of Smolensk's Second District:
In a response to Your 30 January 1917 directive (No. 115), I have the honor of reporting that at this point the I. Sokolov Lumber-mill Plant has in reserve the following amount of consumers goods: 4,000 *puds* of sugar, 500 *puds* of treacle, and 500 *puds* of soap. We wish to inform You that these amounts are not sufficient.[38] We have supplies of timber, but there is a shortage of labor . . .

The mill's workers live in their own houses and need flour, buckwheat groats, and sugar. Their monthly need for goods is: 900–1,000 *puds* of rye flour; 180–200 *puds* of buckwheat groats, and 15–20 *puds* of sugar.

—Plant manager A. Khar'khov
1 February 1917

Smolensk, 31 January 1917
To His Honor, the FACTORY INSPECTOR of Smolensk's 2nd DISTRICT:
In answer to Your inquiry, it is our honor to inform You that there is need:
Among workers—for sugar, wheat flour, various kinds of groats, kerosene, and other goods;
On the part of the factory—for barley, for which there is acute need. We produce various sorts of pearl barley groats, barley that is machined, and other sorts of fodder for cattle.
There also is a shortage of rye, from which we make rye flour. . . . And also of wood: We need 1 cubic *sazhen* daily to make the steam-powered machines work.[39]

—Owner of the Enterprise: E. Borobnikov

1 February 1917

To the Gentleman Factory Inspector of Smolensk's 2nd District:

We hereby provide You with information that there is an acute need for the following products and staples.

For the factory's needs:

Benzine	3 *puds* per day
Coal	1 *pud* per day
Kerosene	2 *puds* per month
Candles	10 *funts* per month[40]
Oil for Spindles	25 *funts* per day

For the needs of employees and workers at our factory:

For all employees and workers, per day:

Rye flour	20 *puds*
Wheat flour	2 *puds*
Sugar lumps	1 *pud* 30 *funts*
Sugar (granulated)	1 *pud* 30 *funts*
Kerosene	7 *puds*
Candles	20 *funts* per month
Soap	3 *puds* 20 *funts* per month
Matches	20 dozen per month
Butter	1 *pud* 30 *funts* per day
Sunflower oil	1 *pud* 30 *funts*
Rye bread	16 *puds*
Fine rye bread	6 *puds*
Buckwheat groats	7 *puds*
Millet groats	5 *puds*
Semolina groats	3 *puds*

—William Gerhard

Smolensk, 3 February 1917[41]

To the Factory Inspector of Smolensk's 2nd District:

Esteemed Sir,

In response to Your inquiry (No. 130) of 30/I of this year, we inform you that:

Regarding workers' provisions, we have absolutely no reserves of any products. The principal need is for flour, rye groats, buckwheat groats, and sunflower oil. Per month consumption is from 150–200 *puds*.

For production, there is an acute shortage of flour for glue for the spindles. We are temporarily using glue made from baking flour, which sticks too poorly, so that the spindles are weak. We have a daily need of 10 *puds* of flour for glue.

Regarding fuel. We chiefly use anthracite coal, of which there is absolutely none. We are using wood or wood shavings, which is very difficult to procure. The daily consumption needs for anthracite are 160–200 *puds*.

> With honor,
> [stamped] The Sergei Ivanovich Reshetnikov Company
> Director of Operations, [signed] Reshetnikov

DOCUMENT 2.14
K. M. PETROV IN MOSCOW TO HIS FATHER IN
VORONEZH PROVINCE, 17 FEBRUARY 1917[42]

The following document in an excerpt that police made from a letter sent by K. M. Petrov to his father, a nobleman in Voronezh Province, days before the February Revolution began. The document and appended notes provide no additional information about the Petrovs.

The younger Petrov makes reference to several politicians: Kadet leader Pavel Miliukov, Zemsto Union Chairman Prince Georgii L'vov, State Duma Chairman Mikhail Rodzianko, and ultranationalist leader Vladimir Purishkevich. He also refers to the left-liberal Nikolai Astrov, Chairman of the All-Russian Union of Towns, and Moscow's liberal mayor, the industrialist M. V. Chelnokov.

Miliukov is a swine. Astrov, Chelnokov, L'vov, etc., are scoundrels. Purishkevich has little character, and Rodzianko is a prowling prostitute. But that is all a matter of personalities. The horror is that Russia has been abandoned. There is no sense, no decisiveness, no movement forward, and nowhere for it to wait. The peasants, the merchants, the nobles, the government clerks, and even the clergy—they have all dried up. Where in our national, idealistic state is reason preserved? Where are the signs of that instinct for self-preservation integral for life? Well? The corpse already has stiffened. And what is more, there is a stench of decomposition, worms, and ashes . . .

[He lists heroes who had come to Russia's rescue in the 300 years of Romanov rule, like General Kutuzov, who commanded the army against Napoleon's invasion in 1812. He laments that Russia now has no such men.]

As for the "the official regime"—What midgets!

PART TWO

FEBRUARY–JULY 1917

The End of Tsarist Rule

By January 1917, the strains of war had severely weakened public faith in the tsarist order and aggravated social tensions in Russia's cities and villages. Workers' frustration at low wages, high prices, shortages of goods, and harsh work routines contributed to a wave of strikes in January and February in Petrograd. In late February, workers' demonstrations and strikes triggered events that ended tsarist rule—the February Revolution.

On 23 February 1917, thousands of working-class women (encouraged by the socialist parties) took to Petrograd's streets in demonstrations marking International Women's Day. The demonstrators also protested against high prices and food shortages. At the core of the crowds were women textile workers from the city's Vyborg District, who transformed the protests by goading male factory workers to join them in the streets. The demonstration became a mass strike, and within three days, some 300,000 workers, students, and white-collar employees had joined in a general strike that effectively shut down Petrograd.[1] At first, most strikers made economic demands—for higher wages, shorter work hours, and so on—but as the protests evolved, crowds began carrying banners calling for political change and an end to the tsarist autocracy.[2]

By 25 February 1917, the mass strike and demonstrations overwhelmed Petrograd's police. Liberal leaders called on Nicholas II to form a new government based on the State Duma, as they had repeatedly during the war. Instead, the tsar—who was at the military command staff headquarters (Stavka) in Mogilev—ordered that the State Duma be shut down and directed the Petrograd garrison to crush the demonstrations. Garrison soldiers initially obeyed these orders: on 26 February, troops fired into crowds of protestors. But on the morning of 27 February, the Petrograd Garrison began to mutiny. That day, unit after unit refused to obey orders, and thousands of soldiers joined the demonstrators. By nightfall, virtually the entire garrison was in rebellion. Three politically critical events then happened more or less simultaneously: the tsar's cabinet resigned; a self-selected Temporary Committee of the State Duma called on Nicholas II to abdicate; and a group of socialist party leaders began organizing a Petrograd Soviet [Council] of Workers' Deputies, based on the model of the soviet that existed during the 1905 Revolution. The Petrograd Soviet and the State Duma Temporary Committee—which met in the same building, the Tauride Palace—both assumed tasks as revolutionary "command centers."

The 27 February 1917 mutiny of the Petrograd Garrison spelled the end of tsarist rule. On 28 February, the military high command made clear that it no longer supported Nicholas II. The tsar's staff negotiated with the State Duma's Temporary Committee to arrange for Nicholas' abdication in favor of his younger brother, Grand Duke

Mikhail. On 1 March, though, the grand duke refused the throne, and the Romanov Dynasty came to an end.

The Question of "Spontaneity" in the February Revolution

The documents in chapter 3 of this book illustrate how various political parties and social groups responded to the February Revolution and how they understood the nature of the new revolutionary order in early spring 1917. Despite a widespread sense that a political crisis was imminent, neither the socialist parties represented in the new Petrograd Soviet, nor the liberals in the State Duma's Temporary Committee, had anticipated that the 23 February 1917 strike would snowball into a revolution. Some commentators at the time, and many subsequent historians, described these events as spontaneous. Historians sometimes contrast the February Revolution's "spontaneity"—the idea that it arose from popular protests without direct political leadership—to the "conspiratorial" October (or Bolshevik) Revolution, which often is described as a coup d'état. The idea that the February Revolution occurred spontaneously also contrasts sharply with the "Party line" in histories published in the Soviet Union, which held that the Bolshevik Party led the masses in the February Revolution.[3]

Since the early 1980s, historians in the United States and United Kingdom have debated the accuracy of describing the February Revolution as spontaneous. This debate has been tied closely to disagreements over the roles played by Menshevik, Bolshevik, and Socialist Revolutionary (SR) activists during the crisis.[4] Recent studies, though, tend to qualify references to "spontaneity" by stressing that workers' and soldiers' political attitudes and dispositions had been influenced by years of socialist political agitation and organization; that steps taken by the city's socialist party organizations in January and February helped set the stage for the revolution; and that, although the socialist organizations did not expect a revolution on 23 February, grassroots socialist activists assumed leadership roles in the crowds on Petrograd's streets as the popular rebellion against tsarist rule developed.[5] Several recent Russian-language studies also assert that historians have overrated the importance of leadership by the socialists and the Petrograd Soviet in the February Revolution, and that the liberal State Duma Temporary Committee played as, if not a more, important a role in shaping the popular rebellion as the socialists.

The February Revolution began in Petrograd, but it was not confined to the capital city. Until the 1980s, English-language literature on 1917 focused entirely on Petrograd and Moscow, with very few exceptions.[6] Since the mid-1980s, however, developments in the provinces and in Russia's regions have drawn far more serious attention from historians.[7] In general, the February Revolution "spread by telegraph," as provincial cities received telegrams carrying news that the tsarist government had fallen. In many cities, events echoed those in Petrograd, with mass demonstrations, arrests of police and other tsarist officials, and the almost simultaneous formation of soviets and duma-based provisional executive committees.

"Dual Power" and Political Divisions over the War

On 2 March 1917, the State Duma's Temporary Committee announced that it had formed a Provisional Government, the purpose of which was to rule Russia until the convocation of a democratically elected Constituent Assembly (which then would decide the form of Russia's permanent government). The new government's cabinet was made up of well-known liberals. Prince Georgii L'vov, a respected nonparty liberal activist, served as the government's prime minister. The new government's most influential figures, however, were its foreign minister, Pavel Miliukov of the Party of Constitutional-Democrats (Kadets), and Alexander Kerensky, the only socialist on the cabinet.[8] Kerensky, who took the post of justice minister, was member of the populist socialist Trudovik Party. As a member of both the duma committee and the Petrograd Soviet, Kerensky represented the main link between these two centers of the revolution.

The Petrograd Soviet's socialist leadership agreed to recognize the Provisional Government's legitimacy, but they rejected direct participation in the government. The Socialist Revolutionaries and Mensheviks believed that the February Revolution was a bourgeois revolution—a revolution that would establish democracy, free Russia of the economic and social remnants of feudalism, and move the country along a path of capitalist development. In a bourgeois revolution, they insisted, the function of the socialist parties and the soviets was to organize the laboring classes, defend their class interests, push the government to implement necessary reforms, and act as a watchdog to prevent the bourgeoisie from abusing the toilers' rights. At the same time, they asserted, the socialists would organize workers and peasants toward an eventual second, socialist revolution, which would come once Russia reached an appropriate stage of economic and social development. Therefore the Mensheviks and SRs rejected direct participation in the Provisional Government. Kerensky, the cabinet's only socialist, would function as an intermediary between the "bourgeois" government and the "revolutionary democratic" elements represented by the Petrograd Soviet.

When the Petrograd Soviet endorsed the new Provisional Government, it did so conditionally, only for as long as the government pursued certain policies. The most important of these conditions were that the Provisional Government must grant universal and full civil liberties; work toward a peace agreement that did not reward countries with territorial gains ("annexations") or payments ("indemnities") and that recognized the right of national self-determination; and take steps toward gathering a democratically elected Constituent Assembly, which alone would have authority to draft a constitution and form a permanent government. But the Petrograd Soviet leadership also expected that the new government would implement a broad range of democratic administrative reforms and progressive social reforms to democratize government and improve living conditions, and that it would begin preparations toward the redistribution of land to the peasantry.

Although the socialist leaders of the Petrograd Soviet and the Provisional Government's liberal leadership agreed to work cooperatively, serious tensions between the two groups existed from the revolution's outset. One of the most significant initial disagreements involved command and control of Petrograd's military garrison. On 1 March 1917, the Petrograd Soviet issued Order No. 1 to the revolutionary soldiers, which stated that soldiers should obey directives from the State Duma's Military Commission *unless* these ran counter to directives from the soviet. Liberals viewed declarations of this sort as undermining the government's authority and subverting order. On 8 March 1917, the Petrograd Soviet established an Organizational Committee (sometimes called the Contact Committee) to "oversee" the government's actions. This relationship between the soviet and the government became known as "dual power"—the division of authority between the Provisional Government, which ran the state, and the Petrograd Soviet, which had the allegiance of revolutionary masses. Miliukov and other liberal cabinet ministers chafed at the idea that the state was supposed to act within guidelines dictated by the Petrograd Soviet and early on voiced their opposition to dual power. They insisted that firm, centralized state order was necessary to defend the revolution, and that any division or diminishment of the state's unity or authority threatened anarchy and might undermine the all-important war effort.

The conduct of the war was a central point of contention in relations between the liberals in the Provisional Government and the Petrograd Soviet's socialist leadership. The liberals insisted on victory in the war, which they defined as one of the revolution's essential goals. For their part, the socialist parties remained internally divided over the war. The right factions among the SRs and Mensheviks still insisted on fighting to victory over Germany and the Central Powers. The Bolsheviks, and the left—or "Internationalist"—factions among the Mensheviks and SRs, condemned the war as imperialistic and called for an immediate peace. In March 1917, the Menshevik Party Central Committee took a "revolutionary-defensist" position. The leading spokesman for this position, Menshevik leader Irakli Tsereteli, argued that Russia must defend itself from the Central Powers, but also called for "the quickest possible peace, without annexations or indemnities." The SR Central Committee took an identical stance, as did the Petrograd Soviet, which elected Tsereteli as its chair. On 14 March, the Petrograd Soviet enunciated its revolutionary defensist position on the war in a declaration "To All the World's People"; the soviet then pressured the Provisional Government to issue a statement renouncing annexationist war aims and calling for a just, democratic peace.

As historian Rex Wade has pointed out, the February Revolution resulted in a realignment of Russian politics.[9] In spring 1917, the right-wing nationalists virtually disappeared from public life (although they would reemerge later that summer). The Kadets, who in the tsarist political spectrum had occupied the center left, now in effect became the center of a "right bloc," which included the prowar socialist factions (primarily, the defensist right among the Mensheviks and SRs). The revolutionary-defensist Mensheviks and SRs, who controlled a solid majority in the soviets, constituted the core of a "centrist bloc." And the Bolsheviks, together with the Anarchists and the most radical antiwar elements among the SRs and Mensheviks, made up an informal "left bloc."

The Bolshevik Response to the February Revolution and Lenin's April Theses

Because the Russian Revolution culminated in the Bolshevik Party's seizure of power, popular histories and general textbooks often view 1917 entirely from the perspective of "the rise of the Bolsheviks," and focus their attention narrowly on views expressed by Bolshevik leader Vladimir Lenin. Specialists on the 1917 Revolution, however, generally agree that this perspective obscures critical dynamics of revolutionary politics and that, although Lenin certainly was the Bolshevik Party's dominant figure, there were intense and almost constant debates over tactics among the party's leaders and between the leadership and the rank and file.[10]

When the February Revolution removed Tsar Nicholas II from power, most top-level Russian revolutionary party leaders were in exile, either internally (for example, in Siberia) or externally (for example, in Western Europe). Lenin, for example, was in Switzerland. This meant that, for a brief period in early March 1917, lower-level Bolshevik leaders set the direction for their party in Petrograd. Unlike the moderate socialist leaders, the editors of the Petrograd Bolshevik newspaper, *Truth* (*Pravda*), refused to support the "bourgeois" Provisional Government and called for a workers' government.[11] In mid-March, the first top-level Bolshevik leaders (for example, Lev Kamenev and Joseph Stalin) returned to Petrograd, took control of the party organization (and *Truth*'s editorial board), and declared that the Bolsheviks—like the Mensheviks and

SRs—endorsed the Petrograd Soviet's decision to conditionally recognize the new government's authority.

When Lenin returned to Petrograd on 3 April, he immediately set about trying to reverse the stance taken under Kamenev and Stalin's direction. In a series of speeches, and in his famous "April Theses," Lenin rejected any cooperation with the bourgeoisie, repudiated the Provisional Government, and called for creation of a workers' and peasants' state based on the soviets. He also attacked the revolutionary-defensist position on the war and claimed that the overthrow of the bourgeoisie would make an immediate peace possible. The Menshevik and SR press condemned Lenin's arguments, and some critics said Lenin had become unhinged. Most Bolshevik Party leaders considered Lenin's views at odds with Russian reality and sought to isolate him. Over the course of several weeks, though, Lenin managed to win over the Bolshevik leadership circles, and the party adopted the arguments laid out in his April Theses.

Labor Relations, Soldiers' Committees, and the Task of Organizing the Masses

Lenin's April Theses appeared at a critical point in revolutionary labor relations in Petrograd and other major cities. In the first days of March 1917, Petrograd's organized factory workers—having gained great political leverage through the February Revolution—used the threat of further strikes to push for an eight-hour workday and other long-deferred workplace demands. This led to complaints from some soldiers' committees that strikes and other labor actions were choking the supply pipeline to the military front. The Petrograd Soviet's Menshevik and SR leaders—who on principle supported the workers' demands—saw ongoing strikes as endangering revolutionary order at a time when a counterrevolutionary backlash was still possible. Mensheviks and SR leaders wanted workers to focus their energy on building new organizations—not just the factory committees that had organized strikes, but trade unions (guided by the socialist party activists). They called on Petrograd's workers to end their strikes, show restraint, and pursue their aims through arbitration whenever possible.

Against the backdrop of pressure from the workers' movement, on 10 March the Petrograd Soviet and the Petrograd Society of Factory and Plant Owners reached agreement on implementation of an eight-hour workday, as well as the creation of arbitration boards to settle labor disputes. This agreement, together with an April Provisional Government declaration authorizing worker-elected factory committees to conduct negotiations with enterprise owners, established mechanisms for peaceful labor relations in Petrograd's largest factories. Owners of smaller enterprises and provincial factory owners, however, did not universally support these measures. Ultimately, the Petrograd Soviet's efforts yielded only a temporary calm in labor relations. In early April—at the same time as the controversy over Lenin's April Theses—the number and intensity of labor disputes over the eight-hour workday, pay rates, and work control issues began to escalate.

Attempts by the Petrograd Soviet's socialist leaders to guide workers away from "disruptive" behaviors had a corollary in policies regarding soldiers. One of the central issues was the meaning and scope of directives on soldiers' civil rights and their right to form elected committees. On 1 March, the Petrograd Soviet's Order No. 1 instructed local garrison soldiers to obey the government's orders unless those commands contradicted the soviet's directives, in which case soldiers were to follow the soviet's orders. Order No. 1 also instructed soldiers to elect their own committees, and it "abolished" a wide range of practices in the military that soldiers found offensive, such as officers' use of abusive language. Two days later, on 3 March 1917, the Provisional Government decreed that soldiers and sailors had civil rights equal and identical to those of other citizens. Soldiers and sailors responded to these declarations by electing their own committees and soviets, both at the front and in rear garrisons.

Liberal politicians and military commanders alike objected to Order No. 1 and the government's declaration on soldiers' rights as disrupting military discipline. In particular, they complained that soldiers were interpreting Order No. 1 as a directive to elect their officers (a common misunderstanding, even among historians). On 7 March, the Petrograd Soviet issued Order No. 2, which explained that soldiers should elect committees to organize their political activities and coordinate their units' daily needs, but that they were not to elect officers. Rumors quickly spread among soldiers that the government was revoking Order No. 1. The Petrograd Soviet and the Provisional Government then jointly issued Order No. 3, on 9 March 1917. This third directive—intended primarily for front soldiers—explained that the previous two orders applied only to the Petrograd Military District; nevertheless, officers must treat soldiers with respect as citizens, in accord with the government's declaration on soldiers' rights. Despite these clarifications, front soldiers expected that Order No. 1—with its call for elected soldiers' committees and its insistence on soldiers' civil rights and their polite treatment—would be extended to the front. Indeed, front soldiers began implementing this "directive" on their own, despite the efforts of their officers and the Provisional Government.

Soldiers' elected committees and workers' factory committees were part of a mass organizational phenomenon in Russia in spring 1917. People from virtually every segment and sector of Russian society formed their own voluntary organizations, unions, or soviets. This rush to organize focused not only on economic and political concerns, but also on cultural development: groups of all sorts set up social clubs, study groups and reading rooms, and musical and theater groups. In spring 1917, liberals and socialists alike believed that public mobilization and organization was critical to the revolution's success. Both factions vigorously encouraged popular civic and political participation and stressed the importance of "political enlightenment" to create a "politically conscious" public.

Liberals were more cautious, however, about the process called "democratization" in 1917. In Russia in 1917, democratization meant the extension of civil and voting rights to all citizens, but it also referred to the direct participation of "the democracy" (broadly speaking, the common people) in the process of government through representation on state administrative bodies. Socialists, who used the terms "the democracy" or "the revolutionary democracy" to refer to the urban and rural laboring classes, argued that representatives from soviets, unions, and various other nongovernmental public committees and organizations should participate in the work of the state. In scores of cities and towns, "committees of public organizations" made up of representatives from local dumas and zemstvos, voluntary civic organizations, trade unions, soviets, and major political parties, functioned as temporary municipal government executive bodies in spring 1917. Grassroots committees sprang up in the countryside—peasants built on their existing communal organizational structure to form new village committees. The Provisional Government sought to harness and guide this phenomenon: it created rural land committees (as part of a nationwide network), township administrative committees, and other committees meant to extend the state's infrastructure to the local level. Already in spring 1917, however, Kadet Party leaders worried that democratization was undermining the central state's authority and that decentralization and democratization could easily turn into anarchy.

The Aspirations of Social Groups

Previous to the 1960s, few histories of the Russian Revolution paid attention to the role of ordinary people in revolutionary politics. Rather, the focus (especially in English-language studies) was on top-level political leaders.[12] In the 1960s through the 1980s, however, historians in the United States and the United Kingdom began examining popular revolutionary politics and social relations, first in studies of political parties, then in histories of specific social groups and provincial society.[13] These "social histories" of 1917 never really abandoned the study of politics. Instead, they concentrated on the political agency of workers, soldiers, and peasants, in accord with larger trends in the historical profession toward the social history. The scope of topics covered by historians of

1917 then expanded further under the influence of new currents in cultural history in the 1990s.[14] As a result, a large body of scholarship (in several languages, including English) now exists about ways ordinary people understood the revolution, their revolutionary aspirations and expectations, and how people organized and acted on these expectations. Chapters 4 and 5 in this book present documents illustrating many popular aspirations and understandings of the revolution.[15]

Historians of the revolution have devoted more attention to factory workers than to any other social group, and as a result, we know a great deal about their aspirations regarding treatment in the workplace, their economic demands, and their workplace organizations.[16] In 1917, Russia's factory workers almost universally expected and demanded respectful treatment as citizens with equal civil rights. They expected shorter work hours, higher pay rates, and better working conditions. The most contentious of their economic expectations had to do with "workers' control"— the right to review a factory's accounts and to supervise hiring, firing, and disciplinary measures. Such demands were a product of longstanding class tensions and the workers' belief (shaped by socialist discourse) that owners would exploit them if not watched closely. But these demands also reflected political suspicion that the capitalists might deliberately undermine production to cripple the revolution.

Although workers' senses of identity and their world views were by no means one dimensional—depending on circumstances, factors such as gender, religion, ethnicity, education, skill level, place of residence, and so on, all influenced how an individual worker might see himself or herself or understand his or her environment—historians generally agree that class identity was central to workers' politics and public lives in 1917. What class *meant* to workers is not so simple. Although the socialist parties defined class as a matrix of economic relations, for workers, factors as subtle as how someone dressed or spoke might determine whether a person was considered a worker or a *burzhui*—a member of the exploiting classes.

In spring 1917, white-collar employees—from lowly store clerks to bank employees to civil servants—voiced many demands similar to those of factory workers. Like workers, they organized unions and professional societies to protect their common interests and made symbolic declarations of support for the revolution. Many, but certainly not all, employees associated their interests with those of the working class and described themselves as workers. Some employees, though, asserted that their education and skills set them outside (or "above") the working class. (Workers, it should be noted, sometimes excluded white-collar employees from their organizations as "class outsiders.")

In spring 1917, educated professionals—such as teachers, doctors, and lawyers—also formed new organizations and unions to promote their professional and social agendas (for example, expanding public access to medical clinics). Although members of these groups seldom defined themselves as part of the working class, many seemed reluctant to define themselves as "bourgeois." In addition to pushing for greater professional autonomy, educated professionals were among the loudest voices calling for mass "public enlightenment"—programs to expand literacy, increase popular access to the arts and science, and promote political and civic consciousness.

Urban social groups that cut across social economic class lines also mobilized behind the revolution in spring 1917. Students in universities, secondary schools, and even in primary schools formed their own "unions" and associations (often, but not always, in support of specific political parties). One of the many general themes of the revolution shared by students was the call for democratization—in this case, of school administration, through greater student participation. Women's groups also seized upon the revolution to organize and press for reforms. The largely "bourgeois liberal" feminist organizations, for example, succeeded in pressuring the Provisional Government to clarify statements on civil rights and suffrage to specify that the law recognized women's equality in these spheres. In 1917, feminist groups persistently demanded equal opportunity for women in education and professional employment. Working-class women, who had been central to the demonstrations that triggered the February Revolution, did at times enunciate their own gender-specific demands and concerns. Generally, however, women workers' concerns were subordinated to the agenda of trade unions, factory committees, local soviets, and socialist party organizations.

Because historians have paid far less attention to business owners than to workers and employees, we know relatively less about the propertied classes in 1917. Contrary to socialist rhetoric about capitalist counter-revolutionaries, it is clear that, on a whole, the business community welcomed the February Revolution. Merchants and industrialists generally believed that the Russian Revolution's success depended on sustaining and increasing productivity, and thus they associated their own economic interests with the interests of the revolution. Entrepreneurs used existing trade associations, stock exchange commissions, and similar business organizations to promote their political and economic interests, and strongly expected that these would give them influence with the Provisional Government.[17]

In spring 1917, soldiers in urban garrisons and at the front (and sailors as well) expected that, as a result of the revolution, they would be treated with the dignity and respect that they associated with civil equality.[18] As citizens, they believed, they had the right to form their own committees and soviets and to have a voice in the administration of their own affairs. Like workers and students, the soldiers and sailors called for "democratization," in this case, of the armed forces. Because such expectations flew in the face of traditional military discipline, rank, and command procedures, soldiers' demands for equal rights spawned great controversy and considerable conflict.

The war, however, was the central concern of those in uniform. In spring 1917, the general consensus among soldiers and sailors was that revolutionary Russia must defend itself. They expected the civilian population to devote themselves to the war effort as well, by sustaining production of war goods and supplies for the army. But the military rank and file also expected the Provisional Government to energetically pursue a peace without annexations or indemnities—in other words, they took the revolutionary defensists' position. In the course of 1917, war weariness would undermine this consensus. And, because the great majority of soldiers (and to somewhat a lesser extent, sailors) had been conscripted from rural districts, they also were concerned with matters central to peasant life, in particular, the issue of land reform.

Like urban workers, the rural toiling population expected that the revolution would bring civil and legal equality.[19] Peasants—like most social groups—had forms of self-organization (such as the village communes) that predated the revolution and shaped their capacity to organize once tsarist rule collapsed. Some peasants were already active in the Peasant Union or other political organizations, and many more belonged to cooperative societies and other rural voluntary associations. In spring 1917, peasants formed local committees (and in some cases, soviets) in a process that paralleled urban developments. Recent research on the complexity of rural society has made clear that broad generalizations about "what peasants wanted" are problematic. Most historians agree, however, that the peasant population expected "democratization" of zemstvos, school boards, township committees, and other state and quasi-state institutions, meaning that these bodies would include peasant representatives and would be responsive to peasant interests. Peasants— male and female—looked to the Provisional Government to end the war as soon as possible, so that their sons, fathers, husbands, and brothers could return home. And they often expected the state to serve as arbitrator in their disputes with private landowners over access to and use of arable land, meadows, and forests.

One widely shared aspiration among the peasant population was that the revolution would bring land reform. The majority of peasants expected the revolutionary state to take land from large private and institutional owners and redistribute it to peasant communities. One of the most common peasant demands in 1917 was, "Land to Those Who Work It." On 21 April 1917, the Provisional Government issued a decree creating a network of land committees, with a Central Land Committee in Petrograd at the top of a pyramid of provincial, county, and township committees. The function of these committees was to work out temporary land reform measures until the Constituent Assembly could gather, and to assemble data that could be used for drafting later, more comprehensive, legislation. The land committees and related arbitration boards quickly became arenas for peasant-landlord conflicts. In 1917, private land-owners, in particular aristocratic landlords, also organized new commit-tees and associations. Like the peasants, they expected the government to protect their own economic and social interests; as a result, landlords continually called on the state to defend their property from incursions by peasant communities.

The February Revolution and Nationality Groups: The Example of Ukraine

In spring 1917, groups representing the Russian Empire's many national minorities quickly advanced agendas that ranged from asserting national cultural autonomy to insisting on full national political independence. Politics among national minorities were divided along lines of ideology, party, and social class, as were politics among the Russian majority. There was no single "Jewish" perspective, for example. Jews might belong to any of a great number of Jewish socialist parties (some of which endorsed Zionism—the pursuit of a separate Jewish national homeland—and some of which did not), or to liberal party organizations or religious-based parties. At the same time, many Jews belonged to the major "Russian," "Ukrainian," or other "national" political parties.

Of all national minorities, the aspirations voiced by Ukrainians proved most politically explosive in 1917. Ukrainians accounted for some 20 percent of the empire's population, and most lived within a large and clearly defined "historical" territory, Ukraine. Ukrainian political parties almost uniformly insisted on Ukrainian political auton-omy within a Russian federation of states. Russian liberals, especially the Kadets, insisted that Ukrainian autonomy threatened the unity and integrity of the Russian state (which they understood as encompassing all the territories of the Russian Empire). Russian Social Democrats (SDs) and Socialist Revolutionaries (SRs) formally endorsed the right of national self-determination and cultural autonomy, but considered such matters secondary to the revolution's main concerns. Ukrainian SDs and SRs, however, took the issue of national autonomy as seriously as did liberal Ukrainian nationalists.

On 4 March 1917, in Kiev, a gathering of Ukrainian liberals and socialists formed a Ukrainian Central Rada (Council).[20] On 5–8 April 1917, the Central Rada convened a Ukrainian National Congress, which passed a resolution demanding national autonomy. The Provisional Government categorically rejected this resolution. In Petrograd in April, though, any discussion of the Ukrainian Rada's demands was drowned out by debate over Russia's war aims.

The April Crisis and the First Coalition Government

In April 1917, a dispute between the Petrograd Soviet and the Provisional Government over war aims resulted in the revolution's first major political crisis. The April Crisis and public reactions to it are illustrated by documents in chapter 6. The conflict emerged soon after publication of the Provisional Government's 27 March statement of war aims, which (under pressure from the Petrograd Soviet) called for rapid conclusion of a just democratic peace and rejected territorial annexations or indemnities. On 18 April, Foreign Minister Miliukov reassured the French and British governments that Russia would fight on to victory and would abide by treaties signed under the tsar—including agreements on the annexation of Ottoman territories. Publication of Miliukov's note sparked mass demonstrations in Petrograd on 20 and 21 April. Tens of thousands of workers and soldiers came out in protest against the government's apparent repudiation of its own stated war aims. Some protestors carried banners calling for resignation of the "capitalist ministers." Other demonstrators, however, came out in support of Miliukov, and clashes broke out between the two camps.

While crowds clashed on the capital's streets, the Petrograd Soviet— which had supported the government, conditional on its rejection of imperialist war aims—demanded clarification of the Provisional Government's position. For its part, the Provisional Government scrambled to argue that Miliukov's note had not contradicted its 27 March declaration. The soviet and the government patched together conciliatory joint statements, and Miliukov stepped down from his post, but these measures did not end the crisis.

The political situation in late April was especially volatile because the controversy over the Miliukov Note was intertwined with debates about dual power, discipline in the army, and whether the socialists should join a coalition government. At a 27 April meeting of the "Four Dumas" (a ceremonial gathering of deputies of all the State Dumas elected since 1906), War Minister Guchkov accused the Petrograd Soviet of undermining the government's authority. On 29 April, Guchkov quit the government. Also on 29 April, Justice Minister Kerensky, in a widely published speech, told a soldiers' congress that declining morale and fraternization were endangering the Russian Revolution, and the Petrograd Military District commander, General Lavr Kornilov, resigned his post to protest the soviet's intervention in military affairs. That same day, the Petrograd Soviet's leadership announced that its representatives would not join a coalition government.

The soviet leadership, however, soon reversed its position on forming a coalition government. In the first days of May, the Menshevik and SR leadership circles approved their parties' participation in a new coalition cabinet. A new, coalition government was then formed. Prince L'vov remained prime minister and liberals kept the majority in the cabinet. Kerensky became war and navy minister. Two Socialist Revolutionaries joined the government: Viktor Chernov became agriculture minister, and Pavel Pereverzev became justice minister. Two Mensheviks also entered the cabinet: Matvei Skobelev took up the new post of labor minister, and Irakli Tsereteli became the minister of post and telegraph. Aleksei Peshekhonov, a Popular-Socialist, headed the newly created Provisions Ministry.

Formation of a coalition government radically altered the political landscape. As a result, the Mensheviks and SRs would be caught between advocating for the interests of the workers, soldiers, and peasants, and defending the interests of the revolutionary state—positions that often were at odds with one another. Moderate socialist leaders often placed the long-term needs of the state above the short-term expectations and aspirations of the lower classes, and as a result, risked alienating their own political base.[21] Moreover, participation in the government meant taking on responsibility for failures and delays in state policies, which also had great political consequences. The economic problems that had helped create the February Revolution had not subsided with the collapse of the tsarist order—indeed, they had worsened. As prices rose and shortages became more acute, as the war dragged on and the prospects for the year's harvest became gloomier, the Mensheviks and SRs would find themselves preaching moderation and patience to an increasingly impatient urban and rural population. In the meantime, the Bolsheviks, who alone among the major socialist parties vehemently rejected participation in any coalition with the "bourgeois" parties, could stand outside the government as critics who bore none of the burdens of power.

In late spring and early summer 1917, the Bolsheviks focused much of their rhetoric on attacking the Provisional Government and the moderate socialists who, the Bolsheviks argued, were betraying the proletarian cause by cooperating with the bourgeoisie. Lenin juxtaposed the Menshevik and SR "conciliationist" tactics with a call for "All Power to the Soviets"—the idea that a government based on the workers', soldiers', and peasants' soviets would replace the Provisional Government. One of the more dramatic confrontations between views of the moderate "socialist bloc" and that of the Bolsheviks came at the First All-Russian Congress of Soviets, which met in Petrograd from 3 to 24 June. The Mensheviks and SRs held a majority among the delegates, who represented workers', soldiers', and peasants' soviets across the former Russian Empire.[22] On 17 June, during a heated debate over socialist participation in the government, Menshevik leader Irakli Tsereteli argued that a coalition was necessary, and that no one political party was prepared to take power by itself. Lenin shouted that there was such a party—his party, the Bolsheviks. In a later speech, Lenin rejected any coalition with the bourgeoisie and argued that power must be passed directly to the soviets.

The June Offensive and the June Demonstrations

Although the coalition Provisional Government formed in May 1917 was fraught with tensions between liberals and socialists (and between the socialist ministers themselves), Alexander Kerensky was able to cobble together agreements in the cabinet on several issues. Perhaps the most fateful of these was over the need for a new military offensive in June. Since early May, the Kadet Party leadership had been calling for a new Russian military offensive. Kerensky, whose cabinet portfolio now included the War Ministry, also pushed for renewed military operations against the Germans. The Russian press heatedly debated the issue throughout May and early June. The revolutionary defensist Mensheviks and SRs initially opposed any offensive and instead sought to convene an international socialist conference (set for June), which they hoped would result in a coordinated campaign by Europe's socialist parties to end the war. Only when plans for this conference collapsed did the moderate socialist leadership accept Kerensky's argument that an offensive would force the Germans to negotiate a general peace under the soviet's terms—no annexations or indemnities and the right of national self-determination.

The June Offensive proved a dismal failure and seriously undermined the coalition government's credibility. On 16 June, Russian artillery began shelling enemy positions, but Russian soldiers did not leave their trenches to storm the enemy lines until 18 June. The Russians took horrific casualties, and within days, the offensive began to falter, in part because soldiers in many units refused to advance. The documents in the first half of chapter 7 illustrate public debates and popular responses to the June Offensive and to demonstrations held in Petrograd in conjunction with the offensive. The Petrograd Soviet had organized a mass demonstration for 18 June, to show support for the military offensive. It also had issued resolutions prohibiting the antiwar left-socialist factions from holding protests. The Bolsheviks and other left socialists in turn called on their followers to take to the streets on 18 June in a counterdemonstration against the military offensive. To the dismay of the soviet's moderate socialist leaders, counterdemonstrators carrying banners calling for an immediate end to the war and the transfer of "All Power to the Soviets" outnumbered those marching in support of the government.

General text books sometimes depict the Provisional Government as doing little or nothing to forestall escalating economic decline and social conflict in summer 1917, and instead putting off all meaningful reform until convocation of the Constituent Assembly or until the end of the war. There is some justice in this generalization—liberals and moderate socialists alike believed that the government's "provisional" nature constrained the sorts of reforms that it could institute, that major reforms required approval of a nationally elected (and thus, popularly sanctioned) government, and that some structural reforms simply could not be implemented during wartime. Nonetheless, the image of a "do-nothing" government ignores the many programs it initiated in 1917, such as mass education efforts, as well as administrative steps like the extension of zemstvo institutions to the township level. As the economy continued to spiral downward, though, members of the coalition government were deeply divided over the sorts of reforms needed to stem the impending crisis. In contrast to liberals in the government, Menshevik and SR ministers viewed market mechanisms as innately irrational and inequitable, and gravitated toward state intervention to stay inflation; ensure supplies of food, fuel, and raw materials; and keep factories running. Perhaps the most serious rift in the government concerned land reform, something that all factions recognized as necessary, but the substance and timing of which were grounds for heated debate. When, on 5 May 1917, the SR leader Viktor Chernov became Russia's agriculture minister, one of his primary concerns was to speed the process by which peasant land committees implemented temporary reforms. Chernov issued instructions that local land committees interpreted as encouragement to take direct control over the land. For liberals in particular, this was anarchy unleashed. But Chernov's actions also provoked the ire of the government's Menshevik members, who believed that he had placed short-term political exigency ahead of the state's needs. The dispute over land committees and the pace of land reform would contribute to a second government crisis in July.

The July Crisis and the July Days

On 2 July 1917, the coalition government that had been formed in May collapsed. Although the product of multiple disagreements over policy—and in particular, the Kadet outrage at Chernov's directives to the land committees—the break between the liberals and moderate socialists in the cabinet finally came over the question of Ukrainian autonomy. In a 10 June declaration called the "First Universal," the Ukrainian Rada argued that Ukraine must have administrative autonomy within the framework of a Russian federation. The Rada then began establishing the framework for a separate Ukrainian state administration. Although the Russian political parties, foremost among them the Kadets, criticized these steps, their effect was to push the Provisional Government into negotiations. When, on 2 July, the government published an agreement with the Rada that granted the Ukrainians independent administrative authority, the government's Kadet members resigned in protest. From the Kadet perspective, the government was initiating Russia's dismemberment and—in effect—playing into the hands of the German enemy. General accounts sometimes mistakenly blur the July government crisis with the "July Days"—the term used to describe a failed bid for power by Bolshevik and other left-socialist militants in Petrograd on 3–4 July. The documents in the second half of chapter 7 illustrate public and popular reactions to the July Days.

By the beginning of July, garrison soldiers' hostility toward the June Offensive and workers' anger over the declining economy and employers' growing refusal to satisfy their workplace demands seemed to dovetail with frustration at the Provisional Government in Russia's urban centers. Garrison soldiers in Petrograd and several other cities were particularly upset over orders to disband and relocate "revolutionary" units that had refused to participate in the offensive. Although the moderate Mensheviks and SRs still held a majority in all major urban soviets (and had won sizable victories in urban duma elections held in June), the more militant mood among soldiers and workers had expanded the ranks of the left-socialist factions. On 2 and 3 July, grassroots Bolshevik, left SR, and Anarchist activists organized a series of meetings in Petrograd that demanded the Provisional Government's overthrow.

Until the late 1960s, most historians treated the events in Petrograd on 3–4 July as a failed coup attempt engineered by Lenin and the Bolshevik leadership. In what is widely considered the most authoritative study of these events, however, Alexander Rabinowitch demonstrated that the Lenin and other top-level Bolsheviks actually were ambivalent toward the street demonstrations and, in a sense, were pushed into a corner by the militancy of the rank and file.[23] On 3 July, workers' meetings at several factories and soldiers' meetings in several garrison units decided to march to the city center to demonstrate—in some cases, with rifles in hand—for the immediate transfer of "All Power to the Soviets." Through that night, armed workers and soldiers filled the city's streets; in several incidents, random shots were fired. After midnight, a huge crowd of soldiers and workers gathered at the Tauride Palace and demanded that the soviet leadership take power—a demand that the soviet leadership refused to accommodate.

On the night of 3–4 July 1917, leaders of the major socialist parties gathered for an emergency joint session of the All-Russian Central Executive Committee of Soviets and the All-Russian Executive Committee of Peasants' Soviets. (The peasant committee had been elected by the First All-Russian Congress of Peasants' Soviets in May; the soviet committee had been elected by the First All-Russian Congresses of Soviets of Workers' and Soldiers' Deputies in June. Each had been charged with representing the soviets between the convocations of all-Russian congresses.) The joint executive meeting had two purposes. First, it was to discuss the government crisis occasioned by the Kadet ministers' resignation in a dispute over Ukrainian autonomy. Second, it had to decide how to respond to the violent demonstrations on Petrograd's streets. Gregorii Zinoviev, one of the senior Bolshevik leaders, claimed that his party had tried to restrain the righteously angry workers and soldiers. Zinoviev argued that the only way to calm the situation was for the soviet leadership to take power. The SRs and Mensheviks rejected this conclusion and insisted that the Bolsheviks had launched a rebellion in order to seize power.

In the meantime, in early hours of 4 July, the senior Bolshevik leadership in Petrograd (Lenin was not in the city) met to discuss the armed demonstrations with the party's "military organization" (which worked with garrison soldiers) and with Bolshevik delegates from the Petrograd Soviet's workers' section. Grassroots activists and some midlevel party functionaries insisted that the street demonstrations could force the Central Executive Committee of Soviets to take power. The senior Bolsheviks disagreed and tried to rein in the demonstrations. Lenin, who returned to Petrograd a few hours later, also considered an armed uprising premature. Still, he had declared that power must be transferred to the soviets—the slogan being championed by the militants on Petrograd's streets—and could not repudiate the armed demonstrations.

On 4 July 1917, militant sailors from the naval base at Kronstadt joined the armed workers' and soldiers' demonstrations in Petrograd. Again, the demonstration focused on the Tauride Palace, where a group of sailors famously demanded of SR leader and agriculture minister Viktor Chernov, "Take power, you son of a bitch, when it is offered to you!"[24] On 4 July, several shooting incidents took place, with as many as 400 fatalities. In the city center, the demonstration spun out of control and crowds looted shops. That night, as the unrest wound to an end, rumors spread that the government had dispatched loyal troops from the front to put down the uprising. Also on the night of 4 July, several of Petrograd's military units renounced the demonstrations after government envoys presented them with "evidence" that Lenin was a German spy. By late on 5 July the government had regained control over the situation. Lenin went into hiding in Finland, and the government arrested Trotsky and several other Bolshevik leaders. Kerensky set about trying to organize a second coalition government, and the Russian Revolution entered another phase.[25]

CHAPTER THREE
RESPONSES TO THE FEBRUARY REVOLUTION

3.15
LENIN, "ON THE PROLETARIAT'S TASKS IN THE CURRENT REVOLUTION"

3.16
THE MENSHEVIKS ON LENIN'S "APRIL THESES"

DOCUMENT 3.1
PROLETARII, "BOLD IN STRUGGLE"[1]

The following document is a poem from the first issue of Petrograd's Bolshevik newspaper, Truth (Pravda), *on 5 March 1917. On 5 March, Lenin and other top-level Bolsheviks had yet returned to Russia. Under its first editors— Viacheslav Molotov and Aleksandr Shliapnikov—*Pravda *rejected the "bourgeois" Provisional Government. In mid-March, though, two newly returned Bolshevik leaders—Joseph Stalin and Lev Kamenev—took over the editorial board. From 15 March until Lenin's return in April,* Pravda *gave the government conditional approval. The identity of the poem's author, Proletarii ("The Proletarian"), is unknown.*

Bold in Struggle, with New-Born Force

Bold in rule over the new day.
Down with Tsarism. It is dead.
Sliced open. It is dead for certain.
Forward, brigades in the struggle for happiness,
Toward a new Socialist order.

Forward, great proletariat,
Forward in glorious, bold battle.
Crush Capitalism's heavy yoke
With your calloused hands.
Freedom is before you
As the sun brightly rises.

You find creativity in labor.
You are the Tsar of labor, and your palace
Will replace the torn-down prison.
And the old order is finished.

Forward, with youth's power,
To smash winter's harsh ice
With your solar freedom.
We must move forward.

—Proletarii

DOCUMENT 3.2
THE PETROGRAD BOLSHEVIKS' INITIAL POSITION ON THE REVOLUTION[2]

The following document also appeared in Truth (Pravda) *on 5 March 1917 and reflects Molotov and Shliapnikov's militant stance. The editorial foreshadows*

Lenin's call in April for the Bolshevik Party's transformation into a mass organization, but did not anticipate Lenin's insistence on the immediate transfer of power to the soviets.

On 23 February, the great Russian revolution began. After three days of demonstrations and several violent clashes with the police, there was a lull. The old order had gathered all its forces in order to deal with the workers. On 26 February the proletariat, together with the revolutionary soldiers, overpowered those troops who still supported the government. Another 2–3 days and it was clear to all that the invincible old regime had fallen. The Peter-Paul Fortress and the Admiralty were taken, and the old government's staff was arrested. The tsar abdicated under the revolutionary movement's pressure, and events were rolling along toward a Constituent assembly and a Republic.

Two tasks stand before the Russian revolutionary proletariat. The first is to consolidate its position, to ward off any possible counterattack by the old order or by the counterrevolutionary bourgeois classes. There still is danger that the old order will seek revenge. And at the same time, even now, the bourgeois are trying to lead the revolution along a deadly channel—organizing the officers, appealing to the soldiers to subordinate themselves to the officers, and declaring themselves in favor of a monarchical form of government.[3]

The proletariat must remember that it can only stabilize its conquests and achieve the revolution's goals if it has weapons in its hands. Among the moment's tasks is to form a revolutionary, democratic guard that, together with the revolutionary troops, can defend the revolution's conquests whenever necessary.

[Second] among the tasks of the moment is to organize the scattered worker masses. The moment's tasks require propaganda for our political program among the masses. In view of the forthcoming Constituent Assembly, the Social Democrats must mobilize and multiply their forces. It is necessary to reestablish the party and its organizations, and it is necessary to renew the party literature.

And so, comrades:

Enroll in the party
Create a party organization
Create cadres of proletarian and democratic guards
Create a party press
Carry out broad agitation for Social Democratic ideas and slogans
    spelled out on the RSDLP's banner[4]
Collect funds for organization, agitation, and literature

DOCUMENT 3.3
THE LIBERALS ON THE FEBRUARY REVOLUTION[5]

The following document, the liberal Kadet Party's first published response to the February Revolution, appeared in that party's Petrograd newspaper, Speech (Rech), *on 5 March. Because of a strike by the city's typographers,* Speech *had not appeared during the revolutionary uprising. The author refers to three archconservative former tsarist officials: Internal Affairs Minister Aleksandr Protopopov, State Council Secretary Sergei Kryzhanovskii, and Pavel Kurlov of the Internal Affairs Ministry.*

Petrograd, 5 March 1917

During the long week of our involuntary silence, great events occurred that turned a new page in the motherland's history. Just a week ago, the old regime defended its existence with unusual stubbornness. It was nourished by profound faith in its own durability, for which it criminally sacrificed state interests. Crazy Protopopov threatened to cover Russia in blood and studded the capital's rooftops with machine-guns . . . And even in the heat of revolution, Kryzhanovskii arrogantly insisted that it all was a sham and everyone would scatter when Kurlov was dispatched.

By then, however, Kurlov had already been arrested, and it was the old regime that turned out to be a sham. It fell with fantastical rapidity, as if someone had waved a magic wand. Honor and glory and eternal memory to our brothers who, in the final battle against the old regime, gave their lives for motherland's good!

It can be said that our revolution is sharply and decisively different from previous revolutions. Unfortunately, though, it is not completely accurate to say that it was bloodless. On 23 February, the government insolently and self-confidently set out, armed, against the people's movement. On 2 March the tsar abdicated the throne, and Grand Prince Michael, to whom the tsar had passed power, declared that only a Constituent Assembly elected by universal, direct and secret ballot could decide upon the form of government.

The shining achievements of the people's movement were made possible, of course, by the old regime's weakness. The old regime could learn nothing and forgot everything. But primarily and most of all, the Revolution was a stunning success because the people and society (in contrast to the old regime) had learned the lessons of our recent and difficult past. In these critical days, they displayed that high degree of unity and boundless self-sacrifice that signifies a nation in the proper sense of the word. Everyone rallied around the State Duma. Orderly lines of soldiers—troops that had joined the people—hurried to the Tauride Palace. The Soviet of

Workers' Deputies sat in session there. And the Provisional Government emerged, with a program that has universally received full approval.

Unity and organization were the keys to successfully achieving this eighth wonder of the world, which is how history will forever see this Revolution. We must not forget, however, that while the victory was brilliant, it still is not consolidated. [The Revolution must prepare] itself against any attempt by the old regime to restore itself to power, which it undoubtedly will try to do if it finds a suitable opportunity. We cannot forget that those who yesterday directed this great country's fate led it toward total ruin. A great exertion of energy is needed to fight for and establish a normal course of life. But most of all, we must understand that we are at war, that our enemies are on our soil and will exploit our slightest weakness.

And so it seems that everything still lay before us after our shining victory. Achievements must be strengthened and the government's shattered life must be set into normal, peaceful channels. These tasks can be realized only if our spirits remain at the highest levels. They can be realized only if our unity and organization strengthen with each passing day and if each of us, together and as individuals, helps the Provisional Government fulfill its weighty public responsibilities.

Citizens! We are living through a great historical moment. We are a fortunate generation, on whom the duty has fallen to build the motherland's fate in the years to come. We will prove worthy of this great epoch. Not for a minute will we forget our great responsibility to Russia's future. We will strengthen and consolidate all the forces of unity and self-sacrifice that in the last few days magically transformed the picture.

DOCUMENT 3.4
THE MENSHEVIKS ON THE FEBRUARY REVOLUTION[6]

The following document is from editorial in The Workers' Newspaper (Rabochaia gazeta), *the Mensheviks' Petrograd newspaper, on 7 March 1917. The Mensheviks (and the SRs) supported the Provisional Government under the condition that it meet expectations laid out by the socialists and the Petrograd Soviet. In a bourgeois revolution, they believed, the socialists must organize the laboring classes, push the government to implement necessary reforms, and act as a watchdog to prevent abuses of the toilers' rights.*

The [Provisional Government's] tasks are clear and simple. With support from the people and the army, it must quickly and decisively destroy all that remains of the old order and all that hinders the new one. It must quickly and decisively create everything that the new order needs to exist. Since creation of the Provisional Government, the Soviet of Workers' and

Soldiers' Deputies has exerted its influence so that the government's program includes all the measures necessary to create a democratic Russia.

If the Provisional Government fulfills its duty, *if* without restraint or delay it begins to act in accord with the interests of democratic Russia, and *if* it carries out the struggle against the old regime *to the end*, then inevitably it will enjoy the people's confidence and a united struggle will be carried out against the common enemy—the old regime's remnants.

During the revolution's first and most difficult week, the conduct of the proletariat and the revolutionary army demonstrated their readiness to [remain united] and pursue Russia's liberation together with the liberal bourgeoisie. It is now up to the Provisional Government to demonstrate through its actions that it deserves this support.

Members of the Provisional Government! The proletariat and the army await your immediate orders concerning the revolution's consolidation and Russia's democratization. Our support is contingent on your actions. The sooner and more decisively you act, the sooner and more completely preparations will be made for the Constituent Assembly, which will determine Russia's subsequent fate. Let us set about the work of destroying the old order and preserving the new Russia. We demand that you immediate realize your program!

DOCUMENT 3.5
THE MENSHEVIKS ON THE NEED TO ORGANIZE[7]

The following document set presents two editorials in The Workers' Newspaper *(Rabochaia gazeta), the Mensheviks' Petrograd newspaper, on 7 March 1917. The first, titled "The Struggle Is Not Over—Organize!" was aimed at workers and soldiers in general. The second, "Women Workers," is a plea for the government and revolutionary activists to recognize women's full equality and calls on women workers to organize themselves.*

The Struggle Is Not Over—Organize!
The old tsarist regime was rotten from top to bottom and fell at the revolution's first charge. The old structure of slavish Asiatic despotism has been torn down; something new already has sprouted from beneath it: a reborn, free Russia.

. . . The revolution's destructive work still is not complete. The old order still has resources. There still is danger from insidious plots against the revolution by Russia's dynastic oppressors and the many packs of tyrants—big and small—scattered across this immense country and its cities. Destructive work—the complete annihilation of the tsarist bureaucratic cliques that strangled and fed off the people's body—must be carried out to the end. A faint whiff of the old order's foul odor can still be detected in its wreckage. The country needs to clear out that wreckage, to prevent any attempts to rebuild the old structure.

We also must start building a new life now, without wasting a minute. We cannot say: first, we must finish annihilating the old; then we can think about building the new. In the course of our struggle, we must strengthen those positions we have already seized.

We are living through a transitional moment. The old is not yet conclusively crushed, but the new is only just being assembled. . . . We must understand history's lessons, which teach that any revolution contains the danger of reaction. In a revolution, the peoples' spirit and energy may rise to the very highest level. But even at this height, it has to hold its ground.

Today we are absorbed in the struggle against the old regime, but we also must look ahead. . . . The revolution's results depend on the democracy's organization and consciousness. To completely prevent the old order's return, the democracy must immediately being implementing the program that the Provisional Government announced to the revolutionary people. The democracy must organize and create new institutions of revolutionary power in the provinces.

Russia's democratic reconstruction cannot and must not be decreed from above. The organized democracy can only make the revolutionary program a reality if it permeates and penetrates all spheres of public life—city administration, the courts, the militia, schools, and so on. The conscious proletariat, as the democracy's revolutionary vanguard, must actively participate in building the new Russia. It cannot close its eyes. It knows a new bourgeois Russia is already being built. . . . It is deeply concerned that bourgeois Russia be democratic, so the proletariat can freely organize its own forces, organize for class struggle toward realizing its ultimate aim—the Socialist reconstruction of society. . . .

Women Workers
The revolutionary uprising began on 23 February, which an international congress had designated as international proletarian women's day. During the uprising's excellent days, our sisters, wives and daughters were with us. It was their happiness and their woes that ignited the struggle. They faced the tsarist executioners' bullets; they mixed their blood along with ours. They fearlessly looked death in the face, lifting all our faith in the coming victory.

But women's rights, and particularly their equal rights, have not been among the revolution's achievements. The Soviet of Workers' and Soldiers' Deputies should immediately place this issue before the Provisional Government. We were equal in struggle, and we should be equal in rights. Women must obtain these rights. And women workers, who displayed great bravery in the struggle, must take the great work of organizing upon their shoulders.

There are no women representing either female or male workers in the soviet. There should be. Conscious comrades must immediately set about organizing meetings to elect delegates. Meetings must be convened immediately to take up the issue of organizing women workers.

The tsarist regime imprisoned women workers. The serfdom-like spirit in industrial enterprises powerfully oppressed all women workers. In the great struggle for liberation, we must not forget this extra oppression against women. We must make it a special task to eliminate such oppression.

Comrade women-workers—organize immediately!

DOCUMENT 3.6
THE ANARCHIST-COMMUNISTS IN THE PETROGRAD SOVIET[8]

The following document is a statement by Iosif Bleichman, representative of the Petrograd Federation of Anarchist-Communists, to the Petrograd Soviet Executive Committee's Workers' Section on 7 March 1917. The Anarchist-Communists were Petrograd's largest anarchist group and Bleichman was one of their most dynamic speakers. In early March 1917, the Anarchist-Communists had no newspaper, and the Soviet Executive Committee had banned their use of the soviet's press facilities. On 7 March, Bleichman twice demanded that the soviet co-opt Anarchist deputies and give the Anarchists access to their typography. In this document—his second appeal—Bleichman sets conditions under which Anarchist delegates would agree to participate in the soviet's work.

Representing the Petrograd Federation of Anarchist-Communist Groups:
With unbelievable force, we obtained the freedom for which we had so long strived. The Petrograd organization of Anarchist-Communists demands that we be admitted to the soviet. We still have not received this right. The Anarchist-Communist organization has resolved to go arm in arm with the revolution. But to ensure that the new government smashes the chains, we demand:

1. removal of the old regime's adherents;
2. abolition of everything that curtails freedom;
3. execution of the old ministers;
4. freedom for anarchist thought;
5. that the anarchists be given weapons and ammunition, as the revolution is not over;
6. material support for liberated anarchists.[9]

. . . When we heard that freedom was near, we rejoiced. But now we have become disappointed, because freedom is in danger. We want to publish a journal. We have been banned from the soviet's typography, and it seems we will not have the right to publish a newspaper without the Soviet Executive Committee's permission. Where is freedom? We should not be laying down our weapons already, and now we hear that the militia will be disarming us.[10] Is that true?

I hope that we will be given the right to participate in the soviet of soldiers' and workers' deputies. . . .

DOCUMENT 3.7
THE LIBERALS ON "THE DEMOCRACY'S RESPONSIBILITIES"[11]

The following document is an editorial from the Petrograd Kadet newspaper, Rech (Speech), on 10 March 1917. Note that in the first two paragraphs, the author refers to Russia's prerevolutionary "inhabitants." The author then switches to the word "citizens" when discussing the population after 2 March 1917. The editorial voices two of the liberals' constant themes in 1917: that citizens' public activism must be organized through legal channels that strengthen the Russian state's unity; and that the Russian state's interests—particularly in foreign policy—transcend the fleeting interests of whatever government may be in power at the moment.

The Democracy's Responsibilities.

The old regime's overthrow must not only replace people and transform institutions; it must lead to a complete renewal of public legal consciousness. We need both a political revolution and a revolution in our thinking. That can only happen if there is an upheaval in Russia's inhabitants' psychology that parallels the government's overthrow. It can only happen if the people are summoned to become citizens of free Russia. The old order collapsed because it deprived society of this. The new order can be consolidated only if it has support from all the collective forces of organized public opinion.

We see very good signs that our inhabitants have entered a psychological-revolutionary period. The tsarist authorities' alienation from the people, and its leaders' hostility to the public, made Russia's inhabitants feel distant from the state and from government affairs. For people who had risen from the dull comfortable crowd and developed a level of conscious citizenship, this situation was offensive and intolerable. But the tsarist government favored apathy, inactivity, laziness, and a lack of responsibility. . . .

Since the tsarist government was overthrown, no one in Russia has the right to think or act as if they are merely inhabitants. We have no more inhabitants. We all have become citizens. As a result, the tension between "us" and "them" has disappeared. The most powerful absolute monarch might say, "I am the state." But sovereign people who have created a democratic state order say, "We are the state."[12] This gives it enormous legal rights, but also brings enormous responsibility.

In our newspapers we read every day about the powerful development of public activism in all spheres of urban life. This demonstrates that the capital's people know their legal rights and appreciate the responsibility of citizenship. Reports from the provinces say that the same process is underway there. Russia is advancing into an epoch of independent activism and self-government. Naturally, public energy is first directed toward satisfying immediate daily needs and demands. The old police force, with its monstrous apparatus of political investigations and professional bribery, has been destroyed. Society has formed a voluntary militia. The old state institutions that managed food supply matters are bankrupt. Society is creating its own committees, councils, and commissariats, which are working to regulate the population's food supply. In the future, the legislature will face difficulties, but it will have the blessed task of utilizing this public spirit and finding expedient forms and means to direct and channel the "living water" of public energy.

The population's independent activism is encompassing all domestic administration. But foreign policy issues cannot remain outside a free nation's interests and attention. Foreign affairs matters are state tasks. They pursue unified, eternal aims that are unchanging despite variations in their formulation. Therefore, foreign affairs must be conducted with society's direct participation and under its vigilant supervision. In practice, that has not been the case. In no other field of state activity was absolute power so jealously guarded and so thoroughly monopolized as in the conduct of international relations. We all paid for this "tradition" with our flesh and blood. We gave soothsayers boundless, uncontrolled command over the state and nation's greatest and most precious affairs—its international objectives and world interests.[13] We put up with an antinational diplomacy conducted by a closed, swaggering, self-satisfied caste. And too often we obeyed without any criticism or protest. And so we bore all the consequences of their frivolity, short-sightedness, and lack of talent.

In this matter, the victorious revolution doubtless will bring a cleansing and a renewal. The people's state will create a national foreign policy and a national diplomacy. A time of independent activism has begun for the democracy. It has acquired great legal rights, which come along with heavy responsibilities. Henceforth, the democracy will be responsible not only for Russia's internal stability, but also for bringing her international glory.

DOCUMENT 3.8
THE BOLSHEVIKS ON "POWER TO THE DEMOCRACY"[14]

The following document appeared in the Bolshevik's Petrograd newspaper, Truth (Pravda), *on 11 March 1917. By defining the Provisional Government as "counterrevolutionary," the editorial clearly differentiated the Bolsheviks from the Mensheviks and Socialist Revolutionaries, who had given the government their conditional support. On 15 March, Stalin and Kamenev took over* Pravda's *editorial board and adopted a more conciliatory position toward the government. In mid-April, Lenin would steer the Bolsheviks back on to a militant course.*

Power to the Democracy.
The revolution has not ended. It has only entered a new stage. Its first wave washed away those at the helm of political power. The counter-revolutionary Provisional Government then seized the helm. But reaction's foundation, its social bed—the landowning aristocrats on whom it relies—still exists and was not damaged by the revolution.

The Provisional Government is gathering forces to silence the revolution, to stop it from moving forward, to prevent it from spreading to the villages and to army units still loyal to the Provisional Government.

But the revolution is inevitable. It is the result of objective conditions. The Provisional Government can gather all its forces and try to prevent the revolution from spreading to the villages and the army. But it will happen just the same, because it is inevitable. . . . It is in the interest of the proletariat and peasantry that its spread . . . takes an expansive and organized form. Therefore the aims of Provisional Government and all the counterrevolutionary forces gathered around it are profoundly different from the aims of the conscious proletariat, peasantry, and soldiers.

The Provisional Government opposes the army's reorganization on the basis of self-government; they would keep it in the old commanders' hands.[15] Revolutionaries must replace the old commanders and organize the entire army on a democratic basis. The Provisional Government removed the [tsarist] provincial governors, but appointed the chairmen of the noble-dominated zemstvo administrations in their place.[16] The countryside is still under the power of the aristocratic landlords and land captains, and it is not being organized.[17]

The revolution's slogan must be to replace the old authorities in the countryside. The organized peasantry must take local power into its own hands. The district police, land captains, and other old government agents must be arrested and disarmed.

The peasantry must organize local peasant revolutionary committees and transfer power to those committees.

In the towns, too, the old order must be replaced by the new. In place of authorities appointed by the Provisional Government, a new town government must arise from the urban democracy's ranks. In other words, replace power appointed from above with power created from below by the revolutionary urban democracy, the revolutionary army, and the revolutionary peasantry.

Democratic self-government in the army, villages, and towns! Revolutionary soldiers' committees, peasants' committees, and urban communes!

The democratic revolution must be carried out to the end.

DOCUMENT 3.9
THE MENSHEVIKS ON "THE PROVISIONAL GOVERNMENT AND THE WORKING CLASS"[18]

The following document is an editorial from the Mensheviks' The Workers' Newspaper (Rabochaia gazeta) *on 12 March 1917. It develops the Menshevik argument that this was a bourgeois revolution, but that the soviet and the revolutionary democracy must keep close watch to ensure that the Provisional Government enacts progressive policies. Several members of the newspaper's editorial board served on the Petrograd Soviet's "Contact Commission," which interacted with the Provisional Government on an almost daily basis.*

The Provisional Government and the Working Class.

A powerful revolutionary wave toppled the dynastic monarchy and washed away the old order. A Provisional Government, made up of State Duma and State Council members and led by the Zemstvo Union chairman, rode in on the crest of that wave.[19] A revolution begun and sustained by the proletariat and revolutionary army pushed into power a temporary government for Russia made up of representatives from the progressive nobility and bourgeoisie—from the liberal democratic intelligentsia. It includes only a single authentic leader from the democracy—Kerensky.

This repeated a common pattern in European revolutions: the workers overthrew the old regime, but the new order fell into the hands of the liberal bourgeoisie and the liberal-democratic intelligentsia. *This was inevitable in Russia, given our current stage of political and economic development.* The working class is a minority of the population. The democratic peasantry and the peasant-based army might adhere to the proletariat's political slogans. But it might not go along with the proletariat's radical economic demands.

Russia still has a long period of bourgeois-democratic development ahead. It is true that the rural and urban petty-bourgeoisie—the great mass of ordinary inhabitants—received an excellent political education thanks to the war and the old government's criminality. That is why the old regime collapsed easily and painlessly.

But their sympathies would immediately turn away from the revolution if the working class were to take state power. The working class is contemporary society's most revolutionary class, and its interests as a whole oppose those of the entire bourgeoisie as a whole. As long as the population's great majority still has not made the transformation from "loyal" inhabitants to free citizens, and as long as the rapid development of the bourgeoisie and capitalism is still in the future, the proletariat cannot and must not rush after state power.

Under pressure from Petrograd's revolutionary democracy, the Provisional Government published a program for action that includes almost all the political demands of the Russian and world democracy. These only meet the socialist proletariat's minimum program, but they are the most that can be attained within the bounds of a bourgeois social framework. Of course, the road to hell is paved with good intentions, and more than once in the past we have seen excellent promises go unfulfilled.

The workers and the entire revolutionary democracy demand that the Provisional Government's program be implemented. The Soviet of Workers' and Soldiers' Deputies has resolved to support the Provisional Government only so far as the government carries through with this program. The working class must keep a vigilant eye on the government's activities and exert continuous pressure on the government to secure the democratic reforms it has promised. At the same time, the working class must welcome and support the government and clear a path for it in the still-dark masses' consciousness, in the towns and particularly in the villages. The working class must smash all the old order's remnants and manifestations.

So far the Provisional Government has executed its program. We expect it to be bolder and more decisive. Still, we all must recognize that in just one week it published a series of important state acts that already are ushering in a new order in Russia. It arrested the tsar, then gradually replaced the old government's functionaries in the provinces. Our task, the task of the entire working class, *is to help it in its work*. Then and only then will this work be durable and fruitful.

The Provisional Government and its program, adopted in collaboration with the Executive Committee of the Soviet of Workers' and Soldiers' Deputies, has been enthusiastically received across Russia. To fight against it when it is just beginning to function, to distrust its every step, and especially to attempt to take power *in its place* would mean *inciting all bourgeois-democratic Russia against us*. It would mean dividing the Russian Revolution's forces and *playing into the hands of the dark past's not-yet-completely extinguished forces*.

The Provisional Government is a revolutionary government befitting revolutionary Russia's level of development. It was created by a whirlwind of events, an irrepressible historical torrent that washed away the rotting foundations of centuries of slavery in just two weeks. It is a government that, *against the will of its majority, has become a revolutionary government*.

Our task is to help the Provisional Government carry the revolution to its conclusion, while at the same time preventing any attempt by the government to hinder or roll back the revolution. This is best done, not by screaming about treason and trying to seize power for the proletariat, but by organizing pressure on the government and incessantly advocating our views to the population's backwards strata. Organize and undermine the counterrevolution; enlighten those who might still support the old order. Understand that supporting the Provisional Government's revolutionary work also prevents any *counterrevolutionary plans on its part.*

DOCUMENT 3.10
THE SOCIALIST REVOLUTIONARIES ON THE FEBRUARY REVOLUTION[20]

The following document set presents two essays from the Socialist Revolution-aries' (SRs) Petrograd newspaper, The People's Cause (Delo naroda), *on 15 March 1917. In spring 1917,* The People's Cause *was a sounding board for a wide range of views among the SRs. In June, it became the official newspaper of the centrist SR Central Committee, but it continued to run essays by comrades on the party's left and right wings as well. The first document is an unsigned essay, "On the Establishment of a Republic." Despite the article's title, Russia was not declared a republic until late summer. The second essay, Aleksandr Gukovskii's "Socialism, the War, and the Fatherland," gives a strong sense of the role that revolutionary morality played in the SR worldview.*

On the Establishment of a Republic.
. . . A republican form of government has been established in Russia. It was established without any elaborate ceremony and without any dec-larations. It appeared effortlessly, unobtrusively, on its own. This, the world's greatest contemporary historical achievement—the sudden collapse and scattering to the winds of a heavy, three hundred year old geological formation—occurred with almost no impediments and hardly any sacrifices. Or so it seems at first sight. And this is the prevailing opinion. . . .

In fact, however, change did not come so easily. Nothing comes free; nature demands sacrifices. If we consider events, it becomes clear that Russia paid a very high price for liberation from the autocracy's shameful yoke. It paid with millions of lives and torrents of blood, unlike anything that the world had known.

The war's unprecedented bloodletting shook Russia's popular masses to the core and opened their eyes to the old regime's depravity, dishon-esty, and criminality. It completely shattered the old order's influence and standing. It therefore led to events that, under different circumstances, might not have happened for another decade. Old idols were pulled down from their splendid thrones. The happy idea of liberty brightened people's minds. A most important thing happened—a revolution in the people's minds and hearts.

The task of the moment is solid political organization to give form to the freedom that had been realized. This form's vital content must be radical democratic and social reforms. The urban and rural toiling masses have paid dearly for Russia's republic. We hope that they will send representatives to the Constituent Assembly, lest the people's liberty be surrendered again to the monarchy.

Socialism, the War, and the Fatherland.

As a party deeply imbued in socialist ideals—ideals that are above all ethical and humanitarian—we must unconditionally condemn our national enemies in all their manifestations and types. We must not be indifferent to their calls for elemental racial hostility and their struggle for political dominance and economic mastery. Before us shines the light of worldwide brotherhood, so close and glowing so brightly—a world-wide federation of peoples; a new great United States embracing the entire globe.

Socialism's ethical basis requires that we invariably uphold the principle of national self-determination. We pledge to fight oppression and coercion. National self-determination is an indispensible condition for the individual's perfectibility and happiness. It is a precondition for the growth and development of the treasury of national languages, literatures, and art in all its forms. It is a precondition for the organic unity of all mankind's many tribes. Only free peoples can actively and forcefully join hands in a mighty, worldwide brotherly union. A socialist's honor and conscience finds military coercion and invasion as revolting as domestic oppression.

We also understand that there are historical moments when the struggle for national liberation awakens the best, noblest feelings in people. Socialism does not extinguish this brilliant impulse of the human soul. It is deeply concordant with its substance and order. Properly conceived international unity and national self-determination are two sides of the same coin, like morality and the humanitarianism. Indifference is not a proper conception of international unity. . . . The fate of small countries—of Belgium, Serbia, Greece, Persia, which have been barbarically devastated by beasts—raises our indignation. It is a deep and solemn injustice that a socialist's conscience cannot tolerate.

We aspire to a worldwide brotherhood of free peoples with equal rights. Enlightenment, rights, and freedom of self-determination in the diverse and great Russian republic are especially dear to us. International brotherhood does not exclude devotion to the motherland—rather, it encourages it. We desire our great motherland's happiness, and we fear that internal and external aggressors and enemies threaten its freedom.

A great people's powerful movement has amazed the whole world though its gigantic growth, its united and singular will, the power of its unity, and the great fighting strength of its armed brothers. Its internal enemies have gone down in flames. But our foreign enemies have weapons in their hands. They are near—they are at our gates.

Were the unbelievable to happen, were we to become divided when facing the enemy, and were the enemy to be victorious as a result, it would end the bright days of Russian freedom. The old regime would return, assisted by Prussian bayonets and machine guns. Or Russia would become a principality of the Hohenzollerns, who have always supported reaction in Russia. Reaction's triumph would be secure for a long time. And the freedom and social reforms for which so many glorious generations have fought would be set aside for a long, long time. Gallows would be set up from Petrograd to Vladivostok. And a free country again would be transformed into a stagnant, rotten police district, with iron bars over dull windows through which hardly any daylight would pass. Instead of the forthcoming Constituent Assembly, again we would have the rule of Shturmer, Manasevich, and Protopopov.

What a disgrace that would be!

—Al. Gukovskii

DOCUMENT 3.11
THE SOCIALIST REVOLUTIONARIES ON ORGANIZATION, THE SOVIETS, AND THE PROVISIONAL GOVERNMENT[21]

The following document set presents two editorials from the Petrograd Socialist Revolutionary (SR) newspaper, The People's Cause (Delo naroda), *on 19 March 1917. The first essay, "Organize!" reflects the common idea that organization was critical to the revolution's success. The second lays out the SR view on the relationship between soviets and the Provisional Government and rejects the liberal complaint that "dual power" was undermining the state's authority.*

Organize!
The People's Cause's editors consider it their moral and political duty to appeal to all party members on the urgent need to begin energetic organizational work in the provinces.

The Constituent Assembly elections are forthcoming. On 15 March the Provisional Government swore a solemn oath to take all measures to convene the Constituent Assembly as soon as possible, on the basis of a universal, direct, equal, and secret ballot. All the country's democratic organizations are pressing the Provisional Government in this direction, so that the Constituent Assembly elections might begin as soon as possible. And so, those decisive elections grow near.

Our party, whose program and entire past has been devoted to the sacred struggle for the toiling classes' interests, can count among its ranks the very broadest strata of the urban working population and the rural toiling masses, who now are awakening to political life everywhere.

We therefore are obliged to exert all our efforts to organize local party committees in all provincial towns immediately, to organize local party committees in all significant railroad junctions and other populated points immediately, and then set about forming party committees in every township and, when possible, to form village committees.

All local committees—regional, provincial, county, and so on—face urgent tasks, imperatively dictated by life:

1. Arranging meetings, assemblies, public readings and talks to familiarize the broad popular masses with the party's basic program, history, and goals.
2. Arranging permanent organizations based on the party platform: a democratic republic, socialization of land, and radical reorganization of industrial labor.
3. Preparing for the Constituent Assembly elections: clarifying the details and tasks of the Constituent Assembly, so that it is based on elections that are universal, direct, secret and equal for all—including women.

. . . At this great historical moment, no party member has the right to be passive.

The Provisional Government and the Soviet of Workers' and Soldiers' Deputies.

The problem of the relationship between these two institutions in revolutionary Russia, and the relationship between the party and national public opinion about them, has advanced to the very forefront of issues that history has set before the great people. It is discussed at meetings, in the press, and in friendly chats. It already is establishing lines that divide parties and political tendencies.

For the Socialist Revolutionaries, one part of this problem is not particularly difficult to solve. The Socialist Revolutionaries—the party of the toiling masses, which have altered history's course through their vital force—refuse to employ a narrow legalism to the revolution or its institutional scope at this time. We are not interested in which institutions in the new order are legally superior to others. Right now we are completely indifferent to questions of public-legal precedence. . . .

Without expounding at great length on creation of new government institutions, we can state some facts. The Provisional Government grew out of the revolution. Its form was agreed to by the State Duma Temporary Committee and the Executive Committee of the Soviet of Workers' and Soldiers' Deputies. At this transitional moment, it is in fact the country's main republican administrative institution. Its role is that of a tool, one history has put in our hands for the revolution's continuation and for strengthening fundamental freedoms and democratic principles. If it is utilized for those aims—as long as it does not deviate from its fundamental historical tasks—we will support it. We support it not out of fear, but with a clear conscience.

It is not a socialist government. Propertied landowners and various shades of bourgeois financiers, industrialists, and members of the liberal professions are prominent among its members. And there are many among these bourgeois political placeholders who are not even Octoberists or left social reformist Kadets.

That the Provisional Government is not an admixture of democrats and socialists is significant because it speaks to the peculiar logic of recent events. As long as the bourgeoisie, which entered the government in its first days, consistently advances a democratic program of new reforms—beyond already existing decrees—then the party of revolutionary socialism can frankly support the Provisional Government. According to this schema, groupings may be formed to defend and consolidate the revolution's first gains that include active socialist forces, whose ultimate demands doubtless will advance far beyond the boundaries of the government's program.

But this is where the other part of the problem begins. If so far the new bourgeois Provisional Government has been a vehicle for strongly designed reforms, then revolutionary Russia owes this to the fact that the Soviet of Workers' and Soldiers' Deputies emerged as a communications center between popular and socialist forces during the heroic struggle against the old regime. The soviet played a primary role in the revolution's victorious outcome. The people who joined it had already raised workers' spirits in February, in constant meetings February that were little known to the public due to oppressive censorship. They drew the workers and soldiers together as the struggle began. They came forward courageously, without any of the confusing hesitation that the Duma showed at first. In short they, with their hearts and heads, were the engine of the Russian revolution. Yes, and at present, despite separate blunders and individual mistakes, they embody the toiling and socialist elements' revolutionary vigor.

And for precisely this reason, socialists are not concerned about dual power, which so agitates the timid bourgeoisie and their unsophisticated yes-men among the mediocre minds of the progressive intelligentsia. Right now the Provisional Government has power, as long as it implements its program. But the government would quickly waste reform's glow and lose its significance as a vehicle for this revolution, were it not for the constant oversight of that vital—if sometimes impulsive and raging—hearth of public and socialist energy, the Soviet of Workers' and Soldiers' Deputies and its Executive Committee. Stopping the soviet's lobbying and its oversight activities and setting it to "pacify" the masses, as the doctrinaires of order so zealously recommend, would stop it from pressuring the Provisional Government. Then the Provisional Government's first test would be holding back the onslaught of reactionaries, who have by no means been decimated. . . .

[The author warns that any break with the Executive Committee of the Soviet of Workers and Soldiers Deputies would distance the Provisional Government from the revolutionary masses. He makes a cautionary comparison to France in June 1848, when the French provisional government's break with the revolutionary masses led to open class warfare.]

The Provisional Government has power to make reforms, and the Soviet of Workers' and Soldiers' Deputies lobbies and oversees its activities. This settles the question of the interrelationship between these two institutions and the question of their relationship to the vanguard of the democrats and the followers of the socialists.

DOCUMENT 3.12
REPORTS AT THE SEVENTH CONGRESS OF THE PARTY OF PEOPLE'S FREEDOM (KADETS)[22]

The following document set presents two reports given at the Kadet Party's seventh congress, held in Petrograd on 25–28 March 1917. More than 300 delegates from 50 cities attended the congress, which considered dozens of reports and proposals from the party's leading figures. What follows are excerpts from two long reports given at the opening session on 25 March. This first, by Prince Pavel Dolgorukov, laid out the congress's tasks. The second, by Feodor Kokoshkin, focused on the party platform regarding state institutions.

[Prince Dolgorukov's report.]
Dear party comrades! I welcome you on behalf of the Central Committee. This 7th delegates' congress gathers under extraordinary circumstances, at a historic stage in Russia's life. Less than a month has passed since Russia entered this definitive, irreversible stage, which was brought on by the Russian revolution. Our hated autocracy, which for centuries weighed upon Russia like a curse, was pernicious. So was the past decade's absurd, pusillanimous constitutional-democratic order, which has passed forever into memory. But the changes that came so rapidly and spontaneously to our motherland also place demands on all Russian citizens. They demand incredible strength and tremendous work from us in particular. Conditions for our party's work have changed completely. Ours was an illegal, persecuted party; now its members participate in a real government.

[Dologrukov names the several party leaders who hold Provisional Government posts, and the meeting applauds them. He asks that the delegates also applaud Russia's citizens, as it was they who made the revolution.]

If all conscious Russian citizens support the Provisional Government in its labors, support its authority over the entire society and all Russia's peoples, and recognize its complete power—if citizens show strong confidence in the government—then it will lead Russia safely to the Constituent Assembly.

We expect other political and class organizations to do great work. But their work must aid and support the Provisional Government, which was chosen by the Russian people and by the Russian revolution. These organizations can have consultative function, as the government's auxiliaries.

We have a great deal of work before us in the next several days, gentlemen. But we cannot sit in meetings very long, because the country demands that many of us return to the provinces. Before us are issues regarding our program, tactics, and organization. [He explains that the new political situation requires modifications of the party program.]

In addition to program questions, it is particularly important that we take up questions of organization if we want our party to be active and to play a part in the revolution. [He explains that the new political situation calls for the rapid introduction of new organizational efforts.]

In addition to organizational questions, there are very important questions of tactics, particularly given this critical moment for the state. [He explains that party tactics in free Russia must differ from those under autocratic rule. He reiterates this idea several times.]

Gentleman, you know what our position on the war has been since its very beginning, since August 1914. We were the first political party that came out for continuing the war until complete and decisive victory over our enemies. This must remain our slogan. After two difficult years of fighting, which demanded innumerable sacrifices from the country, such strains, such ordeals, it must be the slogan for us all. (*Applause.*) And now, despite these ordeals, despite these sacrifices—or on the contrary, precisely thanks to them—we are obligated to continue the war to the end. The hundreds of thousands who have been sacrificed obligate us and our entire country to continue. (*Applause.*) Therefore, our slogan remains what it has been from the beginning: War to total victory. Now our slogan must grow even stronger: the war must continue until the enemy's complete expulsion from Russia's borders.

Despite our negative attitude toward the old regime, we took the same position as it did regarding the war. Now we must do so all the more, as a democratic state. We must do so while the organized Russian people fight to defend their restored rights and freedom, together with our valorous and freedom-loving allies. We must do so while the Russian people fight to destroy German imperialism and militarism, fight for a lasting international peace. Lasting peace and the brotherhood of peoples is unthinkable without a democratized state, because toiling people everywhere are deeply peace-loving. This is true in our country, among our allies, and—I profoundly believe—in the countries of our enemies. Militarism has been forced on them by the privileged upper classes. We must hope and believe in a durable achievable peace. We must hope that the wave of democratization that raised the great Russian revolution will roll over the Central European Powers and sweep away the last traces of absolutism and feudalism.

[Dolgorukov equates those who have died for Russia in the war with those who died overthrowing tsarism. He calls on the congress to stand in a silent tribute, which it does. Then, to great applause, he leads the meeting in expressing gratitude to the Russian Army and Navy.]

And now, gentlemen, we need to take up our work. I think that you all are singularly aware and understand that the fatherland is in danger. The Russian revolution's success must not intoxicate us and cloud our perception. We must remember the danger that still threatens many countries—from outside and also, perhaps, from the inside. World peace and Russia's radical transformation still demand titanic force. May our party play its own modest but appropriate role in this international feat— the creation of a strong and free Russia. A Russia we can celebrate and take delight in. A Russia where the people's freedom has taken root and will be preserved eternally. (*Applause.*)

[Kokoshkin's report.]
Our party's Central Committee has entrusted me with the responsibility of reporting to the congress on the review of our program's political section. [Kokoshkin explains that the public expects the Kadets to debate and discuss their program, rather than make quick decisions based upon the buoyant mood of the moment.] Regarding the issue of the government's form, they also expect we will not limit ourselves to the one general abstract formula that is on everyone's lips—the formula that proclaims a democratic republic. (*Applause.*) They expect us to introduce several concrete terms to this formula, and they are right to demand this.

Gentlemen, eleven years ago we stated in our program that the desirable form of government for Russia was a parliamentary monarchy. While we established this point, however, we were not monarchists in the precise sense of the word. Our majority never considered monarchy—not even parliamentary monarchy—the best form of government. For us monarchy, be it constitutional or parliamentary, never was a supreme principle, like it was for real monarchists. For us, monarchy was not a question of principle, but a question of political expediency. [Kokoshkin gives examples of congresses and meetings at which the Kadets clarified their ideas regarding monarchy.]

. . . Regarding the state's structure, we have always distinguished between the state's form and the state's substance and content. The question of form concerns the legal summit that crowns the pyramid of government power. The question of substance and content concerns the political structure. For us, this second question was always fundamental and more essential. In our notions about the state, we affirm three fundamental principles. Regarding the state's relationship to individuals, our bedrock always has been, and will inalterably remain, the inviolable principles of civil freedom and civil equality. We will defend these principles, and we will come out against their encroachment wherever they might happen. (*Applause.*) The liberation principle—a liberal principle—is the first foundation stone of our program.

Another basic principle for us—one that regards not the state's relationship to the individual, but the state's internal structure—is the principle of secure, complete supremacy of the people's will, the democratic principle. This is our second foundation stone. (*Applause.*)

And our third principle relates to the state's goals. This is the realization of the principle of social justice: broad reform to satisfy the just demands of the toiling classes. Our [conservative] political opponents reproached us for these sections of our program and said that we stood for socialism. In a sense they were right. In reality, with this program point we did enter the realm of the socialist worldview. Not, of course, the socialist worldview that considers it possible to transform the economic structure though violence or political dictatorship. Rather, we expressed the opinion that mankind will gradually evolve a new social structure. A democratic party's tasks include using the state's influence to promote this process at the quickest, most painless, and most successful pace possible.

These are the three principles on which we have stood. Our stated aim was to realize these; everything has been in service of these aims.

[Kokoshkin dwells at length on the historical and tactical reasons the Kadets previously endorsed a constitutional monarchy with representative institutions instead of a republican form of government. He stresses the symbolic importance of monarchy in Russia's popular political culture, which had no strong tradition of representative institutions. The 1905 Revolution then introduced representative institutions that slowly schooled the people in democracy, and that process undermined the tsarist system.]

This dual process came to its culmination with the Great War. Among the population's broadest circles, the problem of the monarchy took a sharp form during the war. The old formula, "For the Tsar and the Fatherland," was subjected to trial by fire. The war showed that one could not be for both the tsar and the fatherland. The monarchy had come out against the fatherland. One could either be for the tsar, or for the fatherland. (*Applause.*) In choosing, one could not waver. The people and the army came out for the fatherland and against the tsar. (*Voices:* "Bravo!" *Applause.*) The monarchy was irrevocably crushed with one blow. It fell like a rotted-out tree falls in a gust of wind. The war tested the monarchy and the people. The people, in its maturity, passed the exam. They concluded their preparatory political course and graduated to the next epoch of history. But the monarchy failed the exam and remained behind, in the past . . .

[Kokoshkin argues that the monarchy committed suicide by refusing to change, and was assisted in this by the monarchist parties. It cannot be restored. Therefore, the Kadets must adopt a republican platform.]

. . . There is no need to create a republic artificially. A republic already exists in fact. Of course, Russia's legal government form is not yet settled, as that is up to future Constituent Assembly to determine. But the order that now exists is not a monarchical order, but a republican order. And this circumstance must influence the Constituent Assembly's future decision regarding the issue . . .

[Kokoshkin says he can foresee no circumstances under which the Constituent Assembly would restore the monarchy. It almost certainly will favor a republic. Russia has freed itself from the Romanovs, but that the German monarchy still threatens free Russia. Therefore all Russia must unite behind the democratic-republican ideal.]

. . . We cannot be satisfied until our program includes the words "democratic republic." [He explains why this issue had divided the Kadets before 1917 and says that the context has changed.] Of course, our task today is not to work out all the details of the future republican order. Several basic variations exist among the main types of republic, and we must determine a position. We must include several concrete factors in our formula under the heading "democratic republic."

[In discussing these "concrete factors," Kokoshkin repeats the idea that the Kadets have three principles: civil freedom and civil equality, democratic rule, and social justice. He makes analogies to the history of the French and the North American republican systems, explains aspects of each, and discusses the danger that a presidential system might develop into a dictatorship.]

. . . In our program, we must endorse principles that would protect the republican form of government from this danger. From our perspective, it therefore would be correct to unite a parliamentary form of government with the election of the republic's president from among the people's representatives.

And so, on the basis of all I have stated, our program regarding the form of government would chiefly be as follows: Russia must be a democratic parliamentary republic; legislative power must rest with the people's representatives; the head of the government executive must be the republic's president, elected to a fixed term by the people's representatives, with a ministry responsible to the people's representatives. . . .

[Kokoshkin stresses that the greatest threat to Russia's freedom comes from outside its borders, from the German monarchy. He insists that Russia cannot lose the world war and remain free. The German monarchy would crush the people's will and restore the monarchy. Russia must stand by its allies and continue the war.]

. . . In an address to the [US] Congress, the North American United States' President Woodrow Wilson mentioned the Russian revolution.[23] He particularly emphasized that the revolution had made the war's meaning and character clear to the whole world. And when our party—which does not ignore its responsibilities, always carefully weighs and considers its decisions, stands for the broadest circles of the people, and is not disposed to rapid and shallow outbursts—when our party comes out in favor of a republican regime, this brings our country into a new, bright standing in the whole world's eyes. Our decision clearly states that Russia has irrevocably stepped onto a new path. Russia, having set itself on the path of freedom, cannot bear anything other than freedom for other peoples. (*Prolonged applause.*)

DOCUMENT 3.13
THE PETROGRAD SOVIET ON "DUAL POWER"[24]

The following document is an editorial from the Petrograd Soviet's official newspaper, Izvestiia, *on 27 March 1917. It came as a response to editorials in liberal newspapers like* New Times (Novoe vremia) *and* The Moscow Bulletin (Moskovskiia vedomosti) *and statements at the Kadet's congress that accused the soviet of giving orders that weakened the state's authority (thus the term "dual power"). While publically the liberals and socialists argued over "dual power," the government and the soviet's "Contact Commission" quietly negotiated agreements on important policy matters. These included an agreement on foreign policy aims that led to a 27 March 1917 government declaration promising a foreign policy in harmony with the soviet's position.*

The campaign against the Soviet of Workers' and Soldiers' Deputies continues. The bourgeois newspapers and bourgeois congresses are making a number of serious charges against the soviet: the soviet is undermining the government's authority; the soviet is creating dual power in the country; because the soviet has a large and diverse membership brought together by accidental circumstances, it cannot govern the country.

[The author explains that reactionaries had made the same accusations against the State Duma's bourgeois leadership in the last years of the tsarist regime.]

This is no accident. Groups in power always try to monopolize power. Ruling groups always tend to interpret every attempt to control them by the population's broad strata as an encroachment upon their own rights. And they always counter these attempts by instilling fear of dual power and of anarchy.

These are empty fears! Without control, there cannot be confidence. . . . [The author explains that popular oversight ensures more effective governance. The bourgeois parties had argued this under the autocracy, but had "forgotten" this and other truths once in power.]

They have forgotten where their power came from. They have forgotten that the revolution created the Provisional Government, and that they assumed their government positions with the Petrograd workers' and soldiers' consent. They have forgotten that the people remain power's highest source, and that the people, represented by their elected bodies, have the right to control any government. The proletariat remembers this.

[The author reviews the great changes that have taken place since February: the old regime's overthrow, the soviet's formation, and creation of the bourgeois Provisional Government.] Even greater changes lay ahead. The proletariat will meet those changes boldly and directly, and will not drop its banner. The Soviet of Workers' and Soldiers' Deputies will not reject its right and duty to control the government's activities.

DOCUMENT 3.14
THE MENSHEVIK DEFENSISTS ON DUAL POWER
AND THE WAR[25]

The following document set presents excerpts from two editorials that appeared in the Petrograd newspaper, Unity (Edinstvo), *on 29 March 1917. Unity was edited by Georgii Plekhanov and other members of his Menshevik defensist faction, Edinstvo. The second editorial, "The Democracy's Victory," was written in response to the Provisional Government's 27 March statement on war aims, which rejected territorial annexations and financial indemnities. Whereas the revolutionary defensists believed this statement was in concord with their call for "the quickest end to the war," Plekhanov and the defensists saw no contradiction between rejecting imperialism and fighting on to victory over Germany. In April 1917, conflicting interpretations of the government's 27 March statement would precipitate a major political crisis.*

. . . The goal of our bourgeois democratic revolution, unlike that of the overthrown semi-absolutist regime, is to destroy the social basis of Prussian aristocracy's rule [in Germany].

In its essence, our revolution is bourgeois-democratic. . . . Given the country's historical and economic conditions, it cannot be otherwise. Our capitalists are still too weak and our productive forces are still too underdeveloped. The remnants of pre-capitalist forms are still too strong. Our economy's technological level is still too weak to meet our military aims, and we are still too disorganized. This is because we entered the war tied to Asiatic political and economic forms. The armed people have overthrown tsarism, but cannot yet move forward toward a dictatorship of the proletariat and peasantry. They cannot begin to press for a socialist revolution. That would lead only to anarchy. The revolutionary masses knew this instinctively. The proletarian vanguard—the majority of Social Democrats, clearly understood this.

To its great historical merit, the Russian proletariat consciously supported the bourgeois democracy's struggle for power and supports the creation and consolidation of a new democratic order. This support will be steadfast and unwavering as long as the bourgeois democracy, in the form of the Provisional Government, strictly fulfills the revolutionary obligations that it has taken upon itself.

The Provisional Government must be given full power. Only then can the country's economic life become organized. Only then can its great economic problems be solved. Only then can urgent political and general social reforms be implemented.

Both sides may make mistakes, and disagreements are natural. But the moment's seriousness—the danger of counterrevolution has not yet vanished, and there is great external danger—cannot tolerate dual power, which is pregnant with disastrous consequences. Details must be sacrificed for the general cause. Debate about petty, secondary questions must not hinder the implementation of vital measures, must not shake the new government's authority.

The Soviet of Workers' Deputies must openly and fully support the Provisional Government, as long as it honestly makes necessary reforms and firmly upholds the banner of the Constituent Assembly.

The Democracy's Victory

The Provisional Government has issued a declaration defining its position on the war. This has tremendous domestic and international significance, and so we will be devoting a special article to it. For now, we must stress that the new government's action breaks from the old regime on the question of foreign policy. It decisively condemns imperialism . . . and the tsarist government's nationalistic predatory policies. . . . [26]

With this act, the Provisional Government has taken a position that defends Russia's freedom. It has defined the war as a struggle for oppressed nations' liberation, for freedom of national self-determination, and for conditions that will guarantee a long and lasting peace. This is the democracy's tremendous struggle, which all those to whom the revolution is dear must welcome.

DOCUMENT 3.15
LENIN, "ON THE PROLETARIAT'S TASKS IN THE CURRENT REVOLUTION"[27]

The following document is Lenin's famous "April Theses." When Truth (Pravda) *published this essay on 7 April 1917, the editors appended a note saying that "Comrade Lenin" was expressing his own views. On 8 April,* Truth *ran an essay by Lev Kamenev that took issue with some of Lenin's arguments. Lenin, however, eventually convinced the Bolshevik leadership to adopt his theses as the party's new program. I have summarized sections that are readily available in translation, but I have included the entirety of Lenin's often-ignored introduction and the seldom-translated text that follows the theses. These provide a sense of how heated the socialists' rhetoric could become and give a taste of Lenin's method of putting down his critics.*

On the Proletariat's Tasks in the Current Revolution.
Having just arrived in Petrograd on the night of 3 April, I came into the 4 April meetings [of Bolshevik and Menshevik party representatives] with a report on the tasks of the revolutionary proletariat that bore my name alone, and with reservations regarding its insufficient preparation.

The sole thing that I could do to make this work lighter for myself—and for my conscientious opponents—was to prepare written-out theses. I read these aloud and gave the text to Comrade Tsereteli. I read them very slowly and twice: first at a meeting of Bolsheviks and then at a meeting of Bolsheviks and Mensheviks.

I am publishing these, my personal theses, furnishing only the briefest notes, which I developed in more detail in the report.

Theses

1. In our attitude toward the war—which under the new government of L'vov and Co. remains a predatory imperialist war on Russia's part, by virtue of that government's capitalist character—the slightest concession to "revolutionary defensism" is impermissible.
   a. [Lenin argues that the "class conscious proletariat" can fight only if defending a revolutionary state that is controlled by the proletariat and poor peasantry, renounces the territorial annexations, and no longer serves the capitalists' interests. The bourgeoisie is using revolutionary defensism as a cloak for a war of conquest, to enrich the capitalists. The Bolsheviks must convince the masses and front soldiers that a just democrat peace is impossible until the

bourgeoisie is overthrown. They also must urge Russian soldiers to fraternize with the Germans.]

2. The peculiarity of Russia's current situation is that the country is in transition from the revolution's first stage—which, because of the proletariat's inadequate organization and class-consciousness, has put power into the bourgeoisie's hands—to its second stage, when power must pass to the proletariat and the poorest peasant strata.

   a. [Lenin describes three characteristics of this "transition": Russia has become "the freest" of all the war's belligerents, since its citizens now have broad legal rights; the government is not using violence against the masses; and the masses have confidence in a government controlled by their enemies, the capitalists. The Bolsheviks must adapt itself to these conditions and conduct mass propaganda.]

3. No support for the Provisional Government. Expose the complete falseness of all its promises, particularly those regarding the renunciation of annexations. This exposure must replace the impermissible, illusion-breeding "demand" that *this* government, a government of capitalists, cease being an imperialist government.

4. Recognition of the fact that our party is a minority in most workers' soviets (and so far, a small minority). It faces a *bloc* of all petty-bourgeois opportunist elements, from the Popular-Socialists and Socialist Revolutionaries down to the [Petrograd Soviet's] Organizational Committee (Chkheidze, Tsereteli, Steklov, etc.), who have yielded to bourgeois influence and spread that influence to the proletariat.

   a. [Lenin defines the workers' soviets as the only truly revolutionary form of government. For the first time, he argues that state power must be transferred to the soviets. Propaganda must lead the masses toward the idea of Soviet power by "patiently, systematically, and persistently" criticizing the dual power arrangement.]

5. Not a parliamentary republic—compared to the Soviets of Workers' Deputies, a parliamentary republic would be a step backward—but a Republic of Soviets of Workers', Agricultural Laborers', and Peasants' Deputies, throughout the country from top to bottom.

   a. [Lenin calls for abolition of the police, bureaucracy and the army. In a note, he says the army must be replaced by "the universally armed people." All government officials must be elected, subject to recall, and paid an average skilled workers' salary.]

6. The agrarian program's emphasis must be shifted to stress Soviets of Agricultural Laborers' Deputies. Confiscation of all landed estates. Nationalization of all the country's land, which will be distributed by the local Soviets of Agricultural Laborers' and Peasants' Deputies.

   [Lenin adds that poor peasants must have their own soviets, and local agricultural laborers' soviets must set up model farms.]

7. Immediate consolidation of the country's banks into one general, national bank controlled by the Soviets of Workers' Deputies.[28]
8. Instead of "introducing" socialism as an immediate task, immediately put social production and distribution of goods under the control of the Soviets of Workers' Deputies.
9. Party Tasks:
   a. Immediate convocation of a party congress.
   b. Change the party program, mainly:
      1. On the question of imperialism and the imperialist war
      2. On our position toward the state and *our* demand for a commune state. [In a note, Lenin says that the model for the state must be the 1871 Paris Commune.]
      3. Amending our outdated minimum program
   c. Change the party's name. [In a note, Lenin says that the Bolsheviks should call themselves Communists, not Social Democrats, because Social Democrats everywhere had betrayed the proletariat by supporting the war and cooperating with the bourgeoisie.]
10. Renovation of the International.[29]
    Take the initiative in creating a revolutionary International, an International that is against *social chauvinists* and against the "center."

[In a note, Lenin explains that the "center" refers to Social Democratic and Labor Party leaders in Germany, Italy, France, and England. Like Chkheidze and Russia's revolutionary defensists, they had vacillated between "chauvinism" and "internationalism."]

So the reader can understand why (in my introduction) I specified the rarity of "conscientious opponents," I invite you to compare such opposition to the following objections by Mr. Gol'denberg: Lenin "has planted the banner of civil war in the midst of the revolutionary democracy" (quoted in Mr. Plekhanov's *Edinstvo* No. 5).[30] Isn't that truly a pearl?

[Lenin repeats thesis point 1, on unmasking revolutionary defensism, to show that he never mentioned "civil war."] What does [Gol'denberg's comment] mean? How is it different from pogrom agitation? From something you might read in *Russkaia volia*?[31]

[Lenin repeats thesis point 4, on propaganda to explain the need for Soviet power.] But the usual opponents present my view as a call for "civil war in the midst of the revolutionary democracy."

I attacked the Provisional Government for *not* designating an early date—or any date at all—for the Constituent Assembly's convocation, for getting away with making promises. I argued that *without* the Soviets of Workers' and Soldiers' Deputies, the Constituent Assembly's convocation is not guaranteed, and its success is impossible. But the view attributed to me is that I am against the Constituent Assembly's speedy convocation!!!

I would call this a case of "raving," had decades of political struggle not taught me to see conscientious opponents as the rare exception.

In his newspaper, Mr. Plekhanov called my speech "ravings." Very good, Mister Plekhanov! But look at how clumsy, awkward, and slow-witted your own polemics are. If I gave a raving speech for two hours, how did an audience of hundreds of listeners tolerate this "raving"? Further—why did your newspaper dedicate a whole column to an exposition of "raving"? Inconsistent! You turn out to be completely inconsistent.[32]

Isn't it so much easier to cry, curse, and wail than it is to relate, explain, and understand *how* Marx and Engels reasoned in 1871, 1872, and 1875 regarding the Paris Commune and *what kind* of state the proletariat needs?

The former Marxist Mr. Plekhanov in all probability does not want to recall Marxism.[33]

I quoted the words of Rosa Luxemburg, who on 4 August 1914 called *German* Social Democracy a "stinking corpse."[34] But the Misters Plekhanov, Gol'denberg, and Co. "take offense." For whom? For the *German* chauvinists whom she called chauvinists!

The poor Russian social chauvinists—socialists in word, chauvinists in deed—have tangled themselves up.

DOCUMENT 3.16
THE MENSHEVIKS ON LENIN'S "APRIL THESES"[35]

The following document set presents several Menshevik criticisms of Lenin's April Theses. Critiques of Lenin's April Theses briefly became a regular feature of the non-Bolshevik socialist press. The first document, "Danger from the Left Flank," appeared in the Petrograd Menshevik's The Workers' Newspaper (Rabochaia gazeta) *on 6 April 1917. The second, a biting satire titled, "Lenin's Dream," appeared in* Unity (Edinstvo) *on 9 April 1917.*

Danger from the Left Flank.

When Lenin, having returned from exile, read his report at the joint conference of Social Democrats, many listeners perceived a whiff of authentic tragedy. The kind of tragedy that is hidden within every revolution: the revolution's transformation into reaction. Developing revolutions are always menaced by danger, not just from the right, but also from the left. The revolution can only fight reaction successfully if it stays within boundaries that are predetermined objectively by necessity (the state of productive forces, the level of mass consciousness, etc.). One could do reaction no greater service than to disregard these boundaries and try to shatter them.

Lenin arrived among us to render reaction this service. After his declaration, it can be said: any significant success for Lenin will be a success for reaction. Until we secure our left flank, until we decisively render harmless the political tendency headed by Lenin, any fight against counterrevolutionary aspirations and intrigues will be hopeless.

It is true that he came to us alone, that he said he spoke only for himself and did not claim to speak for his party. He proposed such a full reversal of his party's work that he might be in danger of remaining alone. But on that basis alone, it would be premature and risky to underestimate the danger that Lenin represents.

Today his associates are justly confused. You see, he is ruthlessly attacking the ideals before which they had genuflected, the ideals in whose name they joined us in overthrowing the old regime and worked with us in revolutionary days. The democratic republic and the Constituent Assembly— weren't these the slogans we all united around during the revolution? But, you see, Lenin has declared these slogans old trash to be thrown out.

He won't even march under Russian Social Democracy's red banner. This banner must be tossed aside, he tells us, along with the universally treasonous European Social Democrats. The only people who are not traitors are a small group of implacable socialists who sat in Europe's prisons.[36] We may extend our hand only to them. The general cause of socialism is possible only with them. Therefore those who, according to Lenin, wear the Social Democrats' soiled shirt are asked to put on the new clean shirt worn by the Communists.

This is difficult for his associates to digest all at once. Lenin speaks of forces and principles. In principle, Russia can stay on course toward a socialist revolution. In principle, Russia—with its weakly developed productive forces and an industrial proletariat that constitutes a minority (and a small one), a proletariat with no significant political or professional education and insignificant organizational experience—can make the transition toward liquidating Capital's domination and Socialism's gradual realization. But if Russia still needs a bourgeois transformation to develop its productive forces and prepare it for socialism, then it is absurd to try to overthrow the bourgeois government. Not when it still has not exhausted itself and is headed down a path necessary for Russia's renovation. It is absurd and impossible. And so the attempt is doomed to failure.

If Russia tried to make the leap to socialism now, regardless of its economic backwardness (which the war has revealed so sharply), the next step is the dictatorship of the proletariat. That, or else. . . .[37]

It is true that a few voices in the revolution's first days defended this position. They came from Lenin's associates. Even now, he has a well-known collection of loyal supporters. When Lenin arrived, they were weak. A more sober and healthier relationship to reality not only predominated in the ranks of the revolutionary democracy, but was growing significantly stronger. But he can recruit new supporters from among the revolution's unconscious and spontaneous elements.[38] Active struggle and agitation are imperative to protect the revolution from the stab in the back that is being planned.

People who would appeal to the proletariat's highest and dearest aspirations are aiding the cause of reaction. Playing on these aspirations and the illusion that they can be realized, these people will incite the country's backward majority against the revolution. They will pave a sure road toward reaction. The revolution is threatened by an indubitable danger. Lenin and his supporters must be decisively rebuffed, before it is too late.

Lenin's Dream.
Lenin wrote, read, chewed, and then slept. And Lenin dreamed.

He is in Russia. Not in the motherland. Surely, he is no social patriot! He is in Russia. Hands reach out to him. The people's unceasing cries welcome him.

His eight renowned Theses are all implemented. In his hand is a no-less renowned conductor's baton.[39] Everything he dreamed of has happened. It all has been realized.

The first thesis realized: Capital is overthrown. In the active army, "revolutionary defense" has been organized, along with wide propaganda about "capital and the imperialist war." Fraternization. Jabbering.

The second thesis realized: Unprecedented broad masses have come to life, rallied around his Theses, and put power into the hands of the population's poorest strata. They receive special self-education for party work.

The third thesis realized: The Provisional Government, after fully implementing all its promises, still can find no support anywhere. Kerensky, true to his words, puts a bullet in his head.

The fourth thesis realized: All the elements yielding to bourgeois influence, from the Popular-Socialists and the Socialist Revolutionaries to the Organizational Committee (Chekhedzi, Tsereteli, etc., etc.) have all quit their positions. Their work is criticized! Their mistakes elucidated patiently, systematically, persistently, in a manner specially adapted to the masses' practical needs.

Thesis five realized: All state power has been passed to Lenin, i.e., to the New Soviet of Workers', Agricultural Laborers', and Peasants' Deputies. The New Soviet has co-opted deputies from among the Chinese who have wandered into Russia.[40] The Chinese deputies, despite not knowing the Russian language, have become Lenin's enthusiastic supporters. Elimination of the police, the army, and the bureaucracy—they have been eliminated, along with everyone else.

Theses six through eight realized: The agrarian program's central work has been passed to the Soviet of Agricultural Laborers' Deputies. Model farms have appeared everywhere, at the wave of the conductor's baton. All the banks have been merged into one general-national bank under control of the Soviet of Chinese Deputies. The International has been renovated.

[Kaiser] Wilhelm has carried his own baton in a renewed march to Petrograd. The government in Russia, yesterday the world's freest country, takes a step unprecedented in Russia's internal affairs—a step that is an offense against the Russian revolution—and turns the revolution's most loyal sons over to the Germans. The Soviet Executive Committee protests to the English government. It asks the English democracy to support its protest and calls on the foreign affairs minister to take extraordinary measures to liberate Russia from all political émigrés, without exception.

CHAPTER FOUR

WHAT THE REVOLUTION MEANS TO ME, PART I: SOLDIERS, WORKERS, PROFESSIONALS, INDUSTRIALISTS, AND STUDENTS

4.1
O. LOBANOV, "ARISE!"

4.2
A GENERAL ASSEMBLY OF SOLDIERS AND
QUARTERMASTERS OF THE PETROGRAD DISTRICT

4.3
AN ASSEMBLY OF SOLDIERS' DEPUTIES IN THE VIAZ'MA
GARRISON, 9 MARCH 1917

4.4
SOLDIER A. KOROLOZHEVICH'S LETTER TO THE PETROGRAD SOVIET

4.5
SOLDIER VASILII ANIFIMOV'S LETTER TO THE PETROGRAD SOVIET

4.6
A RESOLUTION BY THE 15TH SIBERIAN RIFLEMEN REGIMENT'S
COMMITTEE OF SOLDIERS' DEPUTIES

4.7
MANDATE OF THE EIGHTH SIBERIAN RIFLEMEN REGIMENT'S
OFFICERS

4.8
A RESOLUTION BY THE OREL GARRISON MILITARY PARAMEDICS'
ASSEMBLY

4.9
A RESOLUTION BY THE FIRST CONGRESS OF SOLDIERS' AND
WORKERS' DEPUTIES OF THE WESTERN FRONT ARMY AND REAR

4.10
THE PETROGRAD SOVIET EXECUTIVE COMMITTEE,
"TO COMRADE WORKERS"

4.11
AN AGREEMENT BETWEEN THE PETROGRAD SOVIET AND
PETROGRAD SOCIETY OF FACTORY AND PLANT OWNERS

4.12
TWO LETTERS ON WORKER-SOLDIER RELATIONS

DOCUMENT 4.1
O. LOBANOV, "ARISE!"[1]

In spring 1917, Russia's newspapers published a great number of poems by "ordinary people" celebrating the revolution. The following document is a poem titled "Arise" by O. Lobanov, a peasant-soldier from Bel'skii County in Smolensk Province. In March 1917, Lobanov sent a letter from the front to his home region's largest local newspaper, The Smolensk Bulletin (Smolenskii vestnik). *That letter included the following poem, which (according to a brief note by the newspaper's editor) Lobanov had written on 5 March 1917.*

Arise!

Brothers all born of the same Mother!
We greet you warmly and bow deeply.
From afar the ranks of soldiers listen to You—
We hear Easter in the Motherland's bells.
We have known dishonorable, vile slavery.
You will throw off the Fatherland's chains!
You reveal all that is sacred
In Russia's soul! Your call to warriors
Resounds through the night in the Russian land.
It is dawn in the Russian land, dawn!
From the blood of the people in the old fields—
On the martyrs' graves—flowers bloom!
Freedom and brotherhood shine in colorful rays.

DOCUMENT 4.2
A GENERAL ASSEMBLY OF SOLDIERS AND
QUARTERMASTERS OF THE PETROGRAD DISTRICT[2]

The following document is an excerpt from the records of a soldiers' assembly in the Petrograd Military District on 2 March 1917. This document highlights the importance to soldiers of matters of dignity and social equality, which stood above practical issues like pay and food rations in soldiers' lists of fundamental demands. On 1 March 1917, the Petrograd Soviet had issued Order No. 1, which instructed soldiers to elect their own committees and abolished disciplinary practices that soldiers found offensive.

Protocol of the first general assembly of the Petrograd District's lower ranks and local quartermasters (as a consequence of unified command).

Sent to the State Duma's Executive Committee and the Soviet of Workers' and Soldiers' Deputies for discussion of general questions regarding improvement of living conditions for the lower ranks.

The meeting was attended by 170 people.

The meeting considered it necessary to obtain the following rights:

1. Equal rights—the rights of citizens.
2. Abolition of officers' titles and of ranks.
3. Free third-class passage on all railroads and water transport, and transport in first or second class with purchase of a general ticket. Also, free passage in urban railroad cars and horse-drawn trams on the same level as other citizens.[3]
4. Polite address to the lower ranks by commanders at times of official service.
5. Increased pay (after the war).
6. Improvement of food rations.
7. Improvement of uniforms, i.e., so as to satisfy actual needs.
8. Radical change in the disciplinary code.
9. Abbreviation of the term of military service at wartime, under the condition that it accords with state's interests in maintaining the army.
10. Abbreviation of the general term of service (setting a designated length).
11. In keeping with the Petrograd Soviet of Workers' and Soldiers' Deputies' Order No. 1, Pt. 2, Petr Voronov is unanimously elected representative [to the soviet].

> Chair of the meeting, V. Pervov
> Secretary, N. Vaguliaev
> [Followed by 77 signatures]

DOCUMENT 4.3
AN ASSEMBLY OF SOLDIERS' DEPUTIES IN THE VIAZ'MA GARRISON, 9 MARCH 1917[4]

The following document records the first meeting of the Garrison Committee in Viaz'ma, an industrial town in Smolensk Province about 100 miles southwest of Moscow. Viaz'ma's garrison outnumbered its 20,000 civilians. The document was published in the local newspaper, The Smolensk Bulletin (Smolenskii vestnik), *on 14 March 1917.*

A meeting of the Viaz'ma Garrison Soldiers' Deputies, attended by 50 deputies, opened on 9 March 1917 at 10:00 A.M. at the Soldiers' Teahouse. The meeting elected a chairman, his deputy, and a secretary.

The chairman of the soldiers' deputies addressed the meeting with a call for diligence, because there may be several delays, mistakes, and defects in the titanic work of constructing a new Russia. After the chairman's speech, the meeting discussed soldiers' daily needs. Burning questions close to soldiers' hearts were raised. Among these were questions about the soldiers' mess. The chairman said that soldiers pay a great deal for food, considering how little they receive. This is because much of the food quickly "vanishes to who knows where."

As the next issue for discussion, one speaker proposed the distribution of ammunition, so that soldiers can be "at ready" for any circumstance.[5] However, the meeting did not find it necessary to discuss this question right away, since there now is no possible danger from the old regime's partisans.

Many at the meeting spoke about injustices and biases in dealings with soldiers, particularly in the lower ranks. Several proposed that smoking in the barracks be prohibited not only for soldiers, but also for officers.[6] Many spoke about the lack of order in many precincts. In some places, sick soldiers often go without proper medical examinations and develop complications. The meeting discussed a proposal that soldiers should have to rise in the morning no earlier than 5: 30.

The presidium's following proposals were approved by the evening session of Viaz'ma Garrison Soldiers' Deputies:

1. To get people up no earlier than 5:30 A.M.
2. To prohibit violations of quiet until 6:30 A.M.
3. All daily details must be carried out without urgency.
4. Military duty work is to take place after 8:00 A.M.
5. While on duty, soldiers must strictly execute all orders and instructions by the person in command.[7]
6. Cases of disobedience by subordinates and illegal activity by people in command will be adjudicated by the Soviet Executive Committee.
7. During meal breaks, quiet must be observed.
8. Those who go on duty during rests for meals are not to be assigned to daily detail.
9. The assignments must maintain strict succession.[8]
10. Between evening duties and evening roll call, people free from duties must be granted leave for reasonable or useful entertainments. The presidium will work out the ten remaining points for review at the next session, designated for 10 March at 10:00 A.M.

DOCUMENT 4.4
SOLDIER A. KOROLOZHEVICH'S LETTER TO THE PETROGRAD SOVIET[9]

The following document is a 10 March 1917 letter from soldier A. Korolozhevich to the Petrograd Soviet of Workers' and Soldiers' Deputies, regarding soldiers' rights. Liberal politicians and conservative military officers complained that soldiers interpreted their rights in ways that disrupted military discipline. After negotiations with the Provisional Government, on 7 March the Petrograd

Soviet issued Order No. 2 to clarify that solders' committees could not elect their officers. Rumors quickly spread that the government was revoking Order No. 1. On 9 March 1917 the soviet and government's joint Order No. 3 explained that, while the previous two "orders" applied only to the Petrograd Military District, officers must treat soldiers with respect as citizens.

To the Petrograd Soviet of Workers' and Soldiers' Deputies,
Because of alterations to Order No. 1 in the Petrograd Military District, we might be misled about how the law will soon change. In a constitutional state, is it proper to take away what we have been given, so that we cannot elect our officers? Care was necessary so that soldiers were fed and had water and warm clothes. But nobody took care of this. Instead, all the officers cared about was being saluted. [If Order No. 1 is revoked] almost nothing will have changed for us soldiers. It will be impossible for us to go anywhere, to sit down, to eat, or to relax. We will always need to be on guard, knowing that it would still take very little to cause a scandal over saluting. As much we were gladdened, we now will be miserable. The old apparently will be the new.

With respect and esteem,
A. Korolozhevich.

DOCUMENT 4.5
SOLDIER VASILII ANIFIMOV'S LETTER TO THE PETROGRAD SOVIET[10]

The following document is a 13 March 1917 letter to the Petrograd Soviet from Vasilii Anifimov, a soldier in one of the Army of the Caucasus's engineering units. In March 1917, soldiers' resolutions and letters to authorities usually focused on three issues: dignity and civil rights; material conditions for soldiers and their families; and soldiers' and officers' loyalty to the revolution. Anifimov's letter falls into the third category. He uses the old formal address "You."

Mister Chairman!
I have the honor to inform You and the citizen deputies that in our unit we have many citizen officers, from regimental commanders to corporals inclusive, who have not informed the soldiers about the great events taking place in Russia. They are distorting many of Your directives and the army's commands. The loyalty oath to the Provisional Government is not being read and taken. They make us sign blank sheets of paper, but we do not know why and to what end.

Several soldiers do not know who their enemies really are and will no longer sign the blank sheets. Sick at heart, I ask You to take steps so that the officers' actions do not lead to any clashes and misunderstandings. Such, of course, are unwanted when the foreign enemy stands at our back. Unity and solidarity are needed. But there are cranks of all sorts who probably want go back to the old ways. So many were lost, exhausted to death, or hanged for this holy cause! Is it really possible that they, and those still living, will have it taken away, reversed?

The citizen officers pledged to hold discussions with soldiers, but they did not, and they do not want to. This is especially true in infantry sections. Not a single soldiers' assembly has met. We have done nothing. It is impossible now. The current shortage of supplies and products in our unit has led to all sorts of rumors regarding You, citizen deputies, and regarding the Provisional Government. It is necessary to accelerate the dispatch of special plenipotentiaries to explain and strengthen the soldiers' confidence in the bright future of Russia and the Provisional Government.

—Vasilii Anifimov, Engineer in Company 2, Army of the Caucasus

DOCUMENT 4.6
A RESOLUTION BY THE 15TH SIBERIAN RIFLEMEN REGIMENT'S COMMITTEE OF SOLDIERS' DEPUTIES[11]

The following document, a resolution passed by the 15th Siberian Riflemen Regiment's Committee of Soldiers' Deputies on 15 March 1917, demonstrates soldiers' insistence on democratizing the army as well as their hope that the revolution would improve their material condition and that of their families.

Resolved:

1. To petition for an increase in soldiers' pay and in material benefits for their families, who have lost their labor.
2. To elect officials in the regiment's economic departments and to have control over them.
3. To improve medical treatment without distinction between soldiers and officers.
4. To abolish rising to attention, giving salutes, and "humiliating" commands at the front.

The meeting discussed a resolution by the 15th Siberian Riflemen's Regiment's Officers' Temporary Committee, which rejected the Petrograd Soviet of Workers' and Soldiers' Deputies' intervention in army affairs and called for an end to meetings on general-political questions, as they create discord in the army. The meeting passed a resolution stating that the Petrograd Soviet "represents our demands" and that "no questions of a political character are foreign to an army defending the country's freedom. Any restrictions on freedom of thought and exchange of opinions would drag us back to the old regime."

Soldiers' Committee Chairman Demov
Committee Secretary Solov'ev

DOCUMENT 4.7
MANDATE OF THE EIGHTH SIBERIAN
RIFLEMEN REGIMENT'S OFFICERS[12]

The following document is a set of "instructions" approved by a meeting of the 8th Siberian Riflemen Regiment's Officers' Committee, as published in the Petrograd right-liberal newspaper New Times (Novoe vremia) *on 5 April 1917.*

Mandate of the Officers of the 8th Siberian Riflemen Regiment

1. The bright future of the new, free, and happy Russia—with its people's army and fleet—is founded on full confidence, respect, and admiration for its officer-soldiers.
2. The war against German militarism must be carried to a victorious conclusion, and we must conduct a universal struggle against counter-revolution wherever it might emerge.
3. Full confidence in the Provisional Government until convocation of a Constituent Assembly elected on the basis of universal, equal, direct, and secret franchise, with participation by the active army's representatives.
4. The Provisional Government must demand immediate and unceasing work from the rear to supply the active army with military supplies and provisions. Replenishing these now protects the victory of the people's freedom.
5. We propose that the Soviet of Workers' and Soldiers' Deputies wholly recognize the Provisional Government's exclusive state power. We serve the government, and we trust that it will strengthen our victorious holy freedom and lead our dear motherland on the path to glory and general prosperity.

DOCUMENT 4.8
A RESOLUTION BY THE OREL GARRISON
MILITARY PARAMEDICS' ASSEMBLY[13]

The following document is a resolution by an assembly of military paramedics (feldshers) in the Orel Garrison on 7 April 1917, as printed in the Petrograd Socialist Revolutionary newspaper The People's Cause (Delo naroda) *on 15 April. Orel, some 225 miles southwest of Moscow, was an important staging area for the Western Front. In addition to raising issues of specific importance to paramedics, such as professionalization of their services, the document touches on questions of gender: the paramedics distinguished between their own profession-alism and the "amateur" service of nurses ("sisters of mercy," or "sisters"). Volunteer nursing was one of the few forms of patriotic civic engagement open to women during the war years (members of the tsar's family served as military nurses). But in Russia, as in other countries, insinuations regarding volunteer nurses' morality were common, so that the term for nurse was also a slang term for prostitutes.*

A Resolution by the Orel Garrison's Military Paramedics' Assembly, 7 April 1917.

1. The assembly welcomes the [Petrograd] Soviet of Soldiers' and Workers' Deputies' declaration to the peoples of entire world as a moral summons to democratization and peace throughout the world.[14]
2. The assembly considers it necessary to convene an All-Russian Congress of Military Paramedics to work out programs for army paramedics' schools in all regions, and to abolish the existing curriculum in such schools.
3. The assembly considers it necessary to abolish compulsory bodily inspections of soldiers immediately, as it is incongruous with the rights of free citizens.
4. The assembly unanimously considers the presence of nurses in military hospitals undesirable. The overwhelming majority lack professional training, and there is no relationship between their appointment and their moral stature.
5. The assembly meeting considers it immediately necessary to improve hygienic and sanitary conditions for paramedics, in accord with their profession and chiefly in consideration of their responsibilities as paramedics.
6. The assembly calls on all comrade paramedics to make a maximum effort in their daily work. Always do your highest moral and civic duty. Each day of the war, give your best for our brothers who are protecting us and the fatherland.

DOCUMENT 4.9
A RESOLUTION BY THE FIRST CONGRESS OF SOLDIERS' AND WORKERS' DEPUTIES OF THE WESTERN FRONT ARMY AND REAR[15]

The following document is a resolution on soldiers' rights passed on the last day of the 7–17 April 1917 First Congress of Soldiers' and Workers' Deputies of the Western Front Army and Rear in Minsk. Several Provisional Government members and Petrograd Soviet leaders addressed the congress's 1,600-plus delegates. In its substance and language, this resolution echoes an earlier resolution by the First All-Russian Conference of Soviets in Petrograd.

On Soldiers' Rights:[16]

1. All the positions stated below apply to a standing army organized on the principle of compulsory military service. Therefore, the norms set

are temporary and are subject to reworking as the army is reformed on a democratic basis.

2. The government's declaration giving soldiers full rights as citizens must be implemented with complete consistency. In particular, soldiers must be able to exercise freedom of speech, press, association, and assembly both in and outside their barracks, in the rear and at the front. All restrictions on freedom of conscience, compulsory church attendance, mandatory common prayers, and so on must be abolished immediately. Soldiers, including soldiers at the front, must participate in the Constituent Assembly elections with rights equal to those of all citizens.

3. Soldiers' equality as citizens must be extended to the criminal-court sphere. Special courts and special punishments for soldiers must be abolished. In particular, corporal punishment in the army—both that based on the courts and that performed outside court jurisdiction—must be abolished immediately.

   Note: In active army locales where general courts are established but do not function, the existing military-court institutions should be preserved, but soldiers' representatives must be included in their membership (from privates to junior warrant officers, inclusive).

4. Any limitation on soldiers' lives outside their service is impermissible. Full freedom of leaves must be given, free from duties.

5. Subordination to commanders and external displays of subordination must be limited within the strict boundaries of military-technical necessity. In view of this, giving salutes, in and out of formation, to particular people and upon command, must be abolished, as must other rules regarding "respect for military rank."

6. Institution of batman, orderly, and other types of soldier-servant must be abolished.[17] Exclusions are allowed at the front, but only by voluntary agreement of both sides and the company committee. In such cases, no one may have more than one batman. Cavalry orderlies may be designated on the same basis.

7. Any distinction in rights or responsibilities between various categories of soldiers in private ranks is impermissible. In particular, all privileges for volunteers, noncommissioned officers, army paramedics, and junior warrant officers must be abolished. All above-mentioned temporary-service soldiers of various categories must be treated identically to simple soldiers of corresponding rank. All special privileges for the General Staff's guards units and clerks are to be abolished.

8. In close quarters, strict discipline in the execution of service obligations must be maintained. In cases of breach of discipline not requiring the offender's strict punishment, reprimands may be administered only by an elected disciplinary court.

9. In all cases of injustice or violations of rights, complaints, appeals, and claims can be made directly before the court or committee. All limitations of rights that appear to be proven on the basis of complaints, appeals, or claims will be abolished.

10. Transfer of soldiers from one unit to another and shifting their quarters within the units is possible only with the agreement of the company, regimental, or other corresponding committee.

11. All compulsory forms of greeting and response, such as "I wish you good morning, Sir!" "No, Sir!" and "Exactly as you say, Sir!" must be recognized as incongruous with a citizen-soldier's dignity. They must be replaced with general-purpose phrases like "hello," "yes," "no," and so on.

12. Measures must be taken immediately to make possible the broadest extension of civility among soldiers.

13. The congress considers it necessary to abolish dueling in the army. Resolving questions of honor through dueling is absolutely impermissible because it abases citizen-soldiers' dignity.[18]

DOCUMENT 4.10
THE PETROGRAD SOVIET EXECUTIVE COMMITTEE,
"TO COMRADE WORKERS"[19]

The following document is a 7 March 1917 appeal by the Petrograd Soviet Executive Committee "To Comrade Workers," calling for an end to strikes over the eight-hour workday and other long-deferred demands. It appeared in The News of the Petrograd Soviet (Izvestiia Petrogradskogo soveta) *on 9 March. Soldiers' deputies believed strikes were choking the supply pipeline to the military front. Menshevik and Socialist Revolutionary leaders supported workers' demands, but feared strikes weakened the revolutionary order at a time when a counterrevolutionary backlash was still possible. On 5 March, the Petrograd Soviet asked that workers return to work the next day. It added that workers always could strike again, but in the meantime, they must set about organizing. Workers at some of Petrograd's largest factories, though, pledged to continue striking until owners met their main demands. Therefore, the soviet issued this second appeal.*

To Comrade Workers.

The Soviet of Workers' and Soldiers' Deputies voted to recommend that all Petrograd's workers return to work on 6 March. With minor exceptions, the capital's working class demonstrated remarkable discipline and returned to their work benches with the same unanimity as when they abandoned work several days ago, during the great revolution. But we have reports that the resumption of work was accompanied by a series of misunderstandings and conflicts. In some factories, workers presented employers with economic demands, then stopped work again when those demands were not met. In other cases, workers did not return to work at all.

When it adopted its resolution on the resumption of work, the Soviet of Workers' and Soldiers' Deputies did not believe there would be these kind of sporadic actions in individual factories. We assumed that instead of stopping work over misunderstandings with their employers, our comrades—the workers—would follow an orderly path toward realizing their demands with help from factory and district committees, trade unions, and the Soviet of Workers' and Soldiers' Deputies.

For that reason, the soviet has appointed a special commission to present a list of general economic demands to the factory owners and the government in behalf of the working class. Therefore we urge you, comrades, to remain at work wherever there is still hope for a settlement. At the same time, you must insist upon the satisfaction of your demands and bring them to the attention of the Soviet of Workers' and Soldiers' Deputies.

It goes without saying that excesses such as damaging materials, breaking machinery, and committing violence against persons are absolutely forbidden. They harm the workers' cause, particularly at this dangerous moment.

On the other hand, there are reports of employers firing workers as soon as they present demands and of owners shutting down their enterprises. Such an attitude toward those who fought for the motherland's freedom is completely unacceptable. The Soviet of Workers' and Soldiers' Deputies is obligated to fight such abuses—which are particularly disgraceful at present—with the greatest force. In discussions between workers, the city government, and the Provisional Government, the soviet will propose that closed enterprises be municipalized or turned into workers' collectives.[20]

The Executive Committee of the Soviet of Workers' and
Soldiers' Deputies.

DOCUMENT 4.11
AN AGREEMENT BETWEEN THE PETROGRAD
SOVIET AND PETROGRAD SOCIETY OF FACTORY
AND PLANT OWNERS[21]

The following document is an agreement on the eight-hour workday reached by the Petrograd Soviet and the Petrograd Society of Factory and Plant Owners on 10 March 1917. The agreement was honored in large factories, but small enterprise owners generally believed it would raise their labor costs and refused to reduce work hours. (The same was true in provincial cities.) Opponents of the eight-hour workday argued that it hindered military production and that workers had put "narrow class interests" before those of the country and the army.

The document mentions factory committees and arbitration chambers. In large state-owned factories, workers' committees helped manage production. In privately owned factories, they acted as site-specific trade unions, negotiating agreements on wages and working conditions. The 10 March 1917 agreement led to a proliferation of factory committees that became important instruments of workers' politics. It also created arbitration chambers to settle worker-management conflicts without strikes and disruptions of production. The document also refers to the "violent removal" of foremen from the factories. In early March, workers often beat abusive foremen and managers. In one form of "lynching" (samosud) called "wheel-barrowing," workers put a sack over the victim's head, pushed him into a wheelbarrow, then dumped him outside the factory gate (or into the Neva River).

An agreement has been reached between the Petrograd Soviet of Workers' and Solders' Deputies and the Petrograd Society of Factory and Plant Owners on introduction of an eight-hour workday in factories and plants and creation of factory committees and arbitration chambers.

The eight-hour workday:

>   Until publication of a law on workday norms, an eight-hour workday will be introduced (8 hours of actual labor) in all factories and plants, on all shifts.
>   On Saturdays, the workday will be only seven hours.
>   Reduction in working hours must not affect workers' wages.
>   Overtime is permitted only with the factory committee's consent.

Factory committees:

Factory committees (councils of senior workers), elected by the workers at a given enterprise on the basis of universal, equal (etc.) suffrage, will be established in all plants and factories.

The task of these committees are:

>   to represent workers in dealings with government and public institutions;
>   to formulate positions on issues concerning workers' public-economic lives;
>   to resolve disputes arising from internal problems among workers;
>   to represent the workers in relations with the plant or factory administrations.

Arbitration chambers:

>   Arbitration chambers will be created in all plants and factories, to settle all misunderstandings that arise in worker-management relations.

Note: Based upon need, arbitration chambers can be separated into shop and workshop sections.

Arbitration chambers will be composed of an equal number of elected representatives from an enterprise's workers and management.

Rules for workers' election will be determined by the factory-plant committees.

The arbitration chambers will schedule sessions based upon necessity.

In cases where the arbitration chambers cannot reach agreement between workers and management, the issue will be passed along to the Central Arbitration Chamber.

The Central Arbitration Chamber will be composed of equal numbers of elected representatives from the Soviet of Workers' Deputies and the Society of Factory and Plant Owners.

DOCUMENT 4.12
TWO LETTERS ON WORKER-SOLDIER RELATIONS[22]

The following document set presents two letters that illustrate tensions between workers and soldiers in spring 1917. Both were printed in the Petrograd Socialist Revolutionary newspaper The People's Cause (Delo naroda) *on 31 March 1917. The first is a letter to the editor from workers at Petrograd's Lebedev Aviation Plant, Russia's largest producer of military aircraft. The second is from soldiers in the Communications Service Detachment of the Izmailovskii Regiment National Guard Reserve Battalion. The soldiers mention several large factories and plants that engaged in defense production: the Putilov mechanical engineering complex (with more than 30,000 workers), the Obukhovskii machine-building plant, and the Semiannikovskii foundry all manufactured artillery; the Petrograd Pipe Factory (with 20,000 workers), produced munitions.*

To the editor

Recently workers have been heaped with blame in the press and among comrade soldiers for not returning to work in a timely manner as proposed by the Soviet of Workers' and Soldiers' Deputies. We Lebedev Plant workers indignantly protest the dreadful allegations against us. We protest against malevolent people who want to sow enmity between comrade workers and soldiers. We want to explain to all who will listen: we consider it our moral duty to the free motherland and our comrade soldiers to work without sparing our physical strength and without considering time.

On 8 March we returned to work at the Soviet of Workers' and Soldiers' Deputies' first summons. Production at the plant is based not on a nine-hour workday, not an eight-hour day—it has increased. The plant's internal life flows on completely normally, thanks to the workers' general effort and timely creation of a conflict commission. We have organized a "council of elders" and an arbitration chamber, which has averted all sorts of undesirable excesses.

Considering this moment's importance, and understanding that reaction's forces are not conclusively demolished, we ask comrade workers in other plants not to undermine the workers' good name. May this bring an end to all slander against the working masses in the press.

Chairman of the Council of Elders at the V. A. Lebedev
Actuary Society Aviation Plant, V. Savitskii; Secretary: I. Matvev
For the plant's director: Engineer L. Shul'gin

From Soldiers to the Workers.

Comrades!

Recent articles in the Petrograd newspapers are making people perplexed and might even have nasty aims. These articles said that the workers just do not want to work and that the eight-hour workday is holding back production. These articles made their way to the active army. The soldiers, concerned that the rear was not supporting the army, hurriedly sent deputies to Petrograd. They sent deputies, whose inquiries the workers seem not to have understood. Discord began emerging between the workers and soldiers. We knew well who this discord benefits, and we have not believed these articles. We decided to figure it out for ourselves.

And so the Izmailovskii Regiment National Guard Reserve Battalion's Communications Service Detachment sent delegates to the main factories—to the Putilov Plant, the Pipe Factory, the Obukhovskii Plant, and the Semiannikovskii Plant. Our delegates examined all the workshops in these factories, spoke with workers and foremen, and came away with a positive impression. Work has not been halted—it goes on with greater force. The workers are all at their places. All are at their benches. The most important production in largest workshops— cannon-making and artillery-shell making—is carried out around the clock in three shifts, as is other work.

Under the old regime, workers worked 10-hour shifts. But they took two hours for meals and spent much of their time standing idle at their machines because there was no coal, fuel, or metal. Somebody slowed things up. Somebody stuck a spoke in the wheel.

Now workers work eight hours without taking a break, and their machines never stop for a minute.[23] It's true that not everything is straightened out. It's true that you still hear the cries, "There are no materials! There is no coal!" The workers told us, "We each are making 100 artillery shells a day. Give us materials, and we will make 150." Comrades, there must not be such hold-ups. They are criminal. The workers all want to work, not to hinder work. Our delegates saw entire mountains of artillery shells, entire mountains of awesome weapons.

Comrades at the front! Make quick and glorious victory your cause. You will have no shortage of ammunition. We are convinced that free workers here are working harder than slaves. Comrade workers! Pay no attention to nasty rumors. Work in peace. The army at the front is defending you from the foreign enemy, and we have gotten the better of the old regime's lackeys. Comrades, don't believe those who sow discord between us and the workers—this is provocation. Only through full unity can we achieve total victory. Only in alliance can we make a new free Russia.

DOCUMENT 4.13
WOMEN HABERDASHERY WORKERS' DEMANDS
IN ROSLAVL' (SMOLENSK PROVINCE)[24]

The following document records demands made on 3 May 1917 by women haberdashery workers (hat makers) in Roslavl' (Smolensk Province). In 1917, Roslavl' had a civilian population of around 25,000. Local garment workers (mostly young Jewish women) labored in garrets and sweatshops, in the back rooms of clothing stores, and out of their own homes. They had a strong political and organizational tradition that stretched back to before the 1905 Revolution. In spring 1917, local garment workers reconstituted their union, The Needle (Igla), which held its meetings at the Roslavl' Jewish Workers' Club. The Needle included women hat makers, whose demands echoed concerns of workers in Petrograd's great factories.

We, women hat-makers gathered on 3 May at the Jewish Workers' Club, have worked out the following demands to our employers:

1. An eight-hour workday.
2. A 50 percent increase in wages.
3. No overtime work hours.
4. On our part, we are obliged to work conscientiously.
5. Currently employed skilled women workers will remain in their jobs. If there is a need to increase the number of skilled women workers, then this can be done only by agreement between the owners and the senior skilled women workers.
6. If a skilled woman worker falls ill at work, then her wages will not be deducted for 1–2 days.
7. This year the current skilled women workers are to be given a two-week vacation, and wages for this time will not be deducted.
8. If an owner wishes to dismiss a skilled woman worker, he must give 1 month advanced notice or pay her the equivalent of a month's wages. For her part, if a skilled woman worker wishes to leave her job, she must give her employer 1-month advanced notice.

9. On Saturdays, Sundays, and annual holidays there will be no work, and the shops will be closed.
10. Should any important disagreement arise between owners and skilled women workers, an arbitration chamber will be established. It will include the male or female owner, a skilled women worker, and one neutral person. The arbitration chamber's decision will be compulsory for both sides.
11. We cannot be required to take work home.

This agreement will remain in force until 8 May 1918.

DOCUMENT 4.14
PROVINCIAL WHITE COLLAR EMPLOYEES AND
EDUCATED PROFESSIONALS IN MARCH 1917[25]

The following document set presents the aspirations of clerical employees and educated professionals in the provincial city of Smolensk in March 1917. The first document is a resolution passed by a meeting of women public elementary school teachers on 7 March. The second is a resolution by a 9 March meeting of employees at the State Bank's Smolensk Branch. The third is a resolution passed by an assembly of physicians on 10 March, and the fourth recounts a meeting of government office clerks on the same day. These resolutions appeared in the local newspaper, The Smolensk Bulletin (Smolenskii vestnik), *on 12 March and 17 March 1917.*

Generally, the organizers of meetings would send newspapers their resolutions and meeting minutes, because publication of declarations itself was a symbolic display of public engagement. In 1917, white-collar employees organized unions to protect their common interests. In some cases, white-collar employees described themselves as workers; in other cases, they asserted that their education and skills set them outside (and "above") the working class. Educated professionals (teachers, doctors, lawyers, and others) formed professional associations for similar purposes.

A Resolution by Women Public School Teachers.
On 7 March, a meeting of women teachers at Smolensk's city elementary schools was held at the city school visual aids storehouse, at which the following resolution was approved:

1. Teachers must take an active part in preparatory work for the Constituent Assembly's convocation.
2. Teachers will help in the City Executive Committee's work if such help is requested.
3. Teachers (without distinction by sex) must be invited to participate, with full voting rights, in zemstvo and municipal self-government work on public education issues. Also, the teachers' councils must be reorganized on a new basis.[26]

Among the State Bank Employees.

On 9 March an assembly of the State Bank Smolensk Branch's employees resolved to petition the State Bank's central administration and branch institutions with the following call to organize a Union of State Bank Branch Employees:

The idea of forming a narrow professional-legal organization to amalgamate the individual members of the State Bank employees' family has spread, and many have acted.

The force of circumstances and the specifics of this moment, when "Unity" has become a universal slogan, make forming such an organization both necessary and practical. In view of this, this employees' meeting of State Bank Smolensk Branch enthusiastically requests that you set about preparatory work on the program and tasks for a future All-Russian Union of State Bank Employees.

Among the tasks that might be designated for the future union are:

1. Improving employees' economic life (working out staffing issues, establishing a pension and extending it all employees without exception, standardizing labor and work conditions, providing employees with insurance and medical care, establishing a mutual aid fund and a consumers' store, etc.).
2. Improving employees' legal position (regarding personal and service regulations, union representatives' participation in revising the bank's charter, and forming employees' representative institutions—such as senior workers' councils, comrades' courts, arbitration chambers, etc.).

The points stated above are only examples. A conclusive explanation of the union's tasks and an elaboration of its program must be undertaken by a congress of delegates from all local institutions and the central administration. We consider this conference's convocation absolutely desirable and necessary.

From the Assembly of Doctors.

On 10 March, the Smolensk Society of Doctors convened a well-attended special meeting of doctors. At the session's opening, respects were paid in memory of those who had died for freedom. Then, after an exchange of views, it was resolved:

1. To send a telegram greeting the Provisional Government.
2. To assign 100 rules to the Society to Aid Liberated Political Prisoners' charitable fund.
3. To elect a special commission on the question of expanding the Society's activities.
4. To elect Doctor Vladimir Iosifovich Spasskii as the Smolensk doctors' delegate to the provisional City Executive Committee.

The City Executive Committee has resolved that it will include a total of two delegates, representing all doctors, paramedics, etc. After discussing this question, it was decided to elect a single delegate from the doctors. The other delegate, from the remaining medical personnel, will be elected separately.[27]

From the Assembly of Government Clerks.
The meeting was opened at 8:15 P.M. at the Smolensk Provincial Zemstvo Administration Hall, under the chairmanships of B. A. Gern, with N. O. Voeikov as secretary.

At N. A. Dobianskii's suggestion, the meeting paid respects to the fallen fighters for the people's freedom.

It was decided by a majority vote to approve a resolution that had been proposed by the chairman and discussed by the meeting on the need to refrain from all party political activity until the war's conclusion and the Constituent Assembly's convocation. The meeting voted unanimously to express its desire to organize a Smolensk City Union of State Institution Employees, with the following aims:

1. To defend employees' professional interests and rights.
2. To propose a candidate for the Constituent Assembly,
3. To assist in members' political self-education.
4. To show support for the Provisional Government.
5. To assist in forming an All-Russian Government Employees' Union.

Regarding elections to the union's organizational committee, it was resolved:
Elections should be carried out by each institution. Each institution having no fewer than fifteen members will elect one delegate. Institutions having fewer than fifteen members will join with other institutions for the elections. Representation will be proportional to the number of employees, with one delegate for every 50 people. Elections must be carried out within a week of 10 March. Civil servants, as well as lower-level employees, like postal workers, couriers, servants, etc., also come under the designation "employees."

The meeting's secretary proposed that, to familiarize all employees in Smolensk's governmental institutions with the meeting's resolutions, these should be published in *The Smolensk Bulletin.*

DOCUMENT 4.15
INDUSTRIALISTS SUPPORT THE STATE DUMA'S
TEMPORARY COMMITTEE[28]

The following document is a 2 March 1917 statement by the Russian Council of Industrial and Trade Congresses, declaring its complete confidence in the

State Duma's Temporary Committee (which went on to form the Provisional Government). The document appeared on 3 March in The News of the Petrograd Committee of Journalists (Izvestiia Komiteta Petrogradskikh zhurnalistov).[29] *It is signed by the council's deputy chair, Nikolai Iznar, a representative of the Baku oil industry. In 1917, industrialists used preexisting trade associations like the Council of Industrial and Trade Congresses (formed in 1906) to promote the business community's political and economic interests. They also organized new industrial associations, especially in the provinces. The council primarily represented the oil, coal, and metallurgy industries, but also included members of commercial and trade groups.[30]*

On 2 March the Council of Industrial and Trade Congresses, which unites Russia's public trade-industrial organizations, gathered for the first time since the old government's overthrow, which has rendered the country and its national economy in a state of complete shock. The Council bows in admiration at the State Duma's heroic deeds for the country. The Council strongly believes that the State Duma's feat—guiding the army to victory over the old order and liberating Russia—frees fresh forces in the country to completely repel the enemy invasion. The Council declares that it will place itself at the State Duma Temporary Committee's complete disposal. It henceforth considers the Temporary Committee's orders and directives obligatory until the creation of the new state administration.

At the same time, the Council calls on all Russia's public trade-industrial organizations—the stock exchange committees, trade and manufacturing committee, merchants' societies, societies of plant and factory owners, congresses of separate branches of industry and trade, and all of Russia's trade-industrial class—to forget about party and social differences. Now these can only benefit the people's enemies. Close ranks around the State Duma's Temporary Committee, and put all of your resources at its disposal.

—Deputy Chairman of the Council, N. Iznar

DOCUMENT 4.16
A MEETING OF SMOLENSK'S SOCIETY OF FACTORY AND PLANT OWNERS[31]

The following document is an account of the 14 March 1917 inaugural meeting of Smolensk's Society of Factory and Plant Owners. In spring 1917, trade-industrial associations sprang up not only in major industrial regions, but also in places (like Smolensk) that had little heavy industry. Such associations gave the business community a platform for lobbying the Provisional Government and allowed them to designate representatives to local government committees.

An assembly of Smolensk Province's factory and plant owners convened yesterday to discuss current events and to elect a representative to the Smolensk City Executive Committee. The assembly resolved to organize a Smolensk Provincial Society of Factory and Plant Owners. The society's aim is to have industrial representatives in various institutions. S. I. Reshetnikov was elected the society's chairman and I. G. Esaitis his deputy.[32] S. I. Reshetnikov was elected as the factory and plant owners' representative to the City Executive Committee. Today the province's factory and plant owners will convoke a meeting to organize a local trade-industrial committee and elect two representatives to the All-Russian Trade-Industrial Congress in Moscow.

The Society resolved to ask that all factory and plant owners come to the City Duma Hall today at 7:00 P.M. for an assembly to discuss questions related to the election of representatives to the Moscow congress.

DOCUMENT 4.17
THE FIRST ALL-RUSSIAN CONGRESS OF TRADE-INDUSTRIAL ASSOCIATIONS ON LOCAL TRADE-INDUSTRIAL ASSOCIATIONS[33]

The following document is a draft resolution passed by the First All-Russian Congress of Trade-Industrial Associations in Petrograd on 20 March 1917. The authors refer to themselves as belonging to the "trade-industrial class." Leading industrialists equated their own interests as a class with the greater interests of the Russian Revolution (as did other social groups, particularly workers). Many believed that permanent local trade-industrial administrative institutions must play a role in coordinating Russia's industrial economy. The Provisional Government chose not to grant the trade-industrial associations the broad powers requested in this document.

On local trade-industrial administrative institutions.

1. This historic moment, when the entire old Russian way of life is being radically transformed, truly demands that the trade-industrial class—like all the country's other public and popular forces—establish suitable permanent organizations as quickly as possible. These must be regional trade-industrial self-administration institutions, with compulsory representation from all groups in the trade-industrial class.
2. Trade-industrial self-administrative institutions must have the right of prior review and discussion of all government, zemstvo, and municipal government institutions' measures regarding trade and industry. They must have an equally broad right of universal, independent guardianship over trade-industrial needs and development. In this way, they

can defend the interests of these branches of the national economy and regulate a proper pace of local trade-industrial life.

3. For the new trade-industrial self-administration institutions to fully and genuinely represent trade-industrial interests in a given region, they must include properly elected local trade-industrial class representatives from local branches of trade and industry. These must include both individual traders and industrialists and collective legal persons (shareholders' associations, actuary companies, etc.) that pay industrial taxes on their enterprises.

4. All local traders, industrialists, and self-employed artisans must be granted the right to participate in elections for representatives to the trade-industrial self-administration institutions, proportional to the sum of the industrial tax paid in a given region by each category of trade and industry.

5. The new trade-industrial self-administration institutions must be granted the right to collect voluntary contributions to defray their maintenance costs and satisfy local general trade-industrial needs. All people and institutions exercising the right to vote for representatives to these institutions must contribute to a basic compulsory fund designated for these self-administration institutions. The contribution should be a percentage of each enterprise's total aggregate payment in state industrial taxes.

[The document provides details on how trade-industrial self-administrative institutions should levy and distribute funds to create and maintain arbitration chambers in various local branches of trade and industry.]

6. The new trade-industrial self-administration institutions must bring together all representatives of the trade-industrial class and consider all issues relating to the general needs of traders and industrialists in a given region.

DOCUMENT 4.18
WORKER-MANAGEMENT RELATIONS AT A
PROVINCIAL FACTORY, MARCH–APRIL 1917[34]

The following document set presents materials on labor relations at the A. Khludov Textile Factory in Iarstsevo (Smolensk Province). The small village of Iartsevo was on a major railroad line about 120 miles southwest of Moscow. The factory employed some 7,000 workers (mostly women) and had a long history of labor conflict; in 1916, a large strike had shut down the factory for several weeks. As in many such factory villages, in 1917 the Iartsevo Soviet was simply an extension of the Khludov workers' factory committee.

The first document is the protocol of a meeting between the Iartsevo workers' factory committee and management on 29 March 1917. The second is the

*protocol of a similar meeting held on 10 April 1917. The last two documents
are announcements issued by the factory committee on or about 11 April
1917.*

Protocol of a session of the Factory Workers' Committee, with the factory
administration's participation, 29 March 1917.

1. The Factory Committee announces that workers will vote to strike if
   the administration fires anyone, except in cases of larceny. They also
   will strike unless the registers in which fines and violations are recorded
   are abolished.
   The factory administration explains that it has no objections, but
   wants each suspicious case reviewed with the Committee's participation. The administration informs the Committee that several
   workers have left their jobs, and their positions will be filled. They
   will be returned to their previous occupations and posts at the first
   opportunity. The register of fines will be abolished.
2. The Committee states the workers' demand that pay for work on holidays, including the Easter week holidays, must be calculated at double
   the daily rate set in the new agreement worked out between the workers
   and the administration. Piecework at half.[35]
   The factory administration agrees to the workers' demands.
3. The meeting discusses pay for cleaning before Easter. The meeting
   resolves that pay for departments where cleaning takes place on Thursday
   after 12:00 noon will be calculated according to the average pay for the
   Weaving Department. This is because work ends there earlier and they
   clean for 1/4 of the day.
4. The Committee announces that those workers who were removed
   from the payroll between Easter 1916 and Easter 1917 and then hired
   again in other factory departments must be compensated [for time
   unemployed] at a rate that is 10 percent of the pay for workers who
   worked without interruption. That 10 percent rate also applies to those
   who worked after Easter 1916 but who, according to factory elders,
   left work on account of illness before Easter 1917.
   The factory administration fully accepts these terms.
5. The Committee announces workers' demands regarding the holiday . . .
   [illegible]
6. The Committee demands that staples—such as flour, groats, butter,
   bread, herring, and so on—be distributed equitably and equally among
   workers and office employees.
   The factory administration will consider this demand. It proposes
   election of a provisions committee to work out a rationing system
   for the equitable distribution of products.

7. The Committee demands that, since salaried employees have salary account books, workers' wages must also be computed and entered into individual account books, and not on general account lists.

   The factory administration agrees to this demand.

8. The Committee states the demand of workers in the Construction and Maintenance Departments that all staff in these departments be issued account books that list rules and wage levels, like those given the factory workers.

   The factory administration will satisfy this demand.

Committee Chairman P. Grigor'ev
Secretary, K. M. Simbard

Protocol of the Soviet of Workers' Deputies and Factory Committee, with participation by factory administrators R. E. Balykov, D. I. Gorianov, and N. I. Zharikov, 10 April 1917.

The Factory Committee raises the issue of improving the food distribution system in the factory store. The factory administration explains that it already has taken measures to improve the system. Bookkeeper N. I. Zharikov explains the system that will be introduced after Easter.

   The meeting decides to accept this system.

G. D. Kurosh, a representative of the Employees' Committee, reports that factory store employees want full employees' rights regarding regulation of their labor. In particular, they demand the introduction of holidays and a Sunday rest-day, an increase in the length of meal times, and a shortened working day. Discussion.

   The meeting resolves that the store shall be closed on holidays and Sundays. The employees' meal break is to be lengthened to two hours. . . .

   The meeting proposes that the Employees' Committee petition the Administration Council on improving conditions for store employees and for a shorter workday.

The Factory Committee takes up the complaint against Vatershchits Bankobroshnits.

   He will be relieved of his job and join the day workers.[36]

   The administration explains that more workers will be employed at the first opportunity.

The Factory Committee raises a request by workers who worked at the factory after Easter 1916, but then were mobilized into military service. They have petitioned to receive wages at the compensated percentage.[37]

   The administration will bring this issue to the factory's administrative board.

Committee chairman, [unsigned]
Secretary, K. M. Simbard

Declaration of the Iartsevo Soviet of Workers' Deputies and the Factory Committee.[38]

Comrade workers! All to the benches! All to the machines!

Strengthen your work until the war's end! Do not forget your brothers who suffer in the trenches. They have gone to war, so do all that is necessary for them. If there is a gap between the front and the rear, it will kill our dear freedom.

Don't delight the bloody Kaiser and his accomplices. We now are forging our happiness; our motherland's fate and freedom is in our hands. We still have the strength to bring down German Tsarism, to the world proletariat's delight. Be on guard. Protect freedom. Do not provoke any conflicts at work. Any disorganizing and arbitrary work stoppages or any disregard for our personal responsibilities would reveal a lack of consciousness.

We have won an eight-hour workday. We have won several improvements in work. We will not violate discipline and order. We will not be un-conscious citizens. Any violations of order will be reviewed by a comrades' court of honor.

Committee chairman, [unsigned]
Committee secretary, K. M. Sirmbard

Declaration of the Soviet of Workers' Deputies and Factory Committee, 11 April 1917.

Comrade workers! The shameful practice of searching workers as they leave the factory was abolished when the old regime fell. Comrades, be conscious citizens! Do not set out to alienate the ownership. Understand: not one worker should appropriate a single item of the factory's property. Any unseemly conduct of that sort will be punished by the comrades' court.

Committee chairman, [unsigned]
Secretary, N. M. Sirmbard

DOCUMENT 4.19
ACADEMICIAN V. BEKHTEREV, "FREE RUSSIA MUST BE ENLIGHTENED"[39]

The following document is an essay by neurologist Vladimir Bekhterev, a member of the Russian Academy of Sciences, published in Russia's leading business newspaper, The Stock Exchange Bulletin (Birzhevyia vedomosti), *on 7 April 1917. Russia's universities and other institutions of higher education had been hothouses for prerevolutionary radical student circles. We know relatively little about university politics in 1917, but most faculty (and certainly most students) welcomed the tsarist regime's collapse. Bekhterev's emphasis on the duty to "enlighten" common people reflects beliefs central to the Russian intelligentsia's worldview since the mid-1800s. In 1917, liberals and socialists alike believed that enlightenment would transform Russia, and so set out to "tutor" the population.*

Russia's free people must be educated and enlightened, down to the very lowest strata. We cannot be reconciled to the darkness of Russia's population—which was a direct product and also a weapon of the old regime. Henceforth, the people's free souls must be enlightened. To achieve this, we must not hold back any resources. There is no expenditure more productive. Compulsory universal education must be introduced rapidly in Russia.

Introducing compulsory general education in Russia will face considerable hindrances in the provinces. In many places the population is very sparse, particularly in Russia's eastern and northern regions; also, there are absolutely no roads in several mountainous locations. Such hindrances may be gotten around. This has been accomplished by our neighbor, Norway.

As is known, today some of the world's most productive countries are countries that until recently had little education. In these places, so-called mobile schools were used to overcome natural barriers to the people's education, and were sent to places with sparse populations and to mountain locales without roads. Without doubt, mobile schools can and should do great service in the cause of the Russian people's education everywhere it is hindered by natural impediments.

The principle behind mobile schools is that they travel from place to place, together with the teachers and all the teaching materials that they need.

The teacher comes into a village where there is no school and occupies a room that has been prepared beforehand. . . . Immediately upon arriving, he explains his visit to the population. Then the children, obligated by law to study, gather at the school. The teacher enrolls them and begins lessons. After the conclusion of the last lesson, the teacher gathers his things and moves to another place, where exactly the same pattern of business is followed.

There were a great number of such travelling schools in Norway. These schools, together with travelling teachers, were dispatched all across the country and had great success. . . .

This principle can be applied, not only to grammar schools, e.g., to lower-level classes, but also to specialized schools, for instance, agricultural schools.

There are also traveling teachers in our Finland, teaching the population how to work the land properly. I have become convinced that this will be a most beneficial influence in improving peasant agriculture.[40] [The author explains that he is acquainted with a peasant from Finland, who has told him about mobile agricultural schools' successful impact on farming in remote districts of his native land.]

In Russia mobile professional schools would be no less productive. . . . Their organization is simple, and their usefulness is tremendous. If they are moved from place to place and have equipment and supplies, such schools can teach skilled workers in many important crafts. . . .

I know that under our previous conditions of life, introducing such schools was beyond the old political regime's political understanding. But now, after the end of the centuries-long yoke on the people, it is necessary to give these types of schools the broadest freedom wherever they would be useful and needed. We can be certain that, thanks to their unselfish devotion to the cause, educated youths will go to the people enthusiastically and enlighten the dark people in the most unfavorable local conditions. Thus the people soon will enjoy all the benefits of European culture.

—Academician V. Bekhterev

DOCUMENT 4.20
RESOLUTION OF A STUDENT MEETING AT
PETROGRAD'S ELECTRO-TECHNICAL INSTITUTE[41]

The following document is a broadside published by a meeting of technical students in Petrograd on 2 March 1917. Like other social groups, students at Petrograd's schools, universities, and institutes held meetings and passed resolutions greeting the revolution in early March.

Resolution of a meeting of students at the Electro-Technical Institute, 2 March 1917

The singular tasks of the moment: Defending the country, supplying the army, and organizing transport, food supply, and order. The only institution that can fulfill these tasks is the Temporary Committee of the State Duma in unity with the Soviet of Workers' Deputies. We cannot be disunited when the enemy, hunger, and the old regime are standing at the gates.

We repudiate all attempts by party fanatics and obvious provocateurs to sow disunity. In the name of the country's defense and for victory over our foreign enemies, we are rallying around the Provisional Committee of the State Duma and spreading throughout the city to struggle against provocations that continue from hour to hour.

The Organizational Committee of the Electro-Technical Institute

DOCUMENT 4.21
A STUDENT MEETING IN SMOLENSK[42]

The following document is a resolution passed by a meeting of public school students in Smolensk on 6 March 1917. It was published in The Smolensk

Bulletin (Smolenskii vestnik) *on 9 March. The meeting had been convened with the help of teachers at the local public gimnazium, a high school that pre-pared students for higher-level technical or university education. Like students at higher education institutions, primary and secondary school students across Russia joined the general rush to civic activism in spring 1917.*

A Student Meeting.

On 6 March, the first meeting of students at Smolensk city public schools convened under the chairmanship of V. V. Rudnev and at the initiative of the Public High School's teachers.[43] Nearly 300 people attended. The meeting sent the following telegrams:

To the Chairman of the State Duma, Mikhail Vladimirovich Rodzianko:

Smolensk's public school students send the State Duma warm greetings. At this difficult moment, we are fully prepared to serve the New Government with broad intensive work. We are aware that all citizens and students must remain calm to facilitate opportuni-ties to build the people's happy new bright freedom.

To the Minister of Public Enlightenment:

Smolensk's school students greet You as the face of the New Govern-ment and the new civic order, which is leading the dear Motherland to a free cultural life. We look forward to new, free schools. We express our sincere, warm desire to apply all our effort to serve the renewed Russia and the Motherland's people.

After lively discussion of current events and the tasks for schools that these events had set into motion, the meeting passed the following resolution:

1. Students must be familiarized with what is happening now in Russia's life. The means of doing so should be left to the discretion of the local pedagogical personal.
2. We recognize the need for student organizations to maintain a careful and attentive attitude.
3. It is now necessary to set about calm work and summon all students to such work.
4. We recognize the need to create a pedagogical society to unite all Smolensk's teaching personnel. To this end, we have elected a com-mission with the right to co-opt members. It will draft a charter for the society.

Those attending the meeting made lively comments on the need to aid liberated political prisoners. At a participant's suggestion, the meeting collected more than 200 rubles to aid liberated political prisoners. It decided to create a fund for this cause among students in school institutions.[44]

DOCUMENT 4.22
THE PETROGRAD PROLETARIAN YOUTH
ORGANIZATION "LABOR AND LIGHT"[45]

The following document is a 16 June 1917 manifesto by the Petrograd youth group, "Labor and Light." This organization was created in March 1917, and by June had nearly 50,000 members. Labor and Light's members included Socialist Revolutionaries, Mensheviks, Bolsheviks, and Anarchists. Some were students, but most were working-class youths. In August, the Bolsheviks gained control of the organization and forced out its leader, Aleksi Shevtsov. They then dissolved "Labor and Light" and organized a Bolshevik youth group in its place. In 1917, most of Russia's political parties formed youth groups and clubs, which were important vehicles for mobilizing party political support among urban youth.

Comrade girl and boy-proletarians!
Tsarism has fallen, capitalism is collapsing, and the bourgeoisie is shaking. Our mothers and fathers have won a conclusive victory over them. We, future citizens, sustainers of our mothers' and fathers' cause and heirs to their hard-won rights and cultural wealth, understand that history's inexorable laws will wipe the earth's face clean of the remnants of an uncivilized people.

We, the All-District Council of Proletarian Youth, understand history's harsh but just laws. And we consider it our responsibility to strengthen our knowledge. We take a revolutionary attitude toward labor and light. This is because over the centuries, creative labor and the impartial light of science have been, and will continue to be, the fundamental vital basis on which all that is best about humanity and its culture is founded.

The proletariat's invincibility rests in the organization of labor and the organization of educationally activity. Therefore we, the All-District Council of Petrograd Proletarian Youth, recognize that mighty labor is the true shield, and that science's impartial light is the true sword of Proletarian Freedom, Rights, and Creativity. Together, they open the door and lead to one goal—a life of Beauty.

We can and must work and study. We can and must be educated citizens, as well as skilled workers. To become equal to our western brothers, we must become artists at our jobs. Therefore we, the All-Russian Council of Petrograd Proletarian Youth, proclaim: Young people and young proletarians, join under the banner of "Labor and Light"!

We summon all comrade girl and boy proletarians to labor and to educate themselves. But we also summon them to be ready to rise up at the first call of the proletarian-father—the Soviet of Workers' and Soldiers' Deputies. Be ready to rush to the barricades if the remnants of vile tsarism or the soulless capitalists should try to strike a last blow.

We, the All-District Council of Petrograd Proletarian Youth, proclaim that we will conduct our activities under the slogan "Labor and Light." We do so to develop young proletarians' complete independent pursuit of historical, natural, legal, political, moral, and artistic education, as well as physical conditioning and universal self-defense.

Proletarian-fathers, it is your duty to give your proletarian sons the lamp of mighty science and the diploma of a skilled-worker! Soviets of Workers', Soldiers', and Peasants' Deputies! Socialist ministers! Your duty is to support the motherland's future proletarians with your moral authority and material power.

Comrade boy and girl proletarians, we call on you to join and rally around the district committees of youth. Every girl and boy proletarian has the duty to elect youths to their district committee who manifest real knowledge.

Chairman: Petr Shevtsov
Secretary: Aleksei Sokolov

CHAPTER FIVE

WHAT THE REVOLUTION MEANS TO ME, PART II: CLERGY, PEASANTS, ARISTOCRATIC LANDOWNERS, WOMEN, AND NATIONAL AND RELIGIOUS MINORITIES

5.1
ANONYMOUS, "A NEW NATIONAL ANTHEM"

5.2
FEODOSII, BISHOP OF SMOLENSK, "TO PASTORS AND CHILDREN OF THE CHURCH IN SMOLENSK"

5.3
THE HOLY SYNOD OPPOSES CHURCH REFORMS

5.4
A VILLAGE CITIZENS' MEETING IN DOROGOBUZH COUNTY (SMOLENSK PROVINCE)

5.5
A PUBLIC EXECUTIVE COMMITTEE SESSION IN SPASSKII COUNTY (TAMBOV PROVINCE)

5.6
S. VOLKOV, "ON THE SAMARA PROVINCIAL PEASANT CONGRESS (REGARDING THE LAND QUESTION)"

5.7
A COUNTY LAND COMMITTEE ON LAND REDISTRIBUTION

5.8
A SPECIAL SESSION OF THE UNITED NOBILITY

5.9
A LAND CAPTAIN ON THE TASKS OF THE REVOLUTION

5.10
THE KIEV ZEMSTVO GAZETTE ON THE FEBRUARY REVOLUTION

5.11
THE UKRAINIAN NATIONAL CONGRESS ON NATIONAL AUTONOMY

5.12
THE ALL-UKRAINIAN PEASANT CONGRESS ON UKRAINIAN AUTONOMY

DOCUMENT 5.1
ANONYMOUS, "A NEW NATIONAL ANTHEM"[1]

The following document is a proposal for a new Russian national anthem, published in New Times (Novoe vremia) *on 7 March 1917. As* New Times *was a middle-class, right-liberal newspaper, one might compare this anonymous poet's vision with that of the Bolshevik poet "Proletarii" (see document 3.1) and the soldier-poet Lobanov (see document 4.1). Use of the word "triune" ("being three in one") in the last stanza evokes both the Christian concept of the Trinity and the French Revolution's watchwords: Liberty, Fraternity, Equality.*

A New National Anthem

Happiness, great happiness glows
In the hearts of a resurrected people!
The essence of our victory flies world-round:
Fraternity, love, and freedom!

Brothers! The Free Motherland is our
Happy road and life!
Glory to Russia's free sons!
Glory to our great Fatherland!

The light of re-born pride carries
The free brotherhood of the people!
Our triune mighty stronghold is—
Fraternity, love and freedom!

DOCUMENT 5.2
FEODOSII, BISHOP OF SMOLENSK, "TO PASTORS AND CHILDREN OF THE CHURCH IN SMOLENSK"[2]

The following document is a pastoral letter from Feodosii, the Russian Orthodox bishop of Smolensk, calling on the province's congregations to greet the revolution and the Provisional Government. It was published in The Smolensk Bulletin (Smolenskii vestnik) *on 8 March 1917.*

In the early 1700s, Tsar Peter the Great had implemented policies that made the Orthodox Church an institutional extension of the state, and there were strong ties between the high clergy and the ruling elite. At the same time, in the 1800s and early 1900s, parish priests often supported revolutionary social change. In 1917 in Smolensk Province, for example, one of the leading Socialist Revolutionary activists was a parish priest, Father Kutzov.

To Pastors and Children of the Church in Smolensk.

Our Motherland has stepped onto a new life path. The Russian people await creation of a governmental and social order based on today's principles, principles different from those of previous centuries. The new order has colossal tasks and goals, and realizing those goals will demand long years of effort from our generation and the next. Right now, the first obligation of all citizens of the Russian Lands is to rally around the new government. Their unity shall give the government strength and firmness in the struggle against our bloody enemies. It shall remove many difficulties that have arisen in our life.

Family of the Church! I summon the bishopric's clergy, and I call on all the Church's Orthodox children in Smolensk to devote their thoughts, energy, effort, and labor to the Motherland's aid and welfare. Let each of us do our part energetically in this cause.

Pastors of the Church: calm the people's excited passions with the frank, authoritative and penetrating words of the loving Christ. With your prayers, defend and strengthen the humble and the frightened. With your affection, warm their watchful souls. Let the plowman, who provides bread for our valiant warriors and for all Russia's people, understand that each seed he plants strengthens the Motherland's defenders in their battle against the bloody enemy. His toil means more food for those in the rear working for the Motherland's cause, whose actions will speed the conclusion of this unprecedented war. Let those who buy and sell goods understand that raising the price of one good increases the price of other goods. Let them understand that by striving for larger profits, they make others suffer from the rising cost of living and force millions of poor toilers and their innocent children to bear hunger and starvation.

Let each of us understand that now, in these great historical days, the Motherland expects, not loud proclamations about government reform, but quiet, persistent labor to meet Russia's most vital needs. Labor without hesitation or complaint, out of love for the Motherland.

May the All-powerful Creator and Producer, the Lord God, grant our Government wisdom and strength. May He preserve us in peace, united in defense of His Russian State and the glory of His blessed name.

—Bishop of Smolensk *Feodosii*

DOCUMENT 5.3
THE HOLY SYNOD OPPOSES CHURCH REFORMS[3]

The following document concerns Orthodox bishops who opposed democratic church reform. It appeared in the Petrograd Socialist Revolutionary newspaper, The People's Cause (Delo naroda), *on 15 March 1917, under the heading*

"A Strike by Members of the Synod." Although the Provisional Government recognized freedom of religion, it also confirmed the Orthodox Church's status as the state church. On 2 March, it appointed Vladimir L'vov as lay supervisor (Ober-Prokuror) of the Holy Synod, the Church's apostolic governing board. On 4 March, L'vov met with the Synod's bishops, which subsequently recognized the Provisional Government. On 7 March, however, L'vov endorsed the newly created, "All-Russian Union of Democratic Orthodox Clergy and Laity," which demanded reform of the clerical hierarchy. L'vov's support for reform alienated conservative bishops. In April, L'vov removed several intransigent bishops from the Synod. The government supported democratic reforms proposed by an All-Russian Congress of Clergy and Laity in June. To the frustration of church officials, it also took steps toward secularizing education. In August 1917, an All-Russian Sobor (Church Council) heatedly debated church democratization; the issues continued to divide the Orthodox Church into the early Soviet period.

A Strike by Members of the Synod.

The Holy Synod has issued the following announcement:

At a 4 March celebratory open session of the Holy Synod, the Provisional Government, in the person of Ober-Prokuror Prince L'vov, explained to us the disposition of full administrative freedom to the Holy Orthodox Russian Church. He explained that the government reserves the right to suspend the Synod's decisions, but only if these contradict the law or are politically undesirable. In response, the Holy Synod promised to send a reassuring epistle to the Orthodox people and take other actions that the government sees necessary to calm people's minds. On 7 March, the Ober-Prokuror informed us that, in relation to Church affairs, the Provisional Government considers itself invested with all prerogatives exercised by the tsarist government. He, the Ober-Prokuror, would be both a representative to and participant in the Synod. Furthermore, the Synod would be receiving instructions for a Church reform project.

Thus the Ober-Prokuror not only remains the true master and commander of the Holy Synod, as under the past regime, but as a member of the Synod's Executive Committee, he will convene a council that will interfere categorically in Church matters. Given this radical change in the government's relationship to the Church, we, the undersigned, cannot assume responsibility for measures that the Provisional Government, and particularly the Ober-Prokurer, assert are needed to direct the church administration. The state does not have the right to make such changes without approval from representatives of the Russian clerical hierarchy. The undersigned—maintaining, of course, their filial obedience and proper duty to the Provisional Government—consider it impossible to remain in the Holy Synod without such representatives.

8 March 1917, Holy Trinity Aleksandr Nevskii Monastery, Petrograd.

Signed by: Sergei, Archbishop of Finland; Tikhon, Archbishop of Lithuania; Arsenii, Archbishop of Novgorod; Mikhail, Archbishop of Grodno; Ioakim, Archbishop of Nizhegorod; Vasili, Archbishop of Chernigov.

DOCUMENT 5.4
A VILLAGE CITIZENS' MEETING IN DOROGOBUZH COUNTY (SMOLENSK PROVINCE)[4]

The following document is a newspaper report on a 10 March 1917 meeting in Ovinovshchina, a village in Dorogobuzh County (Smolensk Province). The report's author, "V-n," was probably a zemstvo employee or a village teacher. The document records a township committee election, a typical event in rural Russia in March 1917, and highlights elements common to peasant assemblies. For example, villages often received news about the new government from soldiers or from deputations sent by urban-based public committees, as was the case at this meeting. The document also reveals tensions between peasants and nonpeasants (such as members of the rural intelligentsia, village priests, shopkeepers, aristocrats, and other nonpeasant land owners).

On 10 March, at the Sutkinskii township administration building, there was a meeting of citizens from all over the township to discuss elections to a Provisional Executive Committee. More than 300 people attended. Soldiers and peasants sent by the County Executive Committee (Ia. A. Fokin, N. Ia. Bol'din, and K. P. Belorustsev) spoke about current events. A friendly "Hurrah" went out to the orators, and they were thanked for their speeches. The meeting went on into the evening.

It is a pleasure to note that peasants electing members to an executive committee showed civic spirit, perhaps for the first time. Two people were on the ballot: the former township policeman Vakhmistrov, and a man named I. I. Konashenkov, who had never before been elected to a public post. As soon as the peasants heard the candidates' names, there was commotion and cries of, "We don't need them! Don't need them!" They would only support "their" people. The peasants explained that they do not fear anyone now, and for the first time in their lives they could raise their voices and not give in to people who had abused them mercilessly. Those who care about the peasants' attitude toward elections left the meeting with pleasant feeling.

But enough of that! At the meeting, there were very few of the so-called village intelligentsia. When the township scribe and co. showed up, it was "explained" to them that "they have no right to participate in the assembly, since they do not have property in this township." Most of the people to whom this was "explained" came from the "revolutionary" estate, Batishchevo, which the people hated under the old order.[5] Still, it must be admitted that almost all the personnel at Batishchevo showed up in person to do their civic duty. And when they explained this to the peasants, they were greeted with a "hurrah."

After the elections, at N. Ia. Bol'din's suggestion, the meeting heard a requiem for "the fighters for freedom." In keeping with the wishes of the majority of peasants, the requiem took place on the village square. "So as to be festive," said the peasants.

The following people were elected to the township committee: N. Ia. Bol'din, Ia. I. Osipon, I. V. Sherbakov, K. Ia. Lagutenkov, K. P. Belorustsev, K. N. Simonov, the deacon Dokuchaev, V. T. Volodin, and M. E. Kozlov.

[reported by] *V-n.*

DOCUMENT 5.5
A PUBLIC EXECUTIVE COMMITTEE SESSION IN SPASSKII COUNTY (TAMBOV PROVINCE)[6]

The following is an excerpt from the protocols (meeting notes) of the county-level Executive Committee in Spasskii Country (Tambov Province) on 21 March 1917. Tambov Province, southeast of Moscow, was an important grain-producing region. The excerpt presents a petition by the Executive Committee's Peasant Group enumerating common peasant demands.

Petition of the Executive Committee's Peasant Group.
A committee member submitted the following petition:

The Peasant Group asks that the county committee appeal to the Provisional Government to resolve these issues:

1. Transfer to the toiling peasantry of land held by the aristocratic landowners, the tsarist state administration, the church, and the monasteries.
2. Institution of free universal compulsory education. Schools must have 8-year curriculums. Six years of classes must be general-education, and two years of classes must be specialized.
3. Replacement of the standing army with a people's militia.
4. Conclusion of the war in a manner beneficial to Russia.
5. Separation of the church and state and performance of the church liturgy in Russian.[7]

DOCUMENT 5.6
S. VOLKOV, "ON THE SAMARA PROVINCIAL PEASANT CONGRESS (REGARDING THE LAND QUESTION)"[8]

The following document is an account of the 25–29 March 1917 Provincial Congress of Peasants' Deputies in Samara, a grain-rich region on the Volga

River in central Russia. The author was local Socialist Revolutionary (SR) activist S. Volkov. The article appeared in the Petrograd SR newspaper, The People's Cause (Delo naroda), *on 5 May 1917. The document uses the term* obshchina, *which refers to the village community self-government responsible for collecting taxes and other state obligations. In many regions, it also periodically reallocated village lands to households and made decisions concerning farming practices and daily village life. A circle of male household elders traditionally ran the* obshchina, *but wartime conscription had taken so many adult men that in 1917 women and younger men (particularly returning soldiers) could claim a larger role in village politics.*

On the Samara Provincial Peasant Congress (Regarding the Land Question).
On 25–29 March, after a series of county congresses, a Provincial Peasant Congress was held in Samara. Initiative groups of the Socialist-Narodniks and the Socialist Revolutionaries convened the congress.[9] The Samara Committee of People's Government facilitated the congress to organize and unify the peasantry and give the village peasantry a voice in this revolutionary period. Its results had great significance in organizing the province's peasants. It seems to have been one of the first such congresses in Russia.

A list of the congress's reports, which included discussions and resolutions, is in itself enough to characterize this congress as successful. The reports were as follows: 1) On current events in Russia; 2) On the war and peace; 3) On the agrarian question; 4) On food supply matters; 5) On the Constituent Assembly; 6) On Committees of the People's Government and state administration in this time of transition; 7) On government and zemstvo taxes; 8) On the Peasant Union.[10]

In addition, there was a report on creating provincial and local Soviets of Peasants' Deputies. At its conclusion, at the suggestion of the reporter— the author of this article—the congress declared itself the Provisional Provincial Soviet of Peasants' Deputies. Of course, the congress gave special attention to the agrarian question. It passed a general resolution and special "temporary guidelines on the use of land until the convocation of the Constituent Assembly."

First of all, a few words about the congress's convocation. A list of congress members designating their home townships and documentary evidence about peasants in these townships refutes allegations by the military correspondent Mr. Kondrushkin that the congress was "composed predominantly of townsmen."[11] The protocols of participants' speeches show that these were predominantly "ordinary" peasants, not the wealthy peasants or *kulaks* or *otrubniks* that Mr. Kondrushkin evidently observed.[12]

It is our deep conviction these temporary guidelines contain the people's wisdom. They represent the majority's collective thinking on how to avoid "misunderstandings and clashes." This is expressed in the first five points of the guideline's "General Regulations," which I consider necessary to cite at length here to fend off critics:

1. Land must be in the hands of the toiling population. A final decision about the form of landownership awaits the Constituent Assembly and those law-based institutions that it will create.
2. All sale and purchase of privately owned land outside the towns must stop immediately, and all opting out of the *obshchina*s to form *otrub*s and private farms must be suspended.
3. The land question must be settled temporarily pending future legislative decisions, to provide the motherland with more grain and prevent civil war in the country. All possible steps must be taken *immediately* to increase the land sown as well as that in meadow and pasture, particularly in villages where peasants have insufficient land.
4. Tools and machinery unused by private landowners must be transferred to the people's government's township committees.
5. Unsown private landowners' land must be distributed for sowing.

In addition to this "general statute," the congress issued "directives" on concrete organization . . . to maintain the principle of the people's rule locally, through the revolutionary "township and county committees of the people's government." These are being formed in Samara Province and are regulating villagers' whole local political-social life.

[Volkov gives more details on the congress's guidelines on immediate land redistribution.]

Doing this is necessary. The villages cannot wait for the Petrograd government offices. Meanwhile, peasants in every village in the land are inventing guidelines and laws. . . . Here is a resolution passed by the Samara congress:

The form of the transfer of land to the toiling people must be worked out by a special peasant congress and decisively settled by the legislative order, the Constituent Assembly, on the following basis: Private land ownership must be abolished. Pending this, there must no sales or purchase of land. All crown, monastery, church, and privately owned land, etc., must be put into the toiling people's hands. Land must be given only to those who will work it.

—S. Volkov

DOCUMENT 5.7
A COUNTY LAND COMMITTEE ON LAND REDISTRIBUTION[13]

The following document is a resolution by the Timskii County Land Committee in Kursk Province on 16 June 1917. Kursk, southwest of Moscow in Russia's fertile Black Earth Zone, was a center for grain farming and livestock husbandry. In late April 1917, the Provisional Government authorized a network of central, provincial, county, and township land committees to work out temporary land reform measures pending the Constituent Assembly. When Viktor Chernov became agriculture minister in May, he urged land committees to speed implementation of temporary reforms. Local committees often interpreted Chernov's instructions as permission to take control of the land.

At the opening of the session there was discussion of the land committees' fundamental work. It was unanimously agreed that the starting point for the land committees' fundamental work must be transformation of all land—state, crown, monastery, church, and privately owned land—with all its contents (woods and waters), into general-public property, for use by toilers on an equalized basis, without payments to the former owners.

The final resolution of the land question awaits the Constituent Assembly. Until then, to prevent land seizures and to avert violence and disputes between different groups in the population, all land in Timskii County will be transferred to the management of the county and township land committees. The land will be placed at the disposal of all who need it, to ensure its most complete possible utilization.

On the question of how to allot land to those in need it, it was resolved: the land committees will determine the actual number of landless and under-landed citizens in the county and work out norms for land usage to provide for minimum consumption needs. The first priority must be securing land for those who are in need, based upon these norms. To do this, the committees will take land from private landowners for division on a rental basis. The rental tax payments will be those established by the Timskii County People's Soviet: no fewer than 15 rubles per *desiatin* sown with winter crops, and 12 rubles for land sown in spring and summer crops.[14]

To speed the business of satisfying land needs, it was resolved that the township land committees shall give the poor the necessary amount of land from among unused land in the township, guided by the temporarily established norms: for every 4 people in a family, 1 *desiatin* of land sown in winter crops is necessary. If there is no free land within the township's borders, and if surplus land from other townships does not meet these needs, then the township land committees have the right to take land from large estates of private landowners and transfer the necessary amount of land sown in spring and summer crops to those in need, in accord with established norms. In doing so, they must adhere to the principle that private landowners must be left enough land to maintain their farms. Also, the committees must avoid any measures that might incite disorders or mass dissatisfaction.

It was resolved that to discover the actual state of land affairs in the county, the township land committees must quickly carry out a census of private landowners' land, guided by state and private records and other documentary statistics. This must establish exactly how much land private landowners rent out and at what rate. In addition, there must be an exact accounting of all livestock, tools, and machinery on individual farms. All the work entrusted to the township land committees in taking account of private owners' land and inventory must be carried out under the supervision of the nearest and most active sections of the township executive committees. To make the township land committees' work as productive as possible, all their members must be literate. The presidium of the county land committee is entrusted with drafting forms for the note cards on which information regarding the property and condition of individual farms will be recorded and for distributing these to the township and land committees.

In relation to the use of hay meadows, it was resolved: The redistribution of aristocratic landlords' hayfields must be undertaken, regardless of who the nobleman is or where the hayfield is located, with great attention to the entire local population's needs.

It was resolved to send the Provisional Government and the Main State Land Committee a copy of the Timskii County Land Committee's resolutions on the transfer of all land in the county to the committee's management. . . .

DOCUMENT 5.8
A SPECIAL SESSION OF THE UNITED NOBILITY[15]

The following document presents a resolution passed at a special session of the United Nobility's leadership in Petrograd on 10 March 1917. The United Nobility, a national association of aristocratic landowners representing Russia's provincial-level noble societies, had enjoyed considerable influence at the tsarist court and helped shape government policies in 1906–1914. The purpose of this 10 March session was to draft a resolution stating the association's attitude toward the Provisional Government.[16] The meeting's chairman was Aleksandr Samarin of Moscow Province, a conservative aristocrat who had held several high tsarist government posts. This account appeared in The Stock Exchange Bulletin (Birzhevyia vedomosti) *on 11 March.*

A Special Session of the United Nobility
Yesterday A. D. Samarin, Chairman of the Society of the United Nobility's Standing Committee, convened a special assembly of representatives from twenty-two provinces. He proposed that they speak out on the current situation. After prolonged debate they passed the following resolution:

The Society of the United Nobility's Standing Committee gathered today under circumstances of extraordinary state importance, at a time when Russia is fighting a war of unprecedented scope, bitterness, and force. A great revolution has been accomplished, transforming the foundations of state life. Under such conditions, great danger threatens. Our blood enemies vigilantly follow events in our internal life, in hope that they can take advantage of a time of discord and strike a decisive and deadly blow against us. In these difficult and great days for Russia, we must rally around the Provisional Government as Russia's sole legal authority. It has taken on the tasks of defending the state and order and fighting the war to a victorious end. Convinced of this, this council calls on the entire Russian nobility to recognize the government and universally assist it in completing its tasks. Let each of us, as the motherland's devoted sons, put all our energy into common, harmonious work. Peace within the country is absolutely necessary as the great Russian people sets about accomplishing a great historical task—establishment of a new state order. The nobility trusts God's goodness and the intimate unity of all the Russian lands. May our resolve and unselfish labor help renew Russia and strengthen it for the heavy trials that God has laid before it.

This resolution, with an accompanying letter from A. D. Samarin, was sent yesterday to Chairman of the Council of Ministers Prince L'vov, with the request that it be shown to all the Provisional Government's ministers.

DOCUMENT 5.9
A LAND CAPTAIN ON THE TASKS OF THE REVOLUTION[17]

The following document set presents two 12 March 1917 statements by Land Captain Lozhen of Elatomskii County, Tambov Province. Land Captains—generally local aristocratic landlords—were among the most reviled tsarist officials in the countryside. The first document is an address Lozhin presented to a local village assembly; the second is the cover note he attached to a copy of address he sent to provincial officials.

12 March 1917
To the Citizens of the Great Russian State![18]

A great event has taken place. Russia has stepped onto a new path that promises us a beautiful and happy life. Each of us has become a citizen with equal rights. The entire people is entrusted with a weighty and difficult task—to construct a new state apparatus and summon individuals who enjoy the population's confidence to serve the new state.

With all my soul, I welcome this transformation toward Russia's great future. And I congratulate you for this boundless joy. But we must remember, before all else, that this transformation is taking place when we are at war, when our enemy still is not destroyed, and when he is watching us like a vulture, searching for our weak spot.

Therefore, above all else, all our collective force and activity must be directed toward supplying the army with all it needs. To accomplish this, we need peaceful, productive, and selfless work. I summon you all to these tasks. Only a peaceful and orderly life and unremitting daily work in the country's service will secure the victory that the people have awaited for three years. Remember: every rest break, every suspension of work, means innumerable disasters for our unfortunate brothers sitting in the trenches.

I believe that we all fully understand how serious this moment is. That is why I have worded my appeal to you so carefully. I am not appealing to you with incendiary slogans that have little bearing on the interests of the motherland, the army, or the people. There is no place for buffoonery in such serious matters.

Now you understand your tasks. You know better than I why your efforts are needed. This requires your persistent, tireless, and peaceful toil.

Long live free, harmonious Russia in the name of the people's and army's interests.

HURRAH!

—Land Captain Lozhin

12 March 1917
I consider it my duty to convince you, honestly and personally, of my complete readiness to spare no effort in the cause of a free and harmonious Russia, in behalf of the people's and the army's interests. Enclosed are my words to the district's population, spoken by me personally at the Vysokopoliansk Village Assembly, in front of more than 3,000 people,

Concerning the district, it can be reported that everything remains relatively calm. Matters go along in the normal order. Clearly, I do not have in mind the general mood of the population, which still does not completely understand the particulars of the insurrection that has taken place. Many understand this transformation as meaning that they now can do whatever they want. For peace of mind, and to prevent the country's passage from a bright future to a state of anarchy, immediate measures are needed to explain to the population about its rights and its responsibilities in relation to the Provisional Government and the army.

—Land Captain Lozhin

DOCUMENT 5.10
THE *KIEV ZEMSTVO GAZETTE* ON THE FEBRUARY REVOLUTION[19]

The following document set presents three excerpts from the 18 March 1917 issue of Kiev Zemstvo Gazette (Kievskaia zemskaia gazeta/ Kyivs'ka zems'kha hazeta). *Kiev was Ukraine's largest city and cultural capital. The Gazette's editors saw their paper as a venue for Ukrainian arts and culture, and its pages reflected the Ukrainian intelligentsia's concern for cultural and political autonomy in 1917. Ukrainians made up some 20 percent of the Russian Empire's population; most lived within an established "historical" territory—Ukraine. In 1917 Ukrainian nationalists initially pushed the Russian Provisional Government for national autonomy, then called for Ukrainian independence. Russia's liberals believed that national minorities' demands for autonomy or independence threatened the unity and integrity of "all the Russian lands." The Kadet's rejection of Ukraine's autonomy contributed to a government crisis in July.*

The first document is a statement by Kiev Zemstvo Gazette's *editors that they would begin printing contributions in Ukrainian as well as in Russian—something the tsarist government had banned. The second is a poem by the Kiev-based Russian symbolist poet Iurii Zubovskii. The third is an essay on the meaning of the February Revolution by B. Doroshkevich, a frequent contributor to Kiev newspapers. Doroshkevich's essay makes use of two similar Russian words that have distinctly different meanings,* Russkii *and* Rossiiskii. Russkii *means Russian in the ethnic sense, whereas* Rossiiskii *refers to the territory of the Russian state. Doroshkevich uses both (see endnotes); the reader might consider why he used specific words in specific sentences.*

... For now, we will publish articles in the Ukrainian as well as the Russian language.[20] For now, until the Editors organize a new Ukrainian newspaper, we will make it fully possible to contribute Ukrainian language essays for all the newspaper's existing sections. This decision by the Editors is in full accord with requests made by many of our readers in response to a 1916 questionnaire.

—The Editors of "K.Z.G."

Spring

A great moment of mighty shocks has come
And Rus', rallying, glows with vengeance,[21]
And in the first days of spring, in the azure spring days
A magical flame has been ignited for us.

We long languished in unquenchable thirst
And drank the cup of sorrow to the bottom.
But a bright day has come, and today each person is happy
Beautiful spring has arrived for all.

It is as if the grief and sadness and oppressive, bitter, evil days
Had been a heavy, sinister dream;
The people have taken up the garland of victory for the motherland
And guided it onto the path of love!

—Iurii Zubovskii

Liberated Russia.

> . . . In whose living heart holds,
> That all Russia at this hour
> Will burn with spring's liberty
> And from heart to heart the flames pour
> The summoning call, hurry forward!
>
> —K. Bal'mont[22]

Russia's best people had already come forward in hope of securing the people's freedom, because only a free country can develop correctly.[23] But still the Russian people slept, their arms and legs chained by the arbitrary former government.[24] The Russian people was kept in artificial darkness and denied enlightenment, and it did not know the power it had, hidden within. And the chains of arbitrariness pulled tighter and tighter, and it became more and more difficult for a great people to breathe.

But the world war furnished the country with new tasks and placed it in a new era. The old government could not manage in the trying times of world war, and this revealed its internal weakness. It became clear to all that this government was not Russian and was not national. That it had been imposed artificially on the great country. And that, for victory over the enemy and for future generations' good, the old government had to be taken to account and Russian life completely restructured.[25]

It became clear to all that only a free Russia can realize the universal tasks that lay before it. That free Russia must take its fate into its own hands.[26] And the sleeping warrior-hero—the Russian people—shook its powerful back and found that the terrible chains with which the old government had bound Russian freedom were weak, rusting from the inside.[27] And Russia understood that its future—and it broke the rusty chains and a free Russia was born.[28]

Now we are living through the greatest time in all of Russian history.[29] Now a new people's power is strengthening and organizing, and above all else, each citizen must preserve absolute calm. We recognize the State *Duma*, elected by the entire country's people, until that time when a new popular election will decide into what mold free Russia's life will be poured.[30] We here in the provinces must understand that the bitter enemy does not slumber. He is near, and he wants to exploit any sign of our weaknesses, any disruption in our lives.

Therefore we all must work for the war. In these great historic days we, citizens of a free Russia, must clearly understand that the country's entire future depends on our work.[31] That only by preserving complete calm and doubling and tripling our work efficiency may we secure our motherland's further happy development. Now a single great task stands before us—to work for the war. Now we must cease all political and national disputes and discord. A great free motherland will secure the development of all nationalities and make possible all kinds of open expression of our opinions.

And so, to work! And long live free Russia.

—B. Dorozhkevich

DOCUMENT 5.11
THE UKRAINIAN NATIONAL CONGRESS ON
NATIONAL AUTONOMY[32]

The following document is a resolution on Ukrainian autonomy passed by the 5–8 April 1917 Ukrainian National Congress. Russian liberals opposed Ukrainian autonomy, but most Russian Social Democrat (SD) and Socialist Revolutionary (SR) leaders supported the right of national self-determination and cultural autonomy. Still, they considered the issue secondary to the revolution's main concerns. Ukrainian SRs and SDs, however, took the issue very seriously, as did liberal Ukrainian nationalists. On 4 March 1917, a gathering of Ukrainian liberals and socialists formed a Ukrainian Central Rada (Council). In April, the Central Rada convened the Ukrainian National Congress, which passed this resolution.

[On Ukrainian Autonomy]

1. The Ukrainian National Congress recognizes the Russian Constituent Assembly's right to legislate a new state order for Russia, Ukraine's autonomy, and the Russian Republic's federated structure. The congress believes, however, that adherents of a new order in Ukraine cannot passively await the Constituent Assembly. We must immediately lay the foundations for Ukraine's autonomous existence, in cooperation with the smaller nationalities.

   In keeping with the Provisional Government's wishes regarding the organization and consolidation of social forces, the congress recognizes the pressing need to organize a regional council of representatives from all Ukrainian districts, towns, and social groups. The Ukrainian Central Rada is to take the initiative in this work.

2. [The Ukrainian National Congress insists that the process of re-drawing national borders during the inevitable post-war peace conference must include representatives of all peoples living in borderland regions, in keeping with the principle of national political self-determination.]

3. [In reaction to land claims asserted by the Provisional Polish State Council, the Ukrainian National Congress insists that the Ukrainian people will defend their lands from any claims or encroachments by the Poles.][33]

4. [The Ukrainian National Congress calls for democratization of the Ukrainian Central Rada and an increase in the number of deputies elected to the Rada.]

5. The Ukrainian National Congress entrusts the Central Rada with undertaking immediate initiatives to form a strong union with those peoples in Russia who, like the Ukrainians, are demanding national and territorial autonomy based on the principle of a democratic Russian republic.

6. The Ukrainian National Congress commissions the Central Rada to form a committee of delegates and national minority representatives to formulate draft legislation on Ukraine's autonomous status. This statute will be submitted for approval to a Ukrainian Congress reflecting the will of the Ukrainian territory's entire population. The Russian Constituent Assembly retains the power to approve Ukraine's autonomous state order.

7. The Ukrainian National Congress considers it necessary that, in those regions of the Federated Russian Republic where Ukrainian people constitute a minority of the population, the Ukrainian people are guaranteed the same minority rights that non-Ukrainian minorities enjoy in Ukraine.

DOCUMENT 5.12
THE ALL-UKRAINIAN PEASANT CONGRESS ON UKRAINIAN AUTONOMY[34]

The following document is a resolution passed by the All-Ukrainian Peasant Congress, which met in Kiev on 29 May–2 June 1917 and was attended by some 2,200 delegates from across Ukraine. The All-Ukrainian Peasant Rada mentioned in the document was a 133-member executive council elected by the congress. The document reflects escalating tensions between Ukrainian leaders and the Russian Provisional Government. In spring 1917, the Central Rada envisioned Ukraine as an autonomous state within a Russian federation of republics. Russia's Kadets had categorically rejected this idea. After the liberal Provisional Government collapsed in April, a new socialist-liberal coalition government also came out against Ukrainian autonomy.

Having heard a report on negotiations between the delegation of the Ukrainian Central Rada and the Russian Provisional Government, the First All-Ukrainian Peasant Congress acted as follows:

1. It resolved to join the Ukrainian Central Rada in its petition [for autonomy] and to demand that the Provisional Government immediately satisfy this petition.

2. As only establishment of a federative-democratic republic in Russia that recognizes Ukraine's national and territorial autonomy and guarantees national minority rights can save this region from ruin, the congress designated the Ukrainian Central Rada, in conjunction with the All-Ukrainian Rada of Peasants Deputies, with the responsibility:

   a. to draft a statute on Ukrainian autonomy and a federal-democratic organizational structure for the Russian Republic;

   b. to convene a congress of representatives from other regions and peoples who aspire to a federal-democratic order;

   c. to exert all effort to hasten organization of a Ukrainian territorial assembly.

3. The congress resolved that all self-government and other institutions in our Ukraine must be Ukrainianized. Therefore, it invites all public organizations (peasant, zemstvo, and so on) and administrative institutions, as well as Ukrainian military organizations, to aid the Ukrainian Central Rada and All-Ukrainian Rada of Peasants' Deputies in preparatory work toward an autonomous Ukrainian state.

DOCUMENT 5.13
THE UKRAINIAN CENTRAL RADA'S "FIRST UNIVERSAL"[35]

The following document is the Ukrainian Rada's "First Universal," issued on 10 June 1917, which asserted Ukraine's autonomy. Five days after this document was published, the Central Rada created a general secretariat, which it described as autonomous Ukraine's new government. The Russia Provisional Government quickly rejected Ukraine's right to declare its own autonomy. In a Second Universal issued on 3 July 1917, the Rada (again) recognized that the All-Russian Constituent Assembly alone had authority to confirm Ukraine's autonomy. On 3 November 1917 (after the Bolsheviks took power in Petrograd), the Rada issued a Third Universal that declared Ukraine's complete independence from Russia and repudiated the Bolshevik-led Soviet government. When, in January 1918, the Bolsheviks intervened militarily to support pro-Soviet forces in Ukraine, the Rada issued a Fourth Universal reaffirming Ukraine's absolute independence from Russia and condemning Bolshevik aggression.

People of Ukraine, nation of peasants, workers, and toilers:
By your will you made us, the Ukrainian Central Rada, the guardians of the Ukrainian land's rights and freedoms. Your best sons, elected by people from the villages and factories and soldiers' barracks, from all Ukraine's districts and groups, have chosen us, the Ukrainian Central Rada, and entrusted us to defend these rights and freedoms.

The men that you elected express their will as follows:

Let there be a free Ukraine. Let the Ukrainian people have the right to manage their own life on their own territory, without separating from

Russia or breaking from the Russian state.[36] Let a Ukrainian National Assembly—elected by universal, equal, direct, and secret ballot—establish order and government in Ukraine.[37] Only our Ukrainian Assembly has the right to issue laws that will establish this government. The laws that establish a government for the entire Russian State must be issued by an All-Russian parliament.

No one knows better what we need or which laws are best for us. No one can know better than our peasants how to manage their own land. Accordingly, we desire that—when the Constituent Assembly passes a law on confiscation of all noble, state, crown, monastic, and other lands throughout Russia as national property—the right to control our own Ukrainian lands and their use must belong to us and to our Ukrainian Assembly.

This is the will of those who were elected from across the Ukrainian land.

Having spoken, they selected from amongst themselves members of the Ukrainian Central Rada. And they instructed us to stand at the head of our people, to guard their rights and create a new order for free, autonomous Ukraine. And we, the Ukrainian Central Rada, fulfilled our people's wish and took upon ourselves the heavy burden of building a new life, and we set upon this task.

[The Rada looked to Russia's Provisional Government for support, but the Russian Provisional Government rejected its demands. It rejected the principle of Ukrainian autonomy, refused to recognize Ukraine's right to a cabinet member in the government, and would not grant the Rada the right to use Ukrainian tax revenues for Ukrainian-language schools and cultural institutions.]

And now, people of Ukraine, we are forced to make our own destiny. We cannot allow our land to be ruined and to collapse. If the Russian Provisional Government cannot introduce order in our land, if it does not want to join us in initiating this great work, then we must undertake the task ourselves. It is our duty to our region and to the inhabitants of our land. Therefore we, the Ukrainian Central Rada, publish this Universal to all our people and declare that from now on we will build our own life.

Let each member of our nation, each citizen in the villages and towns understand now that the hour of great work has struck. [Local government must work in close coordination with the Central Rada. If it is still controlled by people "hostile to Ukrainianization," then the population should re-elect the local administration. In places with a mixed Ukrainian and non-Ukrainian population, the Ukrainians should involve minorities in the new state's work.]

The Central Rada hopes that the non-Ukrainian peoples living in our land will also show concern for peace and order in our territory and that, during this trying time of national disorganization, they will join us in fraternal spirit to organize Ukraine's autonomy.

After we complete this preparatory organizational work, we will summon the representatives of all Ukraine's peoples to work out laws for her. Those laws—the entire order that we will prepare—must be approved by the All-Russian Constituent Assembly.

People of the Ukraine, the Ukrainian Central Rada—your elected institution—is facing a great, high wall. To lead the people out onto the road of freedom, it must demolish that wall. For this, we need strength. We need strong, brave hands. We need the people's hard work. And for that work to succeed, most of all we need great resources. Until now, the Ukrainian people have turned over all their resources to the All-Russian central treasury. Until now, the people themselves have never had anything in return. Therefore, the Ukrainian Central Rada orders all organized citizens in villages and towns and all Ukrainian public boards and institutions to levy a special tax on the population for their own affairs, beginning 1 July, and to accurately, immediately and regularly transfer this tax revenue to the Ukrainian Rada's treasury.

Ukrainian people! Your future is in your own hands. Prove your unity and civic-mindedness at this hour of trial, disorder, and collapse. Prove that you, a nation of plowmen, can take your place proudly and with dignity as the equal of any organized, powerful nation.

DOCUMENT 5.14
THE SEMIPALATINSK REGIONAL KAZAKH CONGRESS TO THE PETROGRAD SOVIET[38]

The following document is a resolution approved by a congress of indigenous peoples in Semipalitinsk on 13 May 1917. Semipalatinsk was a large province on Russia's border with China. After it was incorporated into the Russian Empire in the mid-1800s, Russians and Cossacks settled in towns like the provincial capital, Semipalitinsk (population in 1917, 30,000). The indigenous Kirghiz population was pastoral and largely nomadic.[39] The document below is a telegram sent by the Kirgiz-Kazakh congress to Petrograd Soviet and focuses on the question of territorial autonomy.[40]

The Semipalatinsk Regional Kirgiz Congress, with a profound feeling of gratitude, greets the [Petrograd] Soviet, true fighters for the people, who with heroic force hammered out freedom for all Russia's nationalities. The congress believes that at the first Russian Constituent Assembly, representatives of the valiant army and organized labor together will assert the nationalities' rights to cultural-national self-determination and guarantee their political autonomy.[41] The special circumstances of our people's life demand publication of special local laws granting it a separate territorial national unit.

DOCUMENT 5.15
THE FIRST CAUCASUS REGIONAL SOVIET CONGRESS ON
THE NATIONALITIES QUESTION[42]

The following document is a 30 May 1917 resolution by the First Caucasus Regional Soviet Congress, which met in Tiblisi. The congress included delegates from workers' and peasants' soviets in Georgia, Azerbaijan, Armenia, the North Caucasus, and Dagestan. Mensheviks, who were particularly strong in Georgia, held the majority. The Caucasus Mountain region (between the Black and Caspian Seas) came under Russian rule in the early 1800s. More than forty ethnic groups lived here, in distinct ethnic enclaves, towns with mixed populations, and cosmopolitan cities like Georgia's capital, Tblisi.

The interests of the working class and peasantry demand new legal norms to ensure freedom of cultural development. These norms must be based on the firm foundation of peoples' power. They must be introduced into all spheres of the self-governing peoples' public-political life. The entire Russian democracy demands a fully democratic government. For the first time in Russia's history, it is politically possible to solve the nationalities question on a state-wide basis.[43]

The general-political development of national culture can be assured by permitting full internal self-government for each nation and population group in Russia. This includes the right to create local public agencies, entrusted by the state with specific administrative tasks. Local state institutions will fund these public agencies, which will address special cultural, economic, and legal interests. They must be fully autonomous and independent in these spheres. But they cannot have the autonomous right to govern. That power rests with the state alone. The state will review cases in which public agencies infringe on spheres designated to self-government institutions.

In locales with mixed populations where national-territorial self-government units are not possible, a territorial self-government will be created for general affairs and national affairs to satisfy the national-cultural needs of each separate nation. Through this combination of territorial and cultural principles, conflicts over national culture in mixed self-governed areas can be kept to a minimum.

DOCUMENT 5.16
A RESOLUTION BY THE MOSCOW CHAPTER OF
THE LEAGUE FOR WOMEN'S EQUAL RIGHTS[44]

The following document is a resolution passed by the Moscow Chapter of the League for Women's Equal Rights on 6 March 1917. The League, founded in 1907, was one of tsarist Russia's most significant feminist organizations (although it had only a few thousand members, mostly aristocratic and middle-class women). The League had steadily lobbied the tsarist State Duma to recognize women's equal rights and suffrage. On 20 March 1917, it organized a mass demonstration in Petrograd that pushed the Provisional Government toward recognizing women's equal rights. The Provisional Government did not grant women's suffrage, however, until July 1917.[45]

The League for Women's Equal Rights.
On 6 March 1917 a joint session of the Council of the Moscow Society of the League for Women's Equal Rights with representatives of women's organizations and women workers approved the following resolution to the [Moscow] Committee of Public Organizations:

The meeting greets the Committee of Public Organizations on the occasion of the old regime's complete collapse and the installation of a new, free order. The meeting asks the committee to join it in adopting the following resolution:

1. Women must be granted full civil and political rights. All texts that formulate the rights of citizens, for clarity and precision, must include the formulation "for both sexes."
2. Women's labor must be paid equally to men's. Protections for maternity and child-rearing must be introduced.
3. In all future agrarian reforms, peasant women must have full equality of rights with men.
4. All exclusionary laws applying to prostitution and the abasement of women's human dignity must be abolished.
5. Women ministers must be named immediately to the Ministries of Internal Affairs, Justice, Public Education, Trade and Industry, and Agriculture. They must be entrusted with leadership in all matters connected to the female population's interests.
6. Women commissars must be named immediately to all cities and rural locations, to execute state and public duties.
7. Women must be admitted immediately to the factory inspectorate, the practice of law, the notary profession, and universally in all spheres of public service activity.
8. If Russia is to become a free country, all these demands must be implemented without delay. Otherwise it will be an open declaration that the term "free citizen" implies only men, and women will remain in their previous position—without rights.

An analogous resolution has been sent to the [Moscow] Soviet of Workers' Deputies.

DOCUMENT 5.17
THE SMOLENSK INITIATIVE GROUP OF WOMEN
AND MOTHERS[46]

The following appeal appeared in the Petrograd socialist newspaper, New Life
(Novaia zhizn'), *on 5 May 1917.* New Life's *founder was the writer Maxim
Gorky; its editors later formed the United Social Democrat-Internationalists
group. The appeal is signed by the Smolensk Initiative Group of Women and
Mothers. Unfortunately, there is no information about this group or its members
in local Smolensk newspapers or in the regional archives.*

To All Russian Women and Mothers.
We, a group of Russian women and mothers, join the toiling people's
protest against the war. We also extend our hand to all the world's women
and mothers. We are profoundly convinced that our extended hand will
be met by the extended hands of all the world's mothers. No annexations,
no indemnities, can compensate a mother for a murdered son.[47]

No more blood. No more of this horrid bloodshed, which is absolutely
pointless for toiling people. No more giving our sons as a sacrifice to the
capitalists' burning greed. We don't need any annexations or indemnities.
It is better to protect our sons, for the good of the world's working people.
Let them put all their effort into the cause of peace and the brotherhood
between all peoples, not to a fratricidal war. And let us, Russian women
and mothers, be proud in knowing that we are the first to extend our hand
to all the world's mothers.

The Smolensk Initiative Group of Women and Mothers

DOCUMENT 5.18
CENTRAL BUREAU OF RUSSIAN MUSLIMS, "APPEAL TO
RUSSIA'S MUSLIM WOMEN"[48]

*The following document by the Central Bureau of Russian Muslims was pub-
lished in the Russian-language newspaper,* The Voice of Turkestan *(Turke-
stanskii golos), on 26 April 1917. In 1917, more than 14 million Muslims lived
in Central Asia, Siberia, the Caucasus, and the lower Volga, Ural Mountain,
and Caspian Sea regions. In March 1917, the Muslim Union* (Ittifaq al-
Muslimin, *formed in 1905) created the Central Bureau of Russian Muslims. The
Central Bureau included members of several political parties, but its leaders were
Azari, Tatar, and Crimean Tatar intellectuals closely tied to the liberal Kadets.*

Muslim women-citizens! Russia has entered into a bright time when the
fetters of centuries of slavery have finally fallen. The sun of freedom shines

happily. Russia's peoples are living through an epoch of great events and great tasks. The tasks that await us as Muslims are complex and important. The most complex and important tasks are those that await Muslim women.

Russian women already have rushed to join in general civil and political life. They are rushing to make use of freedom's benefits. The sun of freedom's vivid rays must penetrate the dirty windows of the stuffy dwellings where Muslim women's souls have been oppressed these many long years. The happy hymn of freedom and renewal must fall on Muslim women's closed ears! The exalted vision of today's new life must fill Muslim women's eyes!

Can there be full human freedom if women are excluded from the ranks of free people as if they were slaves? A declaration of Muslim women's rights must finally be proclaimed. We must speak boldly against those traditions that have chained Muslim women. We must organize their liberty's free flight, the free brandishing of their strength. The key— dear women!—is that we must create a government unique to our Muslim world. This government will proclaim women's rights universally as human beings and will direct the practical affairs of Russia's Muslims.

We must treat the issue of granting women electoral rights for local and general-state institutions as almost predetermined. Millions of Russian women have entered the electoral rolls and have laid their vote on history's scales! How could we waste millions of Muslim women's votes for good Muslim work in Russia?! Immediate action must be taken to organize Muslim women. Women's organizations, meetings, circles and assemblies must be established. Muslim women must actively enter into the thick of life. They must finally raise their voices as part of the general choir! To work, Muslim women! You understand the great responsibilities laid upon us by recent events. To work, with no hesitation!

The Central Bureau of Russian Muslims calls Muslim women citizens to the most intensive organizational work. Muslim women must join the general movement. The Central Bureau calls on Muslim women's organizations to send representatives to the Moscow All-Russian Muslim Congress in May. Say yes to letting Muslim women's free voices ring out! Say yes to awakening those who still quietly dream of the past, those who have not yet seen the exalted radiant dawning sun of new life rising over them!

Long live free Muslim women—women citizens and women comrades!

DOCUMENT 5.19
A RESOLUTION BY THE FIRST ALL-RUSSIAN MUSLIM CONFERENCE[49]

The following document is a resolution by the 1–11 May 1917 First All-Russian Muslim Conference in Moscow.[50] The delegates, mostly members of Turkic and

Tatar ethnic groups, represented a wide spectrum of the Muslim population. The conference differed from most assemblies of national minorities in that it represented peoples connected by religion rather than ethnicity. Its focus on cultural and territorial autonomy within a Russian Republic organized as a federation of territories, though, paralleled the views of ethnic minority activists.

The All-Russian Muslim Conference, having discussed the issue of the form of state administration in Russia, has resolved:
To recognize that the form of state construction in Russia best suited to the Muslim nationalities' interests is a democratic republic, organized on a national-territorial-federative basis. Nationalities that do not have a definite territory are to exercise national cultural self-determination. To regulate general spiritual-cultural questions regarding Russia's Muslim nationalities, and to advance their solidarity, a central general Muslim institution with legislative powers must be founded for all of Russia. The form, composition, and function of this institution will be determined by the first constituent congress of representatives of all [Russia's] autonomous units.

DOCUMENT 5.20
A RESOLUTION AT THE SMOLENSK JEWISH WORKERS' ASSEMBLY[51]

The following document is a resolution on "the nationalities question" offered at an assembly of Jewish workers in Smolensk on 15 March 1917. Jews accounted for about 15 percent of the city's population. The resolution's author, Solomon Gurevich, was editor of The Smolensk Bulletin (Smolenskii vestnik), *which published the document on 18 March. He was a prominent figure in the local Jewish community and in both the Socialist Revolutionary and Socialist Jewish Workers' Party (SERP) organizations locally. His resolution mentions the "reestablishment of Smolensk's old socialist party organization." As in many provincial cities, in Smolensk, the socialist party organizations had been decimated by arrests in 1906, 1907, and 1916.*

At a 15 March Jewish Workers' Assembly, the following resolution proposed by S. G. Gurevich was discussed and approved:
The Jewish Workers' Assembly greets the re-establishment of Smolensk's old socialist party organizations. It urgently asks that at their party meetings and conferences, these parties discuss and pass resolutions endorsing a fundamental, indisputable, and precise law to fully guarantee the democratic principles of freedom of national self-determination and national development in all the Russian state's realms. We ask that the parties include this as a special point in their party programs. It is our assembly's profound conviction that a true democratic order cannot be

established in our diverse Motherland without these principles. Without these principles, there can be no true peaceful and calm coexistence among Russia's peoples. Without these principles, we cannot ensure their harmonious cultural work for the good of all free Russia.

The program point on the nationality question must say that:

1. Every nationality—even if it is so small or so weak that it still has not successfully manifested its own particular national culture and cultural creativity, as it might were it living in one compact mass, and even if it is scattered across all Russia in small groups and colonies—must exercise full rights of cultural-national self-determination.
2. All citizens of each separate nationality must elect representative institutions by a secret and universal ballot. These must exercise autonomous administrative authority in all matters of the represented nationality's cultural and national life. The sphere of competence of these representative national institutions will be established by legislative order.
3. The establishment of national freedom applies to every Russian citizen and every group of citizens. In view of poor attendance, the assembly will discuss this resolution at a workers' meeting on 20 March.

DOCUMENT 5.21
THREE RESOLUTIONS BY THE 10TH CONFERENCE OF THE BUND[52]

The following document set presents excerpts from three resolutions passed by the 10th Conference of the General Jewish Labor Union of Lithuania, Poland, and Russia (the Bund, or Union), held in Petrograd on 1–6 April 1917. The Bund was a Marxist Social Democratic Party formed in 1897 (before the Russian Social Democratic Labor Party). In the prerevolutionary era, it often aligned with the Mensheviks. The Bund was one of several Jewish socialist parties in the Russian Empire, but it was unique in its complete rejection of the idea that Jews should have their own national territory or homeland—be it in Russia (Zionist territorialism) or elsewhere (for instance, in Palestine). Still, the Bund did strongly support Jews' right to national cultural autonomy.

On the Nationality Question in Russia.
Considering that Russia is a multinational state, the question of forming a democratic republic that will secure norms for the coexistence of different nationalities must be put before the Constituent Assembly as a pressing issue.

In doing so, the following must be taken into consideration: on one hand, the class interests of the country's proletariat as a whole, as well as the revolutionary movement's general interests; on the other hand, historical conditions for the development of nationalities, as well as their aspirations for national self-determination.

The Bund conference considers it necessary to form a special commission with representatives of the RSDLP and the socialist parties of other nationalities to consider this issue in relation to the RSDLP and Bund general programs on the nationality question.[53]

On National-Cultural Autonomy.

1. The Tenth Conference, in accord with the Bund Sixth Congress's resolutions on the nationality question, moves that the immediate realization of national-cultural autonomy must be the actual political slogan of the day.
2. The Constituent Assembly must issue Fundamental Laws that establish local, regional, and state-wide public institutions. These must be elected on the basis of universal, equal, direct, and secret ballot, without distinction by sex. They will organize and lead the entire cultural life of the Jewish nation in Russia on the following basis:
   a. Anyone who considers himself a Jew by nationality can be considered a member of these public organizations;
   b. The sphere of competence of national-cultural organizations will include all aspects of the nation's cultural life: school-educational matters and the development of literature, art, science, and technical knowledge. All such national-cultural organizations and the schools created by them must have an exclusively secular character.
3. The language of these national-cultural organizations will be Yiddish.[54] The budgets of the national-cultural organizations will secure the right of national minorities to have schools in other, non-Jewish languages.
   Note: All aspects of religion and religious-devotional life are outside the sphere of these national-cultural organizations. To satisfy their religious needs, that part of the Jewish nation that needs to may organize religious societies as private institutions. These will exist under the protection of the Russian democratic republic's general laws.
4. The state has the right to review the accounts of national-cultural organizations that receive private and general state funds, and in particular to review their assignment of supplementary taxes.[55]

On Realization of National-Cultural Autonomy.
The Bund's Tenth Conference considers that, pending the Constituent Assembly's convocation, local institutions for the Jewish nation's national-cultural autonomy must be created immediately. These must be organized on the basis of universal, equal, direct, and secret ballot, with participation of all citizens of both sexes over 20 years old who consider themselves part of the Jewish nation. These institutions must be entrusted

with administration of all Jewish primary schools, even as the Jewish school network expands. The Provisional Government must immediately publish a decree including Jewish schools in the general schools network and introducing Yiddish as the language of instruction in such schools.

To facilitate the struggle for autonomous national-cultural institutions, the conference approves participation in a general Jewish congress, if this is elected on the basis of a universal, equal, direct, and secret ballot.[56] ... The conference's Jewish worker delegates feel that any Jewish congress must pass a concrete resolution on the question of national autonomy. The Bund's representatives to that congress must fight resolutely against any attempt to divert it toward other general-national and political tasks. The conference declares that the working class cannot be responsible for that Jewish congress's decisions. Final decision of questions discussed at that congress rests with the All-Russian Constituent Assembly, at which the Jewish proletariat's representatives will carry out their struggle together with the representatives of the entire working class of Russia. The Jewish national-cultural organizations' internal structure will be determined by a Jewish constituent assembly, within a sphere of competence to be established by the All-Russian Constituent Assembly in its fundamental laws.

DOCUMENT 5.22
THE SEVENTH CONGRESS OF RUSSIAN ZIONISTS ON CULTURAL ISSUES[57]

The following document is a resolution on cultural issues passed by the Seventh Congress of Russian Zionists, which met in Petrograd on 11–18 May 1917. More than 500 delegates representing more than 300 towns attended the congress. Although Zionism (the idea that Jews as a nation must have their own national territory) came relatively late to Russia, a wide range of Zionist parties had emerged there by 1917. In addition to liberal Zionists and religious Zionists (the Mizrachi), Russia had three significant socialist Zionist parties. In 1917 two of these, the Zionist Socialist Labor Party and the Socialist Jewish Workers' Party, merged to form the United Jewish Socialist Workers' Party. The third was the Jewish Social Democratic Workers' Party, known as Poalei-Tsion (Workers of Zion). The resolution below reflects the influence of socialists who considered Yiddish (not Hebrew) the Jewish national language.

Resolution on Cultural Issues.
Recognizing the Yiddish language as the Jewish people's only national language, necessary for all Jews' Jewish upbringing, culture, and daily speech, the Seventh All-Russian Zionist Congress proclaims the following demands:

a. That in every general school and educational institution [attended by Jews], the Yiddish language be the language of instruction in all grades, in addition to the state, regional, and other languages;
b. That the Jewish language be established as the official language of all the Jewish people's public institutions.
c. That it is the responsibility of all members of Zionist organizations to introduce these principles in the Jewish *obshchina*s, in all [Jewish] teaching and educational institutions, and in other institutions that serve public needs.[58]

CHAPTER SIX
FLASH POINTS OF CONFLICT: THE APRIL CRISIS

6.1
A RESOLUTION BY A WORKERS' MEETING AT THE L. NOBEL ENGINEERING PLANT

6.2
A LABOR CONFLICT AT MOSCOW'S GRACHEV ENGINEERING WORKS

6.3
THE DITMAR FACTORY ASSEMBLY (KHARKOV) ON WORKERS' CONTROL

6.4
THE PETROGRAD SOVIET'S APPEAL, "TO ALL THE WORLD'S PEOPLE"

6.5
THE PROVISIONAL GOVERNMENT'S DECLARATION ON WAR AIMS

6.6
THE ALL-RUSSIAN CONFERENCE OF SOVIETS OF WORKERS' AND SOLDIERS' DEPUTIES ON THE WAR

6.7
FOREIGN MINISTER MILIUKOV'S "NOTE TO THE ALLIED GOVERNMENTS"

6.8
THE BOLSHEVIKS ON THE 20 APRIL 1917 DEMONSTRATIONS AGAINST THE MILIUKOV NOTE

6.9
THE RESERVE ELECTRO-TECHNICAL BATTALION COMMITTEE ON THE MILIUKOV NOTE

6.10
THE FINNISH GUARDS REGIMENT RESERVE BATTALION COMMITTEE ON THE 20 APRIL 1917 DEMONSTRATIONS

6.11
THE PROVISIONAL GOVERNMENT'S EXPLANATION OF THE MILIUKOV NOTE

6.12
THE PETROGRAD SOVIET ON THE PROVISIONAL GOVERNMENT'S EXPLANATION OF THE MILIUKOV NOTE

6.13
A PARTICIPANT'S ACCOUNT OF PETROGRAD WORKERS' DEMONSTRATIONS ON 21 APRIL 1917

DOCUMENT 6.1
A RESOLUTION BY A WORKERS' MEETING AT THE
L. NOBEL ENGINEERING PLANT[1]

The following document is a resolution passed by a workers' meeting at the large Nobel Engineering Plant in Petrograd on 4 April 1917. It appeared in the Petrograd Bolshevik newspaper, Truth (Pravda), *on 7 April 1917. The engineering plant was founded by Swedish entrepreneur Alfred Nobel and specialized in defense-related production. In early spring 1917, Socialist Revolutionaries and Mensheviks led its workers' committee. The first powerful signs that the euphoria brought by the February Revolution might quickly fade came in Petrograd's factories, where conflicts between organized workers and managers led to a significant increase in strike activity in early April 1917.*

1. Liberation of the working class is the workers' own cause.
2. The proletariat's final aim—Socialism—will be achieved not though compromise, conciliation, and reform, but by unceasing struggle— through revolution.
3. The bourgeoisie considers the proletariat a dangerous threat. Time after time, it has arranged for the working class' bloodletting. In 1905 we had 9 January, in 1912 there was Lena, and after Lena, Kostroma and Ivanovo-Voznesensk.[2]
4. The working class cannot trust any government that is made up of bourgeois elements and that depends upon the bourgeoisie.
5. Our Provisional Government, composed almost entirely of bourgeois elements, cannot be a people's government whose judgment and great achievements we can trust.

Considering these points, the workers' assembly at the Nobel plant demands that:

a. Preparations for convoking the Constituent Assembly's must begin now;
b. The Provisional Government must officially contact the Allied and belligerent powers and propose an immediate peace that renounces all annexations and indemnities and recognizes each nation's right to self-determination.

DOCUMENT 6.2
A LABOR CONFLICT AT MOSCOW'S GRACHEV
ENGINEERING WORKS[3]

The following document is a report on a labor dispute at the Grachev Engineering Works in Moscow in April 1917. The report appeared in The News of

Moscow Soviet of Workers' Deputies (Izvestiia Moskovskogo Soveta rabochikh deputatov) *on 2 May 1917. The newspaper's editors were Mensheviks and Socialist Revolutionaries who hoped such labor conflicts could be solved though mediation. In early April 1917, strikes and labor conflicts escalated not just in Petrograd and Moscow, but it many provincial cities as well. Generally, these involved either enterprises that had not yet implemented the eight-hour workday or enterprises whose owners rejected workers' assertion of decision-making rights in management affairs.*

When the Easter holiday ended on 6 April, the Grachev factory was unexpectedly closed to the workers until 10 April. On that day the workers were told that 11 people had been fired, among whom were members of the factory committee. The dismissals were explained as the result of a decrease in orders, the transfer of the works to new premises, and its reconstruction.

The factory committee appealed to the Moscow [Labor] Commissar and the Soviet of Workers' and Soldiers' Deputies' Investigative Commission, requesting that they clarify the causes of the decline in orders to this factory, which is doing defense work.[4] In addition, the factory committee declared that the only work going on now is setting up equipment at the new premises. There is no production of artillery shells. Accounting for this work is done incorrectly. And piece work pay is so low that [some workers] are not even making 1 ruble per day.

The workers also demanded that the factory rehire those who were dismissed, provide pay for the days that the factory was closed (6 to 10 April), and implement new wage regulations.

The Soviet Investigative Commission performed an on-site study. The workers testified that since November 1916, while the plant waited for equipment, its skilled laborers had been occupied fixing broken heaters and repairing floors. For this work, they received very low wages on a daily basis. The workers dismissed included members of the factory committee and workers who had presented the factory with demands for an increase in pay. Six people had been dismissed in the first days of the revolution, but they were hired back in accord with a resolution of the arbitration chamber. This was because the workforce had been cut, daily wages had been reduced, etc., without proper notification.

The administration testified that it would take two weeks to equip the factory, that workers designated for dismissal would not be dismissed, and that the issue of pay for the five-day layoff would be decided by an arbitration chamber. The administration explained that the factory had been closed from 5–10 April because of the death of the owner's father.

The matter appeared to be settled. However, it soon became clear that five of the workers (including two members of the plant committee) had been dismissed permanently, and none of the workers' demands had been satisfied. Therefore the workers went on strike.

The Moscow Committee of Public Organization's Military Council and the Soviet of Workers' Deputies are now examining the conflict.[5]

DOCUMENT 6.3
THE DITMAR FACTORY ASSEMBLY (KHARKOV) ON WORKERS' CONTROL[6]

The following document is from the Ditmar Engineering Works in Kharkov in Ukraine. It is a resolution passed by a workers' and employees' assembly on 8 April 1917 and published in Kharkov's Bolshevik newspaper, Proletarians (Proletarii), *on 14 April. Workers' demand to oversee enterprise administration was one of the most contentious issues in labor relations. Workers suspected that owners might deliberately undermine production to cripple the revolution; owners insisted that managers alone could supervise hiring, firing, and disciplinary measures and make decisions on production.*

1. After individual speakers made statements on various sides of the issue, the workers and employees unanimously agreed on the issue of the unity and mutual solidarity among the factory's workers and employees. The employees categorically refuse to defend the owner's interests, which are opposed to the workers' interests. This is because the employees are part of the toiling masses and are in solidarity with the working class.
2. It was decided that at the next meeting a committee made up of workers and employees will be elected to investigate the owner's activities in relation to productive work (its successful execution). This committee will not tolerate the sale of raw materials that the factory acquired earlier and then held in reserve. It takes this position to oppose speculation, and also because such sales could potentially result in unemployment. But it does so chiefly as a means to eliminate obstacles to the manufacture of defense goods, as it is our duty to the army and the motherland to produce these at full capacity.
3. It was resolved to organize a factory library with funds collected from the workers and employees.

DOCUMENT 6.4
THE PETROGRAD SOVIET'S APPEAL, "TO ALL THE WORLD'S PEOPLE"[7]

The following document was one of the Petrograd Soviet's most important statements on war aims—an appeal "To All the World's People," adopted on 14

March 1917. During soviet debates, Soviet Chairman Nikolai Chkheidze (a leader of the Menshevik revolutionary defensists) insisted that this declaration would influence German workers and help end the war. The resolution was adopted unanimously. It was published in The News of the Petrograd Soviet (Izvestiia Petrogradskogo soveta) *on 15 March and widely republished and commented on in other newspapers. As labor conflicts were heating up in April, the issue of war aims exploded into a major political crisis.*

To All the World's People.

Comrade proletarians and toilers of all countries!

We, Russian workers and soldiers, united in the Petrograd Soviet of Workers' and Soldiers' Deputies, send you our warmest greetings and inform you of a great event. The Russian democracy has thrown centuries of tsarist despotism into the dust. We have entered into your family [of nations] as an equal member and as a great force in the struggle for our common liberation. Our victory is a great victory for universal freedom and democracy. The main prop of reactionaries worldwide, the "gendarme of Europe," is no more. May there be granite-heavy earth on its grave. Long live freedom! Long live the international solidarity of the proletariat and its struggle for a conclusive victory!

Our work still is not complete. The old order's remnants still have not been scattered, and many enemies are gathering force against the Russian revolution. But our accomplishments are greater than [the enemy's forces]. Russia's peoples shall express their will at a Constituent Assembly— elected by universal, equal, direct, and secret ballot—which shall soon be convened. Now it is already possible to predict confidently that a democratic republic will triumph in Russia. The Russian people possess complete political freedom. It now can speak authoritatively about the country's internal self-determination and its foreign policy. And—appealing to all people destroyed and ruined in this horrible war—we declare that the time has come to launch a decisive struggle against all countries' and governments' aggressive [war] aims. The time has come for the people to take the matter of war and peace into their own hands.

Conscious of its revolutionary force, the Russian democracy declares that it will oppose the ruling classes' policy of conquest with all its might and calls upon Europe's peoples to speak out resolutely for peace.

We appeal to our brother proletarians in the Austro-German coalition, and above all, to the German proletariat. From the war's first days, you were assured that you were defending Europe's culture from Asiatic despotism by taking up arms against autocratic Russia. Many of you saw this as justification for supporting the war. Now this justification no longer exists: democratic Russia cannot be a threat to freedom and civilization.

We will steadfastly defend our own freedom from any reactionary encroachment, both from within and from the outside. The Russian revolution will not retreat before the conquerors' bayonets, and it will not allow itself to be destroyed by a foreign military force. But we appeal to you: Throw off the yoke of your own semi-autocratic order, as we Russian people have shaken off tsarist autocracy. Refuse to be tools for conquest and violence in the hands of princes, aristocratic landlords, bankers. As a harmonious united force, we will stop the horrible butchery that disgraces mankind and darkens the great days of Russian freedom's birth.

Toilers of all countries! We extend our brotherly hand across mountains of our brothers' corpses, across rivers of innocent blood and tears, across the smoking ruins of towns and villages, across the ruined treasures of culture. We appeal to you to restore and strengthen international unity. That is the guarantee of our future victory and of mankind's complete liberation.

Proletarians of all countries, unite!
The Petrograd Soviet of Workers' and Soldiers' Deputies

DOCUMENT 6.5
THE PROVISIONAL GOVERNMENT'S DECLARATION ON WAR AIMS[8]

The following document is the Provisional Government's declaration on war aims, as published in The Provisional Government Bulletin (Vestnik Vremennogo pravitel'stvo) *on 28 March 1917. The government had formulated this statement on 27 March, under pressure from the Petrograd Soviet to renounce annexationist war aims. Although the document was "signed" by Prime Minister L'vov, its primary author was Foreign Minister Pavel Miliukov, who actually opposed making concessions to the soviet on foreign policy matters. The government's position on war aims would spark a political crisis a few weeks later, after publication of a note in which Miliukov reassured the Allies that Russia would abide by treaties signed under the tsar.*

Citizens!
It is the duty of the Provisional Government, having discussed the Russian State's military position, to directly and openly tell the people the entire truth.

The overthrown former government left the country's defense in a terribly disorganized state. With its criminal inactivity and ineffective measures, it disrupted our finances, food supply, transportation, and supplies for the army. It undermined our economic order.

The Provisional Government, through the entire people's vital and active participation, will use all its energy to correct these grievous consequences of the old regime. But time will not stand still. The blood of the motherland's sons has flowed without measure for two and a half long years of war. But the country still remains subject to blows from a powerful enemy who has seized entire regions of our state. And now, in the days of Russian's freedom's birth, the enemy threatens us with a new decisive assault. Defending our inheritance and delivering the country from the enemy who have invaded our borders—this is the first and most vital task of our fighters, who are defending the people's freedom.

In keeping with the people's will, and in close communication with our allies regarding all issues, the Provisional Government by its rights and duty now declares that free Russia's aim is not to master other peoples, not to seize their national property, not to forcibly seize foreign territory. Free Russia's aim is to establish a stable peace on the basis of national self-determination. The Russian people do not intend to increase its world power at other people's expense. Its aim is not to enslave or humiliate anyone. In behalf of the highest principles of justice, it removes the fetters tying down the Polish people.[9] But the Russian people will not permit their motherland to come out of this great struggle humiliated and drained of its vital forces. These principles will be the basis of the Provisional Government's foreign policy. It shall unswervingly carrying out the people's will and defend our motherland's rights, while fully observing the obligations that we have assumed in relation to our allies.

Free Russia's Provisional Government does not have the right to withhold the truth from the people—the state is in danger. We need to exert all our effort to rescue it. Let the country's response to these words of truth be not despair, not dejection, but a unanimous effort to create a single national will. This shall give us new strength for the struggle and lead us to salvation.

In this hour of severe trial, let the entire country find the strength to consolidate freedom's achievements and work tirelessly for the good of free Russia. The Provisional Government, taking a solemn oath to serve the people, firmly believes that the general and unanimous support of all shall allow it to fulfill its duty to the country.

Prime Minister Prince G. E. L'vov
27 March 1917

DOCUMENT 6.6
THE ALL-RUSSIAN CONFERENCE OF SOVIETS OF
WORKERS' AND SOLDIERS' DEPUTIES ON THE WAR[10]

On 29 March–3 April 1917, the Petrograd Soviet's leadership convened an All-Russian Soviet Conference to discuss a range of issues, including the soviets' relationship to the Provisional Government and the soviets' position on the war. Most of the delegates were Socialist Revolutionaries and Mensheviks, and the conference's basic resolutions reflected the revolutionary defensists' positions. That was true in particular of the following document, a resolution on the war passed on 30 March by a majority of 325–57 (with most "no" votes coming from Bolsheviks).

In its 14 March Appeal to All the World's People, the Soviet of Workers' and Soldiers' Deputies declared the Russian democracy's firm determination to realize the same principles of freedom and rights in the sphere of foreign policy that it had proclaimed regarding Russia's internal life.

Numerous workers', soldiers', and citizens' meetings across Russia have confirmed this determination. Expressing the people's will, they have proclaimed that they will defend their own freedom, but they will not allow the people's revolutionary enthusiasm to be exploited for violence against other peoples or for open or secret annexations or indemnities.

When the Executive Committee of the [Petrograd] Soviet of Workers' and Soldiers' Deputies entered into relations with the Provisional Government, it demanded free Russia's immediate public renunciation of all tsarist plans of conquest.

On 28 March the Provisional Government published a declaration to Russia's citizens. It stated: "Free Russia's aim is not to master other peoples, not to seize their national property, not to forcibly seize foreign territory. Free Russia's aim is to establish a stable peace on the basis of national self-determination. The Russian people do not intend to increase its world power at the expense of other peoples. Its aim is not to enslave or humiliate anyone."

The Russian democracy considers this act by the Provisional Government extremely significant. It is an important step toward realizing democratic principles in the sphere of foreign policy. The soviets of workers' and soldiers' deputies will support all the Provisional Government's steps in this direction with all their energy. The soviets call upon all peoples, both in the Allied states and in countries at war with Russia, to exert pressure on their governments to renounce their programs of conquest. In addition, the peoples of both coalitions must insist that their governments persuade their allies to renounce all annexations and indemnities. For its part, the Executive Committee emphasizes the need for the Provisional Government to negotiate with the allies to work out a general agreement along these lines.

Russia's revolutionary people will continue their efforts for a quick peace on the basis of brotherhood and equal freedom for all peoples. An official renunciation by all governments of their aggressive programs is a powerful means for ending the war on such conditions.

As long as these efforts are not realized, as long as the war continues, the Russian democracy recognizes that the army's decline and the weakening of its resistance, strength, and readiness for active operations would be a great blow to freedom's cause and the country's vital interests. For revolutionary Russia's most energetic defense against external invaders, and to decisively rebuff all attempts to interfere with the revolution's further success, the Conference of Soviets of Workers' and Soldiers' Deputies calls on democratic Russia to mobilize all the country's vital forces, in all spheres of public life, to reinforce the front and the rear. The moment Russia is living through imperatively demands this; it is a necessity for the great revolution's success.

The Conference of Soviet of Workers' and Soldiers' Deputies calls on all workers in factories and plants, on railroads, in mines, in postal and telegraph offices, and in other enterprises engaged in defense work in the rear to carry out their work with the greatest intensity. The working class' economic achievements and its aspiration for further reforms must not weaken productive energy. It must increase work productivity to the greatest degree, in the interest of providing the population and the army with all that it needs.

The Conference of Soviet of Workers' and Soldiers' Deputies directs the attention of all citizens, particularly those engaged in agriculture and transport, to the danger of the food supply's disruption—a problem bequeathed by the old regime—and calls on them to exert all their strength to overcome it.

The Conference of Soviet of Workers' and Soldiers' Deputies sends its greetings to the revolutionary army's soldiers and officers, who are defending Russia's freedom within the country and at the front.

DOCUMENT 6.7
FOREIGN MINISTER MILIUKOV'S "NOTE TO THE ALLIED GOVERNMENTS"[11]

Various resolutions in March 1917 did not bring an end to debate over Russia's war aims. When Justice Minister Alexander Kerensky—the Provisional Government's only socialist—told a British reporter that Russia supported internationalizing the Straits of the Bosporus and Dardanelles (in Turkey), Foreign Minister Miliukov rushed to reassure the French and British that Russia stood by secret agreements on the Straits signed in 1915. At the same time, Russia was engaged in unofficial, "back-door," discussions of a separate peace with Germany and Turkey. For Miliukov, these unofficial negotiations raised the importance of reassuring Russia's allies. On 13 April, the Kadet newspaper Speech (Rech) *reported that the Foreign Ministry was working on a note to the Allies "to elaborate its views on issues and aims concerning the current war." On 14 April, the Provisional Government denied this report.[12] On 18 April,*

Miliukov instructed Russia's representatives abroad to deliver a telegram to the governments of the Allied Powers. The following document is the text of that 18 April 1917 telegram.

On 27 March of this year, the Provisional Government published an appeal to citizens that explained free Russia's government's views on the tasks of the current war. The minister of foreign affairs has asked me to impart that document to you and to deliver the following statement.[13]

Our enemies have striven of late to bring discord to inter-Allied relations by spreading absurd reports that Russia is ready to conclude a separate peace with the Central Monarchies.[14] The text of the attached document best refutes such inventions. You will see that the Provisional Government's general position in its declaration fully accords with the grand ideas expressed continually and recently by many of the Allied countries' outstanding statesmen. These are ideas expressed with particular clarity by our new ally, the great republic across the Atlantic, in the statements of its President.[15]

The old regime's government, of course, could not assimilate and share such ideas about the war's liberating character, establishing durable foundations for all people's peaceful coexistence, the self-determination of oppressed nationalities, and so on. But liberated Russia can speak a language understandable to contemporary mankind's advanced democracies. She joins her voice with the voices of her allies. Imbued with this new spirit of liberated democracy, the Provisional Government's pronouncements, of course, cannot give [anyone] the slightest reason to think that the current revolution will weaken Russia's role in the common Allied struggle.

Absolutely to the contrary: the [revolution] has only strengthened the international aspiration to bring the world war to a conclusive victory, thanks to universal consciousness of everyone's common responsibilities. This aspiration has become more effective as [Russia] concentrates on the next task, which is dear to all—repelling the enemy that has penetrated our motherland's borders.

It is self-evident, as stated in the appended document, that the Provisional Government, while defending our motherland's rights, will fully adhere to the obligations taken on in relation to our allies. [Russia's government] remains fully confident that the present war will be brought to a victorious conclusion in full cooperation with our allies. It is absolutely certain that the issues raised by the war will be resolved in the spirit of creating a durable foundation for a lasting peace, and that the leading democracies—imbued with identical aspirations—will find a means to obtain those guarantees and sanctions necessary to prevent future bloody clashes.

DOCUMENT 6.8
THE BOLSHEVIKS ON THE 20 APRIL 1917 DEMONSTRATIONS
AGAINST THE MILIUKOV NOTE[16]

The following document, from the Bolsheviks' Petrograd newspaper, Truth *(Pravda), on 22 April 1917, describes demonstrations that took place in Petrograd in reaction to the Miliukov Note on 20 April. The report specifically mentions protests by the 180th Infantry Reserve Regiment, the Finnish Guards Regiment, the Moscow Guards Regiment, and sailors from several ships in the Second Baltic Fleet (all stationed in Petrograd). It refers to two specific locales. The first is the Mariinskii Palace (located on the square adjacent to Saint Isaac's Cathedral), which at this point was the residence of the Provisional Government. The palace square thus became a focal point for political demonstrations. The second is Nevskii Prospect, Petrograd's most famous street and another important site for demonstrations and marches.*

On 20 April soldiers from the 180th Infantry Reserve, the Finnish and Moscow regiments, several separate infantry companies, sections of fleet crews, and so on gathered at the Mariinskii Palace. At first, the soldiers' main demand was, "Down with Miliukov!" Toward evening placards appeared, reading, "Down with the Provisional Government!"

For a long time, soldiers refused to disperse until they learned that the Provisional Government had resigned. They dispersed toward evening, after meetings at which orators of all political shades spoke.

The following must be duly noted: when on 20 April, the orators— both soldiers and civilians—spoke critically of the government's note to the Allies and explained that this note clearly exposed the bourgeois Provisional Government's aggressive, plundering aspiration, soldiers and workers met them with sympathy and support. The "pure" public along Nevskii Prospect—various officers, merchants, students, government clerks, and so on—however, were hostile toward them.

DOCUMENT 6.9
THE RESERVE ELECTRO-TECHNICAL BATTALION
COMMITTEE ON THE MILIUKOV NOTE[17]

The following document is a 20 April 1917 resolution by the Petrograd Garrison's Reserve Electro-Technical Battalion Committee, published in the Bolshevik newspaper, Truth *(Pravda), on 29 April 1917. Its publication in* Truth *might indicate that the committee leaders were Bolshevik sympathizers, but not necessarily. Soldiers' or workers' committees—and many other groups—often sent resolutions to several newspapers.*

Having discussed the Provisional Government's note to the Allied governments, we consider this note a demonstration that the Provisional Government is the faithful servant not only of the imperialist countries of the Alliance, but also of the German and Austrian governments, as it assists them in strangling the German proletariat's evolving struggle for peace. Therefore we, the representatives of 7,000 soldiers in the Reserve Electro-Technical Battalion, at a general meeting of the battalion committee, resolved to direct an appeal to the Soviet of Workers' and Soldiers' Deputies demanding that the following immediately be excluded from membership in the government: Foreign Affairs Minister Citizen Miliukov and War Minister Guchkov. We demand that the government modify its foreign policy and immediately take the most energetic steps to work out a platform with the Allied governments for peace without annexations or indemnities. We demand that it publish all secret treaties concluded between the former tsar and the Allies. Together, we swear an oath to assure the [Petrograd] Soviet of Workers' and Soldiers' Deputies that we will come to its aid with weapons in hand at the soviet's first call.

> Battalion Committee Chairman, Corporal Zabolotskii
> Secretary, V. Kovalev

DOCUMENT 6.10
THE FINNISH GUARDS REGIMENT RESERVE BATTALION COMMITTEE ON THE 20 APRIL 1917 DEMONSTRATIONS[18]

The following document is from soldiers in a unit that demonstrated against the "Miliukov Note" on 20 April 1917. The Finnish Guards Regiment Reserve Battalion Committee sent this letter to Maxim Gorkii's newspaper, New Life (Novaia zhizn'), *which published it on 23 April 1917.*

Citizen Editor!
Concerning the Finnish Guards Regiment Reserve Battalion's demonstration on 20 April:

Idle-talking city inhabitants have been spreading rumors that the Finnish Guards intended to arrest Foreign Affairs Minister Miliukov or even the entire Provisional Government. In reality, Finnish Guards' demonstration at the Mariinskii Palace was aimed at registering a protest against Citizen Miliukov's 18 April note to the Allied Powers. That note had fully roused an understandable feeling of indignation among the demonstrators. Nevertheless, the demonstration was completely peaceful, and there was no attempt to arrest anybody. In regard to Foreign Affairs Minister Miliukov, the protesters displayed two placards on which were written, "Miliukov—Resign!" and "Down with Miliukov!" There were no placards that read, "Down with Guchkov!" The Finnish Guards did not enter the Mariinskii Palace. And we had not been ordered to demonstrate, either. The demonstration resulted from a resolution by a united meeting of the battalion, company, command, and officers' committees. Its purpose was to show immediate support for the Soviet of Workers' and Soldiers' Deputies and its clearly defined position on the war. The demonstration was organized in less than an hour, and the battalion came out complete with its officers, headed up by the Battalion Commander, who can verify all of this information.

We ask that other newspapers also publish this.

Chairman of the Committee, B. Doroshevskii
Secretary of the Committee, Tsimbanov

DOCUMENT 6.11
THE PROVISIONAL GOVERNMENT'S EXPLANATION
OF THE MILIUKOV NOTE[19]

The following document is a statement drafted at an emergency conference of the Provisional Government and Petrograd Soviet leaders on the night of 20 April 1917, in reaction to demonstrations protesting the Miliukov Note. It was published in The Provisional Government Bulletin (Vestnik Vremennogo pravitel'stvo) *on 21 April 1917.*

In view of emerging doubts about interpretation of the minister of foreign affairs' note, which accompanied transmission of the Provisional Government's 27 March declaration on war aims to the Allied governments, the Provisional Government considers it necessary to clarify that:

1. The foreign affairs minister's note was subject to careful and prolonged discussion by the Provisional Government, and its text was approved unanimously.
2. It is self-evident that this note, in speaking of a decisive victory over our enemies, has in view achieving those aims proclaimed in the 27 March declaration, as expressed in the following words:

> In keeping with the people's will, and in close communication with our allies regarding all issues, the Provisional Government, by its rights and duty, now declares that free Russia's aim is not to master other peoples, not to seize their national property, not to forcibly seize foreign territory. Free Russia's aim is to establish a stable peace on the basis of national self-determination. The Russian people do not intend to increase its world power at other people's expense. Its aim is not to enslave or humiliate anyone. In behalf of the highest principles of justice, it removes the fetters tying down the Polish people.

But the Russian people will not permit their motherland to come out of this great struggle humiliated and drained of its vital forces.

3. On the "sanctions" and "guarantees" for a lasting peace mentioned in the note, the Provisional Government meant limitations on armaments, international tribunals, and so on.

The foreign affairs minister will pass this explanation to the Allied Powers' consulates.

DOCUMENT 6.12
THE PETROGRAD SOVIET ON THE PROVISIONAL GOVERNMENT'S EXPLANATION OF THE MILIUKOV NOTE[20]

The following document is a resolution passed by the Petrograd Soviet in the early hours of 21 April 1917, after its Executive Committee completed discussions with the government toward ending demonstrations against the Miliukov Note.

The [Petrograd] Soviet of Workers' and Soldiers' Deputies warmly greets Petrograd's revolutionary democracy. Their meetings, resolutions, and demonstrations reveal their intense attention to foreign policy issues and their anxiety concerning possible deviations in policy down the old road of imperialist conquest. The foreign affairs minister's 18 April note created this anxiety.

The Provisional Government drew up a document that the Soviet Executive Committee then obtained. This document communicated the text of the government's 27 March declaration renouncing annexations to the Allied Powers. The government issued this declaration out of the need to make a statement to the entire democracy, and to the whole world, concerning annexations and war aims in general.

However, the foreign affairs minister's note to the Allied governments, which accompanied the communication of that declaration, presented an explanation that could be understood differently, as an attempt to undermine the authentic significant steps undertaken. Its tone, expression, and formulations came from the old regime's diplomatic arsenal, which is unintelligible to the people. Therefore this note excited justifiable anxiety that the Provisional Government . . . had strayed from its 27 March declaration renouncing annexationist policies.

The unanimous protests of Petrograd's workers and soldiers have shown the Provisional Government, and the entire world, that Russia's revolutionary democracy will never be reconciled to returning to tsarist foreign policy aims, and that her cause remains the unceasing struggle for world peace.

These protests caused the Provisional Government to issue a new explanation, published for general information and communicated by the foreign affairs minister to the consulates of the Allied Powers. This eliminates the possibility of interpreting the 18 April note in a spirit that opposes the revolutionary democracy's interests and demands. In fact, a first step has been made toward an international discussion on the issue of renouncing military conquests, which must be recognized as a mighty achievement for the democracy.

The [Petrograd] Soviet, declaring its unwavering determination to stand in the front ranks of the struggle for peace, summons Russia's entire revolutionary democracy to rally around their soviets. It expresses firm confidence that the peoples of all belligerent countries will overcome their governments' opposition and compel their governments to enter negotiations for a peace that renounces annexations and indemnities.

DOCUMENT 6.13
A PARTICIPANT'S ACCOUNT OF PETROGRAD WORKERS' DEMONSTRATIONS ON 21 APRIL 1917[21]

The following document is a participant's account of a large workers' demonstration in Petrograd protesting the Miliukov Note, published in The News of the Petrograd Soviet (Izvestiia Petrogradskogo Soveta) *on 22 April 1917. At the end of the report, the author refers to the Petrograd Soviet's statement that "provocateurs" had shot and wounded several unarmed citizens during that day's demonstrations. The soviet therefore prohibited any further street meetings or demonstrations for two days, banned carrying or shooting weapons during demonstrations, and promised to investigate the day's violence.*

Yesterday at 5:30 almost 10,000 people headed toward the Admiralty, where the [Petrograd] Soviet of Workers' and Soldiers' Deputies was meeting, to demonstrate solidarity and show it their support.[22] The crowd included the First City District section of the RSDLP and workers from the Molding Production Association Factory, the Novaia Cotton Spinning Factory, the Kolebov and Bobrov Tobacco Factory, the Kopeika Typography, the Gershun Typography, and the Kozhevnikov Cotton Spinning Factory. The district committee had banners reading, "Full confidence in the Soviet of Workers' and Soldiers' Deputies!" "Down with imperialism!" "Long live Socialism!" and "All Power to the Soviets of Workers' and Soldiers' Deputies!"

At Znamenskaia Square the marchers were stopped by two armored cars, on which were written, "Long Live the Provisional Government!"[23] The armored car [soldiers] demanded that the workers' militia not participate in the march. The militia withdrew. The marchers, however, could not move on; the armored cars blocked them and would not give way. Demonstrators who had walked from the Rozhdestvenskii District to Znamenskaia Square, almost all of them women and without any militia, surrounded the armored cars and put their banners over them. The Roshdestvenskii District banners were taken off the automobiles and torn apart in front of the public.

On Nevskii Prospect we encountered a procession with placards reading, "Full Confidence in the Provisional Government!" "Down with Lenin—the Kaiser's Hireling!" and "Long Live Miliukov!" People from that procession began shouting that supporting the [Petrograd Soviet] was intolerable. Soon their shouts turned into violence. Some of the public on Nevskii Prospect shouted, "Provocateurs!" and "German Hirelings!" and destroyed a banner carried by women cotton-spinning factory workers that read, "Long Live Workers' International Solidarity!" The women workers were driven off and beaten with clubs.

At the Moika Canal there was another clash with an automobile that carried university students, high-school students, and so on. The automobile drove into the marchers, destroying a row of banners. Students from the Military Medical Academy and the Institute of Communications rushed into the crowd shouting, "Provocateurs!" and "Leninists!" and tore banners out of the women's hands. At this moment, members of the [Petrograd] Soviet Executive Committee appeared and informed the crowd about the soviet's resolution.

We returned to the district without incident.

A participant in the march.

DOCUMENT 6.14
THE SOCIALIST REVOLUTIONARIES ON THE 21 APRIL 1917
DEMONSTRATIONS IN PETROGRAD[24]

The following document is another description of the violence on Petrograd's streets on 21 April 1917—in this case, shootings in which several people were killed on Nevskii Prospect. The author, N. Kogan, was a worker at the Triangle Factory. Kogan mentions a Kadet "proclamation" regarding the demonstrations. On 21 April, the Constitutional Democrats distributed leaflets calling for street rallies to support the Provisional Government. Kogan's account appeared in the Socialist Revolutionary newspaper, The People's Cause (Delo naroda), *on 25 April 1917.*

As a witness to the clash at 10:00 P.M. on 21 April, I consider it necessary to provide the following information:

At 3:00 on 21 April, workers' meetings were held at the Putilov Factory and in the yard at the Triangle Factory. These discussed the forthcoming demonstrations. At about 5:00, workers and women workers (women were in the majority) from Triangle, who had one red banner with no writing on it, went to the Putilov Works. There workers from both factories held a common meeting. The mood went back and forth, and people were divided "for" and "against" a street demonstration. They waited until 6:00 P.M. for a decision on the issue by the [Petrograd] Soviet of Workers' and Soldiers' Deputies, but none came. Then a group of workers came from Nevskii Prospect and informed them about the bourgeoisie's violence against the workers, the tearing down of red flags, and the arrests for protesting against the Provisional Government. They also read the workers the Kadets' proclamation about street demonstrations.

This produced a sharp turnabout in the crowd's mood. "So, we are driven from the streets and our banners are torn away. Are we going to watch this in silence!? We are going to Nevskii!"[25] That was the approximate mood after the Kadet proclamation. I proposed a show of hands "for" or "against" the demonstration. An overwhelming majority declared themselves "for." The crowd then formed themselves into columns and moved; a dozen workers with banners walked at the front of the march.

I should say that the banners were old. There were only two new ones: "Down with the Provisional Government!" and "Down with Miliukov and Guchkov!" Despite the crowd's spirit, those two banners did not make it all the way to Nevskii: the banner "Down with the Provisional Government!" was carried rolled up; the second vanished somewhere. So the crowd moved in good order, with a banner reading, "Long live the Soviet of Workers' and Soldiers' Deputies" in the front row.

As the march neared Nevskii, unsuccessful attempts were made to hold us back. So we went in the direction of the Staff Headquarters. There we met marchers from Gal'pern Island and the Vyborg Side. They marched in good order, with men armed with rifles in front. We exchanged greetings then fell in again and joined them. To determine the march's path, I split off from the Putilov workers and walked to the head of the procession. This was at the corner of Sadovaia and Nevskii. There the head of the march rolled on to Sadovaia, and we went together toward Inzhenernaia Street. The entire workers' militia and many of the marchers had already come to Sadovaia.

Suddenly there was confusion, and the workers' armed militia came to a halt. It appears that a crowd had attacked the demonstration. Banners were torn from the marching Putilov workers' hands. The Soviet's banners were ripped down. The remaining banner, which read, "Down with the Provisional Government!" was unrolled. The workers defended this with their fists. Then the sound of revolvers firing could be discerned clearly, coming from the direction of Nevskii toward Sadovaia. First there was one shot, and then several. The armed workers had fallen into a most difficult situation. The crowd was being attacked with weapons. But it was not possible to defend those being attacked, because the workers' armed militia was separated from the crowd on Nevskii. So the workers fired their weapons into the air.

I saw the direction that shots came from, and I can confirm that it was not possible for the workers to shoot anywhere except into the air. Otherwise they would have killed their comrades. When the shooting ended, I looked around. Nowhere did I see evidence that people had been wounded or killed. I still do not know how victims appeared where no shots had been fired. But I can confirm that they were not hit by the workers' bullets. From further down toward Inzhenernaia, it is impossible to hit people standing on Nevskii near the Anichkova Palace.[26]

After hand-to-hand skirmishes, the Putilov workers were driven out and their banners taken away. All that remained were two tattered ones that the pro-Kadet crowd had paraded on the streets.

Who did the shooting? The answer is clear. Shots were fired from Nevskii at the demonstrating workers on Sadovaia. The shooting took place after the armed workers had left Nevskii. The armed workers could not have turned back onto Nevskii, because the marchers behind them already had crossed onto Sadovaia. The shooting, then, took place as another group of people were tearing away the workers' red flags.

—N. Kogan

DOCUMENT 6.15
TWO FACTORY WORKERS' RESOLUTIONS
ON THE MILIUKOV NOTE[27]

The following document set presents resolutions protesting the Miliukov Note passed by workers' meetings at two Petrograd factories: the Dynamo machine-building works and the Russian-Baltic Railcar Factory. Both meetings took place on 21 April 1917. The Dynamo workers' resolution was described in a short notice published in the Menshevik's The Workers' Newspaper (Rabochaia gazeta) *on 22 April 1917. The Russian-Baltic workers' resolution was published in the Bolshevik newspaper,* Truth (Pravda), *on 28 April 1917.*

On 21 April, workers at the [Dynamo] plant passed a resolution that demanded removal of ministers Guchkov and Miliukov from the Provisional Government. In the event that the government refuses to undertake the removal of these two ministers, the workers call for complete replacement of the Provisional Government.

The 21 April Russian-Baltic Railcar Factory workers' general assembly energetically protests against the Provisional Government's antidemocratic policies and its note of 18 April, which contradicts the declaration on war aims published on 27 March. The workers' assembly calls on the

[Petrograd] Soviet of Workers' and Soldiers' Deputies to force the Provisional Government to declare, categorically and to the entire world, that the Russian people do not want any annexations or indemnities. It demands that the government publish all secret treaties concluded between Nikolai Romanov and the Allied Powers, so that all people know what he happily sacrificed millions of the best lives for, what the people's blood is being spilled for, and what Russia's remaining vital force is being destroyed for.

DOCUMENT 6.16
THE STOCK EXCHANGE BULLETIN ON THE MILIUKOV NOTE [28]

The following document is an editorial on the Miliukov Note that appeared in the business newspaper The Stock Exchange Bulletin (Birzhevyia vedomosti) *on 21 April 1917.*

The Note to the Allies.
Having considered the substance of the foreign affairs minister's note to the Allies as it was published, one must ask oneself this painful question: "For whom was this fruit of the minister's creativity intended and why?" If the note's primary goal was to produce domestic calm, then why speak to the democracy—which already is aflame with revolutionary heat—in such an elusive form that the words can carry whatever meaning you like? What was needed was the force and courage to speak to the people clearly and unequivocally, as the Provisional Government spoke in its historic 27 March declaration. How could he not foresee and realize that each grain of disagreement and vagueness would develop into a burden of heavy suspicion? If the note was dictated by foreign policy concerns, then it seems we are going through a difficult time because of a "Talleyrand" note. [29]

If the foreign affairs minister wanted, as he said himself, to enunciate ideas clearly expressed in President Wilson's statements, then he should have stressed the two great democracies' uncompromising wills and firmly repeated the Provisional Government's earlier formula on peace "without annexations or indemnities." This formula in no sense means that the Russian democracy has renounced its obligations to the Allies. It does not mean that Alsace and Lorraine will not be liberated from German rule, or that nations "yoked" for centuries should abandon their dreams of liberation from the Austrians or—in the case of Czechoslovakia— give up hope for the right of national self-determination, or that Transylvanian Romanians should not be reunited with their motherland, etc. Absolutely not.

Everyone understands that the basic obligation that the leaders have proposed is a fundamental demand for the world's future—national self-determination. For there to be free elections among the people of Alsace and Lorraine, the Austrian Slavs, Italians, Romanians, and other yoked nations, decisions must be made. Who belongs united with whom, and who should form absolutely independent states?

If, instead of this laconic note, we had a firm note from our foreign affairs minister, then we think it would have been met with a sympathetic response by the "leading democracies" and would have been supported by the "great republic across the Atlantic."[30] And then everyone would have clearly understood that later references to a "victorious conclusion of the present war" in a way "that creates a durable foundation for a lasting peace" meant that we cannot put down our weapons until the Wilhelmian and Karlovian governments agree to a truly democratic peace.[31] To do so would be an absolute crime against people made wretched and devastated by war, who would be given not a durable "eternal" peace—as formulated by Wilson—but only an interlude. As a result, the globe would be threatened by new torrents of blood and tears.

The note's vagueness spurred interpretations that excited the masses' mood. It moved the meaning of the diplomatic note onto the plane of general-political interrelations between the government and the democracy. This posed a threat to the people's fresh freedom, which all classes unanimously wish to defend.

The minister made a mistake, but with luck this mistake is not irreparable. Through the good will of the people, who hold many opinions, it can be mitigated in the near future, when the circumstances are more favorable. Now the task before us is, above all else, not to aggravate the situation. We each may go down a different path to the same goal. But in the sphere of international relations there cannot be two Russias with two minds. We hope that a healthy state can steer the country around the dangers in its path.

DOCUMENT 6.17
THE MOSCOW SOVIET OF WORKERS' DEPUTIES
EXECUTIVE COMMITTEE ON THE MILIUKOV NOTE[32]

The following document is an excerpt from the minutes of the Moscow Soviet Executive Committee's 21 April 1917 session. Many speakers at this session were significant secondary figures in revolutionary politics in 1917: Menshevik Lev Khinchuk was the Moscow Soviet's chairman from March to September; cooperative activist Viktor Nogin was a leading moderate Bolshevik. The document refers to several of Moscow's districts. In Moscow (as in Petrograd), each city district had its own elected district soviet.

Meeting chaired by L. M. Khinchuk. List of those attending to be appended.
Concerning current events.

Khinchuk: The Provisional Government's note to foreign powers concerning the war has disturbed everyone. There are reports in many of Moscow's factories and plants that workers have quit work and are organizing meetings and issuing calls for a demonstration. Given the fact that neither the [Moscow] Soviet of Workers' Deputies or its Executive Committee have yet issued a resolution on the matter, I suggest that we explain our attitude toward the Provisional Government's note and toward uncoordinated demonstrations and appeals made without the soviet's approval.

[Khinchuk reads a long transcript of a telephone message from the Petrograd Soviet, describing the 20 April negotiations between its executive committee and the Provisional Government. He announces that the Petrograd Soviet leaders asked that the Moscow Soviet not take any independent actions.]

[Khinchuk] offers a proposal: This meeting's agenda must be: to clarify the soviet's position toward the working class' demonstrations, which no doubt are uncoordinated; to pass instructive resolutions concerning this, and to implement them immediately; and then to hold a discussion of the general question. The proposal was approved.

[Other speakers] present reports on events taking place now in the districts. On Serpukhovskii Square, there is a meeting underway with banners that read, "Down with the Provisional Government!" and "Death to the traitors!" Workers have walked out at the Bromlei Plant, the Mikhelson Factory, and the Krylov Brothers' Factory. In the Butyrskii District, workers at the telephone plant are demonstrating and have appealed to military units at the Aleksandrovskii Barracks. Demonstrators have attacked the police at the Piatnitskii District Police Station. They called the police lackeys of the Provisional Government, disarmed them, and confiscated all of the weapons in the station.

Gel'fgot: District soviets are issuing appeals asking that people leave work and organize demonstrations. We must organize our efforts immediately and send people to the districts to explain that the Moscow Central Soviet has passed similar resolutions.

Nogin does not consider it necessary to base political steps on unverified rumors. Current events are agitating the population mightily, and the working class cannot but respond. We should not hesitate: we should join them and declare that the working class can have the necessary impact only through organized activity. We have a guiding institution—the [Moscow] Soviet—with which all our proletarian organizations must act in solidarity to ensure that they come out in an organized fashion when necessary. . . .

Smidovich agrees with Nogin, but thinks that should the people's protest swell and manifest itself in other ways, then we should draft another statement explaining that the soviet has not called for a demonstration now. . . . [33]

Isuv: The [Moscow] Soviet of Workers' Deputies is a responsible organization: it speaks, and there is action. Without a soviet resolution, demonstrations in the districts will be disorganized. The Executive Committee should not limit itself to declaring that it has not called for a demonstration; it should condemn participation in unorganized demonstrations. . . .

Kibrik: Smidovich's proposal is unacceptable.[34] We cannot encourage a disorganized movement and wring our hands. This is the first time I have encountered the idea that a workers' organization should not be told to discontinue activity that the soviet considers incorrect. If we go down that path, then our whole existence loses significance. The [Moscow] Soviet of Workers' Deputies stands guard for the revolution. At this moment, it needs to appeal to comrades, saying that participation in demonstrations right now is intolerable. If we do not do this, we are giving up as the movement's leaders and signing our own death sentence.

Shvarts agrees with Isuv and Kibrik. He proposes taking decisive measures to end unorganized demonstrations. To do this, he proposes sending agitators to the districts to explain the soviet's view. There can be meetings and assemblies where opinions and resolution on current events are drafted, but the soviet's task is to prevent unorganized demonstrations.

After this exchange of opinion, it was resolved: To declare that right now the Executive Committee of the [Moscow] Soviets of Workers' Deputies and Soldiers' Deputies is not calling for strikes.

On the question of what else to do, two proposals were considered: one proposed a directive that demonstrations must take an organized form, that they can be held only at the soviet's request, and that there should be no more demonstrations; the other agreed that demonstrations must have an organized form, but added that demonstrations already begun should not be hindered. The first proposal was approved, 89 votes to 15, with 7 abstaining.

A proposal then was approved to draft a leaflet right away with 10–15 phrases that explain the moment's seriousness and explain that the struggle must be carried out in an organized fashion. The leaflet also must explain that the Executive Committee is confident that, when it is necessary, the workers and the revolutionary army together will answer the soviet's call and stand in defense of freedom.

Kibrik read the draft leaflet. Several corrections were made to the draft, and Romanov and Kibrik will work to produce a final text. . . .

The following proposals were considered:

1. To immediately send one or two representatives, together with comrade soldiers from the districts, to the districts to pacify the population and explain our decisions. The rest of the meeting will go on discussing the general issue of the Provisional Government's [18 April] note.

2. As an addendum to the first resolution, it was proposed to immediately send a telephone message to the Petrograd Soviet's Executive Committee informing it of our declaration to the district soviets.
3. To close this meeting. Everyone will go to the districts. . . . To hold the next meeting at 7:00–8:00 P.M.

It was resolved: To close the meeting and send everyone to the district soviets, where they will explain our decisions. To reassemble at 9:00 P.M. to draft a resolution that will be published in our newspaper.

On methods to be used by people sent to the districts to implement the Executive Committee's decision, two proposals were considered:

1. To clarify the state of things at a meeting, and to persuade people not to display banners with slogans that the soviet has not approved, for instance, "Down with the Provisional Government!"
2. To explain the state of things only, with no reference to banners and slogans. . . . The first proposal was accepted.

Sablin proposed that the Executive Committee pass a resolution calling for peaceful workers' and revolutionary soldiers' demonstrations, mediated by the district soviets.[35] A committee member proposed going out to the districts to implement this resolution. The chairman explained that, since an opposing resolution had been approved, Sablin's proposal would be dropped.

DOCUMENT 6.18
A WORKERS' MEETING AT KHARKOV'S GENERAL ELECTRIC COMPANY PLANT[36]

The following document is a resolution passed by a workers' meeting at the American-owned General Electric Company factory in Kharkov, Ukraine, on 22 April 1917. The GE plant had opened in 1915 and was engaged in defense-related production. This meeting's main subject was the Miliukov Note, and its resolution was published in the Kharkov Bolshevik newspaper, The Proletarian (Proletarii), *on 25 April 1917.*

We, 4,000 workers at the G. E. C. plant meeting on 22 April, having discussed the events that have played out in Petrograd over the past few days, approve the following resolution:
The Provisional Government, created by the revolution under armed people's protection, had agreed to exercise the people's will, but it clearly has deviated from this. Disregarding the Petrograd Soviet of Workers' and Soldiers' Deputies' manifesto "To All the World's People," the Provisional Government continued to pursue imperialist war aims. It also

has ignored the people's demand that it publish secret treaties concluded with the Allies.

Considering that the Provisional Government at present refuses to exercise the people's will, and that it has conducted an independent policy of aggression that clearly would lead to counterrevolution, we ask that the Petrograd Soviet of Workers' and Soldiers' Deputies immediately form a new government that will implement the people's will. We declare ourselves ready at any time to support all the Soviet of Workers' and Soldiers' Deputies' pronouncements.

DOCUMENT 6.19
LENIN, "LESSONS OF THE CRISIS"[37]

The following document is an essay by Lenin that appeared in the Bolshevik newspaper, Truth (Pravda), *on 22 April 1917. Lenin employed his usual rhetorical devices to attack his socialist opponents. He describes the Mensheviks and Socialist Revolutionaries (SRs) as "petty-bourgeois" and calls the SRs "Narodniks"—revolutionaries from a previous and, by implication, no longer relevant era. In contrast, he defines the Bolsheviks as "the party of the proletariat."*

Lessons of the Crisis.
Petrograd and all Russia have lived through a serious political crisis, the first political crisis since the revolution. On 18 April the Provisional Government agreed to its infamous note, confirming its aggressive-predatory war aims with sufficient clarity to arouse the indignation of the broad masses, who conscientiously trusted in the capitalists desire (and the capacity) "to renounce annexations." On 20 and 21 April, Piter was seething.[38] The streets overflowed with people. Crowds and groups held meetings of various sizes all through the day and night. Mass protests and demonstrations continued nonstop. Yesterday evening, 21 April, the crisis apparently ended. Or at the very least, its first phase had concluded. The Soviet Executive Committee, and then the soviet itself, recognized the government's "explanation," its amendments to the note, its "clarifications," as satisfactory. All the explanations amount to idle talk, saying precisely nothing. Nothing changed. They are phrases that carry no obligations of any sort. But the soviet declared "the incident settled."

The future will show if the broad masses consider "the incident settled." Our task now is to carefully study the *forces* and classes revealed by the crisis and to extract lessons from it for the party of the proletariat. Because the great significance of all crises is that they expose that which has been concealed. They toss aside the incidental, the superficial, the petty.

They brush aside political litter and disclose the true well-springs of the *class struggles* that are actually emerging.

In essence, on 18 April the capitalists' government only repeated its former notes, investing imperialist war diplomacy with minor diplomatic reservations. The soldier-masses became so indignant because they had conscientiously trusted the capitalists' sincerity and peace-loving intentions. The demonstrations began as *soldiers'* demonstrations, with the contradictory, consciousness-lacking, ineffectual slogan, "Down with Miliukov." As if changing people—or even small groups—in the government could change the *core* of the policies!

The demonstrations mean that the broad, unstable, vacillating mass—which is closest of all to the peasantry and, according to scientific-class characteristics, is petty bourgeois—is wavering *from* the capitalists *to the side of* the revolutionary workers. This wavering—or movement—of the masses has the force *to decide everything*. It created a crisis.

At that very moment, others began to move and went out in the streets and organized. *Not* the center, but the radical elements. *Not* the intermediate petty-bourgeois mass, but the bourgeoisie and the proletariat.

The bourgeoisie seized Nevskii Prospect—or Miliukov Prospect, as one newspaper called it—and the neighboring wealthy district of Piter, the home of Piter's capitalists and government clerks. The officers, students, the "middle classes," demonstrated *for* the Provisional Government, with banners that often bore the slogan, "Down with Lenin."

The proletariat set off from *their* centers—from the workers' districts—having organized around appeals and slogans of our party's Central Committee. The Central Committee issued resolutions on 20 and 21 April that were immediately passed along through the party's organizational apparatus to the mass of the proletariat.[39] The workers' demonstrations overflowed from the city's *poorer*, less central, districts. Then sections of the crowd set off down Nevskii Prospect. The bourgeois demonstration was sharply distinguished from the proletariat's larger and more harmonious demonstration. The proletarians' banners read, "All Power to the Soviets of Workers' and Soldiers' Deputies."

There were clashes on Nevskii Prospect. The "hostile" demonstrators tore down banners. The Soviet Executive Committee received telephone messages from several locations, saying that the crowd had come under fire and that there were dead and wounded—reports that were radically contradictory or unconfirmed.

The bourgeoisie's cries about "the specter of civil war" expressed their fear that the authentic masses, the actual people's majority, would take power into their own hands. The soviet's petty-bourgeois leaders, the Mensheviks and the Narodniks—having failed to elaborate any party line since the revolution began (particularly during the crisis)—allowed themselves to be intimidated. The Executive Committee—where on the crisis' eve almost half the votes cast were against the Provisional Government—gathered 34 votes (against 19) *for* returning to a policy of confidence in and cooperation with the capitalists. The "incident" was considered "settled."

And what of the class struggle's *core*? The capitalists are *for* dragging out the war, for covering this up with phrases and promises. They fling themselves into the nets of Russian, Anglo-French, and *American* finance capital. The proletariat, in the form of its conscious avant-garde, is *for* transferring power to the revolutionary classes, to the working class and the semi-proletariat. It is *for* development of a worldwide workers' revolution, which clearly is developing in Germany. It is *for* ending the war *through this* revolution.

The broad masses, who are predominantly petty-bourgeois, and who still believe in the Menshevik and Narodnik leaders, are thoroughly intimidated by the bourgeoisie and carry out *its* line with minor reservations. They waver first to the right, and then to the left.

War is terrible. And it is the broad masses that feel this most of all. Although it still is not clear, there is an awareness developing among its ranks that this war is criminal, that it is being conducted because of the capitalists' interests and squabbles and for the division of *their* spoils. The worldwide situation is becoming much more complicated. *There is no exit* other than a worldwide workers' revolution. Russia *now* leads the other countries in this revolution, but its development in Germany is obvious (strikes, fraternization). And the masses are wavering. They waver between confidence in and bitterness toward their old masters, the capitalists. They waver between confidence that a new path that will open a bright future for all toilers who follow the revolutionary class—the proletariat—and an unclear awareness of the proletariat's world historical role.

This was not the first time that the petty-bourgeois semi-proletarian masses have wavered, and it *will not be the last!*

The lesson is clear, comrade-workers! Time does not stand still! This first crisis will lead to others. Comrades, give *all* your strength to the cause of enlightening the backward among the masses. Do so directly (not only through meetings) by coming together with each regiment, with each group of toilers who still cannot see. Put *all* your effort into uniting your own people, to organizing workers from the ground up in every district, every factory, and every apartment building in the capital and its environs! *Do not* be misled by those petty-bourgeois who "conciliate" with the capitalists. Do not be misled by the defensists, the henchmen government's "supporters." And do not be misled by isolated people who are inclined to rush out and shout, "Down with the Provisional Government!" before the people's majority have solidly united. The crisis cannot be overcome violently by individual groups or armed people in a Blanquist attempt to "seize power," "arrest" the Provisional Government, and so on.[40]

The slogans of the day are: Explain the proletariat's line and *its* path toward ending the war more precisely, more clearly, and more broadly. Build strong, broad, ranks and columns of the proletariat everywhere! Rally around your soviets. Persuade the comrades in them. Reelect individual members. Strive to rally the majority around the party!

DOCUMENT 6.20
THE MOSCOW BULLETIN ON "THE MOB AND THE PEOPLE"[41]

The following document is an editorial from Moscow's main business newspaper, The Moscow Bulletin (Moskovskiia vedomosti), *on 22 April 1917. The author repeatedly uses the Russian word for "the mob"—"chern"—which also means "the common people" and is based on the root word for "dark." He equates antigovernment demonstrators with the "mob" and suggests that the forces behind the mob work for the German Kaiser. Readers would have understood this as pointing a finger of blame at Lenin, who had returned to Russia with the aid of the Germans and was rumored to be a German agent. The author makes mythological and literary references that might seem obscure, but that would have been at least superficially familiar to educated readers in Moscow. For instance, the author mentions Ormuzd and Ahriman, the gods of good and evil in the ancient Persian religious system of Zoroastrianism. He mentions American writer Edgar Allan Poe, best known for his psychologically complex Gothic horror tales, and the Russian writer Feodor Dostoevsky, who was famous for portraying psychologically complex characters and situations. The essay also makes a passing reference to the French Enlightenment political philosopher Baron de Montesquieu, who stressed the importance of constitutional separation of powers to preserve liberty.*

The Mob and the People.
Events in Petrograd, of course, have captured the entire country's close attention. Not only is the resolution of the events playing out in Petrograd important and of great significance, but the possible emergence of similar crises also is important. This will be settled. But tomorrow, or the day after, a new crisis can arise. To live that way is impossible. We now are comforted by the fact that the regrettable Petrograd events resulted from a misunderstanding. But here is something less comforting: if, on the least occasion, misunderstandings can lead to street clashes, then what will happen when some serious principled disagreement arises, which at present is entirely possible? Wouldn't such a conflict invariably be accompanied by street demonstrations, by furious cries of "down with one or the other," by the appearance of armed forces on the scene—and maybe violence and killings? Then life in Russia, the prosperity and culture of the state, will end, and we will return to revolutionary chaos.

Too many pronouncements are made now in the people's name. Too many people venture to speak for all Russia. We accept that Russia is great and contains opinions of the most diverse character. But it does not follow that every group, every clique of people, can describe themselves as expressing *the entire* country's opinion and permit themselves to commit violence.

After the old order's fall, supreme power passed to the Russian people. In his speech, Foreign Affairs Minister P. N. Miliukov was profoundly correct in defining our Provisional Government's situation:

> The Provisional Government is equipped with the fluttering sails of fate, which can move it forward only when filled with wind. We await your confidence, which will be like a favorable wind that moves our ship along its course. Your confidence will give us the strength to guide Russia toward freedom and prosperity and to preserve a free and great Russia.

In reality, the Provisional Government strength consists entirely of the people's confidence in it. And the government's fundamental task amounts to exercising the people's will. But it is not so easy to come to discern the people's *true* will among the many voices of contemporary opinions and solicitations. And we need to know for certain from which side that fair wind can be found, so that the ship of state may set a course that agrees with it.

There are the *people*, and there is the *mob*. It is impossible to confuse these two forces, just as it is impossible for black to become white, for bitter to be considered sweet, or for good to be recognized as evil. The mob comes from the dark Ahriman, while the people are servants of the eternally sacred Ormuzd. Do not be mistaken—the mob is not simply the dark people, not simply the common people. We find the elements of the mob everywhere. We often even find them in society's highest strata, wearing the refined clothing of the worldly man, while underneath are the coarse clothes of the peasant.

What is it about this mob that determines its understanding and shapes it fundamental characteristics? That is not difficult: the mob is drawn from that layer of society that opposes lofty spiritual values with base material wealth. Members of the mob oppose the general good, the motherland's good, and the state's good, with their own personal good. The mob embodies the lowest and the darkest human instincts. It is the collective of national inadequacies and defects, tripled by the extent of the current situation's monstrousness. It is the embodiment of radical and insolent egoism in its most cynical manifestations.

This mob is freedom's most frightening enemy. It is not for nothing that Edgar Poe, representative of that most freedom-loving people, that most advanced of the democracies, wrote in one of his stories: "Who is the most dreadful despot in all of world history? We know this despot's name—the mob." The writer was correct. Always, if even a particle of power should fall into the mob's hands, the mob will try *through fear* to seize power. For surely, as Montesquieu wrote, despotism's fundamental principle is fear. A despot creates nothing. He sees that his ideas and qualities cannot exercise even a particle of authority in the people's eyes. But power is sweet for the tyrant, and he is blinded by its force. He has no means to hold the obedience of those around him other than violence and fear; these are his resources, and he sets them in motion. He would reduce those around him to slaves, who would only heap praise on him. He would crush anyone who thinks for himself or wants and expects rights.

No, the people have nothing in common with the mob. The people create the sublime; the mob creates nothing. The people are talented; the mob has no talent. The people are magnanimous; the mob is envious. The people can see into the future and live not only for their own interests, but for the interests of future generations; the mob is short-sighted and only considers its own self-interest. The motto of the mob is "After me, the deluge." The people's humility and calm are great—it raises its voice rarely and only in decisive cases; the mob meddles in everything. It is inopportune. Its shrill, ringing voice is deafening and its logic irrational. The people are wise; the mob is senseless. The people possess the quality of sublime sacrifice; the mob has none of this quality and only demands that other make sacrifices for it. The people are courageous and unwavering; the mob is cowardly. As soon as power is taken from it, it turns to dust before the eyes of those who, minutes before, had been subjected to its force and influence.

In days of great historic crisis, the mob always appears on the scene. If it seems that power is wavering, the mob is the first to stretch out its dirty hand. It waits for the chance to stroll in at its will. And woe to the government that mistakes the voice of the mob for that of the people. When the people are silent and waiting, then the mob will become agitated and appear on the scene. But the mob has never moved history's wheel forward—it only impedes its systematic movement. More than this: no one imitates the people's voice more miserably than the mob. Its lack of restraint and its thoughtlessness leads to reaction. Inevitably, mob rule ends in bloodshed. As it appeared, so it disappears. As Dostoevsky put it, the prophet and the conqueror will appear, station cannon along the street, and give it hot to the just and the guilty alike. They will quiver and obey, these frightened creatures! The mob's despotism leads to the despotism of one man. Can this really await us?

Freedom's field is covered in tender green young crops. A great danger threatens them: they can be trampled, destroyed, torn to pieces, and obliterated by the mob's heavy feet. When we consider the Petrograd events, a restless presentiment of the swarming mob arises from the depth of our soul. There, in Petrograd, crude violence raised its voice. Freedom's first months were darkened by a heavy insult to the people's sensibilities.

Yes, the people were insulted. We say this directly and openly. The people were insulted by their own Provisional Government. This was a blow to the people's sensibilities. We repeat: this insult was a mistake, a misunderstanding. But a slap in the face is still a slap in the face. And the cause does not lessen the offense or the significance of the soul's indignation. The entire people understood that the government had sworn an oath completely voluntarily. Was that a farce, a comedy, an amusement? Such things are not done in jest. And in general, it is impossible to play a joke on the people at one of the most dreadful moments in its existence.

And so they put together a farce. It probably was a joke—the note's attitude to the powers, where it speaks of war and peace. They set up a game with the words: "peace without annexations or indemnities." Should we just add a few words here and cut a few words there, thank you, and say that this is significant? "Peace without annexations or indemnities." Perhaps these words renounce the war? Perhaps they are intended to put our enemy at ease, so that they will be very sympathetic and kind to us at some critical moment? Or maybe this is simply an attempt to smash us into pieces before the battle, so that we find ourselves defeated and begging for Kaiser Wilhelm's mercy? It is necessary to think about what is being said.

Citizens, stand in defense of the people's will. Where there is violence, oppression, and threats, you will not find the people's will. In this truly dangerous time, it is every conscious citizen's duty to support the Provisional Government in its cause of state construction. Above all else, the goal requires the great war's victorious conclusion.

DOCUMENT 6.21
A PROVINCIAL SOVIET ON THE APRIL CRISIS[42]

The following document is an editorial from the News of Rostov-Nakhichevan Soviet (Izvestiia Rostovo-Nakhichevanskago Soveta) *on 25 April 1917. By the early 1900s, Rostov—a prosperous center of trade and manufacturing on the lower Don River, with a population of over 100,000 people—had virtually merged with its industrial suburb Nakhichevan. Therefore the local soviet formed in spring 1917 bore the name of both settlements.*

What do the Petrograd Events Teach?
The conflict between the Provisional Government and the Soviet of Workers' and Soldiers' Deputies has been settled. The government

published a supplementary note. But the revolutionary river had already risen beyond its banks and left corpses on Petrograd's bridges and roads.[43]

What have the Petrograd events taught us, after three days of holding all Russia in the greatest anxiety?

The imperialist bourgeoisie tried to exert pressure on the Provisional Government. They tried to force the government to renounce its 27 March declaration, which the government had been compelled to make under pressure from the revolutionary democracy. The imperialist bourgeoisie was not pleased at this renunciation of plans for conquest. . . . It demands a "decisive victory." It does not want to renounce tsarism's foreign policy methods. We have not forgotten that tsarist diplomats and the Allied states concluded secret treaties to redraw Europe's political map, and did so with our patriotic imperialists' active participation. We well understand the role that the current foreign minister, Miliukov, played in Russia's foreign policy in his capacity as the former Tsarist Minister Saznov's "advocate."[44]

But satisfying the imperialist gentlemen's avaricious appetite is not the Russian revolutionary democracy's goal. Its aim is to consolidate the revolution's achievements, and the best guarantee of this is to end the war quickly by concluding a peace without annexations or indemnities on the basis of national self-determination.

The Provisional Government indicated its agreement on the principles of such a peace in its 27 March declaration. But on 18 April, on the same day that all democratic Russia—encouraged by the hope that peace between peoples was growing near—was celebrating the great holiday of international brotherhood, a blow was struck against the cause of peace.[45] With a little thought, it is clear that the cause of peace is identical to the cause of freedom, and the revolutionary democracy has become the vanguard in defense of peace. The Provisional Government has confirmed that Russia is not conducting, and will not conduct, a war of conquest.

The revolutionary river rose beyond it banks. But the corpses remain. The blood of brothers has been spilled. Unnecessary victims. Needless victims. And on whom does the heavy responsibility fall for the spilling of blood?

It falls on the immediate culprits in the conflict. There cannot be two opinions about this. There is no other way to interpret the meaning of the Petrograd events. The lesson to be extracted from the events of 18–21 April, we must tell ourselves, is that our Provisional Government— bourgeois by birth—yields too easily to pressure from imperialist circles. Russia's revolutionary democracy, loyal to its ideals, still stands in defense of freedom and peace. And the democracy's forces are still insufficiently complete or disciplined for the organized stabilization of its position.

These lessons must be learned and internalized. We cannot please ourselves with the hope that this conflict can only lead to a "happy" arrangement and never reoccur. As for our forces' confused organization, we must immediately unify and solidify our ranks, so that we can rebuff any reactionary plots. These are the revolutionary democracy's urgent tasks.

DOCUMENT 6.22
TWO SOLDIERS' RESOLUTIONS IN THE AFTERMATH
OF THE APRIL CRISIS[46]

The following document set presents two soldiers' resolutions passed in the days following the 20–21 April 1917 demonstrations in Petrograd. The first, from a meeting of military units that included the Reserve Electro-Technical Battalion in Petrograd, bears no date and was published in the Bolshevik newspaper, Truth (Pravda), *on 26 April. The second is a 27 April resolution by the Second Siberian Riflemen's Division in Petrograd. The second document mentions the tsarist government's December 1916 "guarantees" and sanctions—its secret agreements with the Allies confirming previous agreements over postwar disposition of territory. It also notes the "German democracy's" opposition to the war—a reference to the antiwar movement among German left socialists.*

Having heard explanations from Soviet Executive Committee members and opinions from several of our comrade soldiers about the conflict between the Provisional Government and the Russian democracy over their attitudes toward the war, we 500 men—soldiers from the youth command, the employees' command, the Reserve Electro-Technical Battalion Third Company, and the 10th and 12th Automobile Squadrons—resolve that the recent sad events in Petrograd's streets were the result of Provisional Government's duplicitous 18 April note to the Allies. And so, proclaiming that complete responsibility for this civil disorder lay with the Provisional Government, we resolve:

1. To ask the [Petrograd] Soviet of Workers' and Soldiers' Deputies to establish strict control over the Provisional Government's activities in all spheres of the country's administration.
2. To approve those measures taken by the Soviet of Workers' and Soldiers' Deputies in these trying days of civil disorder.
3. To declare to the Soviet of Workers' and Soldiers' Deputies that if in the future the Provisional Government violates its obligations to the democracy or tries to get itself out from under the control of Soviet of Workers' and Soldiers' Deputies—which is the sole defender of the toiling people's interests—we will all come out as one man for the Soviet of Workers' and Soldiers' Deputies.
4. We demand that the government and the Allies immediately work out a platform for peace without annexations or indemnities.

5. We insist that all secret treaties between the former tsarist government and the Allies be made public. We must reveal the hidden meaning of the capitalists' and noble landlords' policies, so that in the future the bourgeoisie cannot use our many less-conscious soldier comrades to carry out its imperialist policies.[47]

Meeting Chairman K. Strievskii

[From the Second Siberian Riflemen's Division]

The Petrograd Soviet of Workers' and Soldiers' Deputies' appeal, "To the Peoples of the Entire World" (which all Russia's soviets endorsed), the Provisional Government's declaration, "To Russia's Citizens," and the All-Russian Conference of Soviets' resolution on the war (endorsed by the Western Front Congress of Soldiers and Workers) all showed the world the resolute will of revolutionary Russia's people and army. Revolutionary Russia refuses to carry out the old aristocratic government's violent and aggressive policies. It wants speedy conclusion of a universal peace based upon freedom of self-determination for all peoples.

The Provisional Government's foreign policy, which remains loyal to the treaties secretly concluded between the tsarist government and the Allies and [remains dedicated] to the December "guarantees" and "sanctions" (that have hidden aggressive aims), and Foreign Affairs Minister Miliukov's duplicitous pronouncement (which could be interpreted as a rejection of the 27 March declaration) do not allow for a coalition with the German democracy in an energetic struggle against imperialism and for the war's termination. If the German democracy announced that it would no longer prolong the war, then peace could become possible on equal conditions for all belligerents. The Provisional Government's 18 April note conclusively revealed to everyone that the government has preserved an imperialist foreign policy.

For our part, we soldiers consider it necessary for all the world's peoples that peace be concluded only on the principle of all belligerents' equality, i.e., without annexations or indemnities, and without encroachments on national self-determination from either side. Therefore those of us gathered at this meeting appeal to the Soviet of Workers' and Soldiers' Deputies to resolutely demand that the Provisional Government:

1. Immediately publish secret treaties that the old government concluded with the Allies and that they radically restructure the entire system of foreign affairs on a democratic basis.
2. Without a day's delay, direct an appeal to the Allied governments delineating the Russian people's will in relation to the war.
3. Work out a new peace program with the Allies now, based on the self-determination of peoples, without annexations or indemnities— conditions that we hope will paralyze the German imperialist offensive and secure peace for the entire world.

4. We demand immediate revision of the Provisional Government's membership and immediate removal of those ministers who are clearly hostile to the popular masses' interests. This will prevent further arbitrary public pronouncements by individual Provisional Government ministers against the interests of the revolutionary people and army, such as War Minister Guchkov's statement about postponing the Constituent Assembly until the war's end. And it will prevent repetition of the threat to freedom's cause posed by excesses like those that followed Miliukov's 18 April note.

Meeting chairman, soldier-citizen Leont'ev
Deputy chairman, soldier-citizen Vakhmistrov

DOCUMENT 6.23
THE MENSHEVIK LEADERSHIP'S RESOLUTION,
"ON A COALITION MINISTRY"[48]

During the political crisis triggered by the Miliukov Note, the moderate socialists again faced the question whether to join the government. The following document is a resolution opposing creation of a coalition government, passed by the Menshevik Party's Organizational Committee late on the night of 24 April 1917 and published in The Workers' Newspaper (Rabochaia gazetta) *on 29 April. The authors use the term "social maximalism." Political party programs often contained "minimal" and "maximal" demands—what they expected to be done right away, and what lay as their goals in the more distant future. Among socialists, "maximalism" referred to calls to immediately realize "maximal" demands like creation of a socialist economic order.*

On a Coalition Ministry
On 25 April the Organizational Committee discussed the issue of a coalition ministry, in connection with the acute crisis arising from the 18 April Miliukov Note. Based upon this crisis and the country's social-political situation at the moment, the committee accepted the following fundamental resolution:

1. By entering the government, the socialist parties' representatives or members of the soviets of workers' and soldiers' deputies—who enjoy authority among the popular masses for leading the revolutionary struggle against the old regime's hidden forces and the new bourgeois order's mobilized forces—would exert their influence over the government and provide it with the opportunity to lead the masses.
2. In all the social conflicts that inevitably lay in the revolution's path, responsibility would rest with the government's socialist members, who would stand outside the masses and objectively confront these masses as the state power—this is an element of the revolution.

3. The socialist representatives' participation in the government on one hand would strengthen social maximalism, creating the illusion that radical demands will be realized. On the other hand, it would undermine the popular masses' confidence in leaders who intend to defend civil peace, leading to heightened anxiety among the masses and strengthening anarchy from the left.

4. The entry of soviet representatives in the government would fuse the soviet to the government and extinguish the soviet's role as a revolutionary democracy's institution that exercises control over the government. This would undermine the soviet's whole revolutionary significance and convert it into a regular apparatus of government power. In addition, if the popular masses move further along the path of the revolution, they would be in revolutionary opposition to the soviet—which would be a prop of the government.

5. Participation of socialist representatives or soviet representatives in the government under these conditions would create a radically unstable situation. It would enable anarchy's development from the left and the right, resulting in either a struggle against counterrevolution or a proletarian dictatorship, which is doomed to failure.

6. All this acquires particular urgency under the conditions of the world war, when the Provisional Government's foreign policy has fallen under the influence of the imperialist governments in the Allied countries, the proletarians of which still have not opposed their governments' will for a war of conquest, a war their ruling classes desire.

Based upon these considerations, the Organizational Committee has resolved that the entry of socialist party or soviet representatives into the government ministry is politically undesirable at this moment and would be injurious to the democracy's cause. It considers it the responsibility of the party's representatives on the Soviet Executive Committee to uphold this point of view.

In addition: While the Organizational Committee considers soviet control over and pressure on the government necessary, it also believes that the soviet and its institutions must energetically assist the government in the struggle against counterrevolution and anarchy. Right now, the government's activities in provisions, transport, the regulation of production, etc., are of growing importance.

DOCUMENT 6.24
THE SOCIALIST REVOLUTIONARIES ON
"THE CRISIS OF POWER"[49]

The following document is an editorial published in the Petrograd Socialist Revolutionary newspaper, The People's Cause (Delo naroda), *on 26 April*

1917. The author refers to two documents that appeared in that same issue of the newspaper: a declaration by the Provisional Government reviewing its accomplishments and appealing for support from Russia's "vital forces"; and a declaration by Alexander Kerensky insisting that other representatives of the "toiling democracy" be added to the cabinet. Near the document's end, the author notes the need to transform "organizational dualism into organizational monism," meaning that "dual power"—the de facto division of functional authority between the soviet and the Provisional Government—must come to an end.

The Crisis of Power.

We have just received information on two documents of extraordinary importance. These documents are signs of the times.

A crisis of power has come, a moment that was not completely unexpected and could scarcely be averted, given events. In any case, it has come earlier than the toiling democracy would have wanted. Had matters depended on the toiling democracy, it would have tried to postpone the crisis. The Miliukov Note is what sped the crisis along and forced its advance. Forced it, but did not create it. For events have their own logic.

Who created this government? Duma elements, census Russia, the old regime's *pays légale.*[50] They played an *active* role in forming new state institutions. The soviet of workers' and soldiers' deputies, conversely, played a *passive* role. It *recognized* the new government. True, it did so under condition that the new government accept a designated public program guiding its actions. The government was "accepted" because it "accepted."

This designation of active and passive roles was clear and natural. Duma/census Russia already possessed the privilege of organization under the old regime. In various forms, it had participated in factual management of public affairs of state importance. And so, when the old order fell, census Russia was ready to provide ministers at full battle-readiness. In less than 24 hours, census Russia could form a "cabinet" with solidarity. It created this government.

The toiling democracy is another matter. Denied the possibility of real party organizations by the old regime, driven underground, concentrating on the struggle, but not participating in administration, it was taken unprepared by events. It successfully followed the path of revolutionary improvisation and created a local "workers' parliament"—the [Petrograd] Soviet of Workers' and Soldiers' Deputies. It did this when the State Duma's Temporary Committee already existed and was about to give birth to the new Provisional Government.

Under these conditions, the toiling democracy preferred *to consciously remove itself* from direct participation in the government. Having been granted several guarantees regarding the government's political program, it made way for census Russia. It concentrated on matters of self-organization. It had to make up as quickly as possible for losses from the time of the autocracy. It first had to establish a press, legal party organizations that were democratically reorganized "from the bottom up," and a system of interparty institutions that would concentrate the country's revolutionary will in the soviets of workers' and solders' deputies. It had to consolidate itself. Of course, it also had to mobilize its political, organizational, and scientific-technical forces.

This process has moved forward very powerfully, of course. If at the moment the toiling democracy still does not stand fully armed for the task of creating a new revolutionary government, it is because this task is so great. To be "armed" for it is difficult. However, the toiling democracy is infinitely more prepared now than it was when the new government had only just been formed.

If we must recognize that the old combination (the Provisional Government's current composition) is outdated, that urgent tasks call for a Provisional Government built on a broader foundation, that we can no longer postpone the government's reorganization in the name of a more complete and multifaceted representation by people capable of rallying the country's collective social-political forces—then this means we will be entering a new era in revolutionary Russia's life.

Besides conditional approval based on agreement between toiling Russia and census Russia, an infinitely more difficult task arises: changing organizational *dualism* into organizational *monism*. This cannot be settled by hasty decisions based on optimistic simplifications of a complex matter. All the difficulties, all the complications associated with the transformation from one phase in our development to another, must be clarified. Nothing can be artificially lubricated or smoothed over. There must be exact and point-blank solutions to every question. Only by looking reality directly in the eye can we make responsible decisions about how the toiling democracy should respond to the government declarations that we have just received.

The question has been raised. It must be decided. The toiling democracy cannot avoid—it must not avoid—making a decision. Russia truly is in too serious a position for that. Toiling Russia will not run away from responsibility, although it precisely sees all the negative sides of shifting from its current position to a new one. But such a shift is possible for her only under certain conditions. And the question of the other side's reception of these conditions, perhaps, is more complicated than may appear at first glance.

These public declarations are signs of the times. They attest to a new geological shift in Russia's life. The Revolution continues—not in a narrow, superficial, and crude meaning of the word, but in its most profound sense.

DOCUMENT 6.25
A SPEECH BY CONSERVATIVE VASILII SHUL'GIN[51]

The following document is a speech by the prominent right-liberal Vasilii Shul'gin at a gathering of current and past State Duma deputies to celebrate the Duma's 10th anniversary on 27 April 1917. (The press called this the meeting of the "Four State Dumas.") In the wake of the crisis occasioned by the Miliukov Note, the gathering became a stage for political polemics. A detailed account of the meeting was published in the Kadet newspaper, Speech (Rech), *on 28 April 1917.*

[Shul'gin begins by saying he did not want a revolution and had feared that confrontation between the legislature and the tsar's government would undermine the war effort.]

The revolution began two months ago, and I cannot hide from you that many of us have been filled with doubt. The question is whether these two months, which have brought Russia and its peoples many great achievements, have not also profited the Germans. (*Voices:* "Very much!") It seems to us that our military situation has grown much worse. Trying to account for it, the first thing that occurs to me is that the government that is sitting here now before us—a government that we regard as honorable and talented and that we would like to see invested with full power—is under suspicion.[52] This is not to say that their position is much different from that of the old regime's government, which is imprisoned in the Peter-Paul Fortress.[53] I would say that the Provisional Government is, so to speak, under house arrest. (*Voices:* "Correct!") It is as if a guard had been posted over them and instructed, "Watch them, they are *burzhui*! Watch them closely, and if they try anything, you know your duty." Gentlemen, since 20 April it is clear to everyone that the guard knows his duty and performs it well. But, gentlemen, this raises the great question— have those responsible for stationing the guard done the right thing? This question refers to the socialist parties. I ask them openly: Gentlemen, are you doing the right thing when you place this government under guard? Would it not be better to find some other method of control?

But that certainly is not our only concern. The socialist parties— fortunately not all, but several among them—have habits and manners that remind one of the historic words spoken in this very hall on 1 November 1916, when it was asked, "Is that stupidity, or treason?" This question was put to Shturmer when the principal charge against him was that he was trying to create bad feelings between Russia and her allies, particularly England. And what is happening now? A few days ago, an open and very bitter propaganda battle against England was waged in the streets. It was claimed that England is the nest of all sorts of capitalist and imperialist tendencies and that Russia's task is to free the world from this monster.

I ask you, is that stupidity, or treason? (*Voices:* "Treason!") No, I think it is stupidity. When agitators are sent to bring anarchy and confusion to the villages, so that Petrograd, Moscow, the army, and the Northern provinces will go without grain—I ask you, what is that? And I think that it is stupidity, too, after all. Or when our brave soldiers are stirred up against their officers—I understand that there are all sorts of misunderstandings, and not all our officers are worthy—when soldiers are stirred up against all the officers, just like [the workers are stirred up] against the intelligentsia, I ask you: What is this campaign that can turn our army into a mish-mash mess? What is it, stupidity or treason? Gentleman, that is also stupidity. But when these three things are all brought together, and it is said: "You are on the verge of a break with the Allies; you have no army, and you have no food; therefore, conclude peace at any cost"— that is treason. (*Applause, shouts of* "Bravo!")

Tsereteli, from the floor: "Who is saying this?"[54]

Voice from the left: "Shul'gin says it!" (*Loud disturbance.*)

Chairman of the Presidium: I ask you not to interrupt the speaker.

Shul'gin: I will answer. Gentlemen, let me tell you. Go over to the Petrograd Side and listen to what is being said there.[55] I live in that district, and I have heard it with my own ears many times. Lenin is well known there, and there is a whole crowd of people around him who preach anything that comes into their heads. Do not forget, gentlemen, that our people are not yet fully prepared for political activity. Only with difficulty can they find their way through such questions. And so, unfortunately, these doctrines have an effect.

Gentlemen, I am happy that you allowed me to say these things. I see that now, as before, this tribune is free and incorruptible.

DOCUMENT 6.26
G. PLEKHANOV, "THE FATHERLAND IS IN DANGER"[56]

The following document is an editorial by Georgii Plekhanov in Unity (Edinstvo) *on 2 May 1917. By 2 May, the government crisis sparked by the Miliukov Note had become intertwined with debates over dual power, discipline in the army, and whether the socialists should join a coalition government. Miliukov had resigned his position as foreign minister, and members of the government had openly accused the Petrograd Soviet of undermining the government's authority. War Minister Guchkov and Petrograd Military District Commander General Lavr Kornilov had resigned their posts to protest soviet intervention in military affairs. On 29 April, the Petrograd Soviet resolved that its representatives would not join a coalition government. Plekhanov gives a Menshevik defensist perspective on this multiple crisis in prose laden with literary, mythological, and religious references. He also parodies Lenin's own rhetorical flourishes.*

The Fatherland Is in Danger.

I know that my article's title will give cause for mockery: "He is going to talk about the fatherland. He loves it! And he calls himself a Social Democrat!" I have never feared such mockery, however, and I never will. It invariably makes me recall Nekrasov's words: "Those who laugh will be thought fools/To vulgarize such feelings!"[57]

I am an old internationalist. [Plekhanov argues that there is a difference between internationalism and antinationalism. He claims that Marx founded the Socialist International based upon the idea that nations exist, and their workers must cooperate, not upon the principle of destroying nations. Therefore his patriotic position is consistent with Marxism, and the left socialists' positions are not.]

I cannot be reconciled to the violation of legitimate interests . . . and therefore I do not have the right to disregard my own country's legitimate interests. To reason otherwise would mean that antinationalists would be mistaken for internationalists. They would be mistaken for the likes of the Zimmerwaldists, like Grim or Platen, who assert that socialists betray themselves whenever they take arms to defend their motherland.[58] Let us protect ourselves from the grief brought on by these immortal gods of Olympus! Thus, I do not fearing our antinationalists' toothless mockery, and I consider it my responsibility to defend our fatherland's rightful interests. I call the readers' attention to their own great responsibility to Russia, which is in deadly danger.

But I am not alone in saying this. It is said by other people who fully understand the drift of public opinion. Our military power is rapidly declining. Our army is demoralized, and its dissolution is not far off. Then Russia will be absolutely ruined. This is what Army and Navy Minister A. I. Guchkov said at the commemorative session of the Four State Dumas. His speech sounded an alarm about the approaching disaster and appealed for help. Unfortunately, Guchkov was inappropriately polemical in his speech, which weakened its somber significance and gave some people a reason to suggest that he was exaggerating the great danger to our country.

But several days later at a congress of delegates from the front, our justice minister spoke in exactly the same spirit as Guchkov, calling attention to the danger facing the country: "I am saddened," Kerensky said, "that I did not die two months ago. Then I would have died with the great dream that a new life would burn in Russia forever, that we would treat one another with respect, without the whip and the rod, and that our state would never again be run by despots."

Now Kerensky has lost that confidence he had during the successful revolutionary events. Now his heart is filled with anxiety, and he openly and loudly appeals: "We will create a tragic and hopeless situation today if we do not grasp that responsibility rests with all of us now, if our state mechanism does not act correctly, like a well-oiled machine. Then everything we dreamed of, all we have aspired to in the past several years, will be wasted and perhaps drowned in blood."

This is a frightening and—regrettably—incontestable truth. I would add another formulation (although I cannot say this as well as A. F. Kerensky might). To express this exactly: If we do not act according to the principles and conditions noted by the justice minister, then everything we dreamed of, all we aspired to, will be drowned in blood and wasted, not only for several years, but continually—who knows?—probably for a very long time.

[Plekhanov says that current events in Russia threaten complete disaster. He cites the resignations of Guchkov and Kornilov.]

There are indications that the army's dissolution has begun. These include fraternization between Russian and German soldiers at the front and the resignation of people from the former command staff. Needless to say, under such conditions Russia's military strength will be destroyed completely in a very short time. Those who are not accessories to the subsequent military defeats will find themselves asking this question: What must to be done to prevent the complete destruction of Russia's ability to mount a military resistance?

First of all, there must be an end to fraternization, which profits only the Germans and, in any case, is being practiced only by Russian soldiers. This is only repeating what basic declarations by the Soviet's Executive Committee have already said. But better late than never! Second, our army's high command staff must be given the ability to exercise their responsibilities. This is not the position that they are in now.

[During the April crisis] the Petrograd Military District Commander could not order a single battalion from its barracks. I repeat: not a single unit came out. They remained in their barracks because they had no decision from the Soviet's Executive Committee. They did not do their duty and obey Kornilov's orders. It is understood that Kornilov's post will be taken by someone [favorable to the soviet], like Lavrent'ev or Petrov. But if the new district commander conducts his duties seriously, he will soon conclude that he must follow his predecessor's example. In a word, it is the Tale of the White Bull.[59]

Here is one possible end to this absurd fable: Upon the hearing that Russia may perish, the Petrograd Soviet decides to take military power into its own hands. Taking military power into its own hands, it will begin the dictatorship of the proletariat, about which Lenin's supporters speak, but which up to now has been considered untimely, and therefore harmful, by the representatives of other tendencies.[60] And this dictatorship will . . . take the form of a dictatorship of the Petrograd Soviet Executive Committee. In the place of the dictatorship of the working class, we will have the dictatorship of several dozen people.

Since currently we do not have the political and social conditions for a working class dictatorship, and therefore it is dangerous for Russia— and especially for working class' interests—then it is no more appropriate (and even more dangerous) to have a dictatorship of a few dozen people.

Consider this. Perhaps even take it to heart. Having given it thought, you must realize that I speak the truth. The Petrograd Soviet cannot aspire to take military power unless it loses its political sense. So it follows that it must take all steps necessary so that people in the high military command staff can exercise their duties.

The best means would be to create a coalition ministry that includes representatives of the toiling masses. But here again we confront a Petrograd Soviet resolution saying, chiefly, that such a ministry will not be formed. As long as this decision remains in force, the Tale of the White Bull will continue. Our military power will be at a level that greatly pleases Kaiser Wilhelm II's subjects and our personal enemies. Who will answer, if this decision remains in force for long?

The soviet's decision was passed by a vote of 23 to 22, with 8 abstaining. There is nothing to say about the people who could not decide how to cast their votes. As Dante wrote: "Gaze on them and walk past."[61] And so it appears that entry into a coalition ministry was prevented by one vote. Know this: the tedious and radically damaging fable of the white bull will go on and on in Russia until the owner of the vote who decided the fate of coalition ministry changes his mind. We will be waiting! But it is difficult to wait, knowing that our fatherland is in danger. Therefore, do not be inactive. All those radical left party members who have finally returned to Russia have gone down a blind alley. As much as possible, they must join one another and begin to organize tirelessly and plan agitation to propagate their views among the toiling masses.

For Paul the Apostle there were no Jews, no Hellenes, none who were isolated, none who were ignorant: there were only the enemies of Christianity.[62] For us, there must be no Mensheviks, no Bolsheviks, no *Edinstvo* members, no Social Democrats, no Socialist Revolutionaries. There must only be people who know the fatherland is in danger. And they must know that the fatherland's salvation requires a powerful appeal to revolutionary energy that takes us beyond sectarian dogmatism and party squabbles.

[Plekhanov laments that Kerensky's own party did not endorse his participation in the government.]

All this must be clarified. All this must be purged of contradictions. All this must be agreed upon.[63] And there must be a planned, definitive, and cooperative effort by those radical left party members who do not want to disgrace the public's dignity at this fatal time!

—G. Plekhanov

DOCUMENT 6.27
THE MENSHEVIKS JOIN THE COALITION GOVERNMENT[64]

The following document is a resolution from the Menshevik Party's All-Russian Conference held in Petrograd on 7–12 May 1917. On 3 May the Menshevik and Socialist Revolutionary (SR) leaderships agreed to a coalition government. Prince L'vov remained prime minister and liberals kept a majority in the cabinet. Kerensky became war and navy minister. Two SRs joined the government: Viktor Chernov became agriculture minister and Pavel Pereverzev became justice minister. Alexei Peshekhonov of the Popular-Socialists headed a new Provisions Ministry. And two Mensheviks entered the cabinet: Matvei Skobelev took up the new post of labor minister and Irakli Tsereteli became the minister of post and telegraph.

On the Provisional Government and the Coalition Ministry.

1. As a result of the revolutionary process and the development of deep social conflicts, the government created in the revolution's first days lacked the strength to act on the protracted war, reorganize the country's productive life, or halt the army's disorganization. Because it was incapable of adequately energetic revolutionary steps in spheres of internal construction, and because it was unable to carry out consistent political measures in the sphere of international relations, it aroused the mistrust of the broad democratic masses. Therefore it has not commanded the necessary full authority.

2. This provoked a government crisis that posed the problem of creating a strong revolutionary government. This crisis cannot be solved by the Soviet of Workers' and Soldiers' Deputies seizing power. The objective conditions have not matured, and a [seizure of power] would push much of the bourgeois democracy and peasantry from the revolution. Without participation by the Social Democrats, a government that answers to the revolutionary proletariat's interests cannot be created. The government cannot be turned over to the most right-wing bourgeois elements; that would threaten the country with civil war.

3. We recognize all the political danger connected to the socialists' entry into a bourgeois government under these conditions, but it would threaten the revolution with disintegration were the revolutionary Social Democrats to reject an active role in a Provisional Government founded on a resolute democratic platform in the foreign and domestic policy spheres. It would cut the government off from the interests of the working class and the entire revolutionary democracy.

4. If socialists enter the government on a platform of energetic policies directed toward the world war's quickest democratic conclusion, it will be a powerful factor toward ending the war in the international democracy's interests.

5. Therefore the conference resolves to give its full and unconditional support to the new Provisional Government, which firmly guarantees a policy realizing the democracy's domestic and foreign policy demands. We summon the working class and party organizations to plan active work to consolidate the new revolutionary government's power, both in the center and in the provinces.

6. Having accepted responsibility for the actions of those party members who, at the soviet's instruction, are joining the Provisional Government, the conference considers it necessary that Social Democrat ministers answer not only to the soviet, but also to the party. . . .

DOCUMENT 6.28
DEM'IAN BEDNYI, "THE COALITION"[65]

The following poem by the Bolshevik Dem'ian Bednyi appeared in the Petrograd Bolshevik newspaper, Truth (Pravda), *on 3 May 1917. Bednyi uses two comments by Menshevik leader Irakli Tsereteli to deride Tsereteli's entry into the new coalition government.*

Coalition

The First Faint Note

> ". . . Again the bourgeoisie is
> anxious to save Russia,
> and there can be no doubt,
> that they can be
> trusted."

> Tsereteli

> Such a faint note was sounded!
> Not bad for starters, it's true.
> And all it cost was a "good" little word.
> But . . . we are waiting for the last part.

Readiness for the Ministry

> "If you vote in favor
> of Comrade Zinoviev,
> then you are disorganizing
> the revolution. Because
> what matters is not
> what is wanted, but what
> can be realized, and from this
> point of view it must

be recognized that a huge portion
of Russia is not Socialistic."

Tsereteli

Tsereteli, according to recent
News, is to be named Minister
of Labor.
"The Russian country
Is not Socialistic."
So says the wise woman,
And she is such a practical woman!

After this point, the conclusion will come quickly.
What do you think? Won't there be a ministerial portfolio?
Long live Minister
Irakli Tsereteli!

—Dem'ian Bednyi

DOCUMENT 6.29
THE KADET PARTY'S EIGHTH CONGRESS, "DRAFT
RESOLUTION ON THE CURRENT POLITICAL SITUATION"[66]

*A few days after announcement of the new coalition government, the Kadets—
Russia's most important liberal party—opened their eighth party congress in
Petrograd. The congress, held on 9–12 May 1917, and attended by more than
300 delegates from across Russia, discussed a broad range of issues, including the
party's agrarian program and Ukrainian autonomy. The following document
is the first draft of the conference's resolution, "On the Question of the Current
Political Situation," from 9 May 1917.*

The revolutionary struggle's second phase, marked by awareness of the
government authority's powerlessness in the struggle against anarchy, and
by the weakening of the army's battle-readiness, ended with creation
of a government that includes representatives of the Menshevik Social
Democratic fraction, the Socialist Revolutionaries, and the Popular-
Socialist Party. The Kadet Party's basis for agreeing to this change in
the government's composition, however, had been resolved [beforehand].
Given the danger the motherland faces from the army's collapse at the front
and from internal anarchy, the party considered it its duty to overcome
our recent internal doubts and difficulties, to remain in our posts, and not
to recall our representatives from the government's composition.

As the guardians of the state principle—without the reinforcement
of which the people's freedom would be threatened with inevitable

destruction—we are persuaded that participation in the government provides us a more promising means to protect the country against counter-revolution. We expect that entry into the government of groups on the left, who now become responsible for directing the state's life, will give the government force and stability. We expect this will remove the pernicious element of dual power, both at the front and in the country. We welcome the Provisional Government's declarations on the necessity of an offensive at the front and unwavering faith in our Allies. Therefore the Party of People's Freedom declares its support for the Provisional Government in all undertakings directed toward realizing these stated aims.

DOCUMENT 6.30
A PROCLAMATION BY THE PETROGRAD
ANARCHISTS' CLUB[67]

The following document is a one-page leaflet by the Petrograd Anarchists' Club. Leaflets like this would have been passed along by hand or pasted to walls. Although it bears no date other than "May 1917," the document provides a sense of the anarchist view in the period of the first major crisis that faced the Provisional Government.

Proclamation No. 1.

Citizens! We appeal to you. We are Anarchists who negate private property and the state. The revolution, by crushing our chains, released us from the hated underground, where the people's conscience, freedom, and honor had gasped for air. Now we will teach our lessons loudly. What are these, in a few words?

Workers, soldiers, and peasants, there are those before you who would distort anarchism's principles and aims. Do not believe those who say that anarchism is dangerous. Anarchism is salvation. Do not listen to those who maintain that anarchism is violent. Anarchism's task is to consolidate freedom and happiness in the land. You are taught that anarchy is chaos, but that is how it is understood by those who defend oppression. We who are anarchists understand it differently.

Anarchy—is the harmonious work of free people. It is respecting someone else if he respects you. Like socialists, we strive for labor's complete emancipation: factories, plants, the land, and palaces must be made the entire people's property. But this is not the final goal. This gives economic liberation; it does not, however, give full freedom. Socialism breaks the chains, but only anarchism releases us from prison. Because it alone fights the government authority that creates prisons and oppression. It is not Capital that is frightening, but government. It is government that makes one man a slave and the other the master. We understand history as the individual's struggle against the state, as the struggle of the powerless against power. Understand that if you want to live freely, then in addition to Capital, your enemy is the state system, which is based upon force.

We, the Anarchists, deny the idea of the state, because we consider it ruinous for society. The people do not need a tsar, and so they do not need a president of a republic. The will spoken by the deputy is not the will of those who voted for him. Whenever there is government, there are rulers. The foundation of evil in contemporary life is the state system.

Workers, soldiers and peasants! States incited this fratricidal war, and rivers of blood have flowed from it. If the war is not to be repeated, then governments must not exist. When there is a state, there will be war. And we want no more of any war. The European war would soon be brought to an end if we did not permit ourselves to be dragged, like a bull that has dug in its heels, into the bloody war. Peace must be concluded by the people themselves, in spite of the governments.

Workers, soldiers, peasants—all who are oppressed! Prepare to settle accounts with Capital and the state. Every people must have self-determination, but do not confuse what is done in the people's name with what is done in the state's name. We will aspire to create a European United States, a Great European Federation, entered on the basis of autonomy by all peoples who previously did not have autonomy. That is how we, the Anarchists, would act in the sphere of international relations. In the domestic sphere, we strive to overthrow the state system. It would be replaced by free unions of all branches of the public. These are the ideas expressed by anarchy. Organize in city, village, and professional associations. Prepare to judge the fate of Capital and the state. Unite in groups, in anarchist clubs. Do not let go of each other's hands, and do not let your righteous anger fade.

But remember, Citizens: the Anarchists are for order, not for disorder. Those who want to fish in troubled waters distort our mottos.[68] That only sustains the old government, based on oppression and theft. We will destroy such people as our enemies.

Down with the state!
Down with Capital!
Long live the Social Revolution!

The Petrograd Anarchists' Club
May 1917

CHAPTER SEVEN

FLASH POINTS OF CONFLICT: THE JUNE OFFENSIVE AND THE JULY DAYS

THE MENSHEVIK-INTERNATIONALISTS OPPOSE
REVOLUTIONARY DEFENSISM[1]

The following document is an excerpt from a "flyer" (letuchkii listok) published by the Menshevik-Internationalists in Petrograd, in which they explain their general program and criticize both the revolutionary defensists and the Bolsheviks. Two antiwar factions coalesced in 1917: the Menshevik-Internationalists (associated with Martov) and the United Social Democrat-Internationalists (associated with the Novaia zhizn'). The authors of this flyer associate political positions with social class attributes. They not only label liberals "bourgeois," but also define their socialist opponents' positions as "petty-bourgeois." In 1917 this sort of social class labeling (an inheritance of prerevolutionary socialist rhetoric) was typical in socialist politics, not just among the Bolsheviks.

. . . In the April Days the revolutionary democracy rose up against counter-revolutionary bourgeois groups who sought to impose annexationist aims on the revolution. But while the revolutionary democracy departed from the path chosen by the servants of Russian and British imperialism, it remained on a path that did not create a revolutionary government that is a real instrument of the people's will for peace.

The proletariat was taken by surprise by the revolution and was weakly organized. The world socialist crisis created profound ideological disorder in its ranks.[2] The proletariat was cut off from the international communication so necessary to the maturity of its class politics. Under these conditions, the socialist proletariat, which leads the popular masses, fell under the ideological influence of petty-bourgeois elements. It dissolved into the revolutionary democracy. . . . Up to this point in the Russian revolution, it has only partially and inconsistently carried out its own class policies. This inconsistency, this dissolution into the revolutionary peasant-soldier democracy, resulted in the triumph of "revolutionary defensism." Revolutionary defensism tries to combine socialist internationalism with defense of a national revolution by militaristic methods. It tries to reconcile the socialist struggle against imperialism with the imperialist countries' diplomatic influence. It mixes appeals to international class solidarity with calls for interclass solidarity in the cause of military defense.

The "revolutionary-defensist" policy that a significant portion of the conscious proletariat is following has only brought the proletariat political defeat. It has led them down a blind alley. The revolutionary defensists cannot see that the only way out is to rouse the Western European proletariat to revolution. Instead, they actually lend assistance to the bourgeois Provisional Government. They send representatives to enter a bourgeois government that has taken a duplicitous position on the question of ending the war immediately. Their representatives joined the government based on an agreement that bound the socialist proletariat's struggle for peace to the bourgeoisie's policy of continuing the war. The democracy has capitulated to the petty-bourgeois elements, and so it staggers between an internationalist and a nationalist line, between the struggle for peace and "war until victory."

This only weakens the revolutionary influence that Russian events can have on the European proletariat. It only hampers their liberation from captivity under nationalist dispositions and illusions. It delays the approaching revolutionary explosion in other countries. Aiding a Provisional Government connected to the bourgeois and petty-bourgeois democracy at this time weakens the vanguard's potential influence on the developing revolution. More than that: it promotes a split in the ranks of the worker masses, which strengthens anarchic and maximalist tendencies that feed on general disorder and the aggravation of class distrust.

It is on this ground that the seeds of a utopian idea are being planted among the proletarian masses—the idea that the proletariat can pass immediately from the bourgeois democratic revolution to a socialist revolution before first gathering its strength for the historic tasks that lay before it, before the Russian revolution has been carried forward by the European revolution. On this ground, Blanquist plans are produced for a seizure of power by an active minority of the proletariat. The idea that the revolution can be saved through violent-insurrectionary measures is being knocked around.

The opportunism of one segment of the Social Democrats unfailingly produces the adventurism of the other, which tempts the worker masses to seek escape from the economic crisis and ruinous war through a miracle: the seizure of power and immediate socialism. . . .

DOCUMENT 7.2
THE SMOLENSK SOVIET DEBATE ON THE
MILITARY OFFENSIVE[3]

The following document is an excerpt from the minutes of the Smolensk Soviet's 26 May 1917 session, as published in the local newspaper The Smolensk Bulletin (Smolenskii vestnik). *In early May, War Minister Kerensky and most Russian liberals began pushing for revived military operations against the Germans. The Menshevik and SR revolutionary defensists hoped that a June international socialist conference would make such operations unnecessary. But when the conference plans collapsed, the Petrograd Soviet accepted Kerensky's pro-offensive argument: an offensive would force the Germans to negotiate for a general peace with no annexations or indemnities and the right of national self-determination. In Smolensk, as across Russia, debate over the offensive exacerbated divisions between socialist factions. The question of supporting an offensive came up at the Smolensk Soviet's 26 May 1917 session. The session was attended by 84 soviet deputies, with the revolutionary defensists in the majority.*

. . . The meeting moved on to the soviet's attitude toward the war. *Comrade Iakubovich* reported.[4] He painted a picture of the country's difficult position in connection to the prolonged war and explained that an international-scale struggle for peace is necessary: "But meanwhile, the war continues, and we cannot waver in restoring the army's resources and power. We must strive mightily at this precious moment; the revolution's interests demand it."

Comrade Smol'ianinov (for the Bolsheviks): "We also are fighting for peace on an international scale, and we steadfastly oppose a separate peace.[5] There is one true means to end the war: convening a 3rd International, which will be free from the poison gas of defensism. If we believe in the International's ideals, it will succeed. But it is impossible to lift the International's banner to support this battle between barbarians, or to support your side's battle cries. What justifies your warmongering?

. . . If we agree that the revolution's salvation and the salvation of this devastated culture's remnants lies in the international proletarian revolution and creation of the [Third] International, then we must move directly toward that aim by the shortest and surest road. Any detour toward bourgeois politics or uncertain step drags out the war and essentially endangers the revolution. As a practical step, we demand immediate publication of treaties—the people must know what they are summoned to die for. Is this really an unjust demand? Why are you silent about this? If, as you say, we must fight for the revolution and for freedom, then throw away the old criminal treaties concluded by Nicholas II. This would at least relieve you of some guilt before future generations.

Rest assured, comrades: if we were convinced that the revolution's salvation lies in an offensive, we would join you in your appeals. But we think it is the other way around. Chauvinism will drag out the war and destroy freedom, and it never can be free Russia's salvation. The country is on the verge of complete ruin. The signs of hunger have appeared. We must rescue what remains. That necessitates moving toward peace along the surest path open to the revolutionary democracy. Only a sincere, firm, democratic policy of freedom and a strong faith in the Russian people's rightness can save the revolution's fruit. I do not see this in your policies.

We do not propose anything that could possibly lead to disorganization of the army and the rear. We are for organizing a workers', peasants', and soldiers' government. We think that only a democratic government can save the country from complete disaster. We are clearly aware and understand that this historic moment demands we put forward a resolution of our aims.

Comrade Maizel agreed in principle with Comrade Iakubovich's proposed resolution and added that "it is necessary to stress more vividly our negative attitude toward 'fraternization,' which in fact is a kind of separate truce."[6] He called for a vote on Iakubovich's resolution.

The vote's result was that a majority of 58 against 20 (with 7 abstaining) approved Comrade Iakubovich's resolution, as follows:

a. A peace worthy of all countries' democracies cannot be reached through the military destruction of belligerent countries, but only through the general agreement of all countries' toiling classes, their governments' renunciation of all annexations and indemnities, and recognition of national self-determination.

b. The struggle for peace can be carried out only on an international scale. It must be secured against attempts by imperialist circles in either coalition to use the Russian revolution in their own interests. The struggle's true method is to organize all countries' toiling classes to pressure their governments into immediate peace negotiations on the basis of the formerly stated lofty principles. An international socialist conference, convened at the Petrograd Soviet of Workers' and Soldiers' Deputies' initiative, will establish the proper path for organizing the toiling classes' peace demonstrations. We call on all socialist factions and groups to participate in the conference, which will provide a necessary broad discussion of the issue.

c. The decision by the Provisional Coalition Government and the Petrograd Soviet to restore the Russian Army's offensive capacity is necessary, given the immediate need to support the struggle of all countries' toilers for peace and international brotherhood. It is in keeping with the general spirit of the position held by the Russian revolutionary democracy. And it strengthens our situation in the cause of the international struggle for peace.

d. Demonstrations that disorganize the army's ranks and reduce its battle-readiness are harmful and intolerable precisely from the perspective of the revolutionary democracy's interests and all Europe's future.

DOCUMENT 7.3
KERENSKY'S ORDER FOR A MILITARY OFFENSIVE[7]

The following document is Kerensky's 16 June 1917 order launching the June offensive, as published in The Provisional Government Bulletin (Vestnik Vremennogo pravitel'stvo) *on 20 June 1917. The offensive would begin on 18 June 1917. The Petrograd Soviet's leadership called for patriotic demonstrations on that day to show support for the offensive.*

Having thrown off the chains of slavery, Russia firmly resolved that it would stand up for its rights, honor, and freedom. Believing in international brotherhood, democratic Russia has appealed sincerely to all belligerent countries to end the war and conclude the honorable peace necessary for all. In response to our call for brotherhood, however, the enemy asked us to be traitors. The Austro-Germans proposed a separate peace with Russia. They are trying to disrupt our diligence with fraternization, while at the same time throwing their forces at our allies. They think that once they have destroyed our allies, they then will punish us. But now the enemy, convinced that Russia will not let itself be deceived, threatens us and is amassing forces along our front.

Warriors, the fatherland is in danger. Freedom and the revolution are threatened with destruction. The time has come, and the army is ready to do its duty. Your Supreme High Commander, the glorious victorious chief, understands that each day's delay only strengthens the enemy.[8] Only by an immediate blow can we disrupt the enemy's plans. Therefore, in complete awareness of my great responsibility to the fatherland, and in the name of the free people and its Provisional Government, I call on the army—strengthened by the revolution's force and spirit—to go on the offensive.

Do not let the enemy celebrate victory over us prematurely. Let all peoples know that it is not out of weakness that we speak for peace. Let them know that freedom has increased our might. Officers and soldiers! Know that all of Russia blesses you in this military exploit. In the name of freedom, in the name of the bright future of the motherland, in the name of an enduring and honorable peace, we all call on you—Forward!

—Minister of War and the Navy Kerensky

DOCUMENT 7.4
PAVEL AFANAS'EV-ARSKII, "FOR THE HONOR
OF MOTHER RUSSIA"[9]

The following poem was written by Pavel Afanas'ev-Arskii, a soldier in the Pavlov Guards Regiment of the Second Guards Infantry Division in Petrograd. The author personifies Russia as the people's "mother" and refers to men using diminutives ("little soldiers"— soldatushki, and "little fathers"— batiushki), magnifying their innocence. It appeared in Pravda *on 18 June 1917.*

For the Honor of Mother Russia

For the honor of Mother Russia
Little soldiers go into battle.
They go without complaint,

Go into who knows what.
They go, boldly,
At home they leave little children,
They leave behind
Wives and orphans.

Little soldiers, little sirs,
With carefree smiles,
Come though the watery swamp—
Fighting without complaint,
Fighting who knows what.
Gone away from your young home
To the cold and hunger.

In battle, matters are clear,
The fate of a soldier is dangerous:
A well-aimed bullet will destroy him,
Fleas will bite.
When the machineguns fire
They shoot with the company,
And the entire unit
Is under heavy shellfire.
For the honor of Mother Russia,
Flies cover the little soldiers.

For the honor of Mother Russia,
"Hurrah" cry the little soldiers,
Running into terrible battle,
Hand to hand with the enemy,
Slashing madly.
Pale white masses,
Laid out in rows, in groups.
Corpses beaten black and blue
For the honor of Mother Russia—
Unlucky little soldiers.

For the honor of Mother Russia,
Services are read for the little fathers.
Christ's doctrine forgotten
When called to arms.
Given benedictions
In the cause of destruction.
The unsheathed sword
Brought crucifixion.
And the little fathers believed the Word.
The fallen little soldiers.

A time of peace is coming.
Boys, you will miss
All the fat of the land.
Little workers and little soldiers
Will overthrow the landlords,
But you will lie beneath little crosses.
And you will lie still for years,
Heads buried
For the honor of Mother Russia.
Brave little soldiers.

—Pavlov Regiment Soldier Afanas'ev-Arskii

DOCUMENT 7.5
BOLSHEVIK PARTY SLOGANS FOR THE 18 JUNE 1917
DEMONSTRATIONS[10]

The following document is the Bolsheviks' appeal to workers and soldiers, explaining slogans they should carry in marches to counter the Petrograd Soviet–sponsored demonstration in support of the military offensive on 18 June 1917. The soviet leaders had prohibited antiwar demonstrations.

To All Who Toil, To All Petrograd Workers and Soldiers.

Comrades! Russia is living through a difficult trial. The war, which has countless victims, still continues. Its purpose is to rake in profits for the *robbers and the blood-drinking bankers.* Industrial ruin brought by the war is leading to stoppages in the factories and unemployment. Their purpose is to increase the fantastic profits of *the lock-out capitalists.* Shortages of supplies brought on by the war are growing much worse. Rising prices strangle the city poor. Prices are rising, and it is all for the whims of the *marauder-speculators.* The ominous specter of hunger and ruin hangs over us. . . .

The black clouds of counterrevolution are moving in. The Third-of-June Duma, which helped the tsar oppress the people, now demands an immediate offensive at the front.[11] Why? To drown freedom in blood, to please the "Allies" and the Russian robbers. The State Council, which supplied the tsar with minister-hangmen, silently weaves a treacherous web. For what? So that, at the proper moment, it can throw a net over the people, to please the "Allies" and the Russian oppressors.

The Provisional Government, caught between the Tsar's Duma and the Soviet Deputies, with 10 *burzhui* among its members, clearly has fallen under the influence of aristocratic landlords and the capitalists. Instead of securing soldiers' rights, Kerensky issues a "declaration" violating these rights.[12] Instead of strengthening the liberty that soldiers won in the days of the revolution, there are new "orders" threatening arrests and disbanding our military units. Instead of guaranteeing the freedom won by Russia's citizens, there are political searches in the barracks, arrests without courts or trials, and threats of imprisonment based upon Article 129.[13] Instead of an armed people, there are threats to disarm the workers and soldiers. Instead of the liberation of oppressed peoples, there are objections to Finland and Ukraine's independence and fear of giving them freedom.[14] Instead of a decisive struggle against counterrevolution, there is connivance in the revelry of the counterrevolutionaries, who are openly arming themselves for a struggle against the revolution. . . .

And everywhere the war continues. And there are no real, serious measures to end it. And nothing is done to offer *all* peoples a just peace. And ruin is spreading everywhere, but there are no measures of any kind against it. And hunger is on the move, but there are no real measures of any kind against it. And it is astonishing, but counterrevolution can be seen everywhere, inciting the government to new acts of repression against workers and peasants, soldiers and sailors.

Comrades! It is impossible to tolerate this in silence, to be silent after all of these crimes! You are free citizens; you have the right to protest, and you must exercise this right of yours now, and not later. Let tomorrow (18 June) be a day of peace demonstrations; transform it into a day when revolutionary Petrograd protests thunderously against the revival of oppression and slavery! Tomorrow, let the banners of victory fly over the enemies of freedom and socialism! Let your shouts, the shouts of fighters of the revolution, fly across the whole world and gladden all who are oppressed and enslaved!

There, in the West, in the belligerent countries, a new life is dawning; it is the dawn of a great workers' revolution. Tomorrow, let your brothers in the West know that you are bringing them not war, but banners of peace, banners of liberation and not of enslavement!

Workers! Soldiers! Join fraternal hands with one another. Go forward under the banner of socialism! Everyone to the streets, comrades! Rally around your banners! Form ranks and march through the streets of the capital! Calmly and firmly declare what it is that you want:

Down with Counterrevolution!
Down with the Tsarist Duma!
Down with the State Council!
Down with the Ten Capitalist Ministers!
All Power to the Soviets of Workers', Soldiers', and Peasants' Deputies!
Revise the "Declaration of Soldiers' Rights"!
Abolish the Orders" against Soldiers and Sailors!
Down with the Disarming of Revolutionary Workers!
Long Live the People's Militia!

Down with Anarchy in Production and with the Lockout-Capitalists!
Long Live Control and Organization of Production and Distribution!
Against the Policy of the Offensive!
It is Time to End the War! Let the Soviet Declare Just Terms for Peace!
No Separate Peace with [Kaiser] Wilhelm, No Secret Treaties with the
   French and English Capitalists!
Bread! Peace! Freedom!

The RSDLP Central Committee
The RSDLP Petersburg Committee
The RSDLP Central Committee Military Organization
The Central Council of Petrograd Factory and Plant Committees
The Petrograd Soviet Bolshevik Fraction
The Editors of *Pravda*
The Editors of *Soldatskaia Pravda.*

DOCUMENT 7.6
NEW TIMES ON "RIOTS AND A SEPARATE PEACE"[15]

The following document is from the Petrograd right-liberal newspaper, New
Times *(Novoe vremia), which vigorously supported the June Offensive. Its
author, who used the pseudonym "Independent" (Nezavisimyi), wrote the essay
on the night of 17 June 1917; it appeared in* New Times *the next morning.*

Toward Riots and a Separate Peace.
The Bolsheviks have been completely open about their wish to use the
18 June demonstration for propaganda against the war. Every day *Pravda*
shouts out a new slogan that demands examination: "Against the offensive" and "Bring the war to an end." This is the nastiest demagoguery,
and it is being disseminated successfully behind the battle lines, where
our heroes are fighting: "Abolish discipline against soldiers and sailors"
and "Follow the declaration of soldiers' rights."
    Agitators spread out across the city last night and today. They are
giving speeches in the military barracks and to crowds that have gathered,
telling them what they dare not say in print, not even in *Pravda.* They are
repeating the vile call of the March days—they are inciting against the
officers and the intelligentsia. "Beat the officers!" was heard at meetings
last night. "Smash the intelligentsia!" "Down with the *burzhui*!"
    And who will they include as *burzhui*? Perhaps a banker, or perhaps a
student, or a doctor, or a writer? Anyone who is not wearing oily boots?
Anyone who is wearing an over-coat and a hat? Above all, they do not
like "hats."[16]
    The Bolsheviks deliberately foster counterrevolution by searching for
nonexistent counterrevolution, by pointing to the State Duma and secret

intrigues involving some un-named and undetected people who, of course, inevitably want to restore the unnatural old order. They call out in exasperation, trying to inspire discord between the right and the democracy and among the entire people. Their dream: class against class, social estate against social estate, soldier against officer, Kadet against Menshevik, factory against factory, son against father, and all against Russia.

With each day the Bolsheviks' intent becomes clearer: they are working for Kaiser Wilhelm, for a separate peace. They are working against the Allies and against the Russian people. Freedom and order are their enemies; anarchy and destructive violence is their dream. Look at the slogans that they pronounce for tomorrow's demonstrations. Under Nicholas II, the Black Hundreds fraternized with the Germans and organized pogroms. After the revolution, it is the Red Hundreds who are the provocateurs. The International's banner is held by demagogues and *pogromshchiki*—like those gathered in the Union of Russian People.[17]

DOCUMENT 7.7
FIVE SPEECHES ON THE JUNE OFFENSIVE AT THE
FIRST ALL-RUSSIAN CONGRESS OF SOVIETS[18]

The following document set presents excerpts from speeches at the 19 June 1917 session of the First All-Russian Congress of Soviets. The congress, which met in Petrograd on 3–24 June, was attended by more than 1,000 delegates from soviets across Russia.[19] *Nearly every delegate who wished to speak was given the floor, so the meeting aired significant differences in opinion on most current issues.*[20] *The selection below features speeches by the three Menshevik revolutionary defensists (Irakli Tsereteli, Matvei Skobelev, and Vladimir Voitinskii); one SR revolutionary defensist (Viktor Chernov); and one Menshevik-Internationalist (Iuli Martov).*

Tsereteli: Comrades, our revolutionary army has gone on the offensive. (*Applause.*) It will show the whole world, comrades, that the Russian revolution has strengthened democratic principles, not weakened them, and has strengthened the might of the army. It will show the whole world, comrades, that democratic ideals in domestic and foreign policy have not demoralized the army, as the revolution's enemies try to claim, but have enthusiastically strengthened the army's battle-readiness. A turning point in the Russian revolution has come, comrades, when were must reveal all the power and all the strength of the new democratic ideals that the revolution has realized. . . .

. . . Comrades, a new chapter has opened in the history of the great Russian revolution. Our revolutionary army has gone on the offensive. For what ideals are our brothers spilling their blood at the front? We know that the revolutionary army is one with the entire revolutionary democracy, with all Revolutionary Russia and its aspirations. We know that the Provisional Government has resolved that the foreign policy goal for the revolutionary democracy, for all revolutionary Russia, is universal peace on principles that exclude coercion from either side. In accord with this goal, the representative institutions of the revolutionary democracy and the Provisional Government have recently rejected the old tsarist policies. We have made a complete break from all the old tsarist policies and all the imperialistic tendencies that Russia had promoted at the war's beginning. Henceforth, revolutionary Russia firmly and unwaveringly aspires to defend its freedom and its territory from any encroachments. It also seeks to guarantee all peoples caught up in the war that not one drop of Russia soldiers' blood will be spilled for the imperialist gang's interests.

. . . It is from exactly this perspective, comrades, that we must greet our heroic revolutionary army as one of our Russian democracy's great accomplishments. We know that because the revolution strengthened the army, the army will defend each inch of land. We know that the task confronting the army is the entire revolutionary democracy's task as well. We must prove worthy of the heroes of the Russian revolution who are defending our freedom. And we must exert all our effort so that here, in the rear, we prove worthy by showing support for our revolutionary army. We must fortify the entire country internally, based on the principles for which all Russia is now fighting—at the front and in the rear.

This, comrades, is the offensive's significance. This is our attitude toward the offensive. We must not doubt our revolutionary troops for even a moment. We cannot doubt that all their efforts will strengthen our revolution. . . . An uncertain attitude toward the offensive would liquidate the revolutionary army's shining advances, which have opened a new era in our revolution.

. . . You all must prove worthy of this confidence, comrades, the confidence that the entire people have invested in the revolutionary organizations, in the Soviets of Workers' and Soldiers' Deputies. This great confidence exposes us to great danger. Everyone at this assembly now is in some measure responsible for Russia's fate, for our revolution's fate, comrades. We are responsible for the future, and we must prove worthy . . . We must pursue the one great task that is before revolutionary Russia— the salvation of the revolution. Russia must, can, and will realize this goal. (*Applause.*)

Chernov: Comrades, the moment's business is, in many ways, decisive for the Russian revolution's history.

. . . We have said it before, and we now repeat a thousand times, if necessary: As soon as peace becomes possible on the principles formulated by revolutionary Russia's urban and rural working class and army, then the war must not continue for a single moment. (*Applause.*)

Comrades, we know—we know all too well—that there is no way for any participants to leave this war separately. Either everyone gets out of this war—this dead end, this bloody nightmare—or no one does. That is where matters stand. And that is why, in addition to international socialist action as an effective lever, we must boldly defend all our initiatives, both in Russia's foreign policy and in the strategy of its revolutionary army. We will explain this repeatedly. For Russian troops, for the Russian armed forces, there is a single strategic front: the united political front. The Russian government's foreign policy is guided by the Russian revolution's slogans—by these, and only by these.

The revolutionary army is the tool for these policies and not for any other policies. We can say confidently, comrades, that each success of our revolutionary army will demonstrate this. And so revolutionary Russia's voice and its foreign policies will be heard by all—by combatants and noncombatants, neutrals and allied. Everyone will hear the revolution's voice. And revolutionary Russia's voice will have more weight, will have more real influence, and may be able to lead Europe away from the world war and onto the path of liquidating war. The is the only possibility for salvation, and it can only come through revolutionary internationalization of our conscience.

. . . And therefore, I believe and hope, comrades, that we all—with unanimous willingness and unanimous decisiveness—will make those sacrifices needed for the revolutionary army. We give a socialist salute to the revolutionary army. We are obliged to, based upon our position—the position of the people strengthening the revolution's accomplishments in the rear, at a time when it stands in the flames of danger. We salute them as a way of saying that their fears are our fears; their aims are our aims; their hearts and ours beat in unison. There can be no misunderstandings between us. Just as they trust us, we trust them. This faith is strong, and we value their sacrifices.

And so, before all Russia—the entire proletariat, the toiling peasantry, and all those who have served us in days past, through baptism by blood—we salute them. (*Applause.*)

Skobelev: Comrades, the inevitable has occurred. For two and a half years the Russian people's blood flowed; the Russian democracy's blood flowed, sacrificed before the altar of the god of war. And we here in the rear worked, so that these sacrifices would not be in vain. We watched indignantly as a barbarous government compounded the sacrifices and used up the Russian people's strength, health, and life. They told us: there is no time to be indignant; sacrifices must be made, silent sacrifices. A revolution, they said, will destroy the country and stab the army in the back. Then came 27 February, and a lightning-quick revolution took place. And from stones thrown here in Petrograd into the boundless sea of Russia, infinite circles spread. And the frozen old regime melted away. And the old frozen, despotic discipline that had bound the Russian Army melted away.

Dear comrades, there is no need to hide that in the revolution's first days many of us worried that the army might devour the revolution. Only inexhaustible faith in our fine and hallowed ideals, inexhaustible faith in the democracy's internal strength, quelled this worm of doubt. We awoke to the belief that the war will not snuff out the revolution; the revolution will snuff out the war. So let our comrade brothers dying in the first trenches, and their comrades who will follow in the second trenches, know that the revolution's sacred flame will burn off the stench that the god of war has left in the battle field.

Comrades, henceforth blood will not be sacrificed on the altar of the god of imperialism. Rather, we make a conscious sacrifice at the altar of those exalted ideals that the Russian revolution has written on its banners. . . .

Our comrades expect, of course, that we will do all we can so that they can move forward. They expect that weapons and materials will be delivered in time . . . materials to heal the wounds they receive in battle. To the weighty wartime tasks must be added difficult, tireless, and incessant labor. Peasants who deliver grain understand that their own brothers will eat this bread. Brothers who are defending not only their lives, but also those freedoms and ideals by which the Russian democracy lives. . . . In the factories, at the machines and work benches where the army of labor toils, let them understand that their brothers in the trenches depend on them. Let them know that, for each delay in work, each wasted drop of sweat at their benches, each unproductive moment, a drop of blood is lost at the front. Let all the citizens who are still celebrating the revolution's victory here in the rear know that they must stop celebrating and do their sacred duty to the end.

And as for those who, in two and a half years of war, have only learned to pursue their own selfish interests, those who profited off the people's common grief, let them know that the revolution's sacred flame will not tolerate them, just as it did tolerate tsarism.

Everyone must do their duty to the end and remain at their posts: factory owners, who must realize that they have profited enough from two and a half years of war; the engineers, who still have not come to a complete accord with workers and are not reconciled to the new constitutional environment in the factories; and workers who would want more than the country can give at the moment. Comrade workers: you, who remain in the rear, must understand that your brothers at the front are marching under red banners with the sacred slogan: "Long Live the Revolution!" Anyone in the rear who does not support them will not join in the sacred rapture at death, because he has renounced the sacred word. We who have been fulfilling our duty since the revolution's first days must let our comrades at the front know that we will fulfill it to the end.

Voitinskii: Comrades, in the name of the SD-Menshevik fraction and the SR fraction, I propose a resolution that the All-Russian Congress of Soviets should send a greeting to our comrades and brothers at the front. In this greeting, we must express all those feelings that the news from the front has elicited in us. We must say to our brother soldiers and officers at the front that while they are doing their revolutionary duty in the field of combat, all other citizens—workers, soldiers, and peasants—will do their duty in the rear. We must say that we here will be defending our comrades at the front.

Here, comrades, is the text of the resolution, proposed by the SD-Menshevik faction and the SR faction:

Soldiers and Officers.

Revolutionary Russia's Provisional Government has summoned you to an offensive. You have courageously advanced into battle, organized along democratic principles and tempered by the revolution's flames.

The All-Russian Congress of Soviets of Workers' and Soldiers' Deputies and the Executive Committee of the All-Russian Soviet of Peasants' Deputies send their fraternal greetings to you who are defending the revolution's cause on the fields of combat, who are spilling your blood for freedom and universal peace.

The Russian revolution has summoned all the world's peoples to struggle for a universal peace. Our call has not been taken up by Europe's peoples, and so it is not our fault that the war continues.

Your offensive is demonstrating revolutionary Russia's organization and power. By communicating this to those whom you are battling, and to the neutral and Allied countries, you will bring the war's end nearer. All our thoughts are with you, sons of the revolutionary army.

At this decisive hour, the All-Russian Congress of Soviets of Workers' and Soldiers' Deputies and the Executive Committee of the All-Russian Soviet of Peasants' Deputies calls on the country to exert all its efforts to aid the army. Peasants, give the army bread. Workers, let the army never worry about a shortage of ammunition. Soldiers and officers in the rear, march your companies and whole regiments to the front at the first summons. Citizens, understand all your duties. In these days, no one can refuse to fulfill their duty to the revolution.

The Soviets of Workers', Soldiers', and Peasants' Deputies will guard Russia's freedom. Soldiers and officers! Let there be no doubt in your hearts. You are fighting for Russia's freedom and honor. You are fighting to bring universal peace.

We greet you warmly, brothers. Long live the revolution! Long live the revolutionary army.

Martov: Comrades, three members of the Provisional Government have spoken here about a turning point that has been reached in the Russian revolution's history. We agree with them completely, but we part ways profoundly over this turning point's political significance. The tone in which the ministers spoke here, the tone of Kerensky's order for the offensive—it all reminds us of other days. It sounds like words said at the war's beginning. In reality, the state of things is that the war could destroy all that the Russian revolution has accomplished since the February days. Alas, that would not be difficult, given events that have already passed, the announcements and appeals that have accompanied them, and the nonrevolutionary way that the people are being roused for war.

In his announcement, War Minister Kerensky used the same rhetorical devises used in appeals from the Supreme Command in late July and August 1914, when they had to rouse the people for the war that was then beginning. He incites hatred of the enemy and would even go so far as to prosecute soldiers for fraternization and prosecute those who propose peace, a separate peace. Such incitement was necessary if Kerensky was going to explain to soldiers why now—exactly now—we need to go on the offensive.

After today's speeches—after listening to our speeches—it is impossible to say that the offensive is a purely strategic issue. The very comrade ministers who spoke here approached the issue from a political angle. They sought to explain to us the political meanings and the political results that this general offensive could and must have. And it is exactly from that angle that all the internal manifestations that have accompanied this offensive become comprehensible. The intent, perhaps, is to show that revolutionary Russia now will take an active part in this old and ongoing war, a part that formally had not ended, but that in fact had almost disappeared under the force of revolutionary events.

Here we have the right and are obliged to move from a political critique to an examination of the strategic issues. . . . The Russian revolutionary Provisional Government, having ordered an offensive, must clarify this war's aims. Above all, the Russian government must answer the question that is foremost for the revolutionary democracy: Will the Allies agree to renounce annexationist war aims? Until this happens, let us say here that not one drop of Russian soldiers' blood will be spilled for annexationist aims. (*Applause from the left section of the assembly.*)

The truth is contrary to this. . . . (*A voice:* "You cannot say that!") The truth, contrary to this—the bitter and insulting truth—is that until the war's aims are revised, every drop of blood spilled and mourned over is spilled for shameful aims. . . . (*Applause from part of the assembly. Commotion. Voices shout,* "Nonsense!") We must state what appears true to us. . . . (*Commotion.*) We are expressing our opinions here, not insulting the opinions of others . . . (*A voice:* "That is simply a lie.")

Chairman: I ask you not to make comments from the floor.

Martov: I am explaining that, from precisely the viewpoint that we have had the honor of serving and continue to serve—the perspective of revolutionary Socialism—so far Russia has agreed to secret treaties and has not been forced to revise them in spirit. So far, objectively, independent of the wishes of our army or other armies that are battling without knowing what the results will be. . . . (*A voice:* "We know what will come from these battles.")

Those in battle may think that they know, but history is stronger than individual people, stronger than entire nations. Comrade Skobelev tells us with confidence—and of course, with sincere faith—that we will no longer throw new sacrifices onto the bonfire of burning militarism. But I see other people—people who are not as close as Comrade Skolelev—I see people who are the face of world imperialism, who chuckle listening to this speech, and who know that freedom loving nations already have thrown their own children into this fire, into the flames with their own hands based upon such words. (*Applause and commotion.*)

Comrade Chernov guarantees us that no one will think the Russian democracy's offensive has aggressive aims. But isn't that contrary to its slogans and appeals? Moreover, we are told, the new sacrifices will not be exploited by world imperialism. If Comrade Chernov and other government members would carefully investigate this and resolutely fight for that position, then of course they would enjoy our support. But this does not free us from our responsibility, here and now, to speak facts. And the fact is that this offensive began before we have received any adequate, objective guarantee that the Russian revolution has not taken up arms for a new campaign in an old war that still has not ended, the war led by Lloyd-George and the other imperialists.[21]

Comrade Tsereteli expressed with equally profound confidence that the offensive is a new political stage in the revolution. As he puts it, this offensive should be welcomed by the opposition—by the revolutionary internationalist minority in the Allied and belligerent countries. The odd thing is, at the same time that we still do not know what this opposition has said or will say, we *do* know what the chauvinist majority in the Allied countries have demanded and will demand of this offensive. It is strange that this offensive is presented as if it were a confirmed fact that it had sympathetic supporters of two hostile camps, the imperialists and the anti-imperialists in the Allied countries. But it appears that in those countries, as here, some think that an offensive under current conditions is a gift to German imperialism.

Of course, Comrade Tsereteli's position is based on the idea that the German imperialists now can no longer tell the German proletariat what they have been repeating for two and a half years—that they are being strangled by the iron ring of advancing armies, and if the German people do not rally round the German government, they can expect ruin, devastation, and dismemberment. But when, after several days, we learn that the Allies have supported the Russian offensive with their own offensive on the Western front, then this period, this pause, will come to an end. And then the forces of German imperialism will have favorable conditions to stupefy Germany's masses as they have in the past.

Until now, the Russian revolution has not had the force or the will to instruct the coalition government on its desire for war aims that do not contradict its ideals. . . . The offensive has gone forward with absolutely no guarantee that the Russian people's interests won't be sacrificed for the Allied imperialists.

And so we are compelled to say that we have no confidence in this political action. And so we must bow before the victims who have joined our people's army, who are forced to stand at the border, the victims who are carrying out this offensive. We cannot join in decadent revelry at the rapture of death that was just spoken of moments ago. Socialism cannot comprehend these ruthless deaths and will never capitulate to this rapture. We will hold ourselves responsible for what has been done here. We demand an accounting when we see this latest overthrow of the Russian revolution's policy. And so now we reject any greetings to the people and the army, and we reject the new slogans. Now we repeat our key slogan: "Down with the war, and long live the International." (*Applause and noise.*)

DOCUMENT 7.8
A LIBERAL EDITORIAL SUPPORTING THE OFFENSIVE[22]

The following document is a 20 June 1917 editorial in the Kadet newspaper, Speech (Rech). *The essay reflects the liberals' initial hopes for a military breakthrough and their hostility toward Bolshevik antiwar agitation. Russian artillery began shelling enemy positions on 16 June, but Russian soldiers did not leave their trenches to storm the enemy lines until 18 June (the same day as the demonstrations in Petrograd). The Russian Army took enormous casualties, and within days the offensive began to falter, in part because soldiers in many units refused to advance.*

Petrograd, 20 June.
18 June undoubtedly will play an important role in the history of the great Russian revolution. Some awaited that day's demonstration with fear and anxiety, some with great bitterness against this new display of powerlessness and compliance to the Bolsheviks. A third group—German spies and those whose methods serve the Germans' interests—firmly hoped that [the demonstration] would strike a blow and transform anxiety into open clashes that would give a strong impulse to counterrevolution.

Instead, on the evening of 18 June a full-scale demonstration went on without much enthusiasm. It was dull and perfunctory, like all official demonstrations were under the old regime. Here, in the capital, the gentlemen Bolsheviks with their banners rejoiced for German imperialism and wished for Germany's victory; there, at the front, our courageous army launched a decisive offensive, and our sons and brothers sacrificed their lives for the motherland's honor and future.

In the last week everyone was astonished by the news that Minister Kerensky had gone to Kazan. In reality, he had gone to the front to be with the active army while the great event took place—the event nervously awaited by everyone in whom the spark of patriotism glows, everyone for whom the word "motherland" is never said in vain.

If 18 June had been chosen deliberately as the day to launch the decisive offensive . . . or if this was a happy coincidence, in either case, the day has extraordinary significance. The Bolsheviks bitterly tried to fan the flames of rebellion. They called for a civil war that would cut the head off the revolutionary army's great new advance, which has been justly awarded with red banners.

To those who did not see yesterday's events in Petrograd, it is difficult to relay the happy excitement that dominated the mood on the streets all day.[23] For a week there had been an irresistible impression that we were flying toward disaster, that we would be carried off by a spontaneous course of events like the old regime had been, that we were aware of an approaching danger, but no matter what we said or did, we were powerless to oppose it and could only wait humbly for the blows of fate.

But good news about the decisive and successful offensive gave us hope. Hope that we will restore moral discipline. Hope that the motherland's interests and fate will rise above our class-based disagreements and our self-centeredness. Hope that thanks to these principles, the revolution's great achievements will be saved.

It is difficult, of course, to doubt that German agents are now going to redouble their energetic work. The gentlemen Bolsheviks will be no less energetic in aiding them by opposing our successfully begun shining offensive. There already were indications of this during yesterday's demonstrations. The struggle against these treasonous efforts will not be simple, and will demand great energy. But for precisely this reason, there can be no doubt that this coincidence—that displays of broad silk banners [supporting the government] came on the same day as the army's self-sacrifice—is as heavy a blow for our internal enemy, the Bolsheviks, as it is for the foreign enemy.

All Russia's patriots bow low and send a warm greeting to their glorious army, and they join the army in the happiest hope for the motherland's bright future.

DOCUMENT 7.9
P. DNEVNITSKII, "LONG LIVE THE OFFENSIVE"[24]

The following document is an essay by Menshevik Feodor Tsederbaum, who used the pen name P. Dnevnitskii. It appeared in the defensist newspaper Unity (Edinstvo) *on 20 June 1917.*

Long Live the Offensive!

Today the great Russian revolution won two victories. The first, by General Brusilov's advancing army, was over imperial Austro-Hungarian forces on the South-Western Front. The enemy lines were breached in several places. Three lines of enemy trenches were captured. Many soldiers and officers were taken prisoner, and war materials also were taken. The other victory was in the rear, in Petrograd, over those who would spread disagreement and discord. Over those who day after day subvert faith in the government. Over those who, in the name of separate groups or circles, have fully forgotten their duty to the revolutionary motherland. Over those who, in their behavior and their slogans, have pulled many people who otherwise would still want to serve the revolution away from it.

On Sunday [18 June] it was dark in Petrograd's streets. Rows of demonstrators went by with grey faces that reflected the mood. Of course the slogans under which a significant part of the crowd marched—all those exclamations of the "peace to the world" sort, those weary dead-end slogans—showed a lack of faith in our strength, in our ability to simply defend ourselves against the enemy's armed might. It was insulting and shameful to see young and healthy soldiers demonstrating against the government that has called them to arms in the revolution's defense.

But when notice came of the first breath of military victory, this heavy mood was blown away like a puff of smoke. Petrograd's revolutionary citizens, the whole crowd on the streets, all abandoned their business without previous preparations, without being summoned by anyone from any side. They did this out of one common feeling, one call that united them in groups and then formed a single great, inspiring demonstration. There was no more worrying, no more anxiety. There was common trust and happiness.

And where were these people headed, these citizens conscious of their ties to the motherland? They were headed first and foremost to the Provisional Government, to express their faith in it, to support this united government, this national center. They were headed to the Soviet Congress, that institution of revolutionary democracy on which the revolutionary government leans. They were headed to the Allied consulates, to demonstrate the feelings that tie the Russian people to those in the European democracies who are struggling along with them. And finally, they were headed to us, having justly recognized our editor [Plekhanov] and our group [*Edinstvo*] as those who will defend the revolution's common interests to the end.

Victory at the front gave a first push toward a change in the mood at the rear. We firmly believe this mood will endure, that this demonstration and the feelings it expressed will be followed by practical steps. We believe the rear is enthused for action and will support the front with all its strength. We believe that, in turn, enthusiasm in the rear will spread to the front and give it new energy for the decisive and glorious struggle.

There were moments in the great French Revolution's history similar to what we are now experiencing. France was worn out internally and exposed to invasion by the same reactionary Prussian and Austrian forces that threaten us now. . . . Yet revolutionary France found in itself the strength and courage to move forward, to develop its revolution, and to defend its freedom. Throwing himself into battle at Valmy, a revolutionary general called out, "Long Live the Revolution—Forward!" This filled all hearts with enthusiasm, which spread to all France and the world.[25]

Long live the revolutionary nation! Long live the people's unified force!—Here is a slogan for our own great days. Unity is a necessity. Russia wants to defend the revolution's achievements. Unity is necessary for the offensive to succeed on all fronts, so it can soon bring us the peace we want. And so, long live the revolutionary nation and government! Long live the victorious offensive of the Russian revolution's soldiers!

—P. Dnevnitskii

DOCUMENT 7.10
V. R. IVANOV-RAZUMNIK, "HE WAS INSOLENT TO ME"[26]

The following document is by Razumnik Vasilevich Ivanov (who used the pen name V. R. Ivanov-Razumnik), an editor at the Petrograd Socialist Revolutionary (SR) newspaper The People's Cause (Delo naroda). *Though Ivanov-Razumnik was close to the SRs, he never officially joined the party. In this 24 June 1917 essay, he lampoons a senior Menshevik defensist, Aleksandr Potresov, whom he calls a "social patriot"—a derisive term internationalists applied to socialists who had allegedly abandoned "democracy" in favor of "patriotism." The essay's title, "He was insolent to me," is a line from Feodor Dostoevsky's novel,* The Idiot. *At the end of the essay, Ivanov-Razumnik quotes the epigram to Alexander Pushkin's novella,* The Queen of Spades.

"He Was Insolent to Me"
Among the social-patriots who are exuberantly happy at the new torrents of the toiling people's blood, special note should be made of A. Potresov's comments in the so-called socialist newspaper, *The Day* [*Den*]. He is exuberantly happy that it is not his blood being spilled. For

this, his own SDs rebuked him in *The Workers' Newspaper* [*Rabochaia gazeta*]. Now he responds that *The Workers' Newspaper* has insulted him: "They are angry because I am happy the offensive has begun. They call my happiness 'militaristic delight,' the bubbling over of a "barbarian.' They see my hopes for the offensive as anti-Marxist."

It seems a "socialist" is shamefully "gladdened" by the bloody war. Could it be that *The Workers' Newspaper* is trying to force our social-patriot into the mold of the "revolutionary defensists," who have gone mad from socialism? (Incidentally, for three years—yes, it is true!—for three years and three or four months, they ardently maintained "defensism" *tout court*—when it meant defending an "autocratic" government and not a "revolutionary" government.)[27]

You cannot force A. Potresov into this mold. Yet despite all Potresov's splendor, his own party colleagues question him. They insolently accuse him. But they do not have authority to make charges "that are founded," he complains, "only on the fact that they very badly need a diversion. On the fact that they must create an ugly monster to distract the readers' attention and hide their own critical condition. On the fact that they are doomed to mumble 'neither yes nor no.' And they would ridicule me!"

How charming! As a hero in one of Dostoevsky's novels said (more literately), "He was insolent to me!" Dostoevsky, by the way, also was a patriot, although not a socialist. It also is charming how Potresov has been shown support by his own sort at *Unity* [*Edinstvo*]. They console him against those who "would ridicule him." They say that the "left Interna-tionalists have abandoned Potresov."

Thus in the troubled days
They did their
Business.

DOCUMENT 7.11
SIBERIAN RAILROAD WORKERS WELCOME
THE OFFENSIVE[28]

The following document is a declaration by a congress of railroad workers in Altai, in southwestern Siberia, published in the Popular-Socialists' Petrograd newspaper, The People's Word (Narodnoe slovo), *on 1 July 1917. The Popular-Socialists solidly supported the June Offensive, and their newspaper printed several letters and declarations from workers and soldiers demonstrating support for the government's military policy.*

Greetings for the Offensive.
The Altai railroad workers delegates' congress, having received the happy news that free Russia's revolutionary army has begun the final offensive,

sends its greetings to those who are consciously defending our freedoms and who are fighting to bring world peace and the triumph of the toiling democracy's ideals. Know that we in the distant rear will devote all of our strength to achieving victory.

The Vladikavkaz Railroad Workers' Union delegates' congress will send this telegram to the Supreme High Command and to its chief, Comrade Kerensky. We express our profound disapproval of all those who are hiding out in the rear to carry out disorganization. In addition, the railroad workers declare outright that they are at the Provisional Government's disposal and ready at the first call to march to the trenches to replace those soldier-deserters who have run away from their duty to the motherland. In addition, we declare that revolutionary Russia's victory is necessary, not to enslave other nations, but to bring peace as soon as possible without annexations or indemnities on the basis of national self-determination.

DOCUMENT 7.12
A REPORT ON SOLDIERS' REFUSAL TO PARTICIPATE IN THE MILITARY OFFENSIVE[29]

As the following document reveals, some military units at the front simply refused to follow orders to advance, particularly once the Russian offensive began to bog down. The document is a report sent on 8 July 1917 from S. L. Markov, an officer on the Western Front Command Staff in Minsk, to General A. S. Lukomskii at the Supreme High Command Staff. Markov describes an incident in which commanders directed artillery fire at their own soldiers, who had refused to follow orders to advance.

The 28th Division has not departed to take its position at the front, having explained that it refuses to sustain losses in the attack. It promises to take its position tonight.

The 1st Siberian Corps has categorically refused to advance, as has the entire 62nd Siberian Regiment, more than half of the 63rd Regiment, and almost 300 men in the 3rd Regiment. In the 175th Division's 689th Regiment, the mood improved after the instigators were arrested.

In the 11th Siberian Division's 42nd Regiment, 246 riflemen refused to advance and have been arrested and dispatched.

It was decided to disband and reform the 169th Division's 673rd and 675th Regiments in light of a series of incidents and their complete refusal not only to advance, but to execute orders in general. This was done with direct participation of the front commissar, Captain Kalinin. When these measures did not help, artillery opened fire on the resistant regiments. Losses were insignificant. On the night of 7–8 July the disarmed regiment was directed to the railroad station, so that it could be transferred to the Third and Second Armies. Neither of the units has moved.

—Markov

DOCUMENT 7.13
BOLSHEVIK LEADERS CALL FOR PEACEFUL
DEMONSTRATIONS IN PETROGRAD[30]

The following document was a drafted in the early hours of 4 July by the Bolshevik Party's leaders, who sought to rein in rank and file worker and soldier activists determined to march on the city center to demonstrate—with rifles in hand—for "All Power to the Soviets."

Comrade Petrograd Workers and Soldiers!

Since the counterrevolutionary bourgeoisie clearly has come out against the revolution, let the All-Russian Soviet of Workers', Soldiers', and Peasants' Deputies take power into its own hands. Such is the will of Petrograd's revolutionary population, which has the right to voice its will through a peaceful and organized demonstration at today's session of All-Russian Soviet of Workers', Soldiers', and Peasants' Deputies' Executive Committee.

Long live the will of the revolutionary workers and revolutionary soldiers!

Long live Soviet power!

The coalition government has fallen into ruin. It has come undone because its members cannot fulfill those tasks for which it was created. Grand and difficult tasks lay before the revolution. We need a new government that—in unity with the revolutionary proletariat, the revolutionary army, and the revolutionary peasantry—will decisively strengthen and expand upon the people's achievements. Only the Soviets of Workers', Soldiers', and Peasants' Deputies can be such a government.

Yesterday Petrograd's revolutionary garrison and workers proclaimed this slogan: All Power to the Soviets. We are asking that this movement, which burst out of the barracks and the factories, be transformed into a peaceful, organized demonstration that reflects the will of all Petrograd's workers, soldiers, and peasants.

The Central Committee of the Russian Social Democratic Labor Party
The RSDLP Petersburg Committee
The RSDLP Interdistrict Committee
The RSDLP Central Committee Military Organization
The Soviet of Workers' and Soldiers' Deputies Workers' Section
Commission

DOCUMENT 7.14
LENIN, "ALL POWER TO THE SOVIETS!"[31]

In the following document, an essay published in the Petrograd newspaper, Truth
(Pravda), *on 4 July 1917 (the second day of the armed demonstrations), Lenin
laid out his argument for the transfer of power to the soviets. Lenin was not in
Petrograd when armed demonstrations erupted on 3 July; he returned to the
city the next day. Unlike grassroots activists, Lenin considered an armed uprising premature on 4 July. Still, he had declared that power must be transferred
to the soviets—the slogan being championed by the armed demonstrators on
Petrograd's streets. In the essay Lenin uses the term "revolutionary democrats"
interchangeably with "bourgeois liberals" to describe the Kadets.*

"Chase nature out the door, and she will fly back in through the window."
It seems that the right wing SRs and Mensheviks require repeated lessons
to "get" this simple truth. They joined with the "revolutionary democrats"
and fell into the position of revolutionary democrats. And now they
find themselves coming to the conclusions that are compulsory for
revolutionary democrats.

Democracy is the rule of the majority. As long as the will of the
majority remained unclear and could be depicted as unclear, a counterrevolutionary government of the *burzhui*s could plausibly be presented to
the people as "democratic." But the people's will could not be delayed
for long. During the several months since 27 February, the will of the
majority of the workers and peasants, the country's overwhelming
majority, has become clear in more than a general sense. Their will has
found its expression in mass organizations—the Soviets of Workers',
Soldiers', and Peasants' Deputies.

So, is it possible to oppose the transfer of all state power to the soviets?
To do so signifies nothing other than a renunciation of democracy! It
signifies nothing but the imposition on the people of a government that
certainly cannot come into being or last following *democratic* means, i.e.,
true freedom and authentic universal elections.

As strange as it seems at first sight, the SRs and Mensheviks in fact
have *forgotten* this simple, self-evident, palpable truth. Their position is so
false, and they are so confused and bewildered, that they are no position
"to recall" this lost truth. After elections in Petrograd and Moscow, after
convocation of the All-Russia Peasant Congress, after convocation of the
Soviet Congress, the social classes and political parties all across Russia
have shown what they stand for so clearly and so specifically that it cannot
be claimed that the people have gone mad or have fallen into confusion.

To tolerate Kadet ministers, or a Kadet government, or Kadet policies
means challenging the democracy and democratic principles. This has
been the source of political crises since 27 February. This is the source of

our governmental system's shakiness and vacillation. At each step, daily and even hourly, appeals are made to the revolutionary people and to their democratic spirit in the name of authoritative government institutions and congresses. At the same time, the government's general policies, especially its foreign policy and its economic policy, represent its retreat from the revolutionary spirit and its violation of democratic principles. This sort of thing will not do.

The tottering from one position to another that is happening is inevitable. And propping it all up is a policy that is not very clever. By fits and starts, the whole matter will come to this: the transfer of power to the soviets, which our party proclaimed long ago, will be realized.

DOCUMENT 7.15
THE SOVIET CENTRAL EXECUTIVE COMMITTEES
ON DEMONSTRATIONS IN PETROGRAD[32]

On the night of 3–4 July 1917, an emergency joint session of the All-Russian Central Executive Committee of Soviets and the All-Russian Executive Committee of Peasants' Soviets gathered to discuss two issues: the government crisis caused by the Kadet ministers' resignation in a dispute over Ukrainian and Finnish autonomy; and how to respond to that night's violent demonstrations on Petrograd's streets. Debate on the second issue led to the drafting of the following document, a joint appeal printed on 4 July in The News of the Petrograd Soviet (Izvestiia Petrogradskogo Soveta).

To All Military Units, Soldiers, and Workers.
Comrade soldiers and workers! Unknown people are calling on you to go out into the streets armed, contrary to the clearly expressed will of *all* the socialist parties, without exception. You are being asked to protest against the disbanding of regiments that have discredited themselves at the front and criminally violated their duty to the revolution.

We, the authorized representatives of all Russia's revolutionary democracy, inform you that:

The disbanding of regiments at the front was carried out at the insistence of the army and the front organizations, in keeping with orders from our war minister, comrade A. F. Kerensky, whom we chose. Protesting in the streets to defend disbanded regiments is the same as protesting against our brothers who are shedding their blood at the front. We remind the comrade soldiers: no military unit has the right to leave its barracks with weapons without a directive from the military's Commander in Chief, who is cooperating fully with us. During these troubled times for Russia, we will denounce anyone who violates this directive as a traitor and an enemy of the revolution.

We will use all means at our disposal to implement this resolution.

The Bureau of the All-Russian Central Executive Committee
of Soviets of Workers' and Soldiers' Deputies
The Bureau of the All-Russian Executive Committee
of Peasants' Soviets

DOCUMENT 7.16
TWO RESOLUTIONS ON THE PETROGRAD
DEMONSTRATIONS[33]

The following document set presents resolutions passed at two of the dozens of meetings held in Petrograd's factories and military barracks on 4 July 1917 to discuss the previous night's demonstrations. The first is a resolution from workers at the huge gunpowder plant on the Shlissel'burg Highway, where anarchists had considerable influence. It was sent to the Bolshevik Party's Central Committee, and a note at the end of the document points out that a local Bolshevik verified its authenticity, but that does not mean that the gunpowder workers were all pro-Bolshevik. The second document is a resolution passed by a meeting of First Reserve Infantry Regimental Committee, in direct response to soviet leaders' attempts to quell further armed demonstrations.

We 5,000 male and female workers and soldiers at the Shlissel'burg gunpowder plant, having discussed the 3 July events in Petrograd, greet and support the comrade Petrograd soldiers and workers who have protested in the struggle against counterrevolution. We declare:
Enough vacillation! In the name of freedom, in the name of peace, in the name of the world proletarian revolution, the All-Russian Executive Committee of Soviets of Workers', Soldiers', and Peasants' Deputies must take power in its own hands! Executive power must be in the hands of those who truly express the people's will. There is no other way out of this blind alley. The policy of collaboration with the bourgeoisie has clearly revealed itself to be entirely unsound and ruinous for the cause of freedom.

Meeting Chairman, N. Chekalov
Verified by the RSDLP Committee Secretary, the
Bolshevik Pushkevich

[First Reserve Infantry Regimental Committee]
. . . The meeting heard a special report by delegates from the Executive Committee of the All-Russian Congress of Peasants' Deputies. Based on discussion of that report, and based on a telephone message from the

joint committee of the All-Russian Soviet of Workers' and Soldiers' Deputies and the Peasant Congress on ending the Petrograd demonstrations, the regimental committee approved the following resolution by a majority of 26 votes:

Having heard a report by delegates from the Executive Committee of the All-Russian Soviet of Peasants' Deputies, the regimental committee finds that the present government crisis can be liquidated only by the immediate transfer of all power to the All-Russian Soviet of Workers', Soldiers', and Peasants' Soviets—which will reorganize the government so that it more fully expresses the revolutionary people's interests. The regimental committee exonerates itself from any responsibility for armed excesses that might take place if this transfer of power to the All-Russian Soviet of Soldiers', Workers' and Peasants' Deputies is delayed by the old government's supporters. We take note of the joint Bureau of the All-Russian Soviets' resolution on abstaining from any demonstrations right now. . . .

On the armed demonstrations: in view of the dominant mood among the majority of soldiers in the regiment, the regimental committee recognizes the necessity of avoiding excess bloodshed. We will permit armed demonstrations by separate companies or groups of soldiers from the regiment. These may participate in peaceful and organized demonstrations, with their weapons, and also with a full complement of choral music. We delegate Corporal Sakharov and comrade Osipov to contact the Executive Committee of the All-Russian Soviet of Soldiers', Workers', and Peasants Deputies. The regiment's soldiers are not to demonstrate until receiving news from these two delegates.

Committee Chairman, Torskii
Secretary, T. Zlatkinskii

DOCUMENT 7.17
THE PETROGRAD SR COMMITTEE, "TO ALL PETROGRAD SOLDIERS AND WORKERS!"[34]

On 4 July 1917, the Socialist Revolutionary's Petrograd Committee issued this declaration in response to that day's armed demonstrations. It appeared in The People's Cause (Delo naroda) *on 5 July 1917.*

To All Petrograd Soldiers and Workers!
At this terrible moment of danger for all the revolution's achievements, the [SR] Party calls on you to gather beneath its banners. The Petrograd Committee has resolved that all party members must use all means to show support for the Central Executive Committee of the Soviets of Workers' and Soldiers', and Peasants' Deputies.

Enough demonstrations! Enough wild unrest! Enough senseless parading on the streets! Enough spilling of fraternal blood!

The revolution needs the disciplined and solid unity of all workers and soldiers in Petrograd. All party members—in the factories, at company and battalion meetings, at street meetings, and in separate groups—are obliged to restrain the masses from thoughtless outbursts that could otherwise lead to criminal bloodshed. All district committees must establish contact with the factories and military units and keep uninterrupted watch. For information and directions, all party members are to go the district committees. All soldier and sailor Socialist Revolutionaries are to inform the district committees about any orders to leave the barracks and are to demand documents from whomever issues those orders. The districts are informing the Petrograd Committee about events. All available agitators and all comrade workers and soldiers who can speak at meetings must put themselves at the committee's disposal. The party demands that all its members fully and completely submit to revolutionary discipline.

This declaration should be explained to workers and soldiers at all party and general assemblies and meetings.

The Party of Socialist Revolutionaries' Petrograd Committee
4 July 1917

DOCUMENT 7.18
THE BOLSHEVIKS ON THE PETROGRAD
DEMONSTRATIONS[35]

On 4 July 1917 the Petrograd demonstration by militant workers, garrison soldiers, and sailors from the Kronstadt naval base spun out of control. As many as 400 people were killed in numerous shooting incidents, and crowds looted shops in the city center. That night, rumors spread that the government had dispatched loyal troops from the front to put down the uprising. Several military units in Petrograd renounced the demonstrations after government envoys presented them with "evidence" that Lenin was a German spy. By late on 5 July the government had regained control over the situation. Lenin went into hiding in Finland, and the government arrested Trotsky and several other Bolshevik leaders.

The following document, a resolution drafted in the late hours of 4 July and published in the Bolshevik newspaper, Truth (Pravda), *on 5 July, was the Bolsheviks' first attempt to "spin" the July demonstrations and blame the shootings on "counterrevolutionaries."*

On the Demonstration.

Comrades! On Monday [3 July] you went into the streets. On Tuesday [4 July] you decided to continue the demonstrations. We summoned you to a peaceful demonstration yesterday. Its aim was to show the entire toiling and exploited mass the force of our slogans, their universality, their significance, and their necessity for the liberation of peoples from war, from hunger, from ruin.

The demonstration's aims were achieved. The slogans of the vanguard of the working class and army were proclaimed convincingly and with dignity. Incidental shootings by counterrevolutionaries could not detract from the demonstration's general character.

Comrades! Our aims in this political crisis have been achieved. We therefore have decided to end the demonstration. Let one and all bring a peaceful, organized end to the strikes and demonstrations.

We are waiting for the crisis to develop further. We will continue to prepare our forces. Life is with us, and the course of events is demonstrating the correctness of our slogans.

The RSDLP Central Committee
The RSDLP Petrograd Committee
The RSDLP Interdistrict Committee
The RSDLP Central Committee Military Organization
The Soviet of Workers' and Soldiers' Deputies'
Workers' Section Commission

DOCUMENT 7.19
G. PLEKHANOV, "HOW CAN THIS BE?"[36]

On 5 July 1917 several Petrograd newspapers carried stories charging that Lenin was a German spy and that the Bolsheviks were German tools. Georgii Plekhanov's newspaper, Unity (Edinstvo), *had frequently said that Bolshevik tactics served the German's interests. In this 5 July 1917 editorial, though, Plekhanov makes no such charge. Instead, in an essay probably written on the night of 4 July, Plekhanov points out that Bolsheviks remained a minority party despite their name—which in Russian means "those in the majority."*

How Can This Be?
There is a minority faction in our revolutionary democracy designated "Bolsheviks." This designation is incorrect because, fortunately, few support this minority's tactics. The Bolshevik's followers are Lenin's personal supporters. On principle, it would be more correct to call them the Leninist faction. However, the issue is not what to call them. If they changed their name to something like "violet," they would keep their previous smell. Based upon its odor, the minority about which I am speaking would not be called a violet. Its odor is very different.

Before the [1903] split in the Russian Social Democratic Labor Party— which greatly damaged the Russian revolutionary movement—Lenin's supporters preached persuasively and doggedly for party discipline whenever they were in the majority. Back then, they actually demanded that the minority abide by all decisions taken by our party congresses. They stigmatized the least wavering from the letter (and even from the spirit) of these resolutions as anarchism. But as soon as they became the minority, they immediately underwent a theoretical transformation. The Leninists ceased talking about the majority's will, and Lenin made himself the chief anarchist.

That was the situation earlier, when we all had to live in the revolutionary "underground." But now it is to be recreated for all Russia. Lenin's supporters are a minority in our revolutionary democracy, and the democracy has repudiated their tactics. But that has not kept them from firmly sticking to their tactical devices, including seizing power through an armed demonstration. Up to now their attempts have been unsuccessful.

First, although they have been unsuccessful, their attempt left a mark. The armed demonstrations frightened the population and shook their confidence in the revolutionary government and the revolution. And what is a lack of confidence in the revolution if not a counterrevolutionary mood? Second, who can guarantee us that one of these Leninist-organized armed demonstrations will not somehow succeed? The absolutely legitimate reason that this cannot be guaranteed is that an armed minority can, without much difficulty, dominate the unarmed majority.

It is true that right now, as I write these notes, we still do not know how the disorders in Petrograd will end. (Everyone knows that these are the Leninists' work.) We hope that the Provisional Government will know how to master them. And we ask ourselves: hasn't such unrest taught our revolutionary democracy who the real majority is? This is a most important lesson, and all you have to do to learn it is to look and listen.

The Leninists shout, "All power to the soviets' of workers', soldiers' and agricultural laborers' deputies!" But do they even consider the Petrograd Soviet's will? No, they only care about their own party's decisions. Do they even respect the will of the Central Committee elected by the All-Russian Congress of Soviets of Workers' and Soldiers' Deputies? No, they only respect their own party's central committee, and they only submit its slogans. In their eyes, revolutionary democracy's majority is simply a barrier they must overcome to move toward their goals. So they strive to overcome its decisions by all means.

They give the impression that all they want is to remove the "capitalist ministers" from the Provisional Government. But the "capitalist ministers'" participation in the Provisional Government is in complete agreement with the revolutionary democracy's majority will. This majority is convinced that the Leninists' demands for a dictatorship of the proletariat and the peasantry would be a disaster for our country, since under existing conditions it would lead to anarchy, which would be followed very closely by counterrevolution.

Understand that when Lenin's supporters aim machine guns at the capitalist ministers, their tactics actually are aimed at the revolutionary democracy's majority. No doubt the Leninists will continue these tactics until they manage to pressure our revolutionary democracy into repudiating the idea of a coalition government. The Leninists are not going to retreat. Yes, they are here and they "are not retreating!" They declare this directly. How can this be?

These days, every conscious revolutionary must shudder at the prospect of civil war. Civil war, you must understand, increases the chances of counterrevolution. Therefore it is exceedingly important that the revolutionary democracy's majority does all it can to prevent civil war. This is our duty to the working class and to the entire country.

But, as the French say, when the wine is poured, it must be drunk. When Lenin's supporters begin civil war, the democratic majority has the duty to defend its position and its government. When an armed attack is made on this position and this government, we cannot be content with good council from the society's peaceful elements and good speeches about maintaining public calm. The tool of criticism becomes powerless when those you criticize take up arms.

Damn those who would start a civil war during this difficult year for Russia! And woe to those who answer them only with good words! Those who are under attack will be able to cope if they believe in the rightness of their cause.

—G. Plekhanov

DOCUMENT 7.20
THE STOCK EXCHANGE BULLETIN ON THE JULY DAYS[37]

The following document is an editorial in Petrograd's The Stock Exchange Bulletin (Birzhevyia vedomosti), *written on the night of 4 July 1917 and published the next morning.*

Petrograd, 4 July
We Are in Danger

Events in Petrograd have cast a black shadow over the capital. Confusion, unrest, shootings, and finally, the spilling of blood.

What remains to be asked is: Has the sudden whirlwind of anarcho-bolshevism that swept down blown open the door for counterrevolution? What more is needed to convince the blind that evil, criminal agitators have roused the spirits of those who follow the Bolsheviks, whose policies substitute irresponsible demagogy for consciousness responsibility?

The Executive Committee of the Soviets of Workers', Soldiers', and Peasants' Deputies has issued a resolution that shows awareness of its great responsibilities. This is important precisely because it finally makes the boundary between revolution and counterrevolution very clear. This resolution recognizes the events taking place in Petrograd as equivalent to treason. An armed demonstration loses any political significance and becomes unworthy. In a blow to the revolutionary democracy's back, it attempts to impose an armed mob on the democracy. This inevitably drags the revolutionary democracy into internecine bloodshed.

What is the source of this activity, which is equivalent to treason and is a criminal blow against the revolutionary rear and the heroic revolutionary army as it strains to press forward against our enemy? It comes from the thoughtless masses, the former policemen and gendarmes, the refuse of society, the hidden *pogromshchiki*, who assume the masters' role. But the inspiration, the "ideology," came to these masses from Bolshevism, from *Truth [Pravda]*, from *Soldiers' Truth [Soldatskaia Pravda]*. A Soviet Executive Committee resolution appealing to the soldiers even stated this—it said this directly and clearly.

And where is all this headed? So much is clear, yet so much is hazy. A counterrevolutionary stream flows from this source; it widens and rises. It is dividing the democracy's ranks . . . and threatens to undermine the revolution's foundation. There are organized counterrevolutionary forces everywhere ready to return to the past. Yesterday's events opened up broad possibilities for the hidden reactionaries, who are waiting to seize a favorable moment. Reaction has not come up from the underground yet. Powerless and incapable, it remains where it is hidden, half-dead. But its path was prepared by the anarcho-bolshevist uprising of 3 July, the true substance of which was counterrevolutionary and, it follows, treasonous. . . .

DOCUMENT 7.21
P. OREKHOV, "ON HELPFUL BEARS, WHO THREATEN THE DEMOCRACY NO LESS THAN DO BOURGEOIS WOLVES"[38]

The following document is a poem in the SR Petrograd Military Organization's newspaper, The Revolutionary People (Revoliutsionnyi narod), *published on 5 July 1917. The Petrograd Military Organization was a stronghold of right SRs who viewed the July Days as a betrayal of the revolution. The poem's title refers to stock characters from Russian folk tales. Bear is always clumsy and dull-witted—in the tale of "Masha and the Bear," a little girl tricks Bear into helping her deliver a pie. Wolf is always greedy.*

About Helpful Bears, Who Threaten the Democracy No Less Than Do
Bourgeois Wolves.

Pravda and *Soldatskaia*[39]
Hide their plans in the open.
On gloomy days they
Would hit us with a brotherly cudgel.

In their comfortable offices
There are many sundry delights.
Petrograd has been informed
By the ambiguity of their advice.

No soldier or worker
Committed yesterday's grievous sin.
Last night's gun shots
Were made in the Bolsheviks' workshop.

Manufactured, in every case,
Out of the honeyed "perhaps."
That is why the dark clouds of
Pravda's family has grown.

And will these "chiefs of the people"
Now sit in their office again,
To calm the rising force,
And to grumble and to squeak? . . . No!

No to the demagogues in the bear's den.
We say that too much
Brothers' blood has been spilled!
The democracy will not trust them again!

—P. Orekhov

DOCUMENT 7.22
THE JULY DAYS IN NIZHNI NOVGOROD[40]

*The following document is a local newspaper report on disorders among gar-
risoned soldiers in the provincial city of Nizhni Novgorod on 4–5 July 1917.
Garrison soldiers' opposition to the offensive, and especially to the threat of being
shipped off to the front, had been an important factor in the 3–4 July events in
Petrograd. Events in Nizhni Novgorod suggest just how volatile the situation
had become in provincial garrisons.*

On 4 July at 6:00 in the evening, a directive was read to the garrison
ordering the muster of 62nd Infantry Reserve Regiment soldiers who had

refused to be dispatched to the front. Soldiers then gathered—with red banners, but not with weapons—near the Kremlin Palace. They also sent delegates to the garrison commander and the soviet of workers' and soldiers' deputies with a petition to revoke the directive. The garrison commander explained that the directive would not be revoked. Shouts went up among the evacuated soldiers: "Arrest the garrison commander and the chairman of the Soviet of Soldiers' Deputies! Wipe out the Soviet, defender of the bourgeoisie!" Soon, however, the evacuated soldiers calmed down, and they returned to their barracks in an orderly fashion.

That night cadets from the Alekseev School, together with the 56th Regiment's Training Command, arrived from Moscow and surrounded the barracks and the Pushkin Gardens. After arresting the infantry soldiers, they marched them toward the train station. Several soldiers managed to run away and asked for help at the neighboring barracks of the 183rd and 185th Regiments. Those soldiers then came running, rifles in hand. On the Arzamaski Highway, the cadets fired on the soldiers. The soldiers returned fire, and many of the cadets were wounded. The cadets were captured and disarmed. One unit of soldiers headed to the train station; another headed to the Georgian Barracks, where the cadets were being lodged. There also was shooting at the barracks, but fortunately no casualties. The number of soldiers involved increased. Between them, the cadets had rifles and two machineguns.

On arriving at the train station, the soldiers encountered the 56th Regiment's Training Command and opened fire on them. The Command, having suffered the wounding and killing of several men, ran off. Soldiers captured and arrested many of them . . .

On 5 July in the early morning, soldiers headed to the square near the Kremlin Palace, rifles in hand. The Nizhegorod Training Preparatory Battalion cadets were in the square at the time. There was an air of expectation. For a moment, everyone expected an armed clash. The soldiers were ready. Seeing the inequality of forces, the cadets laid down their weapons. Then the evacuated soldiers, the majority of those in the yard, had a private conference with the soldiers and decided to elect a Provisional Committee to defend the city. This committee was made up of 15 soldiers, most of whom were from the infantry reserves: two SRs, two Bolsheviks, two Mensheviks, and five representatives from the Soviet. . . . The committee seized power and arrested the garrison commander, then began issuing directives on various branches of local and state life. It established control over the telegraph and telephone offices; designated its own representative to the provincial commissar; placed rifles and shells at the disposal of workers, militias, and other private individuals; and resolved to enter into communications with Moscow and Sormovo, etc.[41] The banks and several stores closed. Work was partly suspended in government and public institutions. . . .

Because of the situation in the city, there were several emergency meetings of the Soviet Presidium and the City Provisional Committee, as well as a closed conference of the Provincial Committee. Among other things, it was resolved to issue an appeal asking the public to preserve order and calm and urging them not to go out into the streets unnecessarily.

DOCUMENT 7.23
A PEASANT ASSEMBLY RESOLUTION ON THE JULY DAYS[42]

The following document is a resolution on the July Days passed by a peasant assembly in Sychevka County, Smolensk Province. It appeared on 22 July 1917 in The News of the Petrograd Soviet (Izvestiia Petrogradskogo Soveta).

Ivanovsk Township (Sychevka County, Smolensk Province).
The Peasantry on the 3–5 July Events.
On 8 July a general assembly of peasants in Ivanovsk Township discussed the 3–5 July events in Petrograd and passed the following resolution:
Having discussed all sides of the armed demonstrations in Petrograd that began on 3 July—events that were initiated by individuals calling themselves Social Democrat Bolsheviks against the will of the All-Russian Central Executive Committee of Soviets of Workers' and Soldiers' Deputies, which guards all toiling people's interests—the meeting resolves that:

1. No demonstration can go forward without agreement of the All-Russian Central Executive Committee of Soviets;
2. We demand exposure of those individuals who went into Petrograd's factories and called for an armed uprising. We ask that the press inform all Russia that they called themselves SD-Bolsheviks, who by disorganizing the people and spreading discord and unease among the people helped hidden counterrevolutionaries accomplish their vile crimes, such as provoking shootings. Shootings began after the Bolsheviks, who were not enemies before, electrified and stirred up the mob. The result was a mass of victims from among the toiling people.
3. We consider any demonstration that is not called for by the central soviet leadership to be an intolerable disorganization of the Russian revolution's forces that plays into the hands of dark counterrevolutionary forces.
4. We declare full confidence in the All-Russian Congress of Soviets of Workers', Soldiers', and Peasants' Deputies, as represented by its Executive Committee and the socialist government ministers.

DOCUMENT 7.24
A GEORGIAN NEWSPAPER ON THE JULY DAYS[43]

The following document is from an editorial in the Russian-language Georgian newspaper The Tiflis Newspaper (Tiflisskii listok) *on 15 July 1917. In the weeks following the July Days, most provincial newspapers published commentaries on the armed demonstrations.*

On Current Events.

Recent events developed with dizzying speed. Each story that arrived by telegraph was more frightening than the last. There was a counterrevolutionary uprising in Petrograd organized by the Bolsheviks. (Whether they did so willingly or unwillingly, the result is the same). This shifted our attention from the retreat on the Western Front of entire units, the entire army. It shifted attention from the advancing enemy's movements, numbers, and technical resources.

Even a superficial observer can see the clear and definite relationship between the recent Petrograd events and our units' disorganized retreat. Retreating without a fight, entire military units fell back for dozens of miles. Panicking at the first sign of danger, they deserted all the locales that the army had captured weeks ago at the cost of the blood of free Russia's best sons. Many units abandoned their battle positions intentionally after meetings that discussed whether to "advance or retreat." Such treachery wastes the effort of those combat troops loyal to the revolution and free Russia who were moving forward in a successful offensive.

. . . To avoid being overthrown, [the government] must be ruthlessly firm and unwavering in its efforts. At present, it is still possible to kill that which threatens a future catastrophe. The government must be dictatorial in its actions and remember that "when the woods are cut, chips will fall."[44]

—Slavskii

PART THREE

JULY–OCTOBER 1917

The Leftward Shift in Popular Politics

After the failed uprising in Petrograd on 3–4 July 1917, the Bolshevik Party found itself on the defensive, with many of its top leaders jailed or in hiding and its rank-and-file support significantly eroded. By late August, however, the Bolsheviks and other left socialist parties were poised to take a majority in most of Russia's major urban soviets.

One widely credited reason for the Bolsheviks' political "comeback" in late summer is the party's organizational coherence, which allowed it to roll out effective propaganda. When the Petrograd Soviet condemned the Bolsheviks for fomenting violence during the July Days, Lenin temporarily abandoned the slogan "All Power to the Soviets." Other main points of the Bolsheviks' message, however, remained unchanged. The Bolsheviks argued that the "imperialist war" must be ended immediately and that the only way to do so was for workers and soldiers across Europe to rise up in a socialist revolution. They argued that Russia's workers, soldiers, and peasants must reject all cooperation with the bourgeoisie and that no compromise was possible with the coalition Provisional Government. Moreover, they argued, workers' control over production was the only solution to Russia's growing economic crisis because the bourgeoisie was hostile to the revolution. Bolshevik agitation also demanded immediate land reform, which would turn over all land for use by the peasantry. Finally, the Bolsheviks insisted on holding elections for the Constituent Assembly right away and added that the assembly must establish a purely socialist government.

Although the Bolsheviks' opponents frequently accused them of demagoguery, in a fundamental way their tactics followed a conventional political process. Like other political parties, the Bolsheviks tried to define and clarify their own positions, as well as those of their opponents, to high-light differences in the competition for popular support. Actually, many of the Bolsheviks' central arguments closely resembled the positions taken by the left Socialist Revolutionaries (SRs), the Menshevik-Internationalists, and the anarchists. All the left socialist factions—not just the Bolsheviks— strengthened their popular support and gained ground in elections to the soviets and other popular institutions in August and September. By October, all the country's major soviets had left socialist majorities. Additionally, the left socialists were not alone in making social class a central focus of their political campaigns—"class interests" and "class conflict" were also central features of moderate socialist political rhetoric, as documents in chapter 11 illustrate.

As the left socialist parties gained ground, the moderate socialists saw their support wane, as did the "right bloc" of Kadets and prowar socialists. (The more traditional conservative nationalists, however, experienced a resurgence.) Historians in the Soviet Union usually described the radicalization of the masses as an automatic response to economic conditions and paid relatively little attention to the views of workers themselves. Until the late 1960s, historical accounts published outside the Union of Soviet Socialist Republics (USSR) generally portrayed the shift in the popular political mood as an unsophisticated, emotional response to growing misery. In this view, ordinary people gravitated toward simplistic, demagogic arguments that tapped into their pent up anger and social hatred. This echoed the view of many commentators in 1917, represented in documents in chapters 8 and 9, who drew explicit connections between rising crime, the breakdown of public order, and the ascendency of the Bolsheviks. As chapter 9 illustrates, a tone of looming crisis pervaded public rhetoric in summer and early fall 1917.

Not all historians of 1917 consider political radicalization to have been an automatic process or an indication of ordinary people's political immaturity. Since the late 1960s, most social historians have emphasized ordinary people's "agency"—their role in making their own history—and describe workers', soldiers', and peasants' support for the left socialists as the product of rational political choices about which parties best addressed their interests.[1] More recent cultural and social histories, especially those that examine popular rhetoric (discourses), have again emphasized the emotional context of popular political sympathies. A few of these have stressed ordinary people's limited comprehension of politics and the driving significance of class hatred, which is particularly evident in workers' rhetoric.[2] But the sense of escalating crisis in summer and fall 1917 was not entirely a product of discourse—it was rooted in people's perceptions of the very real and serious problems confronting Russia.[3]

Economic and Social Conditions in Summer 1917

The wartime economic pressures that had helped to cause the February Revolution and shaped social and political tensions in the spring did not abate in the summer and fall. Economic breakdown advanced on all fronts: supplies of coal and fuel oil declined, freight traffic on the railroads was severely disrupted, reduced output in mining and in the supply of cotton and flax added to raw materials shortages for factories, and credit for industry dried up. Successive waves of workers' strikes also hastened industrial decline by further disrupting production. Some factory owners deliberately shut down their plants to thwart workers' demands. Most industrialists who closed their plants, though, genuinely believed that they could not sustain operations given plummeting market demand, shortages of raw materials, and inflated production costs.[4] Between the February Revolution and the start of August, nearly 600 factories had shut down, and production had been cut in half even in defense plants (which the state sought to protect).[5]

Plant closings and declining production meant soaring unemployment, which added to workers' anxiety at a time of dramatically rising living costs. In major cities, food prices increased by nearly 30 percent in May and June, and workers' real wages (their buying power) plummeted. Workers blamed the capitalists, who had resisted further wage increases. Factory committees and trade unions (which by June had almost 2 million members) cited 1916 profit levels as proof that owners were lying about their ability to pay higher wages. Workers insisted on the right to examine factory accounts and demanded greater control over production decisions. They also expected that the Provisional Government's socialist ministers would intervene in their behalf. At the same time, employers, whose mistrust of workers also grew more acute, fought to protect their prerogatives and property rights. The result was that the number of workers engaged in strikes rose from approximately 100,000 in May and June, to 400,000 in July and August, to nearly 1 million in September.[6]

In this context, the moderate Mensheviks' and SRs' calls for labor conciliation, and their appeals that workers put the interests of the revolutionary state before their own class interests seemed increasingly out of touch. In contrast, Bolshevik and other left socialist rhetoric about heightened class conflict and workers' control seemed more and more in tune with workers' sentiments. In the unions, Menshevik and SR leaders were losing influence with the rank and file. In August, for example, the Moscow City Central Bureau of Trade Unions voted to boycott the Moscow State Conference (discussed below), against the objections of the Mensheviks and SRs. Gains made by the left socialist factions in city duma and urban soviet elections were further evidence of the moderate socialists' plummeting support among workers. Moreover, worker sentiment for "Soviet power" grew with the perception that "bourgeois" influence over the coalition government was preventing real solutions to the economic crisis.

The inflated food prices faced by workers were one of many ways that the urban economic crisis was linked to the revolution in the countryside. Government programs to ration bread, sugar, and other foods, and the establishment of maximum grain price limits and a state grain monopoly did not solve the food supply problem. Illegal and expensive "black market" trade expanded, as did crime generally. "Bagmen"—men and women who purchased sacks of food and flour in the villages for black-market sale in the towns and cities—crisscrossed the countryside in search of grain. But foodstuffs often were hard to find in the countryside. As the summer wore on, people in the villages became increasingly worried about supplies of bread and other necessary goods.

Since March, peasants had been pushing to increase their access to farmland, largely by claiming the right to unused privately owned land, especially that of aristocratic landlords. Little evidence, however, indicates that the amount of land sown increased in 1917. Given the economic crisis and lack of consumer goods flowing into the villages, many peasant households in "grain-rich" regions like Ukraine and the Volga River provinces (which already were short on labor because of the military draft) saw little reason to increase their sowing of grain. For many households, it made more sense to hold on to their crops (which the authorities condemned as hoarding) rather than put it to market.[7]

The breakdown of railroad traffic also made it harder to ship grain from region to region. In provinces, like Smolensk, for example, that were "grain-poor" even in the best years, villagers—like the urban population—saw food supplies dwindle as fall approached. The peasant population worried, not only about food supplies, but also about where to obtain wood (for fuel) and other basic necessities. Anxiety over supplies fed into existing resentment against private landowners, especially aristocratic landowners.

Since March, Russia's conservative and liberal newspapers had been carrying reports of violent rural disorders, but from late July, the number of such stories increased dramatically. These reports reflected the general mood of crisis, as illustrated in chapter 9. But there was, in fact, a significant increase in the number of documented peasant encroachments on private property rights, including "unauthorized" use of meadows and pastures, unauthorized timber cutting, and organized seizures of estate land and tools. In many cases, villagers defended their actions as according with the decisions by their elected village or township committees, or pointed to rulings by their township land committee authorizing them to take control of unused land and tools. As noted earlier, local land committees interpreted instructions from Agriculture Minister Chernov as permission to "settle" the land question themselves. In scores of incidents, most dramatically, in Tambov Province, peasants destroyed the homes and barns of their perceived enemies, the aristocratic landowners. When the Provisional Government's regional and provincial officials—the provincial commissars, etc.—tried to intervene to prevent land seizures or punish arsonists, the result often was violent confrontations between peasants and government forces.[8] Historians cite many reasons for this escalation of land seizures and violent unrest, but all agree that it reflected peasant frustration with the Provisional Government and the policies of the moderate socialists.

In summer and fall 1917, frustration with the Provisional Government also became more intense among leaders of ethnic "minority" movements for national autonomy, particularly in Finland and Ukraine.[9] The Ukrainian Rada continued its steps toward creating an autonomous Ukrainian state administration, steps that helped to trigger the July Crisis. Although the Provisional Government's socialist members pledged to uphold the principle of national self-determination, the government also staunchly defended the idea that Russia must remain a single (unitary) state, in which groups like the Ukrainians could at most have cultural autonomy and some limited institutional autonomy. By early October, though, many members of the Rada, including Ukrainian Social Democrats, were openly calling for full sovereignty and separate state status. Although Ukrainian nationalists had relatively little support in Ukraine's cities, where ethnic Ukrainians made up a minority of the population (behind Russians and Jews), or among the region's industrial workers and miners, they were able to pressure the Provisional Government into granting several concessions, such as the formation of Ukrainian "national" units in the army.

Compared to its policy toward Ukraine, the Provisional Government moved quickly to silence demands for independence in Finland. In July, the government disbanded the Finns' socialist-dominated legislative assembly after it declared Finland a sovereign state. But the government's steps served only to unite all the major Finnish political parties behind the cause of independence. Political leaders from many other ethnic and religious minority groups, such as the Cossacks of the Don River valley region and the various Turkic and Muslim political parties, similarly chafed at the Provisional Government's refusal to consider turning Russia into a federation of autonomous states. There were, however, many exceptions. Demands for national autonomy and independence were not a significant factor in politics in Latvia and Georgia, for instance. Moreover, nationality and religious issues were tightly intertwined with other issues, so that general social tensions added to conflicts between ethnic and religious groups. Documents in chapter 8 that deal with an anti-Jewish riot in Smolensk Province in October illustrate how explosive these conflicts could be.

Members of the Kadet Party who staunchly opposed minority demands for autonomy and independence also believed that these demands served the interests of the German enemy and would contribute to Russia's dismemberment. The June military offensive, rather than strengthening Russia's position in the war, had been a wholesale disaster. Entire units had been destroyed, and a sense that the Russian campaign was hopeless further undermined morale and discipline in the army. Liberals and those on the right blamed the collapse of the offensive on the soldiers' committees, the relaxation of discipline, and the influence of the Bolsheviks, who promoted fraternization with the enemy. Deserting soldiers, who fled the front but kept their weapons, became bogeymen for the liberal and conservative press. Newspapers blamed deserters for the offensive's collapse, and for the escalation of crime in the cities and rising violence in the countryside.[10]

Subsequent steps to restore military discipline reinforced soldiers' distrust of their officers, their frustration with the Provisional Government, and their determination that the war must end as quickly as possible.

Increasingly, this brought soldiers (and sailors) into conflict with the Menshevik and SR revolutionary defensists whom they had elected to run their committees in spring and early summer. As was the case with workers, a growing number of men in the military gravitated toward the antiwar arguments of left socialists—the Bolsheviks, left SRs, Menshevik-Internationalists, and Anarchists.

The Resurgence of the Right

After a 7 July 1917 German assault routed three Russian armies in Tarnopol, a city in Galicia, false reports circulated that Russian soldiers had simply abandoned their positions. On 8 July, General Kornilov, then commander in chief of the Southwestern Front, ordered that all deserters be shot. In a 9 July telegram to the Provisional Government, Kornilov threatened to resign unless the death penalty was restored for deserters on all military fronts. On 12 July, the government, at Kerensky's insistence, restored the death penalty for soldiers who deserted or disobeyed orders at the front. Then, on 18 July, Kerensky named Kornilov to replace General Brusilov as supreme commander. "Kornilov," as historian Allan Wildman explained, "was instantaneously transformed into a figure representing the hopes of the resurgent right, overshadowing the Provisional Government, now perceived to be weak and vacillating."[11]

The high point of Kornilov's popularity came at the State Conference held in Moscow on 12–15 August 1917. Despite its title, this conference had no formal, institutional authority. It was attended by some 2,500 delegates from government agencies, military units, soviets, unions and cooperatives, public voluntary organizations, and political parties. Conference attendees represented a broad political spectrum, including right-wing nationalists, but excluding the Bolsheviks, who boycotted the meeting.[12] Kerensky hoped to use the conference to consolidate his position and stave off challenges from the left socialists. In his opening address, Kerensky called for national unity in the face of mounting crises, a theme to which he returned repeatedly during the conference. The star of the conference, though, was General Kornilov, who warned that Russia would disintegrate unless the government stopped all political interference in military affairs and let the military commanders impose strict discipline. Kornilov (and after him, General Aleksei Kaledin) insisted that the country's salvation required iron-willed leadership, not only at the battlefront, but for all Russia, and that the government must put an end to the destabilizing influence of the left socialist parties in the soviets. The subtext was clear to all: Kerensky and the Provisional Government lacked the firmness to save the country, but Kornilov did not. Several conservative newspapers heralded Kornilov's speech as the "the State Conference's most arresting moment."[13]

While Kornilov's speech grabbed the headlines, the centrist Menshevik leaders at the State Conference, led by Nikolai Chkheidze and Irakli Tsereteli, pushed the meeting to create a united democratic front. "The United Democracy," as they called it, was supposed to join all political factions in the common cause of protecting the revolutionary state. The Mensheviks presented the conference with what they called a "Democratic Program," to reorganize the army, shore up state finances, reform local government administration, improve food supply, revitalize trade and industry, plan land reform, and solve the nationalities question. Although the conference's majority approved this program, tensions between Kerensky and Kornilov undercut this largely symbolic display of nonpartisan unanimity. In the weeks that followed, the rivalry between the prime minister and the supreme commander, and not (as the Mensheviks warned) the influence of the Bolsheviks, posed the most immediate threat to civil peace.[14]

The Kornilov Rebellion

When Kerensky appointed him as Russia's supreme commander in July, Kornilov immediately demanded a rollback of revolutionary reforms in the army. After succeeding in restoring the death penalty at the front, he insisted that the death penalty also be established for soldiers in garrisons in the rear. Kornilov repeatedly demanded that officers' disciplinary powers be restored, the soviets abolished, and the socialists' influence on the government brought to an end. When Kerensky failed to grant these demands, Kornilov pressed the issue at the State Conference, where the conservative right greeted him as Russia's savior. As rumors of a military coup spread, Kerensky's proxies, especially Vladimir L'vov and Boris Savinkov, clumsily sought to establish a deal between Kerensky and Kornilov. According to the proposed agreement, Kerensky would declare martial law in Petrograd, and Kornilov would then use the army to crush any Bolshevik resistance in the capital. These negotiations, the subsequent confrontation between Kerensky and Kornilov, and public reactions to the Kornilov rebellion are illustrated in chapter 10.

Discussions between Kerensky and Kornilov broke down because of a combination of bungled communications and mutual mistrust. On 27 August, Kerensky, who was certain that a military plot to overthrow the government was in the works, removed Kornilov from his command. Kornilov responded by denouncing Kerensky and ordered troops to march on Petrograd to overthrow the Provisional Government.[15] On 28 August, the Third Cavalry under General Krymov's command began advancing on the capital. Kerensky countered by ordering that all trains carrying pro-Kornilov troops be stopped, and he directed all military district and garrison commanders to disregard Kornilov's instructions. In reality, however, it was the Petrograd Soviet, and not Kerensky, that successfully organized the capital's defense. The soviet set up a special Committee for People's Struggle against Counterrevolution. This committee, together with the city's district soviets, dispatched armed workers' Red Guards units to defend strategic points in and near the city. In the weeks that followed the Kornilov rebellion, the committee evolved into the Petrograd Soviet Military Revolutionary Committee, the key organization that the Bolsheviks and left SRs would use to take power during the October Revolution.

Ultimately, Kornilov lacked any deep support in the army, even among the officer corps. Few officers were willing to follow his orders, and his attempted *coup d'état* collapsed on 31 August. The Provisional Government arrested Kornilov that same day. Kerensky then hoped to use Kornilov as a foil, to strengthen the legitimacy of his own actions. The government cabinet set up a special commission to investigate the conflict, but the commission actually found Kornilov innocent of fomenting a rebellion. This fueled popular suspicion that the prime minister was implicated in counterrevolutionary plots. In the wake of the Kornilov rebellion, Kerensky was weakened, the Kadets were tainted as alleged accessories, and the Bolsheviks emerged with greater political authority.

The Directory and the Third Coalition Government

On 30 August, during the rebellion, Kerensky held a meeting of his cabinet to discuss removing military commanders and government officials who were supporting Kornilov. Although that cabinet session marked the end of the second coalition government, the coalition actually had started to fall days before: the SR leader Viktor Chernov, for example, had stepped down as agriculture minister on 28 August. On 30 August, Kerensky assumed the post of supreme commander, appointed trusted assistants to key military administrative posts, and laid the groundwork for a temporary five-member "emergency" cabinet, known as the Directory, to run the country until he could organize a new coalition government.[16]

Kerensky's attempt to put together a new coalition faced great political resistance, and not only from the Bolsheviks (who, after all, had long rejected any cooperation with the bourgeois parties). Many Kadets no longer trusted Kerensky, and they spurned any further cooperation with the socialists or the soviets. Many moderate SRs and Mensheviks similarly distrusted Kerensky and believed that the Kadets had been complicit in the Kornilov's counterrevolutionary rebellion. Like the second coalition formed in July, this third coalition took weeks to assemble and was weak from the start. Kerensky won approval for the new government, which was to include members of the "bourgeois parties," from the moderate socialist leaders at a mid-September "Democratic Conference," a meeting of the groups who had supported August's United Democracy platform.

In the days after the Kornilov rebellion, Lenin briefly admitted that the Bolsheviks might be agreeable to creation of an all-socialist coalition Provisional Government, one that excluded all "bourgeois liberals" from the cabinet, with the understanding that the socialist coalition would then turn over power to the soviets. By mid-September, though, Lenin and the Bolsheviks had fully resurrected their demand for "All Power to the Soviets." The Bolshevik press began to call for a "second revolution," to replace the Provisional Government with Soviet power. The Menshevik-Internationalists and left SR faction refrained from talk about a second revolution, but did demand an all-socialist coalition government based on the parties in the soviets. The moderate SRs and Mensheviks expressed outrage at the Bolshevik position, and at the Democratic Conference they rejected both Soviet power and an all-socialist government. Instead, they agreed to create a Pre-Parliament, called the Provisional Council of the Republic, to exercise "democratic control" over Kerensky's coalition government. In return for endorsement of his new coalition government, Kerensky recognized the Pre-Parliament and promised that it would have the right to propose laws and question government ministers.

It took a bit longer for Kerensky to convince members of the Kadet Party to join his new coalition government. The Kadets were deeply divided. Party leaders debated three paths toward the formation of a government in September: creation of an all-bourgeois government led by the Kadets, which they deemed impossible given the country's political mood; formation of an all-socialist government, which the Kadets found intolerable and which the moderate socialists themselves rejected; and a formation of a third coalition government that included Kadets. As Kadet leaders later explained at their party conference in mid-October, they agreed to take the third path as the only means to save Russia.

On 25 September, Kerensky announced formation of an unwieldy new coalition cabinet, called the "Government for the Salvation of the Revolution," made up of 17 members. Most cabinet members were nonparty liberals or socialists, members of minor parties, or second-tier figures in the main political parties.[17] The cabinet was never stable. Moderate socialists' relations with their Kadet coalition partners quickly deteriorated, while Kerensky all but cut himself off from the soviets.

The Call for a Second Soviet Congress and Debate over Its Timing

As the Kadets and the moderate socialists debated whether to join a new coalition government, the Mensheviks and SRs steadily lost their majorities in soviets across Russia. In Petrograd, Moscow, and dozens of other cities, informal left socialist blocs made up of Bolsheviks, left SRs, Menshevik-Internationalists, and Anarchists won majorities in soviet elections. The left socialists' ascendance drove a wedge between local soviets and the Russia-wide soviet leadership (the All-Russian Central Executive Committee of Soviets), in which the moderate Mensheviks and SRs still held a majority. As chapter 12 documents, among the central issues over which the moderate and left socialists clashed was whether a new Russia-wide soviet congress should meet before the gathering of the Constituent Assembly, and whether a purely socialist "Soviet" government should replace the socialist-liberal coalition Provisional Government.

As they moved toward a majority in local soviets across the country, left socialists, especially the Bolsheviks, began insisting on convocation of a Second All-Russian Soviet Congress. The moderate SRs and Mensheviks who still controlled the Soviet Central Executive Committee resisted, arguing that the congress would interfere with elections to the Constituent Assembly. First, they insisted, the Constituent Assembly must be elected and gather to discuss Russia's future; then, a new soviet congress might or might not be appropriate. On 23 September, though, the Central Executive Committee agreed to call another soviet congress, set provisionally for 20 October. (It was later delayed until 25 October.) On 25 September, the Bolsheviks took over leadership of the Petrograd Soviet. Trotsky and the Bolshevik leadership subsequently would use the Petrograd Soviet as a platform in their campaign for "All Power to the Soviets."

The Bolsheviks and Debates over an Insurrection

Although one can still find textbooks that describe the Bolsheviks as a tightly organized conspiratorial organization and the October Revolution as a carefully planned seizure of power dictated by the iron-willed Vladimir Lenin, specialized studies of the preparations and execution of the October Revolution tell a more complicated story.[18] Many of the documents in chapter 12 illustrate that story. When, in September 1917, Lenin began arguing that the Bolsheviks must learn "the art of insurrection" and seize power in the name of the soviets, he faced considerable opposition within the leadership of his own party. The Bolshevik Party Central Committee was hesitant to publish letters that Lenin sent from Finland (where he had gone into hiding after the July Days), in which he argued that conditions were ripe for an uprising, that a workers' insurrection in Russia would trigger a socialist revolution across Europe, and that the Bolsheviks had to act before Kerensky could organize his own "Kornilov-style" military coup or turn Petrograd over to the Germans (who would, according to this logic, crush the left socialists to prevent the threat of revolution). Among the top-level Bolsheviks, Kamenev and Zinoviev in particular questioned Lenin's assumptions. Instead, they argued that the party could take control of the government as part of an all-socialist coalition government, which, they predicted, the Second

All-Russian Congress of Soviets would form in late October. To seize power, they argued, was to risk civil war. The Bolshevik press (and the left SR press as well) called on workers and soldiers to organize regional soviet congresses in preparation for the all-Russian congress—the soviet congress (and, by implication, *not* an armed uprising) would be the key to establishing "All Power to the Soviet."

Although most Bolsheviks agreed that the party should take power, Lenin's demand for an uprising had little support among the top party leaders; in early and mid-October, it was the second-tier party leaders and militant grassroots party activists in Petrograd who favored an insurrection. Many observers at the time, though, were convinced that the Bolsheviks might try to seize power at any moment, particularly after a fiery speech by Leon Trotsky on 7 October. At the Pre-Parliament, Trotsky dramatically condemned Kerensky's government as puppets for the counterrevolutionary bourgeoisie, and then led the Bolshevik delegation in quitting the assembly. Many observers feared this was a prelude to a Bolshevik uprising. But in fact the Bolshevik Party leadership still had not settled on a strategy.[19]

On 10 October, Lenin secretly returned to Petrograd to attend a meeting of the Bolshevik Central Committee. After hours of heated debate, the Bolshevik leadership passed a resolution saying that the current situation in Russia and the prospect for revolution in Europe had put the question of an armed insurrection on the party's agenda, and party organizations at all levels should "act accordingly and . . . discuss and resolve all practical questions" related to the matter of an uprising.[20] This resolution said nothing about the details or timing of an armed uprising, nor did it actually begin the process of preparing for an insurrection. But it did trigger more than a week of bitter debates within the Bolshevik Party, not only among the leaders, but among the rank and file. Moreover, talk of an insurrection among the Bolsheviks led to heated public debates involving the left SRs and Menshevik-Internationalists, over how to replace Kerensky's government with Soviet power.

Debate over tactics turned into an open split in the Bolshevik leadership on 16 October. That night, a meeting of party leaders and key Petrograd party activists discussed the question of preparations for an insurrection. Again, there was heated debate, and many speakers argued that conditions were not appropriate for a seizure of power. Lenin's faction was in the majority, however, and the meeting resolved that party organizations should begin active preparations for an insurrection, that the Central Committee should work with the Petrograd Soviet Military Revolutionary Committee, and the final decision about if and when to launch an uprising should be left to the Central Committee and the Petrograd Soviet. Kamenev and Zinoviev, who were among the most fervent opponents of Lenin's position at this meeting, decided that they would continue to fight against the strategy of armed insurrection by appealing directly to rank and file Social Democrats at public meetings and through the press. On 17 October 1917, Zinoviev and Kamenev demanded that the Bolshevik's main Petrograd newspaper print an explanation of their objections to planning an insurrection. When the editors refused, Kamenev sent a brief summary of his position to the city's most important left Menshevik newspaper. Publication of Kamenev's note on 18 October led to a storm of condemnations against the Bolsheviks from across the center and right of the political spectrum, in all the major liberal, moderate socialist, and nonparty newspapers. Lenin immediately demanded that the Bolshevik Central Committee expel Kamenev and Zinoviev, but the party's leadership did not comply. Moreover, "moderate" Bolsheviks continued to voice opposition against planning an insurrection at a series of meetings around Petrograd.

Between 20 and 24 October, the Bolshevik Party's members continued discussing whether and when it would be appropriate to launch an uprising, and the moderate socialist and right liberal blocs continued to blast Lenin's party for threatening revolutionary order. At the same time, the Petrograd Soviet's Military Revolutionary Committee (made up of left SRs, Anarchists, and Bolsheviks) started mobilizing the city workers' militias (called Red Guards), and began sending emissaries to the various units of the Petrograd military garrison to ensure their cooperation or, at the very least, their neutrality in the anticipated clash with the Kerensky government. Kerensky also prepared forces for the anticipated showdown with the Petrograd Soviet. Ultimately, it was Kerensky's own actions to preempt the Bolsheviks on the night of 23–24 October, and not any Bolshevik plan, that launched the October Revolution.

CHAPTER EIGHT
TWO PROVINCIAL STORIES

8.1
THE SMOLENSK PROVINCIAL COUNCIL DEBATES QUESTIONS
OF LOCAL POWER

8.2
A POGROM IN ROSLAVL' ON 2 OCTOBER 1917

DOCUMENT SET 8.1
THE SMOLENSK PROVINCIAL COUNCIL DEBATES
QUESTIONS OF LOCAL POWER[1]

In 1917, the Provisional Government had difficulty projecting its authority into provincial Russia. In March, it appointed provincial zemstvo assembly chairmen as provincial commissars, to run local affairs at the government's direction. Appointed commissars often faced criticism from local socialist activists, who insisted that local government officials should be locally elected. This issue was one of several in which the central government's attempts to consolidate its power clashed with the process of "democratization."

In Smolensk Province in March 1917, liberal nobleman Aleksandr Tukhachevskii became provincial commissar. In exercising authority, he had to negotiate with a provincial executive committee that had been elected by the region's main public and party organizations and that claimed the right to supervise the state administration. At its insistence, Tukhachevskii formed an advisory Provincial Council. In late May, the Provincial Council became the site of intense debates over whether state officials should be elected or appointed.

In Smolensk Province as elsewhere, locally elected committees began usurping the authority of appointed commissars at the county and township level in April and May 1917. In Smolensk, a Socialist Revolutionary–dominated Provincial Congress of Peasants' Deputies resolved that local land committees could redistribute privately owned land; several local land committees issued directives that violated landlords' property rights. On top of all this, in late May the Smolensk Soviet demanded that Tukhachevskii be replaced by an elected official.

This document set contains minutes from the Smolensk Provincial Commissar's Council sessions of 25–28 May 1917, as published in The Smolensk Bulletin *(Smolenskii vestnik). These begin with a report by Deputy Provincial Commissar V. K. Untilov on problems facing local government—a report that illustrates typical problems in provincial Russia in 1917. Discussion of Untilov's report led to debate over whether the provincial commissar should be elected. The debate reveals the sharp contrasts between conceptions of the revolution. Speakers' political party affiliations (when known) are indicated in footnotes after their first statements.*

The Provincial Council.[2]

On 25 May at 2:30 P.M., a session of the new Provincial Council was opened by Provincial Commissar A. M. Tukhachevskii at the Provincial Zemstvo Administration offices.[3] A. A. Iugansen was elected the meeting's chairman.[4] [The meeting transcript lists the meeting's other officials.]

After a brief report on the Provincial Executive Council's activities, Deputy Commissar *V. K. Untilov* read a long report on the state of affairs in the province, compiled on the basis of information collected at a conference of county commissars held on 22–23 May.

The text of the report:

On general conditions in the counties. The general view is that life is finding its own pace, as it will. In several counties conditions are satisfactory (such as Sychevka County) or peaceful (as in Krasnyi County), while in others there are many misunderstandings and extreme problems that must be solved before it is time to mow hay.

Many violations of established order have been associated with the arrival of irresponsible outsiders. In Viaz'ma County, there has been a definite increase in property crimes. In Porech'e County, the food supply crisis is aggravated. In Belyi County, local organizations made up exclusively of the ignorant people have decided to fight against educational measures, and they want to assign school funds to organize political courses. More alarming, frankly, is the situation in El'nia County, where in one township—Bogoroditsk—it has been impossible to establish any semblance of order. Almost the same has been observed regarding Ivanovsk Township. The provincial commissar's requests for information and the Provisional Government's directives are simply ignored. The El'nia commissar requested that the provincial commissar send delegates from the Provincial Executive Committee to visit the county as a moral influence on the population.

Economic conditions. Economic conditions for private landowners are declining. There is a danger that many owners will completely quit their farms (in Sychevka County, landowners Khomiakov, Lobakov, and Rostovskii). Peasants are dividing the owners' land among themselves (in Gzhatsk County). The Latvian single farms [*khutors*] are in a depressed condition and the farmers fear for their land; as state peasants, they received allotments of less than 15 *desiatins*.[5] Local peasants (in Belyi County) are calling loudly for wide-spread cultivation of untilled land. From fear of hunger, there have been resolutions in Belyi County on reducing the acreage sown in flax.[6] There is a significant increase in oats planting in Gzhatsk County. . . .

Organizations in the counties. In some counties, the auxiliary state institutions called for by the Provincial Council's resolutions have not been organized. The plan worked out by the Council only recently reached some counties (Sychevka and Dukhovshchina). The business of organizing the localities is hampered by delays in reforming the *zemstvos*, some of which have no peasant representatives (as in Roslavl' County). In Belyi County, however, all administrative tasks were concentrated in the zemstvo from the revolution's first days, when the zemstvo's membership was replenished by democratic elements.

County committees have been organized in several counties. In Sychevka County there was no delay, and the committees there stand out for their activity compared to other counties. In Viaz'ma County the committees have taken on great significance. There are proposals that land committees replace the township and county executive committees. Township land committees are active in Dorogobuzh County. The Dorogobuzh County Committee expects to hold a zemstvo assembly that will include land committee members. In Iukhnov, the county land committee passed a series of resolutions regulating land relations and regulating the cutting and sale of timber.

Arbitration chambers are not active in some counties. Where they have been organized, they are working well, particularly in resolving disputes between peasants and landowners (as in Sychevka and Dukhovshchina Counties). There have been problems when arbitration committees' rulings conflict with the courts. Special instructions on this must be worked out. In some localities (like Gzhatsk County) the chambers act as township committees. In Dorogobuzh County several chambers have interpreted their authority very broadly, and their resolutions have countermanded existing contracts.

Requisition of cattle and grain in excess of the established living norm has been observed in almost all counties.[7] The peasants in several locales have protested against requisitions. In Dukhovshchina County, the peasant committees decided that only noble landowners' cattle should be requisitioned and that each estate should be left no more than five head. At the same time, it was resolved that no more than five *funts* of grain per *desiatin* of land can be taken from peasants.[8]

Grain requisitions are being conducted urgently. Impassable roads in Belyi County mean that there will be no requisitions there until July and August. Many peasants have stopped hiding grain, thanks to the influence and activities of the renovated *zemstvos*. Few localities have had successful requisitions (e.g., Porech'e County). In Dorogobuzh County, though, requisitions were carried out at the villagers' discretion, and very many localities refused to take part. Requisitioning there will continue with the aid of soldiers.

The Provincial Council. (Conclusion of Untilov's Report.)[9]
Preparation of firewood and lumber work has nearly come to halt. The main reason is that peasants believe the woods, like the land, will be given to them. Things are looking up, thanks to directives against illegal wood cutting and announcements that all firewood will be sent to the military. But this occasionally gets ignored. Several counties (for instance, Dukhovshchina) have failed to provide wood for the railroads and factories and are not allowing firewood to be cut for local demand, so there is a great firewood shortage. In Dorogobuzh County, the county soviet organized a special lumber commission to fight the firewood shortage. During the timber-floating period there were reports of thefts by

peasants (in Belyi County). Right now in Belyi County there are piles of logs sitting on the Vop River's banks because the river has fallen sharply and they must wait for it to rise.[10]

Agrarian misunderstandings have been encountered everywhere. Local disputes have been resolved or prevented by the land committees or arbitration chambers (in Viaz'ma, Dukhovshchina, and Sychevka). Misunderstandings have been discussed in executive committees (in Porech'e). In Belyi, as in many other counties, agrarian disorders have been widespread and are linked to the threat of hunger. In Dorogobuzh, the peasant population in general is calm. They believe that the Constituent Assembly will settle the land question. Most cases of seizure or unauthorized tilling concern disputed land.

In several cases, horseless single householders and soldiers' wives demanded that they be given a section of land for free use. They supplemented their demands with statements like: "If you give it fairly, we won't be forced to take it!" "Now we have rights such as this!" and "Now the courts belong to the people!"

Regarding pastures: there is an extreme shortage of pasture land in Dorogobuzh. Previously, many villages used noble landowners' pastures in exchange for "services." In recent years this has not been possible because of labor shortages, and because the belief has spread that "it will not do to pay the landlord through *service*." In some localities they have begun to use pasture arbitrarily, without any payments. In other localities the matter was reviewed by the township assemblies, which resolved that cattle would be set to pasture without payment, but which also limited the grazing period. In one township (Volochsk), a decision like this was taken at the landowner's proposal. Very big disputes have emerged over renting landowners' meadows. These often involve clashes between several villages' interests. Often the argument is over which village is closer to the pasture. Such quarrels are passed on to the arbitration chambers and land committees for resolution.

County militias have been organized in most counties, in agreement with new statutes.[11] But they remain under the commissars' direction, because the zemstvos have not yet been reorganized. In some localities (like Roslavl') they do not yet include representatives of the democratic strata. There is general agreement that the militias' present state is unsatisfactory. In most counties, the militias do not have horses and go on foot. They do not have weapons, or they have been denied ammunition for their revolvers. In some places, there are not militia commanders because there are no proper candidates. In such cases, local garrison officers are temporarily serving as militia commanders (as in Dorogobuzh). Almost everywhere, the militia ranks initially were filled through elections, but with negative results.[12] The population everywhere is demanding that many elected militiamen be removed and replaced by paid militiamen. The speedy and energetic organization of militias in the counties is closely tied to such questions.

Deserters literally are not given work locally (e.g., in Dukhovshchina County). In some locales (like Belyi County) they are hiding in the woods. The population in Gzhatsk, Porech'e, and Viaz'ma Counties is ready to fight against deserters with determination, and even with harsh measures.

The Provincial Council. (Session of 25 May.)[13]
After [Deputy Commissar] V. K. Untilov finished reading his report, a debate opened.

P. A. Gubkina is interested in the essence of the Provincial Executive Committee's attitude toward the arbitrary grain requisitions.[14]

Untilov explains that . . . in instances where it is clear that arbitrary behavior occurred, the provincial commissar gave appropriate orders to the county commissars.

L. A. Danilov states that he knows of cases of arbitrary legislation by township committees near Smolensk.

Untilov replies the Smolensk Soviet Executive Committee's previous activities in the localities did not conflict with the Provincial Executive Committee. The Executive Committee of Peasants' Deputies, though, only recently began to function.[15]

A. A. Tykotskii testifies that the Belyi County Commissar is not guilty of any illegal acts.[16] To secure bread for the population, he considered it his duty to requisition reserves for two months. He cannot be reproached for this.

O. I. Leliukhin observes that the report made absolutely no reference to any local creative work, which undoubtedly exists and is spreading.

M. S. Zvziulinskii explains that the rural population is engaged now in great organizational work that is unprecedented in Russia's history.[17] They are playing a vital role in building the state, particularly in places where elections for local offices have begun.

Untilov says that the report's apparent one-sidedness is explained by the fact that the county commissars—who perform their duties amidst the whirlpool of life—inform the provincial commissar of events from a purely subjective point of view. A better perspective is only possible from a distance.

V. N. Kaverznev explains that the only illegal measures taken in Smolensk County are those committed by the township committees.

L. N. Telesnin says that in a period of revolutionary construction it is impossible, of course, to demand that the law be executed to the letter. But nevertheless, any self-authorized organization must act in agreement with the Provisional Government's directives, which have been published repeatedly.

Tykotskii thinks that the report is too one-sided and focuses only on the bad and desolate, which the reporter sees as a consequence of ignored instructions. From that perspective, commissars in the localities are struggling against arbitrariness and demagoguery. In general, though, most of the peasantry's action reveals an instinct for governance.

Gubkin considers it the Council's proper task to set plans for further activities that agree with the provincial government's views.

M. A. Davidovich thinks that every effort must be made to extricate the state from a radically dangerous situation. In particular, we must provide firewood immediately, without any hindrance or restrictions. [He endorses a provincial state timber monopoly, to ensure effective delivery of wood for state purposes.][18]

S. A. Aleksandrov says the two main problems are weakness of state power in the localities and the absolute disconnection between local, provincial, and central government institutions. The Council's task is to provide the localities with general directions and point the way that they need to go.

Danilov sees the report's dark sides as helpful, in that the information might be used to help organize the province. Objecting to Kaverznev's statement, he notes in regard to the "timber" question that it was the Smolensk County Committee that made decisions contrary to state needs, not the township committees.

V. F. Egorov says supply questions are not always resolved favorably because local decisions often are made hastily. . . . [19] Now that provisions committees have been organized, there is no excuse for arbitrary behavior. It is unacceptable for the peasantry and the Provisional Government to be hostile toward one another; it is time to have a government that stands for the people.

Father G. Kutuzov is astonished that town officials paint such a frightening picture of the countryside and are so frightened by the specter of anarchy.[20] The real state of affairs in the province is not nearly so bad. All the report demonstrates is that an un-elected commissariat cannot correctly understand the masses' mood. The masses are not frightening; they are just disorganized. For some reason, the commissariat has deviated from organizing the peasantry. Meanwhile, the government lately has not been pursuing legal means to realize the peasants' demands. The intelligentsia needs to be less distant from the people.

A. V. Kostiukevich notes that the state cannot tolerate arbitrary legislation.[21] In its well-known "bulletin," the Smolensk Soviet of Peasants' Deputies calls for organizing the peasantry in a way that undermines the government's authority. It is meddling in matters that are beyond its sphere of competence.

Telesin considers the blame being cast on the intelligentsia baseless. Villages often dismiss the work of intelligentsia workers.

E. I. Mamichev defends the Soviet of Peasants' Deputies. The Peasant Soviet's bulletin was published because the provincial government has done very little and has provided no leadership in organizing the villages.

Zvziulinskii considers it unjust to blame the people, who often work without any clear instructions. Arguing against M. A. Davidovich's earlier statements [regarding a state timber monopoly], he says that the Council instead must make a strong statement about intolerable embezzlement and waste of timber wealth in the province.

The chairman makes a special announcement that A. F. Kerensky will be travelling through Smolensk, and the session adjourns until the next day. The Presidium is delegated to greet Kerensky together with the provincial commissar.

The Provincial Council. Session of 26 May.[22]
The session began with continued discussion of the deputy commissar's report on conditions in the province.

F. N. Gumennikov proposes a special resolution establishing a timber monopoly. This would be a more rational use of public monies than the current system, under which separate organizations market timber at different prices. It would guarantee the public that firewood is used for state needs. As a result, peasants will trust the Provisional Government. In Dukhovshchina County, a grain inventory was carried out successfully. But when the villages learned that their grain would be requisitioned, speculation in grain began. Now the peasants are in an hostile mood.

Danilov protests against accusations by Father Kutuzov and others at the previous day's meeting. They criticize the provincial commissar for slow work in the localities. However, they took a different position when the provincial commissar protested the seizure of the former provincial governor's mansion.[23] The intelligentsia is only guilty of failing to stand by its principles, failing to oppose demagogues. That has cost it the peasantry's support, as was revealed at the Smolensk Provincial Peasant Congress, which tossed the intelligentsia from its presidium. An organization run by deserters cannot pretend to have principles.[24]

D. S. Rostov says that society now is divided into two camps: one thinks the revolution is over and is working to build the new order; the other thinks that the revolution is still continuing and is struggling for power. The solution to this situation is the daily drudgery of hard work. Tossing around the slogan, "Elect the Commissar!" undermines the state's authority. We must declare as fact that certain commissars are unfit to work in the Provisional Government's new institutions.

Kavervnev thinks that the deputy commissar's report was sufficiently objective, but too gloomy. Like an ancient chronicle, the commissar dwelled chiefly on sorrowful events, some of which should have been removed from the report. The positive aspects of life also should be noted.

Iugansen, chairing the session, proposes that the Council close the general debate on this report and discuss other matters.

S. G. Gurevich proposes that they first discuss the Council's relationship to the provincial commissar and to other organizations and government institutions.[25] In particular, they must decide if organizations represented in the Council will accept responsibility for its decisions. Only then can the Council be confident that its resolutions will be implemented locally. If this confidence does not exist, then why are we working here?

[*Secretary's summary*]: A number of proposals were offered. After an exchange of opinions, the Council moved on to discuss the relationship between the provincial government and the counties and townships.

N. I. Glinka announces that Provincial Commissar Tukhachevskii and Deputy Commissar Untilov have decided to resign [because the Provincial Executive Committee had displayed a lack of confidence in their work and had demanded election of a new commissar].[26]

Gurevich says that organizing the government must be the Council's first order of business; they must make a declaration about the commissar. Gurevich declares, in the name of the organizations he represents, that the provincial commissar simply must be elected. If the circumstances were that commissar represented only the Provisional Government, then he could be appointed. However, the commissar must exercise the local population's confidence. Therefore it is necessary to hold local elections to designate a candidate for provincial commissar, who then will be confirmed or appointed by the central government.

Zeziulynskii considers it inappropriate to speak about the need to trust and support the Provisional Government, since everyone present shares that point of view. Under peaceful circumstances, electing the provincial commissar would be appropriate only if carried out according to instructions from the higher authorities. . . . In the revolution's first days the Provisional Government found it necessary to make a purely mechanical appointment of the zemstvo assembly chairman—who had been elected by the propertied elements—to the commissar's post. The population views this negatively. In the seven counties where there now are elected commissars, nothing frightening has happened. Surely the Provisional Government would not disregard the public good by confirming candidates who had recently revealed themselves as antigovernment anarchists.

The Provincial Council. (Session of 26 May.) (Continuation.)[27]
L. Ia. Ianshin explains that under the old regime, people in the opposition developed a habitually negative attitude toward central government institutions. Nonetheless, only a provincial commissar appointed by the Provisional Government can have authority.

A. V. Karneev says that sometimes it is very difficult to support the government in the localities. For example, in Gzhatsk an investigative commission formed by the local Committee of Public Safety discovered that someone had embezzled money from the town government's treasury. The town's mayor then complained to the provincial commissar about the investigative committee. In the end, the mayor was restored to his post without any detailed investigation. The commissar's rash directive led to a storm of public protest in Gzhatsk. [He accuses the commissar of protecting the mayor—a former tsarist policeman—despite the mayor's attempt to cover up a crime.]

Untilov explains what happened in Gzhatsk. The misunderstanding that aggravated citizens' passions resulted from an improper interpretation of the provincial commissar's directive. The matter was passed to the district court to identify the guilty parties. The town's mayor was temporarily relieved from his post so that the court commission could work with all relevant materials. The matter was resolved in a way that was just. . . . Individual people must be judged by legally established courts.

O. A. Dyzku says that designating commissars from the zemstvos has had very limited success. The provincial commissar understands that his responsibilities are similar to the former governor's responsibilities. But the county commissars have not done their work; they have restricted themselves to purely mechanical reproduction and distribution of directives to the townships.

E. F. Popova thinks that only consistent election of officials can build a coherent government structure; the government will become strong and authoritative only when it is in sync with the public's vital forces.[28] [She also claims that the propertied elites dominate the Provincial Executive Committee.]

Davidovich objects to Zeziulynskii's earlier comments and accuses him of recommending anarchic methods of providing firewood. He says necessary tasks can be achieved only by adopting a general state perspective. Those who advocate decentralizing power, of course, do not understand that the Soviet of Soldiers' and Workers' Deputies has resolutely taken [Davidovich's] position. Strengthening centrifugal tendencies inevitably will end up putting full power in the commissar's hands. In response to Popova's statement that the Provincial Executive Committee is made up of the propertied elements, Davidovich asks that the chairman read aloud a list of its members.

Iugansen reads this list.

Kostiukevich in principle does not oppose the idea of an elected Provincial Commissariat. . . . In places where the appointed commissar was not suitable, the government has agreed to public organizations' requests that it confirm a person chosen through elections. The central government seriously considered precisely this in regard to Smolensk. As far as the government is concerned, Tukhachevskii and Untilov were elected. Tukhachveskii took power only after being approved by the City Executive

Committee, which declared that he had the population's confidence. Untilov was elected by the Provincial Executive Committee.

As for the situation in Gzhatsk, the local committee did not follow correct legal procedures, and therefore it created this drama. When the committee dismissed the town's mayor without authorization, the provincial commissar had no other recourse than to turn the matter over to the court and temporarily restore the mayor's powers.

A. D. Grudzinskii says he considers the mechanical designation of a provincial commissar an unacceptable avoidance of responsibility. Again, because the commissar was chosen only by the propertied elements, he does not exercise any authority. He needs to stand for election, since there can be no higher confirmation than election by the people.

[*Someone*—probably Kadet council member S. O. Zhandovskii—then complains that unauthorized soviet members were participating in the Council's sessions.]

Iugansen responds to a question about whether soviet representatives have proper mandates to serve on the Provincial Council. [He reads the lists of soviet delegates with mandates approved for the 25 May and 26 May Council meetings.]

S. O. Zhdanovskii, referring to a point in the Provincial Council's statutes, explains that the Soviet Executive Committee can claim to represent the entire province only once it has gathered a provincial congress. Until that happens, in his opinion, the soviet's representatives cannot participate in fruitful work at the Council's sessions.

M. I. Tsapenko explains a soviet resolution decreeing that, pending a provincial soviet congress's convocation, the Smolensk Soviet Executive Committee will include one representative from each county-level soviet.[29] Therefore the soviet has the right to claim that it speaks for the entire province. There are new representatives at this Council session because the soviet could elect its full slate of delegates only on 26 May; before that, the Soviet Executive Committee sent plenipotentiaries.

[*Secretary's summary*]: The question of the soviet delegates' mandates is considered settled.

Kaverznev, enumerating cases of arbitrary behavior in Smolensk County, considers organized illegality more dangerous than acts by single people. Even if there are elections, the government must confirm candidates.

Zhdanovskii says that elections and collegiality cannot prevent all mistakes. In any case, if there are to be elections, they must be universally based upon [equal, direct, secret, and universal suffrage].[30]

Father Kutuzov declares that although opinion about the county commissars has long been negative in the localities, the provincial government only recently has lost its popularity and authority. In attacking the self-organized activities of peasant organizations, you forget that it is precisely these peasant organizations that saved us from anarchy. As representative of a class-based organization, he says only workers', soldiers', and peasants' deputies can lead Russia to the Constituent Assembly. Peasants see matters as they are. Having already set up elections, they strive to lead the country away from anarchy. The provincial government must be concentrated in the hands of a collective with the soviets of peasants', soldiers', and workers' deputies at its core.

The Provincial Council. (Session of 26 May.) (Continuation.)[31]
Tykotskii does not understand why the propertied elements' representatives see the democratic organizations' actions as the primary cause of disorganization. The democracy's mood favors the state and supports the Provisional Government. But the provincial government especially needs approval. Only if the provincial government gravitates toward the broadest democracy will it have the force that it needs.

Ia. K. Kurnatovskii says that the Smolensk Soviet of Peasants' Deputies' resolutions . . . contradict the rights of the state. Administrative authority cannot be vested in a collective. The example of Kronshtadt gives us the best illustration of what that can bring.[32] Attacks on appointed commissars miss the mark, in that they suppress the freedom-loving intelligentsia element that found shelter in the zemstvo. Moreover, the commissars not only must continue the revolution, but also must carry out state-organizing work. Even established democracies in France and America do not elect all administrators. In the revolution's first days, the confidence necessary to give the government stability and authority suffered several blows. Trust was torn apart in Russia. Based on the list of members of the Provincial Executive Committee that was read aloud, it appears that only three or four are from the propertied elements. . . .

Zezliulinskii says a new life cannot be built successfully if the propertied elements have power because the masses distrust the upper classes. An elected provincial commissar would prop up state organizations. Electing one will result in greater support for the Provisional Government. Having someone from the propertied elements at the head of the province puts a wall between local organizations and the central government. Electing the provincial commissar would bring an end to excesses.

A. P. Sigirskii says that the revolutionary people, who at present are the real source of power, have entrusted full power to the Petrograd Soviet of Workers' and Soldiers' Deputies and to the Provisional Government. Smolensk does not have the right to create its own form of government. Our duty is to strengthen the designated provincial commissar's authority. We can nominate a new candidate only if the present commissar is not appropriate for the position.

A. N. Churakov, in his capacity as official representative of the Ministry of Internal Affairs, informs the Council about the Provisional Government's position on its relationship with its representatives in the localities.

The Provisional Government welcomed the birth of new spontaneous organizations in the localities and recognized their right to make decisions on new issues as they arise. But the government considers such "home-made" methods of building a new life temporary. From the moment that the Provisional Government's directives set a single "common pattern" for all of Russia, all organizations had the moral responsibility to take this common pattern and implement it, without complaining about restrictions on their rights or an inadequate relationship between their government and the public interest.

Regarding local questions of general state significance, the first priority must always be the interest of the whole, not the interest of parts. . . . Of course, if individual government representatives break the laws, it sometimes is necessary to take extraordinary measures. But it is very dangerous to resort to amputation—otherwise it would be easy for such attacks to disrupt life.

In principle, the government needs to build loyalty from the bottom up, not the other way around. But this still does not lead to the conclusion that the provincial commissar must be elected. The coalition government shares these ideas about state construction and thinks that, for now, there must be clear limits to independent activities in the localities. . . . The Provisional Government cannot tolerate powerful independent organizations at the provincial level. Its reaction to antigovernment measures will be to close off credits at the treasury. This is not a threat, but a last resort dictated by the desire to defend indivisible Russia. This meeting itself must give a direct answer: will it take the Bolsheviks' path, or will it support the Provisional Government? I am convinced that at this dangerous moment we all must speak candidly, without masks. From recent personal discussions with the provincial commissar, in the presence of his deputies, I have the impression that work in the province is becoming more difficult and less productive each day. In the provincial commissar's view, local organizations are leading the province on the path toward another Kronshtadt.

[*Secretary's summary*]: When Churakov visited with the provincial conference of county commissars, he learned that the situation in the localities was far from wretched. It became clear to him that "the knot was tied not in the localities, but here, in Smolensk." In order to confirm his first impressions, he familiarized himself with the work of the Smolensk Soviet Executive Committee. But here he confronted failure: at four exhausting sessions he was unable to get any orator to address his questions. The antipublic work of this quasi-democratic organization stunned and stupefied him.

Churakov declares "Nowhere have I encountered such a detestable state of work."

The meeting's chairman stops him.

Churakov apologizes for the unnecessary harshness of his words, then concludes his speech by asking that the Soviet of Soldiers' and Workers' Deputies exchange its revolutionary-bureaucratic spirit for a revolutionary democratic spirit.

The Provincial Council. (Session of 26 May.) (Continuation.)[33]
Telesnin says that when the revolution began everyone could take part in its creative work. But now people are trying to divide Russia into propertied elements and democratic elements. Everyone knows that someone from the propertied elements can be transformed into a member of the democracy by joining the Soviet of Soldiers' and Workers' Deputies. The issue is not property ownership. As the criteria of fitness, it would be better to consider public and political decency. For example: on one hand, the allegedly "propertied" Provincial Executive Committee acknowledged the need for an All-Russian Congress of Peasant Deputies and even assigned zemstvo funds for this purpose. On the other hand, the township committees behave in ways that do not always agree with the people's will. The Smolensk Soviet of Peasants' Deputies' bulletin and the soviet seizure of the former governor's mansion were not acts that support the Provisional Government. Having the soviet's confidence is not identical with having the people's general confidence.

Dyzuk blames the propertied elements for creating excesses, because petty landowners did not want to turn their land over for peasant use. It was local organizations that brought calm to the villages.

Meeting chairman *Iugansen*, summarizing the discussion so far, believes it has not answered necessary questions about how often the provincial commissar must be elected, or if the person elected must be confirmed by the Provisional Government. The discussion also has not answered questions regarding administrative agencies directed by the commissar or whether such questions can be clarified at the local level.

Zeziulinskii says that there is no danger in an electoral system as long as the assembly does not intend to elect anarchists. . . .

Kostiukevich does not deny this . . . We need to take a positive position. That is everyone's civic duty. Replacing the commissar with a collective is impossible. This would not engender the masses' confidence . . .

Tykotskii considers Churakov's comment about cutting off credits [to local government agencies] wrong. Perhaps a temporary compromise can be reached to avoid conflict with the Provisional Government. Reorganize the Provincial Council with a predominance of representatives from the counties and with an elected commissar, and then submit it to the Provisional Government for confirmation.

Zhdanovskii welcomes this formula. It takes a cautious approach toward the elective principle, so that firm power is not disrupted by illegal reelections.

Aleksandrov worries about involving the Council in the squabbles of class-based organizations. Propertied Russia is being stigmatized, but we must not forget about the service of zemstvo activists. This highest of ideals—service to nation—runs like a red thread through the history of all peoples.

I. N. Nikolaev declares that, as a defender of the Smolensk Soviet of Soldiers' and Workers' Deputies, he protests against Churakov's accusations.[34] All misunderstandings evidently stem from the fact that the soviet, which was crammed into four rooms in the attic of a club, could not possibly suspend its work on pressing issues to provide a celebratory greeting for a guest. The difficult conditions of work in these crowded premises led to the seizure of the governor's mansion. The Provincial Executive Committee agreed in principle on turning the mansion over to the soviet. And after the Provincial Executive Committee's resolution, the soviet continued working for two weeks in the old premises. It seems [Churakov] does not know that the Smolensk Soviet fully supported the Provisional Government at a time when Petrograd had done so only "conditionally." The Smolensk Soviet does laborious day-to-day work. Fifty to sixty soviet members are constantly travelling to the counties. The soviet has not refused a single request from the provincial commissar to dispatch members to the localities. . . . Churakov has made a judgment based only upon how he was received personally.

Churakov, in the Provisional Government's name, thanks the Smolensk Soviet for its work in the Motherland's behalf. . . . He does not wish to further aggravate a ticklish situation. He was not speaking of the [soviet seizure of the] governor's mansion when he referred to the knot being tied in Smolensk. All the same, he now considers it necessary to state that if the soviet is against the Bolsheviks' platform, then it should not have seized the building. It is impermissible to say one thing and then do another.

The Provincial Council. (Session of 27–28 May.) (Conclusion.)[35]
[*Secretary's summary*]: Three fundamental tendencies on resolving the question of the relationship between government institutions had become clear. And so the separate groups agreed that Tykotskii and M. P. Iakobovich would speak as representatives of the soviet and county delegates; Kurnatovskii and Ianshin would represent the zemstvo groups; Kostiukovich, Danilov, and Sigirskii would represent zemstvo employees and the county committees.

Tykotskii again declares that only a government founded on the broadest democratic base will have unquestioned authority. As a way out of this un-wanted conflict, he agrees for now with the proposal to submit a locally elected provincial commissar for confirmation by the central government.

Ianshin says that given the formation of a coalition central government . . . we need to support the government without reservation. The Council must approve a mutually acceptable general formula, so that we do not head down a path toward disintegration.

Kurnatovskii says that those who do nothing make no mistakes. No doubt the democracy has made as many mistakes as the central government has. The Council's task is not to repeat the democracy's slogans. Distrust of Provincial Commissar A. M. Tukhachveskii simply because he is a property owner has completely overwhelmed the confidence that he should rightly exercise in his relations with the democratic strata.

Danilov says that relations between the Soviet of Soldiers' and Workers' Deputies and the provincial commissar only broke down after the Soviet of Peasants' Deputies came into being. Before it began casting accusations at the provincial commissar, everyone supported him.

Kostiukevich stresses that the main issue really is support for the Provisional Government. Soviet activities, like the seizure of the former governor's mansion or the Peasant Soviet's instructions, are opposed to the central government's policies. The soviet cannot support the government unless it desists from separate legislation.

Sigirskii notes that in the villages only the Provisional Government and the Petrograd Soviet have strong authority; self-authorized organizations exercise influence only in so much as they support those two institutions. These self-authorized organizations are intolerably falsifying public opinion. Before anyone decides principal questions about elections, a fully authoritative agency—a Provincial Executive Committee—must be created on the basis of the four-tail electoral formula. It then can study the problem and propose decisive solutions.

Iakubovich welcomes attempts to find a formula for general agreement.[36] We cannot tolerate delays in settling the main question of the day—creating firm state authority. A Provincial Executive Committee that is reorganized on the basis of proportional representation will work as a collective, bringing together all tendencies in the province. The provincial commissar must precisely follow the Provisional Government's directives. At the same time, as someone elected by the local population, he must reflect the collective's aspirations and answer to the collective, which has the right to create new revolutionary forms of life.

Churakov makes the concluding speech. He declared his opposition to the views expressed by Tykotskii and Iakubovich. Making the commissar accountable to both the central government and a local committee is unacceptable to the state, and from a legal perspective, creates a blind alley from which there is no exit. [Churakov], the Provisional Government's representative, proposes a decisive solution to the Council: he recommends preliminary work toward electing the commissar by vote of the entire province.

[*Secretary's summary*]: After the debate, a conciliation commission was elected to consider these four positions and work out a single Council resolution. That commission presented the Council with the following, which is presented here in its edited form:

1. Considering that the Provincial Commissar and his deputy have announced their resignations from their posts, the Provincial Commissar's Council considers it necessary to hold elections for candidates to these posts, who then will be submitted to the Provisional Government for confirmation.

2. Given the issue's urgency the Council considers it necessary to conduct this election through the Provincial Commissar's Council's general assembly, with active participation by the Smolensk City Executive Committee, the Smolensk Executive Committee of Soviets of Soldiers', Workers', and Peasants' Deputies, and representatives from every county committee or similar organization (with two representatives from each county). This will ensure representation of all Smolensk Province's population.

3. The commission is now charged with working out details to establish the precise relationship between the Provincial Commissar, the soviets, and the executive committees. It also must address reorganization of the appointed Council's membership through elections, and it must conclude this work before the election of candidates for the post of Provincial Commissar and his deputy.

DOCUMENT SET 8.2
A POGROM IN ROSLAVL' ON 2 OCTOBER 1917[37]

This document set concerns an anti-Jewish riot in Roslavl', a town in Smolensk Province. Roslavl' was an important railroad junction for lines linking Moscow to the west and the south. It also had many small factories, including several glass factories and flax oil pressing plants. Its wartime population included some 10,000 civilians and more than 15,000 soldiers attached to the local garrison. Roslavl' also become a major transit point for war refugees; in 1915–1916 as many as 80,000 Polish refugees were encamped there, and several thousand refugees remained in 1917. Although Roslavl' had the province's second largest Jewish population, it had never experienced any significant anti-Jewish violence before 2 October 1917.

The document set includes material from The Smolensk Bulletin (Smolenskii vestnik), *the Petrograd Kadet newspaper,* Speech (Rech), *two local Bolsheviks' memoirs, and a local history published in 1967. Two editorials from* The Smolensk Bulletin *represent the views of Solomon Gurevich, a local Socialist Revolutionary leader and an important political figure in Smolensk's Jewish community. One selection from the local newspaper, a 4 October 1917 report by*

Ivan Roslavl'skii (probably a pen name), was republished with minor changes in the conservative Moscow newspaper, Morning Russia (Utro Rossii), *and the Petrograd newspaper,* Russian Will (Russkaia Volia), *on 5 October. On 6 October* Speech *carried the story with alterations from the* Morning Russia *text. Accounts based upon the* Speech *version then appeared in* The Stock Exchange Bulletin (Birzhevyia vedomosti) *on 8 October and in the Moscow-based liberal Jewish newspaper,* Jewish Week (Evreiskaia nedelia), *on 15 October. One newspaper report reproduced below is a summary of the Moscow District Court's investigation of the pogrom, first published in* Morning Russia *on 19 October 1917, then reprinted the next day in* The Smolenskii Bulletin.

[Editorial in *The Smolensk Bulletin.*]
Smolensk, 4 October. Pogrom Wave.[38]
We have received the following cup of poison to drink: a pogrom broke out yesterday in Roslavl'. Soldiers and (chiefly, it appears) hooligans in soldiers' overcoats destroyed stores and beat the store owners and employees—most of whom were Jews—and terrorized the defenseless town population. This vileness was perpetrated under the pretense of the struggle against exploitation and speculation and in the name of defending proletarian interests.

Because of these hooligans' deeds, the murdered and beaten had to be locked up in jail to protect them from the brutal mob.

In Sychevka, a mob tried to break into an alcohol warehouse where 15,000 gallons of spirits were stored.[39] Fortunately a riot at the warehouse was avoided. But the local authorities feared a second attempt and destroyed the alcohol, or else the entire town would have ended up drunk, and the next morning there would have been victims of drunken hooligans.

In several villages in our province there have been robberies at noble landowners' estates. There have been arsons, thefts, and destruction of seed and equipment. On one estate there is a large herd of cows that supplies milk for Smolensk's hospitals. It now has no fodder. The landowner has asked the Smolensk city administration to buy the herd to use the milk for the city population's needs, but the neighboring peasants "are not allowing" the herd to be moved. . . .

The people who profit from these separate facts from the chronicle of recent days in our province are the revolution's enemies, the hateful parties on the left and those greedy people who hunger for a return to the old order. . . . Snakes are coming out from all the dark corners hissing, "Here is your praiseworthy democracy; here is the fruit of your socialist agitation."

In their stupidity, the hissing snakes cannot understand that these pogroms and disorders are echoes of the past, stupid violence by a stupid slavish stratum. They do not understand that the revolution and left agitation is creating opposition to pogrom-hooligan ugliness. Everywhere revolutionary democratic organizations exist, they are fighting against pogroms and lending aid to the revolutionary government.

And if they are powerless in the struggle against the dark forces, isn't there evidence that it is because of measures taken to undermine their authority and weaken their significance?

At the start of the revolution, the revolutionary organizations took positions that the progressive-bourgeois elements could agree upon without trouble. All these elements had to do was relinquish their *class egoism*. Even if they had not renounced their *class interests*, that was enough for them to work cooperatively with the revolutionary organizations at the highest state level. It was enough for them to realize that the revolution was inevitable and to be reconciled to it.

But at the same time, from the revolution's first days, the bourgeois ideologists proclaimed war on revolutionary organizations—at the same time that anarchist-bolshevist elements attacked from the left flank.

The combined result of efforts by the revolution's enemies on the right and left could be seen in early July.[40] The organized democracy, weakened by the right, succumbed to pressure from the anarchistic elements. And now we are harvesting the fruit of this struggle by the bourgeoisie and its mirror image [the Bolsheviks], in the form of a frightening wave of pogroms rolling across our province.

Now the bourgeois camp is calling for "a move toward firm power." But really, can a revolution—a revolution in which soldiers participate—move by any power other than the power of the organized democracy?

[News Report in *The Smolensk Bulletin.*]
A Pogrom in Roslavl'.[41] (From our correspondent.)

On 2 October there was a pogrom in Roslavl'.

A pogrom mood had been rising for a while, but it overflowed suddenly because of the shortage of galoshes. In the morning, a crowd gathered in front of Lel'ianov's store demanding galoshes. The store clerks explained that there were no galoshes, but just then the crowd stopped the loading into a cart of crates that were being removed from the store. The crowd broke open one of the crates. In it, they found galoshes. This was enough for some dark agitator to start shouting, "Beat the Yids!"[42] The crowd grew. They immediately looted some of the galoshes. Members of the soviet of workers' and soldiers' deputies sent to calm the crowd sold the rest for seven rubles a pair. The crowd, however, continued to grow. Leaders emerged who demanded a pogrom against the Jews. A soviet member, the Bolshevik soldier Nosov, threatened to shoot into the crowd with a machinegun, but this threat only poured oil on the flames. Nosov barely escaped being killed and hid in Levinson's pharmacy, where he found shelter from the black deeds. Then some provocateur fired two shots. Cries went out that the shots had come from Levinson's pharmacy. The crowd threw itself in that direction. Some of them broke into the pharmacy and searched everyone there, but found no gun. After badly beating Levinson, the pharmacy owner, the crowd dragged him half-conscious to the soldiers' barracks and then headed to the prison.

[In the meantime,] the crowd on the street killed a Jew who apparently had a revolver. It then broke into stores owned by Shafran and Myshlaevskii and looted all the merchandise. Some soldiers had ladies' clothing, shawls, astrakhan hides and boots hidden under their overcoats. Open trading took place on the spot. Soldiers threw stolen items into the crowd, shouting, "Take these, comrades!"

Two Jews were killed in front of the militia headquarters, and for a long time the crowd would not allow their corpses to be removed. The looting subsided at nightfall. But all through the night soldiers—including some soviet deputies—conducted searches of Jews' homes and offices, from which several things were stolen. The homes and offices of Gol'din, Bolotin, and Shafran were searched. At Gol'din's house, the searchers stuffed silverware into their pockets, but the servants caught them, and they were ordered to return the things they had taken.

The panic in town was dreadful: many fled to Smolensk on horseback or ran off along the highway on foot.

On the morning of 3 October, there was no looting. Sentries were posted all around town, and trucks with armed soldiers patrolled the streets. No one approached the ruined stores. The number of guards posted at the railroad station was increased.

It was typical that patrols dispatched during the pogrom did not stop the crowd from looting.

—Ivan Roslavl'skii

[News Report in *Speech*.]
A Pogrom in Roslavl'.[43]

Morning Russia reports from Smolensk that a full-scale pogrom broke out in Roslavl'. (Yesterday the newspaper *Russian Will* mistakenly referred to the town as Perislavl').

In the morning a mob gathered in front of Lelianov's store, ostensibly demanding galoshes. Store clerks explained that there were no galoshes, but at that moment the crowd stopped the loading of crates from the store into a two-horse cart. Someone smashed open a crate, and there were galoshes in it. This was enough for some dark agitator in the crowd to start shouting, "Beat the Yids!"

The crowd grew. Some of the galoshes were looted immediately; deputies sent to the store by the Soldiers' Soviet to quiet the crowd sold the rest for seven rubles a pair. The crowd, however, continued to grow.

Leaders immediately emerged from the crowd and called for a pogrom against the Jews.

Then a member of the soviet, the Bolshevik soldier Nosov, tried to threaten the crowd by warning that he would fire into it with a machine gun. This only added oil to the fire. Nosov barely escaped being killed, and was saved only by the fact that he hid in Levinson's pharmacy, where he found refuge from the black deeds.

At this point, some provocateur fired two shots. Immediately cries went out that the shots had come from Levinson's pharmacy. Part of the mob forced its way in there and searched everyone. Finding no weapons, they badly beat the old pharmacist Levinson and then dragged him half-conscious to the soldiers' barracks. From there, they headed off to the prison.

At the same time, the rest of the crowd seized and killed a Jew who appeared to have a revolver. Simultaneously, the crowd broke into the stores of Sharfon and Myshlaevskii and looted all the goods. Soldiers were seen with women's clothing, shawls, astrakhan hides, and shoes hidden beneath their overcoats. Soldiers threw stolen articles into the crowd, shouting, "Take these, comrades!"

In the whole time that the mob beat the Jews, two men were killed and twelve were wounded. At nightfall, the looting subsided. But all night soldiers—including soviet deputies—searched the homes and offices of Jews, during which several things are known to have been stolen. The homes and offices of Gol'din, Bolotin, and Shafran were searched. At Gol'din's, the searchers hid silverware in their pockets, but they were caught and the confiscated items were returned.

The panic in town was dreadful: many fled to Smolensk on horseback or ran off along the highway on foot.

It was typical that the patrols dispatched during the pogrom did not stop the crowd from looting. The two reserve infantry regiments stationed at Roslavl' are in a state of complete anarchy, so it would appear that the soldiers supported the pogrom.

[News Report in *The Smolensk Bulletin*.]
On the Pogrom in Roslavl'.[44]

Deputy Provincial Commissar V. Ia. Burgonov, who returned from Roslavl' last night after investigating the pogrom that occurred on 2 October, told our reporter that the riot had an entirely incidental character.[45] There had been no antisemitic agitation of any sort, and there was not and is not any ethnic discord in Roslavl'. These were the unanimous conclusions of the provincial administration's representatives, the town's self-government, and Roslavl's revolutionary organizations. The pogrom had been contained thanks to actions taken by the military units, the Roslavl' Soviet's members, and the town administration.

It now is calm in Roslavl', and court authorities are conducting an investigation. They will establish who fired shorts and excited the crowd so that it did not disperse. Three soldiers found with stolen items have been arrested. Burgonov explained that the military units are on full alert to prevent further disorders.

[Editorial in *The Smolensk Bulletin*.]
Smolensk, 5 October.[46]
  The Bolsheviks and the Pogrom.
  On returning from Roslavl', Deputy Provincial Commissar Burgonov is persuaded that the disorders that took place there were not anti-Jewish, as they had been characterized by our correspondent. Contrary to reports, it was not preceded by antisemitic agitation. In general, he observed no ethnic animosity in Roslavl'.
  So how does one explain the fact that the only people killed and wounded in the Roslavl' disorders were Jews? And how are we to make sense of the fact that the only stores looted were those owned by Jews?
  And then there is that cry, so typical of the "dear old days"—"Beat the Yids!"—that inspired the deadly crowd. And the "characteristic auto-cratic provocation" of shots from the crowd that always accompanied anti-Jewish disorders . . .
  We will not argue with Burgonov! The chief particular causes of the Roslavl' pogrom and other similar disorders are the general chaos, the disruption of supplies and, finally, the fact that the town has been flooded by more than 10,000 people who have been torn from their homes, from their traditional labor, and from the soil on which their moral foundation and spiritual personality was born. Years of inactivity, years of an unnatural life have changed them. People in the town have lost their spiritual equi-librium and are open to all sorts of anarchist agitation in general and anti-Jewish agitation in particular. That is why the Bolshevist slogan, "Beat the Bourgeoisie!" has had so much success among them, as well as calls to "Beat the Yids." Wherever the "bourgeoisie" includes a more or less signifi-cant number of Jews, the Bolshevist slogans very often are exchanged for anti-Jewish slogans. It is no surprise that Bolshevism appeals to former servants of the old order. It is no surprise that you find among the Bolshevik ranks more than a few ex-members of the Union of Russian People, ex-gendarmes, and ex-police officers.[47] Oh, they well know that the wave of Bolshevism can, without difficulty, be channeled toward antisemitism and toward criminal disorders. . . .
  The Roslval' pogrom is a typical case of this transformation. Bolsheviks from the gendarmes and the Black Hundreds there used a Bolshevist slogan. And as for the local Bolshevik party organization, its leaders did not claim one single victim from among their Black Hundreds brothers-in-arms.[48] Something happened during the Roslavl' pogrom that is characteristic of

this relationship. When a local Bolshevik, Nosov, tried to stop the looting of Jewish stores, there was a shout from the crowd: "He's been bribed by the bourgeois Yids!" And then the Bolshevik Nosov ran to hide in a neighboring pharmacy, the owner of which thereafter was beaten senseless "for giving him shelter". . . .

There are similar cases in the chronicles of the pogrom-anarchistic movement when the Bolsheviks were unable to cope and fled. It therefore is not astonishing that the Bolshevik leaders who are closest to life on the streets protest against idealizing "spontaneity," the kind of spontaneity that has led to courts and trial. That is why they distance themselves from Lenin's views. The newspapers have reported on the discord dividing the Bolshevik camp in recent days.[49]

The pogrom in Roslavl' and other disorders of an anarchist-criminal character have persuaded the main Bolshevik leader—Lenin—that "the people are on the proper path" and that radical revolutionary parties, with the Bolsheviks at the head, must lead this movement and give it a more organized character. In contrast, Trotsky considers it necessary to fight against the anarchistic movement among the masses.

We hope that our local Bolsheviks will look for a suitable exit from the Roslavl' pogrom.

[News Report in *The Smolensk Bulletin*]
The Roslavl' Pogrom.[50]

The newspaper *Morning Russia* reports:

The Moscow District Court Prosecutor has received the following report from Roslavl':

A crowd irritated by long waits standing in line at the former bazaar learned that the trader Myshlaevskii had received a shipment of 400 pairs of galoshes. When word spread that what they wanted was at Myshlaevskii's, the crowd from the line headed along Moscow Street toward the store. The militia was summoned. The crowd approached the militiamen, shouting curses at them and menacing them. The municipal command and the local reserve regiment, summoned to aid the militia, joined the crowd and participated in the violence that was beginning. The crowd rushed to the store of Lelianov, where supplies were being taken from the store and loaded onto a cart. The crowd broke open a crate and found new galoshes in it. They immediately looted the store. Soldiers helped the crowd. The soldiers beat the militia's commander, Stoianov. A member of the soviet, the Bolshevik Nosov, tried to give a speech and then threatened to use a machine gun. The crowd rushed at him. Nosov barely escaped and ran off toward Levinson's pharmacy, shooting back at the crowd as he ran. The crowd rushed after him and forced their way into the pharmacy. Somebody shouted that shots had been fired by a Jew in the pharmacy. Levinson and two pharmacy employees, Rubinshtein and Rozenburg, were lynched. They were beaten then taken to the [Oster River] bridge, with the intention of throwing them in the water. Instead it was decided to put them on trial at the soviet of soldiers' deputies' office. From there, for their safety, they were secretly taken to the prison. All goods of value were stolen from the pharmacy. The pogrom crowd then spilled into the streets and began to loot Jewish stores. Through it all there were shouts of "Beat the Yids, the *burzhui*, and the militia!" The stores that were looted were those of Lelianov, Myshlaevskii, Sharfran, and Gol'din. The shop clerks Abram Barkan and Meer Relykov were beaten. Barkan died soon afterwards. Both of them were robbed of all their valuables.

This continued through the day on 2 October. Toward evening two units of soldiers that had not participated in the disorders were able to take people caught red-handed with stolen goods to the militia administration. When the crowd learned of this, it approached the militia building and demanded the immediate release of the prisoners. Toward morning on 3 October the mood in the town had calmed. Patrols were dispatched from the [garrison's] artillery brigade, and soldiers patrolled the town providing reconnaissance. The stores were sealed by order of the town administration, which announced that all their goods would be requisitioned.

The court investigation has established that the most active participants in the pogrom were recidivist criminals.

At present there is a commission for the protection of the town active in [Roslavl'], which is charged with carrying out an investigation.

Moscow Court Office Prosecutor A. F. Stablen sent the Smolensk Prosecutor a telegram with a directive to immediately communicate with the Southwestern Front Command about provision of armed support. No information was provided about whether anyone will be prosecuted.

[From a memoir by I. R. Vinslav, a Roslavl' Bolshevik, written in the 1920s and published in 1957.][51]

On 2–3 October, counterrevolutionary elements succeeded in inciting a pogrom against the Jews. Comrade Konopatskii took three squads of soldiers from the local garrison. To bring order to the rioters and arrest the organizers required armed force.

[From a memoir by D. V. Klochkov, a Roslavl' Bolshevik, written in the 1920s and published in the 1957.][52]

On 2 October, agitation by the bourgeoisie and their baiting of the Bolsheviks in Roslavl' led to a big pogrom in which windows were smashed, goods stolen, and inhabitants beaten and bullied. The pogrom continued night and day and caused a great panic in the town.

As a military officer, I was summoned to serve during the pogrom. On my way from the regiment to the soviet's offices, I witnessed this scene: a crowd of a thousand excited women and men, armed haphazardly, carried two beaten, bloody, elderly Jews, whom the crowd had accused of speculation. The crowd had destroyed the Jews' shops and demanded that the soviet jail them as German spies.

Konopatskii, Nikiforov, and others were at the soviet's offices.[53] Konopatskii convinced the crowd to turn the two beaten Jews over to the soviet, which would handle the matter. If the soviet found them guilty it would take measures to punish them. But the crowd was not appeased. They accused the soviet of working for the Germans and demanded a lynching. Nosov came to the rescue. He offered those individuals with orders for galoshes and other goods the chance to present their receipts in exchange for goods. This offer considerably reduced the crowd's violent mood. Konopatskii then ordered me to accompany the two "German spies."

My squad encircled the two injured people and made our way toward the prison, which was about a two kilometer walk across town. The crowd did not retire, but instead followed us with hisses, hoots, and curses.

At the bridge across the [Oster] River we confronted another crowd, organized by the Black Hundreds, who came at us screaming and threatened to throw us off the bridge. We pointed our rifles and threatened to shoot the leaders of this rabble. Only then were we allowed to bring the "guilty" to the prison. The next day they were found not guilty and set free.

[A 1967 local school textbook account by archivist N. P. Galitskaia.][54] There was a pogrom in Roslavl' on 2–3 October. It appears to have been organized by local and visiting counterrevolutionary elements from the Party of Socialist Revolutionaries, as well as by former Black Hundreds. They took advantage of difficulties resulting from shortages of goods. The pogrom's planned character is clear from the fact that it took place on the day after the soviet had discussed the struggle against speculation and resolved to take radical measures against speculators. A politically unreliable group of soldiers from the 136th Infantry Regiment took part in the pogrom, as did an insignificant number of railroad workers and townspeople. Among the crowd there also were active and experienced rioters whose aim was to slaughter the Bolsheviks.

CHAPTER NINE
PERCEPTIONS OF CRISIS IN SUMMER AND EARLY FALL

9.1
THE FIRST CONFERENCE OF PETROGRAD FACTORY COMMITTEES, RESOLUTION ON WORKERS' CONTROL

9.2
IU. VILLIAMS, "A HORRIBLE SIGHT"

9.3
MILIUKOV'S "REPORT ON THE POLITICAL SITUATION" AT THE KADET PARTY'S NINTH CONGRESS

9.4
A PETROGRAD NEWSPAPER ON SOLDIERS' UNREST IN SARATOV PROVINCE

9.5
PAVEL RIABUSHINSKII'S SPEECH AT THE SECOND ALL-RUSSIAN CONGRESS OF TRADE AND INDUSTRY

9.6
GENERALS KORNILOV AND KALEDIN ADDRESS THE MOSCOW STATE CONFERENCE

9.7
EKATERINA BRESHKO-BRESHKOVSKAIA'S SPEECH AT THE STATE CONFERENCE

9.8
THE BOLSHEVIK DELEGATION'S DECLARATION AT THE MOSCOW STATE CONFERENCE

9.9
IRAKLI TSERETELI, "THE POLITICAL SITUATION IN RUSSIA AND THE TASKS OF THE WORKING CLASS"

9.10
PEASANT UNREST IN TAMBOV PROVINCE IN AUGUST–SEPTEMBER 1917

9.11
LIGOVSKII, "INTO THE REALM OF ANARCHY"

9.12
TWO ESSAYS ON ANARCHY FROM *THE ASTRAKHAN NEWSPAPER*

9.13
LOCAL CRIME IN 1917: A STATISTICAL REPORT COMPILED BY SMOLENSK POLICE OFFICIALS

DOCUMENT 9.1
THE FIRST CONFERENCE OF PETROGRAD FACTORY
COMMITTEES, RESOLUTION ON WORKERS' CONTROL[1]

The following document is an excerpt from a resolution on workers' control approved at the First Conference of Petrograd Factory Committees on 3 June 1917. The economic situation worsened steadily in summer and fall 1917, which aggravated tensions between organized labor and the business community. A 23 April government decree had given workers' trade unions and factory committees legal status in negotiations with ownership, but stopped well short of granting workers the right to supervise (kontrol) *management. As the economy declined, workers increasingly saw such supervision as their committees' prerogative. Employers, however, viewed the factory committees' claim to oversee production matters and hiring decisions as impermissible violations of their property rights. It was in that context that representatives of Petrograd's worker-elected factory committees gathered for their first conference in late May and early June.*

On Workers' Control.

1. The complete disintegration of all economic life in Russia has reached such a level that a catastrophe of an unprecedented scale is inevitable. It will halt production in a whole range of important industries, undermine agriculture, disrupt the railroads, and deprive the millions-strong urban working class of food. Indeed, the destruction has already begun, and it already grips many economic sectors. A successful struggle against ruin requires the maximum exertion of the people's effort and the adoption of several immediate revolutionary measures at the local and national level.
2. There can be no salvation in bureaucratic measures that create institutions dominated by the capitalists and state officials and ruled by finance capital, which will preserve the capitalists' profits and their authority over production.
3. Saving the country from catastrophe requires that workers and peasants be fully convinced—not by words, but by deeds—that central and local level government agencies will not hesitate to turn over to the people most of the profits, income, and wealth of the great magnates in banking, finance, commerce and industry. . . .

DOCUMENT 9.2
IU. VILLIAMS, "A HORRIBLE SIGHT"[2]

The following document is a 28 June 1917 commentary by Iu. A. Villiams (Williams), a regular correspondent for The Smolensk Bulletin (Smolenskii vestnik). *His essay sounds a familiar theme in the liberal and moderate socialist press in summer and fall 1917: the alleged relationship between rising violence and the Bolsheviks' growing popularity. In March, crowds in Petrograd and many other cities had hunted down and beaten agents of the hated tsarist police and also had "liberated" the empire's prisons (which set free quite a few hardened criminals). Although the Provisional Government struggled to preserve order, crimes of all sorts increased. Newspapers across Russia frequently noted that the new local police forces (now called "militias") had trouble coping with crime waves. As anxiety over crime increased, so too did concern over lynching (samosud) incidents in which crowds took the law into their own hands and punished suspected criminals. Many liberals and moderate socialists saw mob justice as proof that the lower classes did not understand the rule of law and that Russia was slipping into anarchy.*

A Horrible Sight.

Would any city resident ever have thought that he would have to witness a dreadful street massacre—to witness a savage lynching? We were used to reading about the lynching of horse thieves or arsonists in villages. But that was "out there," in the dark corners of Russia, in the kingdom of "centuries of silence," almost on another planet. Upon reading about this, a city resident would sigh indignantly at the dark people then look around in satisfaction; such things could not happen here. No, such things cannot happen here. Here, the city resident would tell himself, we have officials, and investigations, and courts. Here there is law and order.

But all that has ended. Now, lynching happens in towns, in large cities, even in the capitals. Lynching happens in broad daylight, on crowded streets, and in railroad stations. And these are not isolated, one-time events; they take place daily!

When I first encountered soldiers escorting two unfortunates with placards on their backs reading, "We are thieves," I did not want to fix on the sight, to give it any significance. I could recognize what was happening; I perceived it in the back of my mind. I even tried to find some beauty and truth in the incident: maybe this was a special sort of cooperative honor court. The soldiers were humiliating their comrades in public. Maybe they already had been before a court. Or maybe they were being taken to court and wanted to show their cooperation. Maybe they were going through the streets carrying signs that proclaimed their guilt as a way of saying, "These soldiers are repentant." Maybe that is what they want to say with this procession.

But such processions were repeated systematically, first in one town, and then in another. And the next time it was not a soldier being led, but a shopkeeper with a sign on his back reading, "I am a looter"! And now the public proclamation of criminal guilt—this new variation on being lashed at the whipping post in prereform times—has been complicated and deepened by physical violence.[3]

In the city center's most crowded place, the train station, a thief was literally torn to pieces, in other words, hacked to bits. The other day, in one of Petrograd's markets, a shop was destroyed and the clerks beaten half to death after hidden goods were discovered. At the freight station just a few days ago, two thieves were killed.

Lynching has become a common sight. The newspapers report on lynching in small print in their "crime report section," as an accustomed danger of our times. And what is most frightening of all is that the ordinary public expresses approval of such savage punishments.

Here is an example of the philistine attitude toward mob justice:

On 18 June in Dubesishchakh Village in El'nia County, more than 2,000 people gathered for a village meeting that "tried" a man who had stolen a fancy plow and a peasant woman who purchased this stolen plow. The thief and the purchaser of the knowingly stolen item were harnessed to the plow and made to drag it around the village, while those gathered whistled and hissed.

In describing this episode, the correspondent—a member of the "rural intelligentsia"—added with a sense of great satisfaction that: "It must be hoped that such *reasonable* measures extirpate evil from our lives." And then the editor added the following note: "Through this correspondence, I wish to show the reader that the village is fighting the criminal element in a *very cultured* way that, in general, is not being discussed."

And this was written by a "populist," a very zealous believer in the enlightenment of the people, a very zealous propagator of "culture" and cultured habits in the village.[4] It had not occurred to him that measures he calls "reasonable" and "cultured" deprave the population. . . .

Theft and robbery have frightened and embittered the average man. Thefts and robberies have taken place. Criminals released from prison in the days of the revolution still have not been apprehended. And when thieves are caught and brought in, it often leads to this sort of talk:

"What are we supposed to do with them? Why spend time dealing with them? So they can sit in prison? Why should we stand on ceremony when we're dealing with thieves? No, there is a better way! Don't give it a second thought! It would be better to kill them."

Such things are said frequently by people with pretensions to intelligence. And it is frightening to observe that this attitude toward lynching has begun to permeate society. They forget that a legal trial must be based on a thorough investigation, a study of the crime, without which there cannot be a trial.

If, for even one minute, we tolerate what is essentially intolerable—the idea that thieves, burglars, and looters deserve whatever savage punishments the hard-hearted mob conceives—then we will have beatings, the pillory, and even murder.

And what guarantees that the guilty really will be subjected to punishment and not accidentally slip through the cracks? In lynching the "investigation" is brief. "Beat him!" "I know him!" "I saw him!" And so on. And who cries this out? Perhaps it was the real thief. Perhaps it was the man's enemy. Perhaps it was some malicious person who somehow will profit. There is no way to know the particulars. We know only that someone cried out, "Beat him!" "I know him!" "I saw him!"

We must not forget this: lynching is a contagious infection. It is carried from one region to the next. It already has spread from the realm of criminals into politics! There already have been cases of massacres in which agitators urged on the mob. The other day General Polovtsev, Commander of the Petrograd Garrison, reported that soldiers had arbitrarily broken up a meeting and arrested the orators for attempting to exercise freedom of speech.[5]

But that was only the bloom of arbitrariness. The fruit already is beginning to appear. There have been cases of savage punishments by the Bolsheviks, Bolshevik attacks against those they call "*burzhui*."

Lynching is one of the most frightening sights of our days. The struggle against it is not within the government's power. And the shame is that the government alone is entrusted with this task. All society, every political party, the entire intelligentsia must rise up in arms against the savage cry, "Beat him! I know him!"

—Iu. V.

DOCUMENT 9.3
MILIUKOV'S "REPORT ON THE POLITICAL SITUATION" AT THE KADET PARTY'S NINTH CONGRESS[6]

On 23 July 1917 the Kadets' Ninth Party Congress opened in Moscow in the midst of a political crisis. The first coalition government had collapsed, and Kerensky was trying to convince the liberals to join a new coalition. On 25 July Miliukov, who had been forced out of the government in April, presented the congress with the following report on Russia's political situation. That same day, the Kadets agreed to join Kerensky's second coalition government.

We have gathered for this Ninth Party Congress at a grave time. . . . Russia is living through a grave illness, an internal illness, complicated by an unprecedented external struggle. We now are not just threatened by catastrophe: we are caught in its whirlpool. The seeds of evil sown by Zimmerwaldism and utopian socialism have already yielded a magnificent crop.[7]

[Miliukov blames the Provisional Government's socialist members for Russia's crisis. He claims events since February 1917 prove their guilt.]

When we look back, we see that the process by which the revolutionary democracy seized power led to the creation, not just of dual power, but of multiple centers of power. I will not argue over whether what happened was an inevitable or natural process that could not be opposed or, as I believed at the time, a process that actually could have been halted. But I would not oppose the idea that the coalition government was a natural result of an arbitrary process—the shattering of the government by organizations calling themselves "representative organs of the revolutionary democracy."

I only know that when our comrades first entered into the coalition ministry, we had a clear mandate from the [Kadet] Central Committee to transform a spontaneous process into a conscious process.[8] The Central Committee's directive said that the country's salvation necessitated, first of all, that there be only one government and that all state agencies would remain subordinate to that government and to no other body. [The directive specified that] this government must have real power and, as the highest level of power, must be able to employ force where and when there was sufficient cause. And finally, the war would continue and would be carried out according to agreements with the Allies. There would not be any rash attempts to end the war on the basis of quasi-internationalist principles, which in reality would serve our enemies, the Germans.

What was the basis of the socialist parties' opposition to these truly principled positions? Not only the Bolsheviks, but all the parties that make up the majority in the soviets and the committees? They formally opposed [our platform] on the grounds that socialist ministers were joining the government to strengthen class struggle, not to reconstruct internal peace in the country. As the socialists understood things, class struggle is the means of victory over war and the so-called bourgeoisie, according to the best recipes of Zimmerwald and Kienthal.[9] In other words, they intended to implement the slogan of Zimmerwaldism—transform the international war into a civil war.

[Miliukov claims that the socialist government members' speeches at the June 1917 First All-Russian Soviet Congress prove the socialists view their role as extending the social revolution. He sees this as a recipe for chaos rather than the rule of law.]

. . . Because we struggle against the revolution's extension as they understand it, [the socialists] time and again label us counterrevolutionaries. If being a revolutionary means that you abuse the revolution, then we must be called counterrevolutionaries in the narrowest sense of the term. But, regrettably, this term is cast at us in a much more widely used philistine sense. They call us the party of *pomeshchiki* and capitalists, proponents of the old order's restoration, constitutional monarchists, and so on.

[Miliukov criticizes the socialists' failure to rein in the Bolsheviks. He blames the socialists for allowing the Bolsheviks to spread "chaos in the army" and insists that the socialist government ministers must decide whether they serve the soviets or the Russian state.]

"The soviets or Russia?"—that is where the Bolsheviks' [July] uprising has led us. We must recognize that this situation resulted from the victory of revolutionary spontaneity over consciousness.

Where would a spontaneous path of revolution lead? The classical history of all revolutions shows that this path would lead first to replacement of a mixed government with a purely socialist government, a government of the Soviet majority. Further along, it would lead to the moderate socialist government's replacement by radical socialists of the Leninist type. After that: anarchy, terror, a military coup, and a military dictatorship. But luckily, we might say, the classical revolutionary model is not in store for Russia. In the classical model, the bourgeoisie fears the masses. But we have no bourgeoisie, and there was no persistent opposition from the propertied classes, and the theoretically predicted [class] struggle did not take place. Quite the contrary—no hindrance to radical demands emerged. Only through a misunderstanding or malevolence could the government's first composition be called bourgeois. We had no interest in class struggle; for us, there was only a struggle of ideas and theories. In other words, there was no hindrance slowing the revolution's development.

[Miliukov says that the socialist ministers' policies, particularly regarding nationalities and land reform, posed a threat to the revolution, which is why the Kadets initially rejected Kerensky's invitation to join a new coalition government. Cooperation now was possible, however, because Kerensky had come came around to the Kadet position on several of these questions.]

. . . It is absolutely clear that now, when the primary issue is boiled down to the question, "the soviets or Russia's salvation?" we should not argue about details, even about important details. We disagreed [with Kerensky] over the government's independence from the soviets and the executive committees. And Kerensky has come around to this exact point of view. . . . We have entered a new phase, absolutely new, despite the fact that the negotiations leading to this moment took only a few days. The new phase consists precisely in the acceptance of our fundamental principles. There are two paths. One leads to the motherland's salvation, the other to its destruction. We needed to find a perspective that lets us differentiate between these two paths, a perspective that allows us to tell if the government would be independent of the so-called democratic representative institutions. Weighed down by the burden of the great danger now looming over Russia, we have concluded that the new [government] cabinet that has been formed really has such independence.

Luckily, the Bolshevist uprising pushed Russia off the path of spontaneity and onto the path of rationality. We believe Russia must not stray from this path. If the revolutionary government does not follow the rational path, we will fall back onto the road toward a new insurrection. And if we take that road, no doubt panic will reign in the entire country. But I think that Bolshevism is not so dangerous now; it is possible that it will fade away. The counterrevolutionary movement is very weak and does not have firm ground.

It is important to pick decision makers from circles that don't dream of restoring the old order or harbor fanatical plans for the future, but focus on the problem of saving the motherland.

[Miliukov concludes that on these grounds it is proper for the Kadets to join the government and that events will vindicate their policies.]

DOCUMENT 9.4
A PETROGRAD NEWSPAPER ON SOLDIERS' UNREST IN SARATOV PROVINCE[10]

The following account of an incident in Atarsk—a district capital in Saratov Province—appeared in the Petrograd business newspaper, The Stock Exchange Bulletin (Birzhevyia vedomosti), *on 1 August 1917.*[11] *In summer 1917, liberal and conservative newspapers printed dozens of accounts of soldiers rioting or arresting their officers. These usually involved soldiers rebelling against transfer to the front. The incident in Atarsk was relatively minor; no one was seriously harmed, and "order" was restored quickly. The* Stock Exchange Bulletin's *decision to print this account suggests that the editors considered it instructive or emblematic.*

The Saratov Bulletin [Saratovskii vestnik] reports the following regarding a recent disturbance in Atarsk:

On 19 July, 65 ensigns from the local garrison were to be transferred to the front. The ensigns appeared at the train station in a cheerful mood, but their mood turned sour the moment train No. 1 arrived.

It so happened that several lanterns at the station were broken. When the train started moving, someone in one of the wagons fired a revolver out the window. At this sound, a cry went out in the crowd that the regiment's commander and several officers had slipped away from the assembly and tried to hide. There were screams of "Catch them!" The crowd rushed out, one after another, into the market square, but they soon returned.

In an attempt to restore some semblance of order, a popular ensign named Gruzin declared that he was taking charge. At the soldiers' insistence, he ordered that the regimental commander and the regimental aide-de-camp be arrested. The crowd gave a great cry of "Hurrah!" and lifted Gruzin up in their arms.

After dispatching the arrested men to the guardhouse, the crowd began returning to its barracks. Separate groups of soldiers, however, stayed out on the streets through the night and angrily discussed what had taken place.

During the night, the Cossack cavalry division commander [in Atarsk] took command of the local garrison and issued strict directives on the preservation of order.

DOCUMENT 9.5
PAVEL RIABUSHINSKII'S SPEECH AT THE SECOND
ALL-RUSSIAN CONGRESS OF TRADE AND INDUSTRY[12]

The following document is a 3 August 1917 speech by the prominent industrialist Pavel Riabushinskii, presented to a congress of Russia's industrial and commercial elites gathered in Moscow. Many speakers at this congress voiced frustration at the Provisional Government, the socialist parties, and the soviets. Riabushinskii had consistently opposed socialist participation in government on the grounds that the revolutionaries lacked practical skills necessary to run the country. Riabushinskii's speech is often misinterpreted to suggest that he thought workers should be starved into submission.

Citizens! It is with heavy hearts that we have gathered for this congress. A heavy gloom hangs over our Russian land. After the infamous tsarist government's collapse, we hoped the Russian state would follow a correct path. A range of possibilities opened before the Russian people. But, regretfully, we spoiled it all with our own hands. Regretfully, the wrong people were given power in our Provisional Government. . . . In fact, a gang of political charlatans have acceded to power. (*Stormy applause throughout the hall.*)

The soviet liar-leaders have taken the people down a path toward ruin and brought the entire Russian state to a gaping precipice. If we cast even a cursory glance at the past five months, we see the following: the army that was our pride has become disorganized and devastated. Our enemy has crossed our borders. We have squandered tremendous material wealth necessary to continue the war. Our legal system has become enfeebled. Our food supply problems have been neglected, and Russia's entire economic and financial life has been shattered. . . . [W]e have gone down a blind alley, and it is painful to ponder what the future will bring. When all this comes into sharp focus, we see that our socialist parties, given the nearest thing to power, have not taken adequate measures and are not capable of creative and constructive work. They have gone about work in a one-sided way, based upon a party mindset. . . . Of course, our government has taken measures and made attempts to resist such tendencies. It has tried to reorganize itself. But its attempts have been weak and miserable. Our life has been altered under the pressure of the doctrinaire left groups and their dubious leaders.

And so at this serious moment, we gather here to discuss the situation. The recent changes [in the government] and attempts to create firm authority have come to nothing. First we were told that [Kerensky] was creating a government that would save the revolution, then it was Russia *and* the revolution, and then, finally, simply Russia.[13] But we think these are only pompous words. They do nothing to create a government that can lead us out of this situation. If we are going to work together, first we must have confidence in the government and assurances regarding measures it has planned. Regrettably, the current government's composition demonstrates that it is simply an accidental combination of people. What we see before us, in fact, is a kind of ministerial muddle. This all demonstrates that what just has taken place is not the reorganization of power, but only a transition. What comes next? That is the question. . . .

. . . We have acute shortages in the factories and plants and other manufacturing facilities. This has a perfectly understandable cause—the war, which affected production of all necessities. But our allies and our enemies all have dealt successfully with these same problems. Not one of them has succumbed to difficulties. Our situation comes from the fact that, on one hand we do not have an organized state, and on the other hand our labor productivity has declined terribly.

An objective view regarding productivity reveals that all production problems are closely interrelated. If there is a shortage of fundamental products, it affects the railroads and factories. If our broken locomotives are not repaired, it also affects the railroads and all our factories. All this adds up to the whole country's terrible misfortune. We knew already that, under normal conditions, the Russian worker's labor productivity is low. But at present, at this critical moment in our state's life, already weak productivity has fallen by 25 to 50 percent in some factories. This amounts to a state catastrophe. The Soviet of Workers' Deputies, which pretends to a leadership role in Russia, and the entire working class that it leads have not upheld their fundamental duty to the Russian state. It is true that life required wage increases. But at the same time, we would expect the working class to exercise necessary care to justify the higher pay it currently receives. If we shift our gaze to America, we see that even in normal conditions workers do not accept people into their trade unions who cannot meet minimum levels of productivity.

If we return to our commercial class and its activities, we see that it craves intensive work. But, regrettably, there is no work. The current government, in fact, does not recognize [the commercial class] and actually hinders its work through all sorts of new institutions, on which [the commercial class] has absolutely no representation or is represented in such insignificant numbers as to have no influence. We see the state making more and more demands on us at the same time that we are in no condition to meet our current obligations. And so we gather here, to discuss what measures we must take. . . .

The government . . . thinks that only governmental measures and state monopolies can lead the country out of this painful situation. We know, and the entire country feels, that many of us are not satisfied by the grain monopoly, for example. It has not produced the results that everyone expected. It has only disrupted market exchange . . . and produced no progress. But the government stubbornly sticks to that single path, blind to all its defects. We are witnessing the creation of a whole series of new [state] monopolies. Soon there will be a monopoly on commercial manufactured goods. City administrations and other urban agencies are competing with the central government to impose policies that make trade in many branches of commerce impossible.

All this makes us think about steps we must take to halt this harmful tendency, which can only lead to larger state expenditures. [Riabushinskii argues that the state cannot organize a successful grain monopoly without adequate capital to subsidize grain at prices less than free market levels—capital it simply lacks.]

I consider it essential . . . that we resist the harmful and false tendencies being followed by the government. [Riabushinskii argues that businessmen continue organizing their own class-based associations to lobby and work with central and local government agencies.]

In addition to organizational work, we must engage in general political work to achieve our aim, which is to make it possible for us, the commercial-industrial class, to take an active part in the country's life. We feel that our class, with its long years of experience in loyal service to the Russian state, is the main link in economic life. If we review the entire core of the government's activity in the realms of finance and politics, we see that the Russian government has no clear plan other than state monopolies. If we consider activities in Petrograd, we see no plan of any sort. Everything is in chaos: our government lacks cash resources and does not know how to do any difficult work. (*Stormy applause.*) It simply continues along the same mistaken path that our old government followed. It prints credit bonds. It amasses paper reserves, which are scattered about the entire country and given in exchange for grain. These are piling up and, of course, already hold no attraction to the peasantry. And this all further complicates the progress of our ship of state.

[Riabushinskii points out that the government's "Freedom Loan" campaign was a failure, despite the business community's participation.] All this has not extricated Russia from its difficult situation. And so the first solution the government turns to is taxes. It thinks that taxes should be increased radically. It thinks that the commercial-industrial class, as the propertied class, should be taxed fiercely. But the government has to recognize that the commercial-industrial class has done all it can to meet the country's needs. We feel that on one hand the government demands our financial help, while on the other hand it takes measures that disorganize the commercial-industrial class' activities. In the end, the government not only will fail to collect taxes—it will be insolvent.

All this frightens us, gentlemen. We hear from all sides, starting with Shingarev, that what is needed are sacrifices, sacrifices, and sacrifices.[14] Well, yes, we need sacrifices. But at the same time, we need reason. We need a government that is reasonable. (*Stormy applause.*) We need to bring in people who have life experience, who can understand the particulars in all situations. Surely it is not enough just to make demands—the government must know how to do things.

And so we—who have given the Russian state all that we can and who, of course, will continue to aid it—we must not hide. But we already can hear a voice asking: "But is it expedient to give money to a squanderer? Surely, no matter how much you give a squanderer, it is useless and he will spend it all the same." (*Voices*: "That's right!" *Applause*.) "He will spend all the capital that the state can gather. In the name of self-defense," the voice asks, "wouldn't it be better to impose a tax on squanderers?" (*Voices*: "Absolutely!" *Applause*.) [Riabushinskii points to historical examples of Russian merchants voluntarily sacrificing to aid the state, but complains that Kerensky's government has no representatives from the trade-industrial class.]

We see the country's already-complicated life growing worse and worse each day. Really, gentlemen, we need to see matters through sober eyes. Most of us understand that life cannot stop, that life moves forward and will take on new forms. But we need to act expediently, before the new experiments being tested on the Russian lands completely destroy the state. We must say: this revolution is a bourgeois revolution—something that all the left groups admit. (*Voices*: "That's right!") We must say that the current bourgeois order was, and still is, inevitable and must be taken to its logical conclusion. Those people who administer the state should think like bourgeois and act like bourgeois. Only under those conditions can this state achieve the greatest good for the greatest number.

This does not mean that we cannot have a coalition ministry now. No, a coalition is necessary now, not only to manage all sectors of the national economy effectively, but also (given the psychological moment) to defeat the enemy. We need the harmonious work of all vital forces, but without doctrinarism. Under present conditions, a coalition is necessary to lead the country out of this difficult situation. It must be led by a ministry made up of all groups.

If we return to the state's economic tasks and consider steps the government is taking now, we see that everything being done is inadequate. In Petrograd, an Economic Council has been formed that will address a wide range of state questions. The council includes representatives of different groups, but when our union petitioned regarding participation, the council refused us. (*Voices*: "A disgrace!") We understand perfectly, of course, that this council's work will be one-sided. It will probably propose unrealizable solutions to problems. . . . Think about the resolutions [such organizations] have passed. Really, they have such a naïve, childish character. . . .

[Riabushinskii says that it is the commercial-industrial class' civic duty to participate in local-level government and public organizations and to guide local policy making.] Our commercial and industrial class will see its work through to the end, without expecting anything for itself. But at the same time, it feels now as if it cannot convince anyone or influence individual leaders.

Therefore our task is extremely difficult. We must wait, since we know that life will naturally follow its own course of development. And, regrettably, life harshly punishes those who violate economic laws. Still, it is bad when state interests are sacrificed at the urging of such a small group of people. It is unpardonable. This is true as well of sacrifices we have made at the front. For the Soviet of Workers' Deputies to change its convictions, several armies first had to be destroyed and our brave officers martyred. And so, gentlemen, we must wait, even if it is against our will. A catastrophe, a financial-economic collapse, is inevitable for Russia; we might already be on the verge of catastrophe. Only then it will become obvious to all; only then will they feel that we have been going down a false path. And when that happens, we must stand up and say that our organizations took the higher ground.

We sense that the things of which I speak are inevitable. Regrettably, the boney hand of hunger and the people's misery are necessary; only its grasp at the throat of the people's false friends, the members of the various committees and soviets, will bring them to their senses. The Russian land is groaning under their comradely embrace. At present, the people still do not understand. But they soon will come around and say: "Away with you, deceivers of the people!" (*Stormy applause.*) We have many people who declare themselves freedom's defenders, but who in fact are destroying real freedom. We have many who claim to stand for the people, but who in fact curse the people and disgrace the revolution's purity. We people of commerce understand that our situation is difficult. Each of us agonizes in his soul because under existing conditions he cannot completely execute his civic duty to the state. Involuntarily, we want to cry out: "Great Russian state, you are alone. Where are your defenders?'

All that is sacred and pure has been defamed, the people's entire culture wasted. Spite and hatred rule in tandem, with no feeling of public responsibility, with no concern for life, honor, and unity. When will the free Russian citizen rise up from among yesterday's slaves? He had better hurry up. Russia is waiting for him. In the circles that only listen to

Satan, those who are ashamed to say the word "motherland" are roaring with laughter. At this difficult moment, this new Time of Troubles, all the country's vital cultural forces must join in one harmonious family. Let the merchant's stoic nature become manifest. People of commerce must save the Russian land. (*Thunderous applause. All rise and greet the speaker.*)

DOCUMENT 9.6
GENERALS KORNILOV AND KALEDIN ADDRESS THE MOSCOW STATE CONFERENCE[15]

The following document set presents 14 August 1917 speeches by General Lavr Kornilov and General Aleksei Kaledin at the State Conference in Moscow. Some 2,500 people attended the conference. These included not only representatives from government and military institutions, but also delegates from soviets, trade unions, cooperatives, and public voluntary organizations. The attendees represented a broad political spectrum, including right-wing nationalists, but excluding the Bolsheviks (who boycotted the meeting). Despite its name, the State Conference had no formal institutional standing. Prime Minister Kerensky had hoped that the meeting would bolster his government's popular authority and used his opening address to call for national unity in the face of mounting crises. Ultimately, though, the person who gained the most politically from the conference was the supreme commander, General Kornilov, whose speech is presented below. Liberal and conservative newspapers heralded Kornilov's speech as "the State Conference's most arresting moment."[16] The next speaker, General Kaledin, commander of the Don Cossacks, outlined a program that built on Kornilov's ideas.

Kerensky: Yesterday the Provisional Government gave you a sketch of the army's general condition and the measures the Provisional Government has proposed and will implement. The Provisional Government also considered it necessary to call on the Supreme Commander to lay out the situation at the front and army's condition for the State Conference. (*Addressing L. G. Kornilov*): You may speak, General.

(*Supreme Commander Kornilov takes the rostrum to prolonged, stormy applause from throughout the hall, with the exception of the benches on the left. The entire gathering, with the exception of the representatives of the Workers' and Soldiers' Soviets, rises from their seats to greet him, and there are welcomes and applause for the Supreme Commander, who has climbed the platform. From various corners of the hall there are a growing number of indignant shouts at those on the left benches who are still sitting. Voices cry out: "Cads!" "Get up!" From the left benches, where no one rises, there are shouts, "Toadies!" The noise, which has been continuous, grows even louder. The chairman tries to calm the meeting and, having obtained a degree of quiet, speaks.*)

Kerensky: I ask the audience to remain quiet and to hear out the first soldier of the Provisional Government with the esteem that is due to him, out of respect for the Provisional Government. (*Cries:* "That's right!" *Applause.*)

Kornilov: As Supreme Commander, I greet the Provisional Government, and I greet the entire State Conference on the active army's behalf. I would have happily added that I greet you in the name of all our armies, which stand fast on our borders like a firm and impenetrable wall, defending Russian territory and the Russian state's integrity and honor. Instead, with deep sorrow, I must add and openly declare that I do not have confidence that the Russian army will remain steadfast in its duty to the motherland.

Everyone knows of my telegram concerning the restoration of the death penalty against traitors and those committing treason in the theater of military operations. The immediate object of this telegram, the reason for sending it, was the disgrace of the breakthrough at Tarnopol'.[17] And that collapse, the likes of which no Russian army had ever known, continues to this day. The shameful Tarnopol' disaster was a direct and inevitable consequence of the unprecedented chaos brought to our once-glorious and powerful army by external influences and by imprudent measures taken in the army's reorganization. The steps taken by the government after my telegram undoubtedly led to several improvements in the army, but the destructive propaganda that previously disorganized the army continues to this day. I will give you the facts.

In the short period since August began, soldiers have brutally killed their commanders, without any semblance of being soldiers at war. [Among the murdered were] Colonel Bykov, the Strelkov Guard Regiment's commander (*A voice:* "We will honor his memory by rising!") and Captain Kolobov of the same regiment. The Abramovich brothers, both officers, were killed at Kalinichi Station; the 437th and 43rd Siberian Regiments' commanders were severely beaten and wounded; soldiers from the Dubnenskii Regiment hoisted their commander, Purgasov, into the air at the end of their bayonets. (*Voices:* "Were the guilty hanged?") But when that regiment, which refused to give up the instigators and criminals, was surrounded by loyal units and the commissar threatened to fire upon them unless they immediately turned the guilty men over to him, they wailed and begged for mercy. (*Voices:* "Shameful!") The criminals all were surrendered. They faced a military-revolutionary court and now await their fate, which they cannot escape. (*Voices:* "As is proper!") After that, the regiment pledged to wash away the shame of their treason. And so, in the face of steadfast revolutionary authority, a crime was punished without shedding one drop of blood, and further possible crimes were prevented. Soldiers committed all these murders in a nightmare of irrational, hideous arbitrariness, boundless ignorance, and abominable hooliganism. Several days ago, when it became clear that the Germans were launching an assault on Riga, the 56th Siberian Rifles Regiment—a regiment that had become famous in previous battles—voluntarily gave up its positions and ran, leaving behind its arms and ammunition. . . . (*Voices:* "Disgraceful!") The regiment returned only when threatened by weapons, after I sent an order by telegraph to exterminate the regiment.[18] (*Voices:* "That was the correct thing to do!" *Applause from the benches on the right.*) And so it is that the army. . . . (*The chairman interrupts Kornilov with the following words*):

Kerensky: Excuse me, General. I ask the assembly to hear those sections of the report that speak of Russia's great misfortune and suffering without any further unworthy outbursts.

Kornilov: And so it is that the army is carrying out a ruthless struggle against anarchy in the army, and anarchy will be crushed. But the danger of new disasters still hangs over the country. The threat of losing new territories and cities still looms; immediate danger still hangs over our capital. Conditions at the front are such that, as a consequence of our army's collapse, we have lost all Galicia and all Bukovina—all the fruits of our victories in the past and present years. In several places the enemy already has crossed the border and threatens the most fertile provinces in our south. The enemy is trying to smash the Romanian Army and drive Romania from the Allied ranks. The enemy already is knocking at Riga's gates. And if our army's instability makes it impossible for us to hold our lines on the coast along the Gulf of Riga, then the road to Petrograd will be open.

Free Russia inherited an army from the old regime that was, of course, radically defective in its organization. But nonetheless, that army had fighting capability. It was staunch and ready to sacrifice itself. A whole series of legislative measures, implemented after the revolution by people who do not understand the army and are alien to its spirit, transformed that army into an insane mob that cares only about its own life. There have been instances when individual regiments expressed the desire to conclude peace with the Germans and were prepared to return conquered provinces to the enemy and pay an indemnity of up to 200 rubles per head. The army must be restored. If it is not restored, there will be no free Russia, no free motherland. To restore the army, the Provisional Government must immediately take all measures that I have proposed in my report. My report has been submitted, and Assistant War Minister Savinkov and Supreme Command Commissar Filonenko have signed this report without any reservations. (*Shouts of* "Bravo!")

I will give you a brief account of the report's fundamental principles. Historical inference and military experience have shown that without discipline there is no army. Only an army welded by iron discipline, only an army following its leaders' singular uncompromising will, only such an army can achieve victory. Only such an army can endure all battle's trials. Discipline must be affirmed in the army's daily, routine work by granting corresponding authority to the commanders, officers, and junior officers, and by assuring them it is really possible to carry out necessary internal work. [They must be able] to force soldiers to clean and feed the horses, to clean their quarters, which now are unbelievably filthy, to save the entire army from epidemics and the country from pestilence. Those of you who have set the struggle for peace as your goal: let me remind you that, given the army's present state, were we to conclude a peace—to the country's great shame—there still would be no peace, because demobilization would result in an undisciplined mob that would destroy its own country in a torrent of violence. (*Voices:* "That's right." *Applause.*)

Officers' prestige must be raised. The officer corps, who have fought valiantly throughout the entire war, and the great majority of whom early on came over to the revolution's side and remain loyal to its cause, now must be rewarded morally for all the abuse it has endured—through no fault of its own—and for systematic humiliations. (*Voice:* "That's correct!") The material condition of officers, their families, fallen heroes' widows and orphans, must be improved. And by rights it must be noted that up to this point officers are almost the only group in Russia that has not breathed a word about its own needs, has not demanded improvement of its own material position. What this position is like can be illustrated by the example of an ensign taken from Petrograd's streets after collapsing from exhaustion brought on by hunger due to a lack of funds.

I am not opposed to soldiers' committees. As the Eighth Army's commander and Commander in Chief of the Southwestern Front, I worked with them. But I demand that their activities be restricted to the army's economic and internal life, within limits established precisely by law, without any interference in the sphere of operational questions, combat decisions, or selection of officers. I recognize the [government appointed] commissariat as necessary at present. But what guarantees this measure's validity is that the personnel who staff the commissariat are people whose democratic political thinking corresponds with tact, energy, and courage to take on very heavy responsibility. Without the rear, there is no army. Everything done at the front will be fruitless, and the blood that inevitably will flow once order is restored in the army will not be expiated by the motherland's good if the disciplined battle-ready army has no reinforcements, food, munitions, and clothing. Measures taken at the front must also be adopted in the rear, guided by the goal of the motherland's salvation. Meanwhile, according to my information, to the accurate information that I have at my disposal, at present our railroad network is in such a poor condition that by November it will not be able to transport all the goods the army needs, and the army will be left without supplies. I need not explain the repercussions of this fact.

On the Southwestern Front, which should be well supplied now that the harvest is being gathered, conditions are as follows. I will read you a telegram I received from the Commander in Chief of the Southwestern Front:

At the front there is a shortage of flour; there is absolutely no flour in the stores at the base. What has been sent by the provincial provisions committees is negligible. All the hardtack bakeries are closed and idle. For the first time in the entire war, reserves of hardtack will be rationed for rear garrisons. But they won't last long. I consider it my duty to report on this distress, as it is an extraordinary occurrence. For two weeks troops in this military district have resorted to exploiting local resources.[19] To preserve order and prevent food riots, the Southwestern Front's chief of supplies ordered the immediate organization of garrison commissions in Kiev. These, under the provincial provisions committees' direction, are to act immediately to procure supplies in the district's rear, through requisitions if need be. Government intervention nonetheless is required urgently. The front cannot go on living like this.

I could cite several statistics to illustrate the problem of supplying the army. Productivity in our defense industries has fallen such that, if we compare round figures on current production of principal goods the army needs to their production in October 1916–January 1917, weapons production has declined by 60 percent and munitions production by 60 percent. I will cite only these statistics. Consequentially, should this continue, our army will find itself in exactly the position it was in early spring 1915. That situation, as you all know, led to our army's withdrawal from Poland, Galicia, and the Carpathians.

I will cite one more statistic. For the active army's success now, it must have "eyes." I call airplanes "eyes." We also need airplanes for artillery action. The condition of our air force is such that we do not have the resources, either from abroad or from our own factories, to replace destroyed aircraft. We cannot replace the aircraft we have lost, and we are not in a position to replace the pilots we have lost, because we have nothing to teach them in. Currently, productivity in aviation factories has fallen by almost 80 percent. So unless resolute measures are adopted our air force, our valiant air force, which has contributed so much to our victories, will be extinct by spring.

If we are to reorganize the army and raise its fighting capability, then there can be no difference between punitive measures taken at the front and the rear. The country's salvation requires this. In one regard, though, the front must have priority, as it stands directly in the face of danger. If it is fated that we not have enough to eat, let the rear go hungry, but not the front.

There is one more thing that I consider it my duty to report, something that I have always believed in my heart and that I now observe: the country wants to live. The suicidal atmosphere that had overtaken this great, independent country like a spell cast by the enemy, which had been wrought by irresponsible slogans spread among the darkest and most ignorant masses, is being lifted. For the people's will to be realized effectively, the measures that I have outlined must be implemented immediately. I do not doubt for a minute that these measures will be implemented urgently. They must not come as a consequence of defeat and reductions to the fatherland's territory. Decisive measures to raise discipline at the front were taken as a result of the Tarnopol' disaster and the loss of Galicia and Bukovina; we cannot allow order in the rear to come as a consequence of our loss of Riga, or order on our railroads to come at the cost of ceding Moldavia and Bessarabia to the enemy.

I believe in the Russian people's genius, in the Russian people's reason, and in the country's salvation. I believe in our motherland's bright future. And I believe that our army's fighting capacity and her former glory will be restored. But I declare that there is no time to waste. We cannot waste one minute. Decisive, firm, and steadfast execution of the outlined measures is necessary. (*Applause.*)

Kaledin: We have outlined the following fundamental measures for the motherland's salvation:

1. The army must be kept outside of politics. (*Applause from the right; voices:* "Bravo!") Meetings and assemblies, with their party struggles and disputes, must be prohibited completely. (*Voices from the right:* "That's right!")
2. All soviets and committees must be abolished (*Commotion on the left; applause from the right. Voices:* Right!) both in the army and in the rear (*Voices from the right:* "That's right!" "Bravo!"; *commotion on the left*), with the exception of regimental, company, battery, and Cossack committees, whose rights and duties must be strictly limited to internal routines. (*Applause from the right; Voices:* "That's right!" "Bravo!")
3. The Declaration of Soldiers' Rights must be revised (*Applause from the right; voices* "Right!"; *commotion on the left*) and supplemented with a declaration of their duties. (*Voices:* "Bravo!" "That's true!"; *applause.*)
4. Discipline in the army must be raised and strengthened through the most resolute measures. (*Noise; voices from the right:* "Right!")
5. The rear and the front are an indivisible whole, ensuring the army's fighting capability, and all measures necessary to strengthen discipline at the front must also be implemented in the rear. (*Voices:* "Right!" "Bravo!")

6. Commanders' right to impose disciplinary measures must be restored. (*Voices from the right:* "Bravo!" "That's right!"; *a storm of applause; noise and whistles from the left.*) The army's leaders must be given full powers. (*Voices from the right:* "Right!"; *applause.*)

At this menacing hour of grave trials at the front, of complete internal collapse due to the country's political and economic disorganization, the only thing that can save the country from absolute ruin is a really strong government in capable and experienced hands. (*Voices from the right:* "Bravo, Bravo!"*) The hands of people who are not bound by narrow party or group programs. (*Voices from the right* "That's right!"; *applause.*) People who can take steps without having to look over their shoulder at all sorts of committees and soviets. (*Applause from the right; voices:* "Right!") People who understand that the source of the state's sovereign power is the people as a whole, not separate parties and groups. (*Voices from the right:* "Bravo"; *stormy applause.*) There must be one single authority for the center and the localities. The usurpation of state power by the soviets and committees must be brought to an immediate and abrupt end. (*Voices:* "That's Right!") Russia must be an indivisible whole. . . .

DOCUMENT 9.7
EKATERINA BRESHKO-BRESHKOVSKAIA'S SPEECH AT
THE STATE CONFERENCE[20]

The following document is a 14 August 1917 speech to the Moscow State Conference by the right Socialist Revolutionary activist Ekaterina Breshko-Breshkovskaia, the "Little Grandmother of the Russian Revolution."

Thank you, citizens, for the honor that you now are giving me. I have been granted permission to speak for a bit about what I think of the current state of things. Having listened to all the speeches on this third day, I sense that this great assembly can be said to represent all Russia. Here we see that our Russian people—or, it would be better to say, the population of our entire Russian state—has been submitted to an examination and has passed. Despite my deafness, I have not heard—nor have I read in the newspapers—a single contrary note in the speeches given here. Everyone in unison recognizes that we have a motherland and that we must defend this motherland's dignity with all of our strength. (*Applause. Voices:* "Right!")

Citizens, I have lived a long time. I have lived through much of Russian history. I have thought things over; I have experienced life, and I have survived. I know that words and promises sometimes hang in the air for a long time, citizens. I think our numerous responsibilities include setting about actualizing the goals we have set here, and doing it immediately, right after this meeting. I think our army must find its leaders, comrades, from among the persons present here. Surely our army faces misfortune not only at the front, but also in the rear. Our rear has gone without for three years. It is hungry and demoralized. There are people at this meeting who have made wise decisions, like those made in various soviets in Petrograd and Moscow. Understand that half these people, the better half, must go to the army and immediately head for the rear to organize our garrisons. Otherwise, you will achieve nothing. The army has no teachers, no friends, no mentors. At the same time, there are so many men occupied in daily affairs in Petrograd and Moscow that they are like vermicelli. So get out there and go to the army. (*Voices:* "It's true!" *Applause.*) Prepare the army for its great work.

Citizen workers, you also must go to work among the people and the army. Don't just talk. In Russia now, every last man must work only for the army. We have twenty million healthy young people in the army. They need to be trained, fed, clothed, and supplied with weapons. It is important that all Russia, and all Russia's women, work only for the army. Therefore, comrade workers—I do not know where your gaze is fixed now, but I am addressing you—remember that your labor is the salvation of republic and of our army. (*Voices:* "Correct!" *Applause.*)

Citizen *tsenstoviki*, you are gifted with such intellectual capabilities that you have spent the entire year studying.[21] Go and help Russia. Where are you? Where is your sense, where is your self-sacrifice, where is your work for the good of the motherland? We have not felt it! Now, when you know that the people need enlightenment, where is this enlightenment? Who is teaching the people? Who is speaking to the people or preaching to the people? I do not see it, I do not hear it. The people, like the army, remains without friends, without teachers, without mentors, without elders. That is a great mistake, citizens! Citizens, throughout tsarist times we all spoke of the Russian people: "Oh, the Russian people, it is a great people, a talented people, a self-sacrificing people! But tsarism holds it back and prevents it from manifesting its qualities." Citizens, now there is no one holding back the valiant Russian people! (*Applause.*)

I was only given 10 minutes for my speech. Citizens, this concerns our capitalists, big and small, and I am saying this before all Russia: they bear a great sin in their souls, a bloody sin! Citizens, I am not a biased person. You know where I come from and that I have many friends from among the propertied classes and among all sorts of different people.[22] I am not a biased person, but I tell you that the capitalists and the big and small traders are Russia's real internal enemies and truly deserve the government's most energetic and strictest attention.

THE BOLSHEVIK DELEGATION'S DECLARATION

And so, I ask that our government send all educated people to the army. Those who are intelligent and can teach the people must go to them, because we remain in such darkness. What is happening now in Russia comes out of that darkness—a frightening darkness that calls out to the counterrevolutionaries. It is intolerable that the country remains uncultivated, unenlightened, uneducated. In Petrograd and Moscow there are meetings every day, but in the villages there are none. Citizens, teachers have spent three years at the front, but until now female teachers have not been employed in any significant numbers. And so Russia relies upon a hundred million illiterates. You must understand this, citizens: this is your responsibility, the responsibility of the *tsentoviki*. You already have all the resources, all the literature, all the writers. The funds are available. You are obliged to accept this responsibility. If you do not, you will have to answer to all Russia, just as the capitalists now must answer before her. Because, citizens, [education] is your treasure, your capital, which you are obliged to give the people.

Citizens, I tell you that it makes my heart glad to hear unanimity, absolute unanimity, on issues concerning Russia and its welfare. But at the same time my heart falters, just as it faltered on 4 March when, sitting in [Siberia], I received a telegram saying that the revolution had been accomplished, the people were free, and I could return. Yes, I was at the highest level of happiness, and all the same my heart faltered. So, [I said to myself], we will go and find out about this revolution. And when we arrive there, what can we give it? I now repeat the words I said to myself then. From tomorrow on, citizens, we must turn our words into deeds. (*Applause.*)

DOCUMENT 9.8
THE BOLSHEVIK DELEGATION'S DECLARATION AT
THE MOSCOW STATE CONFERENCE[23]

The following document is a declaration by the Bolshevik delegation to the Moscow State Conference justifying their decision to boycott the meeting. This statement began to take shape at the Bolshevik Central Committee's 5 August 1917 session, and the final text was prepared between 5 and 12 August. It appeared in the Moscow Bolshevik newspaper, Social-Democrat (Sotsial-demokrat), *on 15 August 1917.*

A deadly danger threatens the revolution: the aristocratic landowners and the bourgeois parties are preparing a bloody punishment for the workers, soldiers, and peasant poor. They are gathering to restore unrestricted repression over and violence against the popular masses. Their aim is to return to power over the people.

At this hour the government, which calls itself the government for the "Salvation of the Revolution," has not come out against counterrevolution, against the parties behind the restoration of the aristocratic-bourgeois cabal, against the parties that demand the continuation of the predatory war. On the contrary, the government has invited notorious counterrevolutionaries to the State Conference in Moscow. It has guaranteed that they will have the majority, and is gathering them to negotiate with them and openly lean on them in furthering its work. Of all people, the Provisional Government has designated the people's branded enemies as the country's saviors; it declares that gravediggers of the revolution are the revolution's vital force. And so the Provisional Government reveals the aim of all its policies—of its struggle against the workers, whose newspapers and organizations it smashes; of its struggle against soldiers, for whom it has restored the death penalty; of its struggle against the peasants, to whom it will not give the land.

The Provisional Government has become a weapon of the counterrevolutionaries and international reaction. It convened the Moscow conference to rally its new power for a new campaign against all the revolution's achievements.

Encouraged by this cooperative policy, the people's enemies—the aristocratic landowners, bankers, and industrialists—have rallied around the Kadet Party for salvation of their war profits, estates, and capital. The Moscow conference provides the counterrevolutionary hangmen a convenient opportunity to reach an agreement, a convenient screen for organizing all-Russian counterrevolutionary negotiations. Before the conference, the Kadets already made up the counterrevolution's permanent political center, leaning on the armed support of the army high command and reactionary Cossack elements.

The Moscow conference reveals a plan to bypass and distort the people's will. At the moment it was convened, the convocation of the Constituent Assembly—the authentic people's government—was deferred again for two months. This was thanks to intrigues by the bourgeoisie, which unswervingly pursues its own aim—the Constituent Assembly's total disruption and its replacement with an institution in which the bourgeoisie could secure a majority.

Having undermined the Constituent Assembly, the bourgeois counterrevolution openly sets the Moscow conference against the workers' and soldiers' soviets. With the conference's help, the counterrevolution hopes to strike a decisive blow against the institutions that the working class has entrusted with responsibility for defending the revolution's interests, responsibility for the struggle for peace, land, and bread. The Socialist Revolutionaries and the Mensheviks, however, who now hold a majority in the Central Executive Committee of Soviets, haven't resisted the Moscow conference's convocation. They haven't tried to fight this trick, which so clearly benefits the counterrevolution. And they can't fight it, because they themselves stand for conciliation, for cooperative work with the bourgeois-aristocratic coalition. They have been making concessions to that coalition all along, by refusing to transfer all power to the workers, soldiers, and peasants and by proposing to share power with the bourgeois counterrevolutionaries.

For the broadest strata of urban and peasant poor, the Moscow conference demonstrates the need for an energetic struggle against counterrevolution. The working class—sure defenders and strong-hold of the revolution—have openly protested against the parade of counterrevolutionary forces organized by the Provisional Government in Moscow.[24] The Moscow proletariat's general strike expresses the thoughts and will of Russia's entire conscious proletariat, which has solved the riddle of counterrevolution. The working class answers the battle cry of the mobilized bourgeoisie with its own slogan: proletarian-peasant revolution.

We, members of the revolutionary party of the proletariat, came here not to negotiate with the revolution's enemies, but to protest on behalf of the workers and poor peasants against convocation of this counter-revolutionary conclave. We came to expose its true character for the entire country to see. But we were ordered to shut our mouths, and the SRs and Mensheviks in the soviet majority helped implement that order.[25] Still, we believe our voices and our protest will reach the popular masses, which will rally around us, the revolutionary party of the proletariat. . . . [T]he proletariat will not tolerate the bourgeois oppressors' triumph. The proletariat will lead the revolution to its conclusion. It will secure land for the peasant, and peace, bread, and freedom for the people.

Russia's proletariat, together with the international proletariat, will bring an end to capital's rule over toiling humanity.

DOCUMENT 9.9
IRAKLI TSERETELI, "THE POLITICAL SITUATION IN RUSSIA AND THE TASKS OF THE WORKING CLASS"[26]

Irakli Tsereteli presented the following report at the Mensheviks' "Unification Congress" on 19 August 1917, as published the next day in The Workers' Newspaper (Rabochaia gazeta). *At the State Conference, Menshevik leaders Tsereteli and Nikolai Chkheidze had proposed a united front, "The United Democracy," to protect the revolutionary state. The conference endorsed a "Democratic Program" to reorganize the army, shore up state finances, reform local government administration, improve food supply, revitalize trade and industry, plan land reform, and solve the nationalities question.*

By the time the Menshevik congress met, though, this "united front" had evaporated.

The Political Situation in Russia and the Tasks of the Working Class

The great historical task of radically reconstructing Russia on a democratic basis fell to the proletariat and its party under difficult circumstances. The Russian Revolution happened at a time of war, and war has been the main impediment to consolidating its achievements. The first task facing the revolution and the proletariat was mustering strength to end the war. This was vital to the democratic country and proletariat. The revolution therefore faced a problem that is international in its nature, which the Russian Revolution's force alone could not solve.

At the same time, devastation from the war demanded great effort in domestic affairs and great sacrifices from the most revolutionary social classes. Marshalling resources to consolidate the democratic revolution made it impossible to increase the toiling classes' material prosperity or to distribute the burden equally on all strata of the population. . . . Attitudes about the war have sharply divided democratic elements. . . . The proletariat had to unite with the bourgeoisie strata in the cause of obtaining peace. Ending the war became a question of life or death for the country.

These details dictated the methods of struggle: the proletariat's leading elements dominated the [soviets], which became the focus of disputes with the democratic organizations. It was impossible to differentiate between the proletariat's tactics and the tactics of [the soviets]; the proletariat had to become the center of the revolution. Had the proletariat refused to participate in forming a national government, no government could have been created. Even before the coalition was formed, the government could not exist without sanction of the democratic organizations.

To give the Russian Revolution direction, a stance toward the war had to be defined. The proletariat, in unison with the democracy, laid out a platform that seemed to represent the entire nation. Sections of the bourgeoisie that would not accept these tasks and the revolution's mission then fell away. The result was the first government crisis [in April 1917].

One of the Russian Revolution's peculiarities is that it was impossible to form a government from the bourgeoisie's ranks that could communicate with the democratic movement and accomplish general-national tasks. The proletariat faced a dilemma: should it allow power to remain in the hands of the bourgeoisie, which had become hostile toward the revolutionary democracy's institutions, or create a new government that included representatives of the proletariat?

We did all we could to create a government that was radical-democratic without the proletariat's participation. But neither the peasants nor the petty-bourgeoisie had sufficient strength to take power without the workers. And so it fell to the working class to take formal responsibility for creating a government. But given objective conditions, this government could not accomplish creative work. The difficulty rested in the mood of both the bourgeois elements and the democracy. Among the proletariat, the peasantry, and the army—other than those aware of the movement's real tasks—there was an anarchistic mindset, fostered under the old order, and fed by the demoralization brought about by the war.

We did not succeed in organizing all toilers around our platform. Constant clashes impeded the work of a government that was revolutionary in composition and had a democratic program. The 3–5 July events were the culmination of this process. The government faced a question of life and death: could it repel the counterrevolution? Could it have anticipated an attempt like that of 3 July?

At the Moscow State Conference, the first [national conference held] after 3 July, representatives of all the toiling elements tried to open a conversation about a unified revolutionary front. The danger that the working class would be isolated from the rest of the democracy, which was spoken of in Moscow, was ended by agreement on a general platform. This platform, drafted by working class' leading elements, makes it possible for the working class to consolidate its vanguard role. This platform must become the single standard for our relations with all strata and with the government. A real coalition that is united can successfully preserve unitary state authority. But we would still repudiate the coalition were it not able to realize the Democratic Program.

. . . The revolution must close its ranks in unity. The time has come for a decisive and forceful policy to prevent civil war and the disintegration of the front. At this moment, the democracy and the proletariat must categorically demand that all the government's actions have one purpose: saving the revolution. Up to this point, the revolutionary government's actions have not guaranteed this. It has not had full support from the revolution's organized elements. In Moscow, for the first time, the organized democracy stood up against propertied Russia. For the first time, an all-national formula for salvation was proposed. This is the formula that all the democracy's organized forces are defending.

Mensheviks will remain in the government under the condition that they can implement the general-national platform advanced and approved by the country's great majority. They will remain under the condition that the revolutionary government pursues the revolution's creative tasks and fights using revolutionary methods against the forces of demoralization. Under these conditions, we must guarantee the government support.

The Social Democrats' tasks include struggling and achieving better real conditions for its class, but also ensuring the propertied classes that we will come out fearlessly against anarchy. . . . One of the Social Democrats' great tasks—as a dangerous mood swells, and as the rash actions of one section of the working class threaten to harm common goals—is to struggle, along with the propertied ranks, against anarchy.[27] [We must] struggle, in the name of unity, around proper notions of revolution's tasks and proper notions of the class movement.

DOCUMENT 9.10
PEASANT UNREST IN TAMBOV PROVINCE IN AUGUST– SEPTEMBER 1917[28]

The two documents in this set concern peasant unrest in Tambov Province in the Black Earth Region. In July and August 1917, local peasant committees began claiming the right to privately owned properties, including both large estates and small farms. In August and September, disputes over land turned violent: peasants destroyed several manor houses, burned barns, and wrecked farm machinery. In one widely publicized incident, peasants in Umansk County killed a landowner, Prince Viazameskii. The first document is an appeal by the Council of the Tambov Union of Private Landowners ("The Union of Unfortunate Landowners") complaining of violent peasant attacks in August.

Such appeals did nothing to alleviate hostility between villagers and landowners. In Kozlovsk County on 6 September 1917, a freeholder named Romanov shot and killed two villagers. The village assembly retaliated by lynching Romanov. Over the next two weeks, peasants in Kozlov County attacked more than a dozen other freeholds and destroyed more than 50 aristocratic estates. Tambov's provincial commissar dispatched 200 soldiers to quell the violence, but they proved inadequate. On 15 September the government sent 300 Cossacks from Moscow as reinforcements. These military detachments arrested some 1,500 peasants. Peasant committees, Tambov garrison soldiers, and the Tambov Soviet protested against this use of force, and the government withdrew its troops. Not surprisingly, landowners called on the government to take an even firmer hand against peasant land seizures. The second document is a list of properties destroyed and burned in Kozlovsk County in early September, compiled by a local state official.

August 1917
To a future in which the proletariat and the Russian landowners are united.
Only in God's fiery vengeance will you find consolation.

Through serfdom, the aristocratic serf owners, with the tsar at their head, gnawed away at the corpse of our wretched land and at the people's fortune. After liberation, the land was almost freed of these gnawers, who, without access to slave labor, lost interest and instead began to gnaw away at state power and big industry.

We and our parents acquired the land that the serf owners abandoned through our blood, toil, and money. We, the new landowners who come from all social strata, are sober and thrifty people, lovers of the land who know how to organize and improve our farms. What is most important in agriculture is not simply labor at the reaper and plow—any drunkard can do that—but toil by thoughtful, sober, hardworking, and attentive builders of farms, by diligent farmers.

Until recently we have lived very badly in our careless and disorderly state. But then our musty old state collapsed because of a war that was beyond its strength. The rotten autocracy has fallen, and the cowardly peasant-soldiers have run away from the front.

And now ruthless fate, as if for a joke, has called on the wise and honorable socialists to save the doomed state. . . . Already they are busy trying to save their own skins, which they did not spare in the struggle with the autocracy, but which became wretched when they seized power. And so they have not so much led the people as dragged along behind them, all the while spouting ignorant slogans.

The socialists, without laughing, talk about our people as if they were drops in the sea. To them, the people are weak, poor, faded, and cowardly. They pay no heed to the cost of property ruined or to the destruction caused by our participation in an international conflict between great nations, nations that have an abundance of force and which despise our poverty and lack of culture.

It is bitter, but equally true, that the solution to this unbearable situation that the socialists offer is to shout about the Russian proletariat's power and abilities. Using absurd expressions, they dictate lessons and make demands to the great cultured nations of Western Europe. Meanwhile, they deceive their own people with rumors about the right to seize our land for free, which is possible only through the complete abolition of private property.

If the land had been seized 60 years ago, as part of the dark people's liberation from the aristocratic serf owners, when the people really had the right to compensation for centuries of torment and labor, then it would have been justified. But it is senseless and criminal to do this now, at the expense of people who are not guilty, when almost no traces of the aristocratic serf owners remain.

The people, having abolished the death penalty as a murderous crime, are themselves introducing another crime into law—criminal seizure—as the foundation of their lazy prosperity. The people know nothing about governing. They are unfit and cannot have their own state. So, just as socialists would not acknowledge the criminal autocracy . . . we cannot acknowledge the criminal, thieving republic; we thirst for a republic of justice and culture.

Under such conditions, we cannot escape ruin, nor can our children escape hunger. Because we will never obey the orders and laws of a criminal state that wants to legalize criminal seizures. We can find no place for ourselves in our reckless state, just as the socialists previously could not. The socialists use terror because they have no other resources. They clearly want to take us and our children down this dreadful path.

. . . This is inevitable, although it is bitter and terrible: from among hundreds of thousands of impoverished landowners, a tenth will have their property taken permanently. That is, tens of thousands of the most unfortunate and the most ardent will lose their land. And one dark night, in tens of thousands of thieving villages, there will be single-minded sessions of soviets of workers', soldiers', and peasants' deputies, led by people who have fled to the countryside after bankrupting the factories and plants. And then they will appear at the properties of these tens of thousands of unfortunates, with boxes of matches and kerosene. And they will light all Russia afire, not sparing the houses, woods, or crops. It will be just that easy for the wicked robbers to divvy up a backwards land.

. . . We face this horror alone, but there will be consolation in God's fiery vengeance.

The Union of Unfortunate Landowners

7 October 1917

List of Privately Owned Estates Wrecked or Burned in Kozlovsk County, 18 September 1917.

Number	Name, Patronymic, and Last name of the ruined owner	In which township	Condition of portions of the estate
1	Natalia Antovna Kozena[29]	Nikol'sk	Wrecked
2	Ivan Alekseevich Shubin	Nikol'sk	Same
3	Mark Makovich Liuboshchinskii	Nikol'sk	Wrecked and burned
4	Aleksei Nikolaevich Volinskii	Nikol'sk	Wrecked
5	Aleksei Vasil'evich	Nikol'sk	Same
6	Palen	Nikol'sk	Same
7	Vasilii Akimovich Sviridov	Nikol'skaia	Same
8	Ivan Minaevich Kurochkin	Bogoivlensko-Surensk	Wrecked and partly burned
9	Petr Ivanovich Rogov	Novo-Degtiansk	Wrecked
10	Ivan Ivanovich Pozniakov	Novo-Degtiansk	Wrecked and burned

11	Ol'ga Nikolaevna Panteleimonova	Novo-Degtiansk	Wrecked
12	Dmitrii Mil'sonovich Safonov	Novo-Degtiansk	Same
13	Vasilii Aleksandrovich Leont'ev	Novo-Degtiansk	Wrecked and burned
14	Naslednikov Strel'nikova	Novo-Degtiansk	Wrecked
15	Ivan Ivanovich Dlugokanskii	Novo-Degtiansk	Wrecked and burned
16	Ol'ga Sergeevna Zhikhareva	Chelnask	Same
17	Sofiia Nikitichna Fursova	Bibikovsk	Wrecked
18	Teacher Petr Erofeevich Popov	Selinsk township and village	Destroyed buildings, wrecked property in village of Stekhkii
19	Former township scribe Pavel Mikhailovich Shushkin	[same]	[blank]
20	Peasant Vasilii Potapovich Kovylin	[same]	[blank]
21	Fedosa Pavlovna Iamshchikov	[same]	[blank]
22	Iakova Pavlovicha Iamshchikov	[same]	[blank]
23	Lavrentiia Petrovicha Nenasheva	[same]	[blank]
24	Ivan Fedorovich Iakushkin	Spassk	Estate wrecked and burned
25	Nikolai Nikolaevich Mil'tsin	Spassk	Wrecked
26	Princess Belosel'skaia-Beloserskaia, Troitsko-Ivanskii village property	Spassk	Wrecked and burned
27	Her property in Skobelevko village	Spassk	Wrecked
28	Evgenii Pavlovich [no last name]	Spassk	Same
29	Dmitrii Nikolaevich Voronin	Spassk	Same
30	Mikhail Nikanorovich Kirillov	Bogoliubsk	Same
31	Roman Pavlovich Riakhovskikh	Pavlovsk	Insignificant damage
32	Vasili Pavlovich Riakhovskikh	Pavlovsk	Insignificant damage
33	Iakov Terent'evich Riakhovskikh	Uspensk	[blank]
34	Nikolai Vasil'evich Sarantsev	Uspensk	[blank]
35	Petr Fedorovich Rakhmaninov, Two estates	Novo-Garitovsk	[blank]

(Continued)

List of Privately Owned Estates Wrecked or Burned in Kozlovsk County, 18 September 1917. *(Continued)*

Number	Name, Patronymic, and Last name of the ruined owner	In which township	Condition of portions of the estate
36	Sergei Danilovich Korovanov	Novo-Garitovsk	[blank]
37	Lev Petrovich Cheremisov	Novo-Garitovsk	[blank]
38	Nikolai Semenovich Rusinov	Novo-Garitovsk	Wrecked
39	Ivan Ivanovich Rakhmaninov	Novo-Garitovsk	[blank]
40	Nikolai Aleksandrovich Dmitriev	Novo-Garitovsk	[blank]
41	Aleksei Nikolaevich Davydov	Iaroslavsk	[blank]
42	Konstantin Petrpvich Kovrigin	Iaroslavsk	[blank]
43	Aleksei and Viktor Ivanovich Petropavlovskii	Iaroslavsk	Wrecked and burned
44	Ivan Iakovlevich Kozhevnikov	Iaroslavsk	Wrecked and burned
45	Konstantin Petrovich Romanov	Iaroslavsk	Wrecked and burned
46	Konstantin Fedorovich Popov	Iaroslavsk	Wrecked and burned
47	Vasilii Nikolaevich Sobolev	Ekaterinoslavsk	Wrecked and burned
48	Stepan Fedorovich Popov	Ekaterinoslavsk	Wrecked and burned
49	Abram Abramovich Ushakov	Ekaterinoslavsk	Wrecked and burned
50	Ekaterina Konstantinovna Beliaeva	Ekaterinoslavsk	[blank]
51	Sergei Sergeevich Desnitskii	Ekaterinoslavsk	Wrecked
52	Vasilii Egorovich Volosatov	Ekaterinoslavsk	Wrecked and burned
53	Efim Efimovich Kopyrin	Izosimovsk	[blank]
54	Nikita Efimovich Losev	Izosimovsk	Wrecked

Detailed information on the wrecking and burning of the estates indicated, with separate listings of losses, specifications, and clarifications will be in a forthcoming report.

[signature]

DOCUMENT 9.11
LIGOVSKII, "INTO THE REALM OF ANARCHY"[30]

The following document is an editorial on rural violence in Tambov Province (see document 9.10). For Ligovskii, author of this commentary in the 22 September

1917 issue of The Moscow Bulletin (Moskovskii vedomosti), *rural unrest was emblematic of general anarchy.*

Into the Realm of Anarchy.

We have not just come recklessly close to the most desperate anarchy; we have crossed into its realm.

The horror is clear from one description of pogroms in Kozlovsk County. The rioters not only stole and burned, but they showed absolutely no mercy for property that creates cultural value. They destroyed seed grain and breeding cattle. According to telegraph reports, nearly 25 estates were burned and looted. But what is really more significant is that the wave of riots has not ended; instead, it has spread to other regions. And is there any way to get accurate telegraphic reports from regions where the rioters control everything, and the telegraphs?

We had all sorts of detailed official information on the unsuccessful and absolutely insignificant Kornilov "uprising."[31] But the government that informed us about this "uprising" says nothing about unbridled and wild pogroms against estates. Not unless they are connected to real hardships, like attacks on some old man's elderberry grove in Kiev.

The official *Telegraph Agency* reports nonsense about gangs of convicts leading the pogroms. Supposedly, terrorized peasants are blindly submitting to these alleged convicts. But these same telegrams, which report that the rioters *not only rob, but also burn*, show that the riots are not led by convict gangs. A convict gang wants to steal; a gang of peasant rioters wants to smash and burn. What is behind these fables about convict gangs?

For instance, did convicts terrorize the peasants who destroyed the estate of Prince Viazemskii, who had shown them much charity? Here, too, nothing at all was stolen, but everything was smashed and burned. No, you can look up convicts in the archives and know who they are.

From the time fieldwork ended in early September, the peasants set themselves to "pogrom work." And unless it is nipped in the bud, this wave of pogroms most certainly will roll across all *Rus.*[32] The rioters are destroying and burning with almost complete impunity, to the absolute bewilderment of the authorities. Consider this strange fact: we all have read about tens, even hundreds, of pogroms. But have you read about any trials of the rioters? No, you have not, because there have not been any trials. Why is that? Can it really be that destroying an estate isn't a criminal offense?

Instead of being the work of convicts, one should see the pogroms as the work of the former Minister-Rioter V. M. Chernov, who issued instructions on land while agriculture minister that have been deemed improper and cancelled.[33] And who allowed those improper instructions to be enacted?

Anarchy on the land is not caused by alleged convicts. It is caused by fear that the government will be strict regarding the land question; fear that the government will declare authoritatively that no plunder will be allowed in our future civilized state. Declare that not a single estate that has been destroyed will be given to the peasants as ransom, and the wave of pogroms will cease. Instead, the various soviets and committees, and even provincial land committees and provincial commissars (as in Tambov) try to calm the provocateurs' passions simply by "appealing to their good will": "Soon, on 29 November, the Constituent Assembly will meet and transfer all property to you. Therefore, do not destroy it, and do not burn it. It all will be yours."

But to the peasants' way of reasoning, isn't it clear—absolutely clear—that it is best if estates are run as "theirs"? And that "The Constituent Assembly will transfer all property"?

But can the will of the Constituent Assembly be anticipated? What if it does not transfer all property? What will happen then? Will there be a new wave of pogroms, arsons, thefts, and murders? And, after these impractical promises about "appeals for calm" to the savages, wouldn't the people have the right to say, "I have been deceived!"

If firm authority is needed anywhere, it is in the struggle against pogroms. If this firmness is not displayed, then Russia will be overcome by waves of flames and blood.

—Ligovskii

DOCUMENT 9.12
TWO ESSAYS ON ANARCHY FROM *THE ASTRAKHAN NEWSPAPER*[34]

In late summer and fall 1917, newspapers across Russia carried story after story suggesting that disaster and complete collapse were inevitable. Newspapers informed readers of growing food shortages and the threat of famines and epidemics, peasant attacks on landlord estates, the breakdown of law and order in the towns, and the decay of discipline in the army and fleet. Such reports contributed to the widespread impression of a government powerless in the face of anarchy. This was true even in far-flung provincial centers such as Astrakhan, where the two following newspaper commentaries appeared in September 1917.

The first is a fel'eton—*a commentary in the form of a satirical sketch—by the local writer Peter Smuglov, published in the nonparty liberal daily,* The Astrakhan Newspaper (Astrakhanskii listok), *on 26 September 1917. Aspiring authors used the fel'eton to showcase their literary skills. The second is an unsigned commentary from the 29 September number of* Astrakhan Newspaper, *which takes a similarly jaundiced view of the collapse of order.*

In Our Times.

On the table there is a wealth of newspaper materials from which to choose. The newspapers contain one sensational story after another. In Kursk and Kaluga Provinces, people are beginning to starve. In Saratov, there is typhus, in Ufa, a pogrom, in Orel, the same. In Orel, the decisive factor is the crowd's contact with a state alcohol storehouse.

All of these stories dwell on human deaths. Here is a story about our army's preparations for its winter campaign, which shows that it still lacks necessary winter gear; there, a story in which Hindenburg resolves something grandiose and very promising for the Kaiser. Every bit of news leaps off the pages as historic. But all this has become so familiar and so ordinary that it does not hold our attention.

Then, rifle shots are heard from somewhere nearby. At first they are rare, each sound distinct. Then they become more frequent and blend into a drum-roll.

A voice outside the window quietly says "A splendid shot!"

There is the sound of the tram, the rattle of carts, the beep of an automobile horn.

A piano clinks in the neighbors' apartment. A young voice artlessly sings:

The tunes that I feel in my heart/ Float through the open window.
They are carried to you, to you/ And I wait for your answer.

Again, shots—scattered and distinct, like desolate, solitary, memorable blows of a hammer, but close, as if they will soon be under the window.

A conversation is heard:

"Why is there shooting? What's going on over there?"
"Well, it looks like they've reached the alcohol storehouse, and there's a riot going on . . ."
"So, what are they doing, shooting in the air?"
"Yeah, well, that's how it goes . . ."

The conversation quiets.

"It's time to sleep" a lazy voice says reluctantly, and then adds "The alcohol storehouse . . . Well, that's what everyone expected. I didn't think it was anything in particular . . ."

"Good night!"

The shots continue. The tram thunders by. There are peaceful footsteps. The young woman's voice competes melodically with the sound of the piano. And on the table the inexhaustible reserve of newspaper material: this is not news—it is the sensation of authentic history.

The midnight hour approaches. As it grows nearer, the sound of rifle fire swells.

—P[eter] Smuglov

Anarchy.

In recent days, various offices have received reports from the provinces on the anarchy that reigns in almost all branches of government administration.

Information from the Justice Ministry is particularly interesting. A number of reports from prosecutors testify that Justice Ministry agents cannot cope with the responsibilities entrusted to them. For example, the prosecutor in one court district issued an order to arrest some character for embezzling state property, purloining private property, and so on. Immediately, on the same day, some unknown people searched that very prosecutor's dwelling and arrested him. And it is up to these prosecutors to implement the Justice Ministry's directives.

In several localities, the workers' and soldiers' soviet executive committees assist in prosecutorial investigations, but in most such cases the committees themselves are at a loss about how they can render any help. In many Russian provinces the authority of the workers' and soldiers' soviet committees is in serious decline.

DOCUMENT 9.13
LOCAL CRIME IN 1917: A STATISTICAL REPORT COMPILED BY SMOLENSK POLICE OFFICIALS[35]

On 17 October 1917, the Provisional Government's Ministry of Internal Affairs requested that police administrators in Russia's provinces send the ministry statistics comparing the number of crimes reported in March through September 1917 to that reported in March through September 1916. The following document is a statistical table prepared by the Smolensk City Militia enumerating crimes in several categories as well as the number and percentage of crimes "solved." The table, it should be noted, counts only those crimes reported to the local police. Although such statistics are not an absolute measure of crime in 1917, they help us understand why many commentators believed public order had broken down.

Regarding categories of crimes: "hooliganism" generally referred to acts of vandalism. "False documents" or "No documents" referred to people who did not present police with valid identification upon request. Police also could arrest soldiers found in civilian clothing, or could detain people for "administrative purposes" as ordered by regional or central state authorities.

Smolensk City Militia Statistics Comparing Reported Crime in 1916 to That in 1917

Type of offense cases	March–September 1916			March–September 1917		
	No. solved	No. solved	Percent cases	No. solved	No. solved	Percent
Theft < 300 rubles	375	203	54%	696	428	62%
Theft > 300 rubles	28	12	43%	51	26	51%
Burglary	40	24	60%	197	63	35%
Horse/Cattle theft	12	9	75%	26	17	73%
Murder	0	0		1	1	100%
Attempted Murder	0	0		3	3	100%
Armed Robbery	0	0		16	12	75%
Armed Offense	2	0		11	8	73%
Infanticide	0	0		13	1	7%
Fraud	11	6	56%	14	13	93%
Swindling	2	1	50%	14	14	100%
False Documents	8	8		18	18	
No Documents	18	18		5	5	
Selling Spirits	14	14		55	55	
Drunkenness	0	0		58	58	
Sale of State Goods	1	1		11	11	
Hooliganism	1	1		3	3	
Out of Uniform	0	0		1	1	
Unregistered Weapons	1	1		3	3	
Totals	513	298	59%	1178	740	63%

(Continued)

Smolensk City Militia Statistics Comparing Reported Crime in 1916 to That in 1917 *(Continued)*

	March–September 1916	March–September 1917
Number Jailed as Criminals	156	242
Number Registered as Criminals	800	1,447
Number Held for Lacking Documents	173	653
Number Held as Repeat Offenders	36	93
Number Held as Deserters	83	275
Number Held for Administrative Purposes	0	64

FLASH POINTS OF CONFLICT: THE KORNILOV REBELLION

342

DOCUMENT 10.1
BORIS SAVINKOV'S ACCOUNT OF A CONVERSATION WITH GENERAL KORNILOV[1]

In late July 1917, Russia's new supreme military commander, General Lavr Kornilov, demanded that Kerensky roll back revolutionary reforms in the army. Having restored the death penalty at the front, Kornilov insisted on its establishment in the rear. He also called for restoration of officers' disciplinary powers, abolition of the soviets, and an end to the socialists' influence on the government. When Kerensky failed to grant these demands, Kornilov pressed the issue at the State Conference. Rumors of a military coup spread.

Vladimir L'vov and Deputy War Minister Boris Savinkov clumsily sought to negotiate an alliance between Kornilov and Kerensky. When bungled communications and mutual mistrust foiled their efforts, Kerensky removed Kornilov from his post on 27 August. Kornilov then denounced Kerensky and ordered troops on Petrograd. Kornilov, though, lacked the army's support, and his attempted coup d'état collapsed on 31 August. In its wake, Kerensky was weakened, the Kadets were tainted as alleged accessories, and the Bolsheviks emerged with greater political authority.

The following document is Savinkov's account of a 23 August 1917 discussion with Kornilov, as presented in testimony before the Provisional Government's Special Commission to Investigate the Matter of General L. G. Kornilov on 15 September 1917.

Savinkov:[2] Mister General, I come to inform you in the Provisional Government's name that the Provisional Government has decided to detach Petrograd city from the Petrograd Military District and to declare martial law in the city. The district will be subordinated to the Supreme Commander. Martial law is being implemented in light of possible disorders in the city, to protect the Provisional Government from any attack. The Prime Minister has entrusted me to ask you for a cavalry corps. This cavalry corps should be sent to Petrograd in the next few days. It will be under the Provisional Government's command. But before we go into detail about the commission entrusted to me, I would like to speak with you privately. (*With these words Filonenko and General Lukomskii, who were present, got up and left the room.*)[3]

Lavr Georgievich, here is how matters stand. The War Ministry recently received telegrams signed by various people—officers at Stavka—I am not hiding anything from you—that alarm me.[4] These telegrams frequently concern political questions; moreover, their tone is intolerable, and they express views that are not always friendly toward the Provisional Government. As I already have said, I trust you and do not fear you, meaning that I trust that you are loyal to the Provisional Government and will not go against it. But I cannot say the same about your staff.

Kornilov: I must tell you that I no longer have faith in Kerensky and the Provisional Government. There are people like Chernov among the Provisional Government's members and also ministers like Avksent'ev.[5] The Provisional Government does not have the strength to stay on the path to firm authority, which is the country's only salvation. It has paid for each step with a piece of the fatherland's territory. This is shameful. Kerensky not only seems weak and vacillating, but insincere. He undeservedly insulted me at the Moscow State Conference. In addition, he carried out discussions with Cheremisov behind my back and wanted to appoint him Supreme Commander.[6]

Savinkov: It seems to me that there is no place for personal grievances in matters of state. Were you or Kerensky to insult me today, I would not try to get even. As for Cheremisov, Kerensky did not want to appoint him, the Workers' and Soldiers' Soviet did. I consider Chernov's presence on the Provisional Government undesirable. I consider Avksent'ev unprepared to be a minister. As for Kerensky, I cannot agree with you. I know Kerensky. I like him and trust him. Kerensky is a person with a big and generous soul, sincere and honest. But you are right about one thing—it is understood that he is not strong.

Kornilov: The government's composition must be changed.

Savinkov: As far as I know, Kerensky shares that opinion.

Kornilov: Kerensky must not meddle in [military] affairs.

Savinkov: That is not possible at present, even were it necessary. In the future, in the natural course of things, Kerensky in all likelihood will become the President of the Russian Republic. I would welcome his presidency.

Kornilov: Alekseev, Plekhanov, and Argunov must be in the government.[7]

Savinkov: Rather, socialists from the soviets must be replaced by non-soviet socialists. Is that what you want to say?

Kornilov: Yes. The soviets have demonstrated their lack of vitality, their inability to defend the country.

Savinkov: But they are not military organizations.

Kornilov: Military organizations are better.

Savinkov: Lavr Georgievich, these all are matters for the future. You are dissatisfied with the government. But nonetheless you must agree that without Kerensky, without him at the head, any sort of government is inconceivable.

Kornilov: Of course, you are correct. Without Kerensky at its head, a government is inconceivable. But Kerensky is indecisive. He wavers. He makes promises and then does not act upon them.

Savinkov: That is not accurate. Permit me to inform you that in the six days after the Moscow Conference, after Kerensky announced the government would take the path of firm authority, the War Ministry worked out and presented the Provisional Government with draft legislation against squandering state property and weapons, prohibiting card games in the military, and abolishing military district courts. You should know that the Provisional Government already has agreed to all three pieces of draft legislation.

You may say these are legal matters of secondary importance. But permit me to explain to you that, beyond what I have already reported, the War Ministry already has declared Petrograd under martial law. In addition—and this is all important—it has worked out a preliminary draft law on military revolutionary courts at the rear. This draft legislation was prepared according to Kerensky's directives, which I delivered myself. It has been reviewed positively and will soon be presented to the Provisional Government.

Kornilov: When exactly?

Savinkov: When I return to Petrograd.

Kornilov: On that very day?

Savinkov: Or the following day.

Kornilov: I trust you, but I have no faith in Kerensky's firmness.

Savinkov: When I deliver it to the ministers, perhaps then you will be assured that Kerensky stands precisely for firm authority. If I see that he changes policy, I will resign on that day.

Kornilov: [The government] will put in place regulations on committees and commissars?

Savinkov: Yes, they are favorably disposed toward that.

Kornilov: Good. You spoke about my staff. If there are conspirators there, I will arrest them.

Savinkov: I'm very glad to hear that. I have no doubt about that.

Kornilov: Come dine with me today. After dinner we can speak about the Petrograd Military District. I must say that for me, separating Petrograd [from the district] is unacceptable strategically.

Savinkov: Mr. General, besides strategic issues, there are political considerations that cannot be ignored. In addition to revisiting staff questions, would you agree to ask Filonenko to issue an order transferring the Union of Officers to Moscow and forbidding the staff from rendering them technical aid?[8]

Kornilov: Yes, I will speak with Filonenko.

Savinkov: And could you also abolish Stavka's Political Department, to avoid misunderstandings?[9]

Kornilov: I need the Political Department. I must know about what is going on among my troops, not only from the commissars, but the front-line commanders. But I will talk about this with Filonenko. He will look into the Political Department's activities.

Savinkov: Thank you, Lavr Georgievich. This has been an honor. Until this evening.

DOCUMENT 10.2
KERENSKY'S CONDEMNATION OF KORNILOV;
KORNILOV'S RESPONSE[10]

Kornilov came away from conversations with Savinkov and V. N. L'vov think-ing that Kerensky had agreed to disband the Petrograd Soviet and form a new government. He plotted with officers in Petrograd to stage a phony Bolshevik uprising, at which point the Third Cavalry would go into action and crush the soviet. If nothing else, Kornilov expected that Kerensky would yield at the threat of military force. Kerensky, however, believed the general meant to seize power for himself, and ordered Kornilov's dismissal as supreme commander on 27 August 1917. Kerensky's telegram relaying this order is the first document below. Upon news of Kerensky's order, Kornilov apparently became despondent and threatened suicide. He had made no detailed plans for a coup d'état *and had not coordinated actions with the army's front commanders. Kornilov sent his own telegram appealing to the country for support (the second document). But the general quickly found himself isolated, and the "Kornilov Rebellion" collapsed.*

To the Entire Country
I hereby announce:

On 26 August General Kornilov sent State Duma member Vladimir L'vov to me with a demand that the Provisional Government surrender all civil and military power so that he might, at his personal discretion, form *a new government* to rule the country. In a conversation with me by direct wire, General Kornilov subsequently confirmed that he had authorized L'vov to make such a proposal. The Provisional Government considers the presentation of such demands, addressed to me as the Provisional Government's representative, an attempt by certain circles in Russian society to take advantage of the state's grave condition, to establish a regime in the country that is hostile to the revolution's achievements. Therefore, the Provisional Government has found it necessary:

For the salvation of our motherland, liberty, and our republican order, to authorize me to take immediate and resolute measures to extirpate any attempt to usurp the state's supreme power or the rights that citizens have gained through the revolution.

I am taking all steps necessary to protect the country's liberty and order. The population will be informed regarding these measures in due time.

At the same time, I hereby order:

General Kornilov to surrender the post of supreme commander to General Klembovskii, commander in chief of the Northern Front, which blocks the way to Petrograd. I order General Klembovskii to assume the post of supreme commander temporarily, while remaining in Pskov.

Petrograd city and county are under martial law, and regulations regarding regions under martial law are extended to Petrograd (under the Comprehensive Code, Vol. 2, General Administration of Provinces, Statute 23, amendment published in 1892 and extended in 1912).[11]

I call on all citizens to remain completely calm and maintain the order so necessary for the country's salvation. I call on all ranks in the army and navy to carry out their duty of defending the country against the external enemy with calm and self-sacrifice.

A. F. Kerensky
Prime Minister, Minister of War
27 August 1917

The entire first part of the Prime Minister's telegram no. 4163 is a complete lie. I did not send State Duma member Vladimir L'vov to the Provisional Government; he came to me as the Prime Minister's emissary. State *Duma* member Aleksei Alad'in is a witness to this. A *great provocation* therefore has taken place that jeopardizes the motherland's fate.

People of Russia!

Our great motherland is dying.

The final hour is near.

Compelled to speak openly, I, General Kornilov, declare that the Provisional Government—working under pressure from the Bolshevik majority in the soviets—is acting in complete agreement with the German general staff's plans. It is destroying the army and undermining the country's foundations at the same time that enemy forces are preparing to land on the Riga coast.

At this ominous moment, the heaviest awareness of the country's inevitable destruction commands that I summon all Russia's people to aid the dying motherland. Let all in whose breast a Russian heart beats, all who believe in God and in His church, pray to the Lord for the greatest miracle: our native land's salvation!

I, General Kornilov, the son of a Cossack peasant, declare to all that I want nothing for myself but to preserve Great Russia. I vow that through victory over the enemy I will lead the people to the Constituent Assembly, at which they themselves will decide their own fate and chose their new form of government. It is absolutely impossible for me to betray Russia into the hands of her ancient enemy, the German tribe, and so to turn the Russian people into slaves of the Germans. I would rather die on the field of honor than see the Russian land in shame and infamy.

People of Russia! Your country's life is in your hands!

27 August 1917

General Kornilov

DOCUMENT 10.3
MENSHEVIK DECLARATIONS AT A JOINT SESSION OF
SOVIET CENTRAL EXECUTIVE COMMITTEES[12]

In Petrograd at 11:00 P.M. on 27 August 1917, a joint session of the Central Executive Committee of Soviets of Workers' and Soldiers' Deputies and the Executive Committee of Peasants' Deputies convened to formulate a coordinated response to the Kornilov revolt. The following documents are declarations made early in this joint session by Mensheviks. This first statement, by Semen Vainshtein (Zvezdin), an antiwar Menshevik from Siberia, set in motion creation of a "Committee for the People's Struggle against Counterrevolution." This committee included representatives from the socialist parties; the Petrograd, Kronshtadt, Vyborg, and Helsinki soviets; Petrograd's factory committees and the trade unions; and the Baltic Fleet. The second document is a summary of Menshevik-Internationalist leader Iulii Martov's statements concerning Kerensky's plan to put government power in the hands of a five-member Directory.[13] Martov also responded to a proposal by Menshevik leader Feodor Dan that a conference of democratic elements should act as a quasi-parliament until the Constituent Assembly's convocation. (A Democratic Conference was subsequently convened, in September 1917.)

Declaration of S. L. Vainstein for the Mensheviks
The Supreme Commander has dared, not only to speak against the revolution, but to send troops to kill the revolution. This counterrevolutionary front must be opposed by a revolutionary front. The revolutionary democracy must rally around the Provisional Government because—and this is the main thing—General Kornilov's forces are moving against it at this very moment. At such a decisive moment, the Provisional Government must be flexible. We fully agree with the Party of Socialist Revolutionaries, and we also propose to Comrade Kerensky that he preserve the cabinet's current composition while bringing democratic elements into the government to replace Kadet ministers who are leaving. The revolutionary democracy must remain flexible and strong. We must understand that we can repel the counterrevolution only by combining our forces with those of the Provisional Government.

The Mensheviks propose a Committee for the Struggle against Counterrevolution. It should include 3 representatives each from the Bolsheviks and Mensheviks; 3 from the SRs and Popular-Socialists; 5 people from [Soviet Central Executive Committee] and the [Executive Committee of Peasant Deputies]; 2 from the Central Council of Trade Unions; and 2 from the Petrograd Soviet (1 from the workers' section and 1 from the soldiers' section).

Finally, we must recognize right now that Comrade Kerensky is the only person who can assemble a government. A blow has been struck against him and against the Provisional Government. If they perish, the revolutionary cause perishes.

No matter how the Provisional Government is composed, we have one requirement: the Provisional Government must stand for the platform agreed to on 8 July, for the consolidation of the entire revolutionary democracy. The Provisional Government also must use language in today's published declaration about General Kornilov saying that any necessary urgent and decisive measures it implements will without a doubt follow legal guidelines.

If the Provisional Government's declaration mentions these decisive measures for the struggle against counterrevolutionaries, then we will find the statement satisfactory.

Statement by I. I. Martov

Comrade Martov made a statement in the Internationalists' name. In that faction's name, he rejected the idea of creating a Directory, because any Directory would give birth to counterrevolution. At this terrible moment, the masses' independent action must be developed. The masses must know that the Provisional Government has begun a decisive struggle against the counterrevolutionary forces and will direct all its energy to satisfying the revolutionary democracy's vital demands. [The Internationalists] support the idea of creating a new institution (a Conference of Democratic Elements), but only under the condition that it be free of reactionary elements and that the soviets of workers' and soldiers' deputies be at the conference's center.

DOCUMENT 10.4
THE SOCIALIST REVOLUTIONARIES ON
THE *KORNILOVSHCHINA*[14]

The following document is an editorial from the Socialist Revolutionary Central Committee's newspaper, The People's Cause (Delo naroda), *on 28 August 1917. Russia's socialists immediately began referring to Kornilov's revolt as the* Kornilovshchina. *The Russian suffix "shchina" means a type of order or rule, but it also suggests violence, misfortune, or tyranny. Adding "shchina" to Kornilov's name was a way of referring negatively to his attempt to take power. Editorials and articles using the term* Kornilovshchina *began appearing in major newspapers on 28 August.*

At last, the revolution's enemies have moved openly to execute programs that they obviously have planned carefully and meticulously. The conspirators already defined the essence of their plans in statements at the Moscow State Conference, where the "Kornilovites" unambiguously threatened to use armed force. Motivated by a *possible* assault on Riga, they had decided that a sharp turn from the gradualist course was inevitable and required a military dictatorship.

And then preparations began. [The Kadet's newspaper] *Speech*, the conspirators' real leader, opened a bitter campaign against the Provisional Government. Riga and the entire Riga district passed into German hands. Stavka released information about the soldiers' traitorous flight. A panic was created in the capital. Rumors were launched about preparations for evacuation and about explosions at ammunition factories. Rumors spread about a street uprising by "Bolsheviks." Finally, there was an artfully created new "crisis" of power. And when the moment seemed favorable, the Military League released a proclamation—"Support the Leader"—calling for an open uprising against the revolution.

Then the "leader" issued demands in an ultimatum to the Provisional Government. Demands motivated by the government's powerlessness in the expectation of an alleged Bolshevik uprising that threatened to bring civil war and that automatically would open the front [to the Germans].

At the same time, troops were moved on Petrograd. . . . The counter-revolutionaries have coordinated between the rear and the front, and their tactics now are revealed in full clarity. Their cynicism and their lack of even the smallest drop of human understanding is striking. This is the face of the real traitors to the motherland, for whom no means of achieving their criminal aims is too disgusting.

All this is an exact imitation of the methods used by the abolished monarchy. It is all there: the provocative rumors, the threat of violence, and direct treason. It is not an intricate, direct reproduction of monarchy, its natural child. Consider the conspirators. But it is connected to the monarchy, to its "moral" traditions and its class interests. Half a year ago the monarchy would only threaten the revolution with opening the front to the Germans. Now they are really ready to resort to such means. Here are the country's saviors, the motherland's defenders! They finally have revealed their faces, and they are even viler than we had predicted.

Now there can be no doubt about with whom we are dealing. Traitors against the people, the country's betrayers—those are the true names of the counterrevolutionaries. They are not principled enemies of democracy, doing their public duty by defending their views in the revolution's name. They must be treated as conspirators against their own country. The government and the revolutionary democracy must take decisive and ruthless measures against them. The revolution has been too indulgent toward its enemies—let her show them her inexorable terrible face!

DOCUMENT 10.5
THE LITHUANIAN GUARDS RESERVES REGIMENTAL
COMMITTEE ON THE KORNILOV REBELLION[15]

The following document, one of many anti-Kornilov resolutions passed by military units during the crisis, is from the Lithuanian Guards Reserve Regiment (also known as the Moscow Guards Regiment) on 28 August 1917. The regiment was barracked in Petrograd's heavily industrial Vyborg District, and the Petrograd Soviet dispatched it to the city's environs for an anticipated battle against pro-Kornilov forces.

Resolved:

1. Comrades Zhiliaev and Il'in shall be delegates to the garrison assembly.
2. Elements of 4th, 9th, and 10th Companies dispatched from Petrograd each should include the following commands: machine gun, communications, and reconnaissance units, along with one member of the regimental committee.
3. People dispatched from Petrograd should be given sufficient rations for two days (2 *funts* of bread, 1 *funt* of meat, and 12 *zolotniki* of sugar per day).[16]
4. Regimental committee members Egorov and Kniazhov shall be delegated for communications with the workers' factory organizations.
5. Any soldier free from service assignments who does not have a medical certification of illness must be dispatched together with the designated units.

Any officer and soldier clearly derelict in his assigned duties will be brought before a revolutionary court.

Signed: Committee Chairman Corporal Bush
Verified: Committee Secretary Corporal Sosnovskii

DOCUMENT 10.6
THE SARATOV SOVIET EXECUTIVE COMMITTEE
DEBATES RESPONSES TO THE *KORNILOVSHCHINA*[17]

The following document is a transcript of the Saratov Soviet Executive Committee's 28 August 1917 session. Saratov, on the Volga River southeast of Moscow, was the Russian Empire's 11th largest city, with a population during World War I of nearly 250,000. Nearly half its residents were wage laborers, and in 1917, its military garrison fluctuated between 30,000 and 70,000 soldiers. Saratov had a strong tradition of worker activism, and the socialist parties (particularly the Socialist Revolutionaries [SRs]) had well-established local organizations. When word of the Kornikov affair reached Saratov, the provincial commissar banned all street meetings, an injunction that the moderate socialists did not wish to break. When local Bolsheviks proposed a rally, the meeting quickly turned into a confrontation between the Bolsheviks and SRs. In reelections held soon after the Kornilov affair, the Bolsheviks and other left socialist factions won a majority in the Saratov Soviet. I have indicated participants' party affiliations (when known) in an endnote and in bracketed text.

28 August Executive Committee Session
Present: Didenko, Antonov, Guterman, Semenov, Lin'kov, Baranovskii, Vasil'ev, Neimichenko, Vorob'ev, Vasil'ev, Terent'ev, Nikanorov, Shchedrovitskii, Tumanov, Lazarov, Pokrovskii, Sokolov-Cheredin, Maksimov, Tugarinov, A. Minin, Lebedev, Motovilov, Sadaev, Plaksin, Telegin.[18]
Agenda: (1) Report of the Bureau. Discussion of the political moment. (2) Demonstration by the garrison. (3) Session of the city *duma*. (4) Proposal of the provincial commissar. (5) Current events.

Comrade Didenko [a Socialist Revolutionary (SR)] reports on the plans for a demonstration by the garrison. There will be a revolutionary parade on Moscow Square, then a resolution on current events will be passed, which will be sent as a telegram.

Comrade Antonov [a Bolshevik]: We need to agree upon tomorrow's demonstration, and we must ensure that it takes place without incidents. Didenko wants to organize a parade. Isn't that just disguising a demonstration as a parade? Will there be a demonstration? The Socialist Revolutionaries think we don't need a demonstration. Instead, should we keep quiet and wait until it is clear who is on which side? We must decide if a demonstration is needed or not. We are for a demonstration.

Tomorrow, a special soviet of workers' and soldiers' deputies session will resolve the issue of the demonstration. The Executive Committee should prepare for this. Slogans against counterrevolution should be proposed. I propose that on the day of the demonstration, all the largest buildings be used for meetings, so that dark activists can't use the meetings to carry out provocations.

Comrade Didenko: Comrade Antonov offers a new proposal for a demonstration.

Comrade Antonov: It is no secret to anyone that the garrison wants to respond to the Kornilovshchina.

Comrade Telegin [an SR]: My opinion has not changed. We have an Executive Committee, which should pass a definite resolution. We can't tolerate any separate demonstrations by the soviet soldiers' section.

Comrade Guterman [a Menshevik] proposes a resolution: "None of the [soviet] sections has the right to hold a separate demonstration."

[Secretary's note]: His proposal is accepted. The resolution is debated.

Comrade M. Vasil'ev [a Bolshevik]: I am positively against this resolution, which represents a kind of police action. We are for organizing a demonstration. Tomorrow is a holiday, and it will be impossible to scatter the crowd. The soviet military organization should take steps to prevent provocations.

Comrades Minin [an SR] *and Vasilev* (the SR) call for a purely military parade with no speeches.

Comrade Minin: If the local garrison has a demonstration tomorrow, it must follow revolutionary order and must not become a meeting.

Comrade Didenko: We want to invite the chairmen of the *zemstvo*, the city administration, and the soviet.

[Secretary's note]: Agreed.

Comrade Guterman: We will send a representative from the Executive Committee to the different parties.

[Secretary's note]: It was proposed that there be orators from each party. It was resolved to pick 7 men: M. Vasil'ev, Lebedev, Antonov [all three Bolsheviks], Telegin, Lin'kov, Minin [all three SRs], and Guterman [a Menshevik]. Agreed.

Comrade Guterman: We all must carry out the Executive Committee's resolution.

Comrade M. I. Vasil'ev: This will depend upon the slogans that are adopted. In the interest of unity, the Executive Committee Bureau worked out these slogans: (1) Long live the Revolution; (2) Down with all counterrevolutionaries, both open and hidden; (3) Down with the slanderous bourgeois press; (4) We demand that the counterrevolutionaries be arrested and not sent abroad.

Comrade Telegin: I welcome these slogans, but the Provisional Government must be defended against threats from both the right and the left.

Comrade Antonov: Are you certain that the bourgeoisie and the Provisional Government are not supporting Kornilov together?

Comrade Telegin: Can we now vote? Either (1) for the slogans of the Executive Committee, or (2) for those of the military organization.

Comrade Trius: Are the comrades against a slogan in favor of the government? They should make that clear.[19]

Comrade Guterman: I do not understand those who want tomorrow's demonstration to be against the Provisional Government. A struggle is going on between Kornilov (a counterrevolutionary) and Kerensky. Our demonstration must take a side. To whom should the revolutionary army listen? We must say, "Long live Kerensky." Why not the slogans of the Executive Committee? I am for the Provisional Government, and long live the Executive Committee of the Soviet of Workers' and Soldiers' Soviets.

Comrade Semenov [a Trudovik]: We cannot go on without the Provisional Government. We will stick by them. The regiment swore an oath to the Provisional Government. We will gather there out of solidarity with the government.

[Secretary's note]: The military section's secretary proposed a demonstration based on these slogans: (1) In free Russia, there is no place for a dictator; (2) Ruthless struggle against attempts to overthrow the government; (3) Long live the leader of the revolutionary troops, Prime Minister Kerensky; (4) Long live the Government for the Salvation of the Country and Revolution.

Regarding the first slogan, it was proposed that it be changed to "personal dictatorship." Slogan 1 was then accepted, 13 for and 10 against. The second slogan was approved, 22 for and 4 against. The third slogan was approved, 18 for and 4 against. The fourth slogan was approved, 24 for and 4 against.

Comrade M. Vasil'ev: I withdraw my slogans, and I will refuse to speak at the demonstration, as I cannot speak for the approved slogans.

[Secretary's note]: It was pointed out to Vasil'ev that the slogans were voted on by the Executive Committee Bureau and that therefore these would be the slogans. They had been voted on and approved.

Comrade Guterman proposed that one more slogan be added: "Long live the united revolutionary front and the Soviet of Workers', Soldiers', and Peasants' Deputies."

[Secretary's note]: Accepted. After this, *Comrades Lebedev* [a Bolshevik] and *Antonov* refused to speak at the demonstration. It was proposed that the meeting protocols be amended to state that "having heard the Bolsheviks' regrettable refusal, the meeting returned to its agenda." It was proposed that this be changed to "baseless refusal." Accepted.

Comrade Shchebrovistkii [a Bolshevik] says a Bolshevik demonstration is necessary on 29 August.

Comrade Neimichenko [an SR]: If the Bolsheviks do not want to take part, then they bear responsibility for any incidents.

Comrade M. Vasil'ev: A coward is someone who wants to lay responsibility for his own actions on someone else.

Comrade Lin'kov: I propose that there be no demonstration by the Soviet at all tomorrow. One would be possible only were there unity. Otherwise, it is dangerous and harmful.

Comrade Telegin is for the demonstration and against Lin'kov's proposal. Let there be a demonstration that demonstrates the unity of those who are really united.

Comrade Lin'kov withdraws his proposal and asks that his name be taken off the list of orators. He will not speak. Pokrovskii, Baranovski, Kitavin, Sadaev, and Vasil'ev (the SR) are chosen to speak in place of those who have withdrawn.

Comrade Lebedev declares that he is not making excuses for Comrade Vasil'ev's sharp tone, which he did not like, but . . .

Comrade Telegin [cutting off Lebedev] urgently says that there has been a joint meeting of the public organizations, the *duma*, and the *zemstvo* with Provincial Commissar Topuridze. That meeting had discussed banning spontaneous meetings on the streets, where the Black Hundreds often demonstrate, because these could easily result in incidents. Therefore that joint meeting agreed to the following compulsory decree:

> From the provincial commissar of the Provisional Government. A compulsory decree:
> All street demonstrations, meetings, or manifestations against the Provisional Government's authority are henceforth prohibited in the city of Saratov and in the entire province by special directive. Any violation of this compulsory decree will immediately be stopped by force and the guilty parties held criminally responsible.

Comrade Neimichenko declares that, in view what has occurred here, he can no longer remain. He will leave the session and withdraw from the Executive Committee.

Chairman Didenko states that he did not hear what Comrade Vasil'ev said, or else he certainly would have stopped him. He asks that Vasil'ev repeat his words.

Comrade Vasil'ev clarifies that he did not use the word "coward" to refer to Comrade Neimichenko personally, but to a faction that would hide its responsibility behind another faction.

Comrade Didenko: You are lying. I did not hear what you said, but I clearly saw the look you gave Comrade Neimichenko. Consequently, the word "coward" was meant for him. This is something, of course, that we will not tolerate. All the soldiers will leave together with Neimichenko. If this conflict is not settled, we will not stay here.

Comrade Neimichenko (directed to Vasil'ev): If I had a weapon, I'd make you answer for your words.

Comrade Vasil'ev: Please, I am not a coward, and I am always ready to answer for my words. I repeat that this word was directed toward you only as the representative of a faction. Definitely.

[Secretary's notes]: After this, all the soldiers leave. *Lin'kov* is elected the meeting's chairman. There is discussion of the incident. The provincial commissar enters and declares that Vasil'ev's actions are intolerable. He must apologize to Neimichenko right now, in the presence of all the Executive Committee's members.

Comrade Vasil'ev explains the meaning of his words. After discussion, the following was put to a vote: (1) the Executive Committee considers that this matter should be settled by an arbitration court; (2) To censure Vasil'ev. The first proposal passed. The second also passed. were for censure, 5 against. Comrade Vasil'ev quit the session.

Comrade Lebedev considers it necessary that the same measures be applied to Didenko for his insult against Comrade Vasil'ev. He must go before an arbitration court and be censured for the insult. This was voted down, 7 to 5. The remaining Bolsheviks then quit the session.

DOCUMENT 10.7
A MENSHEVIK APPEAL "TO ALL MALE AND FEMALE WORKERS, TO ALL CITIZENS OF PETROGRAD"[20]

On the morning of 29 August 1917, the Menshevik Central Committee gathered to discuss the Kornilovshchina.[21] *It agreed to issue an appeal to Petrograd's workers and citizens, to be drafted by Isaak Astrov. The following document is that appeal, as published in* The Workers' Newspaper (Rabochaia gazeta) *on 29 August 1917.*

To All Male and Female Workers, To All Citizens of Petrograd.
Comrades and citizens!

A great danger threatens Russia and all freedom's achievements. A gang of generals—the tsar's former servants, the old regime's adherents who oppose land and freedom for the people—have risen up against the revolution, against the Provisional revolutionary government.

The same generals who—led by Kornilov—again and again proclaimed their love for the motherland while accusing the Soviets of Deputies and the army committees of disrupting the army and ruining the country, now would use our defeats at the front to strike another heavy blow at the motherland and the revolution. They have deceived the front soldiers, ordering them without explanation to advance on Petrograd, against their brothers, Petrograd's workers and soldiers, to drown our revolution and freedom and all our hopes for a better, brighter future, in fraternal blood, to restore the hated old order.

General Kornilov says that he wants what is good for the people and is not acting for himself. *Do not believe him*, citizens and comrades; he is a wolf in sheep's clothing.

Today he issued a vile slander against our Government, saying the government wants to conclude a separate peace with our enemies. Tomorrow he *will threaten to leave the front open.* Tomorrow, he will worm his way into the good graces of the weary, exhausted soldiers and tell them that obeying him will bring peace more speedily.

Whatever he promises, this uprising against the revolution and government by [Kornilov] and his conspirators has struck a terrifying blow against our army and already has done Germany a great service. At this moment—when the enemy has taken Riga and stands near Petrograd, the revolution's heart, and when Russia needs the greatest unity and cohesion—General Kornilov instead creates a civil war within the army and in the country, instead undermines the soldiers' trust in the command staff.

All this weakens our army even more. All this helps [Kaiser] Wilhelm's army strike new blows against us. Kornilov, all the generals who support him, and all those in the propertied classes who sympathize with him are *traitors and betrayers of the motherland*.

This is more than a military strike against us. Kornilov promises us order, but instead he gives us civil strife and a fratricidal war that will bring violence, theft, murder, the disgrace of our wives, sisters, and daughters, total disruption of our entire life, and hunger.[22]

And they do all this for the benefit of the tsarist butchers and lackeys, the landlords, and all those who rode the people's backs for centuries and whom the people threw off in one mighty convulsion just half a year ago. They do all this so that they can reenslave the people and restore the old, odious, hated tsarist order.

DOCUMENT 10.8
THE UNION OF THE KNIGHTS OF SAINT GEORGE
ON GENERAL KORNILOV[23]

The Union of Knights of Saint George, also known as the Union of George's Cavaliers, was a patriotic organization of officers who had been awarded the Saint George Cross for distinction in battle. The following document is a 29 August 1917 proclamation by the Union's Central Committee, in response to Kornilov's appeal to the Russian people. The Union referred to its members as "Georgites" (Georgievtsy). The "liar," "coward," and "traitor" referred to in the document is Kerensky. Few military units actually took up arms for Kornilov's cause.

Brother Georgites! The hour of final judgment has arrived. It still is not too late to save Russia. Our people's leader, General Kornilov, has taken up this great, courageous, and manly deed. Our exhausted motherland has fallen into unskilled and criminal hands, which have brought it to almost complete ruin. If we, Russia's honest sons, do not take a stand for the country, then it will spell the inevitable end of independent Russia and its freedom. The treachery will be complete. Under the slogan of "saving the revolution's achievements," the motherland will be turned over to the Germans, Slavdom's archenemies.

All the Georgites' activities are pure and frank, guaranteed by the sea of blood we have shed for the motherland's honor and freedom and by our cross' sacred valor. A contemptible coward reproaches us as counter-revolutionaries to cover up his own dark treachery against the country and the army. Here is our answer to that contemptible liar and traitor and our appeal to all Georgites and all honest Russian people: At this terrible hour, rally around the people's leader, and make every sacrifice for Russia's salvation. Down with the traitors and cowards!

Long live truth, freedom, and honor. Long live our first Russian people's leader, General Lavr Georgievich Kornilov.

The Central Committee of the Union of George's Cavaliers
29 August 1917

DOCUMENT 10.9
A SOLDIERS' COMMITTEE DEMANDS PROSECUTION OF KORNILOV[24]

On 29–31 August 1917, soldiers' committees and soviets across Russia denounced Kornilov. The following document is a resolution by a joint assembly representing the regimental committees and divisional committee of the Ninth Army's Seventh Rifle Division, passed on 30 August. The Provisional Government arrested Kornilov on 31 August. It formed a special commission to investigate the affair (the Shabalovskii Commission), but the commission proved sympathetic to Kornilov and declared him innocent of fomenting a rebellion. This further undermined Kerensky's authority and fueled rumors of his involvement in counterrevolutionary plots.

A united session of the Seventh Rifle Division's regimental committees with the division committee, having discussed General Kornilov's usurping and traitorous attempt to overthrow the state, resolves:

1. To assure the Provisional Government of our complete support and our readiness to see the Motherland's salvation through to the finish.
2. To demand that General Kornilov and his accomplices be brought before a revolutionary court that considers the death penalty.

Seventh Rifle Division of the Ninth Army
Comrade Chairman Asakhov
Secretary [signature illegible]

DOCUMENT 10.10
THE ROSLAVL' SOVIET ON THE KORNILOV AFFAIR[25]

The following document is a resolution passed by a special general assembly of the Roslavl' Soviet (in Smolensk Province), as published in The News of the Central Executive Committee and the Petrograd Soviet (Izvestiia

Tsentral'nago Ispolnitel'nago Komiteta i Petrogradskago soveta rabochikh i soldatskikh deputatov) *on 30 August 1917.*

General Kornilov's Conspiracy and the Provinces.
Roslavl'.

Having discussed Kerensky's telegram, a special general assembly of the Roslavl' Soviet of Workers', Soldiers', and Peasants' Deputies unanimously revolved that:

In this terrible moment of great danger, the entire democracy as one is prepared to support the Provisional Government, weapons in hand and to the last drop of blood, in its fight against counterrevolution. At the same time, the soviet demands that the Provisional Government display iron firmness against those who would usurp freedom. The death penalty must be carried out against all participants in the conspiracy against the Provisional Government.

The State Duma, that hearth of counterrevolution, must be disbanded immediately. Its leading members must be jailed and placed under guard. All the socialists held in prisons must be freed.[26] The Provisional Government must modify the direction of its policies to immediately actualize all the revolution's achievements. In all its activities, it must cooperate fully with the revolutionary democracy's authorized institutions.

We in the provinces are ready to answer the call. We demand powerful, decisive revolutionary measures.

DOCUMENT 10.11
A KADET EDITORIAL ON KORNILOV[27]

During the Kornilov crisis, the Kadets found themselves indirectly implicated in what appeared to be a military coup against the government. The Kadet's Petrograd newspaper, Speech (Rech), *proposed that the dispute between Kerensky and Kornilov was the product of a misunderstanding (which, from the point of view of history, was at least partly the case). In the following document, an editorial published on 29 August, the Kadets placed the greater burden on Kerensky and warned that the crisis would play into the hands of Lenin and the Bolsheviks.*

Petrograd, 29 August 1917
Never has Russia faced such horror as it does today. The newspapers report regiments moving on Petrograd from the south and north—Russian regiments under General Kornilov. Hurried defensive measures are being taken against them, and other Russian regiments are preparing for battle under the Provisional Government's banner. This comes at a time when a new enemy breakthrough threatens the front, which will immeasurably increase the danger to the country's vital centers. At the same time, both

sides sincerely maintain that they care only for the dying motherland's welfare and salvation.

What is going on? What grandiose misunderstanding is dividing the two sides—if this is only a misunderstanding? Why are they unable to join hands with one another, before the split becomes too deep to end the discord tearing the country into two camps?

Alas, what is being repeated here in free Russia is a scene all too familiar from the old regime's psychology. Even clearly justifiable demands are not met with satisfaction, because that would symbolically undermine the government's "prestige." Concessions are finally made, but . . . they are made too late. Or, even worse: instead of conceding to reality, the government strikes a haughty pose and acts according to the principle that it is better to perish than to concede, forgetting that the struggle affects Russia's living body, which suffers along with the government. Little by little, the motherland's defense is transformed into the government's self-defense. The government gradually loses touch with reality and becomes obsessed with imaginary phantoms. This government stops seeing what everyone else sees and is last to learn what everyone else knows. It scatters its blows against imaginary opponents without seeing the growing danger around it.

Three days ago, reconciliation was still easy; yesterday, it was still possible. All day members of the Party of People's Freedom made every effort to reestablish relations between the antagonists in this struggle, to find a way to halt the civil war that had already begun. These efforts came up against all the familiar formulaic arguments. How could the legal government possibly enter into negotiations with rebels? How can concessions be made without undermining the government's prestige? And shouldn't the government treat today's opponents the same way it treated the Bolsheviks [in July]?

One can answer by stating that first, the Bolsheviks have always been treated with extreme indulgence, and the government never dared to declare them criminals or rebels. Second, it is impossible . . . to ignore the difference between Lenin's adherents and Kornilov's adherents: it is the difference between anarchy and support for the state.

Yesterday it was still possible to guide this spontaneous struggle into conscious channels. All it took was that the logic of living demands not be dismissed as a violation of proper form. Yesterday it still was possible to end the "misunderstanding," to agree on essentials. But the government's stubborn refusal to consider action on the basis of principles prevented it from proving its own case.

Whether or not today brings a clash, Russia will suffer. The enemy at the front greedily waits for brothers to grapple with one another. This will bring misfortune to all, regardless of who is right and wrong. Everyone will be subjected to the law of force. Those who have declared it impossible to prevent this struggle must understand that it has to end as soon as possible. It must end in a way that will not sow new seeds of unprecedented evil or leave an unquenchable thirst for vengeances. Everyone must understand that it is not enough to win; one must be able to hold on to victory. They must understand that victory can be preserved only when the country recognizes that the cause for which it is fighting is the right cause. That among the horrors of civil war awaiting us is the slaughter of all true civil feeling, which is the basis for the principles of civic solidarity and citizens' individual responsibility. Then, perhaps, the thunderstorm that hangs over us will discharge the accumulated electricity and refresh the atmosphere. Then we will better appreciate the value of our welfare and freedom, which they would put at risk. Then we will understand the complex tasks that we face together: to preserve the people's rights with greater consciousness and seriousness than the dark people and their blind leaders have shown up to this point.

DOCUMENT 10.12
TWO POPULAR-SOCIALIST EDITORIALS ON KORNILOV[28]

The People's Word (Narodnoe slovo) *was the Petrograd daily newspaper of the Party of Popular-Socialists, a right socialist group that had broken from the Socialist Revolutionaries in 1906 and merged with Kerensky's Trudovik faction in 1917. The following documents are editorials published in* The People's Word *on 29 August 1917.*

Petrograd, 29 August 1917
The Provisional Government placed enormous trust in General Kornilov. It knew that reactionary circles had vested great hopes in Kornilov. It had abundant evidence of this. It is enough to recall the demonstrative ovation given Kornilov at the Moscow State Conference. It is enough to recall the declarations by the Cossack congress and the Union of St. George's Cavaliers in response to rumors of Kornilov's dismissal. And nonetheless, the Provisional Government trusted General Kornilov. He continued to hold the post of Supreme Commander. It was intended that he would be given military power in Petrograd, with the government remaining in place. At his insistence, it is said, several revolutionary regiments were transferred away from Petrograd.

Events in recent days have shown that the Provisional Government was too trusting. General Kornilov justified all the hopes that the reactionary circles had placed in him. His troops are advancing on Petrograd. At this moment, as we are writing these words, they may already be clashing with units sent by the Provisional Government, and a fratricidal war may have begun.

According to reports, General Kornilov has declared that he is acting to save the motherland. What sense does that make? Raising the banner of rebellion in the name of saving the motherland? The onset of civil war lay buried beneath this claim. And when is this being done? At the very moment when the enemy is headed down the road toward the capital, when the country's position is more dangerous than ever. That is when our general—the general to whom the country's fate was entrusted—strikes a new blow at the motherland. He has aimed his blow not at our enemy, but at the government, the institution that raised him up.

No. There cannot be two opinions about General Kornilov's adventure. It is an open uprising. It is a betrayal of the free country and the revolutionary people. And if the people really appreciate their freedom's value, then they must stand together as one man to smother the counterrevolution.

"People of Russia, your country's life is in your hands," says General Kornilov. Yes. We say the same thing. But the country's real life is not that which General Kornilov sees. Without freedom, a country cannot live. And an uprising, General, is a rebellion against Russian freedom, which will be choked if this is not stopped.

Lunacy or Criminality?

"Is this stupidity or treason?" Miliukov asked in regard to the acts of Shtumer and Sukhomlinov. A story in *Speech* [the Kadet newspaper *Rech*] that describes General Kornilov's surprising, stupefying maneuver as a "misunderstanding," prompts an analogous question: Is this lunacy or criminality? Right now, this is a practical and not hypothetical question.

What reason is there not put out a fire? When a building is burning, you must take measures to extinguish the flames. A man who was not involved in starting the arson still must report it, and he must participate in the safety operations, to prevent the spread of the evil. And still, we cannot avoid the question—is this a criminal adventure or an act of mighty lunacy?

Beyond the moment's tasks, the public must demand an explanation of this terrible event, to comprehend its causes and its motives, to know about all its wellsprings. This is not idle curiosity; public conscience demands this. The public must know who is involved and whether the selfish power-lovers' criminal plan is motivated by private or group interests or by the insane fanaticism of people who imagine they have been called to save the fatherland.

... From a practical perspective, the nature of these nightmarish events must be clarified, if not immediately, then in the coming days. It is one thing to defy a criminal adventure; it is another matter to fight against insane fanatics who are convinced their cause is just. Struggling against adventurism is far easier than fighting lunacy. Adventurism quickly loses its supporters, but fanaticism is always contagious. From that perspective, we must determine the precise meaning of the surprise that Generals Kornilov, Lukomovskii, and company had prepared for the revolution's six-month anniversary.[29]

Were it discovered that the whole gang of adventurers is motivated by the love of power or by their group or class interests, that would be best for the motherland. The struggle will be immensely more complicated if their plan was based on blind conviction that it was necessary to save the motherland.

It is easy to fight criminals; it is dramatically more difficult to deal with lunatics. So today's task is to make this diagnosis: how will we describe those who struck this blow—as criminals or as political lunatics? *Speech*, as we have seen, considers it possible to say that it is neither a crime nor lunacy, but a "misunderstanding."

Some amazing "misunderstanding"! To declare yourself dictator is a misunderstanding. To condemn the Provisional Government is a misunderstanding. And to send the Wild Division, together with Hindenburg, after Kerensky, that is a misunderstanding.[30] Of all the misunderstandings that have filled Russian life, this would be the most amazing.

We think Kornilov's actions were not the product of a misunderstanding, but one of these two: Criminality or lunacy.

—Smirnyi

DOCUMENT 10.13
A LIBERAL MOSCOW NEWSPAPER ON THE KORNILOV AFFAIR[31]

The following editorial appeared in the right liberal newspaper The Moscow Bulletin (Moskovskiia vedomosti) *on 30 August 1917.*

The Motherland's Salvation.

Time and time again, in the newspapers and in public, we have encountered the opinion that we are approaching a civil war. And now this sad prediction has come true. We are not just approaching civil war; we are not even just on its threshold: we have crossed over, and a civil war has begun.

We are reminded of Prime Minister A. F. Kerensky's comment at the Moscow State Conference, that "superhuman" words were needed. We could make do without "superhuman" words then, but now a great tragic moment has come when we need "superhuman" words and when without "superhuman" words, we cannot get by.

Has the tongue gone numb in the face of the horror that is about to happen, or perhaps has already happened? In the face of the culmination of all the misfortunes and shame that have befallen Russia? When Russian blood is to be spilled, not only by the Germans, but also at our own brother's hands?

The mind is tormented by the idea that everything happening is some fatal misunderstanding, that the people who have evoked the civil war have not understood one another, that some agreement is possible, some compromise that recognizes the common enemy and ends the fratricidal fighting.

Or is this groundless hope? Incorrigible optimism when the time for agreements has slipped by, and time for compromise has passed?

And how many voices warned about dragging the military into politics? About divisions among soldiers, who have a single responsibility—defending the fatherland against foreign enemies? How many warned about the political parties, with their divisive platforms and aggressive attitudes, which often treat one another as mutual enemies? About the danger of the country being divided into SRs, SDs, KDs [Kadets], and so on?

On the eve of this real catastrophe, there was a new declaration on freedom of propaganda in the army. And the Bolsheviks—with all their radicalism, preaching the end of the war and conclusion of a separate peace, preaching fraternization with the Germans and various ravings about our allies' imperialist and self-interested aims—were openly allowed to enter our troops' barracks. Recent events have revealed how injudicious these steps were and how vitally necessary it was that the country's defenders, instead of being dragged into politics, be completely shielded from political struggle.

The revolution's salvation—that should be the only slogan, the only slogan they should follow. In these catastrophic times, the revolution's salvation is more important than any rebellious rage, more important than any power struggles or clashes among those who feel insulted or whose pride is wounded.

We believe a day will come when motherland's salvation will take priority and will not be forgotten. It is sad that [the combatants] do not see the forest through the trees. But it is sadder that they do not see that the whole catastrophe taking place will bring the motherland unprecedented suffering.

—M. A-v

DOCUMENT 10.14
LENIN'S 30 AUGUST 1917 LETTER TO THE BOLSHEVIK CENTRAL COMMITTEE[32]

The Bolsheviks are often mistakenly described as a "monolithic" party; they actually had "left," "center," and "right" factions like the other socialist parties. On the night of 27 August 1917, right Bolsheviks in the Petrograd Soviet Executive Committee joined with Mensheviks and Socialist Revolutionaries (SRs) in offering Kerensky support against Kornilov. At a Bolshevik Petersburg Committee meeting that same night, left Bolsheviks completely rejected cooperation with the Mensheviks, SRs, and Kerensky and called for an immediate seizure of power. Centerists rejected this as rash; although they were against rushing to support Kerensky, they claimed that the Bolsheviks would have to aid him should Kornilov gain the upper hand. Lenin, watching events from the Finnish border, two days by mail from Russia's capital, believed the Kornilovshchina *might clear a path toward Bolshevik rule. He explained this in the following document, a letter to the Bolshevik Central Committee.*

To the Central Committee of the RSDLP

These lines might arrive late, because events are developing so quickly that at times, frankly, it makes your head spin. I am writing this on 30 August, and it will be read by the recipients no sooner than Friday, 2 September. But given all that is at risk, I consider it my duty to write the following.

The Kornilov uprising comes as a dramatic surprise (unexpected in its timing and form); it really is an unbelievably sharp turn of events. As with any sharp turn, it demands a change and revision in tactics. And, as with any revision, we must be exceedingly careful not to fall into an unprincipled position.

I am convinced that those (like Volodarskii) who slide into defensism or who (like other Bolsheviks) are for a *bloc* with the SRs and for *supporting* the Provisional Government have fallen into an absolutely false and unprincipled position. We will become defensists *only after* power is transferred to the proletariat, *after* peace is offered, *after* the secret treaties and ties to banks are broken. *Only after.* Neither the fall of Riga *nor the fall of Petrograd* will turn us into defensists. (I ask very insistently that this be given to Volodarskii to read through.) Until we achieve the proletarian revolution, we are against the war, and we are *not* defensists.

Even now, we cannot support Kerensky's government. That would be unprincipled. They may ask: won't we fight against Kornilov? Yes, of course! But that is not the same thing. There is a line here, and it is being crossed by some Bolsheviks who are falling into "collaborationism," who are letting themselves be *carried away* by the course of events.

We will fight—we are fighting—against Kornilov, *as do* Kerensky's forces, but we do not support Kerensky. We expose his weakness. There is a difference. The difference is very subtle, but it is absolutely essential, important, and must not be forgotten.

How then do our tactics change after the Kornilov uprising? We vary the *form* of our struggle with Kerensky. Without reducing our hostility to him one iota, without taking back one word said against him, without renouncing the task of overthrowing Kerensky, we say: we must *consider* the moment. We cannot overthrow Kerensky now. Now we approach the struggle against him *differently*. Namely, we explain Kerensky's *weakness* and *vacillation* to the people (who are fighting against Kerensky). We *had* done that previously, but now it becomes the *main* thing: this is the variation.

Further, there is a variation in that now the *main* thing has become intensifying agitation for our "partial demands" to Kerensky—arrest Miliukov; arm the Petrograd workers; summon troops to Petrograd from Kronshtadt, Vyborg, and Helsinki; disband the State Duma; arrest Rodzianko; legalize the transfer of the aristocratic landlords' land to the peasants; introduce workers' control over grain and factories, and so on. We must present these demands not only *to* Kerensky, not *so much* to Kerensky, as to the workers, soldiers and peasants *enthused* by the struggle against Kornilov. We must build on their *enthusiasm*, we must encourage them to deal with the generals and officers who came out for Kornilov. Guide them so *they* demand immediate transfer of land to the peasants. Lead *them* to the need to arrest Miliukov and Rodzianko, disband the State Duma, shut down and hold criminal investigations of *Speech* and other bourgeois newspapers. The "left" SRs particularly must be pushed in this regard.

It would be wrong to think that we have moved *further away* from the goal of the proletariat taking power. No. We have come extraordinarily close to it, *not directly*, but from the side. And *at this moment* we must agitate, not so much *directly* against Kerensky, as *indirectly* against him, namely, by demanding a more and more active, truly revolutionary war against Kornilov. The war's development alone may carry *us* to power, but we must *say* as little as possible about this in our propaganda (firmly understanding that should tomorrow's events bring us to power, we will not let it go.) It seems to me that this must be passed along in a letter to agitators (not in the press), to inform groups of agitators and propagandists, and members of the party generally. We must struggle relentlessly against phrases about the country's defense, about a united front of the revolutionary democracy, about defending the Provisional Government, and so on and so forth, because these are *only phrases*. We must say: Now is the time for *action*. Gentlemen SRs and Mensheviks, you have worn these phrases thin. Now is the time for *action*. The war against Kornilov must be carried out as a revolutionary war, engaging the masses, stirring them up, inflaming them. (Kerensky *fears* the masses; he *fears* the people). And the war against the Germans now truly needs *action: to propose immediate unconditional peace* on *precise* terms. If this is done, then *perhaps* a speedy peace can be obtained or the war will be transformed into a revolutionary war. If not, all the Mensheviks and SRs will remain lackeys of imperialism.

P.S. Having read through six issues of *The Worker* after writing this, I must say that our views fully concur. With all my soul, I welcome the excellent editorials, reviews of the press, and articles of V. M-n and Vol-skii.[33] About Volodarskii's speech—I have read his letter to the editor, which also "liquidated" my concerns. Again, best greetings and wishes!

—Lenin

DOCUMENT 10.15
R.V. IVANOV-RAZUMNIK, "TWO ENEMIES"[34]

The following document is from R. V. Ivanov-Razumnik's column, "Diary of the Revolution," which appeared in many Socialist Revolutionary newspapers. It was written on 31 August 1917.

Yes, it is easy to deal with honest and straightforward enemies. General Kornilov did not shuffle along; he did not sneak into the revolution through the back door; he did not speak ringing revolutionary phrases. He openly raised the banner of rebellion against the revolution and sent his "Wild Division" against the soviet of workers' deputies. His role was high-minded compared to those of the "revolutionaries" complicit in his affair, who would serve us all by destroying Revolutionary Socialism while preserving their revolutionary innocence!

To his misfortune, he was doomed—doomed already on the first day of March, when the "great chain" tethering the Russian Army "was broken." Tell me, was it broken for both the officers and the soldiers in one decisive blow? No . . . in mid-July, General Kornilov picked up the chain again and succeeded in introducing the death penalty at the front. But how did that happen? How was he able to reverse the military's success, to reverse the soldiers' uprising?

In any case, he rebelled openly. He was vanquished, and the soviet was victorious. But having vanquished him, did they also defeat the people who stood behind him? Those who, with revolutionary phrases on their lips, reintroduced the death penalty? Those who, with an "internationalist" brochure in their pocket, reignited the extinguished flame of the world war? No, these enemies they did not vanquish. And they are dangerous; they are strong. Therefore I am not as apprehensive about the enemy outside the walls as at the enemy within.

DOCUMENT 10.16
G. PLEKHANOV, "AND NOW?"[35]

The following document is a 31 August 1917 editorial on the Kornilov affair from the Petrograd newspaper, Unity (Edinstvo), *by Menshevik defensist leader Georgii Plekhanov. Plekhanov makes a play on words using General Kornilov's first name, Lavr, which is Russian for laurel.*

And Now?

His Excellency Lavr Kornilov no doubt intended to crown himself with laurels for a triumph over Russia's revolutionary government. The power-loving general's uprising is near its sad end. He has been made an offer, and though he still has not responded, one can guess that his answer will not resemble that given him by the Government when he demanded complete power. The Deputy Prime Minister says that Kornilov and the other generals will be prosecuted for their criminal uprising, the end of which is at hand.

Know this—the danger of civil war that threatened Russia has almost passed. But for how long? That is the question that inevitably arises for all to whom Russia's fate is dear.

It is impossible to answer this question with any certainty now. General Kornilov may have imitators who flatter themselves with the hope that they will avoid his mistakes. All that can be said now without vacillating is that our revolutionary government's position seems much more durable than its enemies had supposed. This, of course, will gladden the soul of our entire revolutionary democracy.

The Democracy cannot but be gladdened by the Provisional Government's victory over the rebellious generals, but should avoid excessive optimism. Having survived this radically difficult moment, the Provisional Government's condition might not be durable enough.

We are obliged even more, then, to dedicate all our efforts toward stabilizing it. In doing so, the revolutionary democracy will relieve pressure on the government and help it master a unifying tactic that will defend it against the numerous difficulties that lay ahead.

Furthermore, we know General Kornilov certainly was not revolutionary Russia's only enemy. She has other, far more dangerous enemies. There is still the foreign enemy. We all know that the foreign enemy has an excellent view of what happened here in the last several days; without any doubt, it will seize on our troubles—which fortunately were not deep and are almost concluded—for its own aims. Our terrible economic disorder is the most precious of the enemy's absolutely irreplaceable accomplices. To ward off the foreign enemy, we must first cope with this. But the revolutionary democracy is not strong enough on its own. We can feel sorry about this; we all regret it. The only people who deny it are those born blind, who would blind our toiling masses by throwing the dust of revolutionary phraseology in their eyes.

So, while welcoming the Provisional Government's victory over Lavr, who will not wear laurels, we again appeal to its members with our "tiresome" request: Broaden the social basis of your political power; draw representatives of the commercial-industrial classes into the government. Pursue victory!

—G. Plekhanov

DOCUMENT 10.17
A JOINT DECLARATION BY THE MENSHEVIK DEFENSISTS, RIGHT SOCIALIST REVOLUTIONARIES, AND TRUDOVIKS[36]

The "right" or "defensist" bloc of Mensheviks, Socialist Revolutionaries (SRs), and Trudoviks who believed that Russia's future depended on defeating Germany often displayed greater cohesion than did the moderate socialists or left socialists. The following document is a 1 September 1917 joint declaration on the Kornilov affair by the editors of the major defensist newspapers: the SR's The People's Will (Volia naroda), *the Menshevik's* Unity (Edinstvo), *and the Popular-Socialists'* The People's Word (Narodnoe slovo).

Female and Male Citizens.

We, the editors of *The People's Will, Unity* and *The People's Word*—the voices of the democratic revolutionary press—appeal to you at this terrible hour, when our long-suffering motherland, already horribly wounded by foreign enemies, appears to have received fresh wounds from a person to whom the Provisional Government had entrusted supreme command of all its military forces.

To the Russian people's great fortune, General Kornilov's sedition has come to an end. The unworthy commander, who has betrayed his duty, could draw few soldiers to his side. He and his accomplices deserve to be punished. We believe that none of you for whom the revolution's achievements are dear will raise a voice to defend rebels who boldly took up arms against the revolutionary government. General Kornilov's victory would have been the revolutionary democracy's defeat. The revolutionary democracy's defeat would have been the beginning of counterrevolution. The revolutionary cause, for which the revolutionary democracy furnished the stage, must be protected.

Senseless and bitter people do not understand this, nor do they want to understand. Even if they are not the counterrevolution's willing servants, they serve it all the same, even if unconsciously.

We call on you to dedicate all your energy to supporting the Provisional Government's struggle against attempts to limit its authority. Russia must have a firm revolutionary government capable of quickly and ruthlessly putting down a rebellious uprising, be it under anarchy's boldly unrolled banner or counterrevolution's cowardly cloaked flag. Anarchistic ventures pave the road for counterrevolutionary uprisings. Counterrevolutionary uprisings increase the strength and influence of anarchistic elements.

You must serve the government with all your heart and all your thoughts. You must be ready and able to fight for it. By consciously supporting the government, not only out of fear, but also out of conscientiousness, you will carefully avoid steps that might push it onto a false track. You must not be angry at it for consolidating and broadening the social basis of its political power. On the contrary, with all the legal resources at the disposal of a free country's citizens of a free country, you stand to gain from such a broadening.

It is absolutely necessary for the struggle against the anarchists and counterrevolutionaries, and also for the elimination of our truly unprecedented economic disruption. Should it fail to cope with this disruption, Russia will be in absolutely no condition to withstand the foreign enemy's terrible pressure. For the sake of the struggle against the enemy, you cannot let the government fall into the hands of people who have drawn the wrong conclusions from the lessons of the international brotherhood of toilers.

Russia is a country defending itself. A German victory threatens it with continual economic subservience and humiliating political dependency. To impede Russia's self-defense is to inflict harsh damage on it and on the international revolutionary democracy as well. Our motherland has no choice: it must either persevere and continue the war together with its allies, or perish.

And so we ask that you rally around the government of revolutionary self-defense, to facilitate its march down the path toward energetically suppressing internal sedition and decisively rebuffing our foreign enemy. If you love the motherland and value freedom, you will feel compelled to answer our call.

The editors of the following newspapers:
The People's Will—the Socialist Revolutionaries
Unity—the Social Democratic organization Unity
The People's Word—the Trudovik Popular-Socialist Party
Petrograd, 1 September 1917

CHAPTER ELEVEN
ELECTORAL POLITICS: CAMPAIGNS FOR LOCAL DUMAS AND THE CONSTITUENT ASSEMBLY

371

DOCUMENT 11.1
AN EDITORIAL CARTOON ON THE U.S. ENTRY INTO THE WAR[1]

The United States declared war on Germany in April 1917, but few American troops engaged in actual fighting in Europe that year. This 5 September 1917 editorial cartoon reassured readers of the nonparty liberal newspaper The Stock-Market Bulletin (Birzhevyia vedomosti) *that the United States would help turn the tide against Russia's foreign enemies. The doves in the foreground are labeled "Stockholm" and "Vatican": Sweden and the Vatican were neutrals in World War I. The legend reads "The United States prepares to answer the Germans and the Doves of Peace."*

"The United States prepares to answer the Germans and the Doves of Peace." (*Birzhevyia vedomosti*, 5 September 1917, p. 4.)

DOCUMENT 11.2
"MOLOCH": A BOLSHEVIK CARTOON AND POEM[2]

The following cartoon by A. Z. Sharzheris and the accompanying doggerel by M. V. appeared in the Petrograd Bolshevik newspaper The Workers' Path *(Rabochii put') on 22 September 1917.[3]*

In the Old Testament, Moloch was a god to whom the Ammonites and other peoples sacrificed children. The term has come to mean a thing or a person that demands awful sacrifices. In the cartoon, soldiers feed bags of money to a pig-like creature (labeled "War"), which then excretes money into the pockets of a stereotypical capitalist. The "loan" referred to in the text's last line is the Freedom Loan, in which the Provisional Government sold bonds to raise money for state expenses. In September 1917, Kerensky's government (which had already pumped millions of new banknotes into circulation) allowed use of state bonds and Freedom Loan certificates as cash, which contributed to hyperinflation and sped the decline in living standards.

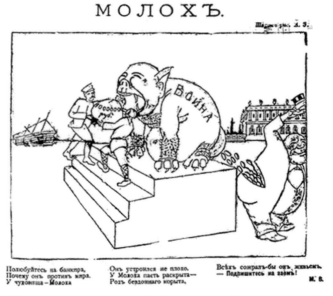

Moloch cartoon by A. Z. Sharzheris. (*Rabochii put'* 22 September 1917, p. 3.)

Moloch

> Just look at the banker,
> Why is he against peace?

Nearby is a monster—Moloch,
He's got an arrangement that's not bad.
Moloch's open jaws are
Some kind of bottomless pit.
He would gobble up everyone, alive.
Subscribe to the loan!

—M. V.

DOCUMENT 11.3
A LIBERAL EDITORIAL ON THE MOSCOW DUMA ELECTIONS [4]

Under the tsarist regime, only propertied residents voted for members of city councils (dumas). The February Revolution democratized local government; a 15 April 1917 Provisional Government directive gave voting rights in duma elections to all city residents age 20 or over (including garrison soldiers). The first elections under the new rules took place in Petrograd in May and in Moscow in June. In Petrograd, residents elected members to 12 district dumas. The Socialist Revolutionaries (SRs) and Mensheviks, who ran together as a Socialist Bloc in 10 districts, received a combined total of 57 percent of the nearly 750,000 votes cast. The Kadets won 22 percent and the Bolsheviks 20.5 percent. In elections to the Moscow central city duma, the SRs won 58 percent of roughly 650,000 votes cast, the Kadets 17 percent, the Mensheviks 12 percent, and the Bolsheviks 11.5 percent.

The following document is an editorial on the Moscow duma elections from the 28 June 1917 issue of the nonparty liberal newspaper, The Moscow Bulletin (Moskovskiia vedomosti), *in which the author claims that pro-socialist voters were "foreign" to Moscow, "transients," as opposed to "native Muscovites."*

Elections.
Elections to the Moscow City Duma have concluded and have given the socialists a decisive majority. The Party of Socialist Revolutionaries won the most votes. With the addition of the significant minority of Social Democrats—Bolsheviks and Menshevik—it appears that the socialists will have an overwhelming majority in the Moscow City Duma. The Party of People's Freedom [the Kadets], which came in second, will enter our city self-government as a minority, and an isolated minority at that.

The victory of radical tendencies is inevitable in revolutionary times; it would have been astonishing had this not happened. Now that their appetites have been whetted, the crowd thinks, "We must get everything we want now; tomorrow is too late." That is why they now shun those whose platforms promise something positive and real. The SRs have played up the land issue, and as a result—certainly as a result of their slogans—they have attracted the masses.

Revolutionary elections express the people's mood, not their will. And nothing is more accidental, more fleeting than a mood. Accidental factors were strong determinants in the recent Moscow elections. We do not know how many voters were transients, completely foreign to Moscow, with no ties to the city. Absenteeism was very high, and doubtless most absentees were native Muscovites who, out of deep conviction, simply *did not consider it necessary* to vote. The duma will have no roots in the real Moscow; it is an accidental child, nothing more.

We note that even these days, Moscow seems more or less contentedly moderate, particularly in comparison to Petrograd.

DOCUMENT 11.4
M. PETROV, "ELECTIONS TO THE CITY DUMA"[5]

The following document, an essay on the 20 August 1917 elections to Petrograd's central city duma, appeared in the Popular-Socialists' newspaper, The People's Word *(Narodnoe slovo), on 27 July. Trudovik Popular-Socialist candidates received just 1 percent of the vote in the May and June elections. To increase their chances of winning a seat in August, they formed an electoral bloc with Lithuanian, Belorussia, and Georgian socialist groups, the Jewish Poalei-Tsion, and the obscure United Party of Socialist Federalists. Their "Candidate List No. 1," also called "The Bloc of Popular-Socialists and National Socialist Parties," included 156 candidates.[6] The Trudoviks, however, did no better in August than they had in June's elections. The big story of the 20 August Petrograd elections was that the Bolsheviks won 33.5 percent of the roughly 550,000 votes cast, while the combined SR and Menshevik turnout fell to 42 percent.[7]*

Elections to the City Duma.

On 20 August, elections will be held for the members of the central city duma.

Scheduling city elections for one month before the Constituent Assembly elections has put the population and the political parties in a difficult situation. The city duma election promises to take on a purely political character. It is natural that the upcoming Constituent Assembly, the greatest event in our history, will overshadow all other ordinary public tasks. Rather than dedicate their "electoral energy" to city elections, the political parties naturally will focus on the Constituent Assembly elections.

Finally, the closeness of the more significant Constituent Assembly elections undoubtedly will decrease the population's interest in the city elections, and there may be very high levels of electoral absenteeism.

Meanwhile, elections to the city duma in our capital have great significance. An aberrant or happenstance makeup of the Petrograd City Duma could hinder the pace of our internal political life.

The capital's duma manages the economy. It administers the country's nerve center and brain. The great Constituent Assembly, the Provisional Revolutionary Government, and the revolutionary democracy's central soviets (the soldiers', peasants', and workers'), the central military organizations and defense organizations—all these are located in Petrograd. All are connected to a great extent to the Petrograd city government.

[The city duma is responsible for] the militia and public safety, food supply, public health, and much else needed for defense in the rear. [It is responsible] for our state center, for making it run in an orderly fashion without interruptions. A catastrophe in [Petrograd] would affect the entire country's life, all our revolution's affairs, and the country's defense.

The Petrograd City Duma is not a parliament . . . but in its substance and its truth, it will have pure governmental and political significance. We, the Trudovik Popular-Socialists, never will forget that local self-government, particularly the capital's duma, is more than a state institution. It also is a political institution. The Petrograd Duma's voice on current political affairs must resound in all Russia. To strengthen the capital, to defend the Provisional Government's revolutionary authority, it must unite the forces of all revolutionary Russia.

In preparing for the forthcoming elections, our party must not for a minute lose sight of two basic tasks that confront the capital: organizing our rear and consolidating the revolution's achievements. One is a practical business task, the other a political task. For us, combining these tasks does not seem impractical. Our party has long years' experience of open parliamentary political work. It has acquired sufficient political experience and skills, and it has more than a few political warriors in its ranks. Our party also has practical workers in the towns and zemstvos who understand the mechanics of creating public culture.

Subjective conditions favor us. We find strength in our duma policies and in real work. The question is, will objective conditions be on our side? Will our banner, on which all toilers' aspirations are inscribed, be met sympathetically? Will the population's democratic strata rally around it and carry it into the duma? We think the previous elections' results were an aberration. . . .

In practice, the Social Democrat-Mensheviks' and Socialist Revolutionaries' slogans seem more and more like the positions on which our party stands and has stood.

In launching the electoral campaign, we must exert all our effort to achieve the most favorable result (which, as things stand now, is fully possible) in the Petrograd City Duma, an institution responsible for great practical matters. Our party—a party of real practical business, not of political phrases and declarations—must receive the duma seats it deserves.

DOCUMENT 11.5
A MENSHEVIK DEFENSIST DISTRICT DUMA
ELECTORAL APPEAL [8]

In advance of Petrograd's 20 August 1917 central duma elections, new elections were held for several city district dumas. The following document is a 5 August editorial in Unity (Edinstvo) *urging workers in the Aleksandr Nevskii District to vote for the Edinstvo faction.* [9]

On Today's Elections.

Today, tomorrow, and the day after, elections will be held for the Nevskii District Duma. Most of the Nevskii District's inhabitants are workers. In electing representatives to their local duma, the Nevskii workers must, of course, keep in mind that their representatives will be called on to decide particularly difficult current problems of local organization. These questions are closely tied to general city economic issues like organizing food supplies, protecting labor, apportioning city taxes among the propertied classes, fighting against unemployment, using city resources to provide free mandatory education, medical care, and legal assistance, and so on.

In voting for their duma representatives, they should not limit themselves to thinking about district and city economic problems that must be solved. They should consider the broader political defense of their rights and interests. In revolutionary times, city local self-government can play a large role. This was true during the great French Revolution, when the city commune became a stronghold in the radical democratic strata's struggle against the royalists (the defenders of the crown's power) and the moderates. It is vitally important that Russia's workers conquer such strongholds, because our revolution still is far from complete. We still await elections to the Constituent Assembly. And we expect that the country will still face great obstacles on the road to organization.

Given the conditions under which duma elections are taking place, the proletariat is obliged to elect only people in whom it has absolute faith, people who can stand up for their class interests without reservations. The representatives of the workers' party, the Social Democrats, are such people. The Nevskii workers must elect members of the Social Democratic Party to the district duma. But many groups and organizations claim to be under the Social Democratic Party's banner, and some of these have actually torn away completely from the party's views.

You must not vote for people who, following Lenin, beckon you to fraternize with the reactionary German Army and struggle against the Russian Revolution's government. There is a reason that the German general staff has sympathized with these people's activities and has tried to aid them. These people arouse the mob's passions. In July's first days, soldiers and sailors who were exhausted or lacked consciousness fired into peaceful crowds of toilers on Petrograd's streets. These people called on you to join that uprising, which could have destroyed all your work.

You also must not vote for the semi-Leninists who, shouting slogans about the international brotherhood of workers, beckon you to negotiate with an enemy who still occupies Russian land. Instead, free yourself from the fog of confusion that Lenin and his friends have wrapped around you.

If you are conscious workers, then you must understand that a German invasion and German victory are the greatest threats to your interests. Not the interests of this or that group of workers, which might benefit from short-term wage increases, but the interests of the entire working class as a whole. A German victory would undermine Russia's economy and halt the economic development of our productive forces. Most of all, it would retard the development of your class, both in regard to its numbers and as relates to its consciousness and capacity for struggle. In addition, a German victory would bring a political reaction that would greatly damage the real Russian proletariat and hinder the development of class struggle.

Therefore, in the name your class' general interests and tasks, you are obliged now to defend the country from foreign invaders. Arm in arm with the other strata and classes of the population interested in the country's free development, you must fight against internal disruption and anarchy. In the name of your interests, which are intertwined with the entire revolutionary country's interests, you are obliged to support the unified Provisional Government.

You must understand that, in defending the fundamental interests of your class and of the revolution, you are at the same time defending the interests of global democracy and the global proletariat. And understand this: in today's elections, you must vote for the representatives of that Social Democratic organization which, from the war's first days, was not confused about the nature of the enemy's aggression or its attacks, and which has constantly called on you to meet all your great tasks and responsibilities.

You must vote for the representatives of the consistently defensist Social Democratic organization "*Edinstvo*."

DOCUMENT 11.6
TWO BOLSHEVIK DUMA ELECTORAL APPEALS[10]

In the first round of Petrograd district duma elections, the Bolsheviks finished third behind the Socialist Bloc and the Kadets. The Bolsheviks devoted considerable attention to the July and August duma campaigns. Their strong showing in August's elections (second after the Socialist Revolutionaries) suggests both the effectiveness of their campaign and a shift in the population's political mood, away from the more moderate socialist factions. The following documents are Bolshevik campaign appeals for the Peterhoff District Duma elections, printed in Worker and Soldier (Rabochii i Soldat) *on 16 July 1917, and for the city duma election, printed in* Proletarians (Proletarii) *on 20 August.*

Elections to the Peterhoff District Duma.

Comrade workers and soldiers!

In the Peterhoff District Duma elections, vote for candidate list No. 2 (Bolsheviks).

The Bolsheviks are the only party that does not cooperate with the people's enemies, with those who preach that Cossack whips are the "revolution's salvation."

With your vote, show that imprisonments and newspaper closures cannot kill the revolutionary democracy's left wing.

Everyone, put list No. 2 in the ballot box.

Workers!   Today in the central city   **Soldiers!**
duma elections
Vote for candidate list No. 6
The Bolshevik Party

Because they are the only ones who, not only in words, but in deeds are

Against The death penalty for soldiers	**For** Transferring power to the workers and poor peasants
The war of aggression	Immediate confiscation of the land
Capitalist plunder	Establishment of workers' control over production
	Limitations on capitalists' profits

DOCUMENT 11.7
THE BOLSHEVIKS ON THE PETROGRAD CITY DUMA ELECTIONS [11]

The following document is a Bolshevik appeal to voters published in the closing hours of the Petrograd City Duma electoral campaign. Unlike slogan-based electoral advertisements, this 19 August 1917 column in Proletarians (Proletarii) *laid out the Bolsheviks' argument in detail. Some of the Bolsheviks' claims distorted the actual positions taken by other left socialist parties; on specific issues, such as the war, the Bolsheviks' stance resembled that of the left Socialist Revolutionaries, the Menshevik-Internationalists, and the Anarchists.*

For Candidate List No. 6.

Our party, the party of the revolutionary proletariat, is running as List No. 6 in the 20 August elections to the Central City Duma.

Every worker, peasant, and soldier must cast their vote for this list only.

For this list only, because only our party is struggling resolutely and bravely against the raging bourgeois-aristocratic counterrevolutionary dictatorship, against introduction of the death penalty, against destruction of workers' and soldiers' organizations, against liquidation of all the freedoms obtained through the people's sweat and blood.

You must vote only for our party's list, because only it is struggling resolutely and bravely with the peasants against the landlords, with the workers against the factory and plant owners, and with the oppressed everywhere against all the oppressors. Only our party has resolutely and bravely pursued the war's speediest end, conclusion of a people's peace, transfer of land to the peasants, and introduction of workers' control over production.

You must vote only for our party, because only it will make truly radical changes to the city economy's administrative system. Only our party will completely transfer the tax burden from the property-less poor's shoulders to the shoulders of the wealthy classes. Only our party wants to solve the housing problem by confiscating the exploiters' grand apartments, exclusive shops, expensive restaurants, and other buildings, and turning them into housing for the poor.

No party but ours raised its voice in protest against restoring the old autocratic police and wants to replace it with an elected people's militia. Of all the parties, our party alone demands introduction of obligatory militia service.

We alone are saying: we must create a new environment for people . . . Let the people, all the people, enjoy clean, safe, orderly streets.

Comrade workers, soldiers, and peasants, understand that questions of the city's welfare are closely connected to questions of all Russia's welfare. Petrograd's supply problems, financial problems, and other problems cannot be solved without solving these problems for all Russia. Understand this, and vote only for the party that is struggling to solve all these problems, that is struggling for the workers, soldiers, and poor peasants.

Anyone who is against the death penalty and against shootings, chaos, and arrests, anyone who is for the revolution against the counterrevolution—must vote for List No. 6.

DOCUMENT 11.8
ARIADNA TRYKOVA, "VOTE!"[12]

The following document is a Kadet electoral appeal in Speech (Rech), *19 August 1917, accompanied by a graphic that accompanied the essay. The author, Ariadna Trykova—a leading Russian feminist and journalist—was a member of the Kadet Party's Central Committee. In spring 1917, the Kadets ran a duma electoral campaign based on the idea that they stood "above" social class divisions and represented Russian state interests, the most fundamental interests of all social classes. Kadet activists went door to door, handing out leaflets and plastered walls with posters. Nonetheless, they placed a distant second behind the socialist bloc in Petrograd and behind the Socialist Revolutionaries in Moscow. The Kadets did not anticipate a stronger showing in Petrograd's 20 August city duma elections. Still, they hoped that their appeal to transcendent state interests and their years of "cultural work" to raise the masses' "political consciousness" would attract voters to List No. 9, the Kadet Party candidate slate.*

Vote!

Elections to the city duma are Sunday. Female and male voters will be putting the city's fate into the hands of those elected for eighteen months. Bridges and trams, schools and hospitals, water and bread—all this will depend on the new duma members' knowledge, wisdom, honesty, and abilities.

In our everyday life, we all will feel the results of their suitability or unsuitability for this work. It is especially important now, when personal energy and thriftiness cannot save individuals or households from absolute deprivation and poverty. It already is impossible to close yourself off, hide, and secure yourself from material troubles.

Civic mindedness and collective-mindedness have become powerful forces in our lives, and so the country should be able to provide real administrators for the work on which all our fates depend. And so Petrograd's fate partly depends on the results of tomorrow's elections.

. . . We bear the dual burdens of war and revolution with all Russia. But a great economic center like Petrograd, with its population of two and a half million, with tens of millions in revenues and 180 million in expenditures, has its own separate, complicated, and difficult life. It is quite a task to put details of city administration in order, to solve problems and handle economic matters with common sense. Since the left parties took control over the duma, we have seen nothing of this sort. True, some of them have been learning. But their education comes at a price, about which the empty city coffers speak no less eloquently than do the empty grocery stores.

Really, they do not speak—they cry out. And those who hear this cry, who understand the enormous significance of the hungry days that are approaching, shouldn't they somehow express their indignation, their protest?

I write this, regretfully, not in the affirmative, but in the interrogative. Many have not yet seen through the [socialists'] promises and the boundless assurances. Magical words—already revealed as empty and black failures and the true source of the things like the July Days—still hold many under their spell. I suppose such people do not need our appeals. It will take more severe lessons for them to recover their sight.

"Tomorrow is the City Duma election. Vote for the list of the Party of People's Freedom, List No. 9. This is the only number for the list in all districts." (A. Trykova, "Golosuite!" *Rech*, 19 August 1917, p. 3.)

But there are others, those who no longer believe the crimson slogans of the revolution's honeyed days. They have turned, cowed, from what is vital and correct. They are ready to stand to the side and let events take their course. . . . They wring their hands and say "No matter what happens, it's all the same."

It is to those people that I want to make an appeal. I want to tell them: go to the polls, cast your vote, gather as many other voters as you can. I urge you, beg you, demand that you not surrender without a fight. Otherwise you will become a deserter from civic life, like soldiers who, with rifles in their hands, run from the Germans like a flock of sheep.

Electoral rights and the ballot—those are your weapon. And you are obliged to use them to battle against those who, through ignorance or through evil, would harm us all—free Russia's citizens—and who would bring shame upon us.

You all must go and vote. Don't hide in your houses and your summer homes. Do your basic and simple duty as a citizen. Pick up your envelope and take it to your polling place.[13] Remember, on the piece of paper that you put in the envelope, you must write: **No. 9**

—A[riadna]Trykova

DOCUMENT 11.9
TWO SOCIALIST REVOLUTIONARY DUMA ELECTORAL
APPEALS [14]

In spring 1917, the Socialist Revolutionaries (SRs) dominated the Petrograd district duma elections as leaders of the Socialist Bloc. Based on the content in their Petrograd newspaper, The People's Cause (Delo naroda)*, however, the SR leadership gave relatively less attention to the Petrograd municipal duma campaign in August. The following documents are SR electoral appeals published in* The People's Cause *on 20 August 1917. The first is an appeal aimed at SR party members, by left SR activist Vladimir Trutovskii. The second is an appeal aimed at voters generally. The SR slate (List No. 3) won a majority in 20 August Petrograd City Duma elections. Their 37 percent, though, was less than they had garnered in June.*

To SR Comrades
Today's elections are being carried out with greater bitterness than the earlier district duma elections, as there is greater indifference among voters.

When the total number of voters is smaller, it magnifies the vote for the bourgeois parties. We all know that these parties gather fewer votes than the socialist parties. But if there is a smaller total number of voters, if the democracy is indifferent to the elections and casts fewer votes, then the bourgeoisie parties will have relatively more votes. The ratio of their votes to the total number of votes cast will favor them.

The bourgeoisie is exerting all its effort to come away from this battle victorious. It isn't skimping on spending and has plastered the city with posters and appeals. These are filled with various slanders against the socialists previously elected to the district dumas. But if there are more voters rather than fewer, then despite all these resources there will be few bourgeois *duma* members, because the bourgeoisie is only a small group when compared to the army of the toiling people.

Therefore the socialists must exert all their efforts, so that not a single vote defending the toiling democracy is wasted. Our Socialist Revolutionary comrades in the province and in the city districts must turn their attention to preventing working class voter absenteeism. We will stun the bourgeoisie with simple, plain signatures written for **No. 3.**

Each party member must feel that we are carrying out a campaign and they are going into a battle. Each SR voter must bring a dozen people along to the polls who will vote for the socialists. Then he can say he did his duty for the party.

Everyone, into the streets! Everyone, to the polls! Everyone, take your positions in the electoral campaign!

—V. Trutovskii

Today's Elections.

Today Petrograd is expected to elect 200 members to the new central city duma. Elections will take place at 163 local electoral commissions. They open at exactly 9:00 this morning and will close today at 9:00 in the evening.

Today's elections are different from the earlier district duma elections in several specific details. Instead of ballot slips on which names of candidates for the duma are printed, voters will be given special ballot slips on which they will write the number under which a specific party candidate list is registered.

The Party of Socialist Revolutionaries appears in today's elections as list No. 3. People voting for the list of the Party of Socialist Revolutionaries must write down the number **3.**

Several difficulties came up in staffing the electoral commissions. Nonetheless, all 163 electoral commissions for today's elections were staffed. Each has a chairman and three members elected by the district *duma* and confirmed by city mayor G. I. Shreider.[15]

The Federated Union of City Employees assigned many of its members to serve as members of the electoral commissions.

Yesterday M. I. Petrov, a member of the city electoral commission, sent the district electoral commission chairmen instructions explaining the election's technical aspects.

At the electoral commission offices, there must be tables that voters can use when filling out their ballots. On the ballot, they must write the number of the party for whom they are voting.

Ballots on which numbers have not been written will not be accepted. These will be wasted votes. So people voting for the Party of Socialist Revolutionaries must not forget to write **No. 3.**

The offices where you will fill out the ballots must have posters with the lists of candidates from each party participating in the election.

No political agitation will be permitted in the polling place, either verbal or in the form of posters.

The ballot slips distributed to voters must not have any marks on them.

Do not lose sight of the fact that the voters themselves are responsible for writing on their ballot slips to cast their vote for the Party of Socialist Revolutionaries, list **No. 3.**

If the voter makes any erasures, marks, or inscriptions, or if the voter signs the ballot, then that ballot will not be counted as a vote.

The voter must pay special attention to this requirement, since a significant percentage of ballots cast in the previous elections were uncountable. Voters can, of course, exchange spoiled ballot slips for new ones before submitting their ballot. In exchange for the spoiled ballot, the local electoral commissioners will provide a duplicate.

Upon entering the room where the ballot box is located, voters will present their voter cards, which will be marked to indicate that they have exercised their right to vote.

Voters who did not receive an electoral envelope must appeal to their housing administration. If the administrator responsible for the envelopes is not there, then they must go to the district commission, with proof of their identity. They should ask if they were included in the voter registration lists. If the voter's last name is on the list, the voter will be given an envelope with a special mark on the ballot slip.

Members of the central electoral commission will be on duty at the city *duma* building all day, from 8:00 in the morning to 9:00 at night. They can be contacted by telephone at the following numbers: 2-73-97; 2-68; 1-38-36; 1-43-23; 15-40, to answer all inquiries and to clarify misunderstandings and questions that may arise.

Electoral envelopes will be provided to military personnel at their barracks, which is where they were enrolled on the district voter registration lists.

Among all the candidate lists, there is only one for which you must vote, for which you must convince others to vote if they care about the interests of the toilers, the interests of the people, and the interests of the revolution—that is the list of the Party of Socialist Revolutionaries, **No. 3.**

DOCUMENT 11.10
A DUMA ELECTORAL APPEAL FROM THE PETROGRAD
COUNCIL OF FACTORY AND INDUSTRIAL EMPLOYEES [16]

In 1917 office employees formed their own unions, joined political parties, and participated vigorously in politics. Employees in government institutions and banks often defined themselves as members of the educated intelligentsia and as liberals. But many others defined themselves as workers and as socialists. The following document is an electoral appeal to employees by the Petrograd Central Council of Elders of Factory, Plant, and Industrial Enterprise Employees, published in The People's Cause (Delo naroda) *on 20 August 1917.*

Comrade Employees!

On 20 August of this year, Petrograd's citizens will do their civic duty by taking an active part in city duma elections. Before we go to the polls, comrades, we must realize who our friends are and for whom we must cast our votes.

We are the population's least secure segment, and our future demands that we take a great interest in our city's proper municipal life. We must vote for those who will stand up for all toilers, who in the days before the revolution never feared prison or death, and who preached equality, brotherhood, and freedom for all toilers and for all the oppressed and exploited.

THE SOCIALIST PARTIES' VICTORY IS OUR VICTORY

Comrades, at this dread hour of political shifts and state financial crisis, we all must rally around freedom's red flag and stand up for the toilers' freedom and rights.

EVERYONE TO THE POLLS! EVERYONE VOTE FOR THE SOCIALISTS' LISTS

Executive Committee of the Petrograd Central Council of Elders of Factory, Plant, and Industrial Enterprise Employees

DOCUMENT 11.11
V. TRUTOVSKII, "PEASANTS AND WORKERS" [17]

In the following document, which appeared in the left Socialist Revolutionary (SR) Petrograd newspaper, Labor's Banner (Znamia truda), *on 24 August 1917, Vladimir Trutovskii explains the difference between the SRs' view of the peasantry and that of the Social Democrats. By late August, differences between the left SRs and the SR Central Committee had grown so significantly that a formal split seemed inevitable. Besides longstanding differences over the war, factions now disagreed about revolutionary government—the left SRs rejected coalitions with the "bourgeois" parties and insisted on an all-socialist government. But the left SRs also had to distinguish themselves from the other left socialist parties. Trutovskii is concerned here with highlighting differences between the left SRs and the left Social Democrats (the Bolsheviks).*

Peasants and Workers.

We Socialist Revolutionaries are constantly explaining the intimate connection between peasants and workers. Both are toiling people, but one sells its labor in factories, and the other sells it to landlords and kulaks.[18] When a peasant goes into a factory, he does so not because he finds it more satisfying, but, on the contrary, because of hunger.

What separates peasants from the workers? Why do some socialist groups divide these two detachments of labor's great army? They even allege that peasants who own 1.5 *desiatins* of land, a wooden plow, a harrow, a milk-cow, and a little horse are "petty bourgeois."[19]

In fact, although the peasants own tools to work the land, they don't use these to exploit and oppress other people, but to feed themselves, which they do just barely. To say that anyone who owns any farm tools is a *burzhui* is exactly like saying that a tailor who has a needle, which surely is his "property," is a *burzhui*.

Clearly the issue is not at all whether one owns or does not own a particular set of productive resources.[20] Clearly some other characteristic identifies the "burzhui." And it is here that we differ radically with the Social Democrats. Because they simply repeat this formula and insist that workers and peasants are on different paths.

We say: The only meaningful difference between people's economic position is whether they toil for others or live at others' expense. True, the rich always live at the poor's expense. But *property* is not always a means for other people's oppression.

Just as a tailor with needle in hand is not oppressing anyone, so peasants sowing their own land, of course, cannot be *burzhui*. For us, peasants are divided into two large categories: the toiling peasantry, which does not live at the wage laborers' expense, and the peasant bourgeoisie, which repeatedly hires workers and lives at their expense.

The toiling peasantry is working class' friend and comrade in arms. This does not apply, of course, to the rural bourgeoisie—the petty aristocratic landowners, the kulaks, the traders, the rural businessmen and so on. When workers conduct their *workers'* politics, they must not forget their millions of village brothers in toil—the toiling peasants. To separate themselves from their brothers, as the Social Democrats do, would commit the great mistake of giving the real bourgeoisie excessive opportunity to break the toiling people's resistance.

The workers must not forget that in our peasant country, where the toiling peasantry numbers in the tens of millions, it is not prudent to separate the workers' liberation struggle from the peasants' struggle. Therefore it is important that urban workers see the land question not as something secondary to their own issues, but, on the contrary, as an issue that touches upon their most essential *class* interests.

DOCUMENT 11.12
A DRAFT OF THE MENSHEVIK CONSTITUENT ASSEMBLY ELECTORAL PLATFORM[21]

In 1917 all Russia's political parties insisted that a Constituent Assembly, chosen in free elections by the entire people, would create a permanent state to replace the Provisional Government. Provisional Government leaders deferred fundamental reforms to the Constituent Assembly, but dragged their feet in preparing for the assembly. In May 1917, a special government commission drafted rules and procedures for the assembly elections.[22] But the coalition government put off elections. Kerensky, reacting to the July Days, set September dates for the assembly's election and opening. In early August, however, the government announced another delay: it set elections for 12 November and the convocation for 28 November 1917. (Elections did take place on 12 November, but the Bolsheviks—who had seized power on 25 October—delayed the assembly's convocation until January.)

The following document is a draft of the Menshevik's Constituent Assembly electoral platform, discussed by the party's Organizational Committee in Petrograd late July 1917. It was published in The Workers' Newspaper (Rabochaia gazeta) *on 29 July. Electoral platforms laid out arguments in greater detail than did electoral advertisements and appeals.*

Russia's people must prepare for Constituent Assembly elections at a difficult time. Russian Army units have faltered and scattered, enemy regiments have penetrated deep into Russia, and great danger threatens the state's very existence. The world war Russia entered three years ago has heavily, almost fatally, wounded the country and revolution. We now must gather and exert all our force to prevent the army's collapse and the country's disintegration, to defend free Russia, to reconstitute its inviolability. In the days to come, Russia's people must make great sacrifices and exert their mighty will so that Russia can reach the Constituent Assembly, which will unshakably affirm the foundations of Russian freedom.

The Great Russian Revolution demolished the tsarist throne and overthrew centuries of slavery that had worn down Russia's people. The revolution proclaimed freedom and equality and ignited hope for a just peace among Europe's exhausted people, bloodied by slaughter. For Russia, the great revolution that stirred the masses in the millions raised questions of extraordinary importance and complexity. Russia's fate, her existence as a civilized country, depends on correctly resolving these questions.

The tsarist regime and three years of unprecedented war left the country at the brink of destruction, and its salvation demands heroic measures and great decisions. To have the free life they dreamed of, the people must determine their own fate. They must decide questions of war and peace; they must work out fundamental laws and determine the state's form. The toiling classes' most vital daily needs and most cherished aspirations must be satisfied. The Constituent Assembly must decide all these great and difficult questions. The Constituent Assembly will take the whole country's administration into its hands. It will express the people's free and supreme will, and all must bow down before that will.

In their programs and slogans, many different parties ask voters to trust them and vote for their candidates.

From its inception the proletariat's party, the Russian Social Democratic Labor Party, made destroying the autocracy its primary task. And 14 years ago it first called for "convocation of a Constituent Assembly, freely elected by all the people" as the means to realize Russia's complete democratic transformation.

Russian Social Democracy is a branch of international socialism. The socialist parties of all countries fight for an order in which all public wealth, all means of production—all land, factories, plants, mines—and all means of communication will be public property; an order in which all society, all citizens, will be obliged to work, but in which all will benefit equally from the blessings humanity procures from nature. In a socialist order the struggle between classes will cease, because classes—rich and poor, exploiters and exploited—will vanish. The struggle for money and the crimes it creates will vanish. Wars—which only benefit the ruling class—will cease. Humanity will become a single family.

But Social Democrats understand that real socialism can be achieved only when industrial development and growing national wealth have prepared the ground and when most people have become conscious socialists. Therefore Social Democrats everywhere are for developing productive forces while also demanding immediate measures to improve conditions for toilers. Everywhere, they fight for all people's complete freedom and power. Everywhere, they seek reforms that will facilitate the struggle for socialism.

The Social Democrats are the party of the working class, the party of the toiling poor. The working class, the proletariat, is contemporary society's most oppressed class. It exploits no one and represents all exploited classes. But individually, each worker is powerless to improve his conditions. Workers can throw off their chains only through mass action, only through an organized uprising. . . .

The working class has taken its first steps toward socialism, and the Social Democrats are the party of the working class. But in capitalist society, life also is hard for small property owners in towns and villages. They suffer from big Capital's power and are ruined, impoverished. They themselves become proletarians. So the Social Democrats ask them to support the workers' struggle for socialism, because socialism is their only salvation.

The more capitalism develops, the more total wealth increases, the more the means of production are concentrated into the hands of powerful unions of capitalists. As the big bourgeoisie become the whole world's masters, the peasants, artisans, and small property owners become less independent. They have less chance to rise in status, and their situation becomes more difficult and more hopeless. They must clearly understand that socialism alone gives them real and total liberation.

The Social Democrats everywhere lead the conscious and organized proletariat in struggle for its own liberation. At the same time, they defend all people's freedom and rights and fight to end ruling class privileges and all injustices. Indeed, Social Democrats everywhere tried to prevent the war. When the world war erupted, the most conscientious and devoted Social Democrats were the first to speak against it. All contemporary society's oppressed classes, all the urban and rural poor who suffer from the war and its burdens, must recognize the tremendous importance of the conscious proletariat's worldwide struggle. The proletariat fights for its own liberation while fighting for liberation of all mankind.

Russia remains a poor country, with weakly developed industry and few proletarians. Therefore, Russia still is far from socialism. Russia first must destroy the remnants of serfdom, create a free form of government, develop its culture, and allow economic forces to flourish.

Until 1905, Russia had no bourgeois party resembling Europe's revolutionary bourgeoisie, where the bourgeois struggle for political freedom and emancipation had prepared the ground for the proletariat's struggle. In Russia, the organized and conscious proletariat began its struggle before any bourgeois parties appeared. Therefore from its inception the Russian Social Democratic Labor Party, in addition to leading defense of the proletariat's interests, had to take on the difficult struggle for Russia's political liberation from the oppressive autocratic police regime and aristocratic rule.

The first worker Social Democrats appeared in Russia thirty years ago. The tsarist government attacked and persecuted them; hundreds and thousands rotted in prisons or were exiled to Siberia. Nonetheless, their numbers grew, and the Social Democrats' influence on the working class increased. In 1905, during the first Russian revolution, the entire working class shouted the Social Democrats' slogans.[23] The Social Democrats also led the general public movement against the autocracy. And when heavy reaction pressed down, when the Stolypin regime strangled the country, the Social Democrat Mensheviks defended what remained of 1905's achievements, consolidated the workers' organizations, rallied the workers' best forces in open arenas, and used the third of June State *Duma* to summon a new generation to struggle for the legacy of 1905.[24]

The Social Democrats sent deputies to all four State Dumas. In the *duma*, they defended the workers' and peasants' interests. They carried out a persistent and genuine struggle against the tsarist government. They exposed the bourgeois parties' weakness, cowardice and indecisiveness, while at the same time supporting their progressive steps. Almost all the Social Democrats in the Second State Duma, including Tsereteli, were sentenced to hard labor or sent into exile, from which they were liberated only by the present revolution.

From the moment war broke out, the Social Democrats in the duma, led by Chkheidze, declared that the people themselves must bring a speedy end to the government's criminal war. From the start, the Social Democrats in the duma demanded a universal peace without annexations or indemnities, with freedom of national self-determination.

When the Great Russian Revolution ignited, the Social Democrat Mensheviks again appeared at its head. They led the soviet of workers' and soldiers' deputies. When it became clear that—despite our revolution's bourgeois character—the purely bourgeois government would not meet the democracy's demands halfway and did not have the confidence of the people and army, the Social Democrats joined the government

. . . [T]he Social Democrat Mensheviks now consider it their duty to defend the country and revolution steadfastly from the external dangers that threaten it. The Social Democrats believe that all the people's strength must be exerted to defend the country from military collapse and save the revolution from impending economic catastrophe, hunger and unemployment, anarchy and counterrevolution. Measures must be taken that alone can save the country: restoration of revolutionary discipline at the front and in the rear, with the help of revolutionary democratic institutions; immediate introduction of urgent labor and land reforms; state regulation of economic life; a new tax on property; appointment of people loyal to the revolution to state offices; and convocation of the Constituent Assembly at the designated time.

In the Constituent Assembly, the Social Democrats will make the following fundamental demands to resolve the important questions raised by the war and revolution.

1. Ending the war.

If, by the Constituent Assembly's convocation, a peace conference has not met, then the Social Democrats—while promoting rebuff of a hostile invasion with all their strength—will propose to the Constituent Assembly an appeal to all belligerent states. This appeal will call for peace negotiations under conditions already advanced by revolutionary Russia and accepted by the great majority of socialists in all belligerent and neutral countries. In the interest of a durable peace and to prevent future wars, the Social Democrats will make the following main demands regarding the peace: armaments limitations in all countries; creation of an international arbitration court to resolve all emerging conflicts; future abolition of all secret diplomacy and secret treaties; and, finally, freedom of economic development in all former belligerent and neutral countries.

In the war's aftermath in Russia, the Social Democrats will obtain state social welfare benefits for war invalids and their families and for families of all war dead, as well as broad state aid for toilers injured due to the war. In addition, the Social Democrats demand the standing army's abolition and its replacement by a people's militia. Until this demand can be realized, the Social Democrats will reorganize the army democratically and recognize that soldiers have full citizens' rights.

2. State building, the nationality question, and citizens' rights

In the sphere of the fundamental laws and the country's constitution, the Social Democrats will secure absolute people's power, i.e., a democratic republic with no president and with one legislative chamber, elected by universal, equal, direct, and secret ballot on a proportional basis, so that all state power in the country rests with the chamber of deputies and the government it forms. This new people's government must hold supreme authority in matters of war and peace and foreign policy.

Further, the Social Democrats will demand that all democratic local self-government institutions, both municipal and zemstvo, be elected in the same manner as the national parliament, and that local administrative institutions—particularly the city and rural militia—be subordinated to them. Finally, the Social Democrats will demand elected law courts. All government officials must be held responsible before the law, equally to other citizens.

The Social Democrats—while declaring themselves against violent suppression of nationality movements, against limitations on the right of national self-determination, and in favor of the proletarian liberation struggle among all Russia's nationalities—stand for an indivisible and unified state. That is because a unitary state guarantees the most favorable conditions for Russia's economic and political development. By preserving a durable unified state, the Social Democrats will secure the broadest degree of self-determination (including even autonomy) for nationally, economically, or domestically distinct regions. Because of Russia's diverse population, neither regional self-administration nor regional autonomy can eliminate conflicts between nationalities. The Social Democrats will fight against any oppression by one nationality over another. They will ensure national minorities the right to education in their native language and the right to use their native language in the courts and other state, regional, and local institutions. For nationalities diffused in various regions and those that do not have a distinct territory, the Social Democrats propose cultural-national autonomy, i.e., the creation of self-administration unions that embrace all members of a given nationality. These unions would function like a state and would administer affairs concerning a given nationality's culture, i.e., public education, and so on.

Regarding all citizens, the Social Democrats will struggle steadfastly against any attempt to curtail or cut back already-achieved freedoms: unlimited freedom of conscience, speech, press, assembly, unions, and strikes. They will secure the inviolability of one's person and home and the abolition of social estate designations, titles, rank, and order. They will achieve complete and unconditional equality of all citizens, regardless of sex, nationality, religion, or social status.

Finally, the Social Democrats will demand separation of church and state, secularization of the schools, and free mandatory education for all children up to age 16.

3. The agrarian question

For the free development of agriculture and the rural economy, and for the peasantry's total liberation from the aristocratic landlords' rule, the Social Democrats will demand a land law under which the government transfers all treasury, crown, and state land to the people. In addition, all church and monastery land and all land of private landowners—petty landowners excluded—will be confiscated and become general-public property. Petty landed property (i.e., peasant allotments) must remain in the current owners' possession.

How to confiscate the land, i.e., how many *desiatins* of land constitute a petty property holding, will be resolved by the largest elected local self-government institutions under the people's supervision through the Constituent Assembly. These local self-government institutions will have the right to administer all land that becomes public property, excluding fields that remain under state administration in the general-state interest (woods, land for resettlement, parcels with mineral wealth, and so on).

In addition, the Social Democrats will demand laws defending agricultural workers from exploitation by employers and will apply all laws on labor defense to agricultural workers.

4. The labor question

To protect the working class from physical or moral injury, and to develop the workers' facility for the liberation struggle, the Social Democrats in the Constituent Assembly will demand: legislation introducing the eight-hour working day for all wage laborers and a mandatory weekly rest period of at least 42 hours; complete prohibition of overtime work; prohibition of night work, except when absolutely necessary; prohibition of labor by children under 16 years old; limitations on the work of teens and women; all-around protection of workers from excessive exploitation; and enterprise responsibility for accidents. In addition, state insurance for illness, old age, disability, and unemployment organized through self-governing insurance funds, and maternity insurance. Also, inspectorates that include people elected by the workers will ensure strict sanitary supervision of work places and workers' living quarters. Employers who violate laws protecting laborers must be held criminally responsible. Finally, arbitration chambers and labor exchange bureaus must be established everywhere.

5. Regulation of production and distribution.

The state faces complex, difficult economic problems: the war has created a sharp economic crisis, industry and transportation are complete disorganized, and the threats of mass unemployment and hunger loom. The Social Democrats will demand decisive state intervention in all spheres of economic life. They will demand state regulation of production, transport, and distribution, and the introduction of state monopolies on important consumer items. To achieve this, the Social Democrats will subordinate the self-interests of the propertied classes to the entire country's interests.

6. Financial policy

Implementing these grand reforms, restoring the losses and healing the wounds inflicted by the war, will require colossal and absolutely extraordinary resources. The Social Democrats in the Constituent Assembly will consider it their duty to warn all the population's classes and groups that—because of Russia's poverty and industrial backwardness and because of its tremendous indebtedness—even Russia's extraordinary public wealth will not cover all necessary expenditures. Therefore all classes of the population must be prepared to make great sacrifices and face deprivation, particularly at first. We must exert all our energy and strength and all our financial resources to pull Russia out of the quagmire into which the old regime and the war has dragged it.

At the same time, the Social Democrats will ensure that the main burden of state expenditures falls on the propertied classes. To this end, besides confiscation of land, the Social Democrats will demand a special one-time property tax. They will propose the complete abolition of indirect taxes and their replacement with a progressive tax on income and profits.

In all their activities in the Constituent Assembly, the Social Democrats will defend urban and rural working class interests; they will fight any attempt at counterrevolution and any pretentions to reverse civic development. We will strive to develop Russia's productive forces and its culture. We will consolidate freedom and people's-power in Russia, thus creating conditions for the successful and unhindered struggle to socialize the means of production, the conditions for socialism.

DOCUMENT 11.13
TWO BOLSHEVIK CONSTITUENT ASSEMBLY ELECTORAL CAMPAIGN DOCUMENTS[25]

Although historians have paid relatively little attention to the Bolsheviks' Constituent Assembly electoral campaign, the Bolsheviks took it quite seriously. This is clear from the following documents, published in the Petrograd Bolshevik newspaper, The Workers' Path (Rabochii put'), *on 28 September and 1 October 1917.*

FOR THE ATTENTION OF ALL PARTY ORGANIZATIONS
All party organizations are responsible for ensuring that all voters are registered.

All voters living in a particular electoral district on the day the voting rolls were compiled must be listed. Those who arrived after the lists were compiled must lodge an appeal for their inclusion in the voting rolls to the city, district, or settlement administration or to the township *zemstvo* administration within the first *five* days after the lists are published.

People who were not included in the lists must appeal to the city or settlement administration or the township zemstvo administration within the first *five days* after the lists are published to ensure their inclusion on the voting rolls. Requests presented during the first five days will be granted directly by the administration. Requests presented in the five days after that will be forwarded by the administration to the county (or capital) electoral commission.

Lists must be published no later than 9 October.

The county commissions will review requests made after the five-day period, and interested people may attend those sessions. The commissions' decisions can be appealed to the district court for administrative affairs within a 10-day period.

The corrected lists must be published at least three days before the election begins.

Because candidate lists must be presented to the district (capital) commissions no later than *12 October*, the Central Committee proposes that all party organizations hurry and send these [to the Central Committee] for review.

In each electoral district, parties may put forward as many candidates as may be properly elected to the Constituent Assembly. It is desirable to put forward the largest number of candidates. The number of [local] candidates, however, must not exceed half the number permissible in a given electoral district.[26] Candidate lists must be signed by at least one hundred people who have the right to vote in the particular district.

According to the instructions, the petitions must include: each proposed candidate's last name, first name, and patronymic [father's name]. Declarations from all the listed candidates stating their agreement to be on the ballot in that particular district must be appended. The list must be submitted in our party's name.

Each organization must make a list of representatives and provide the commission with the address of a local party member (a signatory to that list) as a contact person. That person will be the organization's representative to the county, city, or borough electoral commission and will participate in counting that district's electoral ballots.

To All Comrades:

Comrades, the Constituent Assembly elections are approaching. Defensists of all shades, naïve philistines, and petty-bourgeois utopians, expect this will end all our misery, end the war, give the peasants land, give all people bread and freedom, and cement the Russian revolution's triumph.[27] But the Constituent Assembly can only have such power when it is based on the united force of the people's most revolutionary organizations, when the unified, solid revolutionary detachments of the battle-tested army of revolutionary fighters enter the Constituent Assembly, when the great, unified masses send the Bolsheviks to the Constituent Assembly.

The proletarian revolutionary party—the singularly consistent and implacable party of revolution—the Bolsheviks go to the Constituent Assembly with ranks unified. But achieving the party's final goals demands enormous financial resources and tremendous exertion of the party's full strength now. Delivering and distributing literature, mass agitation activities, serious work examining electoral rolls, work in neighborhood, district, and regional electoral commissions—all this requires money.

The Party's Petersburg Committee and its Central Electoral Commission appeal for help to all comrades—to party members and all who sympathize with the party. *We ask comrades everywhere to immediately organize collections for the commission's fund for Constituent Assembly election campaign needs.*

DOCUMENT 11.14
FROM THE PARTY OF PEOPLE'S FREEDOM: A MOSCOW KADET CONSTITUENT ASSEMBLY ELECTION CAMPAIGN LEAFLET[28]

On 25 October 1917, the Bolsheviks seized power in Petrograd, which transformed the Constituent Assembly electoral campaign. The parties that opposed Lenin's government expected that the assembly would sweep the Bolsheviks from power, and condemning the Bolsheviks became a centerpiece of their campaign literature. This can be seen in the following document, a Kadet campaign leaflet printed in Moscow in early November 1917.

From the Party of People's Freedom.
CITIZENS!
Duty to the motherland requires that everyone participate in the Constituent Assembly elections. DO NOT SHUN THESE ELECTIONS!
By casting your ballot, you will declare your attitude toward current events and help create a government that will reestablish order and legality.
Russia has been the victim of a frightening and vile political crime. The Bolsheviks have stained Petrograd with the blood of civil war. They have shot Russia's heart, Moscow, by criminally and violently seizing power. They are callously trampling citizens' rights. They have begun wrecking the foundations of Russia's state and economic life. And they have declared Russia an enemy of the Allies.
SAVE RUSSIA FROM THE YOKE OF GERMANY'S HENCHMEN, FROM THE TRAITORS AND ENSLAVERS OF FREEDOM! SAVE YOURSELVES FROM STARVATION AND DISGRACE!
Vote for the Party of People's Freedom's candidates in the Constituent Assembly elections. Only the Party of People's Freedom, faithful to its slogans of genuine freedom and rights, has from the revolution's first days unswervingly and resolutely unmasked the Bolsheviks as the people's enemies, warned of their traitorous intentions, unwaveringly demanded suppression of their pernicious activities, and found common ground with them impossible.
CITIZENS, UNANIMOUSLY AND INSISTENTLY CAST YOUR BALLOTS FOR CANDIDATES OF THE PARTY OF PEOPLE'S FREEDOM.
Printed by the Typography of the Riabushchinskii Association, Moscow

DOCUMENT 11.15
A TRUDOVIK POPULAR-SOCIALIST PARTY CONSTITUENT
ASSEMBLY CAMPAIGN PAMPHLET[29]

Like the Kadets, the Trudovik Popular-Socialists made condemning the Bolsheviks a central aspect of their November 1917 electoral campaign. Their literature highlighted socialist aspects of their program while stressing their "defensism." The following document excerpts a four-page supplement to the Moscow news-paper The Popular-Socialist (Narodnyi-sotsialist). *It bears no date (typically such supplements appeared over several days), but it clearly was printed in early November. The Trudovik Popular-Socialist slate appeared as List No. 7 in Moscow.*

No. 7   Who are we?   **No. 7**

WE—are socialists

WE—are a party of toiling people, of all toilers

WE—are for transferring all land to the toiling people (nationalization of the land)

WE—are for the people's complete liberty: all for the people, all through the people

WE—are for state control over all industry

WE—are for the state and against anarchy, arbitrariness, and lynching

WE—are for peace between peoples, an honorable peace, without coercion

WE—are socialists who love their country and do not want to be slaves to [Kaiser] Wilhelm or anyone under his influence. There are no traitors or betrayers among us.

WE—are for the complete equality of all nationalities in the Russian Republic

WE—are for administering the country as a federation

WE—are honest democrats: among us there are no scoundrel dema-gogues who lie to and deceive the toiling people by promising peace and giving civil war, by promising freedom and giving murder and theft, by promising bread and giving hunger.

WE—the Trudovik Popular-Socialists, call on all toiling peoples—peasants, soldiers, workers, and the toiling intelligentsia—under our simple banner, "ALL FOR THE PEOPLE, ALL THROUGH THE PEOPLE"

WE—include in our ranks many warriors for the revolution and socialism, and we have chosen our candidates for the Constituent Assembly from among them.

TO ALL FOR WHOM THE ACHIEVEMENTS OF THE PEOPLE'S FREEDOM IS DEAR

TO ALL WHO LOVE THEIR COUNTRY NOT ONLY IN WORDS BUT IN DEEDS

TO ALL WHO WANT TO DEFEND HER

TO ALL WHO ARE AGAINST THE BOLSHEVIKS!

COMRADES AND CITIZENS!

DO NOT TRUST THE BOLSHEVIKS, and do not believe their promises. They are deceiving us. They will not give the exhausted people peace, bread, or land.

CITIZENS! THE ENEMY IS NOT SLEEPING!

He is ready to make us his slaves. He is ready to give us a new blow, new humiliation, new grief for all the people. And if this happens, there will be no peace, there will be no liberty, there will be no land.

ALL TO THE MOTHERLAND'S DEFENSE, ALL TO FREEDOM'S DEFENSE! THE BOLSHEVIKS ARE RUINING RUSSIA. NOT ONE VOTE FOR THE PEOPLE'S ENEMIES! **THOSE WHO CALL FOR BLOODSHED AND CIVIL WAR MUST BE ISOLATED.**

The blood being spilled is on their hands. The people, who have recovered their sight, curse those who encroach on the motherland's freedom and integrity.

DOCUMENT 11.16
SOCIALIST REVOLUTIONARY ELECTORAL APPEALS
IN SMOLENSK[30]

The following document set presents three Socialist Revolutionary (SR) election appeals from the entire front page of The Smolensk Bulletin (Smolenskii vestnik) *on 11 November 1917.* The Smolensk Bulletin *printed political appeals from several parties, but its editor was a leader of the region's SRs, and its readers understood that it represented a moderate-right SR viewpoint. As elsewhere, in Smolensk national party figures headed up the candidate lists. The local SR list included two national SR candidates: Ekaterina Breshkov-Breshkovskaia and Andrei Argunov. The newspaper's readers also would have recognized the names of local SR leaders like Viktor Podvitskii (1886–1937), Father Georgii Kutuzov, and Solomon Gurevich.*

CITIZENS! Vote for list No. 3 (three)!
12 November is the first day of the Constituent Assembly elections.

You all know there is only one path to free Russia's salvation and the autocratic order's definitive liquidation, and that *path leads through the Constituent Assembly.*

Without the Constituent Assembly, our Motherland will perish. It will suffocate in a miasma of anarchy and counterrevolution. It will drown in blood. It will become a decomposing corpse.

Only the Constituent Assembly can finish the war and give the exhausted people peace. *Only the Constituent Assembly* can give the country a strong government that can overcome economic disintegration and inflation. *Only the Constituent Assembly* can issue laws that will consolidate the democratic order. There is salvation *only through the Constituent Assembly*!

Citizens! The Party of Socialist Revolutionaries and the Central Committee of the Soviet of Peasants' Deputies asks that you divert yourself from daily affairs and prepare yourself for a great civic act—elections to the Constituent Assembly.

Understand that not only Russia's salvation, but the salvation of you and your children depends upon the Constituent Assembly. Understand that there is no turning back. Russia will either perish or it will live as a free country, as a democratic Republic. Understand also, that the government in power cannot establish order in the country or reestablish peace. It will not solve the fundamental problem of our state life, the land question: it will not turn all land into general-public property and will not turn the land over for the toiling people's use. Understand that only by settling the land question can conditions for factory workers be radically improved and our industrial life regulated. Understand that only by settling the land question can the ground be swept from beneath the feet of the all the reactionary classes and groups, all serfdom's secret and avowed advocates, all counterrevolutionaries, all our country's internal enemies, who would set one nationality against another.

Citizen-voters, knowing all of this, on the day of the Constituent Assembly elections—12 November—you must unanimously vote for *List No. 3 (three)*—for the candidates of the Party of Socialist Revolutionaries and the Soviet of Peasants' Deputies.

Citizen peasant men and women! Citizen workers! Citizen-soldiers! Vote for list No. 3 (three)!
If you want the candidates on List No. 3–the ones chosen and endorsed by the Provincial Council of the Party of Socialist Revolutionaries and the Smolensk Provincial Congress of Peasants' Deputies—to go to the Constituent Assembly, then on 12 NOVEMBER all you men and women who are at least twenty years old must put an envelope in the ballot box on which you have written No. 3 (three).

Every peasant man and woman, every worker and soldier must personally cast a ballot. The law forbids handing it to someone else, even your closest relative.

If you do not exercise your right to vote, if on 12 NOVEMBER each of you does not cast a ballot for No. 3 (three), then other candidates will go to the Constituent Assembly instead of your candidates, who all stand for "LAND and FREEDOM."

Citizen peasant men and women! Citizen workers! Citizen-soldiers!
On the day of the Constituent Assembly elections, you are obliged to set aside all your other business and concerns. All of you must go to the ballot box and cast your vote for your list—List No. 3 (three). If you don't, if you remain home on election day, you will commit a crime against the Motherland and the entire toiling people.

Candidates' List No. 3 (three) is your list. Peasant deputies and soldiers— the peasants at the Fourth Provincial Peasant Congress in Smolensk—saw all the candidates enumerated in list No. 3 (three), questioned them in detail, and were convinced that everyone on list No. 3 (three) stands for the defense of the toiling people's interests and needs.

Vote for List No. 3 (three) in the name of "Land and Freedom." Citizen-women! Vote for List No. 3 (three)! At the top of this list is the Russian land's great female citizen, Ekaterina Konstantinovna <u>Breshko-Breshkovskaia!</u>

Smolensk Electoral District No. 3

Name, patronymic and family name (nickname) of the candidate	The candidate's address
1. Breshko-Breshkovskaia, Ekaterina Konstantinovna (the Russian Revolution's Grandmother)	Petrograd, the Winter Palace
2. Argunov, Aleksandr Aleksandrovich	Petrograd, Tikhvinskaia St., No. 8, Apt. 23
3. Podvitskii, Viktor Vladimirovich	Smolensk, Korolevskii St., the Podvitskiis' house
4. Father Kutuzov, Georgii Afanas'evich	Pokrovskoe Village Gzhatsk County
5. Egorov, Mikhail Fedorovich	Iartsevo, Dukhovshchinsk County
6. Burtsev, Safon Ivanovich	Iukhnov County Los'minskaia Township
7. Gurevich, Solomon Grigor'evich	Smolensk, B. Blagoveshchenskaia St., Volkova's house
8. Chubar, Mark Fedorovich	Moscow, M. Molchanova St. No. 8, Apt. 10
9. Tarasenkov, Georgii Nikanorovich (lieutenant)	Moscow, Bol'shaia Gruvinskaia St., No. 25, Apt. 1
10. Kutuzov, Sergei Illiaronovich (ensign)	Smolensk, former Provincial Soviet of Peasant Deputies Bldg.
11. Kuvaev, Mikhail Gavrialovich	Viaz'ma, Vvedenskaia St., Akhromeev's house
12. Kazakov, Minai Nikitich	Zharan, Zharanskaia Township, Roslavl' County
13. Kazakov, Ivan Stepanovich	Smolensk, former Provincial Soviet of Peasant Deputies Bldg.
14. Egorov, Iakov Vasil'evich	Podsosnaia Station, Iukhnov County, Smolensk Province

Every male and female voter will receive this list (ballot) along with the other lists. On 12 November, remember this list, *No. 3 (three)*. Make no erasures or changes (or else your ballot will be thrown out). Place it in the envelope, seal it, and put it into the ballot box (urn).

DOCUMENT 11.17
"WHY MUST YOU VOTE FOR THE PARTY OF SOCIALIST REVOLUTIONARIES, LIST NO. 9?"[31]

After the Bolsheviks seized power in Petrograd on 25 October 1917, the Socialist Revolutionary (SR) Central Committee expelled those in the party's left faction who had cooperated with them. Although the left SRs did not officially form a separate party organization until December, the expulsions effectively meant an SR split. But because SR candidate lists for the Constituent Assembly elections already had been submitted to electoral commissions, they did not reflect the party's division into two competing groups. The following document is an electoral appeal in the SR Central Committee's Petrograd newspaper, The People's Cause (Delo naroda), *on 12 November 1917.*

Why Must You Vote for the Party of Socialist Revolutionaries, List No. 9?

No fewer than four generations of Russian revolutionaries fought for the Constituent Assembly. The Russian Revolution's entire history is the history of the Russian socialists' and revolutionaries' struggle for the Constituent Assembly. But only our generation has the great fortune of participating in Constituent Assembly elections. And among our generation, no socialist or revolutionary party struggled against the old regime for the Constituent Assembly with as much persistence, no party gave as much martyrs' blood, as the Party of Socialist Revolutionaries.

The Party of Socialist Revolutionaries—faithful heirs to the great Party of the People's Will, who, weapons in hand, fought tsarism and executed Alexander II on 1 March 1881—always has stood for steadfast armed struggle against arbitrary rule. Therefore its banner reads: *Through struggle you will achieve your rights!*[32] While the Social Democrats preached about the workers' peaceful economic struggle against the capitalists and opposed all forms of armed struggle, the Party of Socialist Revolutionaries bravely called on all toilers to fight for the socialist cause, called steadfastly for battle to the death against tsarism.

Our party called for struggle not just with its words, but with its deeds. The bold and ruthless hand of the Party of Socialist Revolutionaries' combat organization struck down individual representatives of the old government. The hand of Stepan Balmashov struck down Sipiagin; the hand of Egor Sazonov blew up Minister Plehve; the bomb of Ivan Kalaev tore apart Grand Prince Sergei Aleksandrovich.[33] Thousands of heroes from the Party of Socialist Revolutionaries' ranks undertook acts of combat and died victorious. The deaths of the best and greatest Socialist Revolutionary martyrs demonstrated their loyalty and firmness in struggle for the people's cause—for land and freedom, for socialism!

Of all parties engaged in revolutionary struggle, the Party of Socialist Revolutionaries has been the most courageous, the most steadfast, and the most militant. That is why the old regime cast its most terrible blows against the Party of Socialist Revolutionaries.

The other peculiarity that distinguishes our party from all others is that the Party of Socialist Revolutionaries fights for all the toiling people's interests, not for any individual class. Unlike the Social Democratic Party, which has always been a party of the urban industrial proletariat alone, the Party of Socialist Revolutionaries' ranks unite all urban workers and rural toilers. The fraternal union of urban proletarians and toiling peasants— that is the army of the Party of Socialist Revolutionaries. Because only our party, distinct from all other socialist parties, has written on its banner: *For land and freedom!* The Party of Socialist Revolutionaries was the first to elaborate a detailed land program—the uncompensated transfer of all land to the toiling people for equalized use.[34]

LEV KAMENEV AT THE OPENING SESSION OF THE DEMOCRATIC CONFERENCE[1]

The following document is a 14 September 1917 speech by Bolshevik Lev Kamenev at the opening session of the All-Russian Conference of Democratic Organizations (the Democratic Conference) in Petrograd. The conference had been convened by moderate socialist leaders, and it subsequently formed a "Pre-Parliament" ("The Council of the Republic") to guide the Provisional Government until the Constituent Assembly. The Bolsheviks and other left socialist factions held only a small minority among the conference delegates chosen by soviets, military committees, labor organizations, voluntary associations, and national minority groups from across Russia.[2] Kamenev, a close ally of Lenin's since 1902, had distanced himself from Lenin's "defeatist" stance during the war. In spring 1917, Kamenev endorsed the Provisional Government—a stance Lenin bitterly opposed. He also initially opposed Lenin's call for "All Power to the Soviets." Kamenev had endorsed the idea of Soviet power by September, but he still rejected Lenin's insistence on seizing power.

Speech of L. V. Kamenev

Comrades, the prime minister and supreme commander asked us to speak the truth here. In truth, he accompanied this request with threats. We will ignore his threats, but we agree about speaking the truth. The first word of truth, from the party for which I have the honor to speak, is that the Provisional Government's record over six months compels us to reject any polices now proposed by Minister Kerensky.

(*A voice in the hall:* "Insolent fellow." *Loud noise and applause.*)

Comrades, I assume we live in a republic. At a plenary assembly of the workers' democracy's representatives, the party of the proletariat has the right to declare that it lacks confidence in this or that government. Do not take this statement as overthrowing the Russian state.

Kerensky errs when he claims that lacking confidence in him is the same as lacking confidence in the Russian republic. We must reject the idea that grand speeches can solve the state's pressing problems.[3] Solving problems requires that we realistically appraise the bitter experience of the coalition government's six months. Our lack of confidence is based not on personal distrust of A. F. Kerensky—by no means. It is based upon experience and a reckoning of the class forces that manifested themselves over these six months.

What Kerensky hasn't told you is that his reform project continues proposals that deride the revolution, proposals Petrograd's toiling people will not endure, like introducing martial law and transferring cavalry corps to the Provisional Government's command. (*Loud noises from one side of the hall, applause from the other.*)

We have six months' experience of a certain political party pledging, but not implementing, a democratic program.[4] The issue now is not mistaken programs. This is no time for the democracy to be striking bargains. Review matters yourself. If what you want is a coalition with the bourgeoisie, then include the Kadets in an honest coalition.[5]

But if you've thought about the Kornilov rebellion and pondered what the [Bolsheviks] have said since the revolution's first days, then you must conclude that revolutionary Russia's only salvation—the only means to revive the army's confidence, of soldiers in their officers; the only means to revive the peasants' confidence that they will receive land; the only means to revive workers' confidence that they live in a republic—is to put power in the hands of the workers', peasants', and soldiers' organizations.

. . . Comrades, you heard what I said: we have no confidence in policies symbolically associated with Kerensky. But I say further, it is not just we who lack confidence in Kerensky; so do those who put him in power. That is why they gathered you here to decide questions about the organization of power. That is why they want our conference to create a permanent Pre-Parliament to control the government, to which the government would be responsible. If the Soviet Central Executive Committee trusted [Kerensky's] government, it would not have put forward such slogans.

The revolution's command staff cannot be built around one person, based on good intentions that person does not personify. An irresponsible government cannot be given the right to decide the question of the death penalty. There is no place for confidence in the discretion of a personal regime, an arbitrary regime that the toiling masses will reject.

Kerensky, rescued from a coalition, created a personal regime based on his own dictatorial pretentions. And the revolutionary democracy as represented by the peasants', workers', and soldiers' organizations gathered here has approved this government.[6]

Should a new attempt at a coalition be made? I answer in the negative. Here is why. If we pursue the program approved by the Moscow State Conference, what force, what political group can implement it?![7] Only the propertied elements have such a political party—the Kadets. But they do not approve of the program, as they made clear at the Moscow Conference. We cannot form a coalition with them on that platform. If the Party of People's Freedom is excluded, there are no other political groups with which to enter into a coalition. (*Applause.*) Don't deceive yourselves. Kishkin, Tereshchenko, and Nekrasov cannot substitute for a large political party as the sole representatives of Russia's propertied elements.[8]

Those who consider a coalition necessary, who do not accept our [Bolshevik] program, must step up and say that they reject our program. Agreeing to reject our program is significant, because we are not the ones losing authority among the masses. We represented the masses' interests.

If we stopped mirroring the masses' interests, it would cost us nothing to reach agreement on a coalition with Russia's propertied social elements. But cooperating with the commercial-industrial bourgeoisie is impossible. We tried this already. I recall that Konovalov left the government precisely because questions were raised about the revolution's economic policy.[9]

Thus there is only one way out. The government must not be a coalition. Power must be transferred to the democracy. (*Applause*). Not to the soviet of workers' and soldiers' deputies, but to the democracy as fully represented here today. We must form a government here. We must name the institutions to which that government must answer here. (*Applause*). The responsibility rests on our shoulders. We must reject all fear of responsibility! Form a government. (*Applause from part of the assembly.*)

DOCUMENT 12.2
THE MENSHEVIKS ON "THE SOVIETS AND THE DEMOCRACY"[10]

The following document is a 15 September 1917 editorial in the Petrograd Mensheviks' The Workers' Newspaper (Rabochaia gazeta) *criticizing Lenin's call for Soviet power.*

The Bolsheviks' stand on power was very much in flux in September. Although Kamenev's speech at the Democratic State Conference struck a relatively moderate tone, Trotsky demanded that the conference immediately transfer power to the soviets. Lenin, who in early September had suggested that the Bolsheviks might join an all-socialist government, now insisted on an immediate soviet seizure of power.

The Soviets and the Democracy.

Extremes are converging. Miliukov's newspaper and Lenin's both are doing all they can to undermine the Democratic Conference's importance by alleging that it was "artificially composed" and does not represent the popular majority.

Yesterday, *The Workers' Path* [the Bolsheviks' *Rabochii put'*] claimed that the Soviet Central Executive Committee "at this difficult historical moment has summoned a conference including bourgeois elements instead of a soviet congress. This is more than a crude formal transgression; it improperly substitutes the antirevolutionary classes' will for that of the revolutionary classes." Therefore the Central Executive Committee has "definitively weakened itself" by taking the bourgeois path. . . .

. . . We might ask: Just who are these "propertied elements, directly and indirectly supporting counterrevolution" who supposedly were given the right to participate in the Democratic Conference? Are they the peasant cooperatives? Are they the democratically elected city dumas and zemstvos?

The democratic organizations, like the food supply committees, provisions committees, and so on? The Leninists always claim that all propertied Russia supports the Kadet Party. And as we all know, the Kadets—following the orders of their "Lenin," Miliukov—boycotted the Democratic Conference. So where do these propertied counterrevolutionary elements come from?

But that is not the main issue. Nor is the fact they are preaching "All power to the soviets" and claiming that this alone "can make further development *gradual, peaceful, and calm*" (the italics are Lenin's) while at the same time Lenin and those with him are weakening the central institutions of those very Soviets they claim must take "all power." The main issue is a political question: When deciding the matter of organizing the government, should the Central Executive Committee summon a soviet congress or a congress of the entire democracy?

Since we asked, we must answer. Regarding the organization of state power, power for the entire country, an all-national power, one must appeal to the entire country and as many democratic organizations as possible.

The soviets do not embrace the entire democracy. This is even truer now than in the revolution's first months. Then, the soviets took on heterogeneous functions and substituted for local self-government institutions, government institutions, and trade-union organizations. Now, the lines are clearer, and many of those functions have passed from soviets to other democratic organizations. Therefore the soviets in no way [represent the entire democracy] and cannot rally the entire democracy around themselves.

. . . When the tremendously dangerous Kornilovite conspiracy developed, the soviets did not respond all by themselves. Instead, they created revolutionary committees, committees for the people's struggle against counterrevolution that included representatives from all local democratic organizations and local self-government institutions. It is false to conclude, as *The Workers' Path* does, that the soviets defeated the Kornilovshchina by themselves. No, the soviets were victorious because they managed to gather and unite all the democratic organizations around them. In other words, it was the entire democracy's victory.

In convening the Democratic Conference, the Central Executive Committee took the only path that can rally the entire democracy to resolve national revolutionary tasks.

The other path leads to isolation. It would isolate the democracy from the propertied elements, which are still on the democratic path. It also would isolate the proletariat from the rest of the democracy. That path would alienate the soviets from the other democratic organizations of democracy, which [the Bolsheviks] indiscriminately suspect of "directly or indirectly supporting counterrevolutionaries."

We assert that the Leninists' slogan, "All Power to the Soviets," is insincere. The soviets do not just include "workers and poor peasants," and Soviet power would not be the direct dictatorship of the proletariat and poor peasantry, as Lenin calls it. The Leninists inevitably will oppose the "petty-bourgeois SR and Menshevist elements'" presence in the soviets and talk a great deal about "the counterrevolution." For Lenin, "All Power to the Soviets" is only a compromise formula, a transition period until the hour arrives for the "pure" dictatorship "of workers', soldiers', and landless peasants' deputies."

DOCUMENT 12.3
TWO SOCIALIST REVOLUTIONARY EDITORIALS ON THE SOVIETS AND THE CONSTITUENT ASSEMBLY[11]

The following documents are editorials from The People's Cause (Delo naroda), *the Socialist Revolutionary (SR) Central Committee's newspaper in Petrograd. The first, "A New Revolution or the Constituent Assembly," appeared on 30 September 1917. Lenin seized on language in this editorial and used it to attack the SRs in* The Workers' Path (Rabochii put') *on 2 October (see document 12.4). The second, "The Soviets and the Constituent Assembly," appeared on 6 October 1917. The issue of how power should be constituted deeply divided the SRs in fall 1917. The party's left faction argued for an all-socialist government based on the soviets, a position similar to that taken by the Menshevik-Internationalists and moderate Bolsheviks. The party's right and centrist factions favored a new coalition with the "bourgeois parties" and insisted that the Pre-Parliament could ensure the coalition government's fidelity to the socialist program laid out at the Moscow State Conference. The left SRs demanded convocation of a Second All-Russian Soviet Congress, while the party's Central Committee opposed the idea of a congress that might supersede the Constituent Assembly.*

A New Revolution or the Constituent Assembly?
Elections to the Constituent Assembly take place in a month and a half. In three weeks, a congress of workers' and soldiers' soviets will meet. In a month and a half, a firm, legal, and generally accepted government could finally end the swelling anarchy that is ripping Russia apart. Or, in three weeks a bitter struggle for power could ignite . . . and it is absolutely clear that whoever wins that power struggle will not be generally accepted, and consequently will not have authority in the entire population's eyes.

Those who bury their heads like ostriches at a time of danger serve the democracy and revolution poorly. We must say directly: the only solution might be a combination government that will not satisfy some supporters of the coalition. This combination may be only a temporary exit from a "desperate" situation. It *must be endured* until the moment—which will not be long—when the sovereign representative of the entire Russian people [i.e., the Constituent Assembly] appears on history's stage.

But the Russian democracy might not unanimously recognize and support measures dictated by a desperate situation. The majority's mood and attitude is openly hostile toward the newly formed government. The toiling democracy is holding a leftward course. The soviets in most large cities have gone over to the Bolsheviks. The Moscow elections show that the voters' mood has taken a sharp turn to the left. Almost half the people who voted for SRs three months ago are now for the Bolsheviks. There can be no doubt that a shift is taking place among the toiling democracy. People have begun deserting the "revolutionary center"— the Socialist Revolutionaries and the Mensheviks. And the congress of workers' and soldiers' soviets that will gather on 20 October certainly will strengthen this shift: the congress will have a Bolshevik majority.

But here is something important, something pregnant with great consequence: the Bolsheviks do not intend to "tolerate" the existing government for even the short period that remains until the Constituent Assembly's convocation. They are intoxicated by the masses' support. They speak openly of a new revolution: they preach about it in their newspapers and meetings and call for a new revolutionary uprising. There can be no mistake: this revolutionary "uprising"—if it takes place—will be timed to coincide with the soviet congress.

Everyone must recognize that the situation is extremely alarming and dangerous. The soviet congress will demand "all power" for itself. And, again, make no mistake about it: Kerensky's government has subordinated itself to the will of the All-Russian Democratic Conference, but under no circumstances will Trotsky and Lenin. They will not subordinate themselves. And they will have a foil—the "All-Russian Council of the Democracy," which includes the propertied bourgeoisie's representatives, as well as a majority from the democratic elements. And then? Then a genuine civil war will break out in the democratic camp, and the toiling democracy's ranks will be divided between two "representative" institutions: the Council of the Democracy and the soviets of deputies.

If the Russian Revolution spilled relatively little blood and was carried out with relatively little terror in its first seven months, this "patience" will "be compensated for." Try to give yourself a clear idea about what might take place. Imagine the outpouring of all the poisonous social hatred and evil accumulated over these past seven months of social, party, and group animosity. . . . No power will be able to restrain the accumulated "energy of hatred." Convulsions of spite already pull at the public body; what will happen if, stretched to its limits, it tears apart and bursts? The revolution will perish in blood and devastation, and so will the country.

What a horrifying prospect confronts us now, when only two months remain until the Constituent Assembly's convocation! The struggle about to emerge will, in essence, be an argument about power and to whom power should belong. The people themselves must resolve this question and settle it in a way that secures freedom, exactly according to their will.

In addition . . . even if the Bolsheviks do not try to seize power, *they can* disrupt the Constituent Assembly elections. There are 20 whole days between 20 October and the elections. Ask yourself: Could an election really be prepared, and could elections really take place in an atmosphere of genuine civil war? Of course not. The intense electoral campaign will come to nothing.

More than this. Even if the Bolsheviks' "uprising" turns out to be amorphous, it still will have one incontestable consequence: the extraordinary intensification of party and social conflict. A direct consequence of this intensification may be the *collapse of the elections*. . . .

A Bolshevistic uprising, which they already are calling a "second revolution," in the worst case would bring the revolution's complete ruin and lead to bourgeois counterrevolution's triumph. At best, it will push aside the Constituent Assembly—the sole means to resolve all debates, conclusively and to the point. We must say loudly, in public: The matter stands thus—either revolution or the Constituent Assembly. Choose one or the other. There is no third option!

Let the Bolsheviks think about this. Since they also "summon" the Constituent Assembly, let them prove the truthfulness of their attitude toward it. Those who consider preparing a "new revolution" must realize that postponing the Constituent Assembly until "who knows when"—even in event of a victorious "new revolution"—ultimately will lead to the triumph of counterrevolution. . . .

At this moment, our party bears a great responsibility. We must concentrate all our strength and make the ultimate effort to prevent an irreparable mistake that would border on the criminal. There must be no differences between us Socialist Revolutionaries, no differences of any sort. Realizing this, we must merge all factions: left, center, and right. These distinctions kept us from agreeing about the coalition, as we had different understandings of the government's composition and activities. Saving the Constituent Assembly, and consequently the revolution and country, requires that all differences be set aside.

The government coalition is a fact. And if this coalition's attitude toward the democracy is not hostile, then it is necessary to be patient and wait for the Constituent Assembly!

That is why we must rebuff the preachers of a new revolution as sharply as possible. More than that: We must expend all our energy, all we have, to exert maximum influence over the forthcoming elections to the soviet congress. Let the Bolsheviks come. We must explain the keen importance of all this to the soviets. We must insist that they send delegates to Petrograd with *mandates that resolutely demand they refrain from an uprising and do everything to resist it.*

Yes, resist. Because although the Bolshevik leaders may renounce this "new revolution," the idea, once conjured and put before the masses, can take its own course.

There is a risk that the Bolsheviks, like Heine's Sorcerer's Apprentice, will not be able to control the demons they manage to conjure.[12] We appeal to the democracy, do not give the Bolsheviks demons to raise from the infernal regions . . .

The Soviets and the Constituent Assembly.

The socialist press is again filled with discussion about the relationship between the soviets—which are representative institutions of the revolutionary democracy—and the Constituent Assembly—which is the sovereign institution of the people's will and authority.

The reason is that 20 October has been set as the date for the All-Russian Congress of Soviets of Workers' and Soldiers' Deputies. Because this date falls in the very thick of the electoral campaign, it met heated opposition from the Executive Committee of the All-Russian Soviet of Peasant Deputies (who called the 20 October convocation "untimely and dangerous") and from the army organizations (which declared it, at best, a completely intolerable distraction from preparations for the Constituent Assembly).

Given the grand tasks confronting the revolutionary democracy— drawing tens of millions of men and women who are new to politics into conscious participations for elections, despite the country's great enormity and the poverty of its intellectual forces—political calculation and simple expediency would suggest that the soviet congress meet after Constituent Assembly elections are concluded, but before assembly's opening. But the Bolshevist press has printed a mass of distortions, slanderous insinuations, and garbled facts to present the matter, as if postponing the soviet congress were an attempt to "break" from the soviets, "betray the revolution," "deceive the working class," and even "disrupt the Constituent Assembly." This, as the saying goes, is "the pot calling the kettle black."

Why do this? And beyond all this, there is the general question: should the soviets vanish once the Constituent Assembly opens, or should they exist simultaneously?

The soviets appeared as *class organizations of the workers, soldiers, and peasants.* When the revolution felled the entire tsarist state and all government apparatus supporting the old order in one blow, the soviets took the place of the vanished government machinery. Events dictated that they make themselves into *revolutionary institutions,* i.e., *institutions of state power in the center and in the provinces.* Thus, the toilers' class organizations were invested with state power.

But this extraordinary new organization of power was the exclusive consequence of the disappearance of the old autocratic state's institutions. The popular masses reached out to the soviets because they were the only institutions in the country, the provinces, and the villages addressing economic and administrative chaos. For the popular masses, the soviets substituted for the pillars of our state that had disappeared. But at the same time, new institutions particular to the contemporary democratic state were being created—the city dumas and zemstvos—that raised the issue of limiting the soviets' *state* functions. And that issue will become sharper when the Constituent Assembly becomes as sole possessor of sovereign power.

In the capitalist economic order we live in—and which will be our country's fundamental economic system until the socialist revolution in Western Europe—the soviets can only be class organization of the toiling masses. They will have tremendous might and authority in the country's whole political and economic life, but they cannot constitute the basis for a state in a democratic republic. The slogan "All Power to the Soviets" is incompatible with convocation of a Constituent Assembly elected on the basis of universal, direct, and equal suffrage. It is absolutely appropriate, and indeed necessary, that mighty workers' and soldiers' organizations exist along with the Constituent Assembly. Only their help can ensure that the Constituent Assembly's decisions are implemented; only their existence can guarantee that these decisions will be rooted in democracy and social equality.

The Bolshevistic slander campaign against peasants' and soldiers' organizations and the socialist parties that want to delay the soviet congress to a time between the Constituent Assembly elections and the Assembly's opening testifies to the Bolsheviks' unwillingness to admit that their basic slogan about transferring state power to the soviets is doomed. In opposing the 20 October date for the soviet congress and proposing another date—for example, 20 November—we are not trying to enervate the democracy's revolutionary institutions. On the contrary, we want to connect them with the socialist representatives at the Constituent Assembly, so that the socialist parties, operating as the revolutionary democracy's representatives, can actualize their electoral platforms and promises.

DOCUMENT 12.4
LENIN, "TO WORKERS, PEASANTS, AND SOLDIERS"[13]

In early September, Lenin argued for forming an all-socialist coalition govern-ment that would then transfer power to the soviets. On 12 and 14 September, however, he sent party leaders two letters insisting that the Bolsheviks must seize power immediately. He claimed that "objective conditions" favored the Bolsheviks, but warned that Kerensky might surrender Petrograd to the Germans and render a takeover impossible. Lenin demanded that the party embrace the "fundamental Marxist principle" of "the art of insurrection." The Bolshevik Central Committee ignored Lenin's letters. At a 19 September 1917 conference of socialist leaders, Kamenev supported creation of the Pre-Parliament; at a 21 September Central Committee session, Bolshevik leaders (minus Lenin, still in hiding) again called for an all-socialist coalition government. At the same time, they called for a Second All-Russian Soviet Congress, which they argued could peacefully take power. Lenin then launched a campaign to turn the Bolsheviks toward an armed insurrection. Lenin framed the following 2 October 1917 letter, "To Workers, Peasants, and Soldiers," as a response to the 30 September editorial in The People's Cause *(see document 12.3). The Bolshevik Central Committee chose not to publish Lenin's letter.*

To the Workers, Peasants, and Soldiers.

Comrades! In *The People's Cause* (on 30 September), the Party of "Socialist Revolutionaries," Kerensky's party, calls on you "to be patient."[14]

"It is necessary to be patient," they write, advising that Kerensky's government be kept in power, and that power not be transferred to the soviets of workers' and soldiers' deputies. The tell us: Let Kerensky rely upon the aristocratic landlords, capitalists, and kulaks; the soviets, which made the revolution and defeated Kornilov's generals, must "be patient." Everyone must "be patient" until the Constituent Assembly, which will convene soon.

Comrades! Look around you. Look at what is happening in the countryside and in the army, and you will see that the peasants and soldiers can no longer be patient. A *peasant uprising* is flooding all Russia like a wide river. Transfer of land to the peasants has been delayed fraudulently, and the peasants can no longer be patient. Kerensky has sent *troops* to punish the peasants and defend the *landlords*. Again, Kerensky agrees the Kornilovite generals and officers and stands up for the *landlords*.

Neither the workers in the cities nor the soldiers at the front can tolerate this military suppression of the peasants' just struggle for land.

As for what is happening in the army at the front—a nonparty officer, Dubasov, declared before all Russia "The soldiers will not fight any more." Soldiers are exhausted, barefoot, starving, and do not want to fight for the capitalists' interests. They do not want "to be patient." For months all they have heard are beautiful words about peace, while in deeds, a *proposal for peace*—for a just peace, without annexations, *for all* belligerent peoples—has been delayed (because Kerensky is delaying).

Comrades! Understand that Kerensky is negotiating again with Kornilovite generals and officers *to lead troops against the soviets* of workers' and soldiers' deputies, so that the soviets *do not take power*! Kerensky "under no circumstances will submit" to the soviets—*The People's Cause* directly recognizes this.[15] Go to all the barracks, all the Cossack units, all the toilers, and explain *the truth* to the people.

If the soviets have power, then (if there is a soviet congress on 20 October) *a just peace will be proposed* to all belligerent peoples by no later than 25 October. In Russia, there will be a *worker and peasant government* that *immediately*, without wasting a day, *will propose a just peace to all belligerent peoples*. Then the people will learn who wants the unjust war. Then the people will decide in the Constituent Assembly. If the soviets have power, then the landlords' land immediately will be declared the *property and possession of the entire people.* That is why Kerensky and his government are fighting against the congress, leaning on the kulaks, capitalists, and landlords! It is for their interests that you are told "to be patient"!

Will you agree "to be patient" while Kerensky's military forces suppress the peasants, who now are rising up for land? Will you agree "to be patient" while the war drags on? While peace is delayed? While they delay breaking with the old secret treaties between the Russian and Anglo-French capitalists?

Comrades! Remember, Kerensky has already deceived the people once about convening the Constituent Assembly! On 8 July, he solemnly promised to convene it by 17 September. But he *deceived the people.* Comrades! Those who believe in Kerensky's government are traitors to their brothers, the peasants and soldiers!

No, *not for one day more* will the people put up with more postponements! *Not for one day more* will they put up with using the military to suppress the peasantry or with letting thousands and thousands perish in the war when we can and must immediately *propose a just peace.*

Down with Kerensky's government, which is conspiring with the Kornilovite generals and landlords to repress the peasants, shoot the peasants, and drag out the war. *All power* to the soviets of workers' and soldiers' deputies!

DOCUMENT 12.5
TWO BOLSHEVIK EDITORIALS ON THE SOVIET CONGRESS
AND THE CONSTITUENT ASSEMBLY[16]

From mid-September, the Bolsheviks and other left socialists stressed the importance of the upcoming Second All-Russian Soviet Congress. Bolshevik agitation insisted that the soviet congress form an all-socialist government before the Constituent Assembly's convocation. The Soviet Central Executive Committee reluctantly scheduled the congress for 20 October 1917, then began arguing publically for its postponement. Menshevik and Socialist Revolutionary leaders understood that the left factions had majorities in local soviets across Russia and would dominate the soviet congress. They feared that the congress would disrupt the Constituent Assembly electoral campaign and believed that calls for Soviet power compounded the risk of civil war. The two documents that follow, editorials from the Petrograd Bolshevik newspaper The Workers' Path *(Rabochii put'), present Bolshevik attacks against the moderates' positions. The first was published on 3 October, the second on 13 October 1917.*

The Soviet Congress and the Constituent Assembly
From the revolution's first days, the capitalists and aristocratic landlords have agreed to a Constituent Assembly *in words* but disrupted it *in deeds*, by postponing its convocation on various pretexts "until a better time." Meanwhile, the bourgeois-landlord coalition stubbornly and deftly continued with its own "parliament"—the dark "State Duma"—which hasn't been abolished, and which Kornilov had planned to "put in power" on 15 September in Moscow. That plan was broken up, but the State *Duma* still exists.

Is this because, as Tsereteli explained, it would be wrong to dismiss it when "only weeks remain until the Constituent Assembly"? Other representatives of the "revolutionary democracy" make similar arguments. The leading SR newspaper recently proposed "patience" toward the latest government.[17]

The "unfortunate" government is using all the old regime's Stolypin-style methods, but [the moderate socialists] say we can't create a better government because the Constituent Assembly "is only weeks away"? Petty-bourgeois politicians like this helped *preserve* the Stolypin *duma* and helped *create* the "Stolypin-style" government.

Now these same defensists are carrying out a campaign against the soviet congress "in the Constituent Assembly's name." "The congress is not necessary," they say, because it "calls into question" the Constituent Assembly. And the bourgeois parties and press happily repeat these arguments by the likes of Tsereteli, Dan, and Gots.[18]

The Kadets have transformed themselves into the Constituent Assembly's ardent defenders (!) against all the degenerates fighting for the soviet congress. A "united front" of Kadets and defensist Mensheviks and SRs has come out against the workers, soldiers, and revolutionary peasants.

"A soviet congress is not necessary," they say, because "the Constituent Assembly will meet a few weeks later." At the same that the Tsereteli-Gots crowd is trying to prevent the Soviet revolutionary parliament, it is helping prepare a cozy little Pre-Parliament nest for Kerensky's government. They say the 20 October *Soviet Parliament* is not necessary because "only a few weeks remain," but that the 5 October *Kadet Pre-Parliament* is necessary, even though the Constituent Assembly is "almost here."

The imperialist dictator's government supports a Pre-Parliament where the propertied and kulak bourgeoisie will have a firm majority. And the conciliationist turncoats believe this majority—without a "new revolution"—will call on the Constituent Assembly to make a "peaceful revolution" against the capitalists, landlords, and kulaks, i.e., *against themselves!*

First the Mensheviks and SRs put the Constituent Assembly's convocation wholly into the hands of the bourgeoisie, and now they say: "The only correct thing is to do is to postpone the soviet congress temporarily, because it will hamper the [Constituent Assembly] electoral campaign."

The defensist parties are busily preparing their "electoral campaign" and don't notice the "campaign" that our bourgeoisie is conducting. Meanwhile, the political plan of the revolution's enemies is clear. For months the Kadets have sabotaged the revolution and carried out their plan: take land from the peasants' "property reserve," which ignites a spontaneous agrarian movement everywhere; when flash-fires of hunger and food shortages burn in the cities, give free reign to the counterrevolutionary zealots (or deliberately let loose people like Purishkevich), and they will add their spoon of poison.[19]

These antirevolutionary bourgeois conspirators want the soldiers, peasants, and workers to waste their breath, strength, and blood in this spontaneous movement. Then they won't be able to present any organized political opposition; they will be scattered, and the end result will be that the *revolutionary classes do not come to power. . . .*

The bourgeoisie must prevent the transfer of power to the soviets, and so it does all it can to hinder the soviet congress. The bourgeoisie must hold onto power for itself. When it feels strong enough to do so, it will "postpone" the Constituent Assembly until "after the war," or even later. And the defensist bosses, whether they want to or not, are *helping* the bourgeoisie in this plan.

Our duty—the duty of the party of the proletariat—is to tell the people this: as long as the bourgeoisie and aristocratic landlords hold power (and now it is *entirely* theirs), the Constituent Assembly's convocation is not guaranteed. As long as the bourgeoisie and landlords hold power, there is no guarantee of proper elections in which all people consciously participate. (For example, the bourgeoisie want to "protect" soldiers at the front from the "destructive influence" of electoral agitation). As long as the counterrevolutionaries, landlords, bankers, and factory owners hold power, there is no guarantee that the Constituent Assembly's decisions will be implemented. That is why we tell the people: for the Constituent Assembly to take place, for the masses to participate consciously and freely in elections, for the Constituent Assembly's resolutions to have full force, all intrigues and counterrevolutionary plots must finally end.

The revolutionary workers', soldiers', and peasants' soviet congress must take power; the Constituent Assembly's fate depends on this.

If power is transferred to the soviets, the Constituent Assembly's fate will be in good hands. If the bourgeoisie is able to prevent the transfer of power to the soviets, it will disband the Constituent Assembly. That is why the Kadets are hindering the soviet congress. For them, this is a form of open class warfare. And while the Kadets attack the soviets from the outside, their agents (the Kadet-like socialists) do their bidding by fighting against the proletarian-peasant revolution from within the soviets.

The campaign against the soviet congress shows that some in the "revolutionary democracy" are following the bourgeois political parties' lead more and more closely. At the same time, most peasants' and soldiers' organizations have spoken in powerful support of the soviet congress. Plainly, the rest of them are coming around, pulling closer and closer to the party of the proletariat. . . .

Soviet Power

. . . The moment has arrived when the slogan, "All Power to the Soviets" must finally be implemented. But what is Soviet power, and how does it differ from other kinds of government?

Some believe that transferring power to the soviets means creating a "homogeneous" democratic government ministry, a new cabinet of socialist ministers; in short, making "serious changes" to the Provisional Government's composition. But that is incorrect. The issue is not substituting one person for another in the Provisional Government. . . . The issue is transferring power to the proletariat and revolutionary peasantry. Substituting one person for another in the government is far from adequate. First, all government offices must be radically purged; all Kornilovites must be expelled and replaced by more trustworthy people from the working class and peasantry. Only then, only under those circumstances, can we speak of transferring power to the soviets "at the center and in the provinces."

What explains the well-known helplessness of "socialist" ministers in the Provisional Government? What explains the fact that these ministers are miserable puppets in the hands of people behind the scenes? Most important, not one of them led their administrations; their administrations led them. The reality is that each administrative office is a fortress where tsarist bureaucrats sit, "idly chatting away" in the ministers' offices, preparing to sabotage any revolutionary government measure. For power to pass to the soviets in deeds and not just in words, these fortresses must be taken and the Kadet-tsarist regime's servants removed. Their places must be taken by recruits and courageous people devoted to the revolutionary workers' cause.

Soviet Power means a radical purge of each and every government institution in the rear and at the front, from the top to the bottom.

Soviet Power means all "commanders" in the rear and at the front are subject to election and recall.

Soviet Power means that "government representatives" in the towns and villages, the army and fleet, the "administrations" and the "institutions," the railroads and postal-telegraph offices, are subject to election and recall.

Soviet Power means the dictatorship of the proletariat and revolutionary peasantry.

This dictatorship is a radical departure from the imperialist bourgeois dictatorship that Kornilov and Milukov tried to establish and toward which Kerensky and Tereshchenko are well disposed.

The dictatorship of the proletariat and revolutionary peasantry means the dictatorship of the toiling majority over the exploiting minority—the aristocratic landlords and capitalists, the speculators and the bankers— in the name of a democratic *peace*, workers' *control* over production and distribution, *land* for the peasants, and *bread* for the people.

The dictatorship of the proletariat and revolutionary people means an open, mass dictatorship, created before everyone's eyes without conspiracies or scheming behind the scenes. That dictatorship will not shelter the washed-up capitalists who aggravated unemployment or the banker-speculators who drove up prices and created hunger—there will be no mercy.

The dictatorship of the proletariat and peasantry means a dictatorship without violence against the masses, a dictatorship that represents the masses' will, a dictatorship that will bridle the masses' enemies. That is the class essence of the slogan, "All Power to the Soviets."

Internal events and foreign policy, protracted war and the thirst for peace, defeat at the front and defense of the capital, the Provisional Government's rottenness and its "transfer" to Moscow, destruction and hunger, unemployment and exhaustion—all this is irrepressibly carrying Russia's revolutionary classes toward power.[20] Know this: the country is ripe for a dictatorship of the proletariat and revolutionary peasantry. The moment has arrived to implement the revolutionary slogan, "All Power to the Soviets."

DOCUMENT 12.6
DOCUMENTS ON SOVIET POLITICS IN ASTRAKHAN
IN SEPTEMBER–OCTOBER 1917[21]

Debates in Petrograd on the constitution of state power took place against the backdrop of a powerful shift in the political balance in soviets across Russia. As in Petrograd and Moscow, workers and soldiers in dozens of provincial cities demonstrated their impatience at the government and the moderate socialists by electing a left socialist majority to their local soviets. The following document set illustrates this process in Astrakhan, a city on the Volga River's southern reaches. The first three documents are from the "Local Chronicle" section of The Astrakhan Pages (Astrakhanskii listok) *on 28 September and 6 October 1917. The fourth is a letter to the editor from local Bundist M. D. Naroditskii that appeared in the newspaper's "Party Life" section on 17 October 1917.*

On the Form of Power.

On last night, 18 September, there was a well-attended special joint meeting of the workers', soldiers', and peasants' soviets, the trade unions, the city duma's socialist bloc, and the socialist party committees. The meeting, chaired by K. I. Bakradze, discussed the form of power at the center and in the provinces.[22]

The meeting immediately split into two camps: supporters of the Bolsheviks and supporters of the more moderate left groups. Orators from both persuasions spoke. Two resolutions were proposed and voted upon.

The Socialist Revolutionaries, Social Democrat-Mensheviks, Bundists, socialist duma bloc, and Executive Committee of the Soviet of Peasant Deputies proposed the following resolution:

Russia and the revolution again are experiencing a crisis of power. The causes are the war, economic disruption, and selfish class interests. In the face of all the dangers that threaten the revolution's achievements, all of the country's vital forces—the entire revolutionary democracy—must be unified. Only through such unity can the greater good be achieved in the toilers' interests; only through unity can we end the war and escape the general economic disruption that has grasped the country. The All-Russian [Democratic Conference] opening in Petrograd on 14 September must create a strong and firm government that can defend the revolution from all attacks, from wherever they might come, and carry the country to the Constituent Assembly, which will decide Russia's fate. All vital forces that fought to overthrow the autocratic regime must be drawn into this government. It must include representatives of all the revolutionary democracy's heterogeneous nuances, excluding those groups involved in Kornilov's counterrevolutionary conspiracy.

This resolution gathered 175 votes.

Then the following resolution by the RSDLP (Internationalists) Committee was voted upon:

Considering that economic disorganization has spread not just in Russia, but in all countries; that the central government has taken no energetic measures to end the war, which is the cause of the economic destruction; that the government has made no steps to resolve the growing problems that confront the revolutionary democracy; and that this perpetual mess of a government has been deserted by the representatives of the counterrevolutionary bourgeoisie, which is sabotaging industry, this meeting proposes that:

1. the imperialist bourgeoisie's counterrevolutionary representatives must not have a seat in the government;
2. the counterrevolutionary wolves who howl for the bourgeoisie must be severely punished, as must their newspapers; moreover, the State Duma and the State Council must be liquidated immediately;
3. the death penalty must be abolished, and the military command staff must be purged immediately;
4. an (armed) workers militia (red guard) must be organized immediately;
5. land must be transferred to the toiling peasantry immediately, through the land committees;
6. the government must be subordinated to the All-Russian Central Executive Committee of Soviets, as the controlling institution that has emerged from the revolutionary democracy's bowels, and the executive institutions (the government ministry) must answer to the All-Russian Soviet;
7. locally, power will lay with the soviets of workers', soldiers', and peasants' deputies, the trade unions, and a city duma elected on the basis of universal, direct, secret, and equal suffrage. These true representatives of the democracy will form a single institution—a collegium—to administer local affairs.

This resolution received 276 votes. And so it appears that the meeting endorsed the second resolution.

Election of the Provincial Commissar.
On 4 October, elections for provincial commissar were held at a session of the Provincial Executive Committee with representatives from the soviets of workers', soldiers', and peasants' deputies.

After exchanging views concerning proposed candidates, R. A. Astvatsaturov announced that N. V. Lakhov categorically refused to be nominated for the commissar's post. Representatives from the counties reported that their constituents had directed them to vote for R. A. Astvatsaturov. A vote then was taken. The candidature of V. I. Sklabinskii was not discussed because he had sent a telegram from Moscow asking that his candidacy be withdrawn.[23]

Before the voting, the Muslim group representative Citizen Kapkaev requested in that group's name that the committee choose a Muslim as one of the deputy commissars. He proposed Abdurakhmak Akhmetov as their candidate.

G. I. Krutdikov then raised the issue of whether a practicing attorney might be designated as a deputy commissar. The committee approved this idea.

The Bolsheviks' representative, Citizen Khicher, declared that the Bolsheviks would abstain from voting because they had decided that power must be held only by the soviets. Concerning Citizen Astvatsaturov, the Bolsheviks reminded the meeting he had recently withdrawn his candidacy for the post of local soviet chairman.

A vote then was taken for the provincial commissar. The electors unanimously chose *R. A. Astvatsaturov*.

Elections for the commissar's deputies were set for Saturday.

The committee then took up the issue of naming a new garrison commander. It was resolved to abstain from recommending any candidates for this post.

The Soviet Executive Committee Elections.

The Executive Committee of the Soviet of Workers' and Soldiers' deputies was recently reelected. Workers and soldiers took the elections particularly seriously and elected people who had passed the strictest critique from a civic and moral perspective.

Ensign *Aleksandr Semenovich Parfonov-Perfil'ev*, a Socialist Revolutionary-Internationalist, was elected as soviet chairman.

In his speech, Citizen Perfil'ev provided a short autobiography. He was educated in a seminary and then taught in a city school. From 1905 he was active in the Party of Socialist Revolutionaries and worked primarily in Ural mining establishments in Ufimsk Province. In 1908 he became a member of the Zlatoustovskii District SR committee.[24] He worked in that committee until the war began, and he was mobilized into the army.

When the revolution began, Citizen Perfil'ev was transferred to the local regiment, became closely connected to the Astrakhan Soviet of Workers' and Soldiers' Deputies, and was elected as one of its delegates to the soviet congress in Petrograd. When K. I. Bakradze became soviet chairman, Perfil'ev was elected chairman of the Soviet's Soldiers' Section.

Concerning his program for the soviet, Citizen Perfil'ev explained that he will guide the soviet on strictly businesslike principles. His first step will be to purge the soviet of those employees who had weakened the soviet's authority in the population's eyes. He pledged to carry out this program unswervingly.

The Bund and the Mensheviks (Letter to the Editor).

The following information appeared in *The Astrakhan Pages* on 15 October: "The Menshevik-Bund bloc is dissolving. As is known, the Mensheviks had reserved one spot on its Constituent Assembly candidate list for the Bund, based on their common goals. The majority of Bundists, however, turned out to be Bolsheviks and designated Bolshevik S. A. Gurevich as their candidate. In view of this turnabout, the Mensheviks would rather dissolve the bloc."

This information is not accurate. Doctor S. A. Gurevich, whom the Bund organization put forward as its Constituent Assembly candidate, is not a Bolshevik. He is a member of the United Menshevik group. His many statements in the Soviet of Workers' and Soldiers' Deputies and in other organizations prove this. The Bund organization has absolutely no Bolshevistic tendencies. As the organization's secretary, I do not know of a single Bolshevik. Most Bundists are Menshevik-Internationalists. We did not enter an agreement with the Astrakhan Menshevik organization to bind ourselves to the Menshevik comrades' unacceptable demands.

Secretary of the Bund organization and Soviet of
Workers' and Soldiers' Deputies member, *M. D. Naroditskii.*

DOCUMENT 12.7
THE PETROGRAD SOVIET ON TRANSFERRING
POWER TO THE SOVIETS[25]

In Petrograd, where mounting economic distress fed workers' political militancy, radical soldiers and workers feared Kerensky might surrender Petrograd to the Germans to crush the revolution's left wing. In early October, Kerensky's public attempt to withdraw troops from the capital fed these suspicions. In response, on 9 October 1917, the Petrograd Soviet's Bolshevik-left Socialist Revolutionary (SR) majority passed the following resolution calling for Soviet power. Although the Bolsheviks had the Petrograd Soviet's largest delegation, and Leon Trotsky had been elected as the soviet's chairman, passing resolutions like that below depended upon support from the left SRs and other internationalists.

On the Necessity of Transferring Power to the Soviets
At a moment when the people and revolution face deadly danger, the Petrograd Soviet of Workers' and Soldiers' Deputies declares:

Kerensky's government is ruining the country. It has failed to propose peace while proving completely incapable of conducting the war. Kerensky and the bourgeoisie are preparing to give the Germans Petrograd— the revolution's main fortress. The Allied imperialists clearly are scheming for Wilhelm's movement on Petrograd. Dying sailor heroes, in their own words, call the Bonapartist Kerensky their enemy, not their friend. Because the government hitched itself to the *Kornilovshchina*, because the soldiers, workers, and peasants absolutely distrust the current government, the Petrograd Soviet of Workers' and Soldiers' Deputies can no longer accept any responsibility before the army for the Provisional Government's so-called strategy and especially for the removal of troops from Petrograd.

The transfer of power to the soviets will save Petrograd and the country. The Soviet government must propose an immediate armistice to all nations. Pending the conclusion of peace, however, it must secure the army's fighting capacity and defend Petrograd and the army.

In addition, the Petrograd Soviet of Workers' and Soldiers' Deputies calls on the Petrograd garrison to take all necessary steps to develop and strengthen its battle readiness.

DOCUMENT 12.8
MILIUKOV ON KADET PARTY TACTICS REGARDING STATE POWER[26]

At the Democratic Conference, moderate Socialist Revolutionary and Menshevik leaders agreed to a new coalition including representatives of the "bourgeois parties." On 25 September, Kerensky formed a new coalition—the "Government for the Salvation of the Revolution"—that included three Kadets. Still, the moderate socialists' relations with their Kadet coalition partners deteriorated in late September and October 1917. On 14–16 October 1917, when the Kadets met for their 10th Party Congress in Petrograd, the party was deeply divided over the coalition. Kadet leader (and former Provisional Government member) Vladimir Nabokov told the congress that there had been three paths toward the formation of a government in September: an all-bourgeois government led by the Kadets (impossible given the country's political mood); an all-socialist government (rejected by the moderate socialists themselves); and a coalition that included Kadets. To save Russia, the Kadets had agreed to take the third path. Pavel Miliukov, however, had opposed participation in another coalition. The document that follows is an official summary of Miliukov's 14 October congress report on party tactics.

Report of P. N. Miliukov (Summary).

P. N. Milukov's tactical report, like V. D. Nabokov's statement, shows there are no fundamental differences between factions in the Kadet Party. This is expressed in the report's concluding section, in the platform proposed on the Central Committee's behalf, and in the draft tactical resolution. But P. N. Miliukov did not try to conceal several differences between his views and those of V. D. Nabokov.

P. N. Miliukov proposes that the extraordinary cost of the victories the Party of People's Freedom won in recent negotiations over the coalition government . . . obliges us all the more to reveal the revolutionary democracy's impotence. The revolutionary democracy's leaders do not believe their own slogans. We are living in a period of official hypocrisy; the revolutionary democracy's leaders understand that they must do what the Kadets are proposing, but they do not want to efface their party icons. They would prefer that the work be done by someone else's hands. This is the source of their compliance. In the Provisional Council of the Republic, the hypocrisy and phrase-mongering will continue.[27] Its façade of official hypocrisy probably cannot be smashed, although one cannot exaggerate how much that would improve its health. It is too much to expect a durable majority of SRs and Social Democrats, and therefore to rely on the policy of a government made up of such a majority would be wrong. If the Kadets joined a coalition to compel the government "to be daring" in its affairs . . . then it was utterly pointless. There already is a notable tendency in government circles to solicit the Council's "permission" before acting (General Verkhovskii has said this directly).[28]

The Kadets must not *become what they are not* to secure a majority in the Council [of the Republic]. They must not sacrifice the views and positions that define them—or else the Kadets' positions will become pale and unintelligible. To make the Council into the leading center for defending the state, the Kadets must begin with their basic platform, which must be the national platform. This will shape the basis of agreements and concessions.

Tactical platform of the Kadet Party:

The platform proposed by P. N. Miliulov consists of six points:

1. War to a successful conclusion, in full agreement with the allies. This predetermines the struggle against Zimmerwaldism and all proposals employing [Zimmerwaldian] expressions in Skobelev's directive;[29]
2. Restoration of the army's fighting capacity by reestablishing commanders' disciplinary authority and introducing a proper framework for the functions of the army committees;
3. Unitary government power independent from any specific party organizations;
4. Application of repressive force when necessary to strengthen the government;
5. Restoration of government institutions in the provinces;
6. Independence of the courts as a guarantee of civil liberties that now are trampled on by anarchy. This must be our platform through the Constituent Assembly elections.

DOCUMENT 12.9
THE BOLSHEVIK PARTY CENTRAL COMMITTEE
SESSION OF 16 OCTOBER 1917[30]

On 10–11 October 1917, Lenin—having returned secretly to Petrograd—tried to convince the Bolshevik Central Committee to launch an armed uprising before the Second All-Russian Congress of Soviets. He warned that Kerensky might yet surrender Petrograd to the Germans or organize a "second Kornilov revolt," and argued that an insurrection would spark revolutions across Europe. Kamenev and Zinoviev countered that Lenin had underestimated the Provisional Government's strength and overestimated the Bolsheviks' support; moreover, the working class was too weak to hold power without help from the petty-bourgeoisie. They insisted that the soviet congress should form an all-socialist government and that the Bolsheviks must focus on winning the largest possible representation in the Constituent Assembly. The Bolsheviks then could come into power as part of a left socialist bloc, without risking a disastrous civil war. The Central Committee majority eventually agreed with Lenin and voted to begin discussing "practical details" of preparing and an armed uprising. It did not, however, set a date for the uprising or endorse any specific plan.

Kamenev and Zinoviev were not the only Bolshevik leaders who doubted that Russia was ripe for an uprising. On 15 October, several speakers warned the party's Petersburg City Committee of the masses' "lack of enthusiasm" for an armed uprising. On 16 October the Central Committee met again to discuss the issue. The following document is the published transcript of that important session. The transcript frequently shifts between summarizing speakers' statements in third person and quoting them verbatim in first person.

Present: Members of the Central Committee, Petersburg Committee Executive Commission, Military Organization, Petrograd Soviet, trade unions, factory-plant committees, Petrograd Regional Committee, and railroads.[31]

Session chairman: Comrade Sverdlov

Comrade Sverdlov proposes the agenda: (1) report on the previous Central Committee meeting; (2) short reports by representatives; (3) the current situation.

1. Report on the previous Central Committee meeting.

Comrade Lenin reads the resolution passed by the Central Committee at the previous session. He reports that this resolution was passed with two votes against. If the comrades who opposed it wished to express their views, then it would be possible to open a debate, but for now he explains the resolution's motives.[32]

Had the Mensheviks and SRs broken with conciliationism, it might have been possible to compromise with them. A proposal was made, but they clearly rejected it.[33] On the other hand, by then it was becoming clear that the masses were coming around to us. That was the case even before the Kornilovshchina. As evidence, Lenin provides statistics from the Petrograd and Moscow elections. The Kornilovshchina then decisively pushed the masses toward us. That explains the correlation of forces at the Democratic Conference. The situation is clear: either a Kornilovite dictatorship, or a dictatorship of the proletariat and the poorest peasant strata. We can't be led by the masses' mood, because it changes and defies calculation. We must proceed through objective analysis and estimation of the revolution. The masses trust the Bolsheviks and demand deeds of them, not just words. They demand a decisive policy of struggle against the war and against ruin. A basic political analysis of the revolution makes this absolutely clear, and recent anarchistic uprisings corroborate this.

Lenin further analyzes the situation in Europe and provides evidence that making a revolution is even more difficult there than it is here. So, if matters have reached a stage that revolts are taking place in the navy in a country like Germany, then that means things already have come very far there, too. Certain objective facts about the international situation indicate that the entire European proletariat will be on our side. Lenin gives evidence that the bourgeoisie wants to surrender Petrograd. The only way we can save the city is by taking Petrograd into our own hands. All this leads to the clear conclusion that there must be an armed uprising, as stated in the Central Committee resolution.

As for the practical implications, it is better to discuss this after hearing reports from representatives of the party centers.

Political analysis of the class struggle in Russia and in Europe indicates the need for the most resolute and active policy, which can only be an armed uprising.

2. Representatives' reports.

Comrade Sverdlov of the Central Committee reports for the Central Committee Secretariat on the state of affairs in the localities.[34]

The party's growth has reached gigantic proportions; it can be estimated that now it numbers no fewer than 400,000 people (*he provides evidence*).

Correspondingly, our influence has grown especially in the soviets (*gives evidence*) and also in the army and the fleet. He reports further on facts related to mobilization of counterrevolutionary forces (in the Donets Region, Minsk, and the Northern Front).

Comrade Bokii from the Petersburg Committee.[35] Reports on each city district:

Vasil'evskii Island: Not in a fighting mood, military preparations being carried out.

Vyborg District: The same, but preparing for an insurrection. A Military Council has been formed; the masses will support an uprising but think it must come from above.

1st City District: The mood is hard to gauge. There is a Red Guard.

2nd City District: The mood is better.

Moscow District: The mood is unpredictable. It will come out at the soviet's summon, but not for the party.

Narva District: There's no urge to come out, but there's no decay in the party's authority. The Anarchists are growing stronger at the Putilov {plant}.[36]

Nevskii District: The mood has swung sharply in our favor. Everyone will come out for the soviet.

Okhtenskii District: Things are bad for us.

Petersburg District: There is a mood of anticipation.

Rozhdestvenskii District: There are doubts whether they will come out; the Anarchists have increased their influence.

Porokhovskii District: The mood is strengthening in our favor.

Shlissel'burg: The mood is in our favor.

Comrade Krylenko from the Military Bureau reported that their appraisal of the mood differs sharply.[37]

Personal observation of the regiments' mood suggests they are with us to a man, but the information from comrades working in the districts differ: they say an uprising would require some blow, like withdrawing troops [from Petrograd]. The Bureau believes the mood is declining. The Bureau majority sees no need to discuss practical issues [regarding an uprising], but the minority thinks we must seize the initiative.

Comrade Stepanov from the Regional Organization. Workers in Sestroretsk and Kolpino are arming themselves.[38] There is a fighting mood, and they're ready for an uprising. In Kolpino, an anarchistic mood is developing.

In Narva, the mood is grave because of factory dismissals; 3,000 have already been dismissed.

The garrison appears to be in a depressed mood, but Bolshevist influence is very strong in two machine-gun regiments. In Novyi Petergof, party work in the regiment has declined significantly, and the regiment is disorganized. In Krasnoe Selo, the 176th Regiment is absolutely Bolshevist and the 172nd Regiment nearly so. But there also is a cavalry unit there. In Luga, with a garrison of 30,000, the soviet is defensist but the mood is Bolshevist, and there will be reelections.

In Gdov, the regiment is Bolshevist.

Comrade Bokii says according to his informants things are not so good in Krasnoe Selo.

In Kronshtadt the mood is falling; in respect to fighting, the garrison there is good for nothing.

Comrade Volodarskii from the Petrograd Soviet.[39] The general impression is that no one is tearing out into the streets, but everyone will appear at the soviet's summons.

Comrade Ravich agrees and adds that many say they are at the party's call.[40]

Comrade Shmidt from the trade unions.[41] The total number of organized unionists is over 500,000. Our party has predominant influence. It is weakest in the craft-based unions (particularly among clerks and printers), but even there its influence is growing, especially given discontent over wage rates.[42] The mood is such that we cannot expect active support for an uprising, particularly considering fear of dismissals. To a certain extent, this a restraining factor. Given specific economic conditions, colossal unemployment can be expected in the near future. This adds to the mood of anticipation. Everyone recognizes that there is no way out of this situation except a struggle for power. They are demanding all power to the Soviets.

Comrade Shliapnikov adds that Bolshevik influence predominates in the metalworkers' union, but that a Bolshevist uprising is not popular.[43] Rumors about an uprising cause panic. Across Russia, the mood among metalworkers is predominantly Bolshevist. They are passing Bolshevist resolutions, but they don't understand that they can organize production themselves. The unions are facing a struggle for increased wages, and so there must be a resolution on the issue of workers' control.

Comrade Skrypnik from the factory-plant committees.[44] Everywhere, he finds a strong desire for practical results; resolutions are not enough. [People] think the leadership is more conservative and is not fully expressing the masses' mood. Significant growth in the anarcho-syndicalist influence is noted, particularly in the Narva and Moscow Districts.[45]

Comrade Sverdlov adds that in Moscow steps have being taken to clarify positions on an armed uprising, in keeping with the Central Committee's resolution.

Comrade Movskin from the railroad workers.[46] The railroad workers are going hungry. They are becoming exasperated, and organization is weak, particularly among the telegraph employees.

Comrade Shmidt adds that the railroad workers' strike has reached a crisis. At the Moscow junction especially, there is dissatisfaction with the union committee. On a whole, the Petrograd and Moscow junctions are closer to the Bolsheviks.[47]

Comrade Bokii. About the postal-telegraph employees: they have no separate organization. The majority who work the telegraph apparatuses are Kadets. The postal workers report that they can take control of the post offices at the decisive moment.

Comrade Shmidt. The postal workers' union is more radical than the railroad workers'. The low-level employees are essentially Bolsheviks. But higher-level employees are not; so long as the union is in their hands, there must be a struggle against them.

3. The Current Situation

Comrade Miliutin considers it necessary to have a more concrete resolution based on all these reports.[48] He proposes that the slogan, "All Power to the Soviets" has fully ripened, especially in the provinces, where in some places the soviets in fact have power. The issue really is not agitation. Deeds are what is needed now, not words. The matter won't be settled by moods and bulletins, but by organized forces. Either we take the first step, or our enemies will. The resolution gives too little consideration to a second prospect, i.e., the possibility that objective conditions will result, not in an uprising, which assumes our initiative, but in a clash. [Miliutin] proposes that we are not ready to carry out a first strike. We are not able to depose and arrest the government in the next few days.

Concerning the other prospect, an armed clash, he shows that this is becoming possible and that we must be prepared for this clash. But it is a different prospect from an insurrection. He considers it necessary to develop the resolution to reflect this.

Comrade Shotman says that at the [15 October] city conference the mood in the Petersburg Committee and the Military Committee was much more pessimistic.[49] He argues that we must prepare but are unable to act now.

Comrade Lenin conducts a polemic against Miliutin and Shotman. He argues that armed force is not the issue, struggle against troops is not the issue; the issue is the struggle of one section of the troops against another. He does not see what was said here as grounds for pessimism. He shows that the forces supporting the bourgeoisie are not great; in fact, we have the preponderance over the enemy. Why doesn't the Central Committee begin the insurrection? Based on all the data, this does not make sense. To toss out the Central Committee's resolution, you must demonstrate that there is no ruin, that the international situation is not headed toward complications. If trade union activists are demanding full power, then they understand exactly what they want. Objective conditions demonstrate that the peasantry must be led; they will follow the proletariat.

Some fear that we will not retain power, but just now we have a real chance to hold on to power.

Lenin expresses a desire that debate be confined to discussing the resolution's substance.

Comrade Krylenko declares that the entire Military Bureau agreed unanimously on one point: that the water has boiled long enough. To withdraw the resolution, to take back the resolution, would be a great mistake. Our task is to provide armed support for an insurrection if one flares up anywhere. But the mood as characterized was created by our mistakes.

On the matter of how the insurrection will start and what and who will begin it, [Krylenko] differs with V. I. {Lenin}. He considers it unnecessary to indulge too much in technical preparation for an insurrection. On the other hand, he considers it inexpedient to designate when to begin it. Removing troops—that will be provide the fighting moment when a battle will break out. At the Cheremisov conference, it will be argued that troops must be removed [from Petrograd].[50] We must reply that it will not happen even were it necessary, because there is no confidence in the generals. The fact is, we already have been attacked. Therefore we must

432

make use of this. We must not scale back agitation efforts. There is no point in worrying about who is ready to start [an insurrection], because a beginning already exists.

Comrade Rakh'ia argues that the masses are consciously preparing for an insurrection.[51] Were the Petrograd proletariat armed, it would already be in the streets, no matter what the Central Committee resolved. There is no evidence of pessimism. We cannot wait for a counterrevolutionary attack, because it already is here. The masses expect slogans and weapons. The masses will pour into the streets because they expect hunger. Apparently our slogans have come too late, because there is doubt that we will live up to our exhortations. Our task is not to reconsider, but, on the contrary, to strengthen [the resolution].

Comrade Grigorii {Zinoviev}.[52] It appears the resolution is not conceived as a directive, otherwise it would be impossible to express opinions.

On the resolution's substance, he doubts it is possible for the insurrection to succeed. Above all else, the railroads and postal telegraph apparatus is not in our hands. The influence of the Soviet Central Executive Committee is still sufficiently strong.

The matter must be settled on the very first day, in Petrograd. Otherwise demoralization will set in. One cannot depend on reinforcements from Finland and Kronshtadt. And we are not yet strong enough in Petrograd. In addition, our enemies have a tremendous organized command staff. Our recent chatter [about an uprising] is wrong, even from the perspective of the Central Committee resolution. Why give [the government] a chance to prepare? The mood in the factories now is not what it was in June....

It is said that we are in a situation from which we can find no exit; I think this is not yet the situation. I think our attitude toward the Constituent Assembly is incorrect. Of course, it cannot be seen as the salvation of everything. But the Constituent Assembly will meet in the highest strata of the revolutionary atmosphere. We will keep gaining strength, and the possibility that we will have a majority there, together with the left SRs, cannot be discounted. The peasants will not waver on the question of land. I was for withdrawing from the Pre-Parliament, and I don't think that the masses will never come around to us.

[Kamenev] speaks of the international situation and argues that we also have a responsibility to the international proletariat. We must exercise great caution: our influence is still growing. Petrograd will not be surrendered [to the Germans] before the Constituent Assembly. We do not have the right to take this risk, to stake everything on one card.

I suggest that if the soviet congress gathers on 20 [October], we must propose that it stay in session until the Constituent Assembly gathers. There must be a defensive-anticipatory tactic in the context of the Provisional Government's complete inactivity. We must not take a position that completely isolates us. The Constituent Assembly's convocation alone will not prevent civil war, but it is a very serious stage. The Central Committee resolution must be reconsidered, if possible. We must admit that we cannot organize an insurrection in the next five days.

Comrade Kamenev. A week has gone by since this resolution was passed. That also is evidence that the resolution is an example of how not to make an insurrection. In the last week, nothing was achieved. It only spoiled what should have been done. The week's results demonstrate that the facts do not favor an insurrection now. One cannot claim that the resolution only expressed an intention, as it demanded movement from words to deeds. Well, there have been no deeds. We have no apparatus for an insurrection; our enemies have quite a strong apparatus, and it probably has grown during this week. [Kamenev] gives evidence that nothing was done this week in a military-technical sense or regarding supplies. All the resolution did was allow the government to get organized itself. All the masses not with us now are on [the government's] side. We have made them stronger at our own expense. The situation is more serious than during the July Days. Socially speaking, the crisis has ripened. But there is no evidence at all that we must give battle before the 20th. The issue is not "now or never." I have more faith in the Russian revolution. Social battles lie before us. And preparing for the Constituent Assembly certainly does not mean we are taking the parliamentary path. Our forces are not adequate to ensure victory in an insurrection, but adequate to prevent extreme reaction. There are two tactics at conflict here: the tactic of conspiracy and the tactic of faith in the Russian revolution's motor forces.

Comrade Fenigstein figures that the armed insurrection will come not in weeks, but in days.[53] He agrees about the political position, but not about immediately going to bayonets.

He argues further that we are not technically prepared for an armed insurrection. We do not yet even have an operational center. We are sleep-walking into defeat. There are times when everyone must act. Even if this is not such a moment, we need to adopt a practical perspective.

Comrade Stalin.[54] A day for the insurrection must be picked. This is the only way to understand the resolution.

It may be said that we must wait to be attacked, but we must understand what an attack is: higher prices for bread, dispatching Cossacks to the Donets Region, and so on—all this was already an attack. If there is no military attack, then how long should we wait? The objective result of Kamenev and Zinoviev's proposal would be that the counterrevolution becomes organized; we will retreat endlessly and lose the whole revolution. Why not give ourselves a chance to propose a possible day and circumstances, and take away the counterrevolution's chance to organize? He addresses the analysis of international relations and argues that there should be more faith now. There are two lines: one follows the course to victorious revolution and then Europe's assistance; the second lacks confidence in the revolution and limits us to being an opposition [parliamentary party]. By refusing to agree to troop transfers, the Petrograd Soviet has already set upon the path of insurrection. The fleet has already risen up and come out against Kerensky.

Comrade Kalinin does not interpret the resolution as meaning there will be an uprising tomorrow.[55] But it does move the question from politics to strategy and calls for definitive action. We must not fear conspiracy; conspiracy must always be an option. We do not need to follow the path of parliamentary struggle—that would be wrong. It also does not follow that we should wait until they attack; in fact, an attack improves the chance for victory.

Comrade Sverdlov characterizes the resolution. From one perspective, it was a directive that correctly moved the issue from the political sphere to the technical sphere. He speaks about counterrevolutionary preparations. He criticizes Kamenev's assertion that the resolution's weak point is that it has not yet been implemented. This leads to the conclusion that more energetic work is necessary. Regarding the idea that the majority is against us: he says that this is not so; it just is not for us, yet. We are strong enough in Petrograd. The Junkers are not a threat, particularly if we strike first.[56] He does not share the pessimistic attitude about the garrison expressed here. The correlation of forces favors us. The resolution should not be rescinded, but should be amended to make technical preparations more energetic.

Comrade Skrypnik. If we do not have the strength now, we will not have more later. If now we can't keep power, later it will be even worse. It is said that there is an advantage in defending ourselves—perhaps! But later we will not even have the strength for defense.

Everything brought up here only postpones matters. There is no guarantee of victory. [Kamenev and Zinoviev] are repeating what the Mensheviks and SRs said when power was offered to them. We are talking too much, when what is needed is action. The masses demand this of us. If we give them nothing, they will regard it as a crime. What is needed is preparation for an insurrection and a call to the masses.

Comrade Volodarskii. If the resolution is a directive, then it already has been disobeyed. If the question about the uprising is put in terms of doing it tomorrow, then we must admit that we have done nothing. I have made speeches every day, and I must say that the masses were perplexed by our appeals. But this week something changed.

Were there not a group in the Central Committee that wanted to carry out the class struggle as a parliamentary struggle, we would have been ready for an insurrection by now. But as things stand, we are not. The resolution's positive side is that it compels us to go to the masses with a new slogan. The resolution must be understood as putting us on course to an insurrection. We must not break off our technical preparations.

[Volodarskii proposes] a concrete motion: to continue technical preparations and bring the issue to the soviet congress, but not to regard the moment [for insurrection] as having already arrived.

Comrade Dzerzhinskii argues that Volodarskii is wrong to think our party made a mistake when it carried out, as he put it, parliamentary tactics.[57] As it often turns out, a changing situation led us to change our decisions. Two months ago, illusions still existed and had not been eliminated. So it was impossible to raise the question of an insurrection then. Conspiracy is necessary simply so that everything is technically prepared for an insurrection. When insurrection comes, there will be technical resources. The same goes for supplies.

Comrade Ravich. Rescinding the resolution would rescind all our slogans and our entire policy. The masses truly already have decided that an insurrection is inevitable. If the masses are too revolutionary, then it will begin from below. But were there a call from above, no one can doubt that the masses will support us. There is no turning back.

Comrade Sokol'nikov.[58] Kamenev's objections have lost their persuasiveness. He makes the accusation that we trumpeted our uprising, i.e., that we really demanded a conspiracy. Our greatest distinction and strength lay precisely in our open preparation for an uprising. [Sokol'nikov] recalls February's events, when no preparations were made, yet the revolution was victorious. We cannot expect a more favorable correlation of forces.

Concerning the resolution, it is not a directive ordering an immediate uprising. If events seem to give us a respite, we will of course make use of it. It is possible that the soviet congress will come first. If the congress votes to give all power to the soviets, then it will be necessary to decide what to do—whether or not to appeal to the masses.

Comrade Skalov argues that a transfer of power to the soviets requires the right correlation of forces.[59] Soviet power must resolve the supply question. Now we must become defensists: if we do not take power, the fleet might abandon its position, and the army, too. He talks about breaking treaties and so on. He thinks it is impossible to organize an uprising before convocation of the soviet congress, but that we must take power at the congress.

Comrade Miliutin. The resolution was not intended in the sense given here. It is being interpreted to mean we should set a course toward insurrection. That course was set already in September. Everyone is still talking about political questions and not about technical performance. There is no debate concerning the course. Those talking about insurrection have presented it very primitively. Above all else, we need to take power and replace the old [government]. But to act as if this were a cliché—that is absurd. We gained from the fact that there was no insurrection on 3–5 {July}. And if one does not happen now, we will not be ruined. This resolution must be for internal usage.

Comrade Ioffe argues that the resolution cannot be taken as a directive for an uprising: that would reject the tactic of waiting until an insurrection is recognized as possible; it would reject the responsibility to begin an insurrection at the first opportune moment.[60] . . . On the other hand, it is not true that the issue now is purely technical; even now, the moment for insurrection must be considered from a political perspective. The resolution's sense is that we must take the first opportune moment to seize power. Therefore, it must be welcomed.

Comrade Shmidt. Now the issue is becoming clearer, and there are no objections against preparation for revolution.

Comrade Uncle {Latsis}.[61] It is unfortunate that the resolution has not been implemented already. I am convinced that the resolution will be accepted. I speak so as to introduce a correction in the estimation of the masses' mood. I hold that the masses' eagerness to seize weapons indicates their emerging mood. We have a strange strategy. As for the Junkers, as I have already said, they can be obliterated.

Comrade Lenin. One could only wish that all resolutions failed in this manner. Now Zinoviev says down with the slogan, "Power to the Soviets"; put pressure on the government. To say the moment is ripe for insurrection means there is no need to talk of conspiracy. If an insurrection is politically inevitable, then we must speak about insurrection as an art. And politically, it already has ripened.

It is precisely because there is bread for only one day that we cannot wait for the Constituent Assembly. Lenin proposes that the resolution be confirmed and that decisive preparations be made. Then let the Central Committee and the Soviet decide when.

Comrade Zinoviev. This revolution has been compared to the February revolution. There is no comparison. Then, no one supported the old government; now, it means war with the entire bourgeois world. We did not launch the slogan, "Power to the Soviets" in the abstract. Having the soviet congress put pressure on the Constituent Assembly cannot be compared to the Mensheviks' policy. If we view the insurrection as a long-term prospect, there can be no objection. But if this is a directive for tomorrow or the day after, then it is adventurism. We must not start an insurrection before our comrades have held the soviet congress and there has been consultation.

Comrade Stepanov. The resolution has historical significance; I see it as a barometer indicating a storm. [Stepanov] also objects to Kamenev's arguments about the lack of supplies. Despite the Cheremisov conference, reducing soldiers' rations might trigger the insurrection. The objective conditions ripen with each minute, and this resolution will play an important role. It has clarified much for us. [Stepanov] argues that the masses make a distinction between the Central Executive Committee and the Petrograd Soviet. He proposes that this resolution remain as a barometric index.

Comrade Kamenev argues that the present interpretation of the resolution is a retreat. Before, it was said that the uprising must occur before the 20th, and now the talk is about a course toward revolution. The question proposed is political. Scheduling an insurrection is adventurism. It is our obligation to the masses to clarify that an uprising will not be called in the next three days, but that we consider an insurrection inevitable.

[Kamenev] suggests voting on the resolution and proposes that [*Rabochii put'*] publish a statement saying there will be no call for an uprising before the soviet congress.

Comrade Skrypnik proposes an appeal to the masses, to prepare for an insurrection.

Comrade Lenin, responding to Zinoviev, says this revolution cannot be compared to the February Revolution.

Regarding the resolution's substance, [Lenin] proposes the following:

This meeting entirely welcomes and fully supports the Central Committee's resolution. It calls on all organizations and all workers and soldiers to make comprehensive and intensive preparations for an armed insurrection. It calls on them to support the center that the Central Committee is creating for this purpose.[62] It expresses complete confidence that the Central Committee and soviet will, at the proper time, indicate the right moment and expedient means for the attack.

Zinoviev. Answers Lenin regarding the February revolution: these two months will not be the worst in the pages of our party's history. On the resolution's substance, he proposes: Without postponing reconnaissance or preparatory steps, to consider any uprising before a conference with the soviet congress's Bolshevik section impermissible.

Lenin's resolution is voted on in principle. 20 for, 2 against, 3 abstaining.

Comrade Miliutin proposes an amendment: to substitute the words "armed clash."

Rejected.

Comrade Skrypnik proposes an amendment: to remove the words "expresses complete confidence," etc.

Rejected.

Comrade Fenigshtein proposes an amendment: to substitute the word "attack" with "uprising."

Rejected.

Comrade Volodarskii proposes that Comrade Zinoviev's resolution be considered as an amendment to the accepted resolution.

Rejected.

Comrade Fenigshtein proposes an amendment: "a Center composed by the Central Committee and the Military Committee."

Withdrawn.

[The vote on] the resolution as a whole: 19 for, 2 against, 4 abstaining.

[A vote on] Comrade Zinoviev's resolution: 6 for, 15 against, 3 abstaining.

The Central Committee meets alone [without representatives from the other committees] and accepts the following resolution: The Central Committee organizes a Military Revolutionary Center, composed as follows: Sverdlov, Stalin, Bubnov, Uritskii, and Dzerzhinskii. This center will join the staff of the Soviet [Military] Revolutionary Committee.[63]

DOCUMENT 12.10
THE SOVIET LEADERSHIP ON THE BOLSHEVIKS
AND THE SOVIET CONGRESS[64]

On 17 October 1917, Zinoviev and Kamenev demanded that an explanation of their objections to Lenin's resolution on insurrection be published in The Workers' Path (Rabochii put'). *When the editors refused, Kamenev sent a brief summary of his position to* New Life (Novaia zhizn'). *On 18 October* New Life's *editor, Maxim Gorky, published Kamenev's note, along with his own commentary condemning the Bolsheviks. Kamenev's note sparked a firestorm. Lenin immediately demanded that the Central Committee expel Kamenev and Zinoviev.[65] Still, at an 18 October general Bolshevik meeting in Petrograd, several moderates opposed an insurrection.*

The following document is an editorial from the Soviet Central Executive Committee's newspaper, Izvestiia, *on 18 October. It mentions debates over when the Second All-Russian Soviet Congress should convene. Left socialists had insisted on a 20 October convocation, but moderates argued for a postponement. In the meantime, the left factions organized a Northern Regional Soviet Congress (11–13 October). Lenin hoped the Northern congress would seize power. Instead, it endorsed Trotsky's proposal that the soviets take power at the All-Russian Soviet Congress. It also called on all soviets and soldiers' committees to send delegates to Petrograd for the All-Russian Soviet Congress on 20 October. Under this pressure, on 17 October the Central Executive Committee agreed to set 25 October as the congress's convocation date. The authors of the following editorial seem not to have known of that decision.*

A Split. 18 October.

One can no longer ignore the fact that the Bolshevik Party has created a deep split in our democratic organization. From the moment the Bolsheviks obtained a majority in the Petrograd Soviet, they have converted it into their own party organization. They are using it for intra-party struggle, to take control of all Russia's soviet organizations.

No one can object to the Bolsheviks spreading their ideas in organizations in which they are members. Every party has that right. But if it is done in a violent way, it inevitably leads to a schism and to the organization's break up. No matter how many Bolsheviks there may be in Petrograd, they are by no means the toiling masses' only party. They cannot force all Russia, or even all Petrograd, to become Bolsheviks. That is a utopian idea that—like all such ideas—will end in failure. Unfortunately, however, that failure would affect not just our enthusiastic [Bolshevik] comrades, but the entire Soviets of Workers' and Soldiers' Deputies.

There always have been different parties in the Petrograd Soviet and its Executive Committee. There have always been differences and disagreements between them, but there was also friendly cooperation. At revolution's beginning, fundamental differences never—or almost never—led to violent attacks by one party against another. Now that has become common, and cooperation is no longer possible.

Moreover, the Petrograd [Soviet] Executive Committee is dissatisfied with the Central Executive Committee's policy and has conducted a bitter campaign against it. The Bolsheviks want to force out the current Central Executive Committee and put in their own. They have the right to do this, too. The current members will not oppose new elections. Quite the contrary: they will gladly turn their heavy burden over to comrades who wish to take it on. But that change, should it be necessary, must be carried out legally, with attention to the interests of all military and provincial organizations. It should result from arbitrary grabbing and struggle, which would undermine all confidence in soviet organizations.

The Bolsheviks' Petrograd newspaper makes extremely vicious and hateful references to the Central Executive Committee. And the Bolsheviks' Congress of the Northern Region violated regulations of the All-Russian Soviet Congress by inviting regimental and division committees to the [Second All-Russian Soviet Congress]. They did so after the Central Executive Committee and most army organizations had come out against holding such a congress, in view of the forthcoming Constituent Assembly elections.

The Central Executive Committee has not taken a position on the date of the soviet congress and does not intend to.[66] But the Bolsheviks have already interfered in the matter, without consulting or even notifying the Central Executive Committee.

There is a very basic difference between the Bolsheviks and all the other soviet parties. They have consistently opposed the slogan of national defense, while the others support defense in every way. Unfortunately for the democracy's future, a conflict has emerged between the front and the rear. The Bolsheviks have taken the rear's side, which the front does not support. The army has split: read the recent declarations of the 12th Army and the resolution of the Luga Soviet, and the complete split is clear.[67] The Bolsheviks support a soviet seizure of power, while all other parties oppose it.[68] Still, the Bolsheviks try to impose this tactic on the All-Russian Soviet Congress. To do so, they have taken it upon themselves to convene the congress by circumventing the Central Executive Committee.

The Bolsheviks are trying to overthrow the Provisional Government. They are trying to overthrow the Central Executive Committee. And they want to disperse the Council of the Republic, which has just begun to function.[69] They want to forestall the Constituent Assembly by convening the soviet congress (which means overthrowing it, too, but in a veiled form). And they even want to overthrow the soviet congress itself, by convoking it in violation of regulations. Isn't this too much overthrowing? Might it not all result in their own overthrow?

Izvestiia has always refrained as much as possible from siding with any party, be it openly or implicitly. It will continue to uphold this tradition in the future and will ignore the vulgar speech found in certain extremist newspapers.

But in the present case, what is at stake is a split in the entire soviet—an organization that, until now, has defended the revolution and still has tremendous significance. . . . We cannot fail to warn against a split in this organization. A split never brings strength, it only weakens. And it can only benefit the democracy's enemies.

DOCUMENT 12.11
MOSCOW LIBERALS ON THE THREAT OF A
BOLSHEVIK UPRISING[70]

The following document from the Moscow Gazette *(Moskovskiia vedomosti) on 20 October 1917, responds to the Bolsheviks' mixed signals about a possible uprising. After Kamenev's note in* New Times *(Novaia zhizn'),* Bolshevik *leaders publically denied planning an insurrection.*

There Is Still Danger Ahead.
Well, today, 20 October, was to be a day of great triumph for the Bolsheviks. "Comrade Kollontai," speaking extemporaneously at a Petrograd circus, had predicted that today there would be "an uprising, a successful revolution; the Provisional Government will be overthrown and all power will be transferred to the soviets."[71] The newspapers report great anxiety among Petrograd residents, and the government is taking emergency measures for safety purposes. At the same time, the Bolshevik leaders Trotsky (Bronstein) and Lunacharskii—directly contradicting "Comrade Kollontai"—assure that there are no plans for an uprising and all this fuss is for nothing.[72] Who to believe?

We think there really is no uprising planned, and one won't even be attempted. You don't go around shouting about such things for half a month, the way that we've heard about the ill-fated 20th of October. This is falsification, a distraction, a game of nerves played against the population and government. The Bolsheviks need to keep society in constant tension, and they are succeeding with marvelous ease. They can threaten and squabble because they have a growling, rabid, mongrel dog on a leash—the mob. "Look" they say, "do you want us to let it loose on you? All we would have to do is whistle." Everyone's gaze is fixed on the show, the leash, the animal's jaws. Most have already thought: "Go ahead, let it loose! Let's have the worst and get it over."

Everywhere now you hear: "It's all the same if we let the Bolsheviks have power. It's something we *must* go through. It's inevitable; in every revolution a point comes when a radical party plays on the mob's brutal instincts and grabs absolute power. So, let's get it over with. Things will get worse and then better. The sooner the attack, the sooner it ends."

But the question emerges: what kind of end will it be? The typical answer is some general statement to the effect that, in the end, the people's better judgment will be awakened and they will come to their senses. Everyone clearly knows that one day the Bolsheviks will win a complete victory. But that stage of the revolution is still ahead and can't be seen. All we can see is dense fog and freakish outlines that could be anything you imagine. So people ponder and end up arguing that since a Bolshevik state is the worst thing that could possibly happen, it has to get better after that. Really?

No, we still have not yet reached the nadir of our misfortune. We are told, "The country cannot endure more." Really? Surely those prophets who reassured us that the war would last only three months believed they were right, but the war has gone on for four years and there is no end in sight. The orgy of anarchy is just beginning. Things can get incomparably worse than Bolshevik rule.

The Bolsheviks are flashes, nothings, cast-offs of society. Here is the evidence—their leaders. Most are from the dregs of Jewry, people reasonable Jewry has cast off. They are renegade Jews ashamed even of their given names. To provide a moral lesson, we review a list of this disrespectful company:

Trotsky—Bronshtein
Steklov—Nakhamkes[73]
Martov—Tsederbaum
Zinoviev—Apfel'baum
Sukhanov—Gimmel[74]
Kamenev—Rozenfel'd
Zagrodskii—Krokhman
Bogdanov—Sil'bershtein[75]
Larin—Lur'e[76]
Gorev—Gol'dman[77]

These gentlemen—and we would include Ul'ianov (Lenin)—can in no way be compared to the French Revolution's Jacobins. The Jacobins were men of ideas. Robespierre was a fanatic, which is why he could hold power for so long. He believed his ideas and compelled belief from those around him. There are no such fanatics among our Bolsheviks. They are Jewish businessmen and nothing more.[78] That is why most are on the German payroll. Ul'ianov (Lenin) entered history on a sealed German train. The English arrested Bronshtein (Trotsky)—the Chairman of the Soviet of Workers' and Soldiers' Deputies—as a German agent and sent him to a war-prisoners' camp.[79] Isn't that evidence that we have before us German agents? Such well informed people as Burtsev say the Bolsheviks (and we include Maxim Gorky among them) actively support Germany.[80] Must we say more?

That is why we think the Bolshevik leaders will never hold ministerial portfolios. They are incapable. Moreover, they do not want to. It is very important to the Germans that these gentlemen remain an almost-government. . . . The Bolsheviks will keep pretending. "Here," they will say, "now we are going to take power." But they will not take power. Under current conditions, the Germans have "the right people in the right place" to get a government that will implement the German program. For example, they propound the purely German slogan, "Peace without Annexations or Indemnities." In Russian translation, that means, "I don't know who wrote this, but I am a fool and so I repeat it." And that Russian text will be picked up and recited loudly at the Paris Conference by our "diplomatic"—it is hard to say the word—representatives.[81]

No, the Bolsheviks' triumph would not be the nadir of our misfortunes. Then what would be, you ask? To put it in pure Russian: rule by a Pretender [samozvanstva].[82] Really, the ground has been prepared for this. The Pretender is anarchy's living embodiment. He is the flame and the sword, annihilating everything in his path. He is a leader who moves everything forward and sweeps along the popular masses. Why couldn't this happen? Aren't there many among our people who are ignorant, evil, and disappointed? The air is so saturated, so electrically overcharged, so strange, that a thunderstorm the likes of which we cannot even dream might yet burst over our heads. A storm compared to which the times of the Thief of Tushino, Stenka Razin, and Pugachev will seem like seasons of relative happiness.[83] And a person will emerge who will smile and, in the name of destruction, put himself at the head of the people's blind fury.

The Bolsheviks do not frighten us. What frightens us is ourselves, the intelligentsia, with our passivity and our peaceful disposition. This is a century of iron, a century of struggle, a century of blood and violence. We must adapt to it, or else we will be swept away, without a trace, by the growing wave of exasperation and the people's frightening darkness. Hold to the shore! Unite! Act! Our lives and the lives of our wives and children are at stake.

DOCUMENT 12.12
ALEKSANDR NIKITSKII, "THE SOVIETS AND
THE CONSTITUENT ASSEMBLY"[84]

The following document is an editorial from the Petrograd Menshevik-Internationalist newspaper, The Spark (Iskra), *on 21 October 1917. Iulii Martov and the Menshevik-Internationalists had been urging the soviets to assume power since July 1917, but shunned the Bolsheviks' calls for armed insurrection. In October, they called on the Second All-Russian Congress of Soviets to create an "All-Democratic Government."*

The Soviets and the Constituent Assembly.

According to all the bourgeoisie's socialist yes-men, there is no need for the soldiers', workers', and peasants' soviet congress to meet [two to four] weeks before the Constituent Assembly. After the assembly convenes, the local soviets will simply die out. We, on the contrary, propose that *the soviets' premature burial would create great danger* for our revolution and the democracy. We think that Social Democrats must strengthen the soviets and improve their organization and activities.

Anyone who understands the modern state's development and the legislation that has characterized it must agree with our approach to the soviets.

On one hand, everywhere we look we see that power has been transferred to the people's representatives in the parliaments that have total authority based on laws that apply to everyone. On the other hand, we see growth of bourgeois and proletarian class organizations that—to promote their own interests—at once exert powerful pressure and influence on parliamentary governments and also create a parallel body of extraparliamentary law. More and more, parliaments are relegated to formally confirming laws that classes and interest groups have negotiated among themselves, outside the parliament.

We understand, for example, that everywhere there are "free unions" to defend the capitalists' interests that exercise great influence on government and legislation, like the "trade boards" and "agriculturists' unions" in Germany, the syndicates and trusts in the North American United States, and, of course, the industrialists' and traders' "official" and unofficial organizations in Russia. We particularly understand the reactionary, ruinous role played before our revolution by the Council of the United Nobility and the Union of Landowners.[85]

We would thrice be criminals against the interests of the proletariat and toiling peasantry were we to help destroy their representative organizations, the soviets. Our revolution is far from over, and the people need revolutionary representative organizations to defend labor's political interests.

The Constituent Assembly does not require elimination of the soviets. The soviets have become the main proponents of hastening the Constituent Assembly's convocation. As they gather [for the soviet congress], they will support the assembly. And perhaps the soviets, as a useful source of legislative initiatives by the masses that they have organized, can supervise the Constituent Assembly's legislation and help it fight anarchy and counterrevolution.

In Russia, elections to city dumas and soviets have reflected the people's will and mood as a consequence of the disastrous war. We cannot predict the people's mood during the Constituent Assembly elections or how long that mood will hold. It could be that the people's will and the Constituent Assembly's will soon diverge on a whole range of issues. Unlike the soviets, the Constituent Assembly cannot be reelected quickly; it is doubtful that the Constituent Assembly could be reelected at all. Therefore, the soviets will always express more exactly the active will of the worker, soldier and peasant masses. The soviets' authority among the masses might prove more constant than that enjoyed by legal public institutions. All real policy must be considered from this standpoint. Instead of struggling against the soviets, they should be treated as a political barometer. Break it or smash it at your own risk.

—A. Nikitskii

PART FOUR

THE FIRST MONTHS OF SOVIET RULE, OCTOBER 1917–JANUARY 1918

On 20–24 October 1917, the Petrograd Soviet's Military Revolutionary Committee (MRC) prepared for an insurrection and worked to ensure support from the city's garrison. By late on 23 October, key garrison units either promised to aid the MRC against Kerensky's government or pledged neutrality. Kerensky initially wanted to arrest the entire MRC, but instead simply ordered that the Bolshevik press be shut down on 24 October. In doing so, he set the insurrection in motion. The Bolsheviks, with their left Socialist Revolutionary (SR) and Anarchist allies, claimed that Kerensky intended to disband the Second All-Russian Soviet Congress, which was scheduled to open the next day, so the MRC gradually took "defensive" control of the city's key strategic points. Although there were skirmishes throughout the night, and then during the day on 25 October, only a few military units came to Kerensky's aid, most notably, an officer's training unit and an all-female Women's Battalion of Death.[1] By evening on 25 October, Kerensky's government was isolated in the Winter Palace, besieged by the soviet's forces.

The Second All-Russian Congress of Soviets

Through early October, the left socialists debated whether to seize power in the name of the soviets or to wait for the Second All-Russian Congress of Soviets to declare Soviet power. It was clear that the left factions would be in the majority at the congress, and it was widely anticipated that the congress would name an all-socialist government picked from the parties represented in the soviets. The revolutionary defensist Menshevik and SR leaders, though, not only condemned the Bolsheviks' plans to seize power, but also argued against the creation of an all-socialist government. They insisted that bourgeois participation in the government was still necessary to consolidate the revolution and prevent civil war. Moreover, they argued, the soviet congress had no right to usurp to functions of the upcoming Constituent Assembly. The actions taken by Kerensky and the Petrograd Soviet MRC on 25 October, though, completely altered the nature of the debate over the soviet congress. Now the question became how the other political parties would respond to the Bolshevik seizure of power.

The congress of soviets was scheduled to open on the afternoon of 25 October, but the Bolsheviks delayed it, in hopes that the MRC could first capture the Winter Palace and arrest the Provisional Government. In the meantime, the various socialist parties met in caucuses to work out their formal responses to the insurrection. When the soviet congress finally opened, at about 10:45 P.M. on 25 October, the delegates could hear the shots being fired on the Winter Palace, nearly a mile away. Representatives from the moderate socialist party groups and several military organizations demanded that the Bolsheviks end the fighting. Menshevik and SR speakers condemned the uprising, accused the Bolsheviks of starting a civil war, and then led their delegates out of the congress in protest. Several top Mensheviks and SRs went to the Petrograd City Duma to join a demonstration against the Bolsheviks.

Shortly after the moderate socialists quit the congress, Iulii Martov spoke in behalf of the Menshevik-Internationalists and the Jewish socialist parties. Martov, too, demanded an end to violence and called for negotiations toward a peaceful transfer of power. When Trotsky, for the Bolsheviks, mocked his arguments, Martov led his faction from the hall in protest. In one of the revolution's most famous speeches, Trotsky told them, "Go to where you belong, the dustbin of history!" The left SRs also called for an end to the fighting, but they did not walk out of the meeting. Instead, they voted with the Bolsheviks to pass a resolution declaring Soviet power. Chapter 13 presents important debates and speeches made at the soviet congress on 25 and 26 October, as well as documents that illustrate arguments made for and against the October Revolution in the weeks that followed.

During the day on 26 October 1917, the Petrograd Soviet's MRC consolidated its hold on the capital and moved against the Bolsheviks' liberal opponents. Kadet Party leaders had already started to organize an anti-Bolshevik resistance movement and encouraged government employees to strike in protest against the insurrection. On 26 October, the MRC shut down the Kadet newspaper *Speech (Rech)* and confiscated its printing press. That same day, the Menshevik and SR leaders who had quit the soviet congress formed a Committee to Save the Motherland and the Revolution, which issued declarations denouncing the insurrection. The Menshevik-Internationalists did not join this anti-Bolshevik committee. Instead, they worked with officials from the All-Russian Railroad Workers' Union (Vikzhel) to pressure the Bolsheviks into negotiations on forming an all-socialist coalition government. On the afternoon of 26 October, a small group of Bolsheviks, left SRs, and Menshevik-Internationalists met to discuss the possibility of a left socialist coalition government. These talks, however, produced no agreements. Lenin did all he could to disrupt the negotiations (including ordering the arrest of several senior socialist leaders). The top Bolshevik leaders spent much of that day discussing Lenin's draft decrees on peace and land reform, which were introduced at the soviet congress's evening session.

At its 26 October session, the Second All-Russian Congress of Soviets passed decrees concerning the Russian Revolution's most important unresolved issues—peace and land reform. Lenin presented the congress with a Decree on Peace that offered the warring governments immediate negotiations for a "just, democratic" peace, with no territorial annexations or financial indemnities and with assurance of national self-determination.[2] Lenin's decree also appealed directly to the workers in the belligerent countries—especially the English, French, and German proletariat—to act swiftly and decisively to bring an end to the war. The implication was that, should the bourgeois governments fail to end the war, an international socialist revolution would. With this decree, Lenin's government did something that Provisional Government had failed to do: moved decisively to stop the immensely unpopular war. After the congress voted in favor of the peace decree, Lenin addressed another popular demand that the Provisional Government had failed to satisfy—the call for land reform. Lenin's land decree, much of which was essentially copied from the SR land program, abolished private landownership. All private landed estates, all land owned by church and monastic institutions, and all land owned by the Romanovs, along with all farm buildings, tools, and livestock, would be put under the control of the local soviets and local land committees, without compensating the landowners. Again, the congress voted to pass Lenin's decree. By promising to immediately satisfy the peasantry's central demand—the redistribution of land—Lenin undercut the significance of the Constituent Assembly for the peasant majority and made it easier for the left SRs to agree to cooperate with the Soviet government.

A third decree passed on 26 October formally established the new Soviet government. The new cabinet, called the Council of People's Commissars (known as the Sovnarkom), was charged with implementing soviet congress decrees and pursuing policies according to the "program" set out by the congress. In principle, the Sovnarkom was subordinate to the soviet congress and to the All-Russian Soviet Central Executive Committee. Lenin was designated as Sovnarkom chairman, Trotsky as people's commissar for foreign affairs, and Stalin as the head of the Commissariat for Nationality Affairs. All the people's commissars named in the decree were Bolsheviks. The Mensheviks and SRs had left the congress and cut themselves off from the new government, which they declared illegitimate. The left SRs and the Menshevik-Internationalists refused to participate in the government unless the Bolsheviks formed a coalition with all the major socialist parties—something Lenin and Trotsky would not do. The left SRs and Menshevik-Internationalists, however, did agree to participate in the Central Executive Committee, where they initially made up a small minority. Lenin suggested that left socialists might be given posts as people's commissars. For the time being, though, the Soviet government was a purely Bolshevik enterprise, which contradicted the widely popular idea that Soviet power would mean an all-socialist coalition.

In the early hours of 27 October, a representative from Vikzhel took the podium at the soviet congress. He announced that the railroad workers' union considered all the congress's resolutions invalid, since the walk-out of the Mensheviks and SRs had left the meeting without a quorum.

Vikzhel was taking control over the railroads and would not allow pro-Kerensky troops or counterrevolution forces to move on Petrograd. But it would not recognize the Soviet government and insisted on a "revolutionary socialist government responsible to the entire revolutionary democracy." This set the stage for several days of tense—and ultimately fruitless—negotiations between the major socialist parties.[3]

Reactions to the October Revolution Outside Petrograd

Several documents in chapters 13 and 14 present responses in Moscow and other provincial cities to the October Revolution. In contrast to the relatively regular pattern by which the February Revolution spread, responses to the Bolshevik insurrection varied dramatically from place to place. Some regions outside central Russia immediately fell under the control of anti-Bolshevik military forces. Along the Don River, for example, Cossack leader General Kaledin declared a Don Republic, which rallied anti-Bolshevik forces in the south. In a few cities, particularly Central Industrial Region, left blocs of Bolsheviks, left SRs, and Anarchists reacted to the news from Petrograd by quickly taking power in the name of the local soviet, with little local opposition. Even in such places, though, the advocates of Soviet power envisioned an all-socialist coalition government, not a Bolshevik dictatorship.

In most regions, Soviet power was established only after an armed confrontation. In several cities, the left socialist bloc that controlled the local soviet fought small battles against the moderate socialists, who led city dumas. Most often, these battles concluded with a soviet victory. In Smolensk (and some other cities), however, the new Soviet authorities shared power with "old" local Provisional Government institutions for several months. And in Kharkov (Ukraine), the left socialist bloc that won a battle for power refused to recognize the authority of the Soviet government in Petrograd unless Lenin agreed to an all-socialist coalition. In Ukraine, and in the Baltic states and Finland, the conflict between the Bolsheviks and their opponents was only one thread in a tangled web of political struggles, and the struggle for power became intertwined with the issue of national independence. On 3 November, the Ukrainian Rada in Kiev refused to recognize the Bolshevik government in Petrograd and declared Ukraine independent. In January 1918, Lenin's government sent soldiers to aid the left socialist forces in Kharkov, who were fighting for power against the Kiev-based Rada. The Rada then issued a "Fourth Universal" that condemned Bolshevik aggression and again declared Ukraine's absolute independence from Russia.

In Moscow the soviet's left faction, including the local Bolshevik leaders, expected that Soviet power would mean an all-socialist coalition. Therefore the local Bolsheviks had not prepared for an insurrection. When news came of the seizure of power in Petrograd, the Moscow Soviet was slow to organize an MRC. But the moderate socialists in the Moscow City Duma quickly formed a very well-organized and well-armed Committee of Public Safety. Fighting between the two factions broke out on 27 October. For two days, the Committee of Public Safety completely dominated the conflict, but the tide turned when Red Guards and volunteers from other cities rushed to Moscow to aid the local Bolsheviks. Hundreds of people were killed and thousands wounded in bloody street battles, and both sides murdered prisoners and committed other atrocities. On 2 November, the Bolsheviks emerged victorious and claimed Soviet rule over Moscow.

The Bolsheviks, Their Opponents, Their Allies, and the Constituent Assembly Elections

From its inception, Lenin's government sought to silence socialist opposition. This meant that socialist leaders and newspapers faced harassment similar to that the Bolsheviks meted out to the Kadets. On 27 October 1917, Lenin issued a decree on "Freedom of the Press" that authorized government censorship of opposition newspapers. The Menshevik-Internationalists and left SRs in the Central Executive Committee quickly condemned the censorship of socialist newspapers and denounced arrests of the Bolsheviks' socialist opponents. Several top Bolshevik leaders also decried Lenin's actions and pushed negotiations to create an all-socialist coalition. But the moderate Mensheviks and SRs leaders on one side, and Bolshevik hardliners (primarily Lenin and Trotsky) on the other, insisted on terms that undermined negotiations.[4] The positions taken by the Bolsheviks, the other left socialists, and the major opposition groups are presented in documents in chapter 13.

On 2 November, news of the Bolshevik victory in Moscow reinforced Lenin and Trotsky's conviction that they did not need to negotiate. Two days later, on 4 November, four moderate Bolsheviks resigned their posts as people's commissars after exceptionally bitter exchanges with Lenin and Trotsky in the Central Executive Committee. Since the moderates had been pivotal to negotiations with the other socialist parties, their departure effectively killed any chance for a broad socialist front. It did not, however, end negotiations between the Bolsheviks and the left SRs.

Rifts in the Party of Socialist Revolutionaries had been deepening since the war began in 1914, but all semblance of party unity came to an end when the left SRs decided to remain at the Second All-Russian Congress of Soviets. The SR leadership (like that of the Mensheviks) declared Bolshevik rule illegitimate and rejected point by point the decrees announced by Lenin's government. In mid-November, news that the Soviet government was negotiating an armistice with Germany hardened the SR leadership's position. Conflict within the Party of Socialist Revolutionaries came to a head during the sessions of an All-Russian Peasant Congress in Petrograd on 10–11 November. The center and right SR leaders wanted to use the peasant congress to mobilize opposition against Lenin's government. The left SRs wanted to use the congress to take over the party while avoiding a formal split. Their strategy was to win over the party's centrists, then oust the right wing from the party's leadership. When it became clear that the centrists would not cooperate with them, the left SR faction shifted tactics. On 12 November, the left SRs claimed that the "old" peasant congress had no authority, and the left SR delegates began meeting with Bolshevik delegates for what they called an "Extraordinary" Peasant Congress. The Bolsheviks and left SRs then worked out an agreement that enlarged the All-Russian Central Executive Committee of Soviets by including equal numbers of peasants', soldiers', and workers' deputies—which significantly increased the left SRs' representation. On 15 November, the left SRs joined the Central Executive Committee. Four days after that, they opened a national congress to formally established a new political party, the Left Socialist Revolutionaries.

As the Party of Socialist Revolutionaries was fracturing, its center-right leadership staked their hopes for overturning Bolshevik rule on the Constituent Assembly. Chapter 11 included examples of Constituent Assembly election campaign materials and chapter 14 illustrates debates over the assembly's purpose as its convocation approached. Elections for the Constituent Assembly began on 12 November. The SRs won an absolute majority—nearly 21 million of the approximately 36 million votes cast. With the Ukrainian SRs, they would have at least 370 delegates to the Constituent Assembly. This was more than twice that of the Bolsheviks, who won roughly 9 million votes and 170 seats. Because the elections were held before the formal split in the Party of Socialist Revolutionaries, Left SRs ran as a separate ticket in only a few districts; as a result, they won only 40 seats. The Kadets and Mensheviks each won fewer than two dozen seats, as did several national minority parties and minor party candidates.[5]

The Constituent Assembly elections put Lenin's government in a difficult position.[6] The Bolsheviks had hammered the Provisional Government for delaying the Constituent Assembly, and they had promised that the assembly would meet once Soviet power was established. It was clear, though, that the assembly's elected majority would reject the all-Bolshevik Soviet government. Bolshevik leaders debated means to alter the election results, such as complaining of mass electoral fraud then holding new elections, which they would actively "control." At the same time, the opposition moved to convene the assembly as soon as possible. On 17 November, the handful of Provisional Government ministers whom the Bolsheviks had not yet imprisoned issued a "decree" saying that the Constituent Assembly would open at Petrograd's Tauride Palace on 28 November. The Bolshevik government, however, announced that the assembly would not open until there were enough delegates in Petrograd for a quorum. On 22 November, a joint conference of right and moderate socialists concluded that the Bolsheviks intended to scuttle the Constituent Assembly. The next day they announced creation of a "Union to the Defend the Constituent Assembly," and issued an appeal asking elected assembly delegates to gather on 28 November. Lenin promptly ordered the Union's leaders arrested. The Council of People's Commissars then assigned Bolshevik Mikhail Uritskii to oversee the assembly's convocation.

Uritskii made clear from the start that he would use force to intimidate anti-Bolshevik Constituent Assembly delegates, who had started to arrive in Petrograd. On 28 November, several dozen delegates appeared at the Tauride Palace, where they were harassed by Red Guards and pro-Soviet soldiers. When the delegates were unable to open the Constituent Assembly, they organized a demonstration, which gathered support from many groups hostile to the Bolshevik seizure of power. The Bolshevik government responded by declaring the Kadet Party a counterrevolutionary organization and arresting several of its leaders. The events of 28 November were the first of many confrontations between pro-Bolshevik forces and pro–Constituent Assembly demonstrators, which continued through December and became more violent with each passing week. In early December, Lenin's government created a new police-security institution, The Extraordinary Commission for the Struggle against Counterrevolution and Espionage, known as the Cheka. The Cheka treated the pro-assembly demonstrations as counterrevolutionary acts, and arrested several Menshevik and SR activists, as well as liberal leaders.

Each new repressive measure taken by Lenin's government sparked an immediate protest and harsh criticism from left socialists on the Central Executive Committee. This posed a problem for the Bolshevik leadership primarily because it complicated their relationship with the Left SRs, who were crucial to the work of the MRC and the Cheka. Although the Left SRs agreed to the arrest of Kadet leaders, they were outraged at Bolshevik repression of other socialist parties. Still, they supported the Soviet government's fundamental policies, and Bolsheviks and Left SRs agreed on a number of issues, including the need to delay the Constituent Assembly's opening, so that they could weaken the opposition by recalling and reelecting as many delegates as possible.

On 6 December, the Soviet government decreed that the assembly would begin once 400 or more delegates had arrived and registered. Together, the Bolsheviks and Left SRs warned that, when the Constituent Assembly did open, it must endorse Soviet power and approve all the new government's major decrees, or it would be branded a counterrevolutionary gathering. On 12 December, after weeks of difficult negotiations, the Bolsheviks and Left SRs agreed that Left SRs would assume several posts on the Council of People's Commissars.

As several documents in chapter 14 illustrate, from mid-December 1917, the Bolsheviks and Left SRs defined the Constituent Assembly's role as limited to affirming the legitimacy of the Soviet government and its policies.[7] At the 22 December session of the Central Executive Committee of Soviets, which set the date for the Constituent Assembly's opening as 5 January 1918, Bolshevik and Left SR speakers denounced the assembly's elected majority as hostile toward Soviet power. They agreed that a clash between the Soviet government and the assembly was inevitable and decreed that a Third All-Russian Soviet Congress should meet in early January, as a counterbalance to the assembly.[8]

In the meantime, the Union for the Defense of the Constituent Assembly began preparing a series of demonstrations. According to some sources, right SR military personnel also began planning an armed uprising in case the Bolsheviks moved against the assembly. Soviet authorities responded by declaring martial law in Petrograd. On the morning of 5 January 1918, pro-Soviet soldiers quickly dispersed a number of small demonstrations supporting the Constituent Assembly. When delegates gathered at the Tauride Palace that day for the meetings' first session, they found dozens of armed sailors and soldiers posted to "guard" the assembly.

The Constituent Assembly

When, at 4:00 P.M., the Constituent Assembly finally opened, just over 400 delegates were in attendance, more than half of whom were SRs.[9] In addition, the hall was filled by at least 400 members of the general public who had purchased tickets to watch the spectacle. The meeting began with a tussle. Bolshevik Iakov Sverdlov, chairman of the Central Executive Committee, arrived late, and the SRs tried to open the meeting without him. Sverdlov then pushed his way to the podium and declared the Constituent Assembly open in the name of the Soviet government. Sverdlov's opening speech, presented in chapter 14, called on the assembly to endorse a Declaration of Rights of Toiling and Exploited Peoples, which began by stating that Russia was a Soviet republic in which power rested with the soviets of workers', soldiers', and peasants' deputies. Endorsing the declaration would have entailed supporting all the major decrees and policies of Lenin's government, including a decree recognizing Finland's independence. No sooner had Sverdlov finished than the meeting's majority voted to elect veteran SR leader Viktor Chernov, not Sverdlov, as the assembly's chairman.

Chernov's election was the first in a series of clashes between the majority and the Bolsheviks that night. As Chernov read his long, rambling opening address (excerpted in chapter 14), Bolshevik delegates repeatedly taunted and interrupted him, as did soldiers in the gallery, who according to some accounts were already drunk. Chernov described the tasks that lay before the Constituent Assembly and emphasized that the assembly, not Lenin's government, exercised democratic authority in Russia. The Bolsheviks again demanded that the meeting pass a resolution endorsing the Declaration of Rights of Toiling and Exploited Peoples that Sverdlov had read earlier, which would have recognized the Soviet government's authority. The majority voted against discussing the Bolshevik resolution and instead adopted the agenda proposed by the SRs: to debate the issues of peace and land reform, then to discuss the creation of a new government. The Bolsheviks and Left SRs asked for a recess.

After the recess, the Bolsheviks announced that they were quitting the meeting, and that the Constituent Assembly had revealed itself to be a counterrevolutionary gathering by rejecting the Declaration of Rights. The Soviet government therefore would have to disband the assembly. Although the entire Bolshevik delegation walked out in protest, the Left SRs remained and took part in the meeting's debates on peace and land reform. At about 4:00, however, the Left SR leader Vladimir Karelin interrupted the debate on land reform. He took the podium, denounced the assembly's majority, and said that his delegation was quitting the meeting and would continue working in the Soviet government. Chernov tried to resume the debate on land reform, but within minutes, the soldiers guarding the meeting—whose demeanor had become more menacing as the night dragged on—announced that they were tired and that the session was over. When delegates returned to the hall later on 6 January, they found the doors locked, and the guards refused to admit them to the building. The Central Executive Committee had issued a decree dissolving the Constituent Assembly (which is included in chapter 14).

In the wake of Constituent Assembly's dispersal, the Bolsheviks pushed for more repressive measures against all opposition groups, whom they defined not only as "enemies of Soviet power," but also as "enemies of the people." The consequences of such rhetoric was driven home on 6 January 1918, when a group of sailors from the Baltic Fleet brutally murdered imprisoned Kadet leaders Andrei Shingarev and Fedor Kokoshkin, who were being treated for illness at the Mariinskii Hospital in Petrograd. One of the killers, Stefan Basov—the only man arrested and convicted for the crime—later justified his actions by saying that it meant "two less bourgeois mouths to feed."[10] The Bolsheviks' coalition partners, the Left SRs, considered the lynching of Shingarev and Kokoshkin an outrage and called for greater revolutionary discipline. Still, the Left SRs approved of many other repressive acts taken against alleged counterrevolutionaries.

Despite tensions, the two parties continued working together in the Soviet government (including the Cheka) until spring 1918, when they split decisively over a peace treaty with Germany.

The story of the Constituent Assembly did not end completely with the events of 6 January 1918, although its continuation fits into the context of the Russian Civil War, and not the 1917 Revolution. For several days after the Soviet government's decree dissolving the assembly, its SR, Trudovik, and Kadet members met secretly at a high school in Petrograd. They then moved to Kiev, where they met until Bolshevik forces seized that city in mid-January. In June 1918, an SR-led Committee of Members of the Constituent Assembly (known as Komuch) gathered in Samara, a city on the Volga River, and declared itself Russia's legitimate government. The Bolsheviks had just been driven from Samara by the Czech Legion, a force made up of Czech and Slovak war prisoners in Russia who had volunteered to fight against Germany and Austro-Hungary. The Soviet government had signed a peace treaty with Germany in March 1918 (the Treaty of Brest-Litovsk), but it still agreed to give the Czech Legion safe passage through Siberia, from where the legionnaires were to sail for France. In May 1918, though, Soviet authorities demanded that the Czech Legion disarm. Instead, they rebelled and seized control of Russia's railroad network from the Volga region all the way to Vladivostok on the Pacific coast. The Komuch government took advantage of this circumstance to seize power in Samara. Between June and August, Komuch extended its authority far into Western Siberia. By fall 1918, though, it was losing popular support. It also suffered a series of military defeats to the Red Army. In November 1918, the SR government was overthrown in a right-wing coup led by Admiral Aleksandr Kolchak, which brought a final end to the Constituent Assembly's claim to power.

The Revolution Ends, the Civil War Begins

Historians disagree over when exactly the Russian Revolution ended and the Russian Civil War began. Some scholars argue that the Bolshevik seizure of power on 25 October marked the start of the Civil War. Others argue that the Civil War began with battles between the pro-Soviet "Red" forces and the so-called White Armies (like General Alekseev's Volunteer Army) in Ukraine and the Don River region in December 1917. Some historians consider the May 1918 revolt of the Czech Legion as the war's beginning, while still others consider a series of failed uprisings launched by Left SRs in July 1918 as the start of an all-out civil war.

This book ends with the dissolution of the Constituent Assembly, which reflects another historiographic position that treats 5–6 January 1918 as the turning point between the revolutionary phase of Russia's "continuum of crisis" and the Civil War. By disbanding the Constituent Assembly, the

Bolsheviks made clear that they would not allow themselves to be voted out of power.[11] From that point, whenever opposition socialist parties won majorities in elections to local soviets, as the Mensheviks did in many cities in spring 1918, Lenin's government simply disbanded those institutions and replaced them with temporary "revolutionary committees." Then the government held new elections, which were stacked to ensure a victory for the Communist Party (as the Bolsheviks became known in February 1918).

For all the chaos, crisis, hyperbolic rhetoric, and violent unrest that marked the Russian Revolution, March to December 1917 also witnessed an explosion of vibrant civic engagement. Ordinary people seized on the revolution to voice their hopes and dreams for a new Russia. They created a great variety of groups and organizations to represent their aspirations and to turn them into reality. Each major political party, in its effort to define the revolution and shape its goals, positioned itself as either the champion of popular, class-based aspirations (in the case of the socialist parties) or as the defender of transcendent Russian state interests (in the case of the liberals). Although none of the Provisional Government's various incarnations in March–October were democratically elected, the rise and fall of each had been tightly intertwined with popular politics. The dispersal of the Constituent Assembly in January 1918 did not mean the end of politics or of political debate—indeed, there was no shortage of fighting words during the Russian Civil War— but it did mean the end of the open, peaceful political competition that had characterized the Russian Revolution.

CHAPTER THIRTEEN

FLASH POINTS OF CONFLICT: THE OCTOBER REVOLUTION AND CREATION OF A BOLSHEVIK GOVERNMENT

13.13
AN ANTI-BOLSHEVIK EDITORIAL FROM SMOLENSK

13.14
ZINOVIEV DEFENDS THE OCTOBER INSURRECTION

DOCUMENT 13.1
THE SECOND ALL-RUSSIAN CONGRESS OF SOVIETS
AND THE BOLSHEVIK SEIZURE[1]

On 24–25 October 1917, the Petrograd Soviet's Military Revolutionary Committee gradually took control of the city's key strategic points, so that the Provisional Government found itself isolated in the Winter Palace on 25 October. The Second All-Russian Congress of Soviets was scheduled to convene that afternoon, but its opening was delayed as socialist party leaders discussed the insurrection and the Bolsheviks awaited the government's arrest. When the congress finally began (at about 10:45 P.M.), representatives of several parties and organizations demanded that the Bolsheviks stop the violence on Petrograd's streets and then left the meeting in protest.

The following document presents composite texts of several declarations and speeches made at the congress session of 25–26 October, as compiled from the contemporary press accounts and published stenographic notes. The documents begin with a Menshevik declaration read by Lev Khinchuk, followed by a Socialist Revolutionary declaration read by Mikhail Gendel'man, a Bund declaration read by Henrikh Erlikh, a statement by Bundist Rafail Abramovich, and a speech by Iulii Martov's delivered on behalf of the Menshevik-Internationalists and Poalei-Tsion. Trotsky's famous reply to Martov (the "dustbin of history" speech) is presented here in full. The document selection ends with an appeal, "To Workers, Soldiers, and Peasants," read by Bolshevik Anatoli Lunacharskii.

[Menshevik declaration prepared at a joint meeting with the Socialist Revolutionaries and presented by Lev Khinchuk.[2]]

Khinchuk: Taking into consideration that:

1. The Bolsheviks have organized and carried out a military conspiracy in the soviets' name, behind the backs of all the other parties represented in the soviets;
2. The Petrograd Soviet's seizure of power on the soviet congress's eve is disorganizing and disrupting all other soviet organizations and undermines the congress's importance as the revolutionary democracy's authorized representatives;
3. This conspiracy plunges the country into internecine war, disrupts the Constituent Assembly, and threatens to bring military catastrophe and the triumph of counterrevolution;
4. The only possible peaceful solution to this situation that remains is to negotiate with the Provisional Government to form a government based on all democratic strata;
5. The RSDLP (United) considers it its duty to the working class to absolve itself of any responsibility for the Bolsheviks' actions and to warn the workers and soldiers of the danger this political adventure poses for the country and the revolution.

The RSDLP United fraction is leaving the congress and invites all other fractions that similarly refuse to bear responsibility for the Bolsheviks' actions to gather immediately to discuss the situation.

[As Khinchuk left the podium, pro-Bolshevik delegates shouted, "Deserters!" The SR spokesman Gendel'man took the podium, endorsed the Mensheviks' declaration, and read the following statement.][3]

Gendel'man: The SR fraction at the All-Russian Congress of Soviets of Workers' and Soldiers' Deputies, with the consent of the SR Party Central Committee, declares that:

1. By seizing power before the Constituent Assembly's convocation and on the eve of the All-Russian Congress of Soviets of Workers' and Soldiers' Deputies, the Bolsheviks and Petrograd Soviet of Workers' and Soldiers' Deputies have committed a crime against the motherland and the revolution. This signals the beginning of civil war, disrupts the Constituent Assembly, and threatens to destroy the revolution;
2. The SR fraction, foreseeing an explosion of the people's outrage as they inevitably discover the bankruptcy of the Bolsheviks' obviously unrealizable promises, calls on all the country's revolutionary forces to organize and defend the revolution. That way, when the impending catastrophe comes, they can take the country's fate in their own hands and prevent counterrevolution's triumph. This will ensure the quickest conclusion of a universal democratic peace, convocation of the Constituent Assembly on the designated date, and socialization of land;
3. Because the Bolshevik Party and its leaders in the Petrograd Soviet of Workers' and Soldiers' Deputies seized power, the SR fraction holds them responsible for these mad and criminal steps, which have made cooperative work with them impossible. Moreover, we hold that this congress has no authority, as it lacks representation from the front and from many soviets. Therefore we are leaving the Congress.

[The SR and Menshevik delegation left the hall, to shouts of "Deserters." Several speakers took the podium to argue that the congress either did or did not represent the front soldiers. The Bundist Geinrikh Erlikh then read the following statement.[4]]

Erlikh: In the name of the Bund group, it is my duty to declare that we consider what is happening in Petrograd to be a disaster. Our duty to the Jewish proletariat and the proletarians of all countries demands that we do so. I have been instructed to make the same declaration as the Mensheviks and SRs.

Members of the City Duma have resolved to go unarmed to the Winter Palace Square to see if they can't stop the artillery fire on the palace. The Executive Committee of the Soviet of Peasants' Deputies and the Menshevik and SR fractions have decided to join them.

We are determined to do this, to express our protest against what is happening. We appeal to all who don't want bloodshed to come with us. Perhaps leaving can bring these madmen and criminals to their senses.

[About 75 additional delegates left the hall, accompanied by curses and derisive shouts. Moderate Bolshevik David Riazanov explained that the Soviet's Military Revolutionary Committee was negotiating to end the fighting at the Winter Palace so that further bloodshed might be avoided. The antiwar Bundist Rafail Abramovich then took the podium.[5]]

Abramovich: The Congress must intervene and speak authoritatively about the events unfolding. It is essential that we respond actively to news of the firing on the Winter Palace. I propose that the Congress take decisive steps to end the bloodshed.

Someone retorts: "There is no bloodshed."

Abramovich: I don't know if there has been shooting or not, but 25 minutes ago a message from the Winter Palace said it was under fire and asked that we help those who still remain in the Winter Palace, among whom is a delegation of our own party representatives. I remind you of the severe events of 3–5 July, when our left wing was in similar danger, and we took every step possible to avert that danger.

Someone responds: That's not true!

Abramovich: Yes, it is true. And we must send a delegation to the Winter Palace immediately.

[Abramovich then yielded the tribune to Iulii Martov.]

Martov: The information presented here makes it even more essential that our resolution be considered.

People in the hall, shouting: What information? Who are you trying to frighten? Have you no shame? These are only rumors!

Martov: We've heard more than rumors here! If you go to the windows, you can hear gunfire.

If our congress is going to have real authority, and not just be summoned to suit regulations, then it must answer for today's terrible events. We must adopt a resolution immediately saying that the congress considers peaceful resolution of conflict essential. The congress must say if it wants to end the bloodshed.

[Newspaper accounts summarize what Martov said next. He made a series of accusations against the Bolsheviks for provoking violence and demanded that the congress use its authority to resolve the crisis of power peacefully. He stressed that the congress must negotiate with "all institutions of the revolutionary democracy" to form "a homogenous-democratic ministry," and proposed electing a special delegation to conduct these negotiations. Martov then read the following resolution in the name of the Menshevik-Internationalists and the Jewish Socialist Workers' Party, Poalei-Tsion.]

Martov: Taking into consideration that:

1. This insurrection, which has put power in Petrograd in the Military Revolutionary Committee's hands before the congress opened, was made by the Bolshevik Party alone, as a military conspiracy;
2. This insurrection threatens to cause bloodshed and internecine war and thus the triumph of counterrevolution, which threatens to drown the proletarian movement in blood and destroy the revolution's achievements;
3. The only remaining exit from this situation that can prevent a civil war is agreement between the democracy's insurgent elements and the remaining democratic organizations to form a democratic government, one that includes the entire revolutionary democracy and would peacefully transfer power from the Provisional Government.

The Mensheviks invite the congress to pass a resolution on the need to resolve this crisis peacefully by forming an all-democratic government. The Menshevik-Internationalists propose that the congress appoint a delegation to hold discussions with other democratic organizations and all the socialist parties. The Menshevik-Internationalists ask that the congress suspend its work until results of this delegation's efforts become clear.

[Bolshevik City Duma members then entered the hall and dramatically announced that they had "come to fight and die to with the All-Russian Congress. Trotsky responded to Menshevik, SR, and Menshevik-Internationalist statements.]

Trotsky: An uprising by the popular masses needs no justification. What has happened here is not a conspiracy; it is an insurrection. We tempered the revolutionary steel of Petrograd's workers and soldiers and openly forged the masses' will for an insurrection, not for a conspiracy.

Our uprising has been victorious. Now [the Mensheviks and SRs] tell us, "Renounce your victory. Yield. Compromise." With whom? With whom, I ask, shall we compromise? With those miserable little groups that left? With those who make such proposals? We have seen through them. No one in Russia follows them anymore. And millions of workers and peasants should conclude an agreement with them as equal partners? You are miserable, isolated individuals. Go to where you belong, the dustbin of history!

[According to some accounts, Martov shouted, "Then we'll leave!" and stormed off the platform. Various Menshevik memoirists note that the Menshevik Internationalists did not actually leave the building, but instead held an emergency caucus to plan their next moves. Trotsky, in the meantime, read the following declaration.]

Trotsky: The Second All-Russian Soviet Congress declares:

That the Menshevik and SR delegates' withdrawal from the congress is an impotent and criminal attempt to disrupt the worker and soldier masses' authoritative All-Russian representatives at the very moment that the masses' vanguard, weapons in hand, are defending the congress from counterrevolution's onslaught.

The conciliationist parties, through their own previous policies, have done immense damage to the revolution's cause and hopelessly compromised themselves in the eyes of the workers, peasants, and soldiers.

The conciliationists prepared and approved of the ruinous 18 July offensive that led the army and the country to bloody ruin.

The conciliationists supported the government on the death penalty and betrayed the people.

For seven months, the conciliationists have supported a policy of systematically deceiving the peasants regarding the land question.

The conciliationists supported dismantling revolutionary organizations, disarming workers, introducing Kornilovite discipline in an army, and senselessly continuing the bloody war.

By uniting with the bourgeoisie, the conciliationists helped deepen the country's economic disorganization and doomed millions in the toiling masses to hunger.

Having lost the masses' confidence as a result of these policies, the conciliationists cunningly and unscrupulously retained their positions by preventing reelections in the highest soviet and army organizations.

That is why the Central Executive Committee used every method in an attempt to wreck the soviet congress, with help from conciliationist army committees and direct support from the Provisional Government.

And when the revolutionary classes demanded an end to this wretched bankrupt policy of obstructionism and counterfeit public opinion, when the conciliationist-created Provisional Government fell under pressure from the Petrograd workers and soldiers, when the All-Russian Soviet Congress discovered that the Bolsheviks are the clearly predominant party of revolutionary socialism, when the insurrection obviously unified the revolutionary masses, then the conciliationists made their final exit, tearing away from the soviets, the strength of which torments them.

The conciliationists' withdrawal does not weaken the soviets. It strengthens them by removing a counterrevolutionary stain from the workers' and peasants' revolution.

Having heard the SR and Menshevik declarations, the Second All-Russian Congress continues its work, the goals of which were predetermined by the people's will and by their uprising of 24–25 October.

Down with the conciliationists!
Down with the lackeys of the bourgeoisie!
Long live the victorious workers', soldiers', and peasants' uprising!
Long live the insurgent masses!

[Trotsky's speech drew loud applause and cheers. Several speakers in turn took the podium to protest against the insurrection. Left SR speakers repeatedly echoed Martov's call for an end to bloodshed and talks toward forming a broad-based all-socialist government. The session dragged on into the early hours of 26 October, when word came that the Provisional Government had been arrested. (Kerensky, though, escaped.) Several speakers reported that nearby Northern Front military units fully supported the insurrection. At about 4:00 A.M., Anatoli Lunacharskii read the congress a declaration, "To Workers, Soldiers, and Peasants!" which Lenin had written "on behalf of" the Petrograd Soviet's Military Revolutionary Committee.]

Lunacharskii: To the Workers, Soldiers, and Peasants!

The Second All-Russian Congress of Soviet of Workers' and Soldiers' Deputies has opened. It represents the great majority of soviets. The rule of the conciliationist Central Executive Committee has ended.

Based upon the will of an overwhelming majority of workers, soldiers, and peasants, and on the victorious insurrection of Petrograd's workers and garrison, the congress hereby takes power into its own hands.

The Provisional Government is deposed. The majority of its members are under arrest.

The Soviet government proposes to all peoples an immediate democratic peace and an immediate armistice on all fronts. It guarantees transfer of all landlord, royal, and monastery lands without compensation for disposition by the peasant committees. It will defend soldiers' rights and introduce complete democratization in the army. It will establish workers' control over production. It will ensure the Constituent Assembly's timely convocation. It will supply cities with bread and villages with staple goods.

The congress calls on soldiers in the trenches to be watchful and steadfast. The soviet congress is confident that the revolutionary army knows how to defend the revolution against all imperialist assaults until the new government concludes the democratic peace that it is proposing directly to all peoples.

The new government will take every measure to provide the revolutionary army with all it needs through a resolute policy of requisition and taxation of the propertied classes. It also will improve conditions for soldiers' families.

The Kornilovites—Kerensky, Kaledin, and others—are trying to lead troops against Petrograd. Several units, deceived into action by Kerensky, already have come over to the side of the insurgent people.

Soldiers! Actively resist the Kornilovite Kerensky! Be on guard!

Railwaymen! Stop all troop trains that Kerensky sends against Petrograd!

Soldiers, workers, employees! The fates of the revolution and the democratic peace are in your hands!

Long live the Revolution!

The All-Russian Congress of Soviets of Workers' and Soldiers' Deputies.[6]

[When Lunacharskii finished reading this declaration, the hall burst into applause. Left SR leader Boris Kamkov proposed that the declaration be amended to specify that local land committees would distribute land to peasants. United RSDLP-Internationalists and Poalei-Tsion delegates proposed it be amended "to recognize the necessity of basing the government on the widest possible strata of society." The Ukrainian Social Democrats' representative complained that the declaration did not mention Ukrainian autonomy. An unidentified peasant demanded that it be amended to indicate that the congress included Peasants' Soviet delegates. The congress approved the declaration, with the amendments as offered by the left SRs, Ukrainian Social Democrats (SDs), and the unidentified peasant. (The Internationalist-Poalei-Tsion amendment was rejected.) The session adjourned at 6:00 A.M.]

DOCUMENT 13.2
THE SOVIET CONGRESS DEBATES FORMING A SOVIET GOVERNMENT[7]

On the night of 26–27 October 1917, the Second All-Russian Congress of Soviets discussed the new Soviet regime's first major decrees. Lenin read his "Decree on Peace," which sparked heated debate (particularly among the left SRs and national minority delegates). Next, Lenin read the "Bolshevik" land decree, much of which rephrased the SR land program (a point the left SR delegates made clear). After brief debate over the land decree, the meeting recessed. When it reconvened at 2:00 A.M., the congress discussed forming a new "provisional" government (on the pretense that the Constituent Assembly would create a permanent government). The following document set presents a portion of that discussion, in a composite text based on several contemporary sources. Kamenev read the Bolsheviks' proposal for a new government executive body, the Council of People's Commissars. This is followed by speeches and declarations by Boris Avilov of the United Social Democrat-Internationalists and by left SR, Vladimir Karelin. The document set ends with Trotsky's stinging response to Avilov and Karelin.

[Lev Kamenev, as chair, introduces a decree creating a new government executive body.]

Kamenev: There will be separate collegiums to direct each branch of government activity. The chairmen of these collegiums will be the new government.

[He reads the text.]

The Council of People's Commissars.

The All-Russian Congress of Soviets of Workers', Soldiers', and Peasants' Deputies resolves:

A provisional workers' and peasants' government, to be known as the Council of People's Commissars, is formed to govern the country until the Constituent Assembly meets.

The administration of specific spheres of state activity shall be entrusted to special commissions, whose members will ensure realization of the congress's program in close unison with the workers', soldiers', sailors', peasants', and employees' mass organizations. Government power shall lay in a collegium of these commissions' chairmen, i.e., the Council of People's Commissars.

The All-Russian Congress of Soviets of Workers', Soldiers', and Peasants' Deputies and its Central Executive Committee shall have control over the actions of the [Council of] People's Commissars and the right to overrule its decisions. For the present, the Council of People's Commissars is to be composed of the following people:

Chairman of the Council—Vladimir Ul'ianov (Lenin)
People's Commissar of Internal Affairs—A. I. Rykov
Agriculture—V. P. Miliutin
Labor—A. G. Shliapnikov
For the Military and the Navy—a committee of V. A. Ovseenko (Antonov), N. V. Krylenko, and P. E. Dybenko
Trade and Industry—V. P. Nogin
People's Enlightenment [Public Education]—A. V. Lunacharskii
Finance—I. I. Skvortsov (Stepanov)
Foreign Affairs—L. D. Bronshtein (Trotsky)
Justice—G. I. Oppokov (Lomov)
Provisions Affairs—I. A. Teodorovich
Post and Telegraph—N. P. Avilov (Glebov)
Chairman for Nationality Affairs—I. V. Dzhugashvili (Stalin)
The post of People's Commissar for Railways temporarily remains unassigned.

[After Kamenev finished reading this decree, Boris Avilov spoke on behalf of the United Social Democrat-Internationalists.]

Avilov: The election of [the Council of People's Commissars] predetermines the question of power.[8] At this moment, when the fate of our revolution is being sealed, it is only proper that we ask ourselves calmly, without emotion, what is happening around us and where we are headed.

The ease with which the coalition government was overthrown cannot be explained by the strength of the democracy's left wing, but solely by the fact that the government could not give the people bread and peace. The democracy's left wing can sustain itself only if it solves these two problems. But there are enormous obstacles standing in the way of their solution.

Before all else, the new government must take on these old problems: bread and peace. If it cannot resolve these problems, it will collapse. The new government cannot give the people bread, though, because bread is very scarce and most is in the wealthy and middle peasants' hands. There are only two possible methods of drawing this grain to the cities, industrial centers, and army: either you give the village the industrial products it needs—cloth, iron, leather, agricultural tools, and so on; or you secure the active support of the [wealthy and middle] peasant strata. Taking grain by force is very slow and difficult and could lead to serious complications. At present we cannot supply the villages with industrial products, because there are too few reserves available and too little time to produce more. We don't have enough fuel or raw materials. Productivity in our factories and plants has fallen mightily; anyway, a significant portion of the factories are engaged in defense production. The village can be supplied with the goods it needs only after the war is over and the industrial collapse has been overcome. And we can count on support and sympathy from well-off peasants, who have grain to sell, only if they believe the new government is theirs, that its aims promote their interests.

A government must be formed that will have support from the entire peasantry, not just the poor peasants—a government supported by those who sell grain, as well as those who purchase it. Solving the land question alone cannot guarantee the government's success; poor peasants without tools cannot use the land.

Providing peace will be as difficult, if not more. The Allied powers' governments will refuse to enter into relations with the new government, and in any case will reject its proposal for peace negotiations. Their ambassadors are preparing to leave. This means a break with the Allied powers. The new government will find itself isolated, and its proposals will remain hanging in mid-air. It cannot count on active support from the proletariat or democracy in either the enemy states or the Allied countries, because they are far from a revolutionary struggle and could not even convene the Stockholm [Peace] Conference. The German Social Democrats' left-wing representatives have said very plainly that a revolution cannot be expected in Germany until the war ends.

Russia's growing isolation inevitably will lead to either a German rout of the Russian army and a peace between the Austro-German and Anglo-French alliances at Russia's expense, or a separate peace between Russia and Germany. In either case, the conditions for peace will be burdensome to Russia. And unless we show no resistance to the German conquerors' will, peace will not come soon.

Only the people's majority, if it unites its forces behind these aims, can overcome these incredible difficulties, give the country bread and peace, and preserve the revolution's achievements. At present, however, the leading democratic groups are split into two camps—the left wing at the soviet congress in the Smol'ny Institute, and the right wing gathered at the City Duma that has formed a Committee to Save the Revolution and Country. At the same time, the Kornilovite-Kaledinite reaction is gathering forces and threatens an offensive. To save the revolution, a government must be formed that draws its support from the entire revolutionary democracy, or at least from its majority.

[*Avilov* reads the] Resolution of the United Social Democrat-Internationalists.
Considering that saving the revolution's achievements requires the immediate creation of a government based on the revolutionary democracy, as organized in the workers', soldiers', and peasants' soviets; and recognizing that this government's tasks are to obtain a democratic peace as quickly as possible, transfer land to the land committees for distribution, organize control over production, and convene the Constituent Assembly on the designated date, this congress resolves to elect a Provisional Executive Committee to create a government in agreement with all revolutionary democratic groups represented at the congress.
[Avilov's resolution is rejected by the majority, although it did receive 150 votes in the affirmative. The left SR Vladimir Karelin then took the podium.]
Karelin: Life demands formation of a homogenous democratic government. We support this resolution to create a resolute, direct, firm government of the entire democracy.
[All accounts paraphrase Karelin's next few sentences. He said that a homogenous all-socialist government could not implement policies without support from the parties that left the congress. But Karelin did not consider the Bolsheviks responsible for the moderates' walkout.]
Karelin: In general, the entire revolutionary democracy should be able to unite around the program laid out by the new government. Life has demonstrated this—on the day before the insurrection, when formulas on peace and land were agreed to at the meeting of the Pre-Parliament.[9] But the democracy's two sections were not prepared at all to go forward hand in hand.[10]
[All accounts summarize Karelin's next sentences. He said the left SRs expected that a list of new government commissars would be submitted for approval to a new Central Executive Committee elected by the soviet congress. The list presented by Kamenev would not satisfy the left SRs because it did not include representatives from the peasants' soviets.]
Karelin: We, of course, protest against the fact that instead of temporary committees—which would only pursue temporary answers to the day's urgent questions—we have been presented with a ready-made government.

We do not want to isolate the Bolsheviks, because we understand that the Bolsheviks' fate is inextricably tied to that of the entire revolution; their destruction would be the revolution's destruction.

There could have been some left SRs in the list of the new government's members read aloud here. But had we entered into a coalition, it would have deepened divisions in the revolutionary democracy's ranks. Our task is to find a solution that would include all sections of the democracy.

The left SRs rejected an invitation to enter the cabinet because our presence in a Bolshevist government would create a chasm between the party and those revolutionary army units that left the congress—a chasm that would make it impossible to mediate between those groups and the Bolsheviks. At the moment, the left SRs consider such mediation their chief task and will use all their resources to unite the Bolsheviks with the parties that quit the congress.

[All accounts paraphrase Karelin's next sentences. He reproached the Bolsheviks for arbitrary actions against other socialist parties—local Bolsheviks had closed down the left SR newspaper, *Labor's Banner* (*Znamia truda*) and were violating the free speech of their socialist opponents.]

Karelin: We resolutely declare that we will not tolerate any control over our organization. We will not tolerate any threats against the City Duma, which you want to disband. In general, an aggressive Bolshevik policy toward the other parties is impermissible.

We will support any attempt by the new government to solve the day's urgent problems. But nonetheless, we will vote against formation of a Soviet government.

[Trotsky then took the podium to answer Avilov and Karelin.]

Trotsky: The arguments we have heard here have been leveled against us more than once. We have been warned repeatedly of the left wing's possible isolation. A few days ago, when the question of an insurrection was raised openly, we were told that we were isolating ourselves, that we would meet our ruin. And in the same vein—if the political press came out against the [insurrectionary] class alignment, then the uprising would bring our inevitable ruin. The counterrevolutionaries and all the various defensists stood against us. On the left, only the left SRs joined in courageous work with us in the Military Revolutionary Committee. The others of their sort took a stance of expectant neutrality. And nonetheless, even under these unfavorable conditions, when it seemed everyone had abandoned us, the insurrection was victorious with almost no bloodshed.

If we really were isolated, if all forces really were against us, then how did we achieve victory with almost no bloodshed? No, it was not we who were isolated, but the government and the democrats—or rather, the quasi-democrats. They were isolated from the masses. Through their vacillation, their conciliation, they removed themselves from the ranks of the true democracy. Our great virtue as a party is contained in this fact—we have concluded a coalition of class forces; we have created a coalition of workers, soldiers, and poor peasants.

Political groupings disappear, but fundamental class interests remain. The victorious party, the victorious tendency, is that which can detect and satisfy fundamental class demands. The coalition needed was that of our garrison—made up mostly of peasants—with the working class. We can be proud of such a coalition. It, this coalition, has been tested in the flames of battle. The Petrograd garrison and proletariat came out as one unit in a great struggle that will make it the classical model in the history of all people's revolutions.

We have heard here about the left bloc formed at the Pre-Parliament, but that bloc existed for only one day. Obviously, it was finished before it had begun. Perhaps the bloc was good and the program was good. But all the same, it only took one clash and the bloc flew off to the right.

Comrade Avilov spoke about the great problems that stand before us. To solve all these problems, he proposes to form a coalition. At the same time, he did not disclose the formula: what kind of a coalition—one of groups, of classes, or simply a coalition of newspapers?

As before, those who speak of a coalition, with the old Central Executive Committee, for example, must understand that [this] would help destroy the revolution, not strengthen it. You know that, with the consent of the Central Executive Committee's commissars, we still have no telephone at this moment of intense struggle.

It is said that the schism in the democracy is a misunderstanding. When Kerensky sends shock troops against us, when we are denied telephones with the Central Executive Committee's consent, when we are bearing blow after blow—is it really possible to talk about misunderstandings? If this is a misunderstanding, then I fear all our opponents' statements—Comrade Avilov's and Comrade Karelin's—are also political misunderstandings.

Comrade Avilov tells us that because there is little bread, we need a coalition with the defensists. But will that coalition increase the amount of bread? Certainly the question of bread requires programmatic action. The struggle against disorganization demands a definite system of action, and not just a political grouping.

Comrade Avilov spoke of the peasantry. Again we ask, about which peasants is he speaking? We need to choose between the different peasant elements. Here today—today—a peasants' representative from Tver Province demanded the arrest of Avksent'ev.[11] We need to choose between this Tver peasant, who demand Avksent'ev's arrest, and Avksent'ev himself, who has filled prisons with members of peasant committees. We are with the Tver peasant against Avksent'ev; we are with him until the end and unequivocally.

We reject a coalition with kulak peasant elements. We resolutely reject this in the name of the workers' and poor peasants' coalition. If the revolution has taught us anything, it is that victory can be won only by means of a concord, by a real coalition of these elements. Those who chase after a phantom coalition are absolutely isolating themselves from life. The left SRs will lose the masses' support if they take it into their heads to oppose our party, because any party that opposes the party of the proletariat, which has united with the village poor, isolates itself from the revolution.

We raised the banner of insurrection openly, for all people to see. This insurrection's political formula was All Power to the Soviets through the soviet congress. We are told: you did not wait for the congress. We would have waited, but Kerensky did not want to wait: the counterrevolutionaries did not slumber. As a party, we considered it our task to make it possible for the soviet congress to take power. Were the congress surrounded by Junkers, what means would it have to take power? To achieve that goal, a party was needed that would wrestle power from the grip of the counterrevolutionaries and say to you: "Here is power: it is your responsibility to take it!"

The defensists of all shades fought against us, but we did not stop for them, and we did not give in to them. We proposed that the congress as a whole take power. So, after all this, it takes a distorted perspective to come to this podium and say that we have been irreconcilable! Parties wrapped in a shroud of smoke come to us and say, "We want to govern together," then run off to the City Duma to join with open counterrevolutionaries. They are traitors to the revolution, with whom we will never unite!

To struggle for peace—says Comrade Avilov—a coalition with the conciliationists is necessary. At the same time, he said the allies do not want to conclude peace. But if we unite with those who have betrayed us, then—in Avilov's opinion—all will be well. The marginal democrat Skobelev—comrade Avilov informs us—has been ridiculed by the union of imperialists.[12] But—he advises us—if we secure a bloc with the marginal democrats, then peace will be assured.

There are two paths in the struggle for peace. The first path: the revolution opposes the Allied governments and belligerent countries with moral and material force. The second path: a bloc with Skobelev, which means a bloc with Tereshchenko and complete subservience to imperialism.[13] It has been pointed out that our appeal on peace is directed simultaneously to the governments and to the people. This is just a formal symmetry. We certainly do not think our declaration will influence the imperialist governments. But so long as they exist, we cannot ignore them. We place all our hopes on our revolution unleashing a European revolution. If an insurrection of Europe's people does not crush imperialism, we will be crushed—that is beyond a doubt. Either the Russian revolution raises the whirlwind of struggle in Europe, or the capitalists of all countries will strangle us.

Someone shouts from the floor: There is a third path.

Trotsky: The third path is that taken by the Central Executive Committee. On one hand it sends delegations to the Western European workers, and on the other it forms an alliance with Kishkin and Konovalov.[14] This is a path of lies and hypocrisy, one we will never take.

Of course, we are not saying that there can only be a peace treaty after the European workers' insurrection begins. The bourgeoisie, frightened by the approaching insurrection of all the oppressed, might hurriedly conclude peace. We have given no deadline; it is impossible to envision in concrete form. It is important and necessary to delineate a method of struggle, in principles that apply to foreign and domestic policy equally. An alliance of the oppressed here, there, and everywhere—this is our path.

The Second Congress of Soviets has worked out an entire program of measures. Any group that wants this program realized in deeds and stands on our side of the barricades at this critical moment will be met with only one greeting from our side: "Best wishes, dear comrades. We will take up arms and go with you to the very end!"

[Sources indicate that the audience responded with a prolonged storm of applause.]

DOCUMENT 13.3
A BOLSHEVIK APPEAL AND TWO CARTOONS[15]

The following appeal, "To Russia's Citizens," appeared in the Bolshevik newspaper The Workers' Path (Rabochii put') *on 26 October 1917. It is followed by two cartoons from* Truth (Pravda). *The first, "The Bridge," appeared on 29 October. The second, "The Fate of Foreign Affairs Minister Tereshchenko," ran on 31 October.*

All Power to the Soviets of Workers', Soldiers', and Peasants' Deputies! Peace! Bread! Land!

To Russia's Citizens!

The Provisional Government has been deposed. State power has passed into the hands of the Petrograd Soviet of Workers' and Soldiers' Deputies and its Military Revolutionary Committee, which stand at the head of the Petrograd proletariat and garrison.

The causes for which the people have struggled—immediate proposal of a democratic peace, abolition of the aristocratic landlords' land ownership, workers' control over production, and creation of a Soviet government—these causes will be secured.

Long live the workers', soldiers', and peasants' revolution!

> The Petrograd Soviet of Workers' and Soldiers'
> Deputies' Military Revolutionary Committee

The Bridge. [The young woman is labeled
"The Revolutionary Democracy." The label
"K.-D" refers to the Kadets. The banner on the
building reads, "Constituent Assembly."]

(Dedicated to the memory of the Social-Coalitionists.)

On the way to the Constituent Assembly
You were seduced by a "gentleman"
And—look carefully—
At where he would have taken you!

The bridge over the precipice was nimbly
Crafted from old railroad ties.
You were ready, powerless,
For the Constituent [Assembly] to collapse.

Now we are crossing this precipice
On a bridge of iron
And the working people will be brought
To freedom, truth, and light!

—Dem'ian Bedny

The Fate of Foreign Minister Tereshchenko.
[The puppet's face is Tereshchenko's.]

The Allied capitalists make plans . . ./ The Russian proletariat
disposes of them . . .

DOCUMENT 13.4
THE KADETS ON THE BOLSHEVIK SEIZURE OF POWER[16]

The following document is an editorial from the Kadet's Petrograd newspa-
per Speech (Rech) *on 26 October 1917. Later that day the Bolsheviks shut*
Rech *down and confiscated its printing press. It subsequently reappeared*
under several different titles, each of which the Bolsheviks shut down. Kadet
leaders initially expected the Bolsheviks to collapse quickly, after which the
liberals would emerge as Russia's saviors; they organized strikes by govern-
ment employees against Lenin's government to hasten its fall. By November,
a virtual state of war existed between the Kadets and the Bolsheviks, who
arrested several Kadet leaders and repressed their party organizations.

Petrograd, 26 October.

And so the die is cast. A country exhausted and worried to death by years of war, having survived a revolutionary convulsion, impoverished and led to the final stages of economic and industrial disintegration—a country denied any firm and stable government, a country that has become an arena for anarchistic and riotous movements—this unfortunate, perishing country is performing a new station of the cross.

We already have entered the era of a new experiment: we are vivisecting ourselves. As these lines are being written, we still do not know if the experiment is complete, if in fact all power has been transferred to the soviets, if misters Lenin and Trotsky and their protégés have seized the reins of government. We don't know if Russia still has a government. But we do already know this: a new profound shock has occurred, and its consequences for the country's internal condition and international position are innumerable.

Until recently we did not want to give up hope that our country could escape the crucible of the new experiment. However small this hope, it still seemed to us all that there were limits to blind party fanaticism, beyond which lay the entire country's ruin and the ruin of those "revolutionary achievements" about which so many elevated but dead words have been spoken in these eight months. But this hope proved false. It seems history will repeat itself— and we will not be allowed to forget a single somber and bloody page.

Whatever tomorrow brings, whatever form the government takes and into whomever's hands it falls, it is all absolutely clear that the govern- ment—any government—inevitably must take on the same tasks. These are products of the general aggregate conditions in which we are living, our international situation, our army's condition, our finances, our food supply problems. It will inevitably find that these tasks cannot be accomplished by cheap rhetoric and meetings with empty words, by casting blame and making promises that cannot be fulfilled. This is what awaits misters Lenin and Trotsky if their rebellious designs succeed. Then the country will suffer new convulsions and taste the bitter fruit of political madness and adven- turism—and who knows if it will recover from this new dose of poison.

To the last minute, the Provisional Government understood that it must bear the burden of heavy historical responsibility for the country's fate. We applaud its courageous steadfastness. The government did not capitulate to violence, despite being put in an absolutely horrid, ines- capable situation by the criminal contempt some Petrograd garrison units have shown toward their duty to the country. To the last minute, it believed in the patriotism, honesty, and wisdom of the population's broad strata and appealed to them for support. And if these appeals are in vain—if the government that has called upon the entire country since the February revolution's first days is overthrown—then let all responsibility for the tragic events to come be on the heads of those who, when the motherland faced the greatest deadly danger, plunged her into the abyss of new storms and waves.

DOCUMENT 13.5
THE MENSHEVIK DEFENSISTS ON THE BOLSHEVIK SEIZURE OF POWER[17]

The following document is an editorial condemning the Bolshevik seizure of power from the Petrograd Menshevik Defensist newspaper Unity (Edinstvo) *on 27 October 1917.*

Petrograd, 27 October 1917

A seizure of power has taken place. A civil war has been declared. It has been declared at a desperate moment for Russia, when—it might be said—the armed enemy is at Petrograd's gates.

We will not begin to evaluate these events from a moral perspective. That would be useless. Such events speak for themselves. What faces us is a question not of morality, but of force. In the end, it will be resolved either way through naked force.

The Bolsheviks could realize their plan with little opposition because the masses and a certain segment of the army have become more and more morally deficient. This deficiency had complex causes: the absence of resolute and firm government; exposure of citizens' persons and property to danger; weariness at the prolonged war and, especially, at defeat; and economic disruption tied to food shortages.

The Bolsheviks promised firm power, bread, and an end to the war. Now the time has come to settle accounts. How do matters stand with their promises? Here we shall see.

It is said that the soldiers and sailors listening to Lenin's first speech at the soviet congress were deeply disappointed. We are proposing peace, he said, to all belligerent powers. And what if they reject our conditions? Then what?

Then, it appears, we will go on fighting, not just against Germany and its allies, but also against France, England, and America—or, perhaps, only with the latter. Is that really any better? Is that really what the dark masses expected from the Bolshevik gentlemen?

Lenin promised bread now, bread without delay. But matters stand no better with this promise than with the first promise. On the Bolshevik gentlemen's first day, authoritative institutions like the Food Supply Ministry declared that "under existing conditions, the country and army cannot be supplied with food" and refused to work the Soviet's protégés. Our long-suffering capital city goes hungry from day to day. And we don't need to say any more than that.

Firm power!? To achieve that, a government must rest on the widest possible social foundations, on public organizations of the propertied classes, as well as those of democracy. Not only does no such coalition exist today, but separate government agencies like the Ministries of Labor and Food Supply refuse to submit to the Bolshevik government.

The soviet congress itself did not meet the Bolsheviks' expectations, because an extremely significant portion of the delegates walked out—the representatives of all the socialist parties, front groups, and so on.

The Petrograd City Duma, elected through universal suffrage, has spoken out resolutely against Lenin. And what are Moscow and the provinces saying? What is the overwhelming majority in the trenches saying? What are the Cossacks saying?

One need not be a fortune-teller to predict that the Leninist "experiment" will come to a quick and inglorious end. But in awaiting this end, Russia's citizens cannot and must not remain passive observers. It is their responsibility to help ensure that this "experiment" ends quickly and that the conditions that made the enterprise possible are never replicated.

DOCUMENT 13.6
THE SOCIALIST REVOLUTIONARIES ON THE OCTOBER REVOLUTION[18]

The October Revolution finalized the split in the Party of Socialist Revolutionaries (PSR). On 27 October 1917, the PSR Central Committee expelled the left SRs from the party as punishment for their participation in the Petrograd uprising and for failing to withdraw from the Second Congress of Soviets. The following two documents outline the Socialist Revolutionary Central Committee's attitude toward the Bolshevik insurrection and appeared in The People's Cause (Delo naroda) *on 28 October 1917.*

A Gamble Is Not a Revolution.

As soon as the "proletarian party of Bolsheviks" moved toward victory and tried to seize state power, it became clear that this is not a "workers', soldiers', and peasants' uprising" as the Bolsheviks loudly proclaim, but a successful military conspiracy by some soldiers' regiments and sailors' crews—groups that fell for the political gamblers and fanatics.

A revolution is an insurrection of the *entire people*. It takes place at the state's center, but its victory is secured because it expresses the precepts of the toiling masses' thought, and therefore is supported by *the entire country*. That is what happened in the February Revolution. On the day after its triumph in Petrograd, it was greeted by *all* Moscow, and after that all Russia's cities.

Who has recognized this "second revolution" of Lenin and Trotsky and their ilk? They have deceived small groups of workers, soldiers, and sailors and no one more.

The All-Russian Railroad Workers' Union has refused to transmit the new Bolshevik government's telegrams. One city after another has refused to endorse them or negotiate with them. The All-Russian Soviet of Peasants' Deputies is calling on peasants to struggle against the Bolsheviks. The Party of Socialist Revolutionaries and the Social Democrats—parties that have tremendous countrywide influence and importance—and all the front organizations left the soviet congress, where the Bolsheviks had stacked the deck, and called on all their organizations to struggle actively against the Bolshevik government.

And in Petrograd? Where after the February Revolution thousands joined crowds to celebrate, where workers held meetings and demonstrations and marched down the streets with red flags and victory songs?

In Petrograd, the popular masses are meeting the "second revolution" with tremendous indifference. They are becoming ever more indignant at the gamblers who are playing cards with the revolution's fate. This revolution—if we may call it that—is responsible for a strike in all government offices. The compositors at the state typography have even refused to set the type for *The Provisional Government Bulletin* [*Vestnik Vremennogo pravitel'stvo*], because they do not recognize the Bolshevik government.

Yes, what happened on 24–25 October was not a great workers' revolution—that could be accomplished only after many years of organizing the toiling masses—it was a seizure of power by a clutch of fanatics, and it endangers all the revolution's accomplishments. We are conducting a relentless struggle against this seizure of power, not against a workers', soldiers', and peasants' revolution.

Our Party's Position.

The Bolsheviks' seizure of power in Petrograd has put the revolution in a dangerous situation. On one side, there is the Bolshevist Military Revolutionary Committee, which claims to have started a socialist revolution. On the other, there are the bourgeois classes that are joining up with the counterrevolutionary organizations.

In Petrograd there is a Bolshevik government. In Moscow, Rodzianko and Guchkov are allegedly already organizing a cabinet. On the Don, there is Kaledin's government, and so on and so forth.[19] Finally, Kerensky goes galloping to the army so that it will move against Petrograd. Complete disintegration and decay. A civil war already is developing with all its fury, as is the case in internecine wars.

What line must we follow in these circumstances? Can the revolution still be saved? We think it can be saved only if the entire revolutionary democracy exerts its strength and fully unites in a single, lasting bloc against the Bolsheviks' demagogic lies and against those organizing for counterrevolution.

The Bolsheviks seem to think the other socialist parties did not join them out of "fear to take on legal responsibility for the difficult struggle" and because [we] did not consider the overthrow of Kerensky's government necessary. They are indignant and menacing and threaten us with an "iron gauntlet" because we do not want to share "political responsibility" with them. . . . What is this—hypocrisy or stupidity? We have always rejected Bolshevistic promises, and we won't assume responsibility for their actions. No, Bolshevik gentlemen, you alone must answer for this. If you are angry at others because they do not want to take on your responsibilities, it means you have begun to understand that you cannot fulfill your promises. A few more days' experience and this will be completely clear to you.

The Bolsheviks promised immediate peace. Now they are talking about immediately proposing peace. Only they are forgetting to say openly that their "democratic peace" is possible only after a worldwide socialist revolution.

The Bolsheviks promised immediate transfer of land to the peasantry. As if it weren't obvious that the land that can be snatched away immediately is only enough to suit the needs of the wealthiest and strongest peasants, and the peasant poor—about whom Lenin bangs on and on—will remain without any.

. . . The Bolsheviks promised bread. And now they see for themselves that soon everyone will be without bread.

Although they are still intoxicated by a cheap victory and still imagine they have completed their hard work, the Bolsheviks already can sense the approaching crash. And they are angry that no one is coming to their aid.

No, we will have no part in Bolshevik demagogy. But even less will we be enlisted in the Kaledinite repression. We cannot go along with Kaledin and Rodzianko against soldiers and workers; that would be no more than a substitution for Bolshevik demagogy . . .

What is necessary now? A homogenous socialist ministry, without Bolsheviks or propertied elements, with the following program:

1. Liquidation of the Bolshevist adventure, which will burst like a soap bubble at the first prick by a hard fact.
2. Transfer of all agriculturally significant land to the land committees' authority.
3. An energetic policy to speedily conclude peace with no annexations or indemnities on the principle of the national self-determination.
4. Urgent convocation of the Constituent Assembly. Only such a government can stave off civil war. Only such a government can rally those in the toiling democracy whom the Bolshevik demagogues have not dazzled, as well as those who have begun to come to their senses and understand the true cost of the Bolsheviks' promises.

DOCUMENT 13.7
A MENSHEVIK APPEAL "TO THE PETROGRAD WORKERS!"[20]

On 28 October 1917 the Central Committee of the Russian Social Democratic Labor Party (RSDLP) (United)—the main Menshevik faction—met to discuss ways to overturn the new Bolshevik regime. That meeting approved the following document, an appeal "To the Petrograd workers!" The appeal appeared the next day in The Workers' Newspaper (Rabochaia gazeta). *The Bolsheviks responded by shutting down* The Workers' Newspaper, *which then reappeared under different titles.*

To the Petrograd Workers!

Comrades! Petrograd, and the entire country with it, is living through a terrible moment. A new blow has been struck against the revolution—not a blow to the back by General Kornilov, but a blow to the chest by Lenin and Trotsky.

On the eve of the Constituent Assembly, when everyone should have been discussing the elections to secure liberty, the Bolshevik Party led by Lenin and Trotsky hatched a plot to seize power. Without even waiting for Congress of Soviets of Workers' and Soldiers' Deputies to open, this party initiated a military conspiracy, kept secret from the other socialist parties and revolutionary organizations, and used bayonets and rifles to carry out an insurrection against the state.

They began by using rifles to disperse the Provisional Council of the Russian Republic [the Pre-Parliament], which had been created at the will of the All-Russian Democratic Conference. When it was made clear that a gathering of socialist parties was in progress, they did not stop. They sent soldiers—who they've made into fools—to threaten the Winter Palace, where the Provisional Government was gathering. They committed violence against the government's members, which included the socialists, and imprisoned them in the Peter-Paul Fortress. Not embarrassed by protests from the majority of workers', soldiers', and peasants' organizations, who abandoned the soviet congress, the Bolshevik Party declared themselves the government, and now they seek to subordinate the entire country. We had predicted exactly this. We have always warned about the Bolsheviks.

Bolshevik rule will not lead to the things they have promised the masses. There will not be peace, bread, or freedom, but the opposite. Peace, bread, and freedom can be obtained only by rallying all the democracy's forces, through their organizational efforts, by consolidating revolutionary order in the country.

The country has been ruined by three years of war. Kaiser Wilhelm's troops have penetrated deep into our territory and already threaten Petrograd. Great caution is needed. Every step must be measured. All the people's strength must be rallied so that the country does not fall into a deadly abyss. It is against this ruined country, where the working class is still an insignificant minority, where the people have only just been liberated from centuries of autocratic slavery—it is against this country and at this critical moment that the Bolsheviks planned and carried out their mad experiment at seizing power, which they allege to be a socialist revolution.

Only adventurers or traitors to the revolution would do this. The working class did not have a direct role in this mad undertaking. At the moment the Bolsheviks seized power, they revealed their powerlessness, because they could only do it by bayonet. A government that depends on bayonets alone is guaranteed to fail. A government that depends on bayonets is doomed to employ the tsarist autocracy's methods.

[If the government is to last], it must follow the only correct path—the path our party has walked, that the Soviet Central Executive Committee has walked. That is the path of unifying the entire democracy to defend the country and the revolution's accomplishments. That is the path toward the quickest possible universal peace, in alliance with the entire international proletariat. We need not deceive ourselves. We still support the persistent and systematic struggle for socialism. But first we must save the revolution's achievements; we must save the country from destruction and ruin.

At present what is most necessary is to guarantee *the Constituent Assembly's convocation* on the designated date. It alone can create a lasting revolutionary government and satisfy the people's dreams. We now must concentrate all our thought and efforts on this task.

The Bolsheviks are resurrecting the very worst features of the tsarist autocracy: they are silencing the press, destroying free assembly, and violating personal security. They have threatened to disband and repress democratic city governments that were elected on the basis of universal suffrage.

Such a government elicits only hatred and revulsion. The Bolsheviks allegedly act in the name of socialism, but they have only soiled the Socialist banner and turned the popular masses away from socialism. To prevent this—so that the people do not hold the *working class and socialism* responsible for all the Bolsheviks' crimes—conscious workers must decisively *fence themselves off* from the Bolshevist undertaking. They must reveal to the worker masses all the falsehoods and demagogy of the Bolsheviks, who have bedazzled the worker masses with flattery and promises that cannot be fulfilled.

The Bolsheviks' defeat is inevitable. But we cannot let it become the working class' defeat. Were the working class ruined and defeated, it would mean counterrevolution's triumph. This must not happen.

For this reason, *it is necessary to stop* the rising and worsening *civil war* that will trample the revolution and lead inevitably to the proletariat's defeat and the victory of German imperialism and Russian counterrevolution. It is necessary to rally around democratic self-government institutions and the *All-Russian Committee for the Salvation of the Motherland and Revolution*, and by these means prevent a bloody confrontation.[21]

Comrades, this hour may decide the revolution's fate, the fate of your freedom, which was purchased by several generations' struggles, and the fate of the working class in the years to come. We appeal to your conscience and self-control. Do not give in to provocations. Exert all of your effort to prevent a bloody confrontation and civil war. Remember that we need to guarantee the Constituent Assembly's convocation. In the name of that cause, rally around the Committee for the Salvation of the Revolution and Motherland.

The Central Committee of the RSDLP (United)

DOCUMENT 13.8
THE TRUDOVIK POPULAR-SOCIALISTS CALL FOR
PUBLIC ACTION AGAINST THE BOLSHEVIKS[22]

Like the Kadets, Mensheviks, and Socialist Revolutionaries, the Trudovik Popular-Socialists called on Russia's people to oppose the Bolsheviks. The following document is an appeal that filled the entire front page of The People's Word (Narodnoe slovo) *on 29 October 1917. The Petrograd Soviet's Military Revolutionary Committee shut down* Narodnoe slovo *later that day. Like other opposition newspapers, it then appeared intermittently under different titles.*

Down with the Bolsheviks! Save the Country and the Revolution!
To all for whom the achievements of the people's freedom are dear, to all who love the country in deeds and not just in words—All to her defense, all against the Bolsheviks!

No conciliation with the enemies of the revolutionary people!

Down with the tyrants, the fraudulent usurpers of power! Power must not remain in their hands for one more minute!

Soldiers and workers of Petrograd!

Do not belief the Bolsheviks, do not believe what they are promising you. They are deceiving you. They will give the exhausted people no peace, no bread, no land.

The entire Russian democracy is against them. All Russia is against them. Can you really be against Russia, against the Democracy, against the entire Russian people?

NO! You are revolutionary soldiers, you are workers—loyal friends of freedom who cannot go against your own brothers. You must drop the Bolsheviks!

Citizens! The enemy is not slumbering! He is ready to take advantage of our weakness. He is ready to strike us a new blow, new humiliations, new grief for the entire people. And if this happens—there will be no quick peace, there will be no freedom, there will be no land.

PETROGRAD SOLDIERS AND WORKERS! WE DO NOT NEED BLOODSHED! WE DO NOT NEED CIVIL WAR! LAY DOWN YOUR WEAPONS! The Provisional Government's troops are your brothers. They have come in the name of all Russia to defend the motherland and freedom from the Bolsheviks.

All to the motherland's defense! All to freedom's defense! The Bolsheviks are destroying Russia! Down with the tyrants!

No conciliation with the revolutionary people's enemies! They are calling for bloodshed and for civil war, and they must remain isolated. If blood already has been spilled, and if blood continues to be spilled—the blame falls on their heads. The people curse those who would encroach on the motherland's freedom and integrity.

DOCUMENT 13.9
THE MOSCOW MENSHEVIKS' APPEAL TO
"COMRADE CITIZENS!"[23]

A bloody confrontation over power took place in Moscow on 27 October–2 November 1917. The city's Bolsheviks had not prepared for an insurrection and were slow to organize a Military Revolutionary Committee. In contrast, the moderate socialists in the Moscow City Duma quickly formed a well-organized and well-armed Committee of Public Safety. When fighting between the two factions broke out on 27 October, the Committee of Public Safety initially dominated the conflict. The tide turned, though, after Red Guards and volunteers from other cities rushed to Moscow to aid the local Bolsheviks on 28 October. By 2 November the Bolsheviks claimed Soviet control over Moscow and thousands of people had been killed and wounded. The following document appeared in the Menshevik's Moscow newspaper Forward! (Vpered!) *on 30 October 1917, during a brief cease-fire in the fighting.*

Comrade Citizens!
The irreconcilable positions taken by supporters of both belligerents—the Duma Committee of Public Safety and the Bolshevist Revolutionary Committee—have already borne bitter fruit. Fraternal blood has been spilled needlessly. Moscow has added to the dead and wounded.

Comrade Workers! Comrade Soldiers! You who follow the Bolshevist Revolutionary Committee! Understand that it cannot achieve victory, because it is isolated from the rest of the democracy, from the workers and soldiers. Even should it win—at the cost of blood and corpses—it cannot hold power and will be replaced by organized counterrevolutionaries.

Citizens who hope for the Committee of Public Safety's victory, the armed suppression of the mad Bolsheviks, and the revolution's salvation! Understand that bloody massacres will open the gates wide for counter-revolution! There is a reason Kornilov's evil specter has appeared again on the horizon!

Comrades and citizens! The revolution will perish in the flames of civil war! We cannot let that happen—it must be brought to an end!

Enough blood! Enough victims!

A cease-fire has been formally declared, but in fact is being violated—let this be transformed into an actual peace agreement!

Comrades and citizens! All who are for conciliation, all who want to end this bloody internecine fighting—pressure the faction that you follow, and demand that it bring an end to the civil war.

All democratic organizations—focus all your efforts on creating a general-democratic government that can maintain revolutionary order!

The Committee of the Moscow Organization of the RSDLP
(Mensheviks)

DOCUMENT 13.10
THREE ANARCHIST EDITORIALS ON SOVIET POWER[24]

Although there were relatively few anarchists in Petrograd in October 1917, they constituted an important element in the left-socialist coalition and in Petrograd Soviet's Military Revolutionary Committee. The anarchists soon fell afoul of Lenin's government, because they rejected all forms of state power, including Lenin's "proletarian dictatorship." For his part, Lenin was even more suspicious of the anarchists than of the right socialist opposition. By late December, anarchists were targets of the new Soviet repressive apparatus, the Extraordinary Commission for Struggle against Counterrevolution (Cheka). The three editorials that follow reflect the anarchists' radical social program and their rejection of all government power. The first, "Anarchy is the Mother of Order," appeared in the Moscow newspaper Anarchy (Anarchiia) *on 26 October 1917. The second is from the Petrograd Anarchist newspaper* Labor's Voice (Golos truda) *on 1 November. The third, "Not for Anyone!" appeared in Petrograd's* The Storm Petrel (Burevestnik) *on 14 November.*

Anarchy Is the Mother of Order.

A socialist revolution needs a set period to develop. The revolution begins with the collapse of the autocracy and political power and must end in the collapse of capitalism at every factory, and the struggle against all government, for a free commune. In contrast to bourgeois chaos—with its conquest based on oppression and the exploitation by one man over another—the will of freely organized equals must reign, a new world of free comrades and free workers must be created, a free union of free communes.

Above all else, revolution is great happiness, universal exaltation in expectation of a new life. No pogroms, no excesses, no victims or blood-shed, despite the *extreme* necessity for self-defense. No greedy grabbing! Organized redistribution to each according to his needs, but no more.

Comrades, to this end there must be an *immediate registration* of all property—food, clothes, and housing—and of the number of consumers. This work must be carried out immediately by special initiative groups, or better still, by designated committees of toilers from every enterprise— from the factory committees, the district and all-city unions, and the councils of factory committees. We must use all the information collected by the duma and provisions committees.

Long live revolutionary order! Long live the anarchist commune!

[Editorial in *Labor's Voice*]
... Nothing reveals the diametric opposition between a "seizure of power" and a "social revolution" better than the current disputes among the Bol-sheviks themselves and popular opposition to the government of "People's Commissars." This confirms Anarchism's fundamental principle: the action of parties is no substitute for a social revolution. The Bolsheviks— particularly Lenin and Trotsky—must either admit this truth, abandon the road to power, and follow the road to stateless communism, or fall back to conciliation (that is, reverse the revolution's course). A seizure of political power will inevitably strangle the revolution.

Not for Anyone!
Wretched of the villages and towns, we summon you to independence and to struggle! All power—to anarchy—and thus, to *no one*!
... The Bolshevik Party's banner is a lie. They are resurrecting the old regime.

The Constituent Assembly will be the sword-bearer of the oppressors.

There is too much state intervention. Not one party is offering you "Land and Factories." "Land and Factories" are not being seized by force. This is the workers and peasants cause alone. None of the world's governments will give them to you. The future depends on the soldiers and sailors.

No government will give you liberty. It cannot be given. Liberty must be won through bloody effort.

Building life for all in common takes precedence to individual needs.

All representation restrains freedom. Participating in elections is equivalent to betraying the people. Therefore, don't be confused by party appeals, and boycott the Constituent Assembly elections.

You are the key to the future. Refuse to vote!

DOCUMENT 13.11
ZINOVIEV ON THE BOLSHEVIKS' REJECTION
OF AN ALL-SOCIALIST COALITION[25]

On 3 November 1917, it fell to Bolshevik moderate Grigorii Zinoviev—who had opposed the Bolshevik seizure of power and called for a socialist coalition government—to explain to the Petrograd Soviet why his party would not be entering into such a coalition. Negotiations organized by the railroad union, Vikzhel, had come close to an agreement between the left and moderate socialist parties. The moderates set preconditions for a coalition that most on the left could accept, such as ending press censorship and granting amnesty to arrested Provisional Government members. They also had insisted on excluding Lenin and Trotsky from the government. The Bolshevik Central Committee's majority rejected these conditions and hardened its position with the 2 November Bolshevik victory in Moscow. At that day's Soviet Central Executive Committee session, the Bolsheviks responded to left SR demands for a coalition with their own list of preconditions, which were, in effect, poisoned pills. The following document is Zinoviev's statement to the Petrograd Soviet on 3 November, which faithfully relayed the Central Committee's position (and which ran counter to his own views).

Yesterday the [left] Socialist Revolutionaries gave the Bolshevik fraction an ultimatum on the need for conciliation. They threatened that if we did not agree, they would discontinue joint work with us. You know that at the soviet congress, the Bolsheviks already proposed that the [left] Socialist Revolutionaries enter the government. They did not accept this proposal then. This was not our fault.

Yesterday the great majority in the Central Executive Committee voted to continue negotiations with the socialist parties under the following conditions: The Central Executive Committee must include 100–150 representatives from the Workers' and Soldiers' Soviets; 75 peasants' representatives from the provincial soviets, whom we insisted be authentic representatives of the poor peasantry and not Avksent'ev's men (the sort who arrested the land committees); 80 men from military units and the navy, but not from the army committees; 25 representatives from the united all-Russian trade unions; 10 from Vikzhel; 5 from the postal-telegraph employees; and 50 from the Petrograd City Duma's socialist section. The entire program must remain Soviet. The government must answer to [the Central Executive Committee]. Under all circumstances, Bolsheviks must hold the posts of ministers of foreign affairs, internal affairs, and labor. Petrograd and Moscow Soviet plenipotentiaries will command the Petrograd and Moscow garrisons.

It is unclear with whom we are supposed to negotiate. I think sections of the SRs and Mensheviks will not accept our conditions. But we will not back down. Those who do not accept the program set out by the soviet congress must be excluded.

DOCUMENT 13.12
MENSHEVIK-INTERNATIONALIST AND LEFT SOCIALIST
APPEALS AGAINST A ONE-PARTY DICTATORSHIP[26]

The following documents are appeals printed in the Petrograd Menshevik-Internationalist newspaper, The Spark (Iskra), *on 5 November 1917—two days after Bolshevik leaders torpedoed the all-socialist negotiations. The first appeal, "To All!" filled the newspaper's entire first page; it seems to have been drafted before the Bolshevik victory in Moscow. The second, "To Workers, Soldiers, and Peasants!" was issued jointly by the Menshevik-Internationalists, left SRs, United Social Democrat-Internationalists, the Polish Socialist Party (the "Levitsy"), and the Jewish Socialist Workers' Party (Poalei-Tsion), and probably was drafted on 4 November 1917.*

TO ALL!
Blood is flowing. . . . A civil war is under way. The country has no government. The army does not know who commands it. The Kremlin, embodiment of Russian history, is being bombarded by heavy artillery. Inhabitants anxiously expect pogroms. Petrograd is cut off from Russia and the entire world. No one knows what tomorrow will bring.

In Moscow, Petrograd, and at the front there is no bread. We all face starvation. Because recent events have disrupted rail traffic and the urban economy, there are street disorders and violence by one group of the citizens against another. Because the post and telegraphs are not working, there is no way to communicate with other provinces to find bread. The peasants—intimidated by news of bloody goings-on in the cities—have stopped delivering foodstuffs. At the same time, Kaledin—anticipating the final long-awaited hour—has seized the Southern Railroad to deprive the capital of grain and coal.

Petrograd and Moscow Workers and Soldiers! This is about saving all our causes: salvation of the revolution and the democracy, of freedom and peace. Can't you see now that one-party rule, even if it rests upon the soviet congress and can rely upon 50,000 bayonets and our self-sacrifice, nonetheless cannot manage the tasks of revolutionary power when the country is utterly exhausted, the German army is near our capital, and the internal enemy has forces poised to destroy the revolution?

We, the internationalists . . . again propose the same demand that we laid out on the [soviet] congress's first day: End the conflict through an agreement of the entire democracy.

The All-Russian Railroad Workers' Union's initiated a conference between representatives of all the socialist parties toward this goal. The Party of Socialist Revolutionaries and the Mensheviks agreed to form a government that includes all socialist parties—from the Bolsheviks to the Popular-Socialists. *But the Bolshevik Party, enraptured by military success in Petrograd, demanded conditions for an agreement that made conciliation impossible.* The civil war and ruin will not stop.

The Bolshevik Party wants the new government to answer to the Central Executive Committee, which means to the Bolsheviks. This would mean that, although the government would include socialists from other parties, it would only carry out Bolshevik policies. *And Bolshevik policies are not accepted by a large part of the peasantry and the urban poor or by sections of the army at the front.* Even if SRs and Mensheviks served on it, the peasants and all civil servants in state institutions would boycott such a government, just like the current Leninist [government]. Therefore it also could not master the supply problem or economic disruption, the struggle against Kaledin, or the task of preventing the entire front's collapse. Such a government, like Lenin's, would not provide the capital with bread. Because of its inadequacies, it would not secure peace, convene the Constituent Assembly, or implement the law on the land committees.

The country can only be saved from the ruinous recent policy of adventurism by an authentic cooperative government of the entire democracy. Such a government must rest upon the entire democracy—the Workers' and Soldiers' Soviets, the Peasantry, the City Dumas, the front organizations, and the trade unions. No one party can have a majority in such a government. No one party can lord it over the other parties. They all must agree to work together to defend the country from collapse in the weeks until the Constituent Assembly's convocation. This is the most important thing. Workers and soldiers will have confidence in that government, because they will know that it will conduct an honest policy of peace and freedom because it does not include the bourgeoisie. And it will have the confidence of the democratic strata, because they will know that it does not include adherents of parties that would consolidate power through terror, that it will not be a government of civil war.

Only such a government can raise the forces needed to silence Kaledin and the other counterrevolutionaries and enjoy the full support of all cities and counties in the struggle against them.

Comrade Workers and Soldiers! Making such a coalition possible now depends entirely on the Bolsheviks, who control power in Petrograd. Demand this of them! Strive so that Petrograd does not become an armed camp where violence rules, where all civic life dies, and where the smallest spark can ignite a horrible fire! Demand that Lenin's government transfer power to a government of the entire united democracy.

Long live the revolution!
Long live the democracy!
Long live peace!

—The editors of *The Spark*

To Workers, Soldiers, and Peasants! The revolution is in danger!

The government, created by a portion of the soviet congress, on ground already prepared by an insurrection in Petrograd, is purely Bolshevistic. It cannot win approval from the entire organized democracy. It will be deprived of adequate support in the country as a government of one party alone.

A schism in the democracy's ranks induces its right elements, who still have not realized the full bankruptcy of their coalition policies, into a new rapprochement with the propertied classes.

All this makes the counterrevolution's work easier. Under the pretext of crushing the Bolshevist insurrection, the counterrevolutionaries are mobilizing all their forces to strangle the revolution. Civil war, which threatens the country with awful convulsions and bloodshed, will lead to democracy's wasting away and the revolution's ruin.

Under these conditions only a revolutionary-democratic government, created and supported by all sections of the organized democracy, can manage with economic devastation, lead the country to peace, resolve the land question, and secure the Constituent Assembly's convocation.

We appeal to both camps of the revolutionary democracy with a resolute demand that they cooperate in the name of creating a unified democratic government able to rebuff the propertied classes' counter-revolutionary coalition. We appeal to both camps of the democracy with a resolute demand that they resurrect a united revolutionary front, so that the revolution will not choke on the blood of soldiers, workers, and peasants.

The Menshevik-Internationalists
The Left Socialist Revolutionaries
The United Social Democrat-Internationalists
The Polish Socialist Party (Levitsa)
The Jewish Social Democratic Labor Party (Poalei-Tsion)

DOCUMENT 13.13
AN ANTI-BOLSHEVIK EDITORIAL FROM SMOLENSK[27]

On 30 October 1917, the Smolensk Soviet's left faction battled the Smolensk City Duma's moderate socialists and liberals for control of the city. Unable to vanquish one another, the two camps agreed to a truce and formed a joint Committee of Public Safety.[28] These events took place during a printers' strike that closed the newspaper, The Smolensk Bulletin (Smolenskii vestnik) *from 26 October–4 November. Therefore the newspaper's editor, Socialist Revolutionary activist Solomon Gurevich, had no chance to publish his reaction to the Bolshevik seizure of power until 5 November. The following document is his first editorial on the October insurrection.*

Smolensk, 5 November.
Crimes.

In the dark shadows of bloody Bolsheviks' criminal activity—the dirty stain reveals only the most disgraceful crimes—are crimes against the shining principles of democracy and socialism. We are speaking of Bolshevik violence against democratic dumas. We are speaking of the shocking ignorance that Bolshevik criminals have demonstrated universally—in the capitals and in the provinces—regarding the rights of authorized representatives, representatives invested with entire local population's full confidence. We are speaking of the shelling of duma buildings in Moscow, Smolensk, and Saratov.

We maintain that, in committing these unspeakable crimes, the Bolsheviks have trampled one of the revolutionary democracy's most valuable and reliable achievements in the blood-spattered mud. Isn't it clear to all democrats, revolutionaries, and socialists that democratic self-government is the foundation of a democratic order, the bulwark of public rights? Don't we all understand that without *local* public representation, elected by the entire local population, no democratic government can implant democratic order? That the Constituent Assembly—our all-national representation—would produce fruitless, lifeless decrees? And don't we know that democratic self-government is instrumental to consolidating a democratic order, which is why right reactionary elements have been against it from the start? None of the elements, or lies, or slanders that confronted it could undermine the authority of democratic self-government. And now the Bolsheviks have come to aid the reactionary clique—come with their bloody-violent methods of struggle, with their *Pugachevshchina.* . . .[29]

They have done everything that one hoping to serve old Russia could have wanted. With their criminal demagogy—setting the soviets against "counterrevolutionary" dumas, shelling duma buildings, inciting the semiconscious masses against democratic self-government—they inculcate the masses with the false idea that the duma is a reactionary, antiproletarian citadel. And now they are celebrating their victory, together with "autocracy's lackeys," over the ruined foundations of a new Russia that the revolutionary democracy had built after so many hardships and sacrifices.

Yes, we know how the Bolsheviks justify their shameful campaign against democratic self-government. We know that they have armed themselves for this campaign with arguments from the old arsenal of Plehve and

Sipiagin.[30] Self-government, they say, should manage purely economic local affairs—political struggles and state affairs are not its concern. But isn't that not just stupid, but also hypocritical? It is hypocritical because in their own duma campaign slogans they, the Bolsheviks, howled about state affairs. Didn't they talk about peace, land, social reform, the socialist ministry, the Kadet ministers' crimes, the reactionary Kerensky, etc. at preelection meetings?

Oh, the Bolsheviks assure the duma that if it does not oppose their antidemocratic adventure, which will ruin the workers' cause and the revolution, then it can participant legally in politics and state affairs. That kind of disgraceful political morality was in vogue in the "good old days." When "unreliable" zemstvos and dumas tried to break the chain of "local benefits and needs" that bound them, they were told "hands off!" Whenever they touched upon state matters, they were punished and disbanded. "Reliable" dumas and zemstvos faithfully avoided prohibited state matters. . . .

The horror of the situation is that the Bolsheviks are inoculating the masses with the disgraceful morality of a disgraced past. They are introducing it to crowds of people. And by the time the All-National Constituent Assembly gathers (that is, if it gathers), the Bolsheviks will have made the masses so depraved that they will apply Bolshevist measures to the Constituent Assembly, with Bolshevik cannons and rifles . . .

After this, can we still talk of conciliation with the Bolsheviks? After the scorn the Bolsheviks have shown and the violence they have committed against the democratic duma, can we treat them as democrats? As carriers and disseminators of shining proletarian ideas and ideals? Aren't all parties, all organizations, all political activists who stand for revolutionary socialism obliged to reject those who would stain our shining democratic ideals, drown our bloodless revolution in torrents of blood, and undermine the All-National Constituent Assembly?

DOCUMENT 13.14
ZINOVIEV DEFENDS THE OCTOBER INSURRECTION[31]

In early November 1917, the Socialist Revolutionaries organized an All-Russian Congress of Peasants' Deputies, hoping to mobilize peasants against the Bolsheviks. At this congress's first preliminary session on 10 November, Bolsheviks and left SR delegates split off and formed their own "Extraordinary All-Russian Congress of Peasants' Deputies." On 13 November, the Bolsheviks and left SRs reached an agreement on expanding the composition of the All-Russian Soviet Central Executive Committee. (Until 9 December, though, the left SRs refrained from joining the Council of People's Commissars.) The following document is a brief report that Grigori Zinoviev presented to the Extraordinary Congress of Peasants' Deputies on 12 November 1917. Lenin deliberately selected

Zinoviev—who had publically criticized plans for a conspiratorial insurrection and was a vocal advocate of an all-socialist coalition—to refute charges that the Bolsheviks had seized power through a conspiracy and to explain why an all-socialist coalition was impossible.

[Menshevik leader Irakli] Tsereteli, speaking at a zemstvo conference, declared that the Mensheviks have made every effort to resolve the conflict peacefully and are not to blame if an agreement is not reached. To this, I say that a peaceful solution was possible at the First All-Russian Soviet Congress [in June]. But the Mensheviks and right SRs would not recognize that Soviet power alone could save the country. The moment was missed.

The *Kornilovshchina* again glaringly underscored the need to abandon conciliation. But the conciliationists continued their criminal policy; they believed the solution was to convene the Democratic Conference. We Bolsheviks said from the very beginning that this assembly could do nothing for the country, and we left the Conference. Our comrades, the left SRs, found it necessary to remain, and thus enabled the conciliationist policy's continuation.

We are accused of carrying out a political conspiracy, and it is said that we are prepared for a civil war. But everyone knows that Kerensky's coalition government did nothing to actualize the peasantry's fondest desire—their right to the land. It is natural that the peasantry is rallying more and more around the Soviet government, the government of workers, soldiers, and peasants, which alone can fulfill their desires. The overthrown government could not implement other necessary reforms. It could not establish control over production, defend workers from unemployment, and so on. So an insurrection began. This was a people's insurrection, and only our enemies would accuse the Bolsheviks of a political conspiracy.

Now we are criticized for opposing rapprochement with the socialist parties. Allegedly, we did not want it—this is not true. I was one of those who stood up for an agreement with the socialist parties. But the defensists and conciliationists prevented an agreement with their preconditions—publication of bourgeois newspapers and liberation of arrested former ministers (Tereshchenko, Konovalov, etc.). Although they allegedly wanted an agreement, they distributed leaflets calling for opposition to the new government and approved employees' efforts to sabotage institutions. For us, agreement with them is impossible.

To all who agree to implement the program of the Second All-Russian Soviet Congress, we say: Welcome!

CHAPTER FOURTEEN
FLASH POINTS OF CONFLICT: THE CONSTITUENT ASSEMBLY

14.1
THREE CITIZENS' LETTERS TO SOVIET GOVERNMENT AUTHORITIES, OCTOBER 1917–JANUARY 1918

14.2
A JOINT SOCIALIST APPEAL "TO ALL CITIZENS!"

14.3
AN APPEAL FROM THE UNION FOR THE DEFENSE OF THE CONSTITUENT ASSEMBLY

14.4
TWO LEFT SOCIALIST REVOLUTIONARY RESOLUTIONS ON THE CONSTITUENT ASSEMBLY

14.5
A PROVINCIAL SOVIET CONGRESS ON THE SOVIET GOVERNMENT AND THE CONSTITUENT ASSEMBLY

14.6
LENIN, "THESES ON THE CONSTITUENT ASSEMBLY"

14.7
IULII MARTOV, "THE REVOLUTION AND THE CONSTITUENT ASSEMBLY"

14.8
SPEECHES AT THE ALL-RUSSIAN CONSTITUENT ASSEMBLY

14.9
THE SOVIET DECREE DISBANDING THE CONSTITUENT ASSEMBLY

14.10
THE SOCIALIST REVOLUTIONARIES CALL FOR "ALL POWER TO THE CONSTITUENT ASSEMBLY!"

14.11
THE LEFT SOCIALIST REVOLUTIONARIES ON THE CONSTITUENT ASSEMBLY'S DISSOLUTION

14.12
BORIS KRICHEVSKII, "EITHER-OR"

THREE CITIZENS' LETTERS TO SOVIET GOVERNMENT AUTHORITIES, OCTOBER 1917–JANUARY 1918[1]

After the Soviet Union's collapse, historians gained access to previously secret archival collections of letters ordinary citizens had written to Soviet government officials and Bolshevik Party leaders. Although written to be read by individuals and not for a wider audience, such documents give us a glimpse at what people might have said to one another in political discussions on the street, at work, or in their homes.

The following document set presents three such letters. The first was sent to the Petrograd Soviet by a soldier named M. Venediktov in Pskov Province. It bears no date, but the content suggests that it was written between 25 October and 12 November 1917. The second—an anonymous letter to Lenin—was in an envelope with a stamp cancelled on 15 November 1917 in the Ukrainian city of Ekaterinoslavl' (now called Dnepropetrovsk). The third, an undated letter to the Council of People's Commissars, was marked "received" on 8 December 1917. The signature is illegible. In the first and third letters, the authors use the very formal polite mode of address, the capitalized second person plural "You" (similar to "Vous" in French).

Pskov Province, Kholm County
To the Petrograd City Soldiers', Peasants', and Workers' Soviet Central Executive Committee

Esteemed Comrades.

I appeal to You as one who stands on guard in defense of our dear free motherland and our Revolution's accomplishments. For several days I left the front for the village, where I found many lies. As a soldier in the mighty revolutionary Russian army who wants the best for our dear motherland, the horror of all this drives me to despair. Men in the villages are ignorant, but no one is teaching them. Surely the present will decide the country's fate, its life and death. At this difficult hour I appeal to You, esteemed comrades, with a passionate plea: would it be impossible to send workers to educate our dark villagers? Surely, there soon will be elections to the Constituent Assembly, which needs people who will consider the entire people's interests and express its will. But the village will elect *burzhui* monarchists and whomever the landlords choose. The villagers will not be able to grasp the complex issues on the table. We had elections for the township zemstvo here, and who got sent to it? The landlords and capitalists. I will explain to You how this came to be. The peasant men did not put forward their own candidates. But candidates had already been chosen long before the elections. And our administrators, using threats, forced the men to cast their ballots. And [illegible] how they voted—take one look and that is clear.[2] And so I think this will also happen with the Constituent Assembly elections.

> I remain always ready and at Your service, Mikhail Venediktov, 91st Infantry, Dvinsk Regiment.

[Anonymous to Lenin]

Can't you find time to worry about and include instructions on posting guards in the shrapnel of decrees you have complied!?

Obviously foreign gold, raked out of profits and interest, comes before order in the capital and its inhabitants' welfare!

Where is the peace that was promised?—Is it possible that those who had fraternized with the enemy now fear its cannons or that their disarmed brother-citizens will be robbed, wounded, or trampled? . . .

Where is the bread that was promised?—There is a lot somewhere, but we don't have it!

Where is the land that was promised?—Will it be in equal lots for every citizen, in the cemetery?

These are 3 questions to which not a single soldier or worker will receive an answer from this government of boors.

To the Council of People's Commissars.

Take steps so that here, there, and everywhere in every corner of our immense motherland of the people, the toilers are informed of all Your actions for the betterment of all toiling peoples.

Bourgeois and lying socialist newspapers can be found anywhere you please, but Yours almost nowhere. Your newspaper must be everywhere, in each township, in every city.

Don't spare any resources on this.

In addition, You must devote serious attention to the following. Our people are so confused by the cobweb spun by the bosses of the various parties that they do not understand at all who to follow and who to listen to. Every party tries to persuade the people in its own favor. They're all tugging and tearing the dark people in every direction.

Genuine socialists must have one path.

We can't have more than two parties. There must be only the oppressed and the oppressors.

In addition, freedom must be for the oppressed only. What we need for the oppressors is a club.

In our land, justice can only be done with clubs.

Freedom for the bourgeoisie is death for the proletariat.

This truth must be accepted by all toilers, by all Russian toiling people. 20 million free Russian *burzhui* would make the remaining 160 million into slaves. . . .

Freedom must exist only for the 160 million, and the remaining 20 million must be subordinate to the majority.

Do not hesitate. Take steps so that in every corner of our country all the toilers, be they intelligent or not intelligent, learn and understand that You sincerely want the people's good, and that only You can really bring the people real benefits.

Freedom only for the oppressed.

DOCUMENT 14.2
A JOINT SOCIALIST APPEAL "TO ALL CITIZENS!"[3]

While the Allies ignored the Soviet government's invitation for armistice negotiations, the Germans did not. Soviet-German negotiations on an armistice began on 20 November 1917. The following document is an appeal to Russia's citizens protesting against these negotiations. It was drafted at a joint conference of Socialist Revolutionaries, Mensheviks, and Trudovik Popular-Socialists on 22 November and appeared in the Menshevik newspaper, In the Darkest Night (V temuiui noch') *on 25 November. Opposition socialist newspapers had continued publication despite Bolshevik repression. After the Petrograd Soviet's Military Revolutionary Committee shut down the Menshevik newspaper* Day (Den), *it reappeared as* New Day (Novyi den), *then as* Night (Noch'), *Midnight (Polnoch'),* In the Dead of Night (V glukhuiu noch'), *In the Darkest Night (V temnuiu noch'),* The Dawning Day (Griadushchii den), *and in early 1918, again as* Den *and* Novyi den.

To All Citizens!
Only an immediate peace can save Russia from political and economic ruin and internecine warfare and preserve the revolution's achievements. But to be durable, to guarantee Russia's economic and political independence and the Russian revolution's interests, it must be a general peace, not a separate peace.

Despite this, the Bolshevik government has begun negotiating a separate truce. They do so without waiting for the Constituent Assembly, without approval from the people or its representatives, without any kind of public control, and without consulting other parties or waiting for an answer from our Allies. The Bolsheviks are carrying out negotiations with the enemy's representatives based on secret instructions, hidden from the people.

In light of this, we declare that any separate truce the Bolsheviks conclude is the power-seizing party's work alone. Responsibility for it lay totally and exclusively with them.

Russia is not committed to this truce, or to an agreement made previous to the Constituent Assembly's decision. The Bolsheviks' separate truce cannot bring a real, achievable, universal peace. The conference expresses its resolute confidence that the Constituent Assembly, the proper manifestation of the people's will, will do everything necessary to make a lasting peace that guarantees Russia's interests and those of the international democracy.

The Central Committee of the Party of Socialist Revolutionaries
The Central Committee of the RSDLP (United)
The Central Committee of the Trudovik Popular-Socialist Party
The Central Executive Committee of Soviets of Workers'
and Soldiers' Deputies (first convocation)
The Executive Committee of the Soviet of Peasants' Deputies

DOCUMENT 14.3
AN APPEAL FROM THE UNION FOR THE DEFENSE
OF THE CONSTITUENT ASSEMBLY[4]

In Petrograd on 22 November 1917, a joint socialist conference formed a Union for the Defense of the Constituent Assembly, convinced that the Bolsheviks intended to scuttle the Constituent Assembly. On 23 November, the Union announced that the Constituent Assembly would convene in five days, on the date proposed by the Provisional Government. The Soviet government arrested the Union's leaders and assigned Bolshevik Mikhail Uritskii to oversee the assembly's convocation. Uritskii freely used force against both the Union and those anti-Bolshevik Constituent Assembly delegates who began arriving in Petrograd.

The following document is a protest by the Union for the Defense of the Constituent Assembly against intimidating acts by Soviet authorities. It appeared in the Menshevik newspaper, The New Ray (Novyi luch), *on 3 December 1917. On 18 November the Petrograd Soviet's Military Revolutionary had shut down the Menshevik's* The Workers' Newspaper (Rabochaia gazeta); *in the two weeks that followed, it reappeared eight times under eight different titles:* The Ray (Luch), The Dawn (Zaria), The Call (Plamia), The Torch (Fakel), The Lightning Bolt (Mol'nia), The Hammer (Molot), The Shield (Shchit), *and* The New Ray (Noyi luch).

On the night of 1 December, a Red Guard detachment appeared at the offices of the Union for the Defense of the Constituent Assembly with an order "to take the typography and place it under guard." Considering that there was no typography at the Union's offices, the Red Guard detachment, reinforced by Latvian riflemen, over the course of the entire day detained everyone who came up the stairs to the Union's offices. They interrogated and searched everyone, including boys who were distributing the Union's appeals. They completely destroyed the Union's offices.

The representatives of the following party committees that have joined in the Union for the Defense of the Constituent Assembly (the United Committee of Socialist Parties and Democratic Organizations)—the SRs, the SD Mensheviks, and the Trudovik Popular-Socialists—as well as their representatives in the Petrograd Soviet of Workers' and Soldiers' Deputies, the Central City Duma, the district dumas, the trade unions, the factory committees, the military sections, and so on—protest against the closing and destruction of its offices.

The Union, acting frankly and openly, declares that its aim is to strengthen the popular masses' awareness of the significance of all the revolution's great achievements.

The Union directs the workers', soldiers', and peasants' attention to the overt campaign being conducted against the Constituent Assembly and against all the institutions connected to it. We call on [the workers, soldiers, and peasants] to rally their forces around the Constituent Assembly in its defense.

DOCUMENT 14.4
TWO LEFT SOCIALIST REVOLUTIONARY RESOLUTIONS
ON THE CONSTITUENT ASSEMBLY[5]

On 19 November 1917, the Socialist Revolutionary's left faction opened a hastily organized national congress in Petrograd to formally establish a new political party, the Left Socialist Revolutionaries (Left SRs). Questions about the pending Constituent Assembly dominated the Left SR founding congress. Like the Bolsheviks, the Left SRs wanted to delay the assembly's convocation and looked for a way to alter the election results. Unlike most Bolshevik leaders, though, the Left SRs still took the Constituent Assembly's integrity quite seriously. The following documents are Left SR resolutions on the Constituent Assembly. The first was discussed and passed at the Left SR founding congress on 28 November. The second was published in the Left SR Central Committee's Petrograd newspaper, Labor's Banner (Znamia truda), *on 6 December.*

[Resolution at 28 November 1917 Left Socialist Revolutionary Congress.]

1. The First Congress of Left SRs proposes that the Constituent Assembly's first priority must be to decide questions of peace, land, and workers' control.
2. The congress's standpoint is that a workers' and peasants' government must be realized immediately.
3. The Left SR congress declares that, if the Constituent Assembly proves to be an institution for the construction of such a government and implements the fundamental resolutions of the II Congress of Soviets of Workers', Soldiers' and Peasants' Deputies and the Extraordinary Congress of Peasants' Deputies, then it will support the Constituent Assembly in every way.

4. The congress considers any repetition at the Constituent Assembly of the ruinous experiences of coalition with the bourgeoisie to be absolutely impermissible.

5. So that the Constituent Assembly always authentically reflects the people's will, the Congress considers it necessary to establish the right to recall Constituent Assembly delegates and hold new elections initiated by the Soviets of Workers', Soldiers', and Peasants' Deputies or by sections of the population, according to formulas established by decree of the Soviet Central Executive Committee.[6]

6. The congress considers any attempt to change the Constituent Assembly into a vehicle for struggle against the [Soviet government] an encroachment on the revolution's achievements, and considers it necessary to exert the most resolute resistance against [such attempts].

[Resolution in *Labor's Banner*, 6 December 1917.]
Resolution of the Party of Left Socialist Revolutionaries' Central Committee

1. The Constituent Assembly must convene soon in its full complement.

2. Immediately upon convening, the Constituent Assembly's first priority must be to resolve and decide questions of peace, land, and workers' control in the spirit of the decisions of the recent All-Russian Congress of Soviets of Peasants', Workers', and Soldiers' Deputies.

3. The Party of Left SRs' approach to the Constituent Assembly will be based on the character of its decisions on these questions and its attitude toward the soviets as government institutions.

4. In the struggle against bourgeois counterrevolutionaries, the revolutionary government must not refrain from legal measures of repression against institutions and individual people, in those cases where factual evidence exists of their participation in conspiracies or uprisings against the government and against the toiling people's interests.

5. The government must immediately make the evidence it has available to the public.[7]

DOCUMENT 14.5
A PROVINCIAL SOVIET CONGRESS ON THE SOVIET GOVERNMENT AND THE CONSTITUENT ASSEMBLY[8]

Debate over the Constituent Assembly's fate was not restricted to Petrograd and Moscow. Moderate socialists and liberals in the provinces formed committees that pledged to protect the Constituent Assembly. In many cities, soviets passed resolutions demanding that the assembly accept the Soviet government's program.

The following document, a resolution by the 3 December 1917 Third Novgorod Provincial Congress of Soviets of Workers', Soldiers' and Peasants' Deputies, falls into the second category.

A great event has taken place. The armed people—workers and peasants—having overthrown the autocracy on 27 February, were oppressed by the gentlemen capitalists and aristocratic landlords. In a new successful insurrection on 25 October, they overthrew their oppressors, these same capitalists and landlords. In light of this great people's victory, the congress of Novgorod Province's democratic organizations resolves:

1. To greet the abovementioned revolution and government with all the force of our revolutionary souls:
2. That only this government—the government of the Council of People's Commissars, which is responsible to the Central Executive Committee at the center and the soviets of workers', soldiers', and peasants' deputies in the localities—can consolidate the achievements of the recent worker-peasant revolution: land for the peasants, workers' control over production, and freedom and peace for workers, soldiers, and peasants.
3. That the classes that are the people's oppressors and enemies—the capitalists and aristocratic landlords, embodied by the Kadet Party— must not join the united proletariat and peasantry in the Constituent Assembly, which can realize the people's dreams.
4. That the worker-peasant government will establish real freedom, equality, and fraternity, with the red banner of freedom, equality, and fraternity in one hand and a merciless sword against the people's enemies in the other.
5. To condemn in the most categorical terms and to take the most resolute measures to fight sabotage by government clerks and intellectuals who betray the people. . . .
6. That all Soviet of People's Commissars decrees, especially those on land and workers' control, must be implemented immediately.

DOCUMENT 14.6
LENIN, "THESES ON THE CONSTITUENT ASSEMBLY"[9]

In late November and early December 1917, Bolshevik leaders devoted consider-able attention to the problem posed by the Socialist Revolutionary (SR) victory in Constituent Assembly elections. Few Bolshevik Central Committee members wanted to cancel the assembly outright. Nikolai Bukharin, for example, called for the systematic repression of the opposition coalescing around it.[10] Lenin viewed it as an irritating distraction and proposed having local soviets recall elected assembly delegates. Bolshevik and Left SR leaders settled on demanding that the Constituent Assembly endorse the Soviet government's major resolutions and decrees and recognize its legitimacy. Should it refuse—which the Bolsheviks and Left SRs expected—then the Soviet government could disband the assembly. The following document is Lenin's 19-point "Theses on the Constituent Assembly," prepared after an 11 December 1917 Bolshevik Central Committee discussion of the assembly and published in Truth (Pravda) *on 13 December 1917.*

1. Demanding the Constituent Assembly's convocation was a perfectly legitimate part of the revolutionary Social Democratic program, because under a bourgeois republic the Constituent Assembly represented democracy's highest form, and because Kerensky's imperialist republic, in setting up a Pre-Parliament, was preparing to fix the elections and violate democracy in several ways.

2. While they demanded the Constituent Assembly's convocation, from the 1917 revolution's onset the revolutionary Social Democrats repeatedly stressed that a Soviet republic is a higher form of democracy than the usual bourgeois republic with a Constituent Assembly.

3. Compared to the usual bourgeois republic crowned by a Constituent Assembly, a Soviet republic is both a higher form of democratic institution, and the only form that can secure a painless transition to socialism, from the bourgeois to the socialist system and the proletarian dictatorship.

4. The Constituent Assembly was elected based on candidate lists submitted in mid-October 1917, under conditions that prevented the elections from faithfully expressing the people's will generally and the toilers' will in particular.

5. First: proportional representation can faithfully express the people's will only when the party candidate lists correspond to real divisions among the people, as reflected in party groupings. In our case, however, as is well known, the Socialist Revolutionary Party—the party that in May–October had the largest following among the people and especially among the peasants—presented united Constituent Assembly election lists in mid-October and then split in November, after the elections, but before the Constituent Assembly. Therefore the masses' electoral will and the elected Constituent Assembly's composition have no more than a formal resemblance to one another.

6. Second: an even more important discrepancy between the people's will (and especially the working class' will) and the Constituent Assembly's composition is neither formal or legal, but socioeconomic and class-based. The Constituent Assembly elections occurred at a time when the great majority did not yet know the full scope and significance of the proletarian-peasant revolution begun on 25 October 1917, i.e., after Constituent Assembly candidate lists were submitted.

7. The October revolution has, before our very eyes, passed through successive stages: winning Soviet power, wresting political rule from the bourgeoisie, and passing power to the proletariat and poor peasantry.

8. This began with the 24–25 October victory in the capital, when the Second All-Russia Congress of Soviets of Workers' and Soldiers' Deputies—the vanguard of the proletariat and most politically active peasant elements—gave the Bolshevik Party a majority and put it in power.

9. Then, in November and December, the revolution spread through the army and peasantry. This was expressed primarily by removal of the old leading institutions (army committees, provincial peasant committees, the Soviet of Peasants' Deputies' Central Executive Committee, etc.)—which represented the revolution's superseded, conciliationist phase, its bourgeois (not proletarian) phase, and which were inevitably bound to disappear under pressure from the deeper and broader popular masses—and in the election of new leading bodies in their place.

10. Even now, in mid-December, the exploited people's mighty movement to reconstruct their organizations' leading institution continues; the Congress of Railroad Workers now in session represents one of its stages.[11]

11. Consequently, the alignment of class forces in the class struggle in Russia in November–December in fact was fundamentally different from the class alignments reflected by Constituent Assembly candidate lists compiled in mid-October.

12. Recent events in Ukraine (and Finland and Belorussia, as well as the Caucasus) suggest that a similar regrouping of class forces is taking place there, in the ongoing struggle between the bourgeois nationalist Ukrainian Rada and Finnish Diet, etc. on one hand, and Soviet power and the proletarian-peasant revolution on the other.[12]

13. Finally: the civil war begun by the Kadet-Kaledin counterrevolutionary revolt against Soviet power—against the workers' and peasants' government—brought the class struggle to a head and destroyed any chance for a democratic solution to the acute problems that history has set before Russia's peoples, especially her working class and peasants.

14. The proletarian-peasant revolution's only true safeguard is an absolute workers' and peasants' victory over the bourgeois-aristocratic landlord revolt (as expressed in the Kadet-Kaledin movement) and ruthless military suppression of this slave-owners' revolt. Revolutionary events and the class struggle's development have made the slogan, "All Power to the Constituent Assembly!"—which disregards the achievements of the workers' and peasants' revolution, Soviet power, and the resolutions of the Second All-Russia Congress of Soviets of

Workers', and Soldiers' Deputies and Second All-Russian Congress of Peasants' Deputies, etc.—*in fact* the slogan of the Kadet-Kaledinites and their lackeys. The entire people now understand completely that if the Constituent Assembly parts ways with Soviet power, it is doomed to political extinction.

15. Peace is among our national life's most acute problems. In Russia, a truly revolutionary struggle for peace began only with the 25 October revolutionary victory. This victory's first fruits were the publication of the secret treaties, conclusion of a truce, and initiation of open negotiations for a general peace without annexations and indemnities. Only now can the broad public fully and openly observe the revolutionary struggle for peace and study its results. During the Constituent Assembly elections, the popular masses had no such opportunity. This elucidates the inevitable discrepancy between the elected Constituent Assembly's composition and the people's actual will regarding the war's conclusion.

16. Taken together, all these circumstances mean that a Constituent Assembly based on party electoral lists compiled under bourgeois rule, prior to the proletarian-peasant revolution, must inevitably clash with the will and interests of the working and exploited classes that began a socialist revolution against the bourgeoisie on 25 October. Naturally, this revolution's interests would take precedence over the Constituent Assembly's formal rights, even were those formal rights not undermined by the absence of a provision in the law on the Constituent Assembly recognizing the people's right to recall deputies and hold new elections at any time.

17. Any direct or indirect attempt to consider the Constituent Assembly from a formal, legal perspective—from an ordinary bourgeois democratic framework that disregards the class struggle and civil war—would assume a bourgeois standpoint and betray the proletariat's cause. The revolutionary Social Democrats are duty-bound to warn everyone against this error—an error into which a few Bolshevik leaders, unable to appreciate the October uprising's significance and the proletarian dictatorship's tasks, have strayed.[13]

18. The only way to ensure a painless solution to the crisis caused by the divergence between the Constituent Assembly elections on one hand, and the people's will and the working and exploited classes' interests on the other, is for the people to elect new Constituent Assembly members as broadly and quickly as possible. The Constituent Assembly must accept the Central Executive Committee's decree on these new elections. It must proclaim that it unreservedly acknowledges Soviet power, the Soviet revolution, and the Soviet government's policies on peace, land, and workers' control. And it must resolutely join the camp opposed to the Kadet-Kaledin counterrevolution.

19. Unless these conditions are met, the crisis connected to the Constituent Assembly can only be settled by revolutionary means, through the most energetic, rapid, firm, and determined revolutionary measures by the Soviet government against the Kadet-Kaledin counterrevolution, no matter what slogans and institutions it hides behind (even participation in the Constituent Assembly). Any attempt to hinder Soviet power in this struggle is tantamount to aiding counterrevolution.

DOCUMENT 14.7
IULII MARTOV, "THE REVOLUTION AND THE
CONSTITUENT ASSEMBLY"[14]

The following document is an essay by Iulii Martov published in The New Ray (Novyi luch) *on 15 December 1917. Martov does not refer directly to Lenin's "Theses on the Constituent Assembly," which had just appeared in* Pravda. *But it seems likely that he intended this essay as a response to Lenin's arguments.*

"The Constituent Assembly is so dear to all the revolution's open enemies that they believe they must put a stop to the socialist revolution in Russia." So writes *Izvestiia*.[15]

The RSDLP's program clearly and unambiguously declares that the Russian revolution's aim is to create a *democratic republic*. Therefore it has made the All-National Constituent Assembly its central battle cry.

The party's goals and efforts have fully corresponded with this program. *It therefore is true* that the revolution's aim is a democratic, and not a socialist, revolution. Given the correlation of the country's public forces, fully realizing this goal requires that the Constituent Assembly majority represents the peasantry and urban petty-bourgeoisie. The rural and urban petty-bourgeoisie must assume ongoing revolutionary tasks in . . . the struggle against the surviving aristocratic and serf-holding strata. Therefore the Social Democrats are completely right to expect the Constituent Assembly to fulfill their minimum program.[16]

History has brilliantly confirmed the correctness of the RSDLP's foresight. The fact that the Constituent Assembly's significant majority will be SRs—the party nearest to the middle peasants, which has revolutionary aspirations regarding the land, abolition of legal estates, and establishment of democracy—reveals that the Constituent Assembly *must* be a tool for realizing the democratic revolution's goals.

But there is a reason that when "grey" workers are asked, "Are you Social Democrats?" they habitually answer, "No, we are Bolsheviks."[17] The Bolsheviks broke irrevocably from the RSDLP program when they declared that the revolution's goal is socialism in Russia.

The Russian Constituent Assembly cannot be a vehicle for *socialist revolution*, unless, of course, the cards are stacked. If, like Chekov's hero, you are convinced that "a hare can light matches if you beat it," then the Constituent Assembly can be mastered and driven into accepting a socialist order by repeatedly disbandment and electoral fraud, by Uritsky's manipulation and Larin's hocus-pocus.[18] Talking about *that kind* of Constituent Assembly is like Shchedrin proclaiming that Russia ready for Fourier's *phalanstères*; it is like Arakcheev's military settlements.[19] We speak not of that kind of Constituent Assembly, but of one freely elected by the entire people, reflecting the will of the people's majority.

The Bolsheviks understand this well enough. So they openly proclaim that "Under current conditions, realizing the slogan, 'All Power to the Constituent Assembly!' signifies halting the revolution." And they associate "the victory of Soviet power" as "the victory of socialism."

It is hard to understand the practical significance beneath the sauce of erudition in *Izvestiia*'s reference to the "well-known fact" that in all revolutions "only the revolutionary vanguard can take appropriate measures to secure already-made achievements while also taking revolutionary initiatives toward their further expansion." Surely, our current dispute with the Bolsheviks is not over whether representative institutions must correspond with "public opinion" or whether a certain social class is "more leftist," favors an independent policy, and "urges decisive measures." It is about whether a "more leftist" *state* must be *above* and *independent of* the Constituent Assembly. That, learned *Izvestiia* men, has never happened in any revolution.

This is the first point. The second point is that, in 1792 and 1848 the revolutionary vanguard could move the people's general representatives forward only to the extent that it actually stood for *the same historical goals* as the popular majority's representative assemblies. The Jacobins and *sans-culottes* aspired to the same public transformation in the petty-bourgeois majority's interests as did the Legislative Assembly.[20] They were a vanguard because they were decisive and radical in the cause of realizing *these* tasks. In the current revolution, if the Leninists were to play a "vanguard" role they would dictate to the Constituent Assembly not different goals, but more radical *methods* toward the same goals as the popular majority (peace, a republic, land reform). Instead, they have had done the complete opposite: they act contrary to the popular majority's will and enunciate *utopian* goals.

Conscious worker-socialists understand what this great step forward—achievement of people-power in Russia, consolidation and development of a democratic republic, which Marx considered the very best political form for realizing the proletariat's social liberation—signifies for the cause of authentically liberating the Russian and international proletariat.

Conscious workers reject the sophisms of new utopian "Communists" and—unafraid of being jailed as "counterrevolutionaries"—proclaim, "All Power to the Constituent Assembly!"

DOCUMENT 14.8
SPEECHES AT THE ALL-RUSSIAN CONSTITUENT ASSEMBLY[21]

The Constituent Assembly's first and only session took place in Petrograd on the night of 5–6 January 1918. The following document set presents three excerpts from the Constituent Assembly session transcripts published in 1930: opening comments and a declaration on behalf of the All-Russian Central Executive Committee of Soviets by the Bolshevik Iakov Sverdlov; a welcoming address by the assembly's elected chairman, Socialist Revolutionary (SR) leader Viktor Chernov; and the Left SR's final statement before quitting the meeting, read by Vladimir Karelin.

Sverdlov: The Executive Committee of Soviets of Workers and Peasants Deputies has entrusted me to open the Constituent Assembly. (*A storm of applause from the left. Voices from the right and center:* "There is blood on your hands. Enough blood!")

The Central Executive Committee of Soviets of Workers', Soldiers', and Peasants' Deputies . . . (*Voice from the right:* "Falsification.") . . . hopes that the Constituent Assembly will fully recognize all the Soviet of People's Commissars' decrees and resolutions. The October revolution has ignited the flames of socialist revolution not just in Russia, but in all countries. (*From the right, laughter and commotion.*) Certainly this fire will sweep the whole world (*Commotion*), and the day is not far off when the toiling classes in all countries rise against their exploiters, just as the Russian working class and peasantry rose up in October. (*A storm of applause from the left.*)

Certainly the toiling people's authentic representatives, having gathered at the Constituent Assembly, must help the Soviets do away with class privileges. The workers' and peasants' representatives have recognized the toiling people's right to productive resources and tools—to the property that had allowed the ruling classes to exploit the toiling people in every possible way. Just as in the French bourgeois revolution, the Great 1789 Revolution, a Declaration of Rights of Man and Citizen was proclaimed—a declaration of the right to freely exploit people deprived of tools and productive resources—so our Russian socialist revolution must proclaim its own declaration.[22] (*Applause from the Bolsheviks' benches.*) The Central Executive Committee hopes that the Constituent Assembly—if it properly reflects the people's interests—will endorse the declaration that I shall now read here.

In the name of the All-Russian Central Executive Committee of Soviets of Workers', Soldiers', and Peasants' Deputies, I propose the following (*he reads the declaration*):

1. Russia is a Republic of Soviets of Workers', Soldiers', and Peasants' Deputies. All power in the center and the provinces rests with the soviets.
2. The Soviet Russian Republic is based on a free union of free nations, as a federation of Soviet national republics.

The Constituent Assembly, having set as its fundamental goals the abolition of all exploitation of man by man, complete elimination of the division of society into classes, ruthless repression of exploiters, establishment of a socialist society, and socialism's victory in all countries, resolves the following:

1. To actualize the socialization of land, private landed property is abolished and all land is declared public property, to be transferred to the toilers without any compensation, on the principle of equalized land-usage. All forests, mineral resources, and bodies of water that have state significance, as well as all livestock and farm tools, all estates and agricultural enterprises, are declared national property.
2. To ratify Soviet laws on workers' control and the Supreme Council of the National Economy, to secure the toilers' power over the exploiters, and as a first step toward complete transfer of factories, plants, mines, railroads, and other productive resources and transport, to ownership of the Soviet Worker-Peasant Republic.
3. To ratify the transfer of all banks to the worker-peasant state's ownership, as a means for toiling masses' liberation from capital's yoke.
4. To introduce universal labor duty, to abolish society's parasitical strata and organize the economy.
5. To arm the toilers, form a socialist workers' and peasants' Red Army, and completely disarm the propertied classes, in the interests of securing the toiling masses' complete and full power and eliminating any chance of restoring the exploiters' power.

The Constituent Assembly expresses its uncompromising determination to tear humanity from the clutches of finance capital and imperialism, which has drenched the land in blood in this current and most criminal of all wars. It fully approves the Soviet government's policy of renouncing secret treaties, organizing wide-scale fraternization between workers and peasants in the belligerent armies, and achieving democratic peace between peoples without annexations or indemnities on the basis of free national self-determination at all costs and through revolutionary measures.

Toward this end, the Constituent Assembly calls for a complete break with the barbarian policies of bourgeois civilization that enrich the exploiters in a few chosen nations by subjugating tens of millions of toiling people in Asia, in the colonies in general, and in small countries.

The Constituent Assembly welcomes the Council of People's Commissars' policy granting Finland complete independence, initiating removal of troops from Persia, and recognizing Armenia's freedom of self-determination.[23]

The Constituent Assembly considers the Soviet law annulling (abolishing) the tsarist government's debts a first blow against international banks and finance capital, and is confident that the Soviet government will stay the course until the complete victory of the international workers' insurrection against the yoke of capital.

The Constituent Assembly, having been elected based on party electoral lists compiled before the October revolution—when the people still had not risen as a mass against the exploiters, when they still did not know how strongly the exploiters would defend their class privileges, and when they had still not taken practical steps toward creating a socialist society—would consider it fundamentally wrong, even from a formal perspective, to oppose itself to Soviet power.

The Constituent Assembly proposes that now, during the people's decisive struggle against their exploiters, not a single exploiter can hold a position in government institutions. Power must rest totally and exclusively with the toiling masses and their authorized representatives—the Soviets of Workers', Soldiers', and Peasants' Deputies.

In supporting Soviet power and the Council of People's Commissar's decrees the Constituent Assembly recognizes that its own role is limited strictly to the general elaboration of radical principles for the socialist reconstruction of society.

In addition, in striving to create an authentically free and voluntary—and consequently more complete and lasting—union of the toiling classes of all Russia's nations, the Constituent Assembly confines itself to establishing fundamental principles for a Russian federation of Soviet republics, leaving it to each nation's workers and peasants at their own authorized Soviet congresses to make independent decisions on whether, and under what conditions, they wish to participate in the federal government and in other federal Soviet institutions.

On the authority of the All-Russian Central Executive Committee of Soviets of Workers', Soldiers', and Peasants' Deputies, I declare the Constituent Assembly opened. I propose election of a chairman. (*A voice from the left*: "Comrades, '*The International!*'" They sing *"The International."*)

A voice from the left: "Long live the Soviets of Workers', Peasants' and Soldiers' Deputies! All Power to the Soviets!"

A response from the right: "All Power to the Constituent Assembly!"

[After much shouting back and forth and short speeches from various political party representatives, the assembly elected Viktor Chernov as its chairman. What follows are excerpts from Chernov's introductory address to the Assembly, by far the longest speech given that night.]

Chernov: Citizens, members of the Constituent Assembly! Let me thank you for the display of confidence that you have shown me. I understand perfectly the responsibility and difficulty of the duties entrusted to me. Rest assured, citizens and comrades, rest assured that I will, to the best of my ability, impartially guide this meeting's debates so that they correspond with this Assembly's seriousness and dignity and with the great responsibilities entrusted to it.

Citizens, members of the Constituent Assembly, you have been summoned to exercise your duties at a time when Russia's people are living through uncommon difficulties. . . .

. . . The Russian revolution, citizens, was born with the word peace on its lips. And the Russian revolution must remain faithful to the slogan of democratic peace, peace without annexations or indemnities. Peace, in which the only victors are the people and the only vanquished are those to blame for this war, this unprecedented colossal crime against humanity.

. . . Citizens, we all know that the Russian revolution's grievous situation arises from the fact that the toiling masses are pursuing the most advanced slogans and social dreams in a country that is economically backwards and that finds itself in a most difficult situation. Therefore, we still await the hoped-for response from countries that are more advanced than us in both civic and economic development.

And citizens, the burden of our position has been compounded even more by the last and—as I would call them—desperate attempts toward peace that preceded our assembly.[24] These made imperialism's whole internal essence absolutely clear to us—the imperialism that has triumphed on the war maps, the imperialism of the central empires, who in words alone only half agreed to peace formulas put forward by revolutionary Russia.[25] This was a maneuver to drive a wedge into the [Allied] camp, to steer revolutionary Russia toward separate negotiations. German imperialism's aggressive predatory aims are still in full force.

Perhaps tomorrow they will propose a similar separate peace to other governments. They will find people somewhere who will agree to lay the entire burden for all the war's waste and destruction on Russia. Lay it on revolutionary Russia, which still is dangerous to the imperialist central empires, despite its present weakness at the front. Because our people's strength lies not in the number of bayonets that they can raise or the battle positions these bayonets occupy, but in the power of the Russian revolution's slogans. That power can replenish a country's strength, rouse its people, and move them to defend the Russian revolution's great slogan of peace.

We believe that if these slogans do not decay and collapse, then our country's toilers, represented by this assembly, will gather strength and exert all their effort. And Russia's peoples will rally, join forces, and organize. They will turn the Russian revolution's slogans into the slogans of the Russian state and the slogans of a federated democratic Russian republic—a Russia that is a free union of equal peoples.

. . . Citizens, our situation is dangerous, but we have allies. First among these allies are the socialist toiling masses of all countries, who are exhausted from the nightmarish war and do not want it to continue. . . . Russia's Constituent Assembly, as a union of free peoples and a state institution, will raise its voice and invite all countries' socialists, all who will not lower their banners or their voices before the monster of war, to a conference for a universal war against war. (*Applause.*)

I know, citizens, that there is no precedent for a government to invite political parties from other countries to a universal conference. But citizens, there is no precedent for the Constituent Assembly of a great country—yes, a country that finds itself in a burdensome situation, but still is great in its rudiments and its hidden strengths, which it will not hesitate to demonstrate—it is an unprecedented event in history for a great country's Constituent Assembly to be the first representative institution in world history in which there is a socialist majority. The popular masses, Russia's toiling masses, have a will toward socialism. This, their great will to socialism, is also unprecedented in history. And I dare to hope that in its forthcoming sessions the Constituent Assembly will not hesitate to consider the issue, so that a great peace council . . . will gather at the initiative of state agencies with the supreme authority of the Russian state. (*Applause from the center and from sections of the right.*)

. . . [W]e as a country must not be tempted by the imperialists' overtures. We must not be weak. We must not leave ourselves vulnerable to the imperialists' predatory appetite. They are only waiting for the moment to strike a blow against us—to satisfy this predatory appetite. We must be strong; we must have physical strength. The Russian people's revolution must be mighty inside and out. Citizens, we cannot forget that our soldiers at the front, our men in grey army overcoats, still are carrying a truly superhuman burden. The Constituent Assembly must consider this. There is no other path—you must consider it, because the Russian people command that you do—than creation of a Russian military force based upon a people's militia: a socialist army, a people's territorial militia. Towards this end, you must consider organizing a volunteer army that, under socialism's red banner (*Commotion in the hall.*) can secure the Russian people's opportunity to engage in the work of internal reconstruction. You must do this so that this army, marching voluntarily under the socialist banner, can replace those who are worn out, those who should return to their hearths, who have the right to return to their hearths, who can no longer go hungry and go without food. (*Applause from the center.*)

At this weighty moment, citizens, there is another issue of no less colossal importance. Russia and all its peoples must be a living, lasting, moral, and political united whole. . . . Russia already is a union of many peoples and territories. We envision a central Russian Constituent Assembly working in conjunction with local constituent assemblies. . . . The Constituent Assembly embodies the living unity of all Russia's peoples. Therefore the very fact that its first session has opened proclaims the end of civil war between the peoples who populate Russia. (*Voices from the center and right*: "Bravo!" *Applause. Those on the center and the right stand. A voice from the left*: "So says General Kaledin's telegram.")[26]

Citizens, permit me, in the entire Constituent Assembly's name (*A voice from the left*: "We do not give you permission.") to give you a promise. (*He addresses citizens from Ukraine.*) Henceforth Ukraine need not for a minute fear the hand of Great Russia's soldiers. The Russian state will honor the plowmen of Ukraine.[27] (*Applause from the center and right. A voice*: "Long live Ukraine!") With this, citizens, we lift a weight from the souls of Great Russia's soldiers, to whom you will permit me to say, in Constituent Assembly's name: henceforth no one will dare to make you betray your hearts and stain your hands with Ukraine's fraternal blood. (*Stormy applause from the center and right. A voice from the left*: "Long live the Ukrainian Soviet of Workers' and Soldiers' Deputies!" *Applause from all the benches. Commotion. A voice from the left*: "Down with the bourgeois Rada! Down with the counterrevolutionary Rada! Down with the Kaledinites!")

Permit me also, citizens, to address the toiling Cossacks, sons of the free-flowing Don . . . to say that the Constituent Assembly is lastingly and firmly convinced that toiling Cossacks' legions, sons of the free-flowing Don, will not oppose the Constituent Assembly's will. . . . (*Applause from all the benches except those on the left. A voice from the left*: "Kaledinites"). . . . [W]ith confidence we guarantee the toiling Cossacks that they have nothing to fear from Great Russia's soldiers. (*Applause from all the benches except those on the left.*)

. . . The Muslim population, great and dispersed in all of Russia's cities . . . can expect the Constituent Assembly to recognize its sovereign rights, like any other nationality. (*Applause from the right and center and from the Muslim groups.*) . . . The Jewish people, who do not have their own compact territory, will have equality with all other nations in the Russian republic's territory. They will have the right to organize their own national self-government institutions and speak in their own workers' tongue.[28] (*Applause from the center and right.*)

. . . Citizens, one sphere has national-economic importance that cannot be overestimated, the sphere of agriculture. This is the village sphere, that of toilers who hitherto were at the bottom of the social pyramid. Regarding that sphere, citizens, you must stipulate . . . [that] "All land, without compensation, is the entire people's property." (*Commotion and applause. A voice from the left*: "Long live the soviets, which have given the land to the peasants! The soviets have done this!" *Another voice from the left*: "You're not going to get this from the Kaledinites.") This statement of the people's is so powerful that all parties have bent before it (*A voice from the left*: "Even Chernov's!") even those that previously were not interested in this slogan. (*Applause.*)

Citizens, a colossal task lays before us in this sphere: to pass from bare slogans and general formulas to their realization. (*Commotion and a voice from the left*: "You're too late.") To create real, active, statewide equalized agriculture. (*Loud applause from the right. A voice from the left*: "Didn't you shoot at the peasants?") . . . [E]veryone at this meeting must decide—must understand—that the universal transfer of arable land will not happen in one stroke of a pen. (*A voice from the left*: "But you will have to do without plows.") It will not happen because of any kind of placard, whatever the placard might say. (*A voice from the left*: "So join the Kaledinites.")

. . . All Russia expects the All-Russian Constituent Assembly and the constituent assemblies of all Russia's peoples and territories to work to realize this slogan—that in accord with all Russia's general will, they will really distribute land for usage, equalized usage by all toilers, who have the same right to this land. (*Loud applause from the right.*)

. . . Citizens, regarding the Russian village's affairs—Russia's toiling population does not care just about agricultural affairs and village affairs. It also is concerned about all state affairs, about all the toiling classes. It believes that the great slogan about transferring all the people's property to the people's government institutions for redistribution applies to all sources of wealth and to production of all types. It sees this as the key to the land's productivity, to its wealth—both on the surface and beneath the soil. Land reform will create the foundation for future construction, for further social construction. And in the end, it will properly establish all citizens' equal right to a laboring existence, an existence of compensated labor—a compensated universal labor obligation based on universal utilization [of land and productive resources]. (*Applause.*)

. . . [B]uilding socialism assumes a mighty rise in the country's productive forces; socialism is not a precocious approximation of equality in destitution. (*Commotion.*) During this great construction, the country's productive forces evolve simultaneously with the toiling people's productive might, so that each step toward equality is at the same time a step in the struggle for a more worthy level of human existence. [This] is particularly important for our country, the maximal will for socialism is now paired with maximal disintegration of productive forces—disintegration of transport, declining food supply, declining productivity, financial disorganization. All this stands in ominous contrast to our uncompromising will to socialism.

Citizens, the burden of this situation is unprecedented in history and demands unprecedented seriousness and truthfulness. Citizens, what I have not yet said is this: I can't imagine anyone would harm the Constituent Assembly, harm the popular majority's legitimate will as expressed by their votes. . . . I cannot image that anyone but madmen would oppose or ridicule it or would try to sabotage it. Nonetheless, Citizens, this proper manifestation of the people's will, of the people's freedom, does not fear sabotage. (*Applause from the right and center.*) Russia's people—as a living unity—fear sabotage like a lion fears a mosquito bite. (*Applause.*)

Citizens, our goal in our gigantic, colossal work must be to make breakthroughs on a whole row of questions—on such great issues as unemployment. Unemployment threatens our workers, thanks in significant degree to the civil war, which has disrupted fuel supply and the supply of metal and threatens shortages in all our industries. Our factories have one foot in the grave. Tsar Hunger stares all workers in the face. In this situation, the connection between unemployment and preparations for demobilization, to the extent that demobilization will actually proceed, is a gigantic issue. Our task is to turn all Russia's land over to public usage, to make the land suitable for use, to carry out public work to till the untilled land, irrigate the waterless land . . . (*Laughter from the left. A voice*: "And so on and so forth.")

. . . And, citizens, in taking up such work the Constituent Assembly is right to expect energetic cooperation from all organizations that have the urban and village working class at their core. (*Applause from the right and center.*) All types of organizations, beginning with trade unions, will thrive and grow stronger, will play a giant role in the future society—will take management of enterprises and unite them in great sectors of national production. This must include the powerful trade unions and soviets, which by endorsing the slogan of struggle against the Constituent Assembly have betrayed their own slogans. (*Applause from the center and right.*) (*His words are drowned out.*) . . . The Constituent Assembly has the right to expect support from the entire unified working people, like a chain uniting the country. It has the right to count upon their support.

But, citizens, the Constituent Assembly lacks this. . . .

Of course, should we here not resolve issues in a way that satisfies the people, then the people itself will express dissatisfaction with the results of its own all-national universal election. No one can assume to speak for the people; they will speak for themselves. (*Voice from the left*: "It will recall you.") Should the Constituent Assembly make an unfortunate break from the people's will, it would have to—its duty would require that its own representatives immediately begin new elections. (*A voice from the left*: "That time has come. That time has come for you.") Those who suggest that such a time has come should propose a plebiscite—a plebiscite on whether or not the people continue to have confidence in the Constituent

Assembly. (*Loud applause from the center and right. A voice from the left*: "Recall—there must be a recall.")

Citizens, permit me to speak in my capacity as chairman and remind you that your own inability to hold an orderly meeting does not reflect this assembly's true dignity. . . . [P]eople who would dare assume the lofty authority of Constituent Assembly members must exercise self-discipline. Those who want to do so should propose a plebiscite. The Constituent Assembly's members will wait calmly for the results, because the entire country, the entire toiling people, does not change opinions like someone changing gloves. (*Applause from the right and center. Skortsev*: "So says the former Zimmerwaldist.")[29]

In concluding my greetings to you, allow me also to direct your attention to this circumstance: The right that each of you has to sit at these benches was won through a difficult, bloody struggle, a bloody struggle over several generations. (*Voice*: "The October revolution! The October revolution against Kerensky!" *Voices*: "Quiet!") Citizens, permit me to ask that you maintain an element of composure. This does not seem an excessive request. (*A voice from the left*: "Get to the point.")

Citizens, it is no joke that your right to sit here was purchased with the blood of succeeding generations, the blood of people, the cream of the people. . . . And, citizens, permit me to propose that you honor the memory of all who fell in battle against the arbitrary old order, all who fell in the struggle for the Russian revolution, by standing.

(*The assembly stands. Commotion on the left. A voice from the left*: "We are standing for those who died in the struggle with Rudnev and the Junkers.")[30] Citizens. . . . (*Commotion. A voice from the left*: "For those who died in the struggle against Chernov, Rudnev, and Kerensky.")

Citizens, in addition, let me remind you yet again of the martyrs. (*A voice from the left*: "The soldiers and peasants that Rudnev shot.") We, as the people's representatives, can take up the create constructive work of restructuring all Russia on new principles only thanks to those who have toiling in grey army overcoats at the front, with their countless martyrs. . . . (*A voice from the left*: "You have no right to speak of them." *Powerful commotion and shouting on the left*.) I ask you to come to order. (*The chairman rings a bell*.) I ask you to respect the Constituent Assembly. Citizens, permit me to propose that you stand to honor the memory of all who have fallen defending the Russian revolution's borders. (*Powerful commotion on the left*.) That you stand for their slogans of peace. (*A voice*: "I propose that we honor the memory of the martyrs of 18 June." *A voice from the left*: "Don't you stand: executioners always sit!")[31] Of all who fell defending the Russian revolution's borders. To honor their memory and remember them all in equal measure, the entire assembly will stand in their honor. (*Commotion*.)

Permit me to ask that the meeting observe order. Citizens of the republic, I humbly ask you not to disrupt this assembly. Citizens,

Constituent Assembly members, in concluding my speech, allow me to propose that you elect a secretary.

[After the assembly elected a secretary, several Menshevik and Right SR speakers rejected the Bolsheviks' demand that they endorse the "Declaration of Rights of Toiling and Exploited Peoples" and recognize the Soviet government. The meeting voted to suspend further discussion of the Bolshevik declaration and agreed to an agenda proposed by the SR majority: (1) discussion of peace; (2) discussion of land reform; (3) discussion of forming a new government. The Bolsheviks and Left SRs protested and demanded a recess. After the recess, the Bolsheviks read a statement decrying the majority's refusal to support the Declaration of Rights, warned that the Soviet Central Executive Committee would deal with "counterrevolutionary" assembly, and quit the meeting. The Left SRs remained. Although the Bolshevik withdrawal left the Assembly without a quorum, the meeting went on to discuss and endorse proposals on peace and land reform. At approximately 4:00 A.M. on 6 January, Vladimir Karelin took the podium and made the following statement in the name of the Left SRs.]

Karelin: Our faction considers whatever decisions it pleases the Constituent Assembly majority to pass as a continuation of its policy of hypocrisy and cowardice, as continuing along the path that the majority has taken from the very beginning of this session. . . .

Chairman [Chernov]: I humbly ask that the member of the Constituent Assembly. . . . (*Commotion among the public.*)

Karelin: I will not censure my words here, because I think harsh words are called for. Permit me to be as harsh as circumstances demand. The situation, as it now stands, is that the Constituent Assembly's majority was the product of absolutely accidental circumstances, thanks to which the technical election rules did not allow for change to the electoral lists, even though the alignment of the country's political forces had changed radically. This resulted in an absolutely artificial combination in the Constituent Assembly that does not at all reflect the real correlation of forces in the country. Consequently, this Constituent Assembly does not reflect the toiling masses' mood or will. And consequently, the Constituent Assembly's majority now declares goals and takes official positions that set it on a path toward conflict with the Soviet government, which was tempered in the flames of the October revolution. We consider this situation absolutely intolerable.

We also believe that our further presence here—that even the semblance of our participation in this current session, now that the Constituent Assembly majority has absolutely and definitely stated that it will make those immediate decisions and pass those definite resolutions on issues about which a series of orators have spoken—would be judged as complicity in a sin against the people's will. By our reasoning, that is the path the Constituent Assembly's right majority has taken. Therefore, we are leaving, removing ourselves from this assembly. (*Applause from the left and from the public.*)

We are going so that we can put our effort and our energy into Soviet institutions and the All-Russian Central Executive Committee. At this decisive moment for the great Russian revolution, we are going so that we can put all our effort and might into these institutions and devote ourselves to the toiling classes' cause in this battle between the two irreconcilably clashing camps. We are going so that we can bring about the toilers' victory under revolution's red banner. That is why we are going. We are quitting this meeting, because here. . . . (*Commotion; shouting and applause from the public. A voice from the left*: "We are leaving Avksent'ev, Kerensky, and Chernov!"*)

(*The Left SRs leave the hall.*)

[After the Left SRs walked out, Chernov tried to resume discussion of the land question. He was interrupted by members of the Soviet-appointed guard "protecting" the meeting, who insisted that they had instructions to end the session. They were tired, they claimed, and so the session must end. Chernov argued that the delegates also were tired, but they had to do their duty for the Russian people. After several minutes of hurried votes to confirm earlier resolutions, the session adjourned at 4:40 A.M. on 6 January. Chernov announced that the assembly would resume at 5:00 P.M. That day, however, the Soviet government disbanded the Constituent Assembly.]

DOCUMENT 14.9
THE SOVIET DECREE DISBANDING THE
CONSTITUENT ASSEMBLY[32]

At 11:30 P.M. on 6 January 1918, the All-Russian Central Executive Committee of Soviets held an emergency session to discuss the Constituent Assembly's dissolution. The moderate Bolsheviks, Left Socialist Revolutionaries (Left SRs), and Menshevik Internationalists expressed outrage at the use of violence against pro–Constituent Assembly demonstrators on 5–6 January. The committee agreed to form a special investigative commission to look into these incidents. Lenin then turned the meeting's attention to reasons why the Constituent Assembly had to be disbanded. After some discussion, the Left SR Vladimir Karelin read a resolution declaring the assembly's dissolution. The document below is the text of that resolution, as published on 7 January in Truth (Pravda).

At is very beginning, the Russian revolution brought the soviets of workers', soldiers', and peasants' deputies to the fore as the only mass working and exploited class institutions that could lead the struggle for complete political and economic emancipation of these classes.

During the Russian revolution's first period, the soviets grew in number, size, and strength. Their own experience taught them to abandon illusions of conciliation with the bourgeoisie and to see through bourgeois-democratic parliamentarianism's deceptive forms. From practical experience, they concluded that the oppressed classes' emancipation was impossible unless they broke with these forms and with all conciliation. The October Revolution made just such a break—the transfer of all power to the soviets.

The Constituent Assembly, elected on the basis of electoral lists presented before the October Revolution, expressed the old relation of political forces that existed when the conciliationists and Kadets held power.

When the people voted for the Socialist Revolutionary Party's candidates, they were not in a position to choose between the Right Socialist Revolutionaries—supporters of the bourgeoisie—and the Left Socialist Revolutionaries, supporters of socialism. Thus the Constituent Assembly, which was to crown the bourgeois parliamentary republic, was bound to become an obstacle in the path of the October Revolution and Soviet power.

By giving power to the soviets and—through the soviets—to the working and exploited classes, the October revolution roused the exploiters' desperate resistance. And in crushing this resistance, the October revolution fully revealed itself as the beginning of the socialist revolution.

The working classes must be convinced by experience that old bourgeois parliamentarianism has outlived its day and is absolutely incompatible with the task of achieving socialism, that only class institutions (like the soviets)—not all-national ones—can overcome the propertied classes' resistance and the lay the foundations for a socialist social order.

Any renunciation of the soviets' sovereign power, any retreat from the Soviet Republic won by the people in favor of the bourgeois parliamentarianism and the Constituent Assembly, would be a retreat from the entire October workers' and peasants' revolution and would cause its destruction.

Due to circumstances known to all, the Party of Right Socialist Revolutionaries—the party of Kerensky, Avksentev, and Chernov—obtained a majority in the Constituent Assembly that convened on 5 January. Naturally, this party refused to discuss the absolutely clear, precise, and immutable resolution by the Soviet government's supreme institution, the Central Executive Committee of the Soviets, [that the assembly endorse] the Soviet government's program, the Declaration of Rights of Toiling and Exploited People, the October Revolution, and Soviet power. In doing so, the Constituent Assembly cut its ties with the Russian Soviet Republic. Therefore it was inevitable that the Bolsheviks and the Left Socialist Revolutionaries—who now unquestionably constitute the overwhelming majority in the soviets and enjoy the confidence of the workers and most peasants—withdraw from such a Constituent Assembly.

Beyond the Constituent Assembly's walls, the parties that had a majority there—the Right Socialist Revolutionaries and Mensheviks—are waging an open struggle against Soviet power. Their newspapers openly call for its overthrow. They describe the working class' use of force to crush the exploiters' resistance—which is essential in the cause of emancipating the exploited—as arbitrary and illegal. They are defending the saboteurs, the lackeys of capital. And they have even published undisguised appeals for terrorism, which certain "unidentified groups" have already initiated.

Under such circumstances it is obvious that the remaining part of the Constituent Assembly could only serve as cloak for the bourgeois-counterrevolutionaries' struggle to overthrow Soviet power.

Consequently, the Central Executive Committee resolves: *The Constituent Assembly is hereby dissolved.*

DOCUMENT 14.10
THE SOCIALIST REVOLUTIONARIES CALL FOR
"ALL POWER TO THE CONSTITUENT ASSEMBLY!"[33]

As is clear from the following document—an editorial in the Socialist Revolutionary newspaper The People's Cause (Delo naroda) *on 7 January 1918—the socialist opposition continued to assert the Constituent Assembly's legitimacy as Russia's only duly elected legislative body even after its dispersal.*

All Power to the Constituent Assembly!

The Constituent Assembly's dispersal is an established fact. We understand that the Council of People's Commissars has provided a legal cover for this revolting violence against the revolution's supreme organ, this treachery against the working class.

But the facts speak in our favor. On 6 January the Tauride Palace was shut by the Bolshevist Janissaries.[34] The deputies were not admitted, and the Constituent Assembly session designated for 5:00 P.M. was not allowed to convene. The unambiguous threat contained in the Bolshevik fraction's declaration that the Central Executive Committee would resolve the question of how to deal with the Constituent Assembly's "counter-revolutionary" majority been made real.

Oh, we were not at all surprised or taken unaware by the so-called workers' and peasants' government's tragic tactics. But right now we do not intend to speak bitter words about this affront against the people's supreme will.

On the day the Constituent Assembly convened, we had already predicted in the pages of *The People's Cause* that the Bolsheviks would disband it, because they consider organized armed force the very best system of political administration. Therefore we were not amazed that workers demonstrating peacefully for the slogan, "All Power to the Constituent Assembly!" were fired upon.

Because we have always maintained that the Council of People's Commissars is not a workers', soldiers', and peasants' government—that it is not a socialist government. The Bolsheviks—who seized state power by armed violence and vile, spurious demagogy—are a tyrannical crowd of political adventurers who have committed treason and cannot hold on to power.

Was all this done in the interest of the working class, international socialism, the proletariat's life? If Petrograd's workers take to the streets supporting slogans that deny [the Bolsheviks'] exclusive rule, then the worse for the workers. They are shot at from the rooftops with machine guns, hand grenades are thrown at them, and the tsarist directive to use "bayonets without pity" is realized with all its tragic cruelty.

But using deliberate military force in accord with Bolshevik doctrine to shoot on a workers' demonstration that was defending the Constituent Assembly and to disband the great Russian revolution's highest institution still has not annihilated the Constituent Assembly. It lives and will live, regardless of the autocratic Bolshevik tyrants' violence, because the great Russian toiling democracy lives. It is rallying the entire true proletariat and the peasant masses around itself. Those who remain with the Smol'ny Institute are only declassed imposters, political gamblers, and the *lumpen*-proletarian dregs.[35] And the slogan, "All Power to the Constituent Assembly" will become a greater call to arms than was "Down with the Autocracy," and will summon all the revolutionary democracy's vital and authentic forces!

DOCUMENT 14.11
THE LEFT SOCIALIST REVOLUTIONARIES ON
THE CONSTITUENT ASSEMBLY'S DISSOLUTION[36]

The following document is a resolution on the Constituent Assembly's dissolution and the 7 January lynching of two Kadet political leaders, passed by a joint meeting of the Left Socialist Revolutionary (Left SR) Central Committee and Left SR Constituent Assembly delegates, and published in the Petrograd Left SR newspaper, Labor's Banner (Znamia truda), *on 9 January 1918.*[37]

The Central Committee of the Party of Left Socialist Revolutionaries considers the 6 January resolution by the Central Executive Committee of Soviets regarding the dissolution of the Constituent Assembly to have been expedient and in accord with the interests of the revolution and socialism.

The Central Committee considers it necessary that the Constituent Assembly's Left Socialist Revolutionary members join the Central Executive Committee of Soviets.

The Left Socialist Revolutionaries' Central Committee and Constituent Assembly delegates protest in the sharpest terms against the barbaric lynching of the revolution's political enemies, Shingarev and Kokoshkin. We see this disgusting crime as a blow against the revolutionary cause, and we brand its perpetrators as the revolution's enemies . . .

Let all who would serve socialism's cause put their efforts into the struggle against acts that disorganize the revolution and undermine this socialist revolution's moral greatness.

The Central Committee of the Party of Left SRs
The Left SR Constituent Assembly Fraction

DOCUMENT 14.12
BORIS KRICHEVSKII, "EITHER-OR"[38]

This final document is an essay condemning the Bolsheviks written by one of the Russian Marxist movement's most senior figures, Boris Krichevskii, published in the Menshevik Defensist newspaper, Unity (Edinstvo), *on 11 January 1918.*

Either-Or.

October's nocturnal dealings have led to a fitting conclusion: dissolution of the Constituent Assembly.

The great majority's last hope for salvation of Russia and the revolution is dead. The storms of civil war have extinguished the beacon that shined under the tsarist autocracy and would have illuminated our path to salvation . . .

The Constituent Assembly's death was foretold on the night of 24–25 October. This, of course, is true. But no one, absolutely no one, would have supposed that its death would take place under such circumstances. "The great master of the Russian lands" vanished in the morning twilight, scattered like ghosts of the night, spat upon, stomped into the mud by an armed crowd, shoved shamefully by the coarse and insolent, triumphant victors. . . .

No, not even in the camp of the Constituent Assembly's enemies was there anyone who expected such an easy, cheap "victory"! None of the dictators at Smol'nyi had expected that it would be so much easier to disperse the entire people's young representative body—which only yesterday had been invested with the entire people's confidence—than it was to overthrow Kerensky's rotting government. It was as easy as whistling a tune.

But you knew that Smol'nyi could not tolerate "parliamentary cretinism" anymore.

Do you recall that in their campaign against the Provisional Revolutionary Government the future dictators demagogically accused the government of wanting to "disrupt" the Constituent Assembly? Do you recall that one of Smol'nyi's decrees called for convening the assembly "on the designated date"?

. . . And so the Constituent Assembly was convened, but long after "the designated date." And it was convened under the threat of an ultimatum: "Either obey, or die!" Having firmly decided that they would not allow this universally elected assembly to realize the voters' will, the dictators still were not so bold as to lock down the Tauride Palace before the night of the Constituent Assembly.

The popular masses' "illusion," about which Lenin spoke on the day after the dissolution, had inspired the people with a grain of happiness.[39] The assembly, the highest institution of the people's will, was tied to this "illusion." . . . Out of fear of this illusion's unknown secrets, Smol'nyi decided to hurriedly convene a third so-called, "All-Russian Soviet Congress." Armed from head to toe against the unarmed people's elected representatives, they nonetheless summoned a "Soviet parliament" against it.

What for? Opening this false-parliament seems unnecessary. The violence against the Constituent Assembly was followed a few days later by the opening of the soviet congress, just as the Provisional Revolutionary Government was overthrown on the eve of a soviet congress.

On the Soviet Central Executive Committee, only a couple of odd ducks among the Bolsheviks spoke out against this premature and arbitrary dissolution and opposed measures that contradicted the committee's mandate by the soviet congress.[40] They were two Protestants from among the worst of the Bolsheviks. After two and a half months, all these hangers-on, participants, and accomplices still don't comprehend the dictators' inexorably developing logic. They don't understand that to participate in the unstable dictatorship, they must act according to the "principles" of all adventurers: "seize the moment!"

The spectacle of the powerless, defenseless Constituent Assembly gathering at rifle point, of the malevolent sound of weapons and the crowd's shouts about forming a lynch mob—this spectacle was too great a temptation for the oppressors. They gave in to the temptation and seized the moment. . . .

The forced dispersal was accomplished more quickly than anyone could have expected. And its setting was more humiliating than anyone could have feared. But the results of this unequal struggle were inevitable. It was predetermined by the fact that October's nocturnal dealings continued unhindered right up to 5 January. Nothing substantial changed on the night the Constituent Assembly was dispersed. The country faces the same tragic choice as before: either dictatorship or people's power.

Do the Russian people and its vital forces have the means to secure the free operation of a sovereign institution of the people's will? Or will there be a dictatorship with continually changing personnel, goals, and banners? A dictatorship accompanied by chronic civil war and anarchy, destruction, and starvation, leading to a frightening national people's catastrophe?

There is no third option.

END MATTER

CHRONOLOGY OF MAJOR EVENTS, JULY 1914–JANUARY 1918

Dates are according to calendar in use in Russia.

1914	
28 June	Assassination of Austrian Arch Duke Franz Ferdinand in Sarajevo.
July	Russian government declares military mobilization; Fourth State Duma pledges to support government's war effort.
August	World War I begins; rural unrest and anticonscription riots break out.
September–November	Russia suffers major military defeats.
1915	
March–May	German-Austrian offensive; mass expulsions of Jews from Pale of Settlement begin; anti-Jewish riots occur in Moscow.
May–July	Widespread strikes in Central Industrial Region; political crisis deepens; opposition rises in Fourth State Duma; creation of Town and Zemstvo Unions and War Industrial Committees; Duma demands the tsar replace cabinet members.
June–August	"Great Retreat" of Russian army; shootings of workers in Ivanovo-Voznesensk and in Kostroma; widespread rural unrest.
August	Nicholas II assumes military command; opposition State Duma Progressive Bloc forms.
September	Zimmerwald antiwar socialist congress; State Duma calls for formation of new government; tsar disbands Duma; mass strikes occur in Petrograd, Moscow, Nizhni-Novgorod, and Kharkov.
1916	
June–October	Russian military offensive (the "Brusilov Offensive") fails.
June–August	Kirgiz rebellion in Russian Central Asia.
October	Widespread disturbances among soldiers on Russia's western front.
November	Political crisis; State Duma demands formation of new government.
16 December	Assassination of Rasputin.
1917	
January–22 February	Strikes escalate in Petrograd and other cities.
23–26 February	February Women's demonstrations spark mass strike; troops used against demonstrators.
27 February	Petrograd garrison mutinies; Petrograd Soviet and State Duma Temporary Committee formed.
1 March	Petrograd Soviet's Order No. 1 issued.
2 March	Abdication of Nicholas II; all-liberal Provisional Government formed; Petrograd Soviet conditionally approves Provisional Government.

10 March	Petrograd Soviet and industrialists agree on eight-hour workday.
14 March	Petrograd Soviet issues international appeal for just, democratic peace.
20 March	Provisional Government recognizes universal, equal civil rights.
21 March	Revolutionary defensist Mensheviks and SRs take leadership of Petrograd Soviet.
4 April	Lenin, having returned from Switzerland, issues April Theses.
5–8 April	Ukrainian National Congress demands national autonomy.
18–21 April	Publication of Miliukov Note leads to mass demonstrations; April Crisis.
2–5 May	First Provisional Government collapses; Mensheviks, SRs, and Popular-Socialists create first liberal-socialist coalition government.
3–5 June	First All-Russian Congress of Soviets; creation of All-Russian Soviet Central Executive Committee.
10 June	Ukrainian Rada issues First Universal.
18 June	June military offensive begins; mass demonstrations occur in Petrograd.
1–2 July	Provisional Government and Ukrainian Rada agree on limited Ukrainian autonomy; Kadets resign from government; July Crisis.
3–5 July	Militant Bolsheviks uprising in Petrograd fails (July Days); Bolshevik leaders arrested (Lenin flees to Finland).
5 July	Collapse of the Russian military offensive.
8 July	Kerensky takes leadership of coalition government.
12 July	At Kornilov's insistence, government restores death penalty for soldiers at the front.
18 July	Kerensky appoints Kornilov as supreme commander.
20 July	Provisional Government grants female suffrage.
21–23 July	Kerensky forms second coalition government.
12–15 August	Moscow State Conference.
27–31 August	Kornilov rebellion; collapse of second coalition government.
1 September	Kerensky forms emergency cabinet (the "Directory").
5 September	Left bloc of Bolsheviks, left SRs, and Menshevik-Internationalists win majority in Moscow Soviet.
14–22 September	Democratic Conference; formation of Pre-Parliament.
25 September	Left bloc of Bolsheviks and left SRs win majority in Petrograd Soviet; Trotsky elected Petrograd Soviet Chairman; moderate Petrograd Soviet Executive Committee steps down; Kerensky forms third coalition government.
10–16 October	Bolshevik leaders debate if and when to seize power.
11–13 October	Northern Front Soviet Congress calls for Soviet power.
12 October	Creation of Petrograd Soviet Military Revolutionary Committee.
18 October	*Novaia Zhizn'* publishes Kamenev Note.
21–23 October	Petrograd Soviet Military Revolutionary Committee takes steps to win over or neutralize garrison units.

24 October	Kerensky shuts down Bolshevik newspapers in Petrograd; Petrograd Soviet Military Revolutionary Committee takes control of strategic points in the city; pro-government and pro-soviet forces battle.
25 October	Provisional Government overthrown and arrested (Kerensky escapes to rally forces); Second All-Russian Congress of Soviets holds first session; moderate and right socialists leave congress to protest the Bolshevik insurrection.
26 October	Liberals, and moderate and right socialists form Committee of Salvation; Petrograd Soviet begins arresting opposition leaders and shuts down Kadet newspapers; Second All-Russian Congress of Soviets issues decrees on peace, land reform, and creation of all-Bolshevik Soviet government (Council of People's Commissars); new Soviet Central Executive Committee formed.
26 October– 2 November	Soviets take power in several provincial cities; armed political battles break out in several cities (including Moscow).
27 October	Soviet government issues decree on press censorship.
29 October–3 November	All-Russian Railroad Workers Union (Vikzhel) negotiations on formation of all-socialist coalition government fail.
7 November	Ukrainian Rada issues Third Universal.
12 November	Constituent Assembly elections begin; Bolshevik and left SR delegates quit All-Russian Peasant Congress and form Extraordinary Peasant Congress; agreement expands Soviet Executive Committee.
15 November	Left SRs join Soviet Central Executive Committee.
19 November	Left SRs hold congress and formally break from Party of Socialist Revolutionaries to create a new party.
23 November	Creation of Union to Defend the Constituent Assembly in Petrograd.
28 November	Demonstrations and violent clashes occur in Petrograd; Bolsheviks arrest Kadet leaders and members of Union to Defend Constituent Assembly.
2 December	Soviet government signs armistice with Germany and Austria-Hungary.
7 December	Creation of the Extraordinary Commission for Struggle against Counterrevolution and Espionage (the Cheka).
12 December	Left SRs accept posts in Council of People's Commissars.
Mid-December	Soviet and White forces battle in Ukraine and the Don Region; Soviet power established in several more provincial cities.

1918

4 January	Soviet government recognizes Finland's independence.
5 January	Constituent Assembly meets; Bolsheviks and Left SRs quit in protest after the assembly refuses to endorse the Soviet government.
6 January	Soviet government disbands the Constituent Assembly.

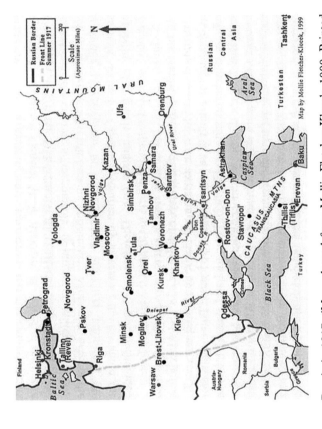

Russia in 1917. (Map adapted from Mollie Fletcher-Klocek, 1999. Printed in Rex A. Wade, *The Russian Revolution, 1917*, Second Edition (Cambridge: Cambridge University Press, 2005), p. 51.)

BIOGRAPHICAL GLOSSARY

Abramovich, Raphael (Rafail Abramovich Rein) (1880–1963). Major figure in the Bund and Menshevik movements. A founder of the Petrograd Soviet in 1917, elected to the Soviet Central Executive Committee in June 1917. After the October Revolution active in Menshevik and Bundist movement in Europe and in New York; published important historical works in Yiddish and English.

Adzhemov, Moisei Sergeevich (1878–1950). Kadet Party leader and deputy to the Second, Third and Fourth State Dumas from the Don Military District. Worked in the justice ministry in 1917. Emigrated to France after October Revolution.

Afanasev-Arskii, Pavel (1886–1967). Poet, lyricist, and playwright. Mobilized in 1915. Arrested in July 1917 for antiwar agitation. Joined the Communist Party in 1918; helped lead the *Proletkul't* (Proletarian Culture) movement in Petrograd in 1918–1922; served in the Petrograd Soviet in 1918–1924 and the Moscow Soviet in 1931–1934.

Alekseev, General Mikhail Vasil'evich (1857–1918). Career military officer; led Russian forces in Galicia in 1914; chief of staff from September 1915 to November 1916. Helped negotiate the tsar's abdication in March 1917, then served as commander in chief in March–May 1917. White Army leader after the October Revolution. Died of natural causes in 1918.

Argunov, Andrei Aleksandrovich (Voronovich) (1867–1939). A founder of the Party of Socialist Revolutionaries (PSR) in 1902; Socialist Revolutionary (SR) leader in St. Petersburg during 1905 Revolution; arrested and exiled repeatedly; led SR defensist faction in exile in 1914–1917. In 1917 helped lead right SR faction and edited *Volia naroda*. Emigrated to Czechoslovakia after the October Revolution.

Astrov, Isaak Sergeevich (Poves) (1877–1922). Joined the Russian Social Democratic Labor Party (RSDLP) in 1902. Elected to Menshevik Central Committee in August 1917. In March 1918 arrested by Bolsheviks for organizing workers' protests in Petrograd; spent the Civil War in Odessa; arrested by Ukrainian Communist authorities. Died in prison in 1922.

Astrov, Nikolai Ivanovich (1868–1934). Kadet activist, chairman of All-Russian Union of Towns in 1916–1917. In 1917 served as mayor of Moscow. After the October Revolution, represented Denikin's White Army in Paris; in 1920 emigrated to France with his partner, Countess Sofia V. Panina (1871–1956); subsequently worked with émigré relief agencies.

Avilov, Boris Vasil'evich (1874–1938). An editor at *Novaia zhizn'* in 1917, was a prominent left Menshevik and a founder of the United Social Democrat-Internationalists.

Avksent'ev, Nikolai Dmitrievich (1878–1943). A founding member of the PSR in 1902; helped lead SRs in 1905 Revolution, arrested and exiled. Helped lead right SR faction in 1917, served as chairman of All-Russian Congress of Peasant Deputies, chairman of Democratic Conference and of the Pre-Parliament, as well as minister of interior in July–September. Served in the Komuch government and the Directory during 1918; emigrated in 1920 to France, where he led émigré populist circles; in 1940 fled to the United States when Germany invaded France.

Bal'mont, Konstantin Dmitrievich (1867–1942). Symbolist poet during Russia's "Silver Age," spent 1905–1916 in Paris, then returned to Russia in 1916. Supported the February Revolution, but not politically active. Emigrated to France after the October Revolution.

Bednyi, Dem'ian (Efin Alekseevich Pridvorov) (1883–1945). Poet. Joined Bolsheviks in 1911; served as medic in the Russian army during World War I. Frequently contributed to Bolshevik newspapers in 1917. Became a major Soviet literary figure during the 1920s–1930s; purged from the Communist Party in 1938.

Beillis, Menachem Mendel (1874–1934). Jewish worker falsely accused of ritual murder in Kiev in 1911. His arrest and 1913 trial were flashpoints for public debate about Jews and antisemitism. Emigrated to Palestine after being found innocent.

Bekhterev, Vladimir Mikhailovich (1857–1927). Neurologist and world authority on brain structure and reflexes; founded psycho-neurological institute in St. Petersburg and was appointed to Russian Academy of Sciences. Stalin later banned his publications. Died under suspicious circumstances in 1927.

Bleichman, Iosif Solomonovich (N. Sol'ntsev) (1862–1921). A leader of Petrograd Federation of Anarchist-Communists. Born in the Jewish Pale of Settlement; emigrated to the United States in the 1890s; became an anarchist in 1904; returned to Russia in 1905; in 1906 arrested and exiled to Siberia. Returned to Petrograd in March 1917, was a key figure during the July Days. Served in the Red Army in 1918–1919, then arrested by Soviet authorities. Died in a labor camp in 1921.

Bobrinskii, Count A. A. (1852–1927). Tsarist agriculture minister from August 1916 to February 1917.

Bogdanov, Aleksandr Aleksandrovich (Malinovskii) (1873–1928). Medical doctor and philosopher. A member of the Bolshevik movement from 1903 to 1909, then broke with Lenin and joined the Mensheviks. Rejoined Bolsheviks in 1918 and participated in the Proletkult' movement.

Bogdanov, Boris Osipovich (Olenich) (1880–1960). Menshevik activist. Served on Central War Industry Board during World War I. In 1917 elected secretary of the Menshevik Organizational Committee, a member of the Petrograd Soviet Executive Committee, and a member of the All-Russian Central Executive Committee of Soviets. After the October Revolution, participated in anti-Bolshevik Menshevik workers' movement; arrested in 1920 and imprisoned until 1955.

Bokii, Gleb Ivanovich (1879–1937). Joined the RSDLP in 1900. In April-December 1917, served as secretary of the Bolshevik Petersburg Committee. During the Civil War, served as a Cheka official and helped establish the network of state prison camps (gulags). Executed in 1937.

Breshko-Breshkovskaia, Ekaterina Konstantinovna (1844–1934). "The Little Grand-mother of the Russian Revolution," a prominent figure in the populist movement. Arrested in 1874; exiled to Siberia in 1878–1896; participated in founding the PSR in 1902; arrested again in 1907 and exiled to Siberia until 1917. In 1917 closely allied with Kerensky. Emigrated to Czechoslovakia in 1918.

Bubnov, Andrei Sergeevich (1887–1938). Joined the RSDLP in 1903; repeatedly arrested and exiled. In 1917 served on the Bolshevik Moscow Committee and the Moscow Workers' Soviet; elected to Bolshevik Central Committee in the fall. Joined Left Communist opposition in 1918 and the Democratic Centrist opposition in 1920; during the Civil War served in railroad and military administrative posts; in the 1930s and 1930s held various posts in military administration and the commissariat of education. Arrested and executed in 1938.

Bukharin, Nikolai Ivanovich (1888–1938). Bolshevik theorist. Joined the Bolsheviks in 1906 and quickly became a leader of the Moscow party organization; arrested in 1911 and exiled in 1912–1917; during World War I, led antiwar Social Democrat circle in New York and edited *Novyi Mir*. In 1917 led the Bolshevik Moscow Committee and served on the Bolshevik Central Committee. In 1918, led the Left Communist opposition; edited *Pravda* in 1918–1929; served on the Communist Party Central Committee in 1917–1937 and the Politburo in 1924–1929; served as chairman of Communist International in 1926–1929; during the Great Terror was arrested, put on a show trial. Executed in 1938.

Burtsev, Vladimir L'vovich (1862–1942). Populist activist, famous for exposing police spies. In 1917 wrote articles naming Bolshevik leaders as German agents. Arrested by Bolsheviks in December 1917, released in 1918; supported the Whites during the Civil War; in 1920, emigrated to France, published volume exposing *The Protocols of the Elders of Zion* as a fraud facilitated by the tsarist police.

Chelnokov, M. V. (1863–1935). Liberal industrialist. Served as mayor of Moscow in spring 1917.

Chernov, Viktor Mikhailovich (1873–1952). Radical populist. Arrested in 1894 and sentenced to internal exile in Tambov; emigrated to Switzerland in 1899; helped found PSR in 1902; SR leader in 1905 Revolution; SR deputy to State Duma and leader of SR antiwar faction in 1914–1917. Helped lead SR revolutionary defensist faction in 1917; served as agriculture minister in May–August 1917. In January 1918, elected chairman of Constituent Assembly, then served in Komuch; in 1920 emigrated to Western Europe then to the United States.

Chkheidze, Nikolai Semenovich (1864–1926). Founder of Georgian Social Democratic movement, leader of Georgian Mensheviks; led Menshevik faction in State Duma in 1907–1914. In 1917 helped lead Menshevik revolutionary defensist faction; chairman of the Petrograd Soviet. In 1920 helped found the Democratic Republic of Georgia; emigrated to France in 1921. Committed suicide in 1926.

Dan, Feodor Il'ich (Gurvich) (1871–1947). Jewish labor activist arrested and sentenced to internal exile in 1896–1899; joined RSDLP in 1899; joined Mensheviks in 1903; active in underground work in 1912–1915; again arrested and sentenced to internal exile in 1915–1916. In 1917 helped lead Menshevik revolutionary defensist faction; served on Petrograd Soviet. During Civil War joined anti-Bolshevik Menshevik opposition; exiled in 1921; lived in the United States, where he wrote a seminal history of the Russian Marxist movement.

Dolgorukov, Prince Pavel Dmitrievich (1866–1927). A founder of the Kadet Party in 1905 and chairman of the Kadet Central Committee in 1911–1915; served as official in the Red Cross and the All-Russian Union of Towns in 1914–1917. In 1917 was leading Kadet organizer among the military. Arrested by the Bolsheviks in December 1917; assisted the White movement in 1918–1920, then emigrated; in 1925 returned to Russia, arrested. Executed without trial in 1927.

Dubnov, Semen Markovich (1860–1941). Important liberal Jewish historian and a founder of the Jewish People's Party (*Folkspartie*). In 1917 supported the February Revolution, then opposed the Bolsheviks. Emigrated to Lithuania in 1922. Executed by the Nazis in 1941.

Dzerzhinskii, Feliks Edmundovich (Dzierżyński) (1877–1926). Joined the Lithuanian Social Democratic Party in 1895; helped found the Polish Social Democratic Party in 1900. In spring 1917 joined Bolshevik Party; served on the Bolshevik Central Committee and the Petrograd Soviet Military Revolutionary Committee in October 1917. Led the Cheka from December 1917–1926. Died of natural causes in 1926.

Erlikh, Genrikh Moseevich (Henryk Erlich) (1882–1942). Jewish Social Democrat and Bund leader. Elected to the Petrograd Soviet in 1917. Emigrated to Poland after the October Revolution, was preeminent figure in Polish Jewish politics; arrested with his wife, Sophia

Dubnov-Erlikh (1860–1941) during Soviet invasion of eastern Poland in 1939; led the Soviet Union's Jewish Antifascist Committee in 1942. Executed on Stalin's orders in 1948.

Fenigshtein, Iakov Genrikovich (Doletsky) (1888–1936?). In 1917 served on the Bolshevik Petersburg Committee and led its "Polish Section." Joined Left Communist opposition in 1918; chairman of Belorussian Soviet government during the Civil War; held several state posts, including that of director of the Soviet news agency TASS in the 1930. Committed suicide in 1936.

Friedman, Naftali (1863–1921). Liberal Jewish deputy to Fourth State Duma.

Gendel'man, Mikhail Iakovlevich (1881–1938). SR activist, helped lead the SR defensist faction in 1914–1917. In 1917 served on SR Central Committee. After the October Revolution, participated in the SR anti-Bolshevik movement; arrested repeatedly in the 1920s–1930s. Executed in 1938.

Gol'denberg, Iosif Petrovich (Roman Meshkovskii) (1871–1922). A Bolshevik leader in 1903–1907 who then broke with Lenin and joined the Mensheviks. In 1917 was among Lenin's harshest Menshevik critics.

Goremykin, Ivan Loginovich (1839–1917). Conservative nobleman. Held several ministerial posts prior to 1914, including prime minister in 1906; appointed chairman of the Council of Ministers in 1914, but was removed from that post in 1916. Lynched in November 1917.

Gorkii [Gorky], Maxim (Aleksei Maksimovich Peshkov) (1868–1936). Prominent Russian novelist and playwright, closely associated with the RSDLP. Favored Bolsheviks in 1905; arrested in 1906, lived abroad until 1913; active supporter of antiwar Social Democrats in 1914–1917. In 1917 edited *Novaia zhizn'* and supported the Menshevik-Internationalists. After the October Revolution, opposed the Bolshevik regime; arrested in 1921; lived abroad in 1921–1933. Lauded by Stalin as a literary hero upon return to Soviet Union.

Gots, Abram Rafailovich (1882–1940). Participated in militant SR terrorist circles in 1905–1914. In 1917 joined SR leadership and served as vice-chairman of the All-Russian Soviet Executive Committee in June-October, then as chairman of Committee to Save the Motherland and Revolution in November. Participated in the SR anti-Bolshevik movement during the Civil War; arrested repeatedly in the 1920s. Died in a Soviet labor camp in 1940.

Guchkov, Aleksandr Ivanovich (1862–1936). Octobrist leader. Helped create the Progressive bloc in the State Duma; served as chairman of the Central War Industrial Committee in 1915–1917. In 1917 served as war and naval minister in March–April. Emigrated after the October Revolution.

Gukovskii, Aleksandr Isaevich (A. Serov) (1865–1925). Radical populist. Joined the PSR in 1902; in 1914–1917 was a member of the right SR faction and the *Prizyv* group. In 1917 served as deputy zemstvo chairman in Cherpovets County, Vologda Province; frequently contributed to *Delo naroda*. Elected to Constituent Assembly, served in a short-lived SR-liberal coalition government in Arkhangel; emigrated to Paris in 1919; active in anti-Bolshevik politics and journalism. Committed suicide in 1925.

Gurevich, Solomon Grigor'evich (dates unknown). Provincial journalist and editor of *Smolenskii vestnik*. In 1917 was a leader of the SR and Jewish Socialist Workers' Party (SERP) groups in Smolensk.

Hrushevskyi, Mykhailo Serhiyovych (1866–1934). Prominent Ukrainian historian. In March 1917, elected chairman of Ukrainian Rada. Led the Rada until July 1918, then emigrated; in 1922 returned to Russia and held top posts in Soviet academic institutions.

Ioffe, Adol'f Abramovich (1883–1927). Joined the RSDLP in 1903. In 1917 belonged to the *Mezhraiontsy* group in Petrograd, then joined the Bolshevik Central Committee in August; elected to the Petrograd City Duma in August; served as chairman of the Petrograd Soviet Military Revolutionary Committee in October. In 1918, led the first Soviet negotiating team at Brest-Litovsk, then held several Soviet diplomatic posts during the Civil War and in the 1920s. Committed suicide in 1927.

Ivanov, Razumnik Vasilevich (V. R. Ivanov-Razumnik) (1878–1946). Writer, journalist, and founder of "Scythians." In 1917 was close to the left SR internationalist faction and served as an editor at *Delo naroda*, but did not join the PSR. After the October Revolution, wrote for Left SR publications and was arrested repeatedly until emigrating to Lithuania; during World War II, spent two years in Nazi concentration camps. Died in Germany in 1946.

Kaledin, General Aleksei Maksimovich (1860–1918). Career tsarist cavalry officer. In June 1917, chosen as *ataman* (chief) of Don Cossacks. After the October Revolution, led anti-Bolshevik forces in the Don. Committed suicide in 1918.

Kalinin, Mikhail Ivanovich (1875–1946). Joined RSDLP in 1898, became a Bolshevik in 1905; worked at a Putilov factory, served on Bolshevik Petersburg Committee in 1914–1916; arrested for antiwar agitation and exiled to Siberia in 1916. In 1917, served on the Bolshevik Petersburg Committee. Served as a member of the Politburo and chairman of the All-Russian Soviet Central Executive Committee in 1919–1946. Survived the Great Terror, but his wife was arrested and sent to a labor camp in 1938.

Kamenev, Lev Borisovich (Rosenfel'd) (1888–1936). Joined the RSDLP in 1901 and allied with Lenin from 1902; served on Bolshevik Central Committee in 1917. Served as chairman of the All-Russian Soviet Central Executive Committee in October–November 1917; chairman of the Moscow Soviet in 1918–1926; belonged to the Bolshevik Central Committee in 1917–1927 and the Politburo in 1919–1925; arrested in 1934, put up on show trial in 1936. Executed in 1937.

Kamkov, Boris Davidovich (Kats) (1885–1938). Helped lead the SR antiwar faction in 1914–1917. In 1917, was a prominent left SR in Petrograd; led efforts to force Bolsheviks into an all-socialist coalition. In 1918 opposed the Brest-Litovsk Treaty and led the anti-Bolshevik Left SR opposition; arrested after failed SR rebellion in July 1918; sentenced to internal exile in 1918–1938. Executed in 1938.

Kartashev, Anton Vladimirovich (1875–1960). Theologian and Kadet Party activist. In 1917 served as procurator of Holy Synod in July and as religious affairs minister in August through October. Emigrated after the October Revolution.

Kerenskii, Aleksandr Fedorovich [Alexander Kerensky] (1881–1970). Prominent lawyer turned politician. Elected as a State Duma deputy representing the SR's Trudovik splinter group. In the 1917 February Revolution served on the Duma Temporary Committee and the Petrograd Soviet leadership group; only socialist to join the first Provisional Government, as justice minister; in May helped form the first coalition government in and served as war and naval minister; in July formed the second coalition government and added prime minister to his portfolio; in September led the Directory and the third coalition government as commander in chief. Emigrated to the United States after the October Revolution; lectured, wrote his memoirs and compiled a document collection on the Provisional Government.

Khinchuk, Lev Mikhailovich (1868–1939). Joined RSDLP in 1898 and the Mensheviks in 1903. In 1917 served as chairman of the Moscow Workers' Soviet in March–September and then elected to the All-Russian Soviet Central Executive Committee in June. After the October Revolution, participated in Menshevik anti-Bolshevik opposition until 1921, then joined the Communist Party and served in several Soviet administrative posts; assigned to the Soviet embassy in Berlin, 1930–1934; purged, arrested, and executed in 1939.

Kibrik, Boris Samiulovich (1885–?). Menshevik activist. In 1917 helped found the Moscow Workers' Soviet, and edited its newspaper.

Kishkin, Nikolai Mikhailovich (1864–1930). Medical doctor and a member of the Kadet Central Committee. In 1917 served as the public welfare minister in September–October. After the October Revolution, active in Kadet anti-Bolshevik opposition; following the Civil War, helped organize famine relief efforts and worked in the commissariat of public health.

Klochkov, D. V. (1893–?). Son of a rural schoolteacher from Vologda Province. Drafted in 1914, and then served in Roslavl' Garrison. In 1917 belonged to the local Bolshevik group and was elected to the local soldiers' soviet.

Kokoshkin, Feodor Feodorovich (1871–1918). Law professor and public education activist. Joined the Kadets in 1905, served on Kadet Central Committee from 1907. Held post of comptroller of Provisional Government in July–August 1917. Arrested in November 1917, imprisoned, and murdered in January 1918.

Kollontai, Aleksandra Mikhailovna (1872–1952). Began participating in radical circles in the 1890s; joined Mensheviks in 1906; became a Bolshevik in 1915. Served on Bolshevik Central Committee in 1917. After the October Revolution, became commissar for social security; resigned in spring 1918; helped lead Left Communist opposition in 1918 and Workers' Opposition in 1920; help post as director of the Communist Party's Women's Bureau (*Zhenotdel*) in 1920s; served in diplomatic posts in 1930s.

Konovalov, Aleksandr Ivanovich (1875–1948). Moscow merchant and a member of the Progressist Party. In 1917 served as minister of trade and industry in March–May, then as deputy prime minister in September–October. Emigrated after the October Revolution.

Kornilov, General Lavr Georgievich (1870–1918). Career infantry officer. In 1917 appointed commander of Petrograd Military District in spring, then commander of Southwestern Front in July; served as supreme commander in July–August; led a revolt against Kerensky in late August 1917, and was arrested. Active in White Army against Soviet government, killed in battle in 1918.

Krichevskii, Boris Naumovich (1861–1919). Founded "legal Marxist" movement in 1897, was a leading figure in Marxist "Economist" movement, and edited *Rabochaia mysl'*, 1900–1903. Remained distant from politics in 1917.

Krupskaia, Nadezhda Konstantinovna (1869–1939). Marxist public education activist, married to Lenin in 1989–1924. Arrested and exiled along with Lenin in 1896; joined RSDLP in 1898; a Bolshevik from 1903. In 1917, worked primarily as a Bolshevik propagandist in Petrograd. In Soviet period served as deputy commissar of enlightenment (education) and as chair of the Communist Party Education Bureau in 1920; belonged to Central Committee in 1927–1939.

Krylenko, Nikolai Vasil'evich (1885–1938). Joined the Bolsheviks in 1905; participated in Petrograd Soviet in 1905; in 1906 arrested and sentenced to internal exile; earned law degree in 1911; served as officer in the tsarist army in 1912–1913; mobilized into the army in 1916. In 1917 elected commander of the 11th Army Committee in March, made a member of the Bolshevik Petrograd Military Organization in May; was an important military organizer during the July Days and the October Revolution. Served as commander in the Red Army from November 1917 to March 1918; chairman of the Revolutionary Tribunal in 1918–1922; deputy procurator of the RSFSR in 1923–1931; and the chief procurator and people's commissar of justice, 1931–1938. Arrested and executed in 1938.

Kryzhanovskii, Sergei Efimovich (1861–?). Served as Tsarist deputy minister of interior in 1906–1911 and as state secretary of the State Council's Chancery in 1910–1917. Supporter of far-right groups.

Kurlov, Pavel Grigorevich (1860–1923). Tsarist interior ministry official for three decades. Reputed arch-reactionary and antisemite.

Kutuzov, Father Georgii Afanas'evich (dates unknown). Russian Orthodox Priest and local SR leader in Smolensk Province in 1917.

Larin, Iurii Mikhailovich (Lur'e) (1882–1932). Joined the RSDLP in 1901; joined the Mensheviks in 1903; was member of Menshevik antiwar faction in 1914–1916. In 1917 joined the Bolsheviks in Petrograd. After the October Revolution, served on the All-Russian Central Executive Committee of Soviets and in several important Soviet economic posts.

Latsis, Martyn Ivanovich (Janis Fredrikh Sudrabs) (1888–1938). Latvian Bolshevik activist and members of Bolshevik Petersburg Committee in 1905–1917. In 1917 served on the Bolshevik Petersburg Committee and was member of the Petrograd Soviet Military Revolutionary Committee in October. Served in the Cheka central administration in 1918–1921, and then in various party and state economic posts. Executed in 1938.

Lenin, Vladimir Il'ich (Vladimir Il'ich Ul'ianov) (1870–1924). Central figure in Russian Marxist theoretical and organizational debates. Founded RSDLP in 1898; led the Bolsheviks from 1903. In 1917, was preeminent figure in Bolshevik Party. In Soviet period was chairman of the Council of People's Commissars and leader of the Communist Party Politburo. Survived an assassination attempt in August 1918, then left political and state posts due to failing health in 1923.

Lukomovskii, Lieutenant General Aleksandr Sergeevich (1868–1939). Career tsarist military officer. In 1917 served as quartermaster general at Stavka and as Kornilov's chief of staff. After the October Revolution, helped lead White Army forces and was chair of General Denikin's White government in 1919–1920; emigrated in 1920.

Lunacharskii, Anatoli Vasil'evich (1875–1933). Joined the RSDLP in 1900, but remained outside Bolshevik and Menshevik camps in 1903–1916; exiled in Western Europe after 1905. In 1917 belonged to Petrograd *Mezhraiontsy* in spring; joined the Bolsheviks and the Bolshevik Central Committee in August; served on Petrograd Soviet Military Revolutionary Committee in October. After the October Revolution, was people's commissar of enlightenment (education) in 1917–1929, and then held diplomatic posts.

Luxemburg, Rosa (1871–1919). Leader of left-wing, antiwar factions in German and Polish Social Democratic parties; broke with the German Social Democrat leadership over the war in 1914. With Karl Liebknecht (1871–1919), founded antiwar Spartacus League, and, in January 1919, the German Communist Party. Murdered by right-wing paramilitary forces in 1919.

L'vov, Prince Georgii Evgen'evich (1861–1925). Liberal zemstvo and public activist. Joined the Kadet Party in 1905; elected to the First State Duma in 1906, then left the Kadets; chairman of the All-Russian Zemstvo Union in 1914–1917. In 1917 served as prime minister in March–July. After the October Revolution, arrested by Soviet government and emigrated to France.

L'vov, Vladmir Nikolaevich (1872–1934). Theologian and a member of the Progressist Party. In 1917 served as Ober-Prokurer of Holy Synod in March–July. Emigrated after the October Revolution, but returned in 1922 and participated in the Orthodox Church renewal movement; arrested and sentenced to internal exile in 1927.

Maklakov, Vasilii Alekseevich (1869–1957). Lawyer and liberal activist. Joined the Kadet Party in 1905, elected as deputy to Second, Third, and Fourth State Dumas. In 1917, served as Provisional Government's ambassador to France. Remained in France after the October Revolution.

Manasevich-Manuilov, Ivan (1869–1918). Journalist, tsarist secret police informant, and member of Rasputin's court entourage. During World War I, protégé and personal secretary to Interior Minister Shturmer; arrested in April 1916 for fraud and accepting bribes.

Manuilov, Aleksander Appolonovich (1861–1929). Economist, Kadet activist, and Rector of Moscow State University. In 1917 served as education minister in March–April. During the Civil War participated in anti-Bolshevik opposition; after the Civil War, worked in Soviet banking institutions.

Markov, Nikolai Evgen'evivh (Markov 2) (1866–1945). Antisemitic ultranationalist political activist. Helped found the Union of Russian People in 1910; editor of its newspaper; and deputy to Third and Fourth State Dumas. Had little influence in Russian politics in 1917. After the October Revolution, emigrated to Germany, led émigré monarchist union, and then supported Hitler.

Martov, Iulii Osipovich (Tsederbaum) (1873–1923). Helped found the RSDLP in 1898 and led the Menshevik faction in 1903; opposed World War I and led the antiwar left Mensheviks. In 1917 led the Menshevik-Internationalists, elected to the Moscow Soviet and the All-Russian Soviet Central Executive Committee. After the October Revolution, led Menshevik-Internationalists in Soviet Central Executive Committee; emigrated in 1920.

Maslov, Petr Pavlovich (1867–1946). Joined Mensheviks in 1905; helped organize Menshevik defensist faction during World War I. With G. Plekhanov, led Menshevik defensists in 1917. Briefly opposed the October Revolution, then pursued career as an economist in Soviet government.

Miliukov, Pavel Nikolaevich (1859–1943). Historian. Founder of the Kadet Party in 1905; member of the Kadet Central Committee from 1905; deputy to the First through Fourth State Dumas; leader of the Progressive Bloc in Fourth State Duma. In 1917, foreign affairs minister in March–April. After the October Revolution, active in the White movement; after the Civil War, emigrated to France and remained an active historian and political journalist.

Miliutin, Vladimir Pavlovich (1884–1937). Joined the Mensheviks in 1903; was a Bolshevik from 1910. In 1917 helped lead the Saratov Bolshevik organization and chaired the Saratov Workers' Soviet; elected to the Bolshevik Central Committee in August 1917. In November 1917 served briefly as people's commissar of agriculture, but resigned in protest of press censorship; during the Civil War was deputy chairman of the All-Russian Council of National Economy; after the Civil War held state economic posts. Arrested and executed in 1937.

Molotov, Viacheslav Mikhailovich (Skriabin) (1890–1986). Joined the Bolsheviks in 1906; repeatedly arrested and exiled between 1909 and 1915; joined Bolshevik Petersburg Committee in 1916. In 1917 served as editor of *Pravda* in early March. Held various party posts during the Civil War; Stalin's right-hand men in 1920s–1950s, served as prime minister in 1930–1939; foreign minister in 1939–1949. Belonged to post-Stalin collective leadership in 1953–1957.

Movskin, Ivan (patronymic and dates unknown). Petrograd Bolshevik activist and a member of the Bolshevik Petersburg Committee in 1917.

Nabokov, Vladimir Dmitrievich (1869–1922). Lawyer and liberal activist. Helped found the Kadet Party in 1905, served on its central committee. In 1917 served as secretary of the Provisional Government's chancellery in March–June. After the October Revolution, participated as part of the White opposition; emigrated in 1920. Killed protecting Miliukov from an assassin in 1922.

Nazarbekov, General Foma (Tomvas Nazerabekian) (1855–1931). Armenian career officer in tsarist army. Commander of the Caucasian Front in 1914; led offensive against Turkey in 1916. In 1917, resisted the army's democratization and lost command in April. After the October Revolution, commanded Armenian national forces; arrested in 1921 when Soviet government took power in Armenia; released and lived in Tbilisi.

Nekrasov, Nikolai Vissarionovich (1879–1940). Kadet activist. During 1917 served as transport minister in March–July; finance minister and deputy prime minister in July–August; and Finland's governor general in September–October. After the October Revolution, was active in the White movement; after the Civil War, worked in Soviet economic institutions. Arrested and executed in 1940.

Nogin, Viktor Pavlovich (1878–1924). Joined the RSDLP in 1898; became a Menshevik in 1903 and a Bolshevik after 1905; worked as cooperative activist. In 1917 served on the Moscow Bolshevik Committee, then joined Bolshevik Central Committee in August; served as chairman of the Moscow Soviet in September–November and as chairman of the Moscow Military Revolutionary Committee in October. After the October Revolution, became people's commissar of trade, but resigned in November 1917 to protest Lenin's refusal to form a socialist coalition; later worked in Soviet trade institutions.

Pereverzev, Pavel Nikolaevich (1871–1944). Lawyer, jurist, and SR activist. As chief court prosecutor in Petrograd in 1917, investigated Lenin's ties to Germany; also served as justice minister in May–July 1917. Emigrated to France after the October Revolution.

Peshekhonov, Alexei Vasil'evich (1867–1933). Economist, teacher, journalist, founder of Union of Liberation in 1903, and active member in the Party of Popular-Socialists. In 1917 was elected to the Petrograd Soviet, served as food supply minister in May–July; deputy chairman of Pre-Parliament in October. After the October Revolution, active in anti-Bolshevik opposition;expelled from Soviet Russia in 1922; worked with Soviet trade institutions in Latvia.

Plehve, Viacheslav Konstantinovich von (1846–1904). Tsarist government official, 1860s–1904; key posts included director of tsarist police administration and minister of interior in 1902–1904. Assassinated by SR terrorist group in 1904.

Plekhanov, Georgii Valentinovich (1856–1918). Russian Marxist theorist, the "Father of Russian Marxism," a populist in the 1870s, then founder of Russia's first Marxist organization in the 1880s. Helped found the RSDLP in 1898; a key figure in the Menshevik movement; from 1914, led the Menshevik defensist faction. In 1917 guided the Menshevik defensists and edited their newspaper *Edinstvo*. After the October Revolution, active in anti-Bolshevik opposition, harassed by the Cheka, and then emigrated to Finland.

Podvitskii, Viktor Vladimirskii (1886–1937). Member of militant SR groups in Smolensk from 1903. In 1917, Smolensk SR leader and key figure in Smolensk Soviet. After the October Revolution, briefly active in anti-Bolshevik opposition. Arrested and executed in 1937.

Polovtsev, General Peter Aleksandrovich (1874–?). Career tsarist military officer. In 1917 served as commander of the Petrograd Military District during the July Days, but was removed from command; then worked in the ministry of internal affairs. Emigrated to Monaco after the October Revolution.

Potresov, Aleksander Nikolaevich (1869–1934). Joined the RSDLP in 1898; sided with Mensheviks in 1903; a staunch defensist from 1914. In 1917, edited the Menshevik newspaper *Den*. After the October Revolution, joined anti-Bolshevik opposition and was arrested repeatedly; expelled to France in 1925.

Protopopov, Aleksandr Dmitrievich (1866–1918). Industrialist, member of the Octobrist Party, briefly vice president of the Fourth State Duma, and acting minister of internal affairs in 1916. Arrested by Provisional Government in 1917. Executed in 1918.

Purishkevich, Vladimir Mitrofanovich (1870–1920). Founded Union of Russian People and Union of Archangel Michael in 1905; served as deputy to Second through Fourth State Dumas; helped assassinate Rasputin in 1916. In 1917 called for dissolution of soviets. In November 1917, helped organized the Committee for the Salvation of the Motherland, arrested and convicted by the Petrograd Revolutionary Tribunal; freed in May 1918; joined the White opposition. Died of typhus in 1920.

Rakh'ia, Eino Abramovich (dates unknown). Finnish worker activist. Joined the RSDLP in 1902. In 1917, served as a member of the Bolshevik Petersburg Committee and as Lenin's emissary from Finland.

Rasputin, Grigorii Efimovich (1869–1916). Charismatic faith healer and advisor to Nicholas and Alexandra Romanov after "treating" the hemophilia of their son Alexei. His influence at court fed scandalous rumors, especially during World War I. Murdered by conservative aristocrats in December 1916.

Ravich, Sara Naumovich (Olga Ravich, Sophia Ravich) (1879–1957). Marxist activist, close friend of Nadezhda Krupskaia; wife of Grigorii Zinoviev. Joined RSDLP in 1898; a Bolshevik from 1903. In 1917 returned to Russia with Lenin and was a Bolshevik propagandist. After the October Revolution, worked in Soviet state educational institutions; removed from state and party posts after 1925, but survived the Great Terror.

Riabushinskii, Pavel Pavlovich (1871–1924). Industrialist, chairman of the Moscow Stock Exchange, liberal activist, and a founder of *Utro Russia*, the Progressist Party, and the State Duma Progressive Bloc. Served as Chairman of the Central War Industrial Committee during World War I. In 1917 opposed socialist participation in the government; fell ill with tuberculosis and retired from public life in September. Emigrated to France after the October Revolution.

Riazanov, David Martin (David Borisovich Gol'dendakh) (1870–1938). Jewish populist activist who joined Marxist movement in 1889. Emigrated in 1900; founded *Bor'ba* group, remained outside Menshevik and Bolshevik factions; arrested and exiled after activity in the 1905 Revolution; joined socialist antiwar movement in 1914–1916. In 1917 was a member of the *Mezhraiontsy*, then joined the Bolsheviks in August and became a member of the Bolshevik Central Committee. After the October Revolution, resigned from the party over the Brest-Litovsk Peace Treaty, but was reinstated in 1921; active in Soviet educational institutions. Purged in 1931 and executed in 1938.

Rittikh, Aleksandr Aleksandrovich (1868–1930). Economist, expert on agriculture and food supply issues. Served as tsarist agriculture minister in 1916–1917. Emigrated after the October Revolution.

Rodzianko, Mikhail Vladimirovich (1859–1924). Career tsarist army officer. Joined Octobrist Party in 1905; elected deputy to Third State Duma, served as president of Fourth State Duma in 1912–1917. In 1917 headed the Temporary Committee of the State Duma and helped negotiate tsar's abdication, then faded from politics. After the October Revolution, supported anti-Bolshevik opposition; emigrated to Yugoslavia in 1920.

Romanov, Aleksandra [Alexandra] Fedorovna (1872–1918). Princess of Hesse, empress of Russia, daughter of Grand Duke Ludwig IV, granddaughter of English Queen Victoria, and wife of Tsar Nicholas II. As staunch autocratic monarchist was a strong influence on state policy, especially during World War I. Arrested in 1917 by the Provisional Government and held under house arrest. Executed in 1918.

Romanov, Mikhail Aleksandrovich (1878–1918). Grand duke of Russia, younger brother of Nicholas II. Designated to succeed Nicholas II on 28 February 1917, but refused to accept the throne on 1 March; arrested and sentenced to internal exile. Executed in 1918.

Romanov, Nikolai [Nicholas] Alexandrovich (1868–1918). Tsar and emperor of Russia, 1894–1917. A staunch autocratic monarchist, was forced to grant constitutional concessions in 1905, but opposed further reforms; assumed post of supreme commander, August 1915. Forced to abdicate in 1917 during the February Revolution, arrested by Provisional Government, and held under house arrest. Executed in 1918.

Romanov, Nikolai Nikolaevich (1856–1929). Russian grand duke, military officer; served as supreme commander of the Russian military in 1914–August 1915 and as commander in chief of the Caucasian Front in 1915–1917. Briefly reappointed supreme commander in February 1917, but removed from command after the February Revolution. After the October Revolution, joined the White Army in Crimea; emigrated to France in spring 1919 and was active in the émigré White movement.

Rudneev, Vadim Viktorovich (1874–1940). Populist activist, joined the SRs in 1902; was a member of the right SR faction during World War I. In 1917 served as the right SR leader in Moscow; Moscow's mayor in July–November; leader of the anti-Bolshevik Moscow Committee of Public Safety in October. Active in the anti-Bolshevik SR opposition, then emigrated.

Samarin, Aleksandr Dmitrievich (1868–1932). Moscow Province marshal of nobility, member of the State Council. Served as Ober-Prokurator of the Holy Synod in 1915; active in wartime voluntary associations in 1914–1917. In 1917 devoted attention to the Orthodox Church. Arrested by Bolsheviks in 1918, spent the Civil War in prison; rearrested in 1925. Died in internal exile.

Savinkov, Boris Viktorevich (1879–1925). Active leader of SR terrorist organizations in 1903–1914; successful novelist. In 1917 served as deputy war minister in July–August. During the Civil War participated in the SR anti-Bolshevik opposition, then emigrated, but was lured back to Russia in 1924, and arrested. Committed suicide or was executed in 1925.

Sazonov, Sergei Dmitrevich (1860–1927). Tsarist minister of foreign affairs in 1910–1916 and last tsarist ambassador to England. Remained in England during 1917. After the October Revolution, served as diplomatic representative of the White armies in England and France.

Shingarev, Andrei Ivanovich (1869–1918). Member of the Kadet Central Committee. In 1917 served as agriculture minister in March–April; finance minister in May–July; also helped post as Kadet Party general secretary from late July. Arrested in December 1917. Murdered in January 1918.

Shliapnikov, Aleksander Gavrilovich (1885–1937). Skilled metalworker who joined the Bolsheviks in 1903; active in the 1905 Revolution; repeatedly arrested then exiled in 1908–1916; was member of the Bolshevik Central Committee in 1915–1917. In 1917 was a Bolshevik organizer in the Petrograd Metalworkers' Union and a member of the Petrograd Soviet. After the October Revolution, appointed commissar of labor; with Alexandra Kollontai, led Workers' Opposition in 1920. Purged in 1933; arrested in 1935. Executed in 1937.

Shmidt, Vasili Vladimirovich (1886–1938). Metalworker; joined the Bolsheviks in 1905; served as secretary of the Bolshevik Petersburg Committee in 1915–1916. In 1917 was a Bolshevik trade union leader in Petrograd. Served as people's commissar of labor in 1918–1928.

Shotman, Aleksandr (1880–1939) Finnish Bolshevik since 1902. Functioned as Lenin's primary emissary from Finland in July–October 1917. Belonged to Stalin's circle in the 1920s and 1930s. Executed in 1939.

Shreider, Grigorii Il'ich (dates unknown). Expert on urban governance; joined the SRs in 1902. Served as mayor of Petrograd in 1917. Arrested by the Petrograd Soviet Military Revolutionary Committee in November 1917, then emigrated to Italy in 1918.

Shteinberg, Issak-Nahman Zakharovich (1888–1957). Joined the PSR in 1906 and was leader of the party's left wing; arrested and exiled to Germany, but returned to Russia in 1910 and practiced law. Helped lead SR antiwar faction in 1914–1917. Was among top left SRs leaders in Petrograd in 1917. Served as people's commissar of justice in December 1917–March 1918, but resigned in protest against the Brest-Litovsk Treaty; led the anti-Bolshevik left SR opposition, persecuted after the failed rebellion in July 1918. Emigrated to Germany in 1923, fled the Nazis for London in 1933, and then led programs to aid Jewish refugees from Nazi Europe, 1933–1947. Emigrated to New York in 1947 and was active in Jewish socialist politics.

Shturmer, Boris Vladimirovich (1848–1917). Reputedly corrupt tsarist official and member of Rasputin's circle; served as prime minister in 1916; minister of interior in March–July 1916, minister of foreign affairs in July–November 1916, and then was removed from office. Arrested for treason by Provisional Government in 1917. Died in prison in 1917.

Shul'gin, Vasilii Vital'evich (1878–1976). Right-liberal constitutional monarchist and leader of the Progressive Bloc in the Fourth State Duma. In 1917 helped convince Nicholas II to abdicate, supported the Provisional Government, then backed Kornilov. After the October Revolution, joined the White movement; emigrated to Yugoslavia in 1920. Arrested by the Red Army in 1944 and spent 12 years in Soviet prisons, then lived in Vladimir.

Shuvaev, Dmitrii Savelovich (1854–1937). Career tsarist army officer, expert in logistics. Appointed war minister in March 1916, but fell out of favor with the Imperial Court for having contact with the State Duma. In 1917 served in military administrative posts. During the Civil War was among the tsarist officers engaged by the Red Army as an expert.

Sipiagin, Dmitrii Sergeevich (1853–1902). Career tsarist bureaucrat; served in various interior ministry posts in 1880s–1890s and as minister of interior and tsarist police director in 1900–1902. Assassinated by an SR terrorist in 1902.

Skalov, Gregorii Borisovich (Sinani) (dates unknown). Bolshevik soldier. Served in Petrograd Soviet Military Section in 1917. Led 1918 Soviet occupation of Turkestan and then served in diplomatic posts in China in 1920s.

Skobelev, Matvei Ivanovich (1885–1938). Social Democrat from the Caucasus, joined the Mensheviks in 1903; was active in 1905 Revolution; went abroad, then returned to the Caucasus, 1906–1912; in 1912–1917 served as a member of the Fourth State Duma; leader of the Menshevik revolutionary defensists in 1914–1917. In 1917 was member of the Menshevik Central Committee; served as deputy chairman of the Petrograd Soviet; deputy chairman of the All-Russian Soviet Executive Committee in June–October and labor minister in May–September. Led the Menshevik opposition in Baku in 1919 and then emigrated to France in 1920; returned to Russia and joined the Communist Party in 1922 and worked in Soviet foreign trade agencies. Arrested and executed in 1938.

Skrypnik, Nikolai Alekseevich (1872–1933). Trade union organizer in St. Petersburg, Moscow, and several provincial cities. Joined the RSDLP in 1899, joined the Bolsheviks in 1903. In 1917 was a Bolshevik trade union organizer in Petrograd; elected secretary of the Petrograd Central Council of Factory Committees in June 1917. Served as an All-Russian Cheka official in 1918–1919, then in party and Cheka posts in Ukraine; opposed Stalin's policies during the 1932–1933 famine. Committed suicide in 1933.

Smidovich, Petr Germogenovich (1874–1935). Joined the RSDLP in 1890, joined the Bolsheviks in 1903. In 1917 served on the Bolshevik Petersburg Committee. Held several Soviet state and party posts in Jewish administrative agencies. Died under suspicious circumstances in 1935.

Smirnov, Sergei Aleksandrovich (1883–?). Kadet activist. Served as comptroller general of Provisional Government in September–October 1917.

Smol'ianinov, Vadim Aleksandrevich (1890–1961). Joined the Bolshevik Party before World War I. Soldier stationed in the Smolensk Garrison in 1917, became leader of the Smolensk Bolshevik organization and Bolshevik faction in Smolensk Soviet. After the October Revolution, held several state and party posts in Moscow.

Sobolev, Vasilii (1893–1928). Member of a prewar Smolensk socialist youth group; helped organize pro-Bolshevik faction in the local RSDLP and local worker sick fund during World War I. In 1917 was a leader of the Smolensk Bolshevik organization and the Bolshevik faction in Smolensk Soviet. After the October Revolution, served in various state, party, and military posts.

Sokol'nikov, Grigorii Iakovlevich (Girsh Iankelevivh Brilliant) (1888–1939). Joined the Bolsheviks in 1905; arrested and exiled to France in 1906. In 1917 served as a member of the Bolshevik Petersburg Committee. Briefly led Soviet delegation at Brest-Litovsk in 1918, then filled diplomatic posts; was people's commissar of finance in 1922–1926. Arrested in 1936 and murdered in prison in 1939.

Spiridonova, Maria Aleksandrovna (1884–1941). SR leader, active in SR terrorist cells, seen as ethical leader of the movement. Assassinated a tsarist police office in 1906 and was arrested, abused by the police, and exiled to Siberia until 1917; while in exile, helped organize antiwar SR faction. In 1917 was leading left SR. Opposed the Brest-Litovsk Treaty, active in the anti-Bolshevik Left SR opposition; arrested after failed rebellion in July 1918, persecuted, repeatedly arrested, and sentenced to Soviet prisons and internal exile. Executed in 1941.

Stalin, Joseph (Iosif Vissarionovich Dzhugashvili) (1878–1953). Principal leader of Soviet Union from 1928 to 1953. Joined Georgian Social Democrats in 1902; a Bolshevik from 1903; repeatedly arrested and exiled in 1903–1916; member of the Bolshevik Central Committee from 1912. Among first Bolshevik leaders to return to Petrograd in 1917; opposed the April Theses, but then fell into line behind Lenin and became involved in party organizational tasks. After the October Revolution, served in multiple party, state, and military posts, primarily as nationalities commissar and Communist Party general secretary.

Steklov, Iurii Mikhailovich (Osip Moiseevich Nakhamkis) (1873–1941). Joined the RSDLP in 1898, but remained outside Bolshevik and Menshevik factions. In 1917, belonged to the *Mezhraiontsy*, elected to the Petrograd Soviet, then joined the Bolsheviks in August of 1917. Edited *Izvestiia* in 1917–1925. Executed in 1941.

Stepanov-Skvortsov, Ivan Ivanovich (1870–1928). Joined the RSDLP in 1898 and the Bolsheviks in 1904. Was a Bolshevik activist in Petrograd in 1917. Served as people's commissar of finance in November 1917–January 1918.

Stolypin, Peter Arkad'evich (1862–1911). Career tsarist interior ministry official and architect of major agrarian reforms. Served as minister of internal affairs and chairman of the Council of Minister in 1906–1911. Assassinated by SR terrorists in 1911.

Sukhanov, Nikolai Nikolaevich (Gimmer) (1882–1940). Joined the SRs in 1903; became a nonfactional Social Democrat after the 1905 Revolution. In 1917 helped organize the Petrograd Soviet and served as a leader of the Menshevik-Internationalists in 1917. After the October Revolution, was the voice of the Menshevik-Internationalists on the All-Russian Soviet Central Executive Committee. After the Civil War, filled Soviet government economic posts; purged in 1930; arrested and imprisoned in 1931. Executed in 1940.

Sukhomlinov, Vladimir Aleksandrovich (1848–1926). Russia's war minister in 1909–1915; removed from that post amid accusations of corruption in June 1915; arrested for corruption and treason in 1916. In 1917 tried as a German spy, found not guilty, but convicted on the grounds that his policies left Russia unprepared for the war. Released from prison and allowed to emigrate to Germany after the October Revolution.

Sverdlov, Iakov Mikhailovich (Movshevich) (1885–1919). Member of the Jewish workers' movement, joined the RSDLP in 1902 and the Bolsheviks in 1903; arrested and sentenced to prison and exile in 1906. Became Bolshevik Central Committee secretary in August 1917. Held that post until 1919, and also served as chairman of the All-Russian Central Executive Committee in November 1917–March 1919. Died of natural causes in 1919.

Tereshchenko, Mikhail Ivanovich (1886–1959). Industrialist, financier, and nonparty liberal. Elected to the Fourth State Duma, aligned with the Progressist Party; active in medical relief organizations and as chairman of the All-Russian Central War Industrial Committee during World War I. In 1917 served as finance minister in March–May and foreign minister and deputy prime minister in September–October. Arrested on 25 October 1917, but escaped in January 1918 and emigrated to Norway, then France.

Trepov, Aleksander Fedorovich (1862–1928). Right wing deputy in the Fourth State Duma, son of notorious St. Petersburg police chief F. F. Trepov, and brother of the equally notorious Moscow police chief D. F. Trepov; served as minister of transportation, then prime minister in 1915, but resigned in December 1916. Had a minor role in the 1917 February Revolution, then faded from politics. After the October Revolution he emigrated to Germany and was active in the émigré monarchist movement.

Trotskii [Trotsky], Lev [Leon] Davidovich (Bronshtein) (1879–1940). A founder of the RSDLP in 1898; arrested, exiled to Siberia, and escaped in 1902 to join the RSDLP leadership abroad. Member of the Menshevik faction in 1903–1917; chairman of the Petrograd Soviet in 1905; arrested, exiled, escaped abroad in 1907; lived in Europe and the United States until 1917, and took an antiwar position in 1914–1917. During 1917, led the *Mezhraiontsy* in Petrograd; joined the Bolsheviks in August, co-opted onto the Bolshevik Central Committee; was a member of the Petrograd Soviet, elected to the All-Russian Soviet Central Executive Committee in June; elected chairman of the Petrograd Soviet in October. Served as commissar of foreign affairs in November 1917–March 1918; during the Civil War, organized the Red Army; held multiple party and state posts. Expelled from state and party posts in 1927; exiled to Kazakhstan in 1928; and expelled from the Soviet Union in 1929. Murdered by Stalin's agent in Mexico in 1940.

Trutovskii, Vladimir Evgen'evich (1889–1937). Economist and expert on local government. Joined the PSR in 1908, belonged to its militant faction; arrested and sentenced to internal exile in 1911; member of the SR antiwar faction in 1914–1917. Was left SR journalist in 1917. After the October Revolution, participated in Left SR opposition; spent most of the 1920s–1930s in Soviet prisons and internal exile. Executed in 1937.

Trykova, Ariadna Vladimirovna (1869–1962). Feminist, liberal journalist. Helped found the Kadet Party in 1905, served on Kadet Central Committee. Frequent contributor to *Rech, Russkiia vedomosti*, other liberal newspapers in 1917. Emigrated to England (home of her husband, journalist Harold Williams) after the October Revolution and helped organize the anti-Bolshevik Russian Liberation Committee in London.

Tsederbaum, Feodor Isaevich (P. N. Dnevnitskii, F. N. Dnevnitskii) (1883–1937). A Menshevik from 1903 and a Menshevik defensist, 1914–1917; Martov's cousin and Plekhanov's personal secretary; was a leading spokesman of the *Edinstvo* faction in 1917.

Tsereteli, Irakli Geogorevich (1881–1959). Georgian Social Democratic leader. Joined the RSDLP in 1902 and the Mensheviks in 1903; served as Georgian deputy to the Second Duma; arrested then exiled to Siberia in 1913; led the "Siberian Zimmerwaldist" group in 1913–1917. In 1917 organized Menshevik revolutionary defensist faction, led the Petrograd Soviet; served as minister of communications in May–July, and as deputy chairman of the All-Russian Soviet Central Executive Committee in June–October. After the October Revolution, led the Georgian Mensheviks and was Georgian representative at the Paris Peace Conference in 1919. Remained in France until 1948, then moved to the United States.

Tukhachevskii, Aleksandr Mikhailovich (dates unknown). Liberal chairman of Smolensk Provincial *Zemstvo* in 1914–1917. Smolensk's provincial commissar in March–June 1917.

Uritskii, Moisei Solomonovich (1873–1918). Joined the RSDLP in 1898 and joined the Mensheviks in 1903; arrested after the 1905 Revolution and exiled until 1917. In 1917, became a member of the *Mezhraiontsy*, then joined the Bolsheviks in August 1917. After the October Revolution, headed the Petrograd Cheka and was a member of the Left Communist opposition to the Brest-Litovsk Treaty. Assassinated on 30 August 1918.

Vainshtein, Semen Lavrovich (Zvezdin) (?–1923). Joined Mensheviks in 1903; arrested and exiled after 1905; became a member of the antiwar Menshevik circle in Siberia. Served on the Petrograd Soviet Executive Committee in 1917. After the October Revolution, active in Menshevik opposition until expelled from Russia in February 1923. Died in Berlin in 1923.

Verkhovskii, Aleksandr Ivanovich (1886–1938). Career tsarist military officer. Served as war minister in September–October 1917. Arrested in 1918 for activity in White Army; released in 1919, joined the Red Army. Arrested and executed in 1938.

Vinaver, Maksim Moiseevich (1863–1926). Jewish lawyer, liberal activist. Helped found the Kadet Party in 1905, and a member of the Kadet Central Committee; also founded Jewish National Group in 1907; arrested and briefly imprisoned while deputy to the First State Duma; member of the Senate. In 1917 served on Kadet Central Committee and directed Kadet agitation and publishing activities; elected to the Petrograd *Duma* in 1917. Served in the White Crimean government in 1919; emigrated to France in 1920.

Vinslav, I. V. (1895–?). Latvian factory worker and Social Democratic activist; drafted into the Russian army during World War I, in the Roslavl Garrison; joined the Bolshevik Party in April 1917 as a member of the Roslavl' Bolshevik Committee and Roslavl' Soviet.

Voitinskii, Vladimir Savel'evich (1885–1960). Economist. Joined the Bolsheviks in 1905; in 1908 was arrested and later exiled to Siberia, where he was close to Tsereteli's circle in 1912–1917. During 1917 joined the Menshevik revolutionary defensist faction in April, was a member of the Petrograd Soviet Executive Committee and the All-Russian Soviet Central Executive Committee; served, on the *Izvestiia* editorial board, and as commissar to the Northern Front. After the October Revolution, was active in the Menshevik movement in Georgia; in 1921 emigrated to Germany, where he was an active trade unionist; in 1935 emigrated to the United States and worked in the Social Security Administration.

Volodarskii, Moisei Markovich (Gol'dshtein) (1891–1918). Joined the Bund and the Mensheviks in 1905; arrested and exiled in 1911; emigrated to the United States in 1913; during World War I, led the internationalist Menshevik faction in New York and was a member of Bukharin's circle at *Novyi Mir*. In 1917 was a member of the Bolshevik Petersburg Committee, a popular activist and propagandist. In November 1917 became people's commissar of press, agitation, and propaganda. Assassinated in 1918.

Zamyslovskii, Georgii Georgovich (1872–?). Prominent ultranationalist and antisemitic deputy to the Third and Fourth State Duma representing Vilna Province.

Zinoviev, Grigorii Eseevich (Ovsei-Gershon Aronovich Radomysl'skii) (1883–1936). Joined the RSDLP in 1901 and the Bolsheviks in 1903; exiled in 1908–1917; close collaborator of Lenin, served on the Bolshevik Central Committee from 1912. In 1917, was leader of the Bolshevik moderate faction, a member of the Bolshevik Central Committee and the Politburo. Served as chairman of the Petrograd Soviet in December 1917–1926; member of the Bolshevik Central Committee in 1917–1927; and member of the Politburo in 1917–1926; held various other state and party posts, including chairman of Comintern. Arrested in 1935, put on a show trial and executed in 1936.

Zubovskii, Iurii (1890–?). Russian poet closely associated with the Symbolist movement. Contributor to newspapers in Kiev in 1917.

NOTES

Part One

1. From 1709 to 1918, Russia followed the Julian calendar instead of the Gregorian calendar used elsewhere in Europe. By 1900, the Julian calendar was 13 days behind the Gregorian calendar. For Russians, the events in Petrograd that led to the abdication of Tsar Nicholas II took place on 23 February–2 March 1917, and were called the "February Revolution" (for the rest of Europe, these events happened on 8–15 March 1917). In this book, dates are given according to the calendar in use in Russia at the time. In February 1918, the Soviet government put Russia on the Julian calendar.
2. Russia's capital city had been called St. Petersburg before World War I, but in 1914, the government changed the name to replace the German word-ending designating town (*burg*) with the Russian equivalent (*grad*).
3. The anarchist socialists were an exception, in that they rejected any form of state.
4. One of the most important examples of this argument was Arthur Mendel's "Peasant and Worker on the Eve of the First World War," *Slavic Review* 24, no. 1 (1965): 23–33. Mendel's essay was written as a rejoinder to Leopold H. Haimson's essay "The Problem of Social Stability in Urban Russia, 1905–1917," *Slavic Review* 23, no. 4 (1964): 619–644 and *Slavic Review* 24, no. 1 (1965): 1–22.
5. For example, Richard Pipes, *The Russian Revolution, 1899–1919* (New York: Knopf, 1990).
6. For example, see Donald J. Raleigh's introduction to Eduard Burdzhalov, *Russia's Second Revolution: The February 1917 Uprising in Petrograd* (Bloomington: Indiana University Press, 1987).
7. The most influential formulation of this view was Haimson's 1964–1965 article on "The Problem of Social Stability in Urban Russia."
8. The social polarization paradigm is often called the "revisionist" or "social history school" of revolutionary historiography. Strictly speaking, however, neither term is accurate. Good history generally is "revisionist," in that historians aim to refine and improve our understanding of the past. And by the 1980s, most new western research on 1917 was influenced, at least partly, by the polarization argument, so it was no longer "revising" a firm consensus. Many historians associated with the social polarization paradigm used social history methods, but some wrote more "traditional" political histories. Also, some excellent social histories have challenged the social polarization paradigm.
9. This phrase was coined by Peter Holquist, in *Making War, Forging Revolution: Russia's Continuum of Crisis, 1914–1921* (Cambridge: Harvard University Press, 2002).
10. Aaron Retish, *Russian Peasants in Revolution and Civil War: Citizenship, Identity, and the Creation of the Soviet State, 1914–1922* (New York: Cambridge University Press, 2008).

Chapter 1

1. *Pravitel'stvennyi vestnik*, 27 July 1914, 1–2.
2. References to applause "from all sides of the hall" or "from all the benches" indicate approval by all political factions.
3. "Deklaratsiia Sotsial-Demokraticheskikh deputatov IV gosudarstvennom dumy v sviazi s nachalom voiny," in *Pamiatniki agitatsionnoi literatury RSDRP*, vol. 6, pt. 1 (Moscow-Petrograd, 1923), 90–91.
4. The "belligerent countries" refers to the Central Powers (Germany, Austria-Hungary, and their allies) and the Entente or Allied Powers (France, England, and Russia and their allies).
5. Socialists used the term "conscious proletariat" to refer to workers with a strong sense of social class identity who actively supported socialist political parties.

6. Ivan Menitskii, *Revolutionnoe dvizhenie voennykh godov (1914–1917). Ocherki i materialy,* vol. 1, *Pervyi god voiny (Moskva) (Moscow: Izdatel'svto Kommunisticheskoi Akademii, 1925), 130–131.

7. This was one of the main slogans of the Party of Socialist Revolutionaries.

8. In 1914, Russia advanced into Austrian-ruled Galicia, which Russian nationalists called "Galician Rus" to stress its historical relationship to the Russian state. Swabia is a territory in southwestern Germany; Russians sometimes used "Schwab" as an abusive term for Germans.

9. "'Pismo-raz"iasnenie' G. V. Plekhanova 17 (30) Sentiabria 1914 g.," *Rech,* 15 October 1914.

10. *Russkovo Slovo (The Russian Word)* was a right-liberal Moscow newspaper. The "Russian professor" may have been Kadet Party leader Pavel Miliukov.

11. "Ententist" refers to a supporter of the Triple Entente (Russia, France, and England).

12. In Alexander Pushkin's *The Captain's Daughter,* a corporal appears at his captain's quarters to report a fight between two soldiers; the captain's *wife* tells him to identify the guilty party but punish both men.

13. In August 1914, the German Army burned Leuven in Belgium and shelled the gothic Notre Dame Cathedral in Reims, France.

14. V. I. Lenin, "Voina i Sotsial-Demokratiia," *Sotsial-Demokrat,* 1 November 1914, 1.

15. The Second Socialist International (1889–1916) dissolved after most member parties supported their countries' national war efforts. Lenin proposed a Third International to unite "revolutionary" socialist parties in opposition to the war. He formed the Third International in 1919; Stalin dissolved it for political reasons in 1943.

16. The Kadets (Constitutional Democrats) were Russia's main liberal party. The Narodniki were populist socialists. The Party of Socialist Revolutionaries (formed in 1902) was Russia's largest and most radical populist-socialist party. Other Narodniki included the Popular-Socialist Party and the Trudoviks (Laborites). Among right Social Democrats, Lenin singled out Mensheviks Georgii Plekahnov and Petr Maslov for criticism.

17. Nikolai Avksent'ev, "God Bor'by," *Prizyv,* 1 October 1915, 1.

18. In 1916, disgraced Russian war minister Vladimir Sukhomlinov was arrested for corruption and treason. In March 1915, secret police agent S. N. Miasoedov was found guilty of espionage and sentenced to hang.

19. In Greek and Roman mythology, Hercules performed a series of tasks ("labors"). The fifth labor was to clean the stables of the King of Elias, Augea (hence the Augean stables) in a single day. They had never been cleaned and were so filled with filth that the task seemed impossible.

20. "Ot Glavnoi Palaty Russkogo Narodnogo Soiuza imeni Mikhaila Arkhangela," *Istoricheskii arkhiv* no. 5 (1994): 36.

21. "Germanophilia" refers to the love of Germany or German culture.

22. These were the royal dynasties of the German and Austro-Hungarian Empires.

23. *Voina. Khronika i otkliki,* no. 15 (1915): 17–18; and no. 6 (1915): cover.

24. In August 1915, the tsar appointed himself supreme commander.

25. V. Maklakov, "Tragicheskoe polozhenie," *Russkie vedomosti,* 27 September 1915, 1.

26. The Greek storyteller Aesop (620–520 bce) used thinly disguised allegories and plays on words to communicate ideas that those in power considered subversive.

27. *Gosudarstvennaia duma. Chetverti sozyv. Sessiia V. Zasedania pervoe. Stenograficheskii otchet* (Petrograd: 1916), 35–48.

28. The Progressive Bloc (a coalition of Kadets, Octobrists, and Progressists group) had formed in August 1915 and made up nearly three-quarters of the Fourth State Duma.

29. Vladimir Sukhomlinov, Russia's war minister in 1909–1915.

30. Criticism by the State Duma opposition had helped to push Ivan Goremykin from his post as prime minister in 1916.

31. Gen. A. A. Polivanov replaced Sukhomilov as war minister in June 1915 and served in that post until April 1916, when the tsar removed him for being "too sympathetic" to the duma.

32. In September 1916, Nicholas II appointed as acting internal affairs minister Aleksandr Protopopov—a favorite of the empress who reputedly favored a separate peace with Germany and was approaching senility.

33. In 1916, the tsar appointed one of the empress' favorites, Boris Shturmer, to replace Goremykin as prime minister; he also briefly served as interior minister (March–July 1916) and foreign affairs minister (July–November 1916). Shturmer's overtures to the Germans regarding a separate peace had outraged the liberals. Ivan Manasevich-Manuilov, Shturmer's protégé and one of Rasputin's entourage, was arrested for fraud and accepting bribes in April 1916.

34. Miliukov refers to Sergei Sazonov, foreign affairs minister in 1910–1916, who was sacked after proposing that the tsar promise Poland autonomy to counter German influence there. Shturmer, whom Miliukov suspected as a German agent, replaced Sazonov as foreign minister.

35. Miliukov refers here to the sacking of Sazonov.

36. Kadet Mosiei Adzhemov, deputy from the Don Military District.

37. Miliukov clearly was speaking of Rasputin. Ultranationalist Nikolai Markov, known as "Markov 2," represented Kursk Province in State Duma.

38. Ultranationalist Georgii Zamyslovskii, a deputy from Vilna Province.

39. Alexander Petrunkevitch, Samuel Northrup Harper, and Frank Alfred Golder, *The Russian Revolution,* published by Harvard and Cambridge University Press in 1918 under single cover with Robert Joseph Kerner, *The Jugo-Slav Movement* (Cambridge, MA: Harvard University Press, 1918), 51–52. I have made minor changes for clarity and consistency.

40. Golder has used the common English spelling of the German name Sturmer. Russian language sources typically used the Russian equivalent "Shturmer." The reference is to Boris Vladimirovich Shturmer.

41. *Letters of the Tsaritsa to the Tsar 1914–1916, with an introduction by Sir Bernard Pares* (London: Duckworth, 1923), 454–456. I have left Alexandra's spelling and syntactical errors unchanged, but replaced her abbreviations with complete words and names.

42. Nicholas Aleksandrovich Romanov spoke near-perfect English, as did Alexandra Fedorovna Romanova, a princess of the German duchy of Hesse who was raised in the household of her grandmother, Queen Victoria of Great Britain.

43. Alexandra distrusted both the newly appointed prime minister, Aleksandr Trepov, and State Duma Chairman Mikhail Rodzianko.

44. Peter I (the Great; reigned 1682–1725) employed violent means in the pursuit of modernization. Ivan (John) IV (the Terrible; reigned 1533–1584) was known for rule by terror. Paul I (reigned 1796–1801) is a rather strange choice, as he was deposed in a palace *coup.*

45. A. D. Samarin chaired a December 1916 congress of noblemen in Moscow that had called on the tsar to form a government "enjoying popular confidence." Liberal Aleksandr Guchkov was a leader of the Progressive Bloc.

46. Mr. Phillipe, who claimed to be a neurologist from France, was among the phony healers (like Rasputin) who had gained Nicholas and Alexandra's favor.

Chapter 2

1. A. Donskoi, "Vpered!" *Zhurnal Kopeika,* no. 32/263 (1914), 1.

2. A. M. Anifimov, ed., *Kresti'anskoe dvizehnie v Rossii v gody pervoi mirovi voiny, iiul' 1914 g.-fevral' 1917 g., Sbornik dokumentov* (Moscow-Leningrad: Nauka, 1965), 72–73, 129.

3. Anifimov, ed., *Kresti'anskoe dvizehnie v Rossii v gody pervoi mirovi voiny,* 432.

4. Zemstvos were introduced in Stavropol' Province on the eve of World War I. As a result of zemstvo teachers' dedicated work, peasant attitudes toward schools improved during the war. Some historians see this as evidence of the rural population's growing sense of national identity.

5. Like other modern bureaucracies, the tsarist police tracked official correspondence by assigning a number to each official document. By "the mobilization period," Kalinin means the first muster of reserves into active service in July 1914.

6. S. P., "Voina," *Novyi voskhod*, 24 July 1914, 3–4.

7. The author uses the hyphenated term Russian-Jews (*russkie-evrei*) to emphasize ties to Russia, in contrast with those who considered Jews aliens resident in Russia.

8. *Novyi voskhod* printed the tsar's manifesto in the 24 July and 31 July 1914 issues.

9. In 1812, Napoleon expected Jews in Russia to greet him as a liberator. Jewish leaders who feared Napoleon as a secularizing force instead aided the Russians.

10. The author is countering the widespread belief that Jews systematically evaded military service.

11. Anton Borovoi, "K tekushchemu momentu. Evreiskii vopros," *Voina i evrei* no. 2 (1914): 1.

12. *Novoe vremia*, 27 July 1914.

13. A *shtetl* was a Jewish village in the Pale of Settlement.

14. In August 1914 Russia's Supreme Commander issued a proclamation promising that Russia would restore Polish unity, but added that "Russia expects only one thing of you: equal regard for the rights of those nationalities to which you are historically linked." Jewish liberals hoped this foreshadowed a broader policy of granting equal rights to Jews in the Russian Empire.

15. Before the war, right-wing Polish parties had endorsed a boycott of Jewish businesses.

16. In 1915, liberals in the State Duma again tried and failed to abolish the Pale. In 1915, the army ordered mass expulsions of Jews from the near-front zone, which aggravated a refugee crisis in the eastern Pale and compounded military supply problems. The government finally suspended restrictions on Jewish residence in Russia's interior in 1916.

17. "Vipiski iz pis'ma s podpis'iu: 'David' Kharkov, ot 30 Iiulia 1914 goda, k A. Z. Rotshteinu, v Smorgon', Vilenskoi gub.," in the microfilm collection *The Department of Police of the Ministry of Internal Affairs. The Fifth Section of the Special Section of the Department of Police (Secret Unit). The Intercepted Letters of Russian Revolutionaries, 1883–1917* (Woodbridge, CT: Research Publications, Primary Source Media, 1998), reel 128.

18. "Ritual histories" refers to the "Blood Libel."

19. "Razvedchik 'Tiapa': Iz pis'ma ofitsera," in *Voina i eia geroi: Nashi chudo-bogatryi na voina 1914 goda* (Petrograd: Gramotnost', 1915), 82–83.

20. The phrase "aerometric war" (*areometicheskaia voina*) suggests war that is rapidly changing technologically. "Areometeric" means something measured by a hydrometer (which determines a liquid's specific gravity). Such terms suggest that the author wanted to sound well educated.

21. Military censors required publications to use an initial, such as "L," rather than a full place name (such as Lodz or Lublin), ostensibly to protect military secrets. The author might have used "L" both as a literary affectation and to suggest that the story relates to Russia's September 1914 victory near the Galician city of L'vov (Lemberg/L'viv/Lwow).

22. "Vipiski iz pis'ma s nerazobrannoi podpis'iu, deistvuiushchaia armiia, c. Radkemen', ot 15 Dekabria 1914 g., k N. A. Rozhanskomu, v Moskvu, Universitet," in the microfilm collection *The Department of Police of the Ministry of Internal Affairs. The Fifth Section of the Special Section of the Department of Police (Secret Unit). The Intercepted Letters of Russian Revolutionaries, 1883–1917* (Woodbridge, CT: Research Publications, Primary Source Media, 1998), reel 132.

23. This might have been physiologist N. A. Rozhanskii, a colleague of Ivan Pavlov.

24. Aleksandr Dneprovskii, *Zapiski dezertira: voina 1914–1918 gg.* (New York: Albatros, 1931), 68.
25. *Novoe vremia (New Times)* was a major progovernment Petrograd newspaper.
26. *Predvestnik* no. 1 (1915).
27. Soviet historians attributed this publication to an illegal Bolshevik Party cell led by Vasilii Sobolev. Sobolev did belong to *The Harbringer* circle, but it also included young antiwar Socialist Revolutionaries, Mensheviks, and Bundists.
28. *Legacies (Zavety)* was a Socialist Revolutionary newspaper. *Russian Wealth (Russkoe bogastvo)* was the best-known journal of the legal moderate populist movement.
29. Article 87 of the 1906 "Fundamental Laws" allowed the tsar to issue emergency decrees when the Duma was not in session. After pledging to support the war effort in July 1914, the Fourth State Duma voted to disband for the duration. The tsarist government then used Article 87 to impose military censorship of the press. Duma leaders successfully demanded the legislature's reinstatement in summer 1915.
30. Black Hundreds refers to the ultranationalist, antisemitic right-wing Union of Russian People.
31. Moscow attorney Alexei Shmakov was famous for defending prominent antisemites, authoring books about the alleged international Zionist conspiracy, and participating in the 1913 Beillis trial (where he insisted that Jews ritualistically murdered Christian children).
32. "Kopia s pis'ma, s podpis'iu: 'liga neschastnykh krest'ianok," Moskva, 14 maia 1916 g., k Voennomu Ministeru Shuvaevu, v Petrograd," in the microfilm collection *The Department of Police of the Ministry of Internal Affairs. The Fifth Section of the Special Section of the Department of Police (Secret Unit). The Intercepted Letters of Russian Revolutionaries, 1883–1917* (Woodbridge, CT: Research Publications, Primary Source Media, 1998), reel 140.
33. "Proshenie krest'ianok-soldatok der. Gavrinoi Ishimskogo u. Tobol'skoi gub. ministru zemledeliia," in *Ekonomicheskoe polozhenie Rossii nakanune velikoi oktiabr'skoi sotsialisticheskoi revoliutsii. Dokumenty i materialy*, pt. 3, *Sel'skoe khoziaistvo i kres'tianstvo* (Leningrad: Nauka, 1967), 54.
34. "1917 g. Ianveria 17—Pis'mo neizvestnogo soldata vzvodnomu komandiru 3-i roy 177-go zapasnogo pekhotnogo polka Filippovu o nastroenii soldat na fronte," in *Revoliutsionnoe dvizhenie v armii i na flote v gody pervoi mirovoi voiny. 1914-fevral' 1917* ed. A. L. Sidorov (Moscow: Nauka, 1966), 281.
35. State Archives of the Smolensk Region (GASO), f. 73, op. 22, d. 912, ll. 10, 12, 15–15 ob, 18.
36. Englishman William Gerhard's textile factory had some 350 workers.
37. Reshetnikov's factory employed about 300 workers.
38. A *pud* is a measure of weight equal to 16.4 kilograms, or 36.1 pounds.
39. A *sazhen* is a unit of length equal to 2.13 meters, or 7 feet.
40. A *funt* is a unit of weight equal to 0.4 kilograms, or 0.9 pounds.
41. The date typed on the letter was 3 January, but it was hand-corrected to read 3 February.
42. "Vipiski iz pis'ma K. M. Petrova, Moskva, 17 fevralia 1917 g., k Ego Prev-vu M. A. Petrovu, v Korotoiak, Voronezhskoi gub.," in the microfilm collection *The Department of Police of the Ministry of Internal Affairs. The Fifth Section of the Special Section of the Department of Police (Secret Unit). The Intercepted Letters of Russian Revolutionaries, 1883–1917* (Woodbridge, CT: Research Publications, Primary Source Media, 1998), reel 143.

Part Two

1. The day before the women's demonstration, a major strike had begun at the giant Putilov Factory, and a few historians have seen that strike as the start of the February Revolution.

2. For detailed narratives, see Eduard Burdzhalov, *Russia's Second Revolution: February 1917 in Petrograd*, trans. and ed. by Donald J. Raleigh (Bloomington: Indiana University Press, 1987), and Tsuyoshi Hasegawa, *The February Revolution: Petrograd, 1917* (Seattle: University of Washington Press, 1981).

3. During a brief ideological "thaw" in the Soviet Union in the 1950s, Eduard Burdzhalov challenged the claim that the Bolsheviks led the February Revolution; he showed that the Bolsheviks were not prepared for the revolution, and that other socialist party groups had been as important as the Bolsheviks in organizing protestors once the revolution began. When the thaw ended, however, Burdzhalov was severely criticized. See Donald Raleigh's introduction to Burdzhalov, *Russia's Second Revolution*.

4. Michael Melancon in particular has challenged the idea that the February Revolution was "spontaneous," in his article "Who Wrote What and When? Proclamations of the February Revolution in Petrograd, 23 February–1 March 1917," *Soviet Studies* 42, no. 3 (1988): 479–500, and in a series of important subsequent articles.

5. For an excellent example, see Rex A. Wade, *The Russian Revolution, 1917*, 2nd ed. (New York: Cambridge University Press, 2005), chapter 2.

6. Some important English language studies published before the 1980s that paid close attention to the revolution in the provinces and regions include works by Andrew Erzegailis, John Keep, Roger Pethybridge, Russell Snow, and Ronald Suny in the list of further readings.

7. For a sample of these studies, see works by Sarah Badcock, Israel Getzler, Michael C. Hickey, Peter Holquist, Hugh Phillips, Donald J. Raleigh, Aaron Retish, and Rex A. Wade in the list of further readings.

8. Four cabinet members were Kadets: Pavel Miliukov, the foreign minister; Nikolai Nekrasov, the transportation minister; Aleksander Manuilov, the education minister; and Andre Shingarev, the agriculture minister. Two were Progressists: the minister of trade and industry, Aleksandr Konovalov; and the religion minister (ober-procurator of the Holy Synod), Vladimir L'vov. War and Naval Minister Aleksandr Guchkov was an Octoberist. Two cabinet members were nonparty liberals: Prince L'vov, the prime minister; and Mikhail Tereshchenko, the finance minister.

9. Wade, *The Russian Revolution*, chapter 3.

10. The works by Alexander Rabinowitch in the list of further readings were seminal in revising historians' picture of the Bolshevik Party in 1917.

11. As a result of the February Revolution, political parties and their newspapers could function legally, and party organizations quickly set up newspapers in Russia's major cities.

12. One of the most important exceptions was William Henry Chamberlin's two-volume *The Russian Revolution*, first published in 1935, which still is one of the best introductions to 1917 (the most recent edition was published by Princeton University Press in 1987).

13. For example, see works by Rex A. Wade, Alexander Rabinowitch, William G. Rosenberg, Diane P. Koenker, Steve Smith, Allan K. Wildman, Graeme J. Gill, Ziva Galili, Donald J. Raleigh, and Orlando Figes in the list of further readings.

14. See, for example, Orlando Figes and Boris Kolonitskii, *Interpreting the Russian Revolution: The Language and Symbols of 1917* (New Haven, CT, and London: Yale University Press, 1999).

15. For an excellent survey of these issues, see Wade, *The Russian Revolution*, chapters 4–6.

16. See, for example, works by Diane P. Koenker, Diane P. Koenker and William G. Rosenberg, David Mandel, and Steve Smith in the list of further readings.

17. See, for instance, Ruth Roosa, *Russia's Industrialists in an Era of Revolution: The Association of Industry and Trade, 1906–1917* (Armonk, NY: M. E. Sharpe, 1997).

18. See works by Evan Mawdsley, Norman Saul, and Allan K. Wildman in the list of further readings.

19. See works by Sarah Badcock, Orlando Figes, Graeme J. Gill, Eric Landis, and Aaron Retish in the list of further readings.
20. Three socialist groups made up the majority in the Rada: the Ukrainian Socialist Revolutionaries, the Ukrainian Social Democrats (Mensheviks), and the Socialist-Federalists.
21. See Ziva Galili, *The Menshevik Leaders in the Russian Revolution: Social Realities and Political Strategies* (Princeton, NJ: Princeton University Press, 1989).
22. Of 784 delegates with full voting rights, 285 were Socialist Revolutionaries, 248 Mensheviks, and 102 Bolsheviks.
23. Alexander Rabinowitch, *Prelude to Revolution: The Petrograd Bolsheviks and the July 1917 Uprising* (Bloomington: Indiana University Press, 1968).
24. See Wade, *The Russian Revolution,* 185.
25. The second coalition, formed on 24 July, included Kadets Piotr Urenov (transport) and Sergei Oldenburg (education), Progressist Vladimir L'vov (religious affairs), Radical Democrat Nikolai Nekrasov (finance and deputy prime minister), and nonparty liberal Mikhail Tereshchenko (foreign affairs). The socialist ministers were Socialist Revolution-aries Viktor Chernov (agriculture) and Nikolai Avksentev (internal affairs), Mensheviks Aleksei Nikitin (communications) and Matvei Skobelev (labor), and Popular-Socialists Aleksei Peshekhonov (supply) and Alexander Kerensky (prime minister and minister of war and navy).

Chapter 3

1. *Pravda* ch 1917, 1.
2. "K momentu," *Pravda*, 5 March 1917, 1.
3. The Petrograd Soviet had issued directives that weakened the officers' authority over soldiers, most famously Order No. 1. Liberal Kadet Party leaders like Pavel Miliukov had hoped to salvage a constitutional monarchy, but accepted that this option was gone after 2 March 1917.
4. The Bolsheviks and Mensheviks both used the title Russian Social Democratic Labor Party.
5. *Rech*, 5 March 1917, 1.
6. *Rabochaia gazeta*, 7 March 1917, 1.
7. "Borb'a ne okonchena—organizuets'," and "Zhenshchina rebotnitsa," *Rabochaia gazeta*, 7 March 1917, 1.
8. O. V. Volobuev, et al., eds., *Anarkhisty. Dokumenty i materialy. 1883–1935gg.,* vol. 2, *1917–1935gg.* (Moscow: ROSSPEN, 1999), 19.
9. Bleichman refers to anarchists just freed from tsarist prisons. Contributing to funds for aiding liberated political prisoners was a common "passive" form of civic participation in spring 1917.
10. The "militia" was the new city police force created after the dissolution of the tsarist police. It should not be confused with the Red Guards or workers' armed militias.
11. "Otvetsvennost' demokratii," *Rech*, 10 March 1917, 1.
12. French King Louis XIV's famously said *"L'etat c'est moi,"* meaning, "I am the state."
13. "Soothsayers" (*avgury*, or augers) may be a reference to charlatans like Rasputin.
14. "Vlast'—Demokratii," *Pravda*, 11 March 1917, 1.
15. This refers to government opposition to Order No. 1 and similar Petrograd Soviet directives.
16. See document 8.1.
17. Land Captains held posts created during the 1880s counterreforms to strengthen aristocratic control over rural politics and administration.
18. "Vremennoe pravitel'stvo i rabochii klass," *Rabochaia gazeta*, 12 March 1917, 1.
19. All-Russian Zemstvo Union Chairman Prince L'vov was prime minister of the first Provisional Government.

20. *Delo naroda*, 15 March 1917, 1.
21. "Organizuites'!" and "Vremennoe pravitel'sto i sovet rabochikh i soldatskikh deputatov," *Delo naroda*, 15 March 1917, 1.
22. O. V. Volobuev, et al., eds., *S"ezdy i konferentsii Konstitutionno-demokraticheskoi partii*, vol. 3, pt. 1, *1915–1917gg.* (Moscow: ROSSPEN, 2000), 362–378.
23. This refers to Woodrow Wilson's 2 April 1917 "War Message" to the U.S. Congress.
24. *Izvestiia*, 29 March 1917, 2.
25. Untitled editorial and "Pobeda demokratii," *Edinstvo* no. 1 (29 March 1917): 1.
26. The Provisional Government's 27 March 1917 Declaration of War Aims renounced the seizure or occupation of foreign territory and called for national self-determination. See document 6.5.
27. N.in, "O zadachakh proletriata v dannoi revoliutsii," *Pravda*, 7 April 1917, 1. Lenin frequently published using the first name Nikolai.
28. "Control" (*kontrol*) in 1917 meant supervision, oversight, and regulation.
29. Lenin refers to the Socialist International (see document 1.5).
30. Among socialists, to call someone "Mister" rather than "Citizen" or "Comrade" was an insult. Menshevik Iosif Gol'denburg (Roman Meshkovskii) broke with Lenin in 1907.
31. *Russkaia volia (Russian Freedom)*, a right wing newspaper, was known for its antisemitism. Gol'denberg, it should be noted, was Jewish.
32. Lenin is throwing back at Plekhanov another comment made about the April Theses in *Edinstvo*, 5 April 1917, 1—that Lenin's statements were "completely inconsistent."
33. Lenin believed that Plekhanov had abandoned Marxism by supporting the war.
34. Rosa Luxemburg broke with the German Social Democratic Party over its support for the war.
35. "Opasnost' s levago flange," *Rabochaia gazeta*, 6 April 1917, 1; "Malen'kii Fel'eton: Son Lenina," *Edinstvo*, 9 April 1917, 2.
36. This refers to Lenin's praise for Rosa Luxumberg and other antiwar left socialists.
37. The ellipses are in the original text, to suggest that the alternative would be disaster.
38. "Spontaneity" inferred thoughtless emotional mob action, whereas "consciousness" inferred disciplined organized actions by class-conscious workers who followed party guidance.
39. The reference to "baton" suggests the author means Napoleon Bonaparte.
40. China and Russia share a long border, so this might suggest that Lenin had to look to Russia's remote corners to find supporters. The wartime press printed sensationalist stories about Chinese criminals, so the point might be that Lenin was a favorite of criminals. Lenin had Kalmuk (Mongolian) ancestors, so this may have been a comment on his "Asiatic" characteristics.

Chapter 4

1. O. Lobanov, "Voskrese!" *Smolenskii vestnik*, 13 March 1917, 1.
2. "Protokol No. 1 obshche sobraniia soldat Petrogradskogo okruzhogo i mestnogo inten-dantstv," in *Revoliutsionnoe dvizehenie v voennykh okrugakh. Mart 1917 g.–mart 1918 g.*, ed. Iu. I. Korablev (Moscow: Nauka, 1988), 16–17.
3. Soldiers had been segregated from the civilian population in urban public transport.
4. "Viaz'ma," *Smolenskii vestnik*, 14 March 1917, 4.
5. Garrison units were not issued weapons or ammunition and had to provide their own food.
6. Soldiers had been prohibited from smoking in the barracks, but officers enjoyed that privilege.
7. The authors repeatedly use the awkward phrase "the person in command" rather than "the commander" to indicate the equality between soldiers and officers.
8. In other words, there must be a regular rotation of such duties.

9. "10 Mart—Pis'mo soldata A. Korolozhevicha v Petrogradskii Sovet rabochikh i soldatskikh deputatove s protestom protiv izmeniia prikaza No. 1," in *Voiksovye komitety deistvuiushchei armii. Mart 1917 g.–mart 1918 g.*, ed. L. M. Gavrilov, et al. (Moscow: Nauka, 1982), 29.
10. "13 marta—Pis'mo soldata saperoi roty otriada generala Nazarbekova V. Anifimova v Petrogradskii Sovet rabochikh i soldatiskikh deputatov," in *Revoliutsionnoe dvizhenie v Russkoi armii. 27 fevralia–24 oktiabria 1917 goda. Sbornik dokumentov*, ed. L. S. Gaponenko, et al. (Moscow: Nauka, 1968), 33–34.
11. "15 marta—Postanovlenie zasedaniia komiteta soldatskikh deputatov 15-go Siberskogo strelkovogo polka o provedenii meropriiatii po demokratizatsii armii i uluchschenuiu material'nogo polozheniia soldata i ikh semei," in *Voiksovye komitety deistvuiushchei armii. Mart 1917 g.–mart 1918 g.*, ed. L. M. Gavrilov, et al. (Moscow: Nauka, 1982), 43.
12. "Nakaz ofitserov 8 Siberskogo strelkago polka," *Novoe vremia*, 5 April 1917, 3.
13. "Rezoliutsiia sobraniia voinnykh fel'dsherov Orlovskago garnizona, sostoiashchagosia 7 aprelia 1917 goda," *Delo naroda*, 15 April 1917, 3.
14. See document 6.4.
15. "17 aprelia—Rezolitusiia I s'ezda voennykh i rabochikh deputatov armii i tyla Zapadnogo fronta o pravykh soldat," in *Revoliutsionnoe dvizhenie v Russkoi armii. 27 fevralia–24 oktiabria 1917 goda. Sbornik dokumentov*, ed. L. S. Gaponenko, et. al. (Moscow: Nauka, 1968), 63–65
16. The original document was amended by hand here, to add the words "and all citizens in military service, from privates to generals, also including army paramedics, military clerks, and so on" (Gaponenko, et al., *Revoliutsionnoe dvizhenie v Russkoi armii,* 63).
17. The Russian "*denshchik*" was equivalent to a "batman" or "soldier-servant" in the British Army.
18. Despite being outlawed in Russia, dueling was still accepted among officers during the war.
19. *Izvestiia Petrogradskogo Soveta rabochikh i soldatskikh deputatov,* 9 March 1917, 1.
20. A "municipalized" enterprise would be owned by the city government.
21. *Izvestiia Petrogradskogo Soveta rabochikh i soldatskikh deputatov,* 11 March 1917, 1.
22. "Pis'mo v redaktsiiu" and "Soldaty rabochim," *Delo naroda*, 31 March 1917, 4.
23. In fact, workers still received a meal break.
24. State Archives of Smolensk Region (GASO), f. 1385, d. 2, l. 140.
25. "Rezoliutsiia uchitel'nits nachal. shkol," "Sobranie vrachei," and "Sobranie chinovnikov," *Smolenskii vestnik*, 12 March 1917, 3; "Sredi sluzhahchikh gosudarsrtvennago banka," *Smolenskii vestnik*, 17 March 1917, 3.
26. Members of committees could have two different types of vote: a "consultative vote" meant they only had the right to voice opinions; a "full" or "decisive vote" meant their vote counted in rendering decisions.
27. In Smolensk in March 1917 doctors, dentists, paramedics, nurses, and wet-nurses argued over professional distinctions and representation in professional organizations and public institutions.
28. "Rezoliutsiia Soveta S"ezda predstavitelei promyshlennosti i torgovli: O polnom doverii Vremennomu komitetu Gosudarstvennoi dumy," *Izvestiia Komiteta Petrogradskikh zhurnalistov*, 3 March 1917, 1.
29. During the uprising, a printers' strike shut down all other Petrograd newspapers, but the Printers' Union agreed to print this special newspaper to inform the public of events.
30. The Bolshevik government liquidated the Council in 1918.
31. "Sobranie zavodshchikov i farbrikantov," *Smolenskii vestnik*, 15 March 1917, 3.
32. Reshitnikov owned and managed a textile bobbin factory. Esaitis was manager of the Vilia Metalworking Plant, which had been evacuated from Vilna (Lithuania) to Smolensk in 1916.
33. *Ekonomicheskoe polozhenie Rossii nakanune velikoi oktiabr'skoi sotsialisticheskoi revoliutsii. Dokmenty i materialy. Mart–oktiabr' 1917 g.,* pt. 1 (Moscow and Leningrad: Izdatel'stvo akademii nauk SSSR, 1957), 162–163.

34. State Archives of the Smolensk Region (GASO), f. 98, op. 2, d. 195, ll. 4, 7–8; and op. 2, d. 199, ll. 1, 2.
35. Either factory committee chairman P. Grigor'ev or committee secretary K. M. Sirmbard underlined the words "at half" and emphatically put question marks after this phrase.
36. Bankoroshnits had been caught stealing. Day workers did unskilled jobs on a day-to-day basis.
37. This refers to the 10 percent rate of compensation agreed to on 29 March 1917.
38. Undated, with an archivist's note indicating 11 April 1917.
39. "Svobodnaia Rossiia dolzhna byt' prosveshchennoi," *Birzhevyia vedomosti*, 7 April 1917, 3.
40. Finland was incorporated into the Russian Empire in 1809, which is why Bekhterev refers to "our Finland." It became independent in December 1917.
41. "Rezoliutsiia skhodki studentov Elektrotekhnicheskoi Instituta," *Harvard Russian Revolutionary Literature Collection* (New Haven, CT: Research Publications, Inc., 1973), reel 47.
42. "Sobranii uchashchikh," *Smolenskii vestnik*, 9 March 1917, 3. *Uchashchie*" refers to students in primary and secondary educational institutions, not to university students ("*studenty*").
43. Rudnev was a popular teacher at the Smolensk Public High School.
44. In spring 1917, collecting money to aid liberated political prisoners and making contributions to such funds became important public symbols of civic engagement. Local newspapers like *Smolenskii vestnik* regularly published lists of contributors to such funds.
45. "Tsarism svergnut, kapiltalizm rushitsia, burzhuaziia triasetsia," *Sbornik dokumentov 1917 g. po istorii leningradskoi organizatsii VLKSM* (Leningrad: VKLSM, 1932), 81–83.

Chapter 5

1. "Novyi narodnyi gim," *Novoe vremia*, 7 (20) March 1917, 6.
2. "K pastyrem i chadem tserki smolenskoi," *Smolenskii vestnik*, 8 March 1917, 3.
3. "Zabastovka chlenov sinod," *Delo naroda*, 15 March 1917, 3.
4. "S. Ovinovshchina sut. v dor. u.," *Smolenskii vestnik*, 16 March 1917, 4.
5. Batishchevo was an experimental farm owned by populist Aleksandr Nikolaevich Engel'gardt (1883–1893), a pioneer of "rational" farming methods in Russia. The document suggests that other peasants took a dim view of Batishchevo and its resident agricultural laborers.
6. "Iz protokol zasedaniia Spasskogo uezda obshchestvennogo ispolnitel'nogo komiteta ot 21 marta 1917 o dovedenii do pravitel'stva zaiavleniia krest'ianskoi gruppy komiteta," in *Krest'ianskoe dvizhenie v Tambovskoi gubernii (1917–1918). Dokumenty i materialy*, ed. V. Danilov and T. Shanin (Moscow: ROSSPEN, 2003), 33.
7. Services in the Russian Orthodox were conducted in Old Church Slavonic.
8. "O Samarskom gubernskom krest'ianskom s'ezde," *Delo naroda*, 5 May 1917, 4.
9. The Socialist-Narodniks were a local populist splinter group close to the Socialist Revolutionaries.
10. Committees of the People's Government were local equivalents to Executive Committees. The Peasant Union was an all-Russian association of peasant organizations created in 1905.
11. A note in Volkov's text refers to Kondrushkin's article in the newspaper *Rech* (nos. 87, 90).
12. *Kulak* ("fist") was a "wealthy peasant" who had more land and livestock than other villagers, hired laborers, or lent money, tools or seed to others for profit. An *otrubnik* had consolidated farm fields separate from the *obshchina* (an *otrub*), but a house in the village.
13. "Postanovlenie zemel'nogo komiteta Tumskogo u. Kurskoi gub. o peredache vsei zemli v uezde v vedenie zemel'nykh komitetov, 16 iunia 1917 g.," in *Ekonomicheskoe polozhenie*

Rossii nakanune velikoi oktiabr'skoi revoliutsii. Dokumenty i materialy, pt. 3, *Sel'skoe knoziaistvo i krest'ianstvo* (Leningrad: Nauka, 1967), 280–281.

14. One *desiatin* is equal to 2.7 acres.

15. "Zhrezvychainoe zasedanie ob"edinnago dvorianstva," *Birzhevyia vedomosti*, 11 March 1917, 4.

16. On the United Nobility and similar associations of prerevolutionary elites during 1917, see the work of Matthew Rendle in the list of further readings.

17. "Obrashchenie zemskogo nachal'nik 3-chastka Elatomskogo uezda Lozhina," and "Preprovoditel'noe pis'mo zemskogo nachal'nika 3-go chastka Elatomskogo uezda Lozhina," in *Krest'ianskoe dvizhenie v Tambovskoi gubernii (1917–1918). Dokumenty i materialy*, ed. V. Danilov and T. Shanin (Moscow: ROSSPEN, 2003), 28–29.

18. Lozhin refers to "the great Russian state" as *"velikoi derzhavy Rossiisko,"* using the root word for autocracy *(samoderzhavie)*.

19. *Kievskaia zemskaia gazeta*, no. 9/10 (18 March 1917): 270, 273–274.

20. A note on page 270 reads: "All articles in the Ukrainian language accepted for publication will be printed in their entirety, as well articles in the Russian language. The Editors."

21. *Rus'* is an archaic term for "the Russian lands." Kiev was capital of the early *Rus'* state. Ukrainian nationalists argued that the *Rus'* civilization of the 800s–1200s was Ukrainian.

22. Konstantin Bal'mont was a significant Russian Symbolist poet. I have not found this fragment celebrating the February Revolution in any collection of Bal'mont's work.

23. The author deliberately uses the phrase *"liudi Rossii,"* people who live in the Russian state.

24. The author repeatedly uses the phrase *russkii narod*, meaning the ethnically Russian people.

25. The author uses *russkoe*, meaning ethnically Russian, and *russkaia zhizn'*, the life of Russians.

26. In this paragraph the author uses *Rossiia*, the territory of the Russian state.

27. The author uses *russkii narod*, the ethnic Russian people, and *russkaia svoboda*, freedom of the ethnic Russians.

28. This sentence twice uses *Rossiia* (the territory of the Russian state).

29. The phrase used here is *"vsei russkoi istorii"*—all of the history of the ethnic Russians.

30. The essay may have been written before the Provisional Government's form had become clear. The author repeatedly uses the phrase *svobodnoi Rossiia*—the free territory of the Russian state.

31. Here and in the last sentence, the phrase used is *svobodnoi Rossiia*.

32. S. M. Dimanshtein, ed., *Revoliutsiia i natsional'nyi vopros. Dokumenty i materialy po istorii national'nogo voprosa v Rossii i SSSR v XX veke*, vol. 3, *1917 fevral'- oktiabr'* (Moscow: Kommunisticheskaia Akademiia, 1930), 136–137.

33. Competing Polish and Ukrainian claims to territory in eastern Galicia had deep historical roots, and led to a border war between the two independent states in 1918–1919.

34. S. M. Dimanshtein, ed., *Revoliutsiia i natsional'nyi vopros. Dokumenty i materialy po istorii national'nogo voprosa v Rossii i SSSR v XX veke*, vol. 3, *1917 fevral'- oktiabr'* (Moscow: Kommunisticheskaia Akademiia, 1930), 150–151.

35. S. M. Dimanshtein, ed., *Revoliutsiia i natsional'nyi vopros. Dokumenty i materialy po istorii national'nogo voprosa v Rossii i SSSR v XX veke*, vol. 3, *1917 fevral'- oktiabr'* (Moscow: Kommunisticheskaia Akademiia, 1930), 161–164.

36. Here the authors use *Rossiia*, meaning the territory of the Russian state.

37. The authors use the Ukrainian *Seijm*, meaning Assembly (often translated as Diet).

38. "Telegramma Semipalatinskogo oblastnogo kazakhskogo s'ezda Petrograskomu Sovety," in *Revoliutsionnoe dvizhenie v Rossii v mae-iiune 1917 g., Iiun'skaia demonstratsiia* (Moscow: Izdatel'stvo Akademii Nauk SSSR, 1956), 448.

39. The Kirgiz, a Turkic-speaking people who had adopted Islam, included the Kara-Kirgiz (Burat) in upland territories and the Kazakh-Kirgiz on the steppes.
40. Some documents refer to the 13 May 1917 meeting as the Regional Kazakh Congress, while others—like this telegram—refer to it as a Kirgiz congress.
41. The authors use the word *Rossiiiskii*, meaning the territory of the Russian state.
42. "Rezoliutsiia I Kavkazskogo oblastnogo s'ezda Sovetov," in *Revoliutsionnoe dvizhenie v Rossii v mae-iiune 1917 g., Iiun'skaia demonstratsiia* (Moscow: Izdatel'stvo Akadamii Nauk SSSR, 1956), 457.
43. *Rossiisskii* and *Rossiia*—referring to the Russian state territory, not ethnic Russians.
44. "Liga ravnopraviia zhenshchin," *Smolenskii vestnik*, 9 March 1917, 4.
45. The League for Women's Equal Rights continued to function through 1917, but it was disbanded by the Bolsheviks in 1918.
46. "K vsem Russkim zhenshchinam-materiam," *Novaia zhizn'*, 5 May 1917, 4.
47. This echoes the socialists' rejection of peace terms that would reward victors with territorial annexations or force the vanquished to pay an indemnity.
48. "Vozzvanie Tsentral'nogo biuro rossiiskikh musul'man k musul'mankam Rossii," in *Revoliutsionnoe dvizhenie v Rossii v aprele 1917. Aprel'skii krizis*, ed. L. S. Gaponenko, et al. (Moscow: Izdatel'stvo akademii nauk SSSR, 1958), 716.
49. S. M. Dimanshtein, ed., *Revoliutsiia i natsional'nyi vopros. Dokumenty i materialy po istorii national'nogo voprosa v Rossii i SSSR v XX veke*, vol. 3, *1917 fevral'- oktiabr'* (Moscow: Kommunisticheskaia Akademiia), 294–297.
50. All-Russian (*Vserossiiskii*) refers to the entire territory of the Russian state.
51. *Smolenskii vestnik*, 18 March 1917, 3.
52. S. M. Dimanshtein, ed., *Revoliutsiia i natsional'nyi vopros. Dokumenty i materialy po istorii national'nogo voprosa v Rossii i SSSR v XX veke*, vol. 3, *1917 fevral'- oktiabr'* (Moscow: Kommunisticheskaia Akademiia, 1930), 277–278.
53. The RSDLP refers to the Russian Social Democratic Labor Party.
54. The Bund considered Yiddish (not Hebrew) to be the Jewish national language.
55. This refers to taxes levied and administered by Jewish communal associations to fund communal institutions and services.
56. The idea of a general Jewish congress had been promoted by the Marxist Zionist party, Poalei-Tsion, as well as by Jewish liberals and liberal nonparty groups. Elections for this congress were held in fall 1917, but the conference never convened.
57. S. M. Dimanshtein, ed., *Revoliutsiia i natsional'nyi vopros. Dokumenty i materialy po istorii national'nogo voprosa v Rossii i SSSR v XX veke*, vol. 3, *1917 fevral'- oktiabr'* (Moscow: Kommunisticheskaia Akademiia, 1930), 279.
58. In the late-tsarist period and under the Provisional Government, every legally recognized Jewish community had an *obshchina* (society) that administered Jewish communal institutions.

Chapter 6

1. *Pravda*, 7 April 1917, 3.
2. On 9 January 1905, Bloody Sunday, soldiers shot down peaceful protesters in St. Petersburg. In April 1912, soldiers killed and wounded hundreds of peaceful strikers at Siberian goldmines on the Lena River. In June 1915, soldiers shot down striking workers at a Kostroma linen factory; in August 1915, soldiers shot 90 striking textile workers (30 of whom died) in Ivanovo.
3. *Izvestiia Moskovskogo Soveta rabochikh deputatov*, 2 May 1917, 3.
4. The city and provincial government committees formed in March 1917 included "commissars" who were members of the local administration and agents of Provisional Government ministries.

5. The issue went to the Moscow Committee of Public Organization's Military Council—which included garrison representatives—because of the strike's impact on munitions production.
6. *Proletarii* (Kharkov), 14 April 1917, 4.
7. "K narodom vsego mira," *Izvestiia Petrogradskogo Soveta rabochikh i soldatskikh deputatov*, 15 March 1917, 1.
8. *Vestnik Vremennogo pravitel'stvo*, 28 March 1917, 1.
9. On 17 March 1917 the Provisional Government announced that it was granting the right of self-government to Poland, which at the time was under German occupation.
10. *Izvestiia Petrogradskogo Soveta*, 31 March 1917, 3; 2 April 1917, 2.
11. *Vestnik Vremennogo pravital'stvo*, 20 April 1917, 2.
12. *Rech*, 13 April 1917, 3; *Vestnik Vremennogo pravital'stvo*, 14 April 1917, 1.
13. The "me" in this sentence was the Russian representative sent to read the statement verbatim.
14. "The Central Monarchies" were Austro-Hungary, Germany, Ottoman Turkey, and Bulgaria.
15. When the United States entered the war, President Wilson stressed the centrality of national self-determination to the postwar order. He incorporated this idea into his January 1918 Fourteen Points peace program.
16. *Pravda*, 22 April 1917, 3.
17. *Pravda*, 29 April 1917, 3.
18. *Novaia zhizn'*, 23 April 1917, 6.
19. *Vestnik Vremennogo pravitel'stvo*, 22 April 1917, 1.
20. *Izvestiia Petrogradskogo Soveta rabochikh i soldatskikh deputatov*, 22 April 1917, 3.
21. *Izvestiia Petrogradskogo Soveta rabochikh i soldatskikh deputatov*, 22 April 1917, 5.
22. The Admiralty was next to the Winter Palace.
23. Znamenskaia Square is on Nevskii Prospect, about halfway to the marchers' destination.
24. *Delo Naroda*, 25 April 1917, 2.
25. To get to Nevskii Prospekt, the workers had to walk more than a mile.
26. Anichkova Palace is at the corner Nevskii Prospekt and the Fontanka Canal, east of Sadovaia.
27. *Rabochaia gazeta*, 22 April 1917, 4; *Pravda*, 28 April 1917, 3.
28. "Nota soiuznikam," *Birzhevyia vedomosti*, 21 April 1917, 3.
29. Charles Maurice de Talleyrand-Perigord (1754–1838) was a French diplomat known for skilled manipulation of language.
30. The quoted phrases in this sentence and the next are from Miliukov's Note.
31. "Wilhelmian" refers to the government of German Kaiser Wilhelm II (1859–1941); "Karlovian" refers to the government of Austro-Hungarian Emperor Karl 1 (1887–1922), who took power upon the death of Franz-Joseph in 1916.
32. V. L. Meller, and A. M. Pankratova, eds., *Rabochee dvizhenie v 1917 g.* (Moscow: Gosizdat, 1926), 135–136.
33. The speaker is Bolshevik Petr Smidovich.
34. Menshevik Boris Kibrik was a founder of the Moscow Soviet.
35. Sablin, a soldier, was a member of the Moscow Socialist Revolutionaries' left faction.
36. *Proletarii*, 25 April 1917, 4.
37. V. I. Lenin, "Uroki krizisa," *Pravda*, 22 April 1917, 1.
38. "Piter" (Peter) was local shorthand for Petrograd/St. Petersburg.
39. Lenin's claim that the workers' demonstrations were pro-Bolshevik is hyperbole.
40. August Blanqui (1805–1881) was founder of one of France's most influential radical socialist parties and President of the Paris Commune in 1871. Among Marxists, the term Blanquist inferred a minority who sought to seize power without any base of mass

support. Lenin's warning about Blanquist behavior was probably a reference to the Anarchists.

41. "Chern' i narod," *Moskovskaia vedomosti*, 22 April 1917, 1.

42. "Chemu uchat Petrogradskiia sobytiia?" *Izvestiia Rostovo-Nakhichevanskago Soveta rabochikh i soldatskikh deputatov*, 25 April 1917, 1.

43. The corpses refer to those killed during the 20–21 April 1917 demonstrations in Petrograd.

44. Miliukov supported Sazonov's policies in the State Duma during the 1912 Balkan Crisis.

45. 18 April 1917 in Russia was 1 May 1917 elsewhere—so the Miliukov Note was published on May Day (International Workers' Day).

46. *Pravda*, 26 April 1917, 3; *Revoliutsionnoe dvizhenie v Rossii v aprele 1917 g. Aprel'skii krizis* (Moscow: Izdatel'stvo akademii nauk SSSR, 1958), 820–821.

47. The Russian *"malosoznatel'nyi"*—a common term in Russian socialists' vocabulary and subsequently part of the Soviet and Communist lexicons—is translated here as "less-conscious."

48. "O koalitsionnom ministerstve," *Rabochaia gazeta*, 29 April 1917, 1.

49. "Krizis vlasti," *Delo naroda*, 26 April 1917, 1.

50. "Census" refers to the propertied groups with electoral rights in tsarist municipal elections. *Pays légale* ("the country as recognized by the law") means those with the privilege of representation before the state.

51. *Rech*, 28 April 1917, 4.

52. Shul'gin was referring to Miliukov, Guchkov, Prince L'vov, and other members of the Provisional Government who attended the State Duma session.

53. Petrograd's Peter-Paul Fortress housed tsarist Russia's most famous political prison.

54. Menshevik leader Irakli Tsereteli responded at length when Shul'gin finished his speech.

55. The "Petrograd Side" was a district in Petrograd with many large factories; the Bolsheviks had their headquarters there.

56. G. Plekhanov, "Otechestvo v opasnosti," *Edinstvo*, 2 May 1917, 1.

57. Plekahnov is quoting "Who Can Be Happy in Russia?" by Nikolai Nekrasov (1821–1877).

58. Plekhanov mockingly refers to Swiss socialists Robert Grimm and Fritz Patten.

59. "The Tale of the White Bull" is a Russian folktale that involves seemingly infinite repetition.

60. Plekhanov's style in this passage is a parody of Lenin's.

61. Plekhanov quotes the *Divine Comedy* by the Florentine poet Dante Alighieri (1265–1321).

62. Plekhanov paraphrases a passage from Paul's epistle to the Romans in the New Testament (16:17), warning against alliances with those who would cause division among the Christians.

63. Again, Plekhanov is parodying Lenin.

64. Z. Galili, and A. Nenarokov, eds., *Men'sheviki v 1917 godu*, vol. 1, *Ot ianvaria do iiul'skikh sobytii* (Moscow: Progress-Akademiia, 1994), 317–318.

65. Dem'ian Bednyi, "Koalitsionnoe," *Pravda*, 3 May 1917, 2.

66. O. V. Volobuev, et al., eds., *S"ezdy i konferentsii konstitutionno-demokraticheskoi partii*, vol. 3, pt. 1, *1915–1917 gg* (Moscow: ROSSPEN, 2000), 501.

67. "Vozzvanie No. 1," *Anarkhisty. Dokumenty i materialy*, vol. 2, *1917–1935 gg*, ed. O. V. Volobuev, et al. (Moscow: ROSSPEN, 1999), 30–31.

68. The Russian idiom "to fish in troubled waters" (*lovit' rybu v mutnoi vode*) means to stir up trouble for the benefit of one's own interests.

Chapter 7

1. "Deklaratsiia Menshevik-Internatsionalistov," in *Letuchii listok Men'shevikov-Internationalistov*, no. 1 (May 1917): 1–4 (the excerpt is from 2–3).

2. This refers to the breakup of the Second Socialist International following disputes over the war.

3. "Biulleten Soveta rabochikh, soldatskikh i krestianskikh deputatov," *Smolenskii vestnik* 31 May 1917, 3.

4. Iakubovich (first name unknown) was a Menshevik activist in Smolensk.

5. Vadim Smol'ianinov was one of the leaders of the Bolshevik faction in Smolensk.

6. Maizel (first name unknown) was a local Bund activist.

7. "Prikaz voennogo i morskogo ministra A. F. Kerenskii deitstvuiushchei armii o perekhod v nastuplenie," *Vestnik Vremennogo pravitel'stvo*, 20 June 1917, 1.

8. This is a reference to Supreme Commander General Brusilov.

9. Soldat Pavloveta Afanas'ev-Arskii, "Za chest' Rossii matushki," *Pravda*, 18 June 1917, 3. This poem later became a popular ballad.

10. *Pravda*, 17 June 1917, 2.

11. On 3 June 1907, Russian Prime Minister Stolypin altered the electoral system to secure disproportional representation for large landowners in the State Duma.

12. This refers to Kerensky's 16 June 1917 declaration announcing the offensive (see document 7.3).

13. Article 129 of the tsarist government's criminal code applied to antigovernment public acts or the dissemination of antigovernment printed material.

14. The Provisional Government promised to grant Poland independence, but would not make similar assurances to Finland and Ukraine. Kadet government members opposed concessions to Finland and Ukraine, which led to a government crisis and resignation of Kadet members in July.

15. Nezavismyi, "K pogrom i separatnomu miru," *Novoe vremia*, 18 June 1917, 3.

16. In 1917, the workers' soft cap became a symbol of the proletariat (versus the "bourgeois" hat).

17. The Black Hundreds were an ultra-right, overtly antisemitic paramilitary organization linked to the Union of Russian People. They were publically associated with anti-Jewish *pogroms*.

18. V. N. Rakhmetov, and N. N. Miamlin, eds., *Pervyi vserossiiskii s"ezd sovetov r. i s. d.*, vol. 2 (Moscow and Leningrad: Gosudarstvennoe sotsal'no-ekonomicheskoe izdatel'stvo, 1931), 82–92.

19. Of 784 delegates with full voting rights, 285 were Socialist Revolutionaries, 248 Mensheviks, and 102 Bolsheviks.

20. At the 17 June 1917, during debate on socialist participation in the Provisional Government, Tsereteli said that no one political party in Russia was prepared to take power by itself. Lenin famously shouted that there was—his party, the Bolsheviks. Lenin then argued that power must be passed directly to the soviets.

21. David Lloyd George (1863–1945) was the prime minister of Great Britain in 1916–1922.

22. *Rech*, 20 June 1917, 1–2.

23. This essay was written on 19 June and published on 20 June 1917.

24. P. Dnevnitskii, "Da zdravstvuet nastuplenie!" *Edinstvo*, 20 June 1917, 1.

25. At the 20 September 1792 Battle of Valmy, Gen. Francois Kellerman (1735–1820) led French troops to victory with the battle cry *"Vive la nation!"*

26. "On menia derznul'," *Delo naroda*, 24 June 1917; reprinted in R. V. Ivanov-Razumnik, *God revoliutsii. Stat'i 1917 goda* (St. Petersburg [Petrograd]: No Publisher, 1918), 65.

27. The French *"tout court"* means "without qualification."

28. "Privetstviia nastupleniiu," *Narodnoe slovo*, 1 July 1917, 4.

29. L. S. Gaponenko, et al., eds., *Revoliutsionnoe dvizhenie v Russkoi armii. 27 fevralia-24 oktiabria 1917 goda. Sbornik dokumentov* (Moscow: Nauka, 1968), 193.

30. "Tovarishhi rabochie i soldaty Petrograda!" *Soldatskaia Pravda*, 5 July 1917, 1.

31. V. I. Lenin, "Vsia vlast' sovetam!" *Pravda*, 4 July 1917, 1.

32. *Izvestiia Petrogradskogo Soveta*, 4 July 1917, 1.

33. *Revoliutsionnoe dvizhenia v Rossii v iiule 1917 g., Iiul'skii krizis* (Moscow: Izdatel'stvo akademii nauk SSSR, 1959), 20–21, 39.
34. "Vsem soldatam i rabochim Petrograda," *Delo naroda*, 5 July 1917, 1.
35. "O demonstratsii," *Pravda*, 5 July 1917, 4.
36. G. Plekhanov, "Kak zhe byt'?" *Edinstvo*, 5 July 1917, 1.
37. "My v opastnosti," *Birzhevyia vedomosti*, 5 July 1917, 3.
38. P. Orekhov, "Ob usluzhlivykh medvediakh, koikh demokratii opast'cia cleduest ne men'she, chem. Burshuaznykh volkov," *Revoliutsionny narod*, 5 July 1917, 4.
39. The Bolshevik newspapers *Truth (Pravda)* and *Soldiers' Truth (Soldatskaia Pravda)*.
40. *Sovremennoe slovo*, 7 July 1917, in *Revoliutsionnoe dvizhenie v voennykh orkugakh. Mart 1917 g.-mart 1918 g*, ed. Iu. I. Korablev (Moscow: Nauka, 1988), 177–178.
41. Sormovo, a suburb of Nizhni Novgorod, was the province's largest industrial center.
42. "Ivanovskaia volost'," *Izvestiia Petrogradskogo Soveta*, 22 July 1917, 11–12.
43. Slavskii, "K momentom," *Tiflisskii listok*, 15 July 1917, 3.
44. This idiom is similar to the idiom, "To make an omelet, you have to break some eggs." In other words, when drastic action is necessary, any harm caused is justified by the greater good.

Part Three

1. See the major "foundational" social histories written in the 1980s by Diane P. Koenker, Steve Smith, David Mandel, Rex A. Wade, Allan K. Wildman, and Orlando Figes, and recent works by Sarah Badcock and Aaron Retish in the list of further readings.
2. The most ambitious version of this argument is Orlando Figes, *A People's Tragedy: The Russian Revolution, 1891–1924* (New York: Viking, 1997). See also Orlando Figes and Boris Kolonitskii, *Interpreting the Russian Revolution: The Language and Symbols of 1917* (New Haven and London: Yale University Press, 1999), and Leopold H. Haimson, *Russia's Revolutionary Experience: Two Essays* (New York: Columbia University Press, 2005). Since 1990, many Russian-language histories of 1917 have heavily emphasized the role of irrationality and social hatred in driving politics.
3. As Christopher Read observed, what mattered most in the process of radicalization was "issues rather than parties." Christopher Read, *From Tsar to Soviets: The Russian People and Their Revolution, 1917–1921* (New York and Oxford: Oxford University Press, 1996), 90.
4. See Steve Smith, "Factory Committee," in *Critical Companion to the Russian Revolution*, Paul Flenley, "Industrial Relations and the Economic Crisis of 1917," *Revolutionary Russia* 4, no. 2 (1991): 184–209.
5. See William G. Rosenberg, "Problems of Social Welfare and Everyday Life," in *Critical Companion to the Russian Revolution*, 638.
6. For a detailed examination of strikes and their impact on the economy, social identities, and politics in 1917, see the work by Diane P. Koenker and William G. Rosenberg in the list of further readings.
7. John Channon, "The Peasantry in the Revolutions of 1917," in *Revolution in Russia: Reassessments of 1917*, ed. Edith Frankel, et al. (New York: Cambridge University Press, 1992), 105–130.
8. For useful statistical tables and an examination of the evidence on peasant unrest, see Maurine Perrie, "The Peasants," in *Society and Politics in the Russian Revolution*, ed. Robert Service (New York: Palgrave Macmillan, 1992), 12–34.
9. There is an excellent brief discussion in Wade, *The Russian Revolution*, chapter 6.
10. The most detailed historical studies of the military, by Allan K. Wildman (see list of further readings), show that the rate of desertion from the army actually declined after May, but then increased dramatically at the end of August.
11. Allan K. Wildman, "The Breakdown of the Russian Imperial Army in 1917," in *Critical Companion to the Russian Revolution*, 75.

12. The Bolsheviks boycotted the conference after its organizers refused to seat representatives of the Bolshevik Central Committee. The Moscow's trade unions' general strike resulted from the Bolshevik call for a boycott.
13. *Russkiia vedomosti*, 15 August 1917, 3.
14. It was in this atmosphere that the Mensheviks held their second party congress of 1917, referred to as the Unification Congress because it brought together the party's several contentious factions. In a 19 August 1917 speech to the Menshevik congress, Tsereteli implicitly recognized the failure of the United Democracy strategy and warned that "rash" elements—a thinly veiled reference to the Bolsheviks—threatened Russia with anarchy.
15. For an excellent brief overview of the Kornilov affair, see James D. White, *The Russian Revolution, 1917–1921: A Short History* (London: Edward Arnold, 1994), chapter 7.
16. The Directory's members were Kerensky, Nikitin, Tereshchenko, and two of Kerensky's military protégées—General Verekhovskii and Admiral Veredevskii. For an overview of changes in the Provisional Government in 1917, see Howard White, "The Provisional Government," in *Critical Companion to the Russian Revolution*, 391–402.
17. The cabinet's Kadet members were Nikolai Kishkin (social welfare minister), Anton Kartashev (religious affairs minister), and Sergei Smirnov (comptroller general). The key nonparty liberals were Aleksei Konovalov (minister of trade), Mikhail Tereshchenko (foreign affairs minister), Aleksandr Liversovskii (transport minister), Sergei Salazkin (education minister), and Sergei Prokopovich (minister of food supply). The Menshevik members were Aleksei Nikitin (minister of internal affairs and minster of communications), Kuzma Gvodzov (labor minister), and Pavel Maliantovich (justice minister). The SR Semen Maslov was agriculture minister.
18. Two studies that largely revised historians' view of the October Revolution were Robert V. Daniels, *Red October: The Bolshevik Revolution of 1917* (New York: Norton, 1967) and Alexander Rabinowitch, *The Bolsheviks Come to Power: The Revolution of 1917 in Petrograd* (New York: Norton, 1976).
19. In October 1917, Trotsky actually argued that the Bolsheviks should wait for the soviet congress to meet, and then seize power in its name.
20. See Robert McNeal, ed., *Resolutions and Decisions of the Communist Party of the Soviet Union*, vol. 1, *The Russian Social Democratic Labour Party, 1898–October 1917*, ed. Ralph Carter Elwood (Toronto: University of Toronto Press, 1974), 288–289.

Chapter 8

1. "Gubernskii Sovet," *Smolenskii vestnik* 27 May 1917, 2; 28 May 1917, 2–3; 31 May 1917, 2–3; 1 June 1917, 2; 3 June 1917, 2; 4 June 1917, 2–3; 8 June 1917, 3; and 9 June 1917, 3.
2. "Gubernskii Sovet," *Smolenskii vestnik*, 27 May 1917, 2.
3. Tukhachevskii was a nonparty liberal, as was Deputy Commissar Untilov.
4. Iugansen was a local Kadet.
5. On a *khutor* farmstead, the land and farm house were separate from the village. "State peasants" refers to those who lived on state-owned lands and paid dues to the state before the Great Reforms. In parts of Smolensk Province, state peasants included ethnic Latvians who, as a result of emancipation, received land allotments of up to 15 *desiatins* (about 40 acres).
6. Flax was the main cash crop in much of Smolensk Province. The war had cut off exports and decreased demand, but the government encouraged its cultivation for fibers and industrial oil.
7. State directives on the requisition of cattle and grain (for the army and other uses) set "living norms"—the amount of grain or number of livestock that peasant households

needed to survive. The claim here is that local provisions authorities were taking grain and cattle beyond that limit.

8. A *funt* is about 4 kilograms; a *desiatin* is about 2.2 acres.
9. "Gubernskii Sovet," *Smolenskii vestnik*, 28 May 1917, 2–3.
10. Timber was one of the region's major exports. Each spring men floated logs down river. Much of western Smolensk's timber harvest was moved to Baltic ports in this fashion.
11. Under the Provisional Government, local police forces were called "militias."
12. All across Russia, the old police force was disbanded as a result of the February Revolution, and there were debates over whether the new "democratic" people's militia should be elected.
13. "Gubernskii Sovet," *Smolenskii vestnik*, 31 May 1917, 2–3.
14. Gubkin was a local Kadet.
15. A recent Peasant Soviet bulletin called on peasants to take over and farm untilled private land.
16. Tykotskii was a local Socialist Revolutionary.
17. Zvziulinskii was a local Socialist Revolutionary.
18. Davidovich was a local Menshevik leader.
19. Egorov was a local Socialist Revolutionary.
20. Kutuzov was a local Socialist Revolutionary leader and a principal author of the policies criticized by the next speaker, Kostiukevich.
21. Kostiukevich was a prominent local liberal.
22. "Gubernskii Sovet," *Smolenskii vestnik*, 1 June 1917, 2.
23. A few days earlier the left factions in the Smolensk Soviet had "requisitioned" the former tsarist governor's mansion and offices as the soviet's new home. After some debate, the soviet leadership agreed to occupy the building. The provincial commissar protested that the seizure was illegal, but he had to back down, which further undermined his authority.
24. In fact, no army deserters had been elected to the Peasant Congress's executive committee.
25. Newspaper editor Solomon Gurevich was a local Socialist Revolutionary leader.
26. Glinka was a liberal noble landowner.
27. "Gubernskii Sovet," *Smolenskii vestnik*, 3 June 1917, 2.
28. Popova, the only woman on the council, was a local Bolshevik.
29. Tsapenko, a local Menshevik labor organizer, was a new soviet delegate to the council.
30. This is what Russians called the "four-tailed" principle of suffrage.
31. "Gubernskii Sovet," *Smolenskii vestnik*, 4 June 1917, 2–3.
32. The Kronshtadt Soviet had declared the city an independent "republic," and for the liberal press, Kronshtadt symbolized anarchy and chaos.
33. "Gubernskii Sovet," *Smolenskii vestnik*, 8 June 1917, 3.
34. Nikolaev was a local Bolshevik. Seizing the governor's mansion had been the local Bolsheviks' idea, and they did so without the soviet's authorization.
35. "Gubernskii Sovet," *Smolenskii vestnik*, 9 June 1917, 3.
36. Iakubovich was a Menshevik member of the Smolensk Soviet's workers' section.
37. *Smolenskii vestnik*, 4 October 1917, 2–3; 5 October 1917, 2–3; *Rech*, 6 October 1917, 5–6; *Vospominaniia uchastnikov bor'by za vlast sovetov v Smolenskoi gubernii*, ed. P. Galitskaia, et al. (Smolensk: Smolenskoe knizhnoe izdatel'stvo, 1957), 87, 93–94; N. P. Galitskaia, "Ustanovlenie i uprochenie sovietskoi vlasti v Roslavl'skom uezde," *Materialy po izucheniiu Smolenskoi oblasti* 6 (1967): 144.
38. "Pogromnaia volna," *Smolenskii vestnik*, 4 October 1917, 2.
39. Sychevka is another of Smolensk's towns.
40. This is a reference to the July governmental crisis and "July Days" in Petrograd.
41. Iv. Roslavl'skii, "Pogrom v Roslavle," *Smolenskii vestnik*, 4 October 1917, 3.
42. In Russian "Yids" (*zhidy*) is a rude term for Jews. The storeowners mentioned were Jews.

43. "Pogrom v Roslavle," *Rech*, 6 October 1917, 5–6.

44. "K pogrom v Roslavle," *Smolenskii vestnik*, 5 October 1917, 3.

45. Burgonov, a member of the Party of Socialist Revolutionaries, had been elected deputy commissar in July 1917.

46. "Bol'sheviki i pogrom," *Smolenskii vestnik*, 5 October 1917, 2.

47. The Union of the Russian People was an ultranationalist, antisemitic political party. Despite Gurevich's claim, there is no evidence that former members of the union joined the Roslavl' Bolshevik organization.

48. The Black Hundreds were militant nationalists associated with the Union of Russian People. There is no specific evidence that former Black Hundreds were involved in the October 1917 Roslavl' pogrom or belonged to the local Bolshevik organization.

49. Divisions among Bolshevik leaders regarding the path to power came into the open in October 1917. The most dramatic display of public tensions came when Kamenev and Zinoviev publically warned that Lenin intended an armed seizure of power.

50. "Roslavl'skii pogrom," *Smolenskii vestnik*, 20 October 1917, 4.

51. I. V. Vinslavl, "Za velikoe delo Oktiabria," in *Vospominaniia uchastnikov bor'by za vlast sovetov v Smolenskoi gubernii*, ed. N. P. Galitskaia et al. (Smolensk: Smolenskoe knizhnoe izdatel'stvo, 1957), 87.

52. From D. V. Klochkov, "Nash vklad v delo revoliutsiia," in *Vospominaniia uchastnikov*, ed. Galitskaia et al., 93–94.

53. Konopatskii and Nikiforov were local Bolshevik leaders.

54. N. P. Galitskaia, "Ustanovlenie i uprochenie sovietskoi vlasti v Roslavl'skom uezde," *Materialy po izucheniiu Smolenskoi oblasti* 6 (1967): 144. Galitskaia cites the memoirs of Vinslav and Klochkov and a report by the Roslavl' Bolshevik Party group (dated 2 October 1917). I have been unable to find this report in the Smolensk regional archives.

Chapter 9

1. *Revoliutsionnoe dvizhenie v Rossi v mae-iiune 1917 g., Iiun'skaiia demostratsiia* (Moscow: Izdatel'stvo akademii nauk SSSR, 1959), 290–291.

2. Iu. V., "Strashnoe iavleniie," *Smolenskii vestnik*, 28 June 1917, 2.

3. Public lashings of people tied to a pillory (a whipping post) were banned in 1863.

4. This refers to *Smolenskii vestnik*'s editor, Solomon Gurevich.

5. General Petr Polovtsev became the object of the Petrograd Soviet's criticism during the "July Days." He was removed from his post on 13 July 1917.

6. *Rech*, 26 July 1917, 3–4.

7. Zimmerwaldism refers to the antiwar positions taken at the international socialist conference in Zimmerwald, Switzerland, in September 1915.

8. The idea that "spontaneity" and "consciousness" (*stikhnost'* and *soznatel'nost'*) were diametrically opposed modes of political behavior—with consciousness the preferred state—is closely associated with Lenin, but was common in Russian political thought in 1917.

9. Kienthal refers to the April 1916 antiwar socialist conference at Kienthal, Switzerland.

10. "Volneniia v Atarske," *Birzhevyia vedomosti*, 1 August 1917, 5.

11. Atkarsk had a civilian population of about 15,000 and a large reserve garrison.

12. "Rech P. P. Riabushinskogo pri otkrytii II Vserossiiskogo torgovo-promyshlennogo s"ezda," in *Ekonomicheskoe polozhenie Rossii nakanune velikoi oktiabr'skoi sotsialisticheskoi revoliutsii, dokumenty i materialy, mart-oktiabr' 1917 g.*, pt. 1 (Moscow-Leningrad: Izdatel'stvo akadamii nauk SSSR, 1957), 196–201.

13. This refers to comments made by Kerensky about the second coalition government.

14. As agricultural minister and then finance minister, Andrei Shingarev had angered commercial interests and industrialists by introducing a state monopoly on grain purchases (in March 1917) and a tax on profits (in June 1917).

15. *Gosudarstvenno soveshchanie. Stenograficheskii otchet* (Moscow-Leningrad: Gosudarstvennoe izdatel'stvo, 1930), 60–66, 73–76.
16. *Russkiia vedomosti*, 15 August 1917, 3.
17. On 7 July 1917, a German assault routed three Russian armies at Tarnopol' (the Russian spelling; in Austrian German, spelled Tarnopol) in Austrian ruled Galicia. Reports wrongly claimed Russian soldiers had deserted en-masse. On 8–9 July, Kornilov (then commander in chief of the Southwestern Front) ordered that deserters be shot and threatened to resign unless the death penalty for deserters was restored on all fronts. On 12 July, the government restored the death penalty at the front. On 18 July, Kerensky appointed Kornilov supreme commander.
18. At Riga, Russian military units fell back in the face of mass German artillery fire and attacks using new "storm trooper" methods. The 56th Siberian Rifle Regiment had retreated when it was overwhelmed.
19. This is a reference to the forcible requisition of food from civilians.
20. *Gosudarstvennoe soveshchanie. Stenograficheskii otchet* (Moscow-Leningrad: Gosudarstvennoe izdatel'stvo, 1930), 227–229.
21. "*Tsenzovik*," refers to the propertied classes but was a less confrontational than "bourgeoisie."
22. Breshko-Breshkovskaia's parents were serf-owning nobles.
23. "Deklaratsiia bol'shevikov-chlenov delegatsii na Moskovskom gosudarstvennom soveshchanii," *Sotsial-demokrat*, 15 August 1917, 1.
24. Moscow's trade unions held a general strike in protest against the conference's convocation.
25. The conference organizers refused to seat members of the Bolshevik Central Committee.
26. *Rabochaia gazeta*, 20 August 1917, 2.
27. This is a barely veiled reference to the Bolsheviks.
28. "Iz obrashcheniia soveta Soiuza chastnovladel'tsev k naseleniiu gubernii," and "Perechen' razgromlennykh i sozhzhennykh chastnovladel'cheskikh imenii po Kozlovskomu uezdu," in *Krest'ianskoe dvizhenie v Tambovskoi gubernii (1917–1918): dokumenty i materialy*, ed. V. Danilov and T. Shanin (Moscow: ROSSPEN, 2003), 175–176, 239–240.
29. Peasants often targeted properties owned by women, who can be identified by last names ending with the letter "a."
30. Ligovskii, "Za predelami anarkhii," *Moskovskii vedomosti*, 22 September 1917, 1.
31. See chapter 10.
32. Ligovskii uses the archaic Russian term *Rus*, referring to the Russian lands.
33. As agriculture minister, Chernov encouraged local land committees to begin "settling" the land question in advance of the Constituent Assembly. His instructions led to tensions with Interior Minister Tseretell and Food Supply Minister Peshekhonov, who argued that Chernov's statements fostered anarchy. The Kadets denounced Chernov; during the July Crisis, they insisted he be removed from the government. Chernov resigned his post on 26 August 1917.
34. Pr. Smuglov, "V nashi dni," *Astrakhanskii listok*, 26 September 1917, 3; "Anarkhiia," *Astrakhanskii listok*, 29 September 1917, 2.
35. GASO f. 578, op. 3, d. 22, ll. 5–6.

Chapter 10

1. *Revoliutsionnoe dvizhenie v Rossii v avguste 1917 g., Razgrom kornilovskogo miatezha* (Moscow: Izdatel'stvo akademii nauk SSSR, 1959), 421–423.
2. Savinkov identifies himself as *Me*; I have changed this to *Savinkov*.
3. Captain Filonenko was the Provisional Government's commissar at the Supreme Command Headquarters in July to August 1917. General Lukimovskii was chief of staff in June to August.

4. Stavka was the Supreme Command Headquarters.
5. Both men were Socialist Revolutionary leaders: Chernov was agriculture minister in May to August 1917; Avksent'ev was internal affairs minister in July to September 1917.
6. General Cheremisov was commander of the Northern Front. In his rendering of this document, Kerensky made a point of saying that he had conducted no such conversation. Robert Paul Browder and Alexander Kerensky, *The Russian Provisional Government, 1917: Documents*, vol. 3 (Stanford: Stanford University Press, 1961), 1557.
7. Right Socialist Revolutionary Andrei Argunov and right Menshevik Georgii Plekhanov were prowar socialists. General M. V. Alekseev had been commander in chief in March to May 1917.
8. The Union of Officers, formed in spring 1917, had sought to mobilize the officer corps politically. It had little influence. For more on patriotic military organizations in this period, see the work of Matthew Rendle in the list of further readings.
9. The Imperial Russian Army, like other armies of the era, had a special Political Department that conducted domestic surveillance and prepared reports on the political mood among soldiers and civilians. This practice continued into the Soviet period.
10. "K vsei strane," *Vestnik Vremennago Pravitel'stva*, 29 August 1917, 1; E. I. Martynov, *Kornilov: popytka voennogo perevorta* (Moscow: Izd. tip. Upr. Del. NKVM, 1927), 110–111.
11. In this parenthetical clause, Kerensky cites as the legal basis of his action tsarist statutes that were universally vilified by revolutionaries before 1917. Kerensky left this clause out of the document in Browder and Kerensky, *Russian Provisional Government*, Vol. 3, 1572–1573.
12. Z. Galili et al., eds., *Men'sheviki v 1917 godu*, vol. 3, *Ot konilovskogo miatezha do kontsa dekabria*, pt. 1, *Avgust-pervaia dekada oktiabria* (Moscow: ROSSPEN, 1996), 109–110.
13. The term Directory had powerful revolutionary historical connotations: it was the title of the "reactionary" government that replaced the Jacobins in France in 1795–1799.
14. "Kornilovshchina," *Delo naroda*, 28 August 1917, 1.
15. "28 Avgust. Postanovlenie komiteta gvardii Litovskogo reservnogo polka," in *Revoliutsionnoe dvizhenie v voennykh okrugakh. Mart 1917 g.-mart 1918 g.*, ed. Iu. I. Korablev et al. (Moscow: Nauka, 1988), 220.
16. A *funt* was equal to 409.5 grams (12 ounces); a *zolotnik* was equal to 4.25 grams (0.33 ounces).
17. "Zasedanie Ispolnitel'nogo komiteta 28 avgusta," in *Saratovskii sovet rabochikh deputatov (1917–1918). Sbornik dokumentov*, ed. V. V. Antonov-Saratovskii (Moscow-Leningrad: Gosudarstvennoe sotsial'no-ekonomicheskoe izdatel'stvo, 1931), 186–189.
18. M. T. Didenko was a Socialist Revolutionary (SR). V. P. Antonov (Antonov-Saratovskii) was a Bolshevik. B. N. Guterman was a Menshevik. N. I. Semenov was a Trudovik, as was A. A. Vasil'ev. Linkov and N. S. Neimichenko were SRs. M. I. Vasil'ev (Vasil'ev-Iuzhin) was a Bolshevik, as was V. N. Sokolov (Sokolov-Cheredin). A. A. Minin was an SR. Pavel A. Lebedev was a Bolshevik, as was Kirill Plaksin. V. M. Telegin was an SR.
19. Trius, whose party affiliation is unknown, was one of several people attending the session who were not included in the list of those present.
20. "Ko vsem rabochim i rabotnitsam, ko vsem grazhdanam Petrodrada," *Rabochaia gazeta* 29 August 1917, 1.
21. Since August, the Mensheviks were called the United Russian Social Democratic Labor Party.
22. "The disgrace of our wives, sisters, and daughters" was a euphemistic warning that Kornilov's soldiers would rape civilian women.
23. "Vozzvanie soiuza georgievskikh kavalerov po povidu vystupleniia gen. Kornilova," in *Kontr-revoliutsiia v 1917 g. (Kornilovshchina)* (Moscow: Krasnaia nov, 1924), Vera Vladimirova 213–214.

24. "30 August. Postanovlenie soedinennogo zasedanii polkovykh i divizionnnogo komitetov 7-i strelkovoi divizii," *Voiskovye komitety deistvuiushchei armii. Mart' 1917 g.–mart 1918 g.*, ed. L. M. Gavrilov et al. (Moscow: Nauka, 1982), 303.

25. "Provintsiia i zagovor gen. Kornilova: Roslavl'," *Izvestiia Tsentral'nago Ispolnitel'nago Komiteta i Petrogradskago soveta rabochikh i soldatskikh deputatov*, 30 August 1917, 8.

26. This is a reference to Bolshevik leaders and activists jailed after the July uprising.

27. "Petrograd, 29 avgust," *Rech*, 29 August 1917, 1.

28. "Petrograd, 29 avgusta 1917 g."; A. Smirnyi, "Bezumnie ili prestuplenie," *Narodnoe slovo*, 29 August 1917, 1.

29. Lt. Gen. Aleksandr Lukomovskii refused to follow Kerensky's 27 August 1917, order that Kornilov be removed from command.

30. The Wild Division ("Savage Division") had moved against Petrograd under the command of General Krymov. Gen. Paul von Hindenburg was Germany's supreme commander.

31. M. A-v, "Spasenie rodiny," *Moskovskiia vedomosti*, 30 August 1917, 1.

32. V. I. Lenin, "V tsentral'nyi komitet RSDRP, 30 Avgust 1917 g," in *Revoliutsionnoe dvishenie v Rossii v avguste 1917 g., Razgrom kornilovskogo miatezha* (Moscow: Izdatel'stvo akademii nauk SSSR, 1959), 511–512 (first published in *Pravda*, 7 November 1920).

33. *Pravda* appeared as *Rabochii* on 25 August–2 September 1917. V. M-n refers to Vladimir Miliutin; Vol-skii refers to V. Volodarskii.

34. R. V. Ivanov-Razumnik, "Dva vraga," in *God revoliutsii. Stat'i 1917 goda*, R. V. Ivanov-Razumnik (St. Petersburg: Izd. Ts. Kom. Partii Levykh Sotsialistov-Revoliutsionerov [Internatsionalistov], 1918), 71.

35. G. Plekhanov, "A teper?" *Edinstvo*, 31 August 1917, 1.

36. "Grazhdanki i grazhdane," *Narodnoe slovo, Edinstvo*, and *Volia naroda*, 1 September 1917, 1.

Chapter 11

1. *Birzhevyia vedomosti*, 5 September 1917, 4

2. "Molokh," *Rabochii put'*, 22 September 1917, 3.

3. M. V. was probably Moisei Volodarskii.

4. "Vybory," *Moskovskiia vedomosti*, 28 June 1917, 1.

5. M. Petrov, "Vybory v Gor. Dumu," *Narodnoe slovo*, 27 July 1917, 3.

6. P. Shaskal'skii, "Gorodskie vybory i blok s natsional'nymi sotsialisti partiami," *Narodnoe Slovo*, 19 August 1917, 1.

7. The Socialist Revolutionaries (SRs) and Mensheviks ran separate tickets. SRs won 37.5 percent, Mensheviks 4.5 percent, and Kadets 21 percent. Nearly 200,000 fewer votes were cast than in June.

8. "K segodniashnim vyboram," *Edinstvo*, 5 August 1917, 1.

9. *Edinstvo* took 1 percent of the district's votes in the 20 August city duma elections.

10. "Vybory na Petrogofskii raionnuiu dumu," *Rabochii i Soldat*, 16 July 1917, 2; "Rabochie, Soldaty!" *Proletarii*, 20 August 1917, 2.

11. "Za spisok No. 6," *Proletarii*, 19 August 1917, 1.

12. A. Trykova, "Golosuite!" *Rech*, 19 August 1917, 3.

13. Voters were sent ballots in envelopes, which they turned in at the polls.

14. V. Trutovskii, "K tovarishcham S.-R.," *Delo naroda*, 20 August 1917, 1; "Segodniashnie vybory," *Delo naroda*, 20 August 1917, 2.

15. Petrograd's mayor in 1917 was the Socialist Revolutionary Grigorii Shreider.

16. "Tovarishche Sluzhashchie!" *Delo naroda*, 20 August 1917, 1.

17. V. Trutovskii, "Krest'iane i rabochie," *Znamia truda*, 24 August 1917, 1.

18. "Kulaks" refers to "rich" peasants who "exploit" their neighbors.

19. 1.5 *destian*s is about 4 acres. Russian Marxists described the peasant population as divided into substrata based upon each household's land, tools, livestock, and labor power. These were as follows: poor and landless peasants (the "rural proletariat"), middle

peasants (the "rural petty-bourgeoisie'), and "substantial" peasants ("kulaks," rural exploiters). In 1917, the Bolsheviks argued that poor peasants were the urban proletariat's natural allies.

20. This refers to the Marxist concept of "relations to the means of production"—the division of social classes on the basis of who owns the means of producing goods (and who, in contrast, owns only their own labor power, which they must sell for sustenance).

21. *Rabochaia gazeta*, 29 July 1917, 2.

22. The rules established 73 civilian and 8 military electoral districts. All men and women age 21 or older could vote. Each district would elect a specific number of the assembly's 800 members. Seats would be granted to parties proportional to their voting returns in each district.

23. In fact, workers supported Socialist Revolutionaries as well as Social Democrats.

24. The "third of June State Duma" refers to dumas convened after 3 June 1907, when Prime Minister Stolypin changed the electoral system to favor landowners.

25. "Vnimaniiu partiinykh organizatsii," *Rabochii put'*, 28 September 1917, 3; "K vyboram v Uchreditel'noe Sobranie," *Rabochii put'*, 1 October 1917, 2.

26. This left places on the local Bolshevik slates for candidates chosen by the Central Committee.

27. The phrase "defensists of all shades" lumps together the defensist ("war to a victorious conclusion") and "revolutionary defensist" factions.

28. *Ot Partii Narodnoi Svobody* (Moscow: Tip. T-va Riabushinskikh, [1917]), in *Russian Revolutionary Literature at the Houghton Library of Harvard University*, reel 47, *Broadsides and Leaflets, 1917–1921* (New Haven, CT: Research Publications, Inc., 1974), no. 1127.

29. *Grazhdane! Golosuite za spisok No. 7* (Moscow: Izdatel'stvo Moskovskii komiteta Tr. n-s partii, [1917]), in *Russian Revolutionary Literature at the Houghton Library of Harvard University*, reel 47, *Broadsides and Leaflets, 1917–1921* (New Haven, CT: Research Publications, Inc., 1974), no. 1127, 3– 4.

30. *Smolenskii vestnik*, 11 November 1917, 1.

31. "Pochemu nado golosovat' za spisok partii sotsialistov-revoliutsionerov no. 9," *Delo naroda* 12 November 1917, 1.

32. *Narodnaia volia* (People's Will) (1879–1883) was one of two parties to emerge from the populist organization *Zemlia i volia* (Land and Freedom). The other, *Chernyi peredel' (Black Repartition)*, rejected terrorism, and its leaders subsequently founded Russia's Social Democratic movement. People's Will, on the other hand, viewed terrorism as an essential tool for political revolution and organized the 1881 execution of Tsar Alexander II.

33. Balmashov shot Internal Affairs Minister Dmitrii Sipiagin in St. Petersburg in April 1902. In July 1904, Sazonov bombed the carriage of Internal Affairs Minister Viacheslav von Plehve in St. Petersburg. Kalaev's bomb destroyed the carriage of Grand Duke Sergei Romanov, commander of the Moscow Military District, in Moscow in February 1905.

34. The phrase used here, "v uravnitel'noe pol'zovanie," suggests redistribution of land according to some kind of "leveling" norm, such as the number of people or workers in a household.

Chapter 12

1. G. I. Zlokazov, and G. I. Ioffe, eds., *Iz istorii bor'by za vlast' v 1917 godu. Sbornik dokumentov* (Moscow: Institut rossiskoi istorii RAN, 2002), 153–157.

2. The Socialist Revolutionaries had 532 delegates (71 from the party's left wing), the Mensheviks 530 (56 from the Menshevik Internationalists), the Bolsheviks 134, and the Trudovik Popular-Socialists 55. There were 17 nonparty delegates.

3. This is a swipe at Kerensky, who was famous for bombastic speeches.

4. This is a reference to the Kadets.

5. On 19 September 1917, the conference voted 776 to 688 (with 38 abstentions) in favor of forming a new government that included Kadets.

6. The conference had resolved to recognize the Directorate, Kerensky's emergency cabinet.

7. This refers to the moderate socialist's programmatic proposals at the Moscow State Conference.

8. Kadet Nikolai Kishkin served as public welfare minister in September–October 1917. Progressist Mikhail Tereshchenko, finance minister in March–May 1917, served as foreign minister and deputy prime minister in September–October 1917. Kadet Nikolai Nekrasov served as transport minister in March–July 1917 and as finance minister and deputy prime minister in July–August 1917, and was Finland's governor general in September–October 1917.

9. Aleksandr Konovalov, minister of trade and industry in March–May 1917, and again on 25 September–25 October 1917, was also deputy prime minister on 25 September–25 October 1917.

10. "Sovety i demokratiia," *Rabochaia gazeta*, 15 September 1917, 1–2.

11. "Novaia revoliutsiia ili uchreditel'noe sobranie?" *Delo naroda*, 30 September 1917, 1; "Sovety i Uchreditel'noe Sobranie," *Delo naroda*, 6 October 1917, 1.

12. In "The Sorcerer's Apprentice" by the German writer Heinrich Heine (1797–1856)—based on an earlier tale by Johan Wolfgang von Gothe (1749–1832)—an apprentice learns how to summon demons but does not know how to control them.

13. V. I. Lenin, "K rabochim, krest'ianam i soldtam," in *Revoliutsionnoe dvizhenie v Rossii nakanune Oktiabr'skogo vooruzhennogo vosstaniia (1-24 oktiabria 1917 g.)* (Moscow: Izdatel'stvo akademii nauk SSSR, 1962), 22–23. First published in *Pravda*, 23 April 1924.

14. See document 12.3.

15. The 30 September *Delo naroda* editorial actually says that Lenin and Trotsky "under no circumstances" would subordinate themselves to the will of the Democratic Conference.

16. "S"ezd Sovetov i Uchreditel'noe Sobranie," *Rabochii put'*, 3 October 1917, 1; "Vlast' Sovetov," *Rabochii put'*, 13 October 1917, 1.

17. This refers to the 30 September 1917 *Delo Naroda* editorial (see document 12.3).

18. This refers to Mensheviks Irakli Tsereteli and Feodor Dan and to Abram Gots of the Socialist Revolutionaries.

19. Vladimir Purishkevich of the Union of Russian People campaigned for the dissolution of the soviets in 1917.

20. In October 1917 the Provisional Government began preparations to move the government to Moscow, to escape an expected German assault on Petrograd. The city's workers and garrison soldiers reacted strongly against these steps, and the Bolsheviks insisted they would protect the capital from the government's treachery. In February 1918 Lenin moved the capital to Moscow, to escape an anticipated German assault after peace negotiations collapsed.

21. "O forme vlasti," *Astrakhanskii listok*, 28 September 1917, 3; "Vybory gubernskogo komissara" and "Perevybory ispolnitel'nogo komiteta soveta r. i. s. deputatov," *Astrakhanskii listok*, 6 October 1917, 3; "Bund i men'sheviki (Pis'mo v Redaktsii)," *Astrakhanskii listok*, 17 October 1917, 4.

22. Bakradze, a left Socialist Revolutionary, was chairman of the Astrakhan Soviet.

23. V. I. Skablinskii had been the editor of *Astrakhanskii Listok* since at least 1902.

24. Zlatoustovskii District is in Amur Province in Siberia.

25. *Rabochii put'*, 10 October 1917, 2.

26. *Rech*, 17 October 1917, 4.

27. The Pre-Parliament was known as the Council of the Republic.

28. Aleksandr Verkhovskii, War Minister in September–October 1917.

29. Menshevik leader Skobelev (as a member of the Pre-Parliament and Soviet Central Executive Committee) drafted instructions for Russia's representatives to an Inter-Allied Conference, scheduled to meet in Paris in early November 1917. These required that the representatives uphold the fundamental principles of "peace without annexations or indemnities on the basis of the right of national self-determination."

30. *Protokoly Tsentral'nogo Komiteta RSDRP (b). Avugst 1917-fevral' 1918* (Moscow: Gospolitizdat, 1958), 93–104.
31. Leon Trotsky was occupied with tasks as the Petrograd Soviet chair and did not attend.
32. I have italicized speakers' names and added full last names and institutional names.
33. In early September, Lenin offered to compromise with the other socialist parties under limited conditions.
34. Iakov Sverdlov was Bolshevik Central Committee Secretary from August 1917 to March 1919.
35. Gleb Bokii was Bolshevik Petersburg Committee Secretary from April 1917 to March 1918.
36. Insertions by the Russian editors are indicated with brackets { }.
37. Nikolai Krylenko was a leader of the Bolshevik Party's Military Organization in Petrograd and played important organizational roles in the July Days and October Revolution.
38. The Russian editor indicates that Kolpino was crossed out in the archival text of this sentence and Narva written in its place.
39. Petersburg Committee member Moisei Volodarskii was a popular activist in 1917.
40. Bolshevik activist Sarra Ravich was a close friend of Lenin and his family.
41. Bolshevik Vasili Shmidt was a trade union leader in Petrograd in 1917.
42. In settling an August 1917 strike, the Menshevik-dominated Petrograd Printers' Union had made significant wage concessions.
43. In 1917 Aleksandr Shliapnikov was a key Bolshevik member of the Petrograd Soviet and the metalworkers' union.
44. In June 1917 the Bolshevik Nikolai Skrypnik was elected secretary of the Petrograd Central Council of Factory Committees.
45. Anarcho-syndicalism is a form of socialist anarchism that envisions "syndicates" of labor unions as replacing the state.
46. Ivan Movskin was a member of the Bolshevik Petersburg Committee in 1917.
47. In late September 1917 the moderate socialist-led All-Russia Executive Committee of Railroad Unions (Vikzhel) organized a nationwide strike of more than 700,000 railroad workers.
48. In 1917 Vladimir Miliutin often took moderate positions on the Bolshevik Central Committee.
49. Finnish Bolshevik Aleksandr Shotman was Lenin's primary emissary to the Central Committee (and his bodyguard) while the Bolshevik leader was in hiding in Finland.
50. In early October 1917, the government directed Northern Front Commander General Cheremisov to remove "unruly" units from Petrograd's Garrison. When soldiers vehemently objected, Cheremisov convened a conference of garrison representatives and front commanders in Pskov on 17 October. Garrison representatives rejected troop transfer as strategically unnecessary.
51. Finnish Bolshevik Eino Rakh'ia, a member of the Petersburg Committee, was one of Lenin's emissaries to the Central Committee while in Finland.
52. Zinoviev's code name in the party was "Grigorii."
53. Iakov Fenigshtein ran the Bolshevik Petersburg Committee's "Polish Section" in 1917.
54. Stalin carried out important behind-the-scenes Bolshevik organizational tasks in 1917.
55. In 1917 Mikhail Kalinin was a leader of the Bolshevik Petersburg Committee.
56. In Russian, Junkers refers to officers in training (in English, these are called "cadets").
57. In 1917 Feliks Dzerzhinskii helped organize the Petrograd Military Revolutionary Committee.
58. Grigorii Sokol'nikov was an important Petrograd Bolshevik activist.
59. Skalov was a member of the Petrograd Soviet's Soldiers' Section in 1917.
60. Adol'f Ioffe, who joined the Bolsheviks and the Central Committee in early August 1917, led the party faction in the Petrograd City Duma.
61. Martyn Latsis, known as "Uncle," was a member of the Bolshevik Petersburg Committee.

NOTES

62. "Center" refers to the Military Revolutionary Center.

63. In 1917 Andrei Bubnov served on the Moscow Workers' Soviet before moving to Petrograd to join the Central Committee in fall. Moisei Uritskii joined the Bolsheviks in early August 1917.

64. *Izvestiia Tsentral'nogo Ispolnitel'nogo Komiteta i Petrogradskogo Soveta rabochikh' i soldatskikh' deputatov*, 18 October 1917, 1.

65. The Central Committee refused to expel Kamenev and Zinoviev. On 20 October, it demanded that they refrain from public statements that contradicted party resolutions.

66. In fact, the Central Executive Committee had just set a date, 25 October 1917.

67. On 17 October 1917, *Golos' soldata* printed a resolution by Executive Committee of the 12th Army Soviet of Soldiers' Deputies calling on rear garrisons to "do their revolutionary duty" by allowing transfer of soldiers to the front "to save the revolutionary capital." In contrast, the Luga Soviet of Soldiers' Deputies rejected the troop transfers.

68. In fact, the left Socialist Revolutionaries also called for "All Power to the Soviets."

69. The "Council of the Republic" was the Pre-Parliament's official title.

70. "Groza eshe vperedi," *Moskovskiia vedomosti*, 20 October 1917, 1.

71. Aleksandra Kollontai was a member of the Bolshevik Central committee in 1917. Urban political meetings often took place at movie theaters and circuses—large public spaces where the lower classes felt comfortable (unlike more formal lecture halls).

72. Anatoli Lunacharskii joined the Bolsheviks in August 1917 and was a member of the Petrograd Soviet's Military Revolutionary Committee in October 1917.

73. Iurii Steklov (Osip Nakhamkis) joined the Bolsheviks in August 1917.

74. Menshevik Internationalist Nikolai Sukhanov (Gimmer) helped organize the Petrograd Soviet.

75. The Bolshevik Aleksandr Bogdanov (Malinovskii) was Belorussian, not Jewish; the birth name of Menshevik activist and Petrograd Soviet leader Boris Bogdanov was Olenich.

76. Iurii Larin (Lur'e) joined the Bolsheviks in 1917.

77. Menshevik B. I. Gorev (Gol'dman) joined the Bolsheviks at the end of the Civil War.

78. The Russian "*liudi geshefta*" incorporates the Yiddish for "business" (*gesheft*), suggesting "Jewish businessmen."

79. In March 1917, British officials arrested Trotsky in Canada. They released him in April at the Provisional Government's insistence.

80. In 1917, Populist activist Vladimir Burtsev wrote several articles accusing the Bolshevik leaders of being German agents.

81. This refers to the November 1917 Inter-Allied Conference in Paris.

82. Pretender (*samozvanets*) also can be translated as "Imposter." In Russian folk culture, the Pretender is associated with the Anti-Christ.

83. In 1607–1610, the Polish-backed "Thief of Tushino" claimed to be Tsar Ivan IV's dead son, Dmitrii. Cossack rebel leader Stepan (Stenka) Razin claimed to be Russia's rightful tsar in 1670–1671. In 1773–1774, Cossack rebel Emel'ian Pugachev claimed to be the dead Tsar Peter III.

84. A. Nikitskii, "Sovety i Uchreditel'noe Sobranie," *Iskra*, 21 October 1917, 2.

85. The Council of the United Nobility, formed in 1905, functioned as a conservative lobbying group during the last decade of tsarist rule. The All-Russian Union of Landowners, also formed in 1905, similarly pressed the tsarist government to protect large landlords' interests.

Part Four

1. In May 1917, War Minister Alexander Kerensky endorsed creation of several all-female volunteer military combat units, called Women's Battalions of Death. Their purpose was to motivate male soldiers, who were supposed to be moved (and perhaps shamed) by the women's patriotism and enthusiasm.

2. For translations of the 26 October decrees, see Rex A. Wade, *The Bolshevik Revolution and the Russian Civil War* (Westport, CT; London: Greenwood, 2001), 166–168.
3. For an excellent set of documents on the Vikzhel negotiations and attempts to form a broad socialist coalition government, see James Bunyan and H. H. Fisher, *The Bolshevik Revolution, 1917–1918* (Stanford: Stanford University Press, 1934), 155–156, 185–209.
4. On the debates in the Central Executive Committee, see the superb annotated translation of its sessions in John H. L. Keep, trans. and ed., *The Debate on Soviet Power: Minutes of the All-Russian Central Executive Committee of Soviets, Second Convocation, October 1917–January 1918* (Oxford: Clarendon Press, 1979).
5. On the elections, see Oliver Radkey, *The Election to the Russian Constituent Assembly Election of 1917* (Cambridge: Harvard University Press, 1989).
6. The most detailed examination is in Alexander Rabinowitch, *The Bolsheviks in Power: The First Year of Soviet Rule in Petrograd* (Bloomington: Indiana University Press, 2007).
7. Nikolai N. Smirnov, "The Constituent Assembly," in *Critical Companion to the Russian Revolution 1914–1921*, ed. Acton, Cherniaev, and Rosenberg (Bloomington and Indianapolis: Indiana University Press, 1997), 329.
8. The Menshevik-Internationalist Nikolai Sukhanov denounced these arguments as cowardly and hypocritical, and alone among Central Executive Committee members defended the Constituent Assembly. Keep, *The Debate on Soviet Power*, 240–251.
9. Because of recall elections, disputes over delegates' mandates, and the existence of several different delegate counts, the exact number of delegates from each party attending on 5 January cannot be determined. The following figures are the most commonly cited estimates: SRs, 237; Bolsheviks, 110–120; Left SRs, 30–35; Mensheviks, 16–20; Kadets, 16–20; Trudovik Peoples-Socialists, 2; and other parties, factions, and organizations, 80.
10. Orlando Figes, *A People's Tragedy, 1894–1924* (New York: Viking, 1997), 536.
11. See Wade, *The Russian Revolution, 1917*, 286.

Chapter 13

1. *Izvestiia*, 26 October 1917, 2; 28 October 1917, 4; *Novaia zhizn'*, 26 October 1917, 3; *Delo naroda*, 26 October 1917, 2; *Rabochaia gazeta*, 27 October 1917, 4; *Pravda*, 27 October 1917, 3; K. G. Kotel'nikov, ed., *Vtoroi vserossiiskii s"ezd sovetov r. i. s. d.* (Moscow and Leningrad: Gosizdat, 1928), 4–9, 34–47.
2. In 1917, Menshevik Lev Khinchuk chaired the Moscow Workers' Soviets' chairman and served on the All-Russian Soviet Central Executive Committee.
3. Lawyer Mikhail Gendel'man was a member of the Socialist Revolutionary Central Committee.
4. In 1917 Bund leader Genrikh (Henryk) Erlich served on the Petrograd Soviet.
5. Rafail Abramovich was a founding member of the Petrograd Soviets and had been elected to the Soviet Central Executive Committee in June 1917.
6. This resolution was first published in *Pravda*, 27 October 1917, 1.
7. Kotel'nikov, *Vtoroi vserossiiskii s"ezd sovetov*, 78–89; *Novaia zhizn'*, 28 October 1917, 3; *Le Journal de Russie*, 29 October 1917, 3; *Pravda*, 28 October 1917, 3; *Rabochaia gazeta*, 28 October 1917, 3.
8. Stenographer's notes published in 1928 state that Avilov said, "election of the Central Executive Committee," not the Council of People's Commissars. Newspaper accounts do not mention this sentence. Kotel'nikov, ed., *Vtoroi vserossiiskii s"ezd sovetov*, 25.
9. At the 24 October 1917, Pre-Parliament session, Kerensky appealed for support against the Bolsheviks. The left Socialist Revolutionaries and Menshevik-Internationalists instead demanded an all-socialist government. The socialist parties (minus the Bolsheviks, who had quit the Pre-Parliament) then agreed on some basic principles.

10. "The democracy's two sections" refers to the "bourgeoisie," represented by the Kadets, and the toiling masses, represented by the socialists.

11. Provisional Government member Nikolai Avksent'ev.

12. Skobelev had been chosen to lead the Soviet Central Executive Committee's delegation to the November Paris conference of Allied Powers.

13. Mikhail Tereshchenko was Foreign Minister in May to October 1917.

14. Kadet Nikolai Kishkin was social welfare minister, and Progressist Aleksander Konovalov was trade minister in Kernsky's last coalition government.

15. "K grazhdam Rossii!" *Rabochii put'*, 26 October 1917, 1; "Rabochim, soldatam i kestianam!" *Pravda*, 27 October 1917, 1; "Most," *Pravda*, 29 October 1917, 3; "Sud'ba ministera Tereshchenko," *Pravda*, 31 October 1917, 3.

16. *Rech*, 26 October 1917, 1.

17. *Edinstvo*, 27 October 1917, 1.

18. "Avantiura—ne revoliutsiia" and "Pozitsiia nashei partii," *Delo naroda*, 28 October 1917, 1.

19. Mikhail Rodzianko was chairman of the Fourth State Duma. Aleksander Guchkov was war minister in the first Provisional Government. General Alexei Kaledin commanded the Don Cossacks.

20. "K rabochim Petrograda!" *Rabochii put'*, 29 October 1917, 1.

21. The All-Russian Committee for the Salvation of the Motherland and Revolution was formed on 26 October 1917 by the city *duma*, the Kadets, and the moderate socialist parties.

22. "Doloi bol'shevikov! Spacaite rodinu i revoliutsiiu!" *Narodnoe slovo*, 29 October 1917, 1.

23. "Tovarshi grazhdane!" *Vpered!* 30 October 1917, 1.

24. "Anarkhiia—mat' poriadka," *Anarkhiia*, 26 October 1917, 1; untitled editorial, *Golos truda*, 1 November 1917, 1; "Ni za kogo!" *Burevestnik*, 14 November 1917, 1.

25. G. E. Zinoviev, *God revoliutsii (fevral' 1917 g.-mart 1918 g.)* (Leningrad: Gosizdat, 1925), 688.

26. "Ko vsem!" and "Rabochie, soldaty i krest'iane!" *Iskra*, 5 November 1917, 1–2.

27. "Pristuplenie," *Smolenskii vestnik*, 5 November 1917, 2.

28. The Smolensk Soviet disbanded the city *duma* in December 1917.

29. The *Pugachevshchina* was a mass uprising led by the Cossack Emel'ian Pugachev in 1774–1775.

30. Viacheslav Plehve and Dmitrii Sipiagin both served as interior minister and police director under Nicholas II.

31. Zinoviev, *God revoliutsii*, 412–413.

Chapter 14

1. A. Ia. Levin, and I. B. Orlov, eds., *Pis'ma vo vlast. 1917–1927. Zaiavleniia, zhalobyi, donosy, pims'ma v gosudarstvennye struktury i bol'shevistskim vozhdiam* (Moscow: ROSSPEN, 1998), 14–15, 24–25.

2. In fact, the Socialist Revolutionaries (not representatives of "capitalists" and "landlords") won the local zemstvo elections in August 1917.

3. "Ko vsem grazhdanam!" *V temuiu noch'*, 25 November 1917, 1.

4. "Ot soiuza zashchita Uchreditel'nogo Sobraniia," *Novyi luch'*, 3 December 1917, 1.

5. "Rezoliutsii vo voprosu ob otnoshenii k Uchreditel'noe Sobranie," in *Vserossiiskoe Uchreditel'noe Sobranie*, ed. I. S. Malchevskii (Moscow and Leningrad: Gosudarstvennoe izdatel'stvo, 1930), 169; "Postanovlenie TsK PLSR," *Znamia truda*, 6 December 1917, 1.

6. The Soviet Central Executive Committee issued a decree on recall on 21 November 1917.

7. This is a reference to the 28 November 1917 decree outlawing the Kadet Party as a counterrevolutionary organization and the subsequent arrest of several Kadet Party leaders.

8. V. Bragin, et al., eds., *Ustanovlenie Sovetskoi vlasti v Novgorodskoi gubernii (1917–1918 gg.)* (Novgorod: UVD akhivnyi otdel, 1957), 70–71.

9. *Pravda*, 13 December 1917, 1.

10. At the 29 November 1917 Bolshevik Central Committee session, Bukharin proposed the party "beat" the Constituent Assembly "bit by bit," expel right-wing socialist delegates, outlaw the Kadets, and turn the left bloc into a "revolutionary convention" like that in Jacobin France.

11. In December 1917 the Bolsheviks organized an All-Russian Congress of Railroad Workers, which replaced the moderate socialist Vikzhel organization with a new union called Vikzhedor (the All-Russian Executive Committee of Railroad Workers).

12. In November 1917, the Ukrainian Central Rada's "Third Universal" declared that Ukraine would soon become an independent republic. In early December, the Council of People's Commissars issued an "ultimatum" to the Central Rada. The Bolsheviks organized a Ukrainian Soviet Congress in Kharkov that proclaimed a Ukrainian Soviet Republic. In January 1918, Lenin's government sent troops to intervene in the civil war between the Kiev-based Rada and Kharkov-based Soviet Republic. In contrast, the Soviet state recognized Finland's independence in December and did not intervene directly in the bloody Finnish civil war.

13. Tensions remained between Lenin and the moderate Bolsheviks. Zinoviev had done penance and returned to the Central Committee, but many moderates opposed Lenin's position on the Constituent Assembly. The Central Committee devoted its entire 11 December 1917 session to discussing how to deal with the party's "right" tendency regarding the assembly.

14. L. M., "Revoliutsiia i Uchereditel'noe Sobranie," *Novyi luch*, 15 December 1917, 1.

15. Martov refers to a 6 December article in *Ivzestiia* by Bolshevik Mikhail Uritskii, justifying the Constituent Assembly's postponement. Uritskii said that under certain circumstances the Bolsheviks would not allow the assembly's convocation.

16. The Mensheviks had a "maximum" program (creating a socialist society) that could be fulfilled only after achieving their "minimum" program (creating a democratic republic).

17. Russian socialists categorized workers as politically "conscious," "semiconscious" (grey), or "ignorant" (dark).

18. In addition to Uritskii's 6 December essay, Martov refers to 24 November and 9 December *Izvestiia* articles by Bolshevik Iurii Larin that compared outlawing the Kadets to measures taken by Oliver Cromwell and Maximilian Robespierre in the English and French Revolutions. The quotation is from Anton Chekov's short story "The Bird Market." The same character states that "An animal is like a man—a man is made wiser by beating him, and so is a beast."

19. While a member of the radical "Petrashevsky Circle" in the 1840s, satirist Mikhail Saltykov-Shchedrin championed the *phalanstère*—a utopian community proposed by French socialist Charles Fourier. *Phalanstères* built in Europe and North America failed miserably. In 1816 Count Aleksei Arkacheev, a senior military advisor to Tsar Alexander I, set up military agricultural settlements that also failed.

20. Jacobins dominated the revolutionary French Legislative Assembly in 1792–1794; the *sans culottes* were radical urban artisans and small shopkeepers in revolutionary France.

21. *Vserossiiskoe Uchreditel'noe Sobranie*, ed. I. S. Malchevskii (Moscow and Leningrad: Gosudarstvennoe izdatel'stvo, 1930), 3–6, 9–23, 109–110.

22. Marx described the 1789 French Revolution as a bourgeois revolution and the August 1789 Declaration of the Rights of Man and Citizen as clearing away feudalism's vestiges to make way for capitalist exploitation.

23. In December 1917, the Soviet government recognized Finland's independence and began withdrawing troops the tsarist government had sent to Persia (Iran). While it also recognized Armenia's right to self-determination, in January 1918 Lenin's government

signed a treaty with Turkey that many historians believe enabled a Turkish attack on the Armenian Republic.

24. This is a reference to the Soviet-German armistice negotiations.

25. "Central empires" refers to the German and Austro-Hungarian Empires.

26. The Cossack General Aleksei Kaledin organized an army to fight the Soviet government. The Bolsheviks called Kaledin's followers "Kaledinites."

27. Chernov is referring here to the Soviet government's dispatch of soldiers to aid the Ukrainian Soviet government against the Ukrainian Central Rada.

28. Chernov is saying the Jewish state institutions will use Yiddish, supposedly the language of Jewish workers, as opposed to Hebrew, the "bourgeois" language of Jewish clerics.

29. The Bolshevik Ivan Stepanov-Skvortsov was people's commissar of finance in October 1917–January 1918. The taunt "former Zimmerwaldist" is a reference to Chernov's participation in the 1915 antiwar socialist conference at Zimmerwald, Switzerland.

30. In late October 1917, right Socialist Revolutionary Vadim Rudneev was a leader of the Moscow Committee of Public Safety; Bolsheviks blamed Rudnev for the execution of dozens of Bolshevik prisoners at the Kremlin on 28 October 1917. Junkers refers to officers in training (cadets).

31. 18 June 1917 was the date that Russia's "June" military offensive began. Kerensky had pushed for the offensive, and the right Socialist Revolutionaries and right Mensheviks had been its strong supporters.

32. *Pravda*, 7 January 1918, 1.

33. "Vse vlast' Uchreditelnomu Sobraniiu!" *Delo naroda*, 7 January 1918, 1.

34. Janissaries were Ottoman Sultan's soldier-bodyguards.

35. The Smolnyi Institute was headquarters for the Bolshevik Party and (in October 1917–February 1918) the Soviet government. The term "*lumpen*-proletariat" refers to criminal elements.

36. "Ot tsentral'nogo komiteta partii levykh s.-r.," *Znamia truda*, 9 January 1918, 1.

37. Kadet leaders Andrei Shingarev and Fedor Kokoshkon were murdered in their prison hospital beds on 7 January 1918.

38. Boris Krichevskii, "Ili-ili," *Edinstvo*, 11 January 1918, 1.

39. This is a reference to Lenin's comments (made repeatedly) that the masses would approve the Constituent Assembly's dissolution because they had cast off their "illusions" about bourgeois parliamentarianism.

40. At the 6 January 1918, committee session, David Riazanov and one unidentified Bolshevik or Left Socialist Revolutionary voted against the decree dissolving the Constituent Assembly.

LIST OF FURTHER READINGS

This list is not intended as comprehensive. It includes English-language books and articles mentioned in the text and a sample of other works on revolutionary Russia.

General Histories, Collections of Essays, and Works on Historiography

Acton, Edward. *Rethinking the Russian Revolution*. New York: Bloomsbury, 1990.

Acton, Edward, Vladimir Cherniaev, and William G. Rosenberg, eds. *Critical Companion to the Russian Revolution 1914–1921*. Bloomington and Indianapolis: Indiana University Press, 1997.

Chamberlin, William Henry. *The Russian Revolution, 1917–1921*. 2 vols. New York: MacMillan, 1935.

Figes, Orlando. *A People's Tragedy: The Russian Revolution, 1891–1924*. New York: Viking, 1997.

Frankel, Edith, Jonathan Frankel, and Baruch Knei-Paz, eds. *Revolution in Russia: Reassessments of 1917*. New York: Cambridge University Press, 1992.

Keep, John. *The Russian Revolution: A Study in Mass Mobilization*. New York: Norton, 1976.

Lincoln, W. Bruce. *Passage through Armageddon: The Russians in War and Revolution*. New York: Simon and Schuster, 1986.

Orlovsky, Daniel. "Russia in War and Revolution, 1914–1921." In *Russia: A History*, ed. Gregory Freeze, 231–262. 2nd ed. Oxford: Oxford University Press, 2002.

Pipes, Richard. *The Russian Revolution, 1899–1919*. New York: Harvill, 1990.

Read, Christopher. *From Tsar to Soviets: The Russian People and Their Revolution, 1917–1921*. New York: Oxford University Press, 1996.

Service, Robert, ed. *Society and Politics in the Russian Revolution*. London: Macmillan, 1992.

Smele, Jonathan D. *The Russian Revolution and Civil War, 1917–1921: An Annotated Bibliography*. London and New York: Continuum, 2003.

Wade, Rex A. *The Russian Revolution, 1917*. 2nd ed. New York: Cambridge University Press, 2005.

Wade, Rex A., ed. *Revolutionary Russia: New Approaches*. New York and London: Routledge, 2004.

White, James D. *The Russian Revolution, 1917–1921: A Short History*. London: Edward Arnold, 1994.

Specialized Studies

Abraham, Richard. *Kerensky: The First Love of the Revolution*. London: Sedgwick and Jackson, 1987.

Badcock, Sarah. "Politics, Parties, and Power: Sormovo Workers in 1917." In *A Dream Deferred: New Studies in Russian and Soviet Labor History*, ed. Donald Filtzer et al., 69–94. Bern: Peter Lang, 2008.

Badcock, Sarah. *Politics and People in Revolutionary Russia, a Provincial History*. New York and Cambridge: Cambridge University Press, 2007.

Baker, Mark. "Rampaging *Soldatki*, Cowering Police, Bazaar Riots and Moral Economy: The Social Impact of the Great War in Kharkiv Province." *Canadian-American Slavic Studies* 35, nos. 2/3 (2001): 137–155.

Burbank, Jane. *Intelligentsia and Revolution: Russian Views of Bolshevism, 1917–1922*. New York: Oxford University Press, 1986.

Burdzhalov, Eduard. *Russia's Second Revolution: The February 1917 Uprising in Petrograd*, trans. and ed. Donald J. Raleigh. Bloomington: Indiana University Press, 1987.

Daniels, Robert V. *Red October: The Bolshevik Revolution of 1917*. New York: Norton, 1967.

Edmondson, Linda. *Feminism in Russia*. Stanford, CA: Stanford University Press, 1984.

Engel, Barbara Alpern. "Not by Bread Alone: Subsistence Riots in Russia during World War I." *The Journal of Modern History* 69, no. 4 (1997): 696–721.

Engel, Barbara Alpern. *Women in Russia, 1700–2000*. New York and Cambridge: Cambridge University Press, 2004.

Erzegailis, Andrew. *The 1917 Revolution in Latvia*. New York: Columbia University Press, 1974.

Figes, Orlando. *Peasant Russia, Civil War: The Volga Countryside in Revolution, 1917–1921*. Oxford: Clarendon Press, 1989.

Figes, Orlando, and Boris Kolonitskii. *Interpreting the Russian Revolution: The Language and Symbols of 1917*. New Haven, CT and London: Yale University Press, 1999.

Flenley, Paul. "Industrial Relations and the Economic Crisis of 1917." *Revolutionary Russia* 4, no. 2 (1991): 184–209.

Fuller, William C. *The Foe Within: Fantasies of Treason and the End of Imperial Russia*. Ithaca, NY: Cornell University Press, 2006.

Galili, Ziva. *The Menshevik Leaders in the Russian Revolution: Social Realities and Political Strategies*. Princeton, NJ: Princeton University Press, 1989.

Gatrell, Peter. *A Whole Empire Walking: Refugees in Russia during World War 1*. Bloomington: Indiana University Press, 1999.

Gatrell, Peter. *Russia's First World War: A Social and Economic History*. London: Longman, 2005.

Getzler, Israel. *Kronstadt, 1917–1921: The Fate of a Soviet Democracy*. Cambridge: Cambridge University Press, 1983.

Gill, Graeme J. *Peasants and Government in the Russian Revolution*. London: Macmillan, 1979.

Haimson, Leopold H. "The Problem of Social Stability in Urban Russia." *Slavic Review* 23, no. 4 (1964): 619–642; 24, no. 1 (1965): 1–22.

Haimson, Leopold H. *Russia's Revolutionary Experience: Two Essays*. New York: Columbia University Press, 2005.

Hasegawa, Tsuyoshi. *The February Revolution: Petrograd 1917*. Seattle: University of Washington Press, 1981.

Hasegawa, Tsuyoshi. "Crime and Police in Revolutionary Petrograd, March 1917–March 1917: Social History of the Russian Revolution Revisited." *Acta Slavica Iaponica* 13 (1995): 1–41.

Hickey, Michael C. "Big Strike in a Small City: The Smolensk Metalworkers Strike and the Dynamics of Provincial Labor Unrest in 1917." In *New Labor History: Worker Identity and Experience in Late Tsarist Russia*, ed. Michael Melancon and Alice Pate, 207–231. Bloomington, IN: Slavica, 2002.

Hickey, Michael C. "Discourses of Public Identity and Liberalism in the February Revolution: Smolensk, 1917." *The Russian Review* 55, no. 4 (1996): 615–637.

Hickey, Michael C. "Local Government and State Authority in the Provinces: Smolensk, February–June 1917." *Slavic Review* 55, no. 4 (1996): 863–881.

Hickey, Michael C. "Moderate Socialists and the Politics of Crime in Revolutionary Smolensk." *Canadian-American Slavic Studies* 35, nos. 2/3 (2001): 189–218.

Hickey, Michael C. "Paper, Memory, and a Good Story: How Smolensk Got Its 'October.'" *Revolutionary Russia* 13, no. 1 (December 2000): 1–19.

Hickey, Michael C. "Peasant Autonomy, Soviet Power, and Land Redistribution in Smolensk Province, November 1917–May 1918." *Revolutionary Russia* 9, no. 1 (1996): 19–32.

Hickey, Michael C. "Revolution on the Jewish Street: Smolensk, 1917." *The Journal of Social History* 31, no. 4 (1998): 823–850.

Hickey, Michael C. "The Rise and Fall of Smolensk's Moderate Socialists: The Politics of Class and the Rhetoric of Crisis in 1917." In *Provincial Landscapes: Local Dimensions of Soviet Power, 1917–1953*, ed. Donald J. Raleigh, 14–35. Pittsburgh: Pittsburgh University Press, 2001.

Hickey, Michael C. "Urban Zemliachestva and Rural Revolution: Petrograd and the Smolensk Countryside in 1917." *The Soviet and Post Soviet Review* 23, no. 2 (1996): 143–169.

Holquist, Peter. *Making War, Forging Revolution: Russia's Continuum of Crisis, 1914–1921.* Cambridge, MA: Harvard University Press, 2002.

Jahn, Hubertus F. *Patriotic Culture in Russia during World War 1.* Ithaca, NY: Cornell University Press, 1995.

Johnson, Robert. *Peasant and Proletarian: The Working Class of Moscow in the Late Nineteenth Century.* New Brunswick, NJ: Rutgers University Press, 1979.

Keller, Shoshanna. *To Moscow, Not Mecca: The Soviet Campaign against Islam in Central Asia.* Westport, CT: Praeger, 2001.

Kenez, Peter. *The Birth of the Propaganda State: Soviet Methods of Mass Mobilization, 1917–1929.* New York and Cambridge: Cambridge University Press, 1985.

Khalid, Adeeb. *The Politics of Muslim Cultural Reform: Jadidism in Central Asia.* Berkeley: University of California Press, 1999.

Koenker, Diane P. *Moscow Workers and the 1917 Revolution.* Princeton, NJ: Princeton University Press, 1981.

Koenker, Diane P., and William G. Rosenberg, *Strikes and Revolution in Russia, 1917.* Princeton, NJ: Princeton University Press, 1989.

Kolonitskii, Boris. "Antibourgeois Propaganda and Anti-'Burzhui' Consciousness in 1917." *Russian Review* 53, no. 2 (1994): 183–196.

Kolonitskii, Boris. "Democracy in the Political Consciousness of the February Revolution." *Slavic Review* 57, no. 1 (1998): 95–106.

Landis, Eric. *Bandits and Partisans: The Antonov Movement in the Russian Civil War.* Pittsburgh: University of Pittsburg Press, 2008.

Lih, Lars. *Bread and Authority in Russia, 1914–1921.* Berkeley: University of California Press, 1990.

Lohr, Eric. "The Russian Army and the Jews: Mass Deportations, Hostages, and Violence during World War I." *The Russian Review* 60, no. 3 (2001): 404–419.

Lohr, Eric. *Nationalizing the Russian Empire: The Campaign against Enemy Aliens during World War I.* Harvard, MA: Harvard University Press, 2003.

Mandel, David. *The Petrograd Workers and the Fall of the Old Regime: From the February Revolution to the July Days 1917.* London: Macmillan, 1983.

Mandel, David. *The Petrograd Workers and the Soviet Seizure of Power: From the July Days 1917 to July 1918.* London: Macmillan, 1984.

Mawdsley, Evan. *The Russian Revolution and the Baltic Fleet: War and Politics, February 1917–April 1918.* London: Macmillan, 1978.

Melancon, Michael. "From Rhapsody to Threnody: Russia's Provisional Government in Socialist-Revolutionary Eyes, February–July 1917." *Soviet and Post-Soviet Review* 24 (1997): 27–80.

Melancon, Michael. *The Lena Goldfields Massacre and the Crisis of the Late Tsarist State.* College Station: Texas A&M University Press, 2006.

Melancon, Michael. *The Socialist Revolutionaries and the Russian Anti-War Movement, 1914–1917.* Columbus: Ohio State University Press, 1990.

Melancon, Michael. "The Syntax of Soviet Power: The Resolutions of Soviets and Other Institutions, March–October 1917." *Russian Review* 52, no. 4 (1993): 486–505.

Melancon, Michael. "Who Wrote What and When? Proclamations of the February Revolution in Petrograd, 23 February–1 March 1917." *Soviet Studies* 42, no. 3 (1988): 479–500.

Morrisey, Susan K. *Heralds of Revolution: Russian Students and Mythologies of Radicalism.* New York and Oxford: Oxford University Press, 1998.

Orlovsky, Daniel T. "Corporatism or Democracy? The Russian Provisional Government of 1917." *Soviet and Post-Soviet Review* 24 (1997): 15–26.

Orlovsky, Daniel T. "The Lower-Middle Strata in Revolutionary Russia." In *Between Tsar and People: Educated Society and the Quest for Public Identity in Late Imperial Society,* ed. Edith Clowes et al., 248–268. Princeton, NJ: Princeton University Press, 1991.

Orlovsky, Daniel T. "The Provisional Government and Its Cultural Work." In *Bolshevik Culture: Experiment and Order in the Russian Revolution,* ed. Abbot Gleason, Peter Kenez and Richard Stites, 39–56. Bloomington: Indiana University Press, 1985.

Orlovsky, Daniel T. "Reform during Revolution; Governing the Provinces in 1917." In *Reform in Russia and the USSR: Past and Perspectives,* ed. Robert Crummey, 100–125. Urbana and Chicago: University of Illinois Press, 1989.

Pethybridge, Roger. *The Spread of the Russian Revolution: Essays on 1917.* London: Macmillan, 1972.

Phillips, Hugh. "'A Bad Business': The February Revolution in Tver." *Soviet and Post-Soviet Review* 23, no. 3 (1996): 123–142.

Posadskii, Anton. "World War I: a Russian National Perspective July 1914 to February 1917." *The Journal of Slavic Military Studies* 15, no. 1 (March 2002): 57–90.

Rabinowitch, Alexander. *The Bolsheviks Come to Power: The 1917 Revolution in Petrograd.* New York: Norton, 1976.

Rabinowitch, Alexander. *The Bolsheviks in Power: The First Year of Soviet Rule in Petrograd.* Bloomington: Indiana University Press, 2007.

Rabinowitch, Alexander. *Prelude to Revolution: The Petrograd Bolsheviks and the July 1917 Uprising.* Bloomington: Indiana University Press, 1968.

Rachaminov, Alon. *POWs and the Great War: Captivity on the Eastern Front.* New York: Berg, 2002.

Radkey, Oliver H. *The Agrarian Foes of Bolshevism: Promise and Default of the Russian Socialist Revolutionaries, February to October 1917.* New York: Columbia University Press, 1958.

Radkey, Oliver H. *The Election to the Russian Constituent Assembly of 1917.* Cambridge, MA: Harvard University Press, 1989.

Radkey, Oliver H. *The Sickle under the Hammer: The Russian Socialist Revolutionaries in the Early Months of Soviet Rule.* New York: Columbia University Press, 1963.

Raleigh, Donald J. *Experiencing Russia's Civil War: Politics, Society, and Revolutionary Culture in Saratov, 1917–1922.* Princeton, NJ: Princeton University Press, 2002.

Raleigh, Donald J. *Revolution on the Volga: Saratov in 1917.* Ithaca, NY: Cornell University Press, 1986.

Rendle, Matthew. "Conservatism and Revolution: The All-Russian Union of Landowners, 1916–1918." *Slavonic and East European Review* 84, no. 3 (2006): 481–507.

Rendle, Matthew. *Defenders of the Motherland: The Tsarist Elite in Revolutionary Russia.* Oxford and New York: Oxford University Press, 2010.

Reshtar, J. S. *The Ukrainian Revolution, 1917–1920: A Study in Nationalism.* Princeton, NJ: Princeton University Press, 1952.

Retish, Aaron B. *Russian Peasants in Revolution and Civil War: Citizenship, Identity, and the Creation of the Soviet State, 1914–1922.* Cambridge, MA: Cambridge University Press, 2008.

Rosenberg, William G. *Liberals in the Russian Revolution: The Constitutional Democrat Party, 1917–1921.* Princeton, NJ: Princeton University Press, 1974.

Rossa, Ruth. *Russia's Industrialists in an Era of Revolution: The Association of Industry and Trade, 1906–1917.* Armonk, NY: M. E. Sharpe, 1997.

Sanborn, Joshua A. *Drafting the Russian Nation: Military Conscription, Total War, and Mass Politics, 1905–1925.* DeKalb: Northern Illinois University Press, 2003.

Saul, Norman. *Sailors in Revolt: The Russian Revolution and the Baltic Fleet in 1917*. Lawrence: University of Kansas Press, 1978.

Seregny, Scott J. "A Wager on the Peasantry: Anti-*Zemstvo* Riots, Adult Education and the Russian Village during World War One: Stavropol' Province." *The Slavonic and East European Review* 79, no. 1 (2001): 90–126.

Smith, S. A. *Red Petrograd: Revolution in the factories, 1917–1918*. Cambridge, MA: Cambridge University Press, 1983.

Snow, Russell E. *The Bolsheviks in Siberia, 1917–March 1918*. Rutherford, NJ: Rutgers University Press, 1975.

Stites, Richard. *The Women's Liberation Movement in Russia*. Princeton, NJ: Princeton University Press, 1978.

Stoff, Laurie S. *They Fought for the Motherland: Russia's Women Soldiers in World War 1 and Revolution*. Lawrence: University Press of Kansas, 2006.

Suny, Ronald G. *The Baku Commune, 1917–1918: Class and Nationality in the Russian Revolution*. Princeton, NJ: Princeton University Press, 1972.

Tirado, Isabel. "The Socialist Youth Movement in Revolutionary Petrograd," *Russian Review* 46, no. 1 (1987): 135–156.

Wade, Rex A. *Red Guards and Workers' Militias in the Russian Revolution*. Stanford, CA: Stanford University Press, 1984.

Wade, Rex A. *The Russian Search for Peace, February–October 1917*. Stanford, CA: Stanford University Press, 1969.

White, James. "Lenin, Trotsky, and the Arts of Insurrection: The Congress of Soviets of the Northern Region, 11–13 October 1917." *The Slavonic and East European Review* 77, no. 1 (1999): 117–139.

Wildman, Allan K. *The End of the Russian Imperial Army: The Old Army and the Soldiers' Revolt (March–April 1917)*. Princeton, NJ: Princeton University Press, 1980.

Wildman, Allan K. *The End of the Russian Imperial Army: The Road to Soviet Power and Peace*. Princeton, NJ: Princeton University Press, 1987.

Document Collections

Ascher, Abraham, ed. *The Mensheviks in the Russian Revolution*. Ithaca, NY: Cornell University Press, 1976.

Avrich, Paul, ed. *The Anarchists in the Russian Revolution*. Ithaca, NY: Cornell University Press, 1973.

Bone, Ann, trans. *The Bolsheviks and the October Revolution: Minutes of the Central Committee of the Russian Social-Democratic Labour Party (Bolsheviks), August 1917– February 1918*. London: Pluto Press, 1974.

Browder, Robert Pail, and Alexander F. Kerensky, eds. *The Russian Provisional Government, 1917: Documents*. 3 vols. Stanford, CA: Stanford University Press, 1961.

Bunyan, James, and H. H. Fischer, eds. *The Bolshevik Revolution, 1917–1918*. Stanford, CA: Stanford University Press, 1934.

Daniels, Robert V., ed. *The Russian Revolution*. Englewood Cliffs, NJ: Prentice Hall, 1972.

Gankin, Olga Hess, and H. H. Fischer. *The Bolsheviks and the World War*. Stanford, CA: Stanford University Press, 1968.

Keep, John L. H. *The Debate on Soviet Power: Minutes of the All-Russian Central Executive Committee of Soviets, Second Convocation*. Oxford: Clarendon Press, 1979.

Kowalski, Ronald. *The Russian Revolution, 1917–1921*. London: Routledge, 1997.

Lenin, V. I. *Collected Works*, Vols. 25, 26. Moscow: Progress, 1972.

McNeal, Robert, ed. *Resolutions and Decisions of the Communist Party of the Soviet Union*, Vol. 1, *The Russian Social Democratic Labour Party, 1898–October 1917*, edited by Ralph Carter Elwood. Toronto: University of Toronto Press, 1974.

Murphy, Brian. *Rostov in the Russian Civil War, 1917–1920: The Key to Victory*. London: Routledge, 2005.

Raleigh, Donald J. translator and editor. *A Russian Civil War Diary: Alexis Babine in Saratov, 1917–1922*. Durham and London: Duke University Press, 1988.

Steinberg, Mark David. *The Fall of the Romanovs: Political Dreams and Personal Struggles in Time of Revolution*. New Haven: Yale University Press, 1995.

Steinberg, Mark David. *Voices of Revolution, 1917*. New Haven and London: Yale University Press, 2001.

Wade, Rex A. *The Russian Revolution and Civil War*. Westport and London: Greenwood Press, 2001.

INDEX

FIGHTING WORDS

Fighting Words is an innovative and accessible new military history series, each title juxtaposing the voices of opposing combatants in a major historical conflict. Presented side by side are the testimonies of fighting men and women, the reportage of nations at war, and the immediate public responses of belligerent war leaders. Together, they offer strikingly different perspectives on the same events.

The extracts are short and snappy, complemented by brief introductions which set the scene. They vividly recreate the conflicts as they were experienced. At the same time, they open up new perspectives and challenge accepted assumptions. Readers will question the nature of primary sources, the motivations of the authors, the agendas that influence media reports and the omissions inherent in all of the sources. Ultimately, readers will be left to ponder the question: whose history is this?

Recent titles in the Fighting Words series
J. Michael Francis, Series Editor

Competing Voices from the Crusades: Fighting Words
Andrew Holt, James Muldoon

Competing Voices from Revolutionary Cuba: Fighting Words
John M. Kirk, Peter McKenna

Competing Voices from Native America: Fighting Words
Edited by Dewi Ioan Ball and Joy Porter

Competing Voices from the Pacific War: Fighting Words
Sean Brawley, Chris Dixon, and Beatrice Trefalt

Competing Voices from the Mexican Revolution: Fighting Words
Chris Frazer

Competing Voices from World War II in Europe: Fighting Words
Edited by Harold J. Goldberg

Edwards Brothers Malloy
Thorofare, NJ USA
May 22, 2012